Insurance Law: Doctrines and Principles

Second Edition

JOHN LOWRY and PHILIP RAWLINGS
University College London

with contributions by

Rob Merkin
University of Southampton, and Barlow Lyde & Gilbert

·HART·
PUBLISHING

OXFORD AND PORTLAND, OREGON
2005

Published in North America (US and Canada) by

Hart Publishing

c/o International Specialized Book Services
920 NE 58th Avenue, Suite 300
Portland, OR 97213-3786
USA
Tel: +1 503 287 3093 or toll-free: (1) 800 944 6190
Fax: +1 503 280 8832
Email: orders@isbs.com
Website: www.isbs.com

Hart Publishing, Salter's Boatyard, Folly Bridge, Abingdon Rd, Oxford, OX1 4LB

Telephone: +44 (0)1865 245533 Fax: +44 (0) 1865 794882

Email: mail@hartpub.co.uk

Website: http//:www.hartpub.co.uk

British Library Cataloguing in Publication Data

Data Available

ISBN-13: 978-1-84113-540-3 (paperback)
ISBN-10: 1-84113-540-2 (paperback)

Typeset by Forewords, Oxford, in Times 10/12 pt

Printed and bound in Great Britain by
Page Bros (Norwich) Ltd

Preface

This new edition of the book is very different from the last. We have rewritten and restructured much of the book. This is due in no small part to the creativity of the judiciary over the last five years or so. Indeed, it is a particularly interesting time to be an insurance lawyer in view of the current strength of the commercial bench. Also, of course, since the publication of the first edition, the legislature has been active. Of particular note in this regard is the Financial Services and Markets Act 2000 which has resulted in the regulatory landscape being redrawn.

The emphasis of the book is upon the general principles underlying non-marine insurance contracts. We do not attempt to make a comprehensive survey of particular types of insurance contracts. Rather, reference is made to certain types of policy as a means of adding context to particular issues which insurance law gives rise to. Our principal aim is to provide a text that combines exposition with critical analysis.

We owe a number of debts. First, to Rob Merkin who, with typical generosity, contributed entirely new chapters covering Conflict of Laws and Reinsurance. Also, to the reviewers of the first edition for their constructive comments. We thank our colleagues at the Faculty of Laws, University College London for their support. It is hard to imagine a better environment in which to undertake serious inquiry. In particular, we thank Michael Bridge. Special thanks are due to Sylvia Lough and Jacqueline Bennett. As always, it has been a pleasure to work with Richard Hart and his colleagues.

We have endeavoured to state the law as it stood in April 2005.

John Lowry and Philip Rawlings
Bentham House
London
May 5th 2005

Contents

Table of cases

Table of statutes

Table of statutory instruments

Table of EC legislation

Table of national legislation

Table of international legislation

The Insurance Contract

1. Insurance contract

Insurance has a history that appears to go back to the Babylonians and certainly it was well established among the town guilds of Europe by the mid-fourteenth century. However, it was the rapid growth in international trade by sea from the fifteenth century, which was centred, in particular, around the great Italian city states, that led to the development by those states of recognisably modern methods of insurance. This trade involved enormous financial risks for the merchant and insurance enabled these risks to be shared, either through an agreement with other merchants to provide cover if one member of the group suffered a loss or through an insurer who, in exchange for the payment of a premium, agreed to cover specified losses and who would then seek to spread that risk among other insureds.[1] By the 1680s, insurance provision for merchants in London centred on Edward Lloyd's Coffee House in Tower Street, where the proprietor had built up a regular clientele among merchants and shipowners. It was from these origins that the present Lloyd's market emerged and, although much has changed, its purpose remains to provide a place in which those who seek insurance and those who provide it can conduct their business. The marine trade represented the core of the early insurance business, but the economic expansion of the eighteenth and nineteenth centuries led to the development of insurance companies, such as the Royal Exchange Assurance, which obtained its charter in 1720, and the popularity of other types of policy. Indeed, the investment by insurers of income from premiums played a key role in that economic expansion and the insurance industry continues to be a major source of funds for business. Insurers provided cover for those private individuals whose wealth was invested in tangible property: so, for instance, from the late seventeenth century a strong market emerged in private fire insurance. All of these policies were contracts of indemnity: that is, the insurer indemnified the insured against loss and, therefore, the insured could not recover more than the actual loss suffered.[2] As a consequence the insured could not recover the same loss from different insurers and the insurer who paid for

---

[1] See W Holdsworth, 'The Early History of the Contract of Insurance' (1917) 17 *Col LR* 85.
[2] See Marine Insurance Act 1906, s 1.

the loss acquired the right of subrogation, which, in effect, meant the insurer could take action against any third party who was responsible for the loss.[3]

The eighteenth and nineteenth centuries also saw the development of life assurance policies under which the payment due on the death of the life insured is determined by the sum fixed in the contract and not by an estimate of the loss suffered. Some of these policies combine life assurance with investment: such as an endowment policy which, for an increased premium, builds up a fund that is paid provided the insured survives beyond a specified date.[4] Since such contingency contracts do not indemnify the insured, there is no rule against double insurance and the insurers have no right of subrogation, which means the insured will retain any payment from another insurer and any damages from a tortfeasor.[5] The insurance industry has expanded the range of such policies. For example, in the nineteenth century specialist insurers began to offer policies that provided a fixed amount in the event of the insured suffering injury or death as the result of an accident,[6] or combined elements of indemnity and contingency insurance: under the accident policy in *Theobald v Railway Passengers Assurance Co*,[7] the insurer promised to pay a fixed sum on death and to compensate for pain and loss suffered up to £1000.

These indemnity and contingency policies provide first-party insurance, which means, broadly, they cover property or a life in which the insured has an interest,[8] but insurers also write third-party insurance against the risk of the insured incurring liability to a third party: third-party motor insurance covers the liability of the motorist for injuries caused to another person.[9]

---

2. Definition

The courts and Parliament have been somewhat reluctant when it comes to defining a contract of insurance.[10] Megarry V-C thought it 'a matter of considerable difficulty,'[11] and, while prepared to discuss the issue in so far as it assisted in the determination of the case before him, declined the opportunity to attempt an all embracing definition, remarking that, 'it is a concept which it is better to describe than to

---

[3] See ch 11.
[4] According to *Fuji Finance Inc v Aetna Life Insurance Co Ltd* [1997] Ch 173, these are still life assurance policies even if their main objective is investment (see below).
[5] On subrogation, see ch 11.
[6] *Dalby v India and London Life-Assurance Co* (1854) 15 CB (NS) 365 at 387, *per* Parke B.
[7] (1854) 10 Ex 45.
[8] The insured must have an interest in the subject matter (the house or the life insured, for instance) at the time of the contract, but, while in indemnity contracts that interest must also be present at the time of the loss, there is no such requirement in the case of life assurance: see ch 6.
[9] A motor policy may also provide first-party cover–referred to as comprehensive insurance. See chs 13 and 14.
[10] MA Clarke, *The Law of Insurance Contracts* (London, LLP, 2002), ch 1; R Hodgin, 'Problems in Defining Insurance Contracts' [1980] *LMCLQ* 14; RL Purves, 'The Expanding (or Shrinking) Scope of "Insurance" in FSA Regulation' [2001] *JBL* 623.
[11] *Medical Defence Union Ltd v Department of Trade* [1980] Ch 82 at 95.

attempt to define.'[12] Similarly, Templeman J believed that a general definition was 'undesirable...because definitions tend sometimes to obscure and occasionally to exclude that which ought to be included.'[13] Nonetheless, some notion of what constitutes insurance is important since, although subject to the general principles of contract law, special rules also apply to such contracts. Moreover, those who carry on insurance business without authorisation are committing a criminal offence.[14]

Legislation provides some guidance for the purpose of regulation. The Financial Services and Markets Act 2000 (Regulated Activities) Order 2001 (as amended) does not define 'contract of insurance', but does set out a list of indicative activities that require authorisation by the Financial Services Authority (FSA). Furthermore, the FSA has recognised that in view of both the general prohibition against unauthorised persons engaging in insurance business and the importance attached to clear and accountable regulation, there is a need for clear guidelines as to how it will exercise its discretion. The FSA has, therefore, issued its own criteria based on the judgment of Channell J in *Prudential Insurance Co v Commissioners of Inland Revenue*,[15] which concerned the application of stamp duty to insurance policies. He said that a contract of insurance is an agreement in which:

> for some consideration, usually but not necessarily in periodical payments called premiums, you secure to yourself some benefit, usually but not necessarily the payment of a sum of money, upon the happening of some event. Then the next thing that is necessary is that the event should be one which involves some amount of uncertainty. There must be either uncertainty whether the event will ever happen or not, or if the event is one which must happen at some time there must be uncertainty as to the time at which it will happen. The remaining essential is that which was referred to by the Attorney-General when he said the insurance must be against something. A contract which would otherwise be a mere wager may become an insurance by reason of the assured having an interest in the subject-matter – that is to say, the uncertain event which is necessary to make the contract amount to an insurance must be an event which is prima facie adverse to the interest of the assured. The insurance is to provide for the payment of a sum of money to meet the loss or detriment which will or may be suffered upon the happening of the event. By statute it is necessary that at the time of the making of the contract there should be an insurable interest in the assured. It is true that in the case of life insurance it is not necessary that the interest should continue, and the interest is not the measure of the amount recoverable as in the case of a fire or marine policy. Still, the necessity of there being an insurable interest at the time of the making of the contract shows that it is essential to the idea of a contract of insurance that the event upon which the money is to be paid shall prima facie be an adverse event.[16]

It is worth focusing briefly on some of the issues that Channell J raised. He suggested that the agreement must relate to a risk which involves uncertainty in that the loss might or might not occur, or it will occur at a time that cannot be predicted: there is uncertainty in fire insurance because the house might not catch fire, and, although in life assurance it is certain that the insured life will die, the time of death is uncertain.

---

[12] Ibid.
[13] *Department of Trade and Industry v St. Christopher Motorists' Association Ltd* [1974] 1 WLR 99 at 101.
[14] See ch 2.
[15] [1906] 2 KB 658.
[16] Ibid, at 663.

In other words, 'a contract of insurance is a contract upon speculation.'[17] Yet, uncertainty is not unique to insurance: the insurer's liability to pay damages in the uncertain event that the insured suffers loss mirrors the liability of any contracting party to pay damages in the uncertain event that it commits a breach.[18]

Channell J's view that this uncertain event had to be one 'which is prima facie adverse to the interest of the assured' might accurately describe most insurance contracts, but it is difficult to understand why it is required and, perhaps, it is not.[19] He may have linked this factor to the requirement that the insured have 'an interest in the subject-matter.' The insurable interest distinguishes an insurance contract from a wager. Furthermore, an insurance contract is void under the Marine Insurance Act 1906, section 4(1) and (2) if the insurer agrees to provide cover irrespective of whether the insured has an insurable interest (known as a policy proof of interest or ppi clause).[20] Of course, in both wagering and insurance contracts the parties make judgments about the occurrence of uncertain events, whether it is a house that might burn down or a horse that might or might not win a race. The difference lies in the fact that the risk of loss to the house owner exists independently of the contract, whereas the risk on the horse race is created by the contract. Moreover, someone with no interest in the house will lose nothing if it burns down and the only risk that person runs is the loss of the consideration paid in exchange for the promise of payment if the house does burn down. In other words, in a wagering contract the risk is created by the agreement for without it the contracting party would have suffered no loss, whereas in an insurance contract the risk exists whether or not there is such a contract.[21] Blackburn J put the matter succinctly: 'I apprehend that the distinction between a policy and a wager is this: a policy is, properly speaking, a contract to indemnify the insured in respect of some interest which he has against the perils which he contemplates it will be liable to.'[22] Interestingly, the courts have tended to set themselves against contracts designed to 'insure' against losses from gaming, even though they would seem to fit the definition of an insurance contract in that the risk arises not from the 'insurance' contract but from the gaming contract.[23]

More difficult is the distinction between a contract of insurance and a contract of guarantee. In terms of regulation, the distinction is less significant than previously, because under the Financial Services and Markets Act (Regulated Activities) Order 2001, contracts of insurance include 'fidelity bonds, performance bonds, bail bonds, customs bonds or similar contracts of guarantee' that are effected by someone not undertaking banking business, are not merely incidental to another business carried out by the person effecting them and are effected in return for the payment of a premium. Nevertheless, there are significant differences between the treatment of contracts of insurance and contracts of guarantee at common law. Harman LJ

---

[17] *Re Barrett; ex parte Young v NM Superannuation Pty Ltd* 106 ALR 549 (Fed Court of Australia), per von Dousa J.

[18] As will be seen, the courts characterise the insurer's liability following a covered loss as a claim in damages: see ch 10.

[19] See the comments on life assurance in *Gould v Curtis* [1913] 3 KB 84 at 92, per Cozens-Hardy MR, at 95, per Buckley LJ, at 98–9, per Kennedy LJ. Buckley LJ commented, 'some people regard [death] as adverse, and some do not.'

[20] *John Edwards and Co v Motor Union Insurance Co Ltd* [1922] 2 KB 249.

[21] *Carlill v Carbolic Smoke Ball Co* [1892] 2 QB 484 at 490, per Hawkins J.

[22] *Wilson v Jones* (1867) 2 LR Exch 139 at 150.

[23] This is the implication of *Hill v William Hill (Park Lane) Ltd* [1949] AC 530.

suggested that the attempt to distinguish between them is fraught with difficulty and has 'raised many hair-splitting distinctions of exactly the kind which brings the law into hatred, ridicule and contempt by the public.'[24] In a contract of guarantee, Alex (the guarantor) promises Toytown Bank (the creditor) that, if it will enter into a contract to lend money to Yasmin (the debtor), Alex will be responsible for Yasmin's debt should she default. Under a contract of guarantee there is a less rigorous duty of disclosure or even no duty at all, and while in insurance the primary liability is on the insurers, in a contract of guarantee that primary liability is on the debtor and the guarantor's liability arises only if the debtor defaults. Furthermore, under section 4 of the Statute of Frauds Act 1677, a guarantee must be in writing, but there is no such requirement in respect of a contract of indemnity.

In *Re Denton's Estate*, Vaughan Williams LJ suggested that the key to distinguishing between these contracts lay in whether it was appropriate to apply the duty of disclosure to the agreement:

> The distinction in substance, in cases in which the loss insured against is simply the event of the non-payment of a debt, seems to be, as I read the judgment of Romer LJ [in *Seaton* v *Heath*[25]], between contracts in which the person desiring to be insured has means of knowledge as to the risk and the insurer has not the same means, and those cases in which the insurer has the same means.[26]

The traditional justification for this approach is that insurance is a commercial relationship in which the insured has knowledge of facts material to the risk, whereas in a guarantee, it has been assumed, the guarantor acts out of motives of friendship and is assumed to be aware of the risk, so that there is no need for disclosure. The problem is that guarantees are common in commercial transactions and guarantors do not necessarily know the facts.

To determine whether an agreement is a guarantee or an insurance the courts will look at the contract as a whole in order to discover its effect, and neither the use by the parties of the terms 'insurance' or 'guarantee', nor the fact that one of the parties is an insurance company will be conclusive.[27] The use of such words may, of course, be indicators and there are others. Insurance will generally involve the payment by the insured of a premium, whereas usually a contract of guarantee is entered into without any payment, although one might expect a fee to be charged by a guarantor in a commercial contract. Moreover, in insurance there are normally two parties (insured and insurer), while in a contract of guarantee there are normally three parties (creditor, debtor and guarantor).

There is also a difficult distinction to be drawn between insurance and contracts of

---

[24] *Yeoman Credit Ltd v Latter* [1961] 1 WLR 828 at 892, per Harman LJ. To add to this confusion, a guarantee entered into by an insurer will be insurance business: *Travellers Casualty & Surety Co of Europe Ltd v Commissioners of Customs and Excise*, unreported, 6 May 2005 (VAT Tribunal).
[25] [1899] 1 QB 782.
[26] [1904] 2 Ch 178. See also *United States v Tilleraas* 709 F2d 1088 (US Court of Appeals, 6th Cir, 1983).
[27] *The 'Zhula K' and 'Selin'* [1987] 1 Lloyd's Rep 151.

warranty. [28] A warranty is commonly given in connection with the sale of goods and might, for instance, involve a promise to repair goods that are defective on delivery.[29] This would seem not to amount to insurance since it is merely a promise to do that which the party had promised to do in the sale contract, which was to deliver goods that were not defective. Yet, it could be insurance if the promise goes further, as where the seller promises to replace goods if they are lost or damaged by the buyer, or if the promise to repair is made by someone who otherwise has no responsibility for the fault.[30]

In the English courts there has been relatively little consideration of this distinction. The judges have, however, declined the invitation to stipulate that for insurance the insurer should have no control over, or responsibility for, the fault that causes the loss.[31] For the purposes of regulation under the Financial Services and Markets Act 2000, the FSA has taken the view that a promise by the seller which relates to defects in the goods is not insurance, but a promise by the seller to extend the warranty beyond the normal period for an additional payment or a promise by a third party to make repairs does amount to insurance.[32] In the US, where there has been a good deal of case law on this issue, no clear principle has emerged. In *Ollendorf Watch Co Ltd v Pink*,[33] a promise by the seller of a watch to provide a replacement if the watch were lost or stolen was held to amount to a contract of insurance because it covered risks that did not relate to defects in the watch itself. Similarly, in *Griffin Systems, Inc v Washburn*,[34] a court in Illinois decided that a contract of insurance existed where Griffin, who had not supplied the car, promised to repair any damage caused to it by weather, collision, vandalism, negligence or failure to have it serviced. On the other hand, a majority in the Ohio Supreme Court in *Griffin Systems, Inc v Ohio Department of Insurance*[35] said that it was not the status of the party offering the warranty that was important, but the promise made: 'warranties that cover only defects within the product itself are properly characterised as warranties... whereas warranties promising to cover damages or losses unrelated to defects within the product itself are, by definition, contracts substantially amounting to insurance.' The fact that Griffin was not the manufacturer or retailer of the car was irrelevant and a promise to compensate the motorist for repairs caused by defective parts was not insurance. In that case, however, there was a vigorous dissenting judgment by Wright J, who argued that the status of the person providing the promise was crucial: 'This case does not involve a warranty because a warranty is a statement of representation made by the

---

[28] *First National Tricity Finance Ltd v OT Computers Ltd* [2004] EWCA Civ653; Competition Commission, *Extended Warranties on Domestic Electrical Goods* (2003);C Twigg-Flesner, 'Consumer Product Guarantees and Insurance Law' [1999] *JBL* 279. See generally GL Priest, 'A Theory of the Consumer Product Warranty' (1981) 90 *Yale LJ* 1297; T Baker, 'On the Genealogy of Moral Hazard' (1996) 75 *Texas Law Rev* 237.

[29] Or are deemed to have been defective on delivery by virtue of s 48A, Sale of Goods Act 1979.

[30] *Re Sentinel Securities plc* [1996] 1 WLR 316. Companies providing roadside breakdown services to motorists are clearly giving undertakings that amount to insurance, however, they are exempted from regulation under the Financial Services and Markets Act 2000 by virtue of the Financial Services and Markets Act 2000 (Regulated Activities) Order 2001, r 10.

[31] *Medical Defence Union Ltd v Department of Trade*, above n 11; *Department of Trade and Industry v St. Christopher Motorists' Association Ltd*, above n 13.

[32] J Lowry and P Rawlings, *Insurance Law: Cases and Materials* (Oxford, Hart Publishing, 2004) 29.

[33] 17 NE2d 676 (New York, 1938).

[34] 505 NE2d 1121 (Illinois, 1987).

[35] 575 NE2d 803 (Ohio, 1991).

seller or manufacturer of goods contemporaneously with and as part of the contract of sale.'

It is commonplace for firms to seek ways of guarding against a risk of loss through, for instance, unfavourable changes in commodity prices or currency exchange rates or adverse weather conditions. Such risks may, of course, be covered by insurance, but there various other methods which, while transferring the burden of risk away from the firm, are not treated as insurance contracts. An airline concerned at the prospect of oil prices rising might take out insurance, or it might hedge by buying oil futures, which would amount to an investment contract. This is not merely a matter of semantics. Insurers are only permitted to undertake insurance business,[36] so an insurer which gets it wrong and writes a risk transfer contract that amounts to an investment rather than insurance will be committing a regulatory breach. Similarly, an insurance intermediary must have authorisation to advise on investment contracts. For the party contracting with the insurer the distinction is less critical since a breach of authorisation will not affect the contract's enforceability.[37]

The difficulties involved in defining the constituent features of an insurance contract or in distinguishing it from other contracts have led most judges to resist generalisations and to turn instead to the particular issue before them. As Professor Clarke has put it:

> Insurance contracts are best seen (and defined, if at all) according to the angle or line of approach, that is, the context or issue before the court. With regulatory statutes, courts are concerned with the purpose of the statute, whether, for example, this is the kind of thing that Parliament intended to regulate, or to encourage...and they examine the terms of the contract in that light.[38]

In the New Zealand Court of Appeal, Richardson J suggested:

> The true nature of a transaction can only be ascertained by careful consideration of the legal arrangements actually entered into and carried out: not on an assessment of the broad substance of the transaction measured by the results intended and achieved or of the overall economic consequences. The nomenclature used by the parties is not decisive and what is crucial is the ascertainment of the legal rights and duties which are actually created by the transaction into which the parties entered. The surrounding circumstances may be taken into account in characterising the transaction. Not to deny or contradict the written agreement but in order to understand the setting in which it was made and to construe it against that factual background having regard to the genesis and objectively the aim of the transaction.[39]

An agreement may have elements that means it resembles an insurance contract, but when taken as a whole it may be clear that it is not: it is common for a publishing contract to contain a term under which the writer agrees to indemnify the publisher

---

[36] Financial Services Authority, *Handbook; Interim Prudential Sourcebook*, 1.3; see ch 2.
[37] See ch 2.
[38] MA Clarke, *The Law of Insurance Contracts* (London, LLP, 1997) 2. See J Hellner, 'The Scope of Insurance Regulation: What is Insurance for Purposes of Regulation?' (1963) 12 *Am J Comp L* 494.
[39] *Marac Life Assurance Ltd v Commissioner of Inland Revenue* [1986] 1 NZLR 694 (Court of Appeal, New Zealand).

against liability for libel, but this does not make it an insurance contract[40]; on the other hand, investment schemes, which include minor elements of life insurance, would seem to be contracts of insurance because 'the right to the benefits is related to life or death.'[41]

The refusal of Megarry V-C in the *Medical Defence Union* case to provide a general definition of an insurance contract might have been wise, but it also allowed him to decide the case according to whether the Medical Defence Union seemed to him to be insurers: 'I also consider that the general nature of the business carried on by the union is too far removed from the general nature of the businesses carried on by those who are generally accepted as being insurers for the union's business to be fairly regarded as the effecting and carrying out of contracts of insurance...'[42] Yet, did he give proper consideration to the objectives of regulation, and in particular to the protection of the members of the scheme? This was a scheme that for all practical purposes must have been regarded by the members as insurance. It is, therefore, reasonable to suggest that he should have erred on the side of finding that the scheme amounted to insurance so that it might be appropriately regulated and the members properly protected, rather than, as he seems to have done, approaching the issue from the point of view of the Union and, therefore, seeing regulation as a burden.

---

3. Insurance law

It might be suggested that too much emphasis has been placed in this chapter on the role of contract in insurance. In the UK, the insurance principle was fundamental in the construction of the modern welfare state during the twentieth century,[43] and as that welfare state comes under pressure the role of both compulsory and voluntary private insurance becomes more significant as an instrument of social policy.[44] Yet, during the course of this book it will become clear that, although in other countries insurance is no longer simply seen as a private contractual relationship between an insurer and an insured, the English courts and legislature continue to approach it in that way and largely disregard social policy considerations.

The early dominance of marine insurance meant that it was through judicial decisions on such policies that the principles of insurance law were developed. Those principles were then transmitted to other types of insurance, so that the bulk of the rules embodied in the Marine Insurance Act 1906 have universal application. This means that principles shaped in a commercial context have been forced into the very different environment of consumer insurance. Successive governments have shown

---

[40] *Medical Defence Union Ltd v Department of Trade*, above n 11, at 85.
[41] *Fuji Finance Inc v Aetna Life Insurance Co Ltd*, above n 4, per Morritt LJ.
[42] *Medical Defence Union Ltd v Department of Trade*, above n 11.
[43] In their original forms state unemployment and pension schemes in the UK were based on insurance (eg, National Insurance Act 1911) and the insurance idea was fundamental to the construction of the post-Second World War welfare state under the Beveridge plan.
[44] On compulsory liability insurance, see chs 13 and 14.

little interest in effecting reform, in spite of the occasional promptings of law reform bodies,[45] and indeed the insurance industry has been exempted from changes in the law that apply to other contracts.[46] This contrasts with countries such as the US where regulators and the courts appear willing to intervene in the insurance contract. As one US judge put it, insurers 'are part of an industry which is affected by the public interest…As a result, they can and should be held to a broader legal responsibility than are parties to purely private contracts.'[47] The difference in approach has been explained in terms of different welfare strategies. [48] The argument is that in the US welfare is seen, primarily, as a matter for the individual to arrange through private insurance, and therefore the insurance industry is regulated to ensure it delivers appropriate provision. In the UK, on the other hand, welfare has been mainly delivered through the state and insurance is seen as a matter of private choice. So, while English law leaves the parties free to choose the content of their contract and is less sensitive to the potential for insurers to exploit their bargaining strength, US law is wary of this inequality between the parties and because of the importance placed on insurance, is more willing to intervene to redress any imbalance. It may also be that the insurance industry in the UK has been relatively successful in resisting intervention because of its significance within the economy, both as a major earner of foreign currency and as a major investor, and because of the position of some insurance companies within the powerful grouping of financial institutions that comprise the City.

Nevertheless, the level of regulation to which the insurance contract is subject is increasing. Although the principal focus of statutory regulation is on those who conduct insurance business, there has been a growing interest in the contract itself. This has come from the FSA, from the industry itself and from European legislation. The Financial Services and Markets Act 2000 gives the consumer (and, to a lesser extent, the commercial buyer) significant protections when buying various types of insurance, but these largely concentrate on providing the consumer with information and a period of reflection rather than interfering with the principles governing the contract.[49] The Unfair Terms in Consumer Contracts Regulations 1999, which originated in an EU directive, does address some aspects of the imbalance in bargaining strength in consumer contracts.[50]

Arguably, it is the introduction by the insurance industry of various schemes that has had a greater impact on the insurance contract. The Statement of General Insurance Practice and the Statement of Long-term Insurance Practice first appeared in 1977 at the same time as the industry negotiated itself out of the Unfair Contract Terms Act, which regulates clauses that limit liability for breach. Those insurers who subscribed to the Statements of Practice agreed not to give effect to their full legal rights under contracts with consumer insureds in various areas where the common law was regarded as harsh, such as the duty of disclosure and the effect of a breach

---

[45] There has been any number of proposals for reform: eg, Law Commission, *Insurance Law: Non-Disclosure and Breach of Warranty*, report 104, Cm 8064, (1980); see ch 4.
[46] Unfair Contract Terms Act 1977, sch 1.
[47] *Continental Life & Accident Co v Songer*, 603 P.2d 921 (Ariz, 1979).
[48] R Hasson, 'The Special Nature of the Insurance Contract: A Comparison of American and English Law of Insurance' (1984) 47 *MLR* 505.
[49] See ch 2.
[50] The directive (93/13/EEC) was originally implemented in 1994. See ch 8.

of warranty or condition. In addition, codes of practice were established in respect of each type of consumer policy and to control the selling of policies. In 2000, the industry, with encouragement from the Treasury, established the General Insurance Standards Council to promote fair dealing with consumers through codes of practice.[51] The GISC was superseded in 2005 by the FSA and general insurance intermediaries became subject to compulsory regulation.[52] The industry also set up the Insurance Ombudsman Bureau in 1981 with the power to hear complaints from insureds and to make awards up to £100,000.[53] These awards bound insurers who were members of the scheme,[54] but not insureds, who, if dissatisfied with the ombudsman's decision, could bring the matter to court. In determining complaints the ombudsman was to consider, not just the law, but also what was 'fair and reasonable.' The result was that the ombudsman was able to mitigate some of the harsher effects that would have resulted from the strict enforcement of the insurer's legal rights. This voluntary scheme has been replaced by a statutory system under the Financial Services and Markets Act 2000, Part XVI, but the Financial Ombudsman Service has continued the tradition of a broader approach to consumer insurance disputes.[55]

These reforms appear to be opening up a division between the commercial and the consumer insurance contract that reproduces the more general separation between commercial and consumer law. Rules on, for example, the duty of disclosure were developed in, and may remain appropriate for, commercial insurance contracts, but they have also been applied to consumer policies to which they are often less well suited. Over the last twenty years this problem has been tackled from outside the common law. This means commercial and consumer insureds are subject to the same legal rule on disclosure, but, in practice, they may enjoy different outcomes because in the consumer's case the ombudsman may ignore or modify that rule. This may allow flexibility, but there are obvious dangers in the construction of a system of consumer insurance 'law' that stands apart from insurance law as determined by the courts.

The picture becomes even more complex when one adds the difficulties of defining the insurance contract. This confusion has been part of the reason for the failure of insurance law to capture the area of risk transfer and that, in turn, has made it difficult to determine which common law and regulatory rules apply to a particular contract.[56]

---

[51] GISC Scrutiny & Consumer Affairs Committee, *Report on GISC Performance against Objectives* (2004): http://www.gisc.co.uk; J Burling, 'The Impact of the GISC' (2001) *JBL* 646–53.

[52] See ch 2.

[53] A relatively small number of insurers set up another scheme called Personal Insurance Arbitration Services under which complaints were subject to the much more formal and less flexible process of arbitration. See ch 2.

[54] Insurers were not even permitted to challenge the ombudsman through judicial review: *R v Insurance Ombudsman Bureau, ex p Aegon Insurance* [1994] CLC 88.

[55] See ch 2.

[56] See further, J Basedown, 'The Case for a European Insurance Contract Code' (2001) *JBL* 569–86; C Crody and R Merkin, 'Doubts about Insurance Codes' (2001) *JBL* 587–604; M Clarke, 'Doubts from the Dark Side – The Case against Codes' (2001) *JBL* 605–15; P Griggs, 'Insurance Codes – A Middle Way' (2001) *JBL* 616–22.

2

Regulation of Insurance Business

1. Why regulate insurers?

The insurance industry in the UK is vast: there are approximately six hundred insurance companies, two hundred Friendly Societies,[1] as well as the Lloyd's of London insurance market and around 40,000 firms who advise customers and insurers. Insurance companies (although, as will be seen later, not insurance intermediaries) have long been subject to a greater degree of regulation than most other types of business. This began with the Life Assurance Companies Act in 1870 and gradually spread to other parts of the industry until by 1946 the whole sector was regulated. At first the main focus of regulation was solvency. The insurance contract is unusual in that, while the insured is required to perform by paying the premium, the insurer is only called on to perform (if ever) at some distant point in the future. This means that, unlike other trading businesses, the solvency of insurers is not immediately obvious on looking at the accounts. Moreover, a large premium income may not indicate a secure company if that income has been obtained by offering policies on terms that prove too advantageous to the insured.[2] The problem is particularly acute in life assurance, which as a long-term business means policyholders must have greater confidence that the insurers will be in a position to pay out when the risk eventually matures than is required in relation to those companies that write short-term policies on, for instance, property fire and theft. The solution adopted was simple: life insurers were required to lodge a deposit of money in the Court of Chancery as a sign that they were 'substantial people.'[3] This strategy was later used in other aspects of insurance business. But being rich did not necessarily make a firm a good insurer and the

---

[1] Small mutual insurers.

[2] *Re North & South Insurance Corp Ltd* (1933) 47 Ll L R 346. A reasonable prediction of the liabilities that an insurer will face can be made and it is the ability to make such a calculation with a high degree of accuracy that is one of the skills of the industry, but this is not a scientific process and complete accuracy is impossible.

[3] *Nelson v Board of Trade* (1904) 84 LT 565 at 567, per Lord Alvestone CJ.

Companies Act 1967 required assessments of the financial state of the company, the adequacy of its reinsurance cover on the risks carried and the fitness of its principal officers and main shareholders. The act gave the Board of Trade the power to intervene in the operation of the company after its initial authorisation.[4] This more comprehensive approach to authorisation and supervision was extended by subsequent legislation.

The history of insurance regulation might be seen as reform prompted by the failure of an insurer. The statute of 1870 followed the failure of some life assurance companies, the provisions in the Companies Act 1967 were included after the collapse of the Fire, Auto and Marine Insurance Company, and the Insurance Companies Amendment Act 1973 was passed in the wake of the failure of Vehicle and General. Yet, while this pattern continues, over the last 30 years other factors have led to and, therefore, shaped reform. Some understanding of these will provide an insight into the objectives of the system now in place.

In the first place, increased competition at home and internationally has forced firms operating in the financial sector to cut costs, develop new products and find new markets. As insurers have found it more difficult to make profits in their traditional areas of business, some have moved into non-insurance business, such as banking. At the same time, other companies such as banks and supermarkets have developed insurance products for their customers. A lot of huge financial conglomerates have emerged and prospered in this environment, but inevitably many firms have been unable to compete and have been swallowed up or disappeared, while others have struggled as a result of entering lines of business or markets in which they have little experience.

There has also been pressure for better consumer protection that has, in part, found its expression in a clamour for improved consumer rights. In the area of financial services, this reflects growing prosperity, but it is also an expression of the fragility of that prosperity. Following its election in 1979, the Conservative government under Mrs Thatcher took a good deal of interest in private investment and, as a consequence, in the financial services industry. For various reasons government wished to promote private investment by, for instance, encouraging people to buy their own homes and to acquire shares. In addition, the government made no secret of its wish to reduce the welfare state. This was presented as a policy aimed at reducing taxation so that people would be able to make their own choices as to how to spend their money, but it was also a response to the alarming prospect that expenditure on the welfare state seemed set to rise beyond the ability of the country to pay for it: for instance, as birth rates fell and people lived longer, the number on state pensions was expected to increase while the size of the working population, whose taxes funded those pensions, shrank. Of course, the danger in giving people a choice to invest for periods of unemployment or ill health or for their retirement is that some may choose not to do so. The government, therefore, encouraged personal investment and insurance to cover events of life, such as unemployment, ill health and retirement, which had previously been seen as largely tasks for the welfare state. Competition in the financial sector was seen as a way of improving efficiency, prices and performance, and of providing investors and consumers with better protection

---

[4] Part II, ss 58–108.

and rights. From the point of view of those investors, much of the enthusiasm for investment in the 1980s was fuelled, not by ideology or improved consumer protection, but by the expectation of profit through buying shares or houses which then seemed almost inevitably to rise in value. Nevertheless, investment was also motivated by a concern about the consequences of not investing or insuring in a post-welfare state: 'How long must I wait for health care through the state system? What will happen to me when I become old if I do not make provision for myself?'

As investment grew, so the consumers of financial services in their various guises (insureds, bank customers, pensioners, shareholders, etc) became politically significant by the sheer weight of their numbers. This meant that when the risks involved in investment emerged (the value of houses and investment fell, or financial companies failed to deliver on their promises or simply failed) the voices of these consumers were heard loud and clear. This is best illustrated by comparing a newspaper of 30 or 40 years ago with one of today: business news is no longer confined to a small section and addressed to those who work in the industry, it is a matter for all and is, therefore, something that frequently appears on the front page–as for instance with the scandals over the collapse of the investment firm of Barlow Clowes and the plundering of the Mirror pension fund.[5] While life insurers have been benefiting by a shift from public to private pension provision, they have suffered as a result of a drop in share prices that has affected their ability to deliver the level of performance expected by customers. There has also been sharp criticism of their products and allegations that some employees were improperly advised about shifting from company pension schemes into private pension schemes or were encouraged to purchase endowment life policies in the expectation that they would produce returns adequate to pay off mortgages on properties. The result has been that customers now have less confidence in long-term savings, such as with-profits insurance contracts.

Investors have often regarded financial failure as the fault of government or a regulator. Not infrequently, the result, as has been seen, is reform, which although often justified does create both the impression that government acknowledges its responsibility and the expectation that it will step in when problems arise. In other words, the problem is characterised as a failure in regulation rather than as an acceptable risk of investing in a free market. Investors–including those who take out insurance–may, therefore, be encouraged to the belief that investment carries no risk, which is rather dangerous since risk (that is, the potential for an investment to fall as well as rise) is regarded as fundamental to the proper functioning of the free market. How does government balance the free market, which requires winners and losers and in which all must bear the consequences of their own choices, with a system where all will be winners or, at least, none will be substantial losers (private pensions will be paid, the sick will be cared for)? The consequence of this dilemma has been that those ministers, who championed the free market and sought to roll back the state, have introduced an unprecedented level of regulation: for instance, the Banking Acts 1979 and 1987, the Building Societies Act 1986, the Lloyd's Act 1982, the Insurance Companies Act 1982, the Financial Services Act 1986 and the Financial Services and Markets Act

---

[5] After much resistance on its part, the government felt compelled to assist those who had lost money through the actions of Barlow Clowes. The scandal involving the removal of money from the Mirror newspaper pension fund by its former owner, Robert Maxwell, rumbles on and seems to be endlessly repeated.

2000.[6] This has led to complaints from the industry about the cost of compliance, although this does not mean the industry opposes regulation: some financial firms clearly welcome regulation where it has reassured customers, and so encouraged investment, and has excluded those firms which, through insufficient skill or poor quality products, are viewed as damaging the reputation of the rest of the market (and perhaps of undercutting the better established firms).

The difficulty has been to translate all these issues into regulation. The central concern of the Insurance Companies Act 1982 remained the financial viability of insurers rather than direct protection for the insured, although the Policyholders Protection Act 1975 did establish a fund to compensate certain categories of insureds in the event of the failure of an insurer.[7] Moreover, insureds were given additional rights: for instance, insurers were obliged to provide certain types of information, particularly, as with some life assurance, where an element of investment was involved; cooling-off periods were instituted allowing some insurance contracts to be cancelled by the insured[8]; and simpler, cheaper and quicker complaints procedures were introduced. Significantly, although some of these changes were the result of law reform, it was the industry itself that introduced the most important measures of consumer protection, such as the ombudsman scheme and the Statements of Insurance Practice, which were self-imposed limits on the contracting power of the insurers.

Further scandals and changes in the financial services industry made it evident to many by the late 1990s that a rethink was required. The regulatory structure had become too complex, it had also failed to keep up with developments in the industry and it was perceived as not providing protection to consumers.[9] The method of regulation used was to divide financial services into different sectors–insurance, deposit-taking, building societies, pensions and so forth–and to give each sector its own supervisory regime and its own supervisor: for instance, insurance business was regulated under the 1982 Act by the Department of Trade and Industry, banking under the Banking Act 1987 by the Bank of England, the building societies under the Building Societies Act 1986 by the Building Societies Commission, and the investment industry under the Financial Services Act 1986 by a number of regulators. This had been the result of the piecemeal development of regulation. By the late 1980s, there were ten financial regulators (more, depending on which bodies were included in the count). This fragmented system of regulation did not work because, as has been seen, the financial industry did not operate in neat, self-contained segments: multi-functional financial conglomerates had emerged. A single financial institution or group was subject to several regulators and the inquiry into problems at Equitable Life indicated some of the difficulties this caused when it noted that two regulators had quite different interpretations of the facts leading to the company's problems.[10]

---

[6] This is only a partial list of the primary legislation and it omits the huge volume of secondary legislation.
[7] See also Policyholders Protection Act 1997. A new scheme has been put in place under the Financial Services and Markets Act 2000, which is discussed in more detail later in this ch.
[8] See below.
[9] The headline scandals concerned the Mirror pension fund, private pension and endowment insurance misselling and the spectacular failures of Bank of Credit and Commerce International and Barings Bank.
[10] Parliamentary Commissioner for Administration, *The Prudential Regulation of Equitable Life*, 4th report, HC 809 (sess 2002–03); The Rt Hon Lord Penrose, *Report of the Equitable Life Inquiry*, HC 290 (2004).

2. International regulation

In addition to purely domestic issues, by the 1970s there were calls for international agreement on the regulation of financial services firms, which led to reforms that have had an important impact on regulation in the UK. Concerns had emerged as a result of the growth of multinationalism (firms operating in more than one country through branches, subsidiaries or direct cross-border selling) and of globalisation (the interconnectedness of financial markets in different countries). In a global market firms are not constrained by the same national boundaries that limit the authority of regulators. The failure of two large international banks in the 1970s brought a realisation of the interdependence of national financial markets and led to efforts to improve (or, in many countries, to establish) regulation and to develop co-operation between regulators. Central bankers and bank regulators from the richest nations set up the Basel Committee in 1974. This committee has no formal legal authority, but the economic and political power wielded by its member countries means that its proposals on bank regulation have acquired a powerful influence over national laws. The committee developed the idea that the supervisor from the state in which the bank is authorised (the home state) should take the lead in supervising that bank's global operations. Left without qualification this would have rested a little too much confidence in the home supervisor for the liking of many countries and so Basel recognised that the host nation (the place where a bank operates) should have a role; in particular, it should be able to restrict the bank's operations if not satisfied about the quality of the supervision. The committee also emphasised the importance of encouraging the exchange of information between supervisors. By the 1980s the committee had, however, become more ambitious and had moved on to establishing minimum standards in various aspects of bank regulation, in particular, in relation to capital adequacy.

The Basel Committee's work encouraged the establishment of the International Association of Insurance Supervisors (IAIS) in 1994. The IAIS has a broader base than Basel with members from around 100 countries supplemented by a large number of observers from the industry and professional associations. Like Basel, the IAIS has issued 28 core principles as benchmarks for an effective supervisory system.[11] These are supplemented by sets of principles on particular issues, such as the supervision of reinsurers, Internet insurers and international insurance companies, and capital adequacy and solvency. The expectation is that national supervisors will use these standards, and certainly the International Monetary Fund employs them when undertaking its Financial System Stability Assessments.[12] The IAIS has also co-operated with Basel and the International Organisation of Securities Commissions through the Joint Forum, which deals with issues of mutual interest, such as the regulation of financial conglomerates.

The European Union has been involved in these initiatives, although the reforms introduced by the EU have often exceeded the requirements imposed by membership

---

[11] IAIS, *Insurance Core Principles and Methodology* (2003) www.iaisweb.org
[12] International Monetary Fund, *United Kingdom: Financial System Stability Assessment*, country report 03/46 (Washington DC, IMF, 2003), Pt VII.

of the global organisations. There have been EU directives on life assurance and general insurance, and on narrower issues, such as motor vehicle liability insurance,[13] legal expenses insurance,[14] aviation insurance,[15] credit and suretyship insurance,[16] accounting[17] and the insolvency of insurers.[18] Much of this legislation has been enacted with the objective of establishing a single market in the European Union.[19] The single market seeks to give EU citizens access to a wide range of insurance products and to enable insurers authorised in one member state to operate freely in other member states, although it has been suggested that this project appears more concerned to facilitate access to markets for insurers than to provide consumer protection.[20] The single market requires the breaking down of regulatory and tax barriers, which inhibited free access to markets. In addition, each state is required to have in place certain minimum standards.[21] This has been prompted, in part, by fear that there might be a 'race to the bottom' in which countries would encourage firms to set up by offering weak regulation and that this might have disastrous consequences if poorly regulated firms were able to operate throughout the EU. The minimum standards also recognise the importance for consumer confidence in the single market of establishing a minimum level of rights. At the same time, setting only minimum standards is an acknowledgement of the difficulty in obtaining the agreement of the member states to a single set of laws that would apply across the EU.

In establishing the single market European law has used separate measures for non-life and life insurance because of the fundamental differences between them, in particular, the role of life insurance in long-term investment. The first wave of directives on non-life insurance in 1973 and on life insurance in 1979 gave insurers established in one member state the right to undertake business in other member states.[22] The directives also prohibited new insurers from offering both life and non-life business,[23] although existing insurers that undertook life and non-life business were permitted to continue, subject to certain requirements with regard to their life business.[24] These directives still obliged insurers to obtain authorisation to operate outside their home state, but prohibited a member state from discriminating against insurers coming from another member state. The Second Directives were influenced by a series of decisions of the European Court of Justice in 1986 that had

---

[13] Eg, directives 73/239, 88/357, 90/232, 90/618, 2000/26.
[14] Dir 87/344.
[15] Reg No 785/2004.
[16] Dir 87/343.
[17] Dir 91/674.
[18] Dir 2001/17.
[19] Generally, R Merkin and A Rodger, *EC Insurance Law* (London, Longman, 1997); A McGee, *The Single Market in Insurance: Breaking Down the Barriers* (Aldershot, Ashgate & Dartmouth, 1998). FSMA, ss 31, 37, sch 3 and 4 and the Financial Services and Markets Act 2000 (EEA Passport Rights) Regulations 2001 (2001/2511) implement some of the key parts of the machinery of the single market.
[20] EC Commission, *Communication from the Commission to the Council, the European Parliament, the European Economic and Social Committee and the Committee of the Regions*, COM (2003) 238.
[21] Dir 92/49, rec 18.
[22] Directives 73/239, 73/240, 79/267 (repealed by 2002/83).
[23] It was commonplace for a UK insurer (but not an insurer elsewhere in Europe) to offer both types of business.
[24] Dir 79/267, art 13.

been aimed to combine liberalisation of the market with consumer protection.[25] These directives developed the passport idea in which an insurer authorised in one member state would be permitted to supply insurance services in all states. Supervision of the insurer was to be conducted mainly by the home state, although the host state retained a role. The directives also aimed to focus on consumer protection by distinguishing consumer from commercial insurance. This was achieved in respect of non-life insurance by separating large risks, which are, broadly, large-scale commercial risks, from mass risks, which are consumer products.[26] In life insurance a distinction was drawn between those policies that originated from an approach made to the insured through, for instance, advertising, and those policies that were initiated by the insured, with consumer protection measures being targeted at the first type.[27] The Third Directives extended the notion of the single passport.[28] An insurer, which is authorised and has its head office in one member state, is permitted to sell its products in another member state, either directly or by setting up a presence in that state, without requiring fresh authorisation. For instance, if an insurer from another member state undertakes business in the UK through a branch, the establishment conditions must be satisfied, which in essence means that the consent of the home state must be obtained to the branch being established in the UK; if the intention is to provide services in the UK from offices outside the country, the service conditions must be met, which merely require the home state to be notified by the insurer of its intention to provide such services.[29] The FSA will be informed of the home state's consent to the establishment of a branch or will receive notification from the home state of the insurer's intention to provide services in the UK. Since the Third Directives, the Financial Services Action Plan has been established to speed up the completion of the single market.[30] Some of the changes introduced as a result of the plan are specific to a particular sector,[31] while others are broader in their impact.[32] In 2001 the Commission sought to improve customer confidence in the single market by establishing a network (FIN-NET) to help consumers, who are dissatisfied with a

---

[25] *Commission v France* [1986] ECR 3663; *Commission v Denmark* [1986] ECR 3713; *Commission v Germany* [1986] ECR 3755; *Commission v Ireland* [1986] ECR 3817. See D Edward, 'Establishment and Services: An Analysis of the Insurance Cases' (1987) 12 *EL Rev* 231; RW Hodgin (1987) *CML Rev* 273.

[26] Dir 88/357.

[27] Dir 90/619 (repealed by 2002/83).

[28] Directives 92/49 and 92/96.

[29] The host state may impose conditions on an insurer seeking to exercise its passport rights when it is 'in the interests of the general good' of that state: see, eg, Third Non-Life Directive 92/49, recitals 19, 20, 24 and 29; arts 28 and 32(4). However, the European Court of Justice has construed this exception narrowly. For a measure to be justified as in the general good it must not have been harmonised at EC level, must not be discriminatory, must be clearly justified as being in the general interest, objectively necessary and proportionate to the aim sought, and must not reproduce the rules applied in the insurer's home state. Practices that may be justified as in the general good include enforcing professional codes of conduct in a particular member state and prohibiting the marketing practice of cold calling.

[30] EC Commission, *Financial Services: Implementing the Framework for Financial Markets: Action Plan*, COM (1999) 232.

[31] For instance, the introduction of new solvency requirements for insurers (Solvency II): European Commission, *Note to the Solvency Subcommittee*, MARKT/2539/03 (2003); the regulation of electronic commerce in relation to insurance: European Commission, *Electronic Commerce and Insurance*, MARKT/2541/03 (2003).

[32] See, eg, the adoption of the Fair Value Accounting Directive, which implemented the International Accounting Standard as from 1 January 2005.

financial service, obtain an out-of-court settlement where the supplier is established in another member state.

Another important reform is the introduction of Solvency II, which will incorporate into EU insurance regulation the method adopted in banking by the agreement on capital adequacy known as Basel II. The hope is that it will bring the regulator's view of what capital and solvency requirements are necessary closer to those that the insurer sees as appropriate to the task of carrying the business forward. This is to be achieved by regulatory measurement systems that are more carefully tuned to the risks each insurer runs and that acknowledge the measures a firm has in place to mitigate those risks. In addition, the discipline of the market is to be given a sharper edge through improvements in the supply of information about risks and risk management within a firm, and the firm's management is to be required to put risk control at the centre of their day-to-day activities. Yet, even ahead of the introduction of these new systems, it has been estimated that the measurements methods in Solvency II together with the new International Financial Reporting Standards will increase capital requirements and may, thereby, expose a massive shortfall among the less capital-rich life assurance companies. It is suggested that companies will be forced to reduce their risk profile by, for instance, reducing equity investments and to change to more conservative products with lower guarantees. It may even push companies into extinction.[33]

One danger with international 'agreements' is that they are controlled by the richest nations and reflect their interests. So, while such agreements have undoubted benefits, it is important that the role of regulation in protecting legitimate national interests is properly considered and not simply dismissed as an obstacle in the way of open markets. The objective of these meetings of international regulators must be to construct methods of regulation that facilitate economic growth and that provide legitimate levels of protection for international systems, for individual states, for firms and for consumers from the problems that can arise across borders through the failure of a firm, or of a financial system, or of a national regulatory process. It might be argued that stepping beyond measures designed to reduce global systemic risks should be resisted since it interferes with legitimate competition between the regulatory regimes offered by different countries and might affect the variety and price of products. On the other hand, differences between regulatory systems might end with consumers being seduced to buy products from a firm established in a state where regulation and consumer protection are weaker than might be expected. A separate problem with these international initiatives–including those in the EU–is that they continue to construct regulatory regimes based on a model of the financial services industry as composed of separate compartments: so, although there are initiatives to cope with multi-functional conglomerates,[34] the form of regulation adopted in European directives and in initiatives from IAIS, Basel and IOSCO adheres to the traditional divisions of banking, insurance, investment and so forth.

---

[33] H Bjerre-Nielsen, *Regulating a Single Insurance Market* (Committee of European Insurance and Occupational Pensions Supervisors, 2004); J Lowry and P Rawlings, *Insurance Law: Cases and Materials* (Oxford, Hart Publishing, 2004) 63–5; *Financial World*, April 2003, 42; KPMG, *Capital Assessment Practice Among UK Insurers* (London, 2004); A Stevens (Mercer Oliver Wyman), *Life at the End of the Tunnel? The Capital Crisis in the European Life Sector* (London, 2004).
[34] See, eg, Dir 2002/87.

3. The Financial Services and Markets Act 2000

3.1 The Financial Services Authority

Shortly after its election in 1997 the Labour government began to reshape the regulatory environment of the financial sector. This led to the Financial Services and Markets Act 2000 (FSMA),[35] which established the Financial Services Authority (FSA) as the regulator for most of the financial services industry and which combined prudential supervision (by which is meant, broadly, supervision aimed at reducing the likelihood of a firm becoming insolvent) with a conduct of business regime (that is, the rules on how the firms deal with those who buy their products).

The FSA is an extremely powerful body with a range of functions that seems to run counter to the idea of the separation of powers.[36] First, it is a legislator. In broad terms, FSMA sets out the functions and powers of the FSA, and the FSA lays down the procedures it will follow and the considerations it will take into account in the exercise of those functions and powers (see Part X, FSMA for the rule-making powers). Secondly, the FSA investigates breaches of the regulatory regime and has powers to gather information. Thirdly, it is a judicial and enforcement authority ruling on breaches and imposing penalties (eg, sections 205–211 and Part XXVI, FSMA). Fourthly, the FSA acts as a prosecutor with respect to offences under FSMA and related legislation (eg, sections 401–2). Finally, it was given responsibility for establishing a compensatory mechanism to cover those who suffer loss when an authorised person is unable to meet claims (sections 212–24). The FSA subsequently set up Financial Compensation Scheme.

Attempts have been made to balance the omnipotence of the FSA, although the effectiveness of some of these is open to debate. The mechanisms created include an independent Complaints Commissioner to whom complaints against the FSA can be brought (schedule 1, para 7) and the Practitioner and Consumer Panels with whom the FSA must consult and whose representations it must take into account (ss 8–11). The FSA is required to engage in public consultation before issuing rules, statements or codes of practice (eg, sections 65 and 155). The Treasury may appoint an independent person to conduct a review of the 'economy, efficiency and effectiveness with which the Authority has used its resources in discharging its functions' (section 12(1)), although this is specifically not concerned with the merits of the FSA's general policy or principles in pursuing regulatory objectives (section 12(3)).[37] The Treasury also has a limited power to appoint an independent inquiry (sections 14–18).[38] A common criticism is that these mechanisms are cumbersome and place huge burdens on industry. A different complaint is aimed at the Financial Services and Markets Tribunal. Under FSMA, a person or firm that has been disciplined or refused authorisation by the FSA may seek a fresh hearing before the Tribunal, which is an

---

[35] Pronounced 'fizma'.

[36] For general provisions about the FSA, its constitution and status, see FSMA, ss 1, 2, 7, sch 1.

[37] On the meaning of 'regulatory objectives', see FSMA, s 2(2), which is discussed below.

[38] In 2003 the Treasury instructed the Office of Fair Trading to conduct a two-year review into the impact of the FSMA and, in particular, to look at the impact of the Act on competition.

independent body[39] and can direct the FSA to take a particular course of action.[40] The infrequency with which this right of appeal has been used appeared to confirm views expressed during the Bill's passage that a regulated firm would be reluctant to avail itself of such an appeal because of the bad publicity it might involve and the consequent effect on its business.[41] However, the recent appeal brought before the Tribunal by the Legal & General Assurance Society Ltd against a fine imposed by the FSA suggests that firms may not suffer the sort of reputational damage that had been feared, indeed the appeal seems to have been seen by Legal & General as a way of restoring its reputation, which it felt had been wrongly tarnished by the imposition of a large fine.

The FSA's rules, statements of principle, directions and general guidance are to be found in the FSA *Handbook of Rules and Guidance* (Handbook), which is available through the authority's website.[42] It is divided into blocks and each block is sub-divided into sourcebooks, which provide sources of the FSA's requirements and guidance, and manuals, which contain processes to be followed. The first block in the Handbook is High Level Standards. This consists of Principles for Businesses (PRIN), Senior Management Arrangements, Systems and Controls (SYSC), Threshold Conditions (COND), Statements of Principle and Code of Practice for Approved Persons (APER), The Fit and Proper Test for Approved Persons (FIT), and General Provisions (GEN). The second block is titled Business Standards and includes Integrated Prudential sourcebook (PRU), Interim Prudential Sourcebook for Insurers (IPRU(INS)), Conduct of Business (COB), Insurance: Conduct of Business (ICOB), Client Assets (CASS), Training and Competence (TC), and Money Laundering (ML). The third block is called Regulatory Processes and includes Authorisation (AUTH), Supervision (SUP), Enforcement (ENF), and Decision Making (DEC). The fourth block is Redress. It includes Dispute Resolution: Complaints (DISP), Compensation (COMP), and Complaints against the FSA (COAF). Next are the specialist sourcebooks, which include Electronic Commerce Directive (ECO), Lloyd's (LLD), and Professional Firms (PROF). References to the sourcebooks and manuals in this chapter will be noted using these abbreviations.

Each sourcebook and manual opens with an explanation of the types of firms and persons to whom it applies and its purpose, and similar information is provided throughout the text. The sourcebook or manual is divided into chapters, the chapters are divided into sections and the sections into numbered paragraphs. Each paragraph has its regulatory status indicated by a letter in the margin. The most common are 'R' and 'G'. 'R' stands for rules made by the FSA under FSMA, section 138 or sections 140–7 and breach of a rule may render the firm liable to an enforcement action. 'G' usually indicates guidance issued under section 157 and is used, among other things, to explain the implications of provisions and to recommend particular courses of action. However, guidance is not binding on those to whom FSMA applies or the courts, nor does it have any evidential effect, so that a breach of the guidance does

---

[39] Established under FSMA, s 132. On the Tribunal's constitution and procedures, see FSMA, 132–137, sch 13; DEC 5 (see below). For an example of a right of appeal to the Tribunal, see s 67.
[40] FSMA, s 133.
[41] A Hayes, 'Open Justice at the Tribunal?' [2002] *Butterworths Journal of Banking and Financial Law* 427.
[42] FSA, *Handbook of Rules and Guidance* (2005) at www.fsa.org.uk. For a guide to the Handbook, see *Reader's Guide: An Introduction to the Handbook* (2005) at www.fsa.gov.uk.

not mean there has been a breach of a rule, although the FSA will presume that a firm which follows guidance is in compliance with the relevant rule.[43] The General Provisions (GEN) manual in the Handbook states that, 'Every provision in the Handbook must be interpreted in the light of its purpose.' (GEN 2.2.1) That purpose is to be gathered from the provision itself and its context. This manual also notes that all communications required by the Handbook to be 'in writing' may, unless a contrary intention appears, be given through electronic media (GEN 2.2.14).

3.2 Regulatory objectives

The FSA must discharge its functions, 'so far as is reasonably possible,' in a way 'which is compatible with the regulatory objectives and which the Authority considers most appropriate for the purpose of meeting those objectives.' (section 2(1)). The regulatory objectives are listed in section 2(2): '(a) market confidence; (b) public awareness; (c) the protection of consumers; and (d) the reduction of financial crime.' These objectives are so broad as to render them impossible to translate into precise responses to particular situations, but that is not their purpose. Their purpose is to set a direction for the FSA. The FSA does not have an entirely free hand in seeking to achieve the regulatory objectives since it is required to have regard to the following considerations (s 2 (3)):

(a)   the need to use its resources in the most efficient and economic way;

(b)   the responsibilities of those who manage the affairs of authorised persons;

(c)   the principle that a burden or restriction which is imposed on a person, or on the carrying on of an activity, should be proportionate to the benefits, considered in general terms, which are expected to result from the imposition of that burden or restriction;

(d)   the desirability of facilitating innovation in connection with regulated activities;

(e)   the international character of financial services and markets and the desirability of maintaining the competitive position of the United Kingdom;

(f)   the need to minimise the adverse effects on competition that may arise from anything done in the discharge of those functions;

(g)   the desirability of facilitating competition between those who are subject to any form of regulation by the Authority.

Each of the regulatory objectives is explained in sections 3–6 in fairly broad terms. Market confidence is hardly defined at all: FSMA refers only to 'maintaining confidence in the financial system [of the UK]' (section 3(1), (2)). Nevertheless, it is clearly regarded by the FSA as a key regulatory objective.[44] The public awareness objective involves the obligation to promote public understanding of the financial system including its benefits and risks (s 4). By protection of consumers is meant 'securing the appropriate degree of protection for consumers' (section 5(1)).[45] This means balancing protection from the risk involved with recognition that it may be appropriate for customers to bear some or all of that risk: FSMA refers to 'the general principle that consumers should take responsibility for their decisions' (section 5(2)(d)). In

---

[43] See also, s 395 and sch 1, para 7.

[44] J. Tiner, 'Reform of the Insurance Industry,' Insurance Sector Conference, April 2005 (www.fsa.gov.uk).

[45] For the definition of consumer: see s 135 (s 5(3)).

construing what is appropriate in this context the FSA must consider the degrees of risk involved in different types of transactions and the degrees of expertise possessed by different types of consumers and their needs for advice and information (section 5(2)(a)–(c)). The reduction of financial crime objective relates to the extent that it is possible for a business[46] to be 'used for a purpose connected with financial crime' (section 6(1)). This addresses the risk of people–those on the inside and out-side–stealing from the firm, or manipulating company accounts in order to create a false oppression ('financial engineering'), or using a firm for crime, such as money laundering (ML).

The FSA has developed its method of working from the regulatory objectives and the principles of good regulation.[47] First, the FSA rests its authorisation and supervi-sion procedures on an assessment of the risks posed by a firm or individual to the regulatory objectives: what is the probability that a risk will materialise and what impact would there be if it did materialise? There will be an assessment of: the degree to which risks related to the firm or individual, if they were to materialise, would damage market confidence; how far–if at all-the firm or individual poses a risk to achieving public understanding; the extent to which consumers may be affected were there to be misconduct or failure within the firm; and the incidence and significance of any financial crime that might be perpetrated through or by the firm. If permis-sion is granted, this risk assessment process will also enable the FSA to be proportionate in its allocation of resources to supervision of the firm (AUTH 1.4.4).[48] Secondly, the FSA ensures that a firm meets certain standards in the conduct of its business. These are explained in the Principles for Businesses part of the Hand-book (PRIN): it must conduct its business with integrity, maintain adequate financial resources, deal with regulators in an open and co-operative way, and treat customers fairly.[49] Much of the FSA's approach is found in this important document and the eleven Principles it propounds; indeed, the other parts of the Handbook can be seen as working through the implications of these Principles. Thirdly, the FSA places responsibility on the firm's management for ensuring that the firm complies with the regulations: 'It is senior management and not the regulator who is engaged in their business day in day out and it is right that they should accept the regulatory responsi-bility which comes with managing their business.'[50] The FSA is primarily concerned with the firm's management of the risks it poses to the regulatory objectives set out in FSMA. This is separate from the firm's interest in its own profitability, even if there is much overlap between these two matters. Fourthly, the FSA does not seek to achieve a zero-fail regime: firms will fail and insureds will be sold the wrong products without there being a flaw in regulation. The FSA is seeking to support a competitive market place, which will encourage insurers to innovate and to be efficient, and to establish a prudential environment in which insureds feel reasonably safe and yet are able to take risks. As Howard Davies put it when he was chair of the FSA, it comes down to the

---

[46] Either one authorised under FSMA or one that is illegally operating without authorisation.

[47] FSA, *A New Regulator for a New Millennium* (2000); J Tiner, 'The FSA's Radical New Approach to Insurance Regulation' in Lowry and Rawlings, *Insurance Law: Cases and Materials*, above n 33, at 54–9.

[48] The FSA also considers the impact of external events and publishes an annual review of its assessment of the risk to the regulatory objectives posed by economic, financial and social developments. The most recent of these is FSA, *Financial Risk Outlook 2005* (2005).

[49] For further discussion of the Principles for Businesses, see below.

[50] J Tiner, 'The FSA's Radical New Approach to Insurance Regulation,' above n 47.

issue of 'just how safe one wishes to make the industry.'[51] The aim of regulation is not to prevent insurers from taking risks with investment or to shield insureds against market risk. So 'a corporate failure is not necessarily a failure of regulation. It may simply be a sign that market forces are working.'[52] Yet this approach is likely to be challenged by the common reaction among investors to loss of money following the collapse of a firm, namely, that it should not have happened, and therefore the regulator must have failed in its duty by allowing it to happen. Fifthly, the FSA places a good deal of emphasis on tailoring its work to different circumstances. For instance, the FSA is more likely to step in to protect consumers than to protect participants in the wholesale insurance market where the parties are skilled. In relation to the latter, the view is taken that a greater reliance can be placed on the market developing solutions to problems as they arise so that the FSA need only intervene if there is clear evidence of market failure. Finally, as has already been seen, the FSA is obliged to be transparent in its work: so, for instance, it must consult and engage in a cost–benefit analysis before implementing rules.

3.3 General prohibition and authorisation

Section 19 of the Financial Services and Markets Act 2000 contains the general prohibition: no one, who is not an authorised[53] or exempt person,[54] may carry on (or purport to carry on) a regulated activity in the UK (see section 418; AUTH 2.4).[55] An authorised person is someone who has obtained Part IV permission,[56] or a European Economic Area (EEA) or Treaty firm that qualifies for authorisation,[57] or someone who is otherwise authorised by a provision of FSMA. A regulated activity is an activity that is within the list in schedule 2 of FSMA, that is specified by the

---

[51] Howard Davies, 'Rational Expectations–What Should the Market, and Policyholders Expect from Insurance Regulation?' Airmic Annual Lecture, 29 January 2002, in Lowry and Rawlings, *Insurance Law: Cases and Materials*, above n 33, at 52.

[52] Ibid, at 53.

[53] The Society of Lloyd's is an authorised person: s 315(1); see below. Someone authorised under the Insurance Companies Act 1982 (s 3 or 4) retains their authorisation: Financial Services and Markets Act 2000 (Transitional Provisions) (Authorised Persons, etc) Order 2001 (2001/2636), art 14.

[54] The term 'person' refers to a legal person and so includes a company . On the definition of an exempt person: see FSMA, ss 38, 39(1); Financial Services and Markets Act 2000 (Exemption) Order 2001 (2001/1201), sch, para 43 (trade unions and employers organisations that provide certain benefits to members) and 14 (someone who ceased to be an underwriter at Lloyd's before 24 Dec 1996); SUP 12.2.2. Those who provide motor breakdown services do not require authorisation: Financial Services and Markets Act 2000 (Regulated Activities) Order 2001 (2001/544), art 12.

[55] On the meaning of regulated activity, see below.

[56] See below.

[57] See ss 31, 34 and 35 and schs 3 and 4. The distinction is between firms from those states which are signatories to the EEA agreement but not members of the EU (EEA firms) and firms from states which are members of the EU (Treaty firms). The EEA agreement was signed at Oporto in 1992 (coming into force in 2004) between the European Community, the Member States of the EU and the seven member states of the European Free Trade Agreement (EFTA). Of the EFTA states, Switzerland later withdrew and three of the other countries subsequently joined the EU, leaving Norway, Iceland and Liechtenstein. In broad terms, the agreement enables these non-EU countries to participate in the Internal Market of the EU, although it precludes them from engaging in the decision-making process. Notification of an EEA firm intending to do business in the UK or a UK firm intending to take advantage of the passport system to do business in Europe is dealt with by the Passport Notification team at the FSA: see AUTH 5 and Supp Appendix 3; also, ECO.

Treasury and that is carried on as a business (section 22).[58] The list in schedule 2 includes a contract of insurance (para 20) and under the Financial Services and Markets Act 2000 (Regulated Activities) Order 2001 effecting or carrying out a contract of insurance is a specified activity.[59] The business element depends on the particular circumstances, but it includes consideration of the degree of continuity of the activity, the presence of a commercial element, the scale of the activity and the proportion it bears to other activities carried on by the person that do not require to be regulated. Insurance mediation is only a business if carried on for remuneration (AUTH 2.3.2(4), 2.3.3).

A person, who is acting in the course of business and who is not either authorised or acting with the approval of an authorised person, may not invite or induce another to engage in an investment activity (section 21),[60] and breach of the general prohibition contained in section 19 is a criminal offence (sections 23–5). An agreement made by someone in breach of the general prohibition is unenforceable against the other party. That other party is entitled to recover any money or property paid or transferred under the agreement and to be compensated for any loss caused by parting with it (sections 26–8. See also, section 30(2)–(4)). Where someone, who is authorised under FSMA, undertakes a regulated activity that lies outside the limits of their authorisation, this amounts to a contravention of the Act, but, while they may be liable to a disciplinary sanction imposed by the FSA, it does not render them guilty of an offence, or make any transaction void, although it may give rise to an action for breach of statutory duty (section 20(1), (2)).[61]

Both the framework within which the FSA must work when granting, suspending, varying and withdrawing authorisation and the rights of applicants or authorised persons affected by decisions on these matters are set out in Part IV of FSMA. The FSA is empowered to give permission (known as 'Part IV permission') to carry on a regulated activity (section 42(2)), but is required to ensure that the authorised person 'will satisfy and continue to satisfy, the threshold conditions in relation to all of the regulated activities for which he has or will have permission' (section 41(2)).[62] These threshold conditions are contained in schedule 6 (see section 41(1)) and are the subject of a sourcebook in the FSA's Handbook titled Threshold Conditions (COND).

The first threshold condition is that, if the regulated activity involves effecting contracts of insurance, the authorised person must be a body corporate, registered friendly society or member of Lloyd's (schedule 6, para 1(1)).[63] Secondly, where the authorised person is a body corporate constituted under UK law, its head office and registered office, if any, must be in the UK (schedule 6, para 2(1); COND 1 Annex 1 and 2). This aims to prevent problems of supervision caused by a company having its

---

[58] See s 419.

[59] SI 2001/544, para 75; also sch 1.

[60] The term 'engaging in investment activity' is defined as, among other things, 'entering or offering to enter into an agreement the making or performance of which by either party constitutes a controlled activity': s 21(8). See further, s 20(9), (10), sch 2, and on 'controlled activity', see below 3.4.

[61] A limited right of action for breach of statutory duty does exist under s 20(3), see Financial Services and Markets Act 2000 (Rights of Action) Regulations 2000 (SI 2001/2256), para 4.

[62] This stipulation does not, however, restrict the FSA from taking such steps as it considers necessary to secure the regulatory objective of protecting consumers: FSMA, s 42(3).

[63] Requirements imposed by the First Non-Life Directive (73/239/EEC), art 8(1) and First Life Directive (79/267/EEC), art 8(1). See also, COND 2.1;

head office in the UK while being authorised elsewhere (COND 2.2.2). There is no definition of 'head office' in any of the relevant legislation, however, the FSA has taken the view that it need not refer to the place of incorporation, or where the firm conducts most of its business, or to the place where its central management and administration are located (COND 2.2.3). If a firm authorised in the UK is carrying on motor vehicle liability insurance business, it must have a claims agent in each of the other EEA states (schedule 6, para 2A).

The third threshold condition is that, if the authorised person has close links with another person, the FSA must be satisfied that this will not inhibit effective supervision and that, if the other person is subject to the laws of a country outside the European Economic Area, those laws will not prevent effective supervision. By 'close links' is meant that the other firm is the parent or subsidiary of the authorised firm, or is the parent of a subsidiary of the authorised firm, or is a subsidiary of the parent of the authorised firm, or the other firm controls 20 per cent of the voting rights or capital of the authorised firm, or the authorised firm controls 20 per cent of the voting rights or capital of the other firm (schedule 6, para 3). It is worth noting that the FSA may have regard to anyone who has, or is likely to have, a relationship that is considered relevant with an applicant or with an authorised person when determining whether to grant permission or to vary or cancel an existing permission (section 49(1)). A key concern here is that the FSA receives adequate information from all these parties to enable it to assess whether the regulatory requirements are being met (COND 2.3 and 2 Annex 1).

The fourth threshold condition requires the FSA to be satisfied that the authorised person has adequate resources to conduct the regulated activity (schedule 6, para 4). By 'adequate' is meant 'sufficient in terms of quantity, quality and availability,' while 'resources' refers not only to financial resources but to, for instance, the systems, staff and anyone related to the firm, such as directors, controllers or those with close links (PRIN 3 and 4, see below). As part of this condition, the FSA will expect an applicant for authorisation to present an appropriate business plan (COND 2.4). Fifthly, the FSA must be convinced that the authorised person 'is a fit and proper person.' Consideration is given to any relevant circumstances, including connections with any other person, the nature of the regulated activity and 'the need to ensure that his affairs are conducted soundly and prudently' (schedule 6, para 5). Obviously, the ability of a firm to satisfy this condition will be affected by the fitness of those who work in the firm and those who are closely connected with it so that, for instance, an unfit director may render the firm itself unfit. A firm will be expected to conduct its business with integrity and in compliance with the relevant standards of the FSA and of any other regulatory bodies. It must have competent and prudent management and must conduct its affairs with due skill, care and diligence (COND 2.5). The sixth threshold condition is that an insurer from a non-EEA state must appoint an authorised UK representative. The non-EEA insurer must be a body corporate formed under the law of the place where its head office is located and the person carrying on insurance business in the UK must comply with the requirements on assets held in the UK; if it wishes to conduct insurance business in other EEA states it must have such assets in those states as agreed between the FSA and the supervisor in those states.[64]

To elicit the information required to make a decision about authorisation the FSA has designed an application pack.[65] The pack reflects the fact that, although the FSA operates a single process for all those seeking Part IV permission, in practice the requirements vary between different applicants according to both the risks a firm poses to the regulatory objectives set out in FSMA, section 2(2) and the unregulated activities (that is, the activities for which authorisation is not required) it is going to undertake.[66] While all applicants must therefore, complete some elements of the pack, other sections are addressed only to firms engaged in certain types of business: so, for instance, there is a section for firms proposing to undertake insurance business. After receipt of the application the FSA may visit premises and arrange discussions with the management, and at this stage the FSA will discuss with prospective insurers the margin of solvency requirements (that is, the stipulation that an insurer must maintain a specified excess of assets over liabilities: AUTH 3.8.6; IPRU(INS) 2). The FSA will not grant permission to an insurer to conduct both long-term and general insurance business, unless the insurer's business is confined to reinsurance or its general insurance business only involves accident or/and sickness policies (AUTH 3.12.4). The FSA may grant or refuse permission, or may grant a narrower permission than is sought,[67] and it must describe the regulated activities for which permission is being given, although it may also specify limitations to that permission and requirements that must be fulfilled.[68] The FSA maintains a public register of those to whom it has granted Part IV permission (FSMA, s 347; AUTH 3.10).[69]

3.4 Approved person

An approved person is an individual within a firm who carries out a controlled function and is approved by the FSA as being fit and proper to carry out that function

---

[64] Financial Services and Markets Act 2000 (Variations of Threshold Conditions) Order 2001 (SI 2001/2507). See COND 2.6 and IPRU(INS), vols 1, 8. These requirements do not apply to a Swiss general insurer.

[65] Under s 51(3), the FSA is empowered to determine the form that the application process takes. For an overview of the expectations the FSA has of someone who is considering applying for Part IV permission, see AUTH 1.6. Note that those seeking permission in connection with insurance business are expected to have pre-application meetings with the FSA: AUTH 1.6.10(3). On the process involved in the application see AUTH 3.9.

[66] Guidance on the way in which the FSA will use its powers in relation to applications for Part IV permission is contained in AUTH 3.

[67] FSMA, s 42. It may also grant a broader permission than sought where, for instance, it becomes clear that the applicant is proposing to engage in activities that require a broader permission: AUTH 3.9.29.

[68] See FSMA, s 42; AUTH 3.6 and 3.7: eg, an insurer may be limited as to the type of business that can be undertaken (AUTH 3.6.3); or a firm may required to take or to refrain from taking a particular action (and such a requirement can extend to its non-regulated business) (AUTH 3.7)–so an insurer might be required to submit financial returns more frequently or engage only in reinsurance business (see AUTH 3.7.6). Before the imposition of a limitation or requirement, the firm is informed so that it can make representations to the FSA before the decision is finalised (AUTH 3.6.5 and 3.7.7). A firm can apply to have a limitation or requirement varied or removed: see AUTH 3.6.6, 3.7.8 and SUP 6.

[69] To deal with questions about, for instance, whether authorisation is required (see generally AUTH 2) the FSA has set up an Authorisation Enquiries team (AUTH 1.8).

(FSMA, section 59).[70] The holders of certain posts in an overseas, non-EEA company, which has UK branches, do not require approval by the FSA, although there must be notification to the FSA ('notified posts'): the worldwide chief executive of a firm where that person is situated outside the UK; the person within the overseas firm who has purely strategic responsibility for the UK; and the authorised UK representative of an insurer.[71] A controlled function is one that the FSA regards as key to the obligations under Part V of the FSMA, which deals with the performance of regulated activities. There are 27 controlled functions listed in SUP 10.4.5 (section 59(3)), and these are divided into categories. The first four of these categories are the 'significant influence functions' and involve the management of the business (SUP 10.5): governing functions (SUP 10.6), required functions (SUP 10.7), systems and controls functions (SUP 10.8) and significant management functions (SUP 10.9).[72]

The application to become an approved person must be submitted by or on behalf of the firm (section 60). Under section 61(1), the FSA can only grant approved person status if satisfied that the individual is fit and proper, and this is the subject matter of a manual titled, the Fit and Proper Test for Approved Persons (FIT). The FSA emphasises the need for honesty, integrity, reputation, competence, capability and financial soundness (FIT 1.3.1 and 2). These matters will be assessed within a context that takes account of the firm's activities and the markets in which it operates (FIT 1.3.2). An authorised person must take reasonable care to ensure that no one who is not approved by the FSA performs a controlled function in relation to the carrying out of a regulated activity by the authorised person, even if the firm has outsourced the performance of the controlled function (section 59(1), (2); SUP 10.12.13–10.12.14).[73] Finally, there are time limits within which the FSA must make a decision on an application, but it has been held by the Financial Services and Markets Tribunal that breach of these limits does not lead to approval by default, and although the applicant could apply for judicial review, the breach will not result in the FSA's authority to determine the application lapsing.[74]

The Statements of Principle for Approved Persons (APER) is issued under section 64(1) and contains seven Statements of Principle relating to the conduct of an approved person. They only apply in so far as the approved person is carrying out a controlled function (APER 1.2.9), that is, the standards do not apply to other aspects of the firm's business, although conduct in non-controlled functions could influence the FSA's opinion of whether someone is a fit and proper person (FIT). They must: (1) 'act with integrity' and (2) 'due skill, care and diligence'; (3) 'observe proper standards of market conduct'; (4) 'deal with the FSA' and other regulators in 'an open

---

[70] The Individual Approvals team at the FSA deals with the issue of whether an individual requires approval under the Act.

[71] There is a fourth type of position, but it relates to banks.

[72] In addition there are customer functions, but the firm that only does general insurance (see below n 75) business is not required to apply for individuals to be approved for consumer functions.

[73] Someone approved for one controlled function is not necessarily thereby approved for other controlled functions (SUP 10.4.3), although approval to undertake certain controlled functions will include other controlled functions (see SUP 10.6.2, 10.10.7 and 10.10.20).

[74] *David Thomas v Financial Services Authority*, 22–23 July 2004, reported at www.financeandtax-tribunals.gov.uk. The Tribunal took the view that, while, in *R (Davies and Others) v Financial Services Authority* [2004] 1 WLR 185, the High Court had said judicial review should be permitted sparingly, this was one situation where it would be appropriate because without a decision by the FSA the Tribunal could not intervene.

and cooperative way' and disclose such information as the FSA would reasonably expect to receive. These first four Statements of Principle apply to all approved persons (APER 3.1.7). In addition, an approved person performing significant influence functions, which means, broadly, managing and overseeing the business (SUP 10.4.5): (5) 'must take reasonable steps to ensure that the business of the firm for which he is responsible... is organised so that it can be controlled effectively,' (6) 'must exercise due skill, care and diligence in managing the business... for which he is responsible' and (7) 'must take reasonable steps to ensure that the business of the firm for which he is responsible... complies with the relevant requirements and standards of the regulatory system.' (See APER 3.3.1) The Code of Practice for Approved Persons is also part of this manual (APER 4; FSMA, section 64(2)). It sets out the types of conduct that will, in the FSA's opinion, constitute a breach of the Statements of Principle or, with regard to Statement of Principle 3, which indicates compliance. The approved person will only be in breach of a Statement of Principle where their conduct was deliberate or below a reasonable standard of behaviour (APER 3.1.4, ENF 11.5.3).

3.5 Appointed representative

An appointed representative (AR), who may be an individual or firm, carries on a regulated activity on behalf of an authorised firm and is exempt from seeking permission under FSMA, section 19 (FSMA, section 39; SUP 12.2.7), although the FSA must be notified (SUP 12.7). Anyone who performs a governing function in a firm that is acting as an AR and is carrying on general insurance business[75] must be an approved person. Where the general insurance business is incidental to the main business of the AR, such as a dentist who recommends a particular dental insurance policy offered by a specific firm, only one person in the firm need be approved, although that person must be a director or partner.

To become an AR the person must not be an authorised person, must have entered into a contract with an authorised person to carry on business described in the Appointed Representatives Regulations and must comply with any requirement in those regulations (SUP 12.2.2). In the contract, the authorised person must expressly agree to the AR acting on its behalf and accept responsibility for the AR's acts or omissions. Indeed, the AR's acts or omissions are deemed to be those of the authorised person (SUP 12.5, 12. 3.1–12.3.3; FSMA, section 39(3), (4), (6)). The authorised person can permit the AR to undertake regulated activities for which the authorised person is authorised in so far as these extend to the pre-contractual advising and arrangement of deals. The AR can also act in concluding and in the administration and performance of general insurance and pure protection contracts,[76] but cannot undertake these functions in relation to investment business.

---

[75] Broadly, general insurance means any contract of insurance other than long-term insurance: for the definition see, Financial Service and Markets Act 2000 (Regulated Activities) Order 2001 (ST 2001/544), sch 1.

[76] A pure protection product is a long-term insurance contract that is not an investment product. More particularly, it is a contract under which the benefit is paid on death (occurring within 10 years of the contract or before the insured life attains 70), or on illness, injury or infirmity and for which there is no surrender value (unless it is a single premium policy and the surrender value does not exceed the value of that premium): eg, critical illness insurance.

Before appointing an AR the authorised person must establish on reasonable grounds that the appointment will not prevent it from satisfying the threshold conditions and that the proposed AR is solvent, suitable and has no close links which would be likely to prevent the effective supervision of the AR by the authorised person. The authorised person must have adequate controls over the regulated activities performed by the AR and sufficient resources to monitor compliance. The authorised person must be ready to comply with the other requirements in SUP 12 (SUP 12.4.2) and make regular assessments as to the suitability of the AR to undertake the particular tasks assigned to it (SUP 12.4.1–12.4.5). The regulatory burden with respect to ARs, therefore, lies with those firms on whose behalf they act. As has been seen, the actions of the AR are deemed to be those of the authorised person, but in addition, such an action may also suggest that the authorised person is in breach of the requirement to maintain adequate systems and controls (see SYSC 3; SUP 12.6.7). The authorised person must ensure that the AR understands the regulatory provisions relevant to the authorised person's business, that the AR will provide sufficient access to its staff, premises and records to enable supervision by the authorised person, that it complies with the requirements of knowledge, ability and good repute set out in PRU 9.1.8 and 9.1.10, and that it is able to deliver the same level of protection to clients as if the clients had been dealt with by the authorised person itself (SUP 12.4.8–12.4.10). Finally, an AR may work for several principals, but a multiple principal agreement must be in place with all the principals and one must act as lead principal for dealing with complaints (SUP 12 12.4.5).

An 'introducer appointed representative' (IAR) is an AR whose appointment is limited to effecting introductions to the firm and distributing non-real-time financial promotions (see below 9.5.2) relating to the products available from the firm (SUP 12.2.8).[77] A dentist, who provides information on dental insurance and then passes details of interested clients to an authorised firm so that firm can arrange insurance, would need to be appointed as an IAR. The full AR regime does not apply, but an IAR must fulfil the qualifications of an AR and the obligations as between the authorised person and an IAR are the same as apply between an authorised person and an AR (SUP 12.2.8–12.2.10; SUP 12.4.6).

For the sake of completeness, and in order to distinguish them from introducer appointed representatives, mention should be made of 'introducers' and 'representatives'. An 'introducer' is an individual appointed by an authorised person or by the AR of an authorised person to effect introductions in the course of designated investment business and to distribute non-real-time financial promotions (see below). An introducer (unless also an IAR) is not an exempt person under FSMA, section 39, and so cannot carry on regulated activities on their own behalf, but must work in the name of the authorised person. Such a person does not come within the Approved Persons regime because they do not perform a controlled function (SUP 12 .2 .13). A 'representative' is someone appointed by a firm or an AR to advise on investments, arrange deals in investments or deal in investments as an agent.

---

[77] Terms of the contract of employment must limit the scope of the appointment to these matters: SUP 12.5.7. On financial promotions, see below 9.5.2.

4. High Level Standards

4.1 Principles for Businesses

The first block in the Handbook is entitled High Level Standards and applies to all those regulated by the FSA. The first manual in this block is the Principles for Businesses (PRIN). [78] Much of the rest of the Handbook rests on these Principles. They 'are a general statement of the fundamental obligations of firms under the regulatory system' (PRIN 1.1.2) and, in particular, they expand on the fit and proper requirement in Threshold Condition 5, although the implications of that requirement are not exhausted by the Principles. A firm applying for authorisation must be able and willing to abide by the Principles, and a breach of the Principles renders the firm liable to disciplinary sanctions, which include fines and the variation, suspension or termination of authorisation, and may lay open the issue of whether the firm is fit and proper (PRIN 1.1.4).

There are eleven Principles (PRIN 2.1.1). An authorised firm or person must (1) 'conduct its business with integrity' and (2) 'with due skill, care and diligence,' (3) 'take reasonable care to organise and control its affairs responsibly and effectively, with adequate risk management systems,' (4) 'maintain adequate financial resources,'" and (5) 'observe proper standards of market conduct'; it must 'pay due regard' both (6) 'to the interests of its customers and treat them fairly'[79] and (7) 'to the information needs of its clients, and communicate information to them in a way which is clear, fair and not misleading' (also ICOB 2.2.3, below); a firm (8) 'must manage conflicts of interest fairly' and (9) 'take reasonable care to ensure the suitability of its advice and discretionary decisions for any customer who is entitled to rely upon its judgment'; (10) 'it must adequately protect those client assets for which it is responsible,' and (11) 'must deal with its regulators in an open and cooperative way, and must disclose to the FSA appropriately anything relating to the firm of which the FSA would reasonably expect notice.'[80] The application of the Principles will vary according to the circumstances: for instance, what will be required to fulfil the obligations imposed under Principles 6, 7, 8, 9 and 10 will depend on the characteristics of each customer (see PRIN 1.2.1).

4.2 Systems and Controls

The second manual in the High Level Standards block is Senior Management Arrangements, Systems and Controls (SYSC). This manual expands on Principle 3 in the Principles for Businesses (SYSC 1.2) in that it aims 'to encourage firms' directors

---

[78] Another manual in this block is Threshold Conditions (COND), discussed above.

[79] See FSA, *Treating Customers Fairly–Progress and Next Steps* (2004), which seeks to ensure that: products sold are appropriate to the customers; the systems in the firm do not encourage misselling (eg, through incentives to salespersons); the customer understands the terms, pricing and risks of the product and is aware of suitable alternatives and of complaint and redress procedures; and subsequent changes in performance of the product are communicated to the customer.

[80] See also, SUP 2.3, below. For the territorial application of the Principles, see PRIN 3.3.1.

and senior managers to take appropriate practical responsibility for their firms' arrangements on matters likely to be of interest to the FSA because they impinge on the FSA's functions under the Act' (SYSC 1.2.1). The FSA, it will be recalled, is 'not primarily concerned with risks which threaten only the owners of a financial business' (SYSC 1.2.2). The firm must take reasonable care to have systems and controls that are sufficient to ensure compliance and counter the risk of financial crime (SYSC 3.2.6) and 'are appropriate to its business' (SYSC 3.1.1). What this means in practice will depend on the nature, size and complexity of the business, the diversity (including geographical diversity) of its operations, the volume and size of its transactions, and the degree of risk associated with its business (SYSC 3.1.2). The larger, more complex firms will have an audit committee and internal audit process charged with monitoring systems and controls (SYSC 3.2.15, 3.2.16). There are also provisions in this sourcebook that relate to whistleblowing under the Public Interest Disclosure Act 1998 (SYSC 4). The systems and controls mechanisms must ensure that all employees are suitable, which includes assessing their honesty and competence in the context of their role within the firm (SYSC 3.2.13, 3.2.14).[81] Delegation of management responsibilities is, of course, inevitable, but the firm must assess the suitability of the person designated to carry out a task (SYSC 3.2.3), and the manual also covers the means by which a firm can apportion responsibilities among directors and senior managers in a way that is clear, enables the flow of information and facilitates adequate control and monitoring by the management (SYSC 2.1, 3.2.11). Outsourcing–that is, contracting someone outside the firm to undertake services–of regulated functions is permitted, but the firm cannot contract out its regulatory obligations so it must take reasonable care to ensure regulated functions are being properly performed by the other party and it must have sufficient information to assess the impact of the outsourcing on its systems and controls (SYSC 3.2.4).

4.3 General Provisions

The final manual in the High Level Standards block is General Provisions (GEN), which, as its name suggests, contains a variety of provisions that do not fit in appropriately anywhere else: for instance, what happens when an emergency makes compliance with a rule impossible (GEN 1.3) and general guidance on interpreting the Handbook (GEN 2). The manual also includes a provision that seeks to prevent the public from being misled by the fact of authorisation: 'a firm must ensure that neither it nor anyone acting on its behalf claims, in a public statement or to a client, expressly or by implication, that its affairs, or any aspect of them, have the approval of the FSA' (GEN 1.2.2(1)). This does not prevent a firm from making a statement explaining that it is authorised or has permission to carry on a specific activity or that the firm's approved persons have been approved by the FSA (GEN 1.2.2(2)). Indeed, firms are under certain obligations to reveal their authorisation in communications with customers (GEN 4.3, 4.4. and 4 Annex 1; ICOB 3.3)[82]: for instance, a firm must take reasonable care to ensure that every letter or electronic communication sent with a view to conducting a regulated activity discloses that the firm is 'authorised and

---

[81] See also the Training and Competence sourcebook (TC), below.
[82] Based on Principle 7 in PRIN 3.

regulated by the Financial Services Authority,' and an appointed representative must in addition to this specify the firm of which they are an appointed representative.[83]

---

5. Business Standards

5.1 Interim Prudential Sourcebook for Insurers

The second block in the Handbook is called Business Standards and consists of prudential sourcebooks dealing with the day-to-day business of firms. The long-term intention is to create a single integrated prudential sourcebook for banks, insurers and investment firms, but although part has been published, it will not be completed before 2007 and until then there are Interim Prudential sourcebooks for each sector: the one for insurers is the Interim Prudential Sourcebook for Insurers (IPRU(INS)).[84] IPRU(INS) applies the Principles for Businesses to insurance, and in particular, the requirements with respect to systems and controls contained in Principles 3 and 4. It also provides prudential rules to protect the insured against the risk that an insurer will fail to meet claims.

All insurers must maintain a margin of solvency appropriate to their business.[85] An insurer which undertakes both long-term and general insurance business must maintain separate margins of solvency for each type, and non-UK insurers undertaking insurance business in the UK must maintain a UK margin of solvency in addition to that which is required in their home state (IPRU(INS) 2.1).[86] Non-UK insurers must maintain records relating to their business here; there are also stipulations about the appointment of a chief executive, who has responsibility for the UK business, and an agent resident in the UK (IPRU(INS), vol 1, 8). Liabilities under contracts of insurance must be covered by assets of appropriate safety, yield and marketability, and there are provisions to ensure that investments made by an insurer are not concentrated into one particular class or type (IPRU(INS), vol 1, 8). Long-term insurers are required to keep assets relating to that business separate from other assets and the sourcebook regulates the application of those assets and the allocation of surpluses to eligible policyholders.[87] There are also provisions on valuing assets and liabilities,[88] on the requirement that insurers match liabilities in foreign currency with appropriate assets in that currency (currency matching),[89] on the preparation of accounts and on

---

[83] GEN 4.3 and GEN 4 Annex 1. For the meaning of appointed representative, see above 3.5.
[84] The counterpart sourcebook for friendly societies is IPRU(FSOC). For guidance on the categorisation of a firm, see SUP Appendix 1.
[85] IPRU(INS), vols 1, 2.4–2.10, App 2.1, 2.2 and 2.3. On an insurer which is a subsidiary of an insurer, see IPRU(INS), vols 1, 10.
[86] IPRU(INS) 2.1. There are exceptions to these requirements: IPRU(INS), vols 1, 2.1(3), 2.1(5). In general, insurers may not carry on both long-term (eg, life) and general insurance business: see below.
[87] IPRU(INS), vol 1, 3; vol 3, Guidance Note P.1.5, P. 1.7.
[88] IPRU(INS), vols 1, 4 and 5, App 4.2 and 5.1; vol 3, Guidance Note P.1.8-1.11, Annex A.
[89] IPRU(INS), vols 1, 7. This chapter also deals with 'localisation' in relation to currency matching, that is, the place where assets must be held. See also, IPRU(INS), vol 3, Guidance Note P.1.5.

the making of statistical returns.[90] Finally, insurers are prohibited from engaging in non-insurance business, either in the UK or elsewhere.[91]

Volume 3 of the Interim Prudential Sourcebook for Insurers contains guidance notes to assist insurers in determining the appropriate course of action in particular situations. The guidance opens with issues arising out of Principle 3 (PRIN), which concerns management systems and controls.[92] Running through these notes is the idea that, 'Overall responsibility for the determination, implementing and monitoring... rests with the board of directors.'[93] The FSA's expectations of management structures will vary according to the nature and complexity of the insurer, so that in general larger businesses will require more sophisticated systems than smaller ones.[94] These systems must 'enable the insurer to implement an appropriate investment strategy,[95] and they must ensure that its investment managers have clear terms of reference and that they are suitably qualified and their work properly monitored.[96] In addition, Principle 3 requires 'a firm to organise its affairs effectively,' including 'keeping adequate and orderly records of its business and internal organisation' (IPRU(INS), vol 3, Guidance Note P. 2.2).[97] Here particular attention is drawn to the need for systems and controls to ensure that the amounts set aside for handling notified and potential claims to the insurer are appropriately established, recorded and monitored (IPRU(INS), vol 3, Guidance Note P. 2).

The FSA has proposed a four-step risk management system. First, the firm's governing body (usually, the board of directors) will set goals and the strategy for achieving these goals; it will then identify and prioritise all the material risks facing the business[98]; next, it will put arrangements in place to control the risks; and finally there will be systems to monitor the operation of the controls and ensure that they remain appropriate and effective.[99] It is contemplated that the day-to-day oversight of risk management will usually be delegated to a risk committee, and in view of this the FSA suggests that it may be appropriate to establish a separate mechanism for advising the governing body. The systems in place should be such as to provide the governing body with relevant, reliable and timely information to enable the

---

[90] IPRU(INS), vols 1, 9 and App 9.1–9.8.

[91] IPRU(INS), vols 1, 1.3; vol 3, Guidance Note P.1.5.

[92] IPRU(INS), vol 3, Guidance Note P.1, P.2 and P.3.

[93] IPRU(INS), vol 3, Guidance Note P.1.6.

[94] The Guidance Note points out the complexities involved where a firm is a member of a group: IPRU(INS), vol 3, Guidance Note P.3.22 and Annex G; SYSC 3. For further provisions on this issue, see The Integrated Prudential Sourcebook (PRU), ch 8, which implements Art 8 of the Insurance Groups Directive.

[95] IPRU(INS), vol 3, Guidance Note P.1.5.

[96] IPRU(INS), vol 3, Guidance Note P.1.12, Annex B. This does not prevent the use of investment managers from outside the insurer, although Annex B draws attention to the need for clear requirements that the manager must follow: eg, 'to invest in whatever the manager considers appropriate' is regarded as inadequate. Instructions must seek 'an appropriate balance between risk and reward, taking due account of the nature of insurer's insurance liabilities and (as appropriate) the interests and reasonable expectations of its policyholders.' (Annex B2)

[97] There are requirements as to record keeping throughout the Handbook; these are summarised in sch 1 of each of the sourcebooks and manuals.

[98] Attention is drawn to the need to take account of legal risk, that is, the risk that 'the law is proved to operate in a way adverse to the interests or objectives of the insurer': IPRU(INS), vol 3, Guidance Note P.3.14 and Annex C.

[99] On internal auditing, see IPRU(INS), vol 3, Guidance Note P.3.16–3.17, Annex D and SYSC 3.2.16.

management of those risks that are identified in section 2(2) of FSMA (IPRU(INS), vol 3, Guidance Note P.3.18, Annex E).

5.2 Training and Competence

The Training and Competence Sourcebook (TC) covers the firm's obligations with respect to its employees in recruitment, training, attaining and maintaining competence and monitoring these issues.[100] These provisions originate in the stipulation in Principle 3 (PRIN) and the requirement in the threshold conditions that firms demonstrate they are organising and controlling their business and they are fit and proper (FSMA, schedule 6, para 5). They must, therefore, ensure both that their staff in general are competent and that those individuals charged with performing controlled functions are, in addition, fit and proper.[101]

---

6. Regulatory Processes

The third block in the Handbook is titled Regulatory Processes and contains four manuals: the Authorisation manual, which, as has been seen, deals with the FSA's powers with regard to those applying for Part IV permission; the Supervision manual sets out the relationship between the FSA and authorised persons; the Enforcement manual covers the FSA's enforcement powers under FSMA; and the Decision Making manual is concerned with the FSA's procedures for making decisions that involve the issue of statutory notices under FSMA.

6.1 Supervision

The Supervision manual (SUP) covers supervision after authorisation or approval has been granted. The FSA applies the same risk-based approach to supervision to all firms, that is, it seeks to mitigate the risks posed by a firm to the regulatory objectives set out in FSMA, section 2(2). At the same time, it must observe the principles of good regulation set out in section 2(3) so, for instance, it may not impose regulatory burdens on a firm that are disproportionate to the benefits expected (section 2(3)(c)). The FSA must also be satisfied that a firm is continuing to fulfil the threshold conditions. The FSA uses a number of tools in performing its supervisory function: diagnostic tools to identify and assess risks; monitoring tools to track identified risks; preventative tools, which limit identified risks and prevent them from crystallising or increasing; remedial tools to respond when risks have crystallised (SUP1.4).

---

[100] See also SYSC 3.1.1 and 3.2.13
[101] For the threshold condition, see FSMA, sch 6, para 5. On the competence and fit and proper requirements for individual members of staff who are charged with performing controlled functions, see FSMA, ss 59 and 61; FIT.

The FSA assesses the probability that the firm will endanger the regulatory objectives against the impact that this would be likely to have and adjusts its supervisory regime appropriately (SUP 1.3.3). This involves consideration of the firm's strategy, the risks inherent in its business, its financial soundness, the nature of its customers and the products it offers, the internal systems and compliance culture of the firm, its organisation and the role played by all staff in mitigating risk (SUP 1.3.4). Insurers will be subjected to an intensive study of how they underwrite risk, including pricing and the contract terms they use, and how they manage other risks (eg, investment risk, operational risk,[102] legal risk). The assessment of the risk posed to the regulatory objectives will also be affected by the degree of confidence the FSA has in the quality of information it has about the firm, on predictions of the likelihood that the impact and probability factors may change and, where a firm's head office is not in the UK, the quality of the home supervisor (SUP1.3.6). The outcome of these analyses enables the insurance industry to be divided into different categories ranged along a sliding scale that determines the level of supervision: at one end of the scale are firms requiring intensive supervision, which involves regular meetings and inspection visits, and at the other end, are firms that can be monitored chiefly through examination of financial returns. Yet, as has been seen, in the final analysis the FSA recognises that the best prospect of achieving its aims rests on the firm itself taking responsibility for ensuring compliance. The FSA, therefore, places great emphasis on the requirement that management (directors and senior managers) take reasonable care to organise and control the firm, maintain appropriate risk management systems,[103] and generally ensure that the firm complies with the regulatory requirements.

In order to monitor a firm's compliance with regulatory requirements, the FSA depends on gathering information.[104] In practice, it seeks to work 'in an open and cooperative relationship with firms' and to obtain information through that relationship rather than by using statutory powers. The FSA also requires firms to disclose, without being asked, anything of which it would reasonably expect notice (SUP 2.1.6; SUP 15.3.8. See Principle 11 (PRIN)). A firm must take reasonable steps to ensure that anyone supplying it with services or outsourcing facilities deals with the FSA in the same spirit of cooperation (SUP 2.3.7). The authorised firm must inform the FSA immediately if it fails to satisfy one of the threshold conditions, or of any matter that might have a significant adverse effect on its reputation or its ability to provide adequate services to customers, or of anything that could lead to serious financial consequences to other firms or the financial system. The firm is also

---

[102] The risk of loss from inadequate or failed internal systems or people, or from external events: eg, computer breakdown, terrorist attack or natural disaster.

[103] See FSMA, s 2(3)(b). There also provisions regarding those who control large blocks of shares: SUP 11. These arise as an obligation under FSMA Part XII, under the directives on the establishment of a single market and as a consequence of the threshold conditions (eg, threshold condition 3; COND 2.3).

[104] FSMA, sch 1, para 6(1). See also, FSMA, s 354. FSA, *Reporting Requirements for Mortgage, Insurance and Investment Firms, and Supplementary Consultation on Audit Requirements* (Consultation Paper CP 197, 2003); FSA, *Regulatory Reporting – A New Integrated Approach* (Consultation Paper CP 198, 2003); FSA, *Reporting Requirements for Mortgage, Insurance and Investment Firms, and Audit Requirements for Insurance Intermediaries* (PS04/9, 2004). Among other things, these documents signalled a shift from reporting based on the type of firm to a system based on the regulated activities of a firm, and also introduced a move towards mandatory electronic reporting. Firms carrying on retail mediation activities will be required to submit retail mediation activities returns (RMAR), which must provide financial information, evidence of compliance with certain threshold conditions, information on advisers and their qualifications, and data on conduct of business and on transactions. See further below 9.3.

required to notify the FSA of any breach of rule or requirement imposed under FSMA (SUP 15.3.11), any civil, criminal or disciplinary proceedings against the firm (SUP 15.3.15), any fraud, errors or other irregularities SUP 15.3.17), insolvency or winding up proceedings (SUP 15.3.21), changes in the accounting reference date (SUP 16.3.17), and changes of controller (SUP 11.3), auditor (SUP 3.3) or among the approved persons (SUP 10.11–10.13). It must give notice of matters such as: proposed changes in business, including restructuring or expansion plans that might have a significant impact on the risk profile or resources; a significant failure of the firm's systems; any proposed action that might affect capital adequacy or solvency; any significant breach of rules or regulatory requirements.[105] Advanced warning of other matters must be given to the FSA (SUP 15.5.1, 15.5.4, 15.5.5, 15.5.7): a change of the firm's name, its principal place of business or its legal status, or a shift to supervision by an overseas regulator.

Information will come, therefore, primarily from the firms themselves (SUP 15–17), including through the work of the firm's auditors (SUP 3).[106] It may also come from requests made by the FSA (SUP 2.1.6), from visits to the firm and meetings with its representatives (SUP 2.3.1), from the Financial Ombudsman Service, and ultimately from the FSA's use of its powers under Part XI of FSMA, which requires the provision of information on demand and also enables a report to be commissioned, an inspector to be appointed, or a warrant to be granted for entry into premises.[107] The FSA can gather information on how a firm sells its products by mystery shopping techniques (SUP 2.4). Special rules on information gathering apply in the following circumstances: where an insurer is failing to meet the threshold condition concerning adequate resources and its margin of solvency or its guarantee fund has dropped below the minimum level at which it has been set[108]; or an insurer has ceased to effect new contracts of insurance; or an insurer is going through a period of uncertainty, as when it has come under the control of a new parent undertaking, or there has been a grant or variation of permission (SUP Appendix 2).

The Supervision manual contains various other provisions. It explains the procedure by which a firm may vary or cancel its Part IV permission,[109] or may seek either a waiver of rules (SUP 8; FSMA, section 148)[110] or guidance on the application of rules (SUP 9).[111] It covers the powers of the FSA to impose additional requirements

---

[105] FSA, *Guide to the FSA Handbook for Small Mortgage and Insurance Intermediaries* (2004), 11.2.3.
[106] This is also covered in IPRU(INS) and, with regard to Lloyd's in LLD (see below 8). In addition, the auditing regime is covered in general legislation on companies (Companies Act 1985 and 1989).
[107] See FSMA, ss 165, 166, 167–9 and 176; SUP 5; ENF 2.3, 2.4 and 2.15.1–2.15.4. These powers are summarised in ENF 2, Annex 3
[108] First Life Directive 79/267/EEC; Second Life Directive 90/619/EEC; Third Life Directive 92/96/EEC; Consolidated Life Directive 2002/83/EC; First Non-Life Directive 73/239/EEC; Second Non-Life Directive 88/357/EEC; Third Non-Life Directive 92/49/EEC. The guarantee fund is based on capital requirements.
[109] SUP 6; Auth 3.6 and 3.7; FSMA, s 44. This does not include the situation where on its own initiative the FSA proposes to vary or cancel a Part IV permission: see ENF (below 6.2).
[110] SUP 8 and 9. A waiver may be granted on application by a firm, or the FSA may consider it appropriate to waive the rule with respect to a number of firms, in which case it will notify the firms and each firm may then consent to the waiver. A waiver will only be granted if the FSA is satisfied that compliance by a firm would be unduly burdensome or would not achieve the objective of the rule, and it would not jeopardise persons whose interests the rule was designed to protect: FSMA, s 148(4). Sch 6 of each sourcebook or manual indicates the rules that can and cannot be waived.
[111] Normally, guidance will be given only to a particular person rather than to a class of regulated persons. The FSA may of its own initiative give guidance.

on a firm or to amend the activities it is permitted to undertake (SUP 7; FSMA, sections 45–7). The manual explains how a UK firm can establish a branch in, or provide cross-border services into, another EEA state (SUP 13; FSMA, schedule 3). It also gives guidance on transfers of insurance business (SUP 18). Part VII of the Act contains certain safeguards in the event of a proposed transfer, including requirements to notify affected parties and to obtain court approval.[112] The FSA controls the appointment of an independent expert, whose function is to report on the transfer (FSMA, section 109(2)), and the FSA has a right to be heard by the court[113] which, among other things, is meant to ensure that appropriate consideration is given to the interests of customers.[114] The court's role is to consider the interests of all those affected. In determining this matter the representations of the FSA and the actuarial judgment contained in the independent expert's report play a vital role. Nevertheless, the court does not impose its own view, it merely decides whether the proposed scheme or schemes of transfer are fair and it is for the company's directors to make a commercial judgment as between those schemes.[115] In the event of a scheme of transfer being approved, the FSA may consider whether there is a need to vary the Part IV permission of, or the regulatory regime applicable to, the transferor and the transferee (SUP 7).

6.2 Enforcement and Decisions

The FSA possesses a range of powers that it can use to enforce the provisions of the FSMA, the rules of the FSA, the Statements of Principle and other relevant legislation. Guidance on the use that will be made of most of these powers is contained in the Enforcement manual (ENF).[116] The FSA may: vary or cancel permission and withdraw authorisation (FSMA, sections 33, 45–8, 56–8; ENF 3 and 5); issue a prohibition order against an individual who is considered not fit and proper to perform functions in relation to a regulated activity (FSMA, section 56; ENF 8); withdraw approval from an approved person (FSMA, section 63; ENF 7); issue a public censure or impose a fine on an approved person (FSMA, section 66; ENF 11–13) or a firm (FSMA, sections 205–6; ENF 12–13). It can intervene in respect of an 'incoming firm' (that is, a non-UK firm exercising passport rights to carry on a regulated activity in the UK) (FSMA, sections 193–9; ENF 4 and 6.8). It can participate in insolvency proceedings[117]; it can apply to a court for an injunction where, for instance, there is a reasonable likelihood of a regulatory breach occurring (FSMA, section 198, 380; ENF 6.3–6.8 *passim*), or under powers in the Unfair Terms in Consumer Contracts Regulations 1999 (reg 12; ENF20); and it can seek a restitution order (FSMA, section 382, 384; ENF 9). Moreover, the FSA can prosecute for an

---

112 FSMA, ss 104 and 111(1). See also, the Financial Services and Markets Act 2000 (Control of Business Transfers) (Requirements of Applicants) Regs 2001 (SI 2001/3625).
113 FSMA, s 110. Indeed, the FSA's views are likely to be sought: SUP 18.2.60.
114 This is pursuant to the regulatory objectives and also Principles 6, 7, 8 and 11 (PRIN). See also, SUP 18.2.46 and 18.2.51.
115 *Re Allied Dunbar Assurance plc* [2005] EWHC 28.
116 For the power under FSMA, s 297 and 298 to revoke recognition see REC, and for procedures related to the issue of supervisory notices and decision notices see the Decision manual (DEC) below.
117 FSMA, ss 356, 357, 359, 362, 362, 365, 367, 371, 372, 374, 375; ENF 10.5–10.13.

offence under the Act and under the rules on money laundering.[118] It should be noted that the Decision manual (see below) permits the settlement of some enforcement decisions through mediation between the FSA and the person affected (DEC, Appendix 1).

The Decision manual (DEC) sets out the procedures to be followed by the FSA on those occasions when it is required to issue statutory notices (FSMA, section 395) as, for instance, it must do when proposing to refuse an application for Part IV permission or to grant permission on narrower terms than those sought in the application (FSMA, section 52(6), (7); AUTH 3). The manual provides guidance on the procedure for the use by the FSA of its powers in relation to insolvency, criminal offences and the Unfair Terms Regulations. Certain decisions must be taken by the Regulatory Decisions Committee (RDC) which, although its members are appointed by the FSA, works outside the FSA structure: members of the committee, with the exception of its chair, are not from the FSA (DEC 4.2). The RDC has responsibility for what are the most serious of the statutory notice decisions, such as where it is proposed to refuse permission (DEC 4.1.4). Other decisions are taken within the FSA by a senior staff committee under what is called the executive procedure (DEC 4.3). The aim of these structures is to separate functions and follows the requirement in FSMA, section 395(2) that a decision giving rise to the obligation to issue a notice must be taken by someone 'not directly involved in establishing the evidence on which that decision is based' (but see FSMA, section 395(2)). Someone affected by such a notice has the right to have it referred to the Financial Services and Markets Tribunal.

The FSA has come in for much criticism over enforcement. Two of the most important methods by which the objectives of the regulatory regime can be achieved are providing redress for consumers, which is quick and cheap, and removing those firms and individuals that are unfit. Although the enforcement process provides a way of achieving these goals, it is a double-edged sword since in exposing incompetence or malpractice the FSA may damage confidence in the industry. This is perhaps inevitable, but the degree of damage done to the reputation of the industry and individuals and firms working within it can be compounded by various problems inherent in the enforcement system. The first of these problems is that the FSA acts as investigator, prosecutor and judge. The fact that only the chair of the Regulatory Decisions Committee is from the FSA may not be sufficient to ensure an impression of neutrality to the outside world. Moreover, that neutrality may be less significant because of the FSA's control over the investigation. This means the FSA governs the pace and scope of the process which, in turn, shapes the role of the RDC as well as the input of those being investigated. This may be inevitable, but it makes it important to recognise the impact that the mindset of an investigator has on the processes of investigation, prosecution and decision-making, and the industry seems concerned that the FSA is focused too much on consumer protection and too little on the reputation of the market. The second problem is that, unless the likely outcome is a serious penalty such as the withdrawal of authorisation, the individuals and firms on the receiving end of an investigation may feel their wish to defend themselves is inhibited, not merely by a concern that to minimise the effect on their commercial

---

[118] FSMA, ss 401, 402; ENF 15. For a list of the criminal offences covered, see ENF 15.2.1 and 15.2.2.

reputation it may be best to seek a quick and relatively private solution, but by their anxiety that a vigorous defence may undermine future relations with FSA officials, particularly in view of the emphasis placed by the FSA on an open and cooperative approach to regulation. The third source of problems with enforcement may come from the regulator's desire to present a particular image of itself as efficient in pursuing consumer protection and industry malpractice or incompetence. This is not an insignificant issue since in many ways the FSA is seen–and sees itself–as representing the regulatory system established under FSMA and, in addition, criticism of the FSA is likely to have a human impact on those who work within the organisation since it is always difficult to take the 'Godfather' approach and see these things as only business and not personal. The FSA faces difficulties in establishing its own image, not least because of what may appear to outsiders–and often insiders as well–to be contradictions in the regulatory objectives between consumer protection and promoting confidence in the market. The complexity of the issues involved may mean the FSA can only hope to create a fleeting impression of itself in the minds of the general public. Certainly, enforcement can be a way of capturing publicity and so generating an image of the FSA as vigorous in the pursuit of redress and the rooting out of malpractice and incompetence. Yet, this may lead the industry to believe that the FSA starts from a pro-consumer position and wishes to demonstrate toughness. Moreover, using enforcement to promote the image of the FSA is problematic. It requires the FSA's actions to be publicised as soon as possible after the relevant regulatory breach because any delay risks the FSA being characterised as inefficient, as adding to the problems faced by consumers and as damaging the industry. This must be balanced against the need to provide the firm or individual affected with the opportunity to respond and not to damage the reputation of such people or of the industry (or a sector) by premature publicity.

7. Redress

This block of the Handbook is concerned with complaints and compensation.[119] The Dispute Resolution: Complaints sourcebook (DISP) stipulates the procedures that firms are required to have in place to deal with complaints from 'an eligible complainant,' that is, someone who would be eligible to refer a complaint to the Financial Services Ombudsman (DISP 1.2.2). These procedures must cover receiving complaints, responding, investigating and notifying complainants of their right (if any) to seek redress through the Financial Ombudsman (DISP 1.2). There are stipulations about the time within which a firm must deal with a complaint (DISP 1.4), the records it must keep and the reports it must make to the FSA (DISP 1.5). The firm must publicise its complaints procedures (DISP 1.2.9–1.2.15). These provisions derive from FSMA, s 2(2)(c), which concerns the protection of consumers, and they aim to ensure that complaints are treated fairly and promptly (DISP 1). Moreover,

---

[119] On the Financial Compensation Scheme, which is part of this block (COMP), see below 10.

under FSMA, section 150(1), a private person (and in certain circumstances, other persons: section 150(3)) may bring an action to recover loss suffered as a result of the contravention by an authorised person of a regulatory rule, subject to any defences applying to actions for breach of statutory duty, unless this right of action is excluded.[120] A private person is any individual, but an individual who suffers loss in the course of carrying on any regulated activity may not bring an action, unless that loss occurs in the course of effecting or carrying out insurance contracts written at Lloyd's.

The Complaints against the FSA (COAF) sourcebook establishes a complaints scheme and an independent Complaints Commissioner. These are designed to deal with a claim brought by someone who has allegedly suffered loss, distress or inconvenience as a direct effect of the misconduct of the FSA in the exercise of its powers or in its failure to exercise them (FSMA, schedule 1, para 7; COAF 1.4).[121] The types of complaints envisaged are mistakes, lack of care, unreasonable delay, unprofessional behaviour, bias and lack of integrity (COAF 1.4.1). The procedure is in two parts. When a complaint is received the FSA must ensure that it falls within the scheme and, if it does, the FSA may take action that satisfies the complainant. If, however, the complainant remains dissatisfied, the complaint is referred to the Complaints Commissioner, who may make a recommendation to the FSA on the form that any redress should take.

---

8. Lloyd's of London insurance market

The Society of Lloyd's of London does not provide insurance, it is a market within which insurance is written: it provides the buildings within which trading takes place and the rules under which that trading occurs. Its history goes back to the late seventeenth century and the practice of merchants meeting at Lloyd's Coffee House to transact insurance business. As the market developed it outgrew the coffee house, but the original name lived on. During the 1970s and 1980s Lloyd's was beset with a range of problems that exposed the flaws in its structure. In particular, the London Market Excess of Loss Spiral, whereby risks were underwritten and then reinsured by a small number Lloyd's syndicates, got into difficulties. This placed enormous pressure on the Members, who constituted those syndicates and who provided the financial backing. Indeed, many Members went into bankruptcy. There followed allegations of negligence in the underwriting practices used in the market, several court cases, inquiries and major reforms.

---

[120] Financial Services and Markets Act 2000 (Rights of Action) Regs 2000 (SI 2001/2256), para 6. No action lies where the rule breached is one that requires the authorised person to have financial resources: s 150(4)(b). Each sourcebook or manual contains rules on the availability of the right to sue (eg, see SYSC 1.1.12) and summarises these in the appendix.

[121] These mechanisms do not cover complaints related to the FSA's legislative functions, or the operation of the Financial Ombudsman Scheme (COAF 1.4.2), or dissatisfaction with the FSA's general policies, or the exercise of its discretion where no misconduct is alleged (COAF 1.4.2A), or where another procedure is more appropriate (COAF 1.4.3).

The Lloyd's Act 1982 provides the framework for the management structure and the rules of the market. The main objective of the Act is to provide reasonable safeguards for Lloyd's policyholders and for members of Lloyd's to give people confidence in the market as a place to do business. This is primarily achieved by ensuring that people trading in the market are solvent, competent and honest, that those who use the market are fairly treated, that the market operates with an appropriate degree of transparency and that there is no abuse. The Council of Lloyd's is responsible for management and supervision of the market, although it now acts under the supervision of the FSA (FSMA, section 314). The FSA has specific powers given to it in relation to Lloyd's under Part XIX of FSMA, and, in addition, since the Society of Lloyd's is an authorised person for the purposes of FSMA (FSMA, section 315(1)), this renders it subject to the various powers that the FSA has with regard to such persons. The FSA relies on Lloyd's to carry out regulation on its behalf, so the Lloyds sourcebook (LLD), which is part of the Handbook, is chiefly concerned with the information that Lloyd's must supply to the FSA.

---

9. Insurance intermediaries

It might seem obvious that the regulation of the insurers who write insurance contracts should be accompanied by the regulation of those who give advice to prospective insureds, but until relatively recently there was no statutory supervision of these insurance intermediaries. This meant that anyone could set up as an intermediary and offer advice to the public on insurance. There was also the conflict of interest that arose as a result of intermediaries, from whom consumers expected impartial advice, receiving secret commissions from insurers. A report by the British Insurance Brokers' Association in 1976 and a government White Paper the following year led to a slow process of reform.[122] The Insurance Brokers (Registration) Act 1977 was limited in its scope, and in particular only applied to those who chose to call themselves insurance brokers and might, therefore, be avoided by the simple expedient of using some other title to describe one's function. Later, most of those involved in life assurance business came within the terms of the Financial Services Act 1986. Key players in the industry established the General Insurance Standards Council (GISC) with encouragement from the Treasury in the wake of the repeal of the Insurance Brokers Registration Act 1977. Its aim was to maintain and indeed improve standards in the general insurance market through a set of rules and codes of practice. Yet, in spite of initial enthusiasm and a good deal of excellent work, various factors conspired against the GISC. Membership was voluntary, but members were required only to undertake business with other members. A campaign was launched against the legality of this rule that diverted the council from the task of establishing effective regulation and undermined its public credibility. In spite of GISC's many achievements, it was clear that statutory regulation of intermediaries was required to

---

[122] Cmnd 6715.

ensure that consumers would not be exposed to unregulated intermediaries.[123] Since January 2005 the FSA has taken over regulation of those intermediaries involved in general insurance business.[124] However, the FSA has stretched its net wider than the GISC and the new regime now applies to many who advise their clients on insurance, but who doubtless have never thought of themselves (or been seen as) part of the insurance industry, such as doctors, dentists, vets, motor car dealers and removal firms. If they engage in a certain level of insurance business, authorisation is required and continuing to act without obtaining such authorisation is a criminal offence. We have already seen how one way around this is to become an appointed representative, but the difficulty with this route is that the responsibility placed on an authorised firm means they will be cautious about selecting appointed representatives and are likely to focus on those with whom they have a long-established relationship, which may affect the ability of new firms to progress their businesses.

As has been seen, the objective of the FSMA is to apply a single regulatory regime to all parts of the financial services industry covered by the Act. This means that, in general terms, the rules already discussed in relation to insurers also apply to insurance mediation.[125]

9.1 Authorisation

All firms must be authorised if they carry out insurance mediation activities in connection with contracts of insurance (AUTH Appendix 5.3) and those activities are carried on by way of business (AUTH Appendix 5.4). Insurance mediation means 'the activities of introducing, proposing or carrying out other work preparatory to the conclusion of contracts of insurance, or of concluding such contracts, or of assisting in the administration and performance of such contracts, in particular in the event of a claim.' (AUTH 5.16.2).[126] The FSA has taken the view that someone will only be required to be authorised to give advice where there is an expression of opinion by the adviser: in other words, where someone recommends a particular course of action. Recommending that someone takes out (or does not take out) the Acme Insurance Company's motor insurance policy is a regulated activity, but recommending that someone take out motor insurance is not. Providing information on a selected – as opposed to a balanced and neutral – basis and thereby influencing the decision of the person to whom the information will also amount to advice. Assisting in the administration and performance of a contract of insurance is a regulated activity and this includes giving someone material assistance in the completion of a claims

---

[123] GISC Scrutiny & Consumer Affairs Committee, *Report on GISC Performance against Objectives* (2004): http://www.gisc.co.uk

[124] This was also a consequence of the Directive on Insurance Mediation (2002/92), which was implemented by the Financial Services and Markets Act 2000 (Regulated Activities) (Amendment) (No 2) Order 2003 (2003/1476) and the Insurance Mediation Directive (Miscellaneous Amendments) Regs 2002 (2004/1473). Although the FSA took over regulation of general insurance intermediaries from 14 January 2005, there are various transitional provisions to ease this change. These will not be dealt with in the discussion that follows, but are contained in the FSA Handbook.

[125] For an introduction, see: FSA, *Guide to the FSA Handbook for Small Mortgage and Insurance Intermediaries*, see above n 105. The parts of the Handbook that are relevant to intermediaries have been edited into a version called the Tailored Handbook for Insurance Intermediaries: www.fsa.complinet.com/fsa_mgi/display/rulebook.html

[126] See Insurance Mediation Directive, art 2.3.

form or negotiating the settlement of a claim on behalf of the insured (AUTH Appendix 5.7. But see, AUTH 5.7.2–5.7.6).

Where someone has engaged in a regulated activity, authorisation is only required if they have done so in the course of business (FSMA, section 19; see above 3.3). In relation to insurance mediation the business test comprises two main elements: does the person receive remuneration and, if so, are the activities undertaken with a sufficient degree of regularity to constitute a business? The test will usually not be satisfied where someone conducts the relevant activity for a member of their family or for employees or club members (AUTH Appendix 5 .4). Finally, authorisation is only required where regulated activities are carried on 'in the United Kingdom' (FSMA, section 19; AUTH 5.12).

As has been observed, these provisions substantially broaden the coverage of the regulatory regime and bring within its compass many who might be surprised to find themselves subject to it. If they become an appointed representative of an authorised insurer or insurance intermediary, the authorised person will be responsible for the firm's activities (AUTH 5.13, 5.15.4; see above 3.5). There are also some important exceptions to these requirements. The first is where a firm, whose main activity is not financial services, supplies information to its customers on policies that are complementary to its main business and the supply of information does not amount to the carrying on of a business in its own right. For example, the dentist who gives information to a client about a particular kind of dental insurance or about insurers offering such policies will not require authorisation, nor will authorisation be required where dental insurance brochures are merely displayed in the reception area (even if the dentist receives a fee for this). But authorisation will be required if the dentist provides information about pet insurance, or recommends that a patient buy a particular company's dental insurance policy, or fills out an application form for the patient, or forwards information about a potential policyholder to an insurer (AUTH Appendix 5.6.5–5.6.9). Authorisation will not be required where an activity is carried on in the course of a business that is not insurance mediation, that does not consist of carrying on regulated activities and that is a necessary part of other services provided as a part of that business: for example, a solicitor who arranges the assignment of a contract of insurance (AUTH 5.11.9–5.11.12). Solicitors, accountants and actuaries may also be allowed to engage in insurance mediation activities in the course of their profession by claiming Part XX exemptions, but this will require them to appear on the FSA register (AUTH 5.14.1),[127] and where a material part of such a firm's business involves acting for claimants in litigation against insurers, authorisation may be required (AUTH 5.14.2). Someone who merely provides the means by which parties to a transaction are able to contact one another, such as the provider of an Internet service or telephone line, will not require authorisation, unless the introducer is not indifferent to whether a transaction takes place (eg, because it may lead to the payment of a commission) and the introduction specifically relates to contracts of

---

[127] Under Part XX where a professional body has been designated by the Treasury to supervise members of the profession in the conduct of regulated activities incidental to their work, those activities are designated as exempt regulated activities and separate authorisation is not required. See the Professional Firms manual: PROF 7.1; also Financial Services and Markets Act 2000 (Professions) (Non-Exempt) Activities Order 2001 (2001/1227), as amended by Financial Services and Markets Act 2000 (Regulated Activities) (Amendment) (No 2) Order 2003 (2003/1476), art 93.

insurance rather than to investments generally (AUTH 5.6.10–5.6.23). Where advice appears in a periodical publication and the principal purpose of that publication is not to give advice on insurance contracts, no authorisation is required (AUTH 5.8–5.9). There are also exclusions from the requirement to obtain authorisation that apply to retailers and travel agents (connected contract of insurance: AUTH Appendix 5.11.13–5.11.15). A retailer of goods other than cars will not require authorisation with respect to a general insurance policy for non-motor goods that is for five years or less, has an annual premium of £500 or less, covers breakdown, loss or damage to the goods, does not cover the liability of the insured to third parties, is complementary to the goods supplied by the retailer, and is in standard form. Travel agents do not require authorisation with respect to a general insurance policy that is for five years or less, has an annual premium of £500 or less, covers risks connected to the travel, does not cover liability risks unless this is ancillary to the main cover, is complementary to the service supplied by the agent, and is in standard form.

9.2 Adequate resources

As has already been seen, the threshold condition 4 and Principles 3 and 4 (PRIN) require the authorised firm's senior management to ensure that it maintains adequate resources and this includes appropriate management and control systems (SYSC) as well as adequate and competent staff.[128] An insurance intermediary with Part IV permission must allocate responsibility for the firm's insurance mediation activity to a director or senior manager, who must be an approved person (PRU 9.1.3). The intermediary must show that a reasonable proportion of those persons in its management structure, who are responsible for insurance mediation activity, and the staff directly involved in that activity have appropriate levels of knowledge and ability and that they are of good repute (PRU 9.1.8-9.1.13; FIT), and the firm must have systems and controls that enable it to be satisfied of the suitability of such persons (SYSC 3.2.13).

Financial resources must also be sufficient 'to reduce the possibility of a shortfall of funds and to provide a cushion against disruption if the firm ceases to trade.'[129] What this means in practice is explained in the Integrated Prudential sourcebook (PRU). The capital resources a firm must hold are calculated as a percentage of its annual income from regulated activities (PRU 9.3).[130] In addition, firms will be required to maintain professional indemnity insurance cover against the risk of incurring liability as the result of, for instance, providing negligent advice that causes loss to a client.[131]

---

[128] The rules on appointment, training, etc are in TC2. An intermediary engaged in non-investment insurance is not required to have passed particular examinations.

[129] FSA, *Guide to the FSA Handbook for Small Mortgage and Insurance Intermediaries*, see above n 105, at 7.1.3.

[130] This would mean that someone who sells cars and is authorised to conduct insurance mediation business would only make the calculation against income derived from the latter activity: FSA, *Guide to the FSA Handbook for Small Mortgage and Insurance Intermediaries*, see above n 105, at 7.2.6. For details on the calculation of income, see PRU 9.3.42–9.3.5. What counts as capital is set out in PRU 9.3.51–9.3.57. Where there is a shortfall in meeting the solvency or capital requirements a sole trader or partnership that does not hold client's money may resort to those personal resources not required to meet other liabilities; a firm that holds client money, or a company must increase its capital resources: PRU 9.3.54.

[131] The stipulations as to the level of cover required under a policy are contained in PRU 9.2. The intermediary may be excused this obligation if a guarantee that is comparable to cover under such a policy is provided by an FSA authorised firm with net tangible assets of more than £10 million: PRU 9.2.1.

9.3 Supervision

As has been seen, the FSA approaches its tasks of regulation and supervision by assessing the risk posed by a firm to its regulatory objectives. Many insurance intermediaries are relatively small operations, and therefore present little risk to the regulatory objectives. The FSA is, however, concerned about the risk that might be posed by widespread failures and this has led it to concentrate on thematic work across the sector.[132] This means that the FSA's supervision of individual firms is largely conducted through returns of regulatory information supplied electronically by those firms through the Retail Mediation Activities Return (RMAR) (SUP 16; see above 6.1). The RMAR covers financial matters, including the balance sheet, profit and loss, regulatory capital, client money accounts and indemnity insurance cover, and issues such as adherence to the threshold conditions, training and conduct of business.[133] In addition, the firm is required to confirm certain basic information, such as the name and registered office. Insurance intermediaries may be required to appoint an auditor by virtue of the FSA's rules: in brief, there is no FSA requirement to appoint an auditor if the firm does not hold client money or title documents, or if it holds client money in a statutory trust (see below, CASS) and the balance of the account never exceeds £30,000 (SUP 3.1). Intermediaries that come within the Companies Act 1985 will be required to appoint an auditor.

Complaints against a firm are dealt with in Dispute Resolution: Complaints (DISP). In addition to the requirements already discussed, an insurance intermediary is required to have procedures for recording and responding to complaints received about insurance mediation from those who are not eligible complainants (that is, those who do not have a right to go to the Financial Ombudsman Service) (DISP 1.2.1A).

Insurance intermediaries, who are engaged in general insurance or pure protection contracts, are not subject to the requirements contained in the Money Laundering sourcebook, but there is a general obligation to maintain adequate systems to prevent the firm from being used for financial crime, which, of course, includes money laundering (SYSC 3.2.6) and the criminal law relating to money laundering applies.

9.4 Client money

The Client Assets sourcebook (CASS) deals with the rules concerning the handling of client funds and other assets and it develops Principle 10, which requires a firm to provide adequate protection for client assets. The sourcebook contains rules on holding client funds, on the segregation of such funds from money held as agent for the insurer and on accounting procedures. It also obliges an intermediary to ensure that its appointed representatives and other agents observe rules on segregating client money (CASS 5.5.18–5.5.25). Client money is that which is received and held for a client by an intermediary acting in the course of carrying on insurance business. Client money received by the firm must be paid out or placed in a client bank account

---

[132] FSA, *Reporting Requirements for Mortgage, Insurance and Investment Firms, and Audit Requirements*, see above n 104.
[133] In addition, product sales data (PSD) is collected on individual transactions in pure protection products, but this comes from the product providers and not the intermediaries.

as soon as is practicable, which will normally be the next business day after receipt (CASS 5.5.5–5.5.6). An insurance intermediary that holds client money must regularly undertake a calculation to ensure there are sufficient funds to meet obligations to clients (CASS 5.5.62). Where the client money resource is less than the client money requirement, the firm must top it up; where the resource exceeds the requirement, the firm must withdraw the excess.

Client money does not include money received and held for an insurer, which funds must not be held in a client bank account unless the insurer has consented to its interest in the mixed funds being subordinated to the interests of clients (CASS 5.1.5). The role of many intermediaries is simply to introduce business to an insurer, but often a binding authority agreement exists under which an intermediary is authorised to enter into insurance contracts on behalf of the insurer. Where the insurer authorises the intermediary to undertake one or more of the following tasks relating to funds, the binding authority agreement must state that the intermediary is acting as the insurer's agent in respect of those tasks: receiving and holding premiums, holding claims money and refunding premiums.

The rules in CASS cover the situation where an intermediary transmits to an insurer a premium paid by a customer, or transmits to a customer claims monies or returned premiums received from an insurer. An intermediary may adopt one of two approaches to its role in the transmission of money: the first is to transfer from the intermediary to the insurer the risk of non-transmission (CASS 5.2); the second is to segregate clients' money in an account that is not available to other creditors in the event of insolvency (see CASS 5.3–5.4).

In the first approach, the funds are not held as client money and the insurer is liable for the failure of the intermediary to transfer funds (CASS 5.2). There must be a written agreement between the insurer and the intermediary that stipulates premiums (and, if the insurer consents, claims monies and premium refunds) are to be held by the intermediary as agent for the insurer. If the insurer consents, such money can be treated as client money and held in the client bank account (CASS 5.2.3; 5.2.4), but clients must be informed of this arrangement and their interests must be made superior to those of the insurer (CASS 5.1.5).

In the second approach, client money is held in a segregated bank account on a statutory trust (CASS 5.3) or a non-statutory trust (CASS 5.4). Under both types of trust the intermediary acts as trustee and both are used for holding premiums received from clients and claims moneys and returned premiums received from insurers. The main difference between the types of trust is that it is only where funds are held in a non-statutory trust account that the intermediary is permitted to advance credit by paying a premium for a client before the premium has been received from the client, or by paying claims or refunding premiums before those funds have been received from the insurer, although the firm must not advance credit to itself (CASS 5.4.1).[134] The intermediary must satisfy a number of conditions before it is allowed to operate a non-statutory trust account: there must be adequate systems and controls to manage any credit risk, an auditor must confirm that these arrangements are adequate and a manager must be given the responsibility of ensuring they are

---

[134] Commission may only be withdrawn from the client bank account when it is received and not simply when it is earned (CASS 5.5.16).

maintained; the firm must observe a minimum capital resources requirement of £50,000 where the intention is to hold client money for retail customers[135]; there must be reasonable steps taken to inform customers of these arrangements and the customer must consent to money being held in such an account (CASS 5.4.4). While a statutory trust arises automatically under the FSA's rules, in the case of a non-statutory trust the firm must execute a trust deed, which, if the firm wishes to advance credit, must state that it has the power to do so (CASS 5.4.6–5.4.8). Although a special type of bank account is not required, the account used must be designated as a statutory or non-statutory trust by written notice to the bank and by the bank's acknowledgement both that money in the account is held by the intermediary as trustee and that the bank may not combine the account with another account or exercise rights of set off or counterclaim against the funds in the account for any moneys owed by the firm to the bank (CASS 5.5.49(1)). The title of the account must also be such as to distinguish it from any other account held by the firm (CASS 5.5.49(2)).

An intermediary who has received a premium from a client may transfer that money to another firm provided this is done to effect the transaction for the client and, if a retail customer, the client was told at the outset that such a transfer might be made (CASS 5.5.34).[136] The intermediary will be treated as a client of the second firm. That second firm must, therefore, hold the money on behalf the intermediary and must place that money in a segregated account (CASS 5.5.7). It is important to note that transferring premium funds to the second firm does not relieve the intermediary of its obligations as trustee for the funds until that money is received by the insurer (or by an agent of the insurer), although the second firm will be liable to account for money not so transferred (CASS 5.5.33).

9.5 Conduct of Business

The Insurance: Conduct of Business sourcebook (ICOB) is concerned with the processes of advising, selling and administering non-investment insurance contracts, that is, a general insurance contract, such as motor or household insurance, or a pure protection contract, such as critical illness or income protection (but excluding a long-term care insurance contract).[137] ICOB includes marketing, sales, literature on products and the handling of claims. It develops the requirement in Principle 6 (PRIN) to treat customers fairly and implements various pieces of EU law, including parts of the Insurance Mediation Directive and the Distance Marketing Directive. The sourcebook covers not only those firms whose business is to advise customers on insurance, but an insurer who advises on its or another's insurance products (ICOB 1.2.1). The whole of ICOB applies to a firm dealing with a retail customer, which, in essence, means someone acting other than in the course of business, but parts do not apply to a commercial customer (ICOB 1.2.4, 1.7.3 and 1 Annex 1).

---

[135] This applies if the funds are held for retail customers, other intermediaries holding client funds in a statutory or non-statutory trust account are required to hold capital resources equivalent to 5% of annual income (minimum £10,000).
[136] The intermediary is also required to take reasonable care in choosing the firm to which funds are paid: CASS 5.5.81.
[137] The ICOB does not apply to reinsurance contracts.

9.5.1 Communications with customers

Under ICOB 2.2.3 a firm must take reasonable steps to ensure that all its communications with customers are clear, fair and not misleading.[138] In determining how to comply with this requirement, the intermediary must have regard to the customer's knowledge of the relevant insurance contract (ICOB 2.2.4). A firm must also take reasonable steps (see ICOB 2.3.9) to ensure that it does not offer, give, solicit or accept an inducement[139] and does not refer any mediation activity to another person on its own initiative if such actions are likely to conflict materially with a duty owed to the firm's customer in connection with a mediation activity (ICOB 2.3.2). Staff must not be offered incentives that encourage them to sell products unsuited to the needs of their customers (ICOB 2.3.8). A firm may not exclude or restrict the duties or liabilities it owes to a customer under the regulatory system, and may only exclude or restrict other duties or liabilities in so far as it is reasonable for it to do so (ICOB 2.5).

9.5.2 Financial promotions

The sourcebook also covers the communication of a non-investment financial promotion to a person inside the UK (ICOB 3).[140] The FSA regards financial promotions as a risk area because of the important part they play in the consumer's decision-making process. Particular concerns are products that are not properly described or are described in a way that creates a misleading impression. As a result, the FSA has established a financial promotions department to review promotions and assess firms' systems and controls.

A person who is not authorised under FSMA must not communicate an invitation or inducement to engage in investment activity, including insurance, in the course of business, unless the content of the communication has been approved by an authorised person (FSMA, section 21; ICOB 3; AUTH App 1.3.1). The FSA has taken the view that an invitation or inducement will come within these provisions if the reasonable person would have considered that the intention of the communicator was to persuade the recipient to engage in investment activity (AUTH App 1.4.4. Generally, AUTH App 1.3–1.8). A distinction is drawn between a non-investment financial promotion, which is regulated, and a real time financial promotion, which is not: factors indicating that it is the former include that the promotion is communicated in the same terms to more than one person, or by a method that creates a record of the communication, or in a way that does not enable the recipient to respond immediately to it (ICOB 3.6.2). A promotion communicated during a personal visit, over the telephone or through another form of interactive dialogue will therefore be exempt,

---

[138] Also, ICOB 2.2.5. This builds on Principle 7 from PRIN. The provision does not apply in circumstances covered by ICOB 3. For the meaning of 'communicate', see AUTH App 1.6.
[139] See AUTH App 1.4.
[140] ICOB 3 does not apply to an authorised professional firm in relation to the communication of a non-investment financial promotion if the firm's main business is the practice of its profession (which is not a regulated activity and which is supervised by a designated professional body: eg the Law Society), if the promotion is incidental to its provision of professional services and if the communication is not effected on behalf of someone who could not lawfully have communicated the promotion: ICOB 3.2.4. ICOB 2.2.3, which requires communications to be clear, fair and not misleading communication, may, however, apply: ICOB 3.2.5.

but a promotion communicated through letters, e-mails, mail shots or advertising on television will be subject to regulation (ICOB 3.1–3.6). Where an exemption applies the promotion may still be subject to other rules, such as the requirement that communications be clear, fair and not misleading (ICOB 2.2.3), or the requirements on advising and selling standards (ICOB 4) or on product information (ICOB 5).

There are certain non-investment financial promotions that are exempt from regulation (ICOB 3.3.5–3.3.6). The first is a generic promotion, which does not identify an insurer or anyone else as carrying on a controlled activity in relation to a non-investment insurance contract: for instance, an advertisement placed by an insurance intermediary advertising mediation services without naming an insurer is not covered by the provisions because the activities of such an intermediary are not controlled activities (AUTH App 1.12.14–1.12.17).[141] Secondly, a promotion that may reasonably be regarded as directed only at commercial customers is exempt (ICOB 3.3.8(1)). Thirdly, certain promotions communicated from outside the UK are exempt. Fourthly, a 'one-off' promotion will be exempt where it is communicated to one recipient or to one group of recipients (who would be expected to engage jointly in the activity), the identity of the contract is tailored to the circumstances of the recipient, and the promotion is not part of an organised marketing campaign. A promotion may be regarded as 'one-off' even though not all, or even any, of these conditions is met. This exemption applies, for instance, to letters and e-mails directed at a particular recipient (ICOB 3.3.8(2)), although not a general campaign that merely addresses information to individuals but is not tailored to those individuals. Where a 'one-off' promotion includes a personal recommendation it will be subject to other obligations (eg, ICOB 4.3, 4.4). Fifthly, a non-investment financial promotion that consists of any of the following information is exempt: the name of the insurer or its appointed representative, the name of the non-investment insurance contract, a logo, a contact point, and a brief, factual description of the firms activities, it fees or its products. The attempt here is to distinguish image advertising, which gives a general description of the company (such as 'life and general insurance business') and which is not regulated, from financial promotion (ICOB 3.3.8. Also AUTH App 1.4.20).

Before the regulated promotion is communicated or approved, the firm must arrange for someone with expertise appropriate to the nature of the promotion to confirm that it complies with the rules (ICOB 3.7.1). The rules do not dictate the content of a promotion, but it must be clear, fair and not misleading (ICOB 2.2.3, 3.8.1, 3.8.3) and it may be subject to the disclosure rules in ICOB 4 and 5 (see below 9.5.3 and 9.5.4), the requirements in Principle 7, which concerns communications with clients, and those in SYSC 3, which relate to systems and controls. The promotion must present any fact, promise or prediction in a clear and fair way (ICOB 3.8.2–3.8.3). For instance, a comparison must compare like with like, it must not create confusion between the firm and a competitor, and it must not discredit a competitor (ICOB 3.8.1).

---

[141] Advertisements that are not regulated by the FSA will, nevertheless, be subject to regulation by the Advertising Standards Authority. Such promotions may also be subject to the regulations of an overseas regulator where the promotion is marketed from the UK into another country, and it may come within the terms of the Privacy and Electronic Communication Regs 2003 (SI 2003/2426).

9.5.3 Advising and selling

The rules on advising and selling in ICOB 4 elaborate Principles 6, 7 and 9.[142] The bulk of the chapter applies to both retail and commercial customers.[143] Its objectives are to ensure (ICOB 4.1.7): the customer has adequate information about the service provided by the intermediary in relation to non-investment insurance contracts, including the scope and type of products on which this service is based; where a personal recommendation is given, it is suitable for the customer's demands and needs; the customer is supplied with a statement of their demands and needs and the reasons for any personal recommendation by the intermediary; the charges to a retail customer are not excessive (ICOB 4.5)[144]; any commission received by an intermediary or by an associate must be revealed to a commercial customer, if requested (ICOB 4.6)[145]; and a retail customer must not be charged for a non-investment insurance contract concluded by distance means unless there is prior consent.

An intermediary must provide all customers with the following information: the name and address of the firm, its statutory status (eg, that it is authorised and regulated by the Financial Services Authority: GEN 4 Annex 1) and that both of these issues can be verified on the FSA's register; any holdings that the intermediary has in an insurer, or if an insurer has more than 10 per cent of the voting rights or capital in the intermediary; the range of insurers from which products are being selected for sale to a particular customer, which may be either a wide range of insurers (called a service on the basis of a 'fair analysis' of the market)[146] or from one or a limited number of insurers[147]; the complaints mechanisms available, including details of the Financial Ombudsman Service; and the possibility of compensation from the Financial Services Compensation Scheme should the intermediary be unable to meet its obligations (ICOB 4.2.8).[148] This information must normally be provided prior to the contract and must be in a durable medium, unless the customer requests that the information be provided orally or immediate cover is required. Customers must be informed of any fee to be charged to them for mediation services before the fee becomes due or before the contract, whichever is earlier (ICOB 4.2.15–4.2.18).[149] A limited amount of information can be given if the contract is made over the telephone and the customer consents: the name of the intermediary, the purpose of the

---

[142] They also implement arts 12 and 13 of the Insurance Mediation Directive and art 9 of the Distance Marketing Directive. ICOB 4 applies to renewals of contracts of insurance even where the terms are identical to the previous contract: ICOB 4.1.5 (but see ICOB 4.2.20, which restricts the requirements in ICOB 4.2 regarding status disclosure, see below 9.5.4).

[143] The exceptions are ICOB 4.2 (status disclosure), 4.4 (statement of demands and needs) and 4.6 (commission disclosure).

[144] This is determined by the charges made in the rest of the market, whether they represent an abuse of the retail customer's trust in the intermediary and whether they have been disclosed to the customer: ICOB 4.5.

[145] No such obligation exists where the intermediary is an insurer: ICOB 4.6.3.

[146] What amounts to a sufficiently wide range for there to be a fair analysis of the market is dealt with in ICOB 4.2.12–4.2.13.

[147] In the latter case the intermediary must offer to provide on request a list of the insurers.

[148] ICOB 4 Annex 1 contains a template document (the initial disclosure document (IDD)) that intermediaries may (but are not obliged to) use in providing status information. The status document in Annex 2 can be used where the intermediary is arranging mortgage and non-investment insurance contracts for a customer: this is the combined initial disclosure document (CIDD). See also www.fsa.gov.uk/mgi for examples of completed status documents.

[149] Fee here does not include a commission that forms part of the premium.

contract (where it was initiated by the intermediary), the name of the person contacting the customer and their relationship with the firm, and the nature of the remaining information that can be obtained on request (ICOB 4.2.2). The full information must be provided immediately after a telephone contract. Where a customer is obtaining a number of quick quotes from intermediaries there is no need at that stage to provide status disclosure information (ICOB 4.2.1(3)). On renewal of a contract the intermediary need only notify the customer of any changes in the original information (ICOB 4.2.20). If the intermediary is merely introducing a customer to another intermediary or insurer, the only disclosure required is the name and address of the introducing intermediary and their statutory status, any fees charged for the introduction, and whether the introducer and the other firm are members of the same group (ICOB 4.2.9).

Where an intermediary makes a personal recommendation to a customer to buy or sell a non-investment insurance contract, the intermediary must take reasonable steps to ensure that the recommendation is based on the scope of the service disclosed in accordance with ICOB 4.2.8 (see above) and is suitable for the customer's demands and needs (ICOB 4.3.1). To assess the demands and needs, the intermediary must seek relevant information concerning the customer's requirements and explain to the customer the pre-contractual duty of disclosure (ICOB 4.3.2) and must issue a statement of the demands and needs and the reasons for any personal recommendation (ICOB 4.4).[150] In the case of a contract concluded over the telephone, the statement must be provided immediately afterwards in a durable medium (ICOB 4.4.2(2)). If a customer is seeking a number of quick quotes from different intermediaries, no statement is required until shortly before the contract conclusion (ICOB 4.4.3(2)). The intermediary must assess the suitability of a contract against the demands and needs (ICOB 4.3.6): is the cover sufficient, what is the cost and are the terms exclusions, limitations and excesses appropriate?

9.5.4 Product disclosure

Insurers and intermediaries are required to provide information about products to their customers. The provisions in ICOB 5 reinforce Principle 7 by aiming to ensure that customers are able to make an informed choice about the purchase of a specific non-investment insurance contract, that they are encouraged to read the information supplied both by the intermediary and by the form in which the information is provided, and finally, that after the contract has been concluded they are provided with complete information about the policy. The information required indicates that the focus is on the situation where a customer is being advised, for instance, about buying a particular household contents policy offered by Acme Insurance Company rather than where the customer is merely being advised as to the general merits of buying a household contents policy.

Where the insurer and intermediary are both authorised and operate from permanent places of business in the UK, it will normally be the insurer that produces the

---

[150] There is no such requirement in relation to a commercial customer, unless the intermediary makes a personal recommendation, and there is no such requirement where the intermediary is an insurer, which makes a personal recommendation, if the commercial customer consented not to receive a statement (ICOB 4.4.2(1)).

information and the intermediary will simply pass it to the customer, but where the insurer does not operate from the UK, the intermediary is responsible for producing and supplying the information (ICOB 5.2.2–5.2.7, 5.2.12). There are distinctions made between the information that needs to be supplied to retail customers and to commercial customers and also between information required in non-distance sales, where there is a degree of face-to-face contact (even if part of the negotiations were by telephone, e-mail etc), and in distance sales (eg, telephone).

Prior to the conclusion of a non-investment insurance contract, which is not a distance contract, a retail customer must be provided with a policy summary (see ICOB 5.5.1–5.5.13), a statement of price (see ICOB 5.5.14–5.5.15) and directive-required information,[151] and the customer's attention must be drawn orally to the importance of reading the policy summary and to the exclusion clauses (ICOB 5.3.1–5.3.3). Once the contract has been concluded the customer must be supplied in a durable medium with the policy document (see ICOB 5.5.27–5.5.28) and information on claims handling, any cancellation rights and the extent of any compensation scheme (ICOB 5.3.4). In the case of a non-investment insurance contract that is a distance contract, where it is possible before the contract the retail customer must be provided with–in a durable form–a policy summary, the price, the policy document, directive-required information, and information about claims handling and any cancellation rights (ICOB 5.3.6(1)). No further information is required after the conclusion of such a contract. If the contract is concluded by telephone, the retail customer may consent to receiving only limited information orally.[152] Similarly, more limited information can be given where the contract is concluded at the retail customer's request by a form of distance communication, which is not the telephone and which does not permit provision of full information in a durable form before conclusion of the contract (ICOB 5.3.6 (2b)). In such cases the full information must be supplied after conclusion of the contract (ICOB 5.3.6(2)–5.3.8).

With respect to commercial customers, there is an obligation to give information before the contract, unless the contract is for a large risk (large-scale commercial risk). The information that is required will vary according to the customer's own expertise and knowledge and need only be such as will allow the customer to make an informed decision, although it must include the premium, any fees and information required by EU law. The customer (including the customer insuring large risks) must be supplied with the policy document promptly after the contract (ICOB 5.4.1–5.4.7)). Where there is reason to believe that a commercial customer wishes to renew a policy, the terms on which the insurer is willing to renew must be provided 'in good time' (that is, sufficient time for the information to be useful to the customer) prior to expiry of the existing policy, or the customer must be informed either that the intermediary no longer deals with that insurer or that the insurer does not wish to renew (ICOB 5.4.10–5.4.14).[153]

---

[151] This is information that is required to be supplied under EU law: see ICOB 5.5.20.
[152] If the customer does not give consent and both parties wish to proceed by telephone, the intermediary must provide orally all the information required before the conclusion of the contract: ICOB 5.3.6(2a)).
[153] On the information required when group policies are sold to retail customers, see ICOB 5.3.29, and when group policies are sold to commercial customers, see ICOB 5.4.8.

9.5.5 Claims

Normally, the insurer handles claims (ICOB 7) and, therefore, the intermediary has no obligations, although where an intermediary arranges a policy for a customer it is quite likely also to be an agent for the customer in handling any claim against the insurer. If, however, the intermediary does act for a customer with respect to a claim, they must do so with due care, skill and diligence and must avoid any conflict of interest by making proper disclosure to a customer and obtaining prior informed consent (ICOB 7.4.5). Where that intermediary also acts for the insurer in relation to claims, the risk of conflict may not be resolved simply by disclosure to the customer and the insurer (see ICOB 7.4.7).

10. Financial Services Compensation Scheme

The Policyholders Protection Acts of 1975 and 1997 were, in broad terms, designed to provide consumer insureds with compensation in the event of an insurer being unable to meet claims. That arrangement has been replaced by a scheme established by the FSA under the provisions of FSMA, Part XV. It is important to note at the outset that there is no protection under these provisions for those whose policies are with an unauthorised firm (section 213(3)), or for those with policies at Lloyd's, although in that case a separate compensation scheme exists (COMP 1.5; LLD 8A.1). The scheme for compensating consumers is administered by the Financial Services Compensation Scheme Ltd (FSCS) under rules laid down by the FSA in the Compensation sourcebook (COMP). The FSCS is obliged to carry out its functions efficiently and economically, it must publish an Annual Report, must have a procedure to deal with complaints against the FSCS and must keep consumers informed about the process of making a claim (COMP 2). Funding for the scheme comes from levies on authorised firms (COMP 13). The sourcebook lays down the conditions that must be satisfied for a claim to succeed, which are, in broad terms, that the claimant must be eligible (COMP 4), the activity that caused the loss and the firm involved must be covered by the scheme (COMP 5 and 6) and the claimant must assign to the FSCS their rights to bring a claim against the firm, although if the FSCS obtains a sum above that which it paid out the excess must be handed to the claimant (COMP 7). As well as payments of compensation to insureds,[154] in certain circumstances the FSCS is obliged to secure continuity of insurance for insureds and may be permitted to assist an insurer that is facing financial problems (COMP 3.3.1–3.3.7).

---

[154] On the time frame within which payment must be made, see COMP 9; on the limits on the amount payable, the method of payment and the calculation, see COMP 10–12.

11. The Financial Ombudsman scheme

If a claim is rejected or not settled to the satisfaction of the insured, the obvious recourse is litigation, but cost, time and probably a sense of fatalism are likely to deter all but the most determined. The Insurance Ombudsman Bureau (IOB) was established in 1981 by a number of leading insurers to provide a cheap, simple means of redress.[155] It was part of a more general enthusiasm for ombudsmen that began in the 1960s. Originally seen as a means of protecting citizens in their dealings with state agencies, they have now spread into all areas of consumer activity. In essence, the IOB dealt with complaints by private individuals against insurers who were members of the scheme. Its aim was to facilitate the settlement or withdrawal of a complaint by a variety of means, including making an award, which the insurer, but not the insured, was obliged to accept.[156] The IOB proved radical in its approach. It was required to consider the terms of the contract, relevant rules of law and principles of good insurance practice, including the Statements of Insurance Practice, however, the IOB tended to give priority to 'a fair and common sense conclusion' if it felt the result produced by the law was not appropriate. In other words, the IOB introduced notions of fairness and held insurers liable in situations where the courts would not have done: so, for instance, the IOB held insurers liable for the defaults of intermediaries in spite of the general rule that they are the agents of the insured; the IOB relaxed the strictness of the duty of disclosure; and it introduced requirements of procedural fairness in, for example, the way insurers investigated claims.[157]

The various ombudsmen and other independent complaints arrangements that existed throughout the financial services industry were replaced by a unified, statutory scheme established by the FSA under Part XVI of FSMA. This provides for a scheme 'under which certain disputes may be resolved quickly and with minimum formality by an independent person' (section 225), and it led to the establishment of The Financial Ombudsman Service (FOS). The scheme is funded by a combination of a levy on each authorised firm and a fee charged to firms linked to the number of complaints brought before the ombudsman (DISP 5). In 2003–4 the ombudsman dealt with more than 500,000 enquiries and just under 100,000 complaints were referred to adjudicators. More than half of the cases that reached the adjudicators were related to endowment policies linked to mortgages and insurance featured high among the rest of the complaints.[158]

---

[155] J Birds and C Graham, 'Complaints Mechanisms in the Financial Services Industry' (1988) 7 *CJQ* 313; A McGee, 'The Insurance Ombudsman and the Unfair Contract Terms Act 1977' (1992) 2 *Insur L & P* 86; P Rawlings and C Willett, 'Ombudsman Schemes in the United Kingdom's Financial Sector: the Insurance Ombudsman, the Banking Ombudsman and the Building Societies Ombudsman' (1994) 17 *Journal of Consumer Policy* 307. Other complaints mechanisms also existed in the insurance industry: the Personal Insurance Arbitration Scheme operated by the Chartered Institute of Arbitrators; the Consumer Enquiries Department at Lloyd's, which did pass unresolved complaints to the IOB; and the mechanisms created by individual firms and particular sectors of the industry.

[156] On the possibility of the insurer challenging the IOB through judicial review: A McGee, 'Challenging the Decisions of the Insurance Ombudsman' (1994) 4 *Insur L & P* 43.

[157] Rawlings and Willett, 'Ombudsman Schemes in the United Kingdom's Financial Sector', above n 155, at 312–14.

[158] See the statistics on the FOS website: http://www.financial-ombudsman.org.uk/publications/ar04/ar04-keyfacts.htm.

The FOS is regulated under FSMA and the rules contained in the Dispute Resolution: Complaints sourcebook (DISP). It has two jurisdictions. The first is its compulsory jurisdiction, which covers those authorised firms that are obliged to participate in the scheme with regard to those complaints specified by the FSA (section 226). The second is the voluntary jurisdiction: if the activity does not come within the compulsory jurisdiction, a firm can voluntarily contract that the FOS will handle complaints relating to that activity (section 227). In the main the procedures in relation to both types of jurisdiction are identical (DISP 1, DISP 4).[159] The sourcebook stipulates the activities and omissions of insurers that are covered by the FOS, the people who may refer a complaint and the time limits (DISP 2; sections 226, 227 and schedule 17, para 13).[160] An eligible complainant must bring the complaint, which means, in essence, that it must be brought by someone who is a private individual or small business (DISP 2.4). It must be brought against a firm and relate to an activity that is subject to the compulsory or voluntary jurisdiction.[161] The firm must have failed to resolve the complaint within eight weeks, and it must have been authorised under FSMA at the time of the relevant action, or it must have been a voluntary jurisdiction participant both at the time of the action and when the complaint is referred to the FOS.

In line with the requirements in FSMA, the FOS aims to resolve complaints 'quickly and with minimum formality.' (DISP 3.1.7).[162] There is jurisdiction to dismiss a complaint without considering the merits in a number of situations, such as where the FOS believes the complainant has suffered no loss, material distress or inconvenience, or the complaint is vexatious, or the firm has made a fair and reasonable offer that is still open for acceptance, or the complaint concerns investment performance or the firm's legitimate exercise of its commercial judgement, or it is a matter that is being dealt with by a court, an independent complaints or dispute resolution process comparable to that of the FOS, or it would be more appropriately dealt with by a court because, for instance, there is a dispute over evidence (DISP 3.3.1 and 3.3.5; see also, DISP 3.4). The FOS has said that if reasonable compensation has been offered, it will not launch an investigation simply to satisfy the complainant's desire for an explanation for the error.[163] Having decided that there is jurisdiction to consider the complaint, the FOS will consider if 'there is a reasonable prospect of resolving the complaint by mediation' (DISP 3.2.9). If an investigation is deemed necessary by the FOS, both parties will be given an opportunity to make representations during those investigations and the FOS will give the parties a reasoned provisional assessment. If either party disagrees with that assessment the FOS will proceed to determination (DISP 3.2.11).

Before arriving at a determination the FOS must receive representations, but need not hold a hearing (DISP 3.2.12). The issues of the evidence that is admissible and

---

[159] See also, *Ombudsman News*, 14 (Feb 2002). For the application of DISP 1 to Lloyd's, see DISP 2.5.3. On the special procedure that must be observed by firms dealing with complaints relating to the sale of endowment policies for the purpose of achieving capital repayment of a mortgage, see DISP App 2. On internal complaints procedures, see also *Ombudsman News*, 33 (Nov 2003). For further information on the scope of the FOS's jurisdiction, see ibid, 32 (Oct 2003).

[160] The time limits are imposed on voluntary jurisdiction participants by virtue of a term in the contract under which the firm agreed to join the scheme. See also, *Ombudsman News*, 28 (May 2003).

[161] On the types of activities covered, see DISP 2.6. On the territorial scope of the scheme, see DISP 2.7.

[162] On the practice of the FOS, see *Ombudsman News*, 18 (Jul 2002)

[163] Ibid, case 41/3 (Nov 2004).

the conclusions that can be drawn from it are largely left to the FOS. There is no requirement to follow judicial rules of evidence, indeed there is a specific power to exclude evidence that a court might admit or include evidence that a court would not admit (DISP 3.5). In view of the requirement that its determination reflects the merits of each case, the FOS does not consider itself bound by its own previous decisions, although a degree of certainty has its advantages and, as with the IOB, a rough jurisprudence is being constructed. The FOS will have 'reference to what is, in his opinion, fair and reasonable in all the circumstances of the case' taking account of 'the relevant law, regulations, regulators' rules and guidance and standards, relevant codes of practice and, where appropriate, what he considers to have been good industry practice at the relevant time.' (DISP 3.8.1; see section 228). So, for instance, this (along with a liberal interpretation of the provisions of the Unfair Terms in Consumer Contracts Regulations 1999)[164] has led to the FOS insisting that insurers will not be permitted to rely on clauses limiting liability unless they have provided a reasonably clear explanation of those terms.[165] It may use codes of practice even though they are not strictly relevant to the particular policy or policyholder.[166] The impact of this approach can be seen in many areas. For example, the strictness of the duty of disclosure on the insured has been alleviated. Where the FOS regards the non-disclosure as innocent and involving genuine oversight or inadvertent error, it will require the insurer to meet a claim even if, had there been disclosure, it would have refused cover or increased the premium. The FOS is likely to hold that the non-disclosure was innocent where the questions posed by the insurer were unclear, or it was reasonable for the insured to have overlooked the particular fact because, for example, it occurred a long time ago and was fairly trivial.[167]

A determination may include an award of 'fair compensation,' or a requirement that the firm take certain steps, or both (section 229(2); DISP 3.9.1); costs may also be awarded to – but not against – the complainant, although such awards are likely to be rare (FSMA, section 230; DISP 3.9.10–11). The reasoned determination must be notified to the parties, and the complainant (but not the firm) may accept or reject it within a prescribed time.[168] Rejection by the complainant means that the firm is not bound by the determination (DISP 3.8.3). Finally, a private person may bring an action for damages under section 150 where, for instance, loss has been suffered as the result of a breach of the rules in DISP on a firm's or the FOS's handling of a complaint (DISP schedule 5).

Clearly, the complaints brought before the FOS may reveal problems relating to individual firms or products, but they may also provide insights into the working of the regulatory system. The FSA and the FOS have, therefore, established a 'wider implications' procedure under which the two organisations meet and also liaise with trade and consumer bodies in situations where a case or a series of cases suggests that a change in regulation may be necessary.[169]

---

[164] Ibid, 36 (Apr 2004).
[165] Ibid, 29 (Jul 2003).
[166] Ibid, 39 (Aug 2004); cases 31/3 (Sep 2003), 39/1 (Aug 2004), 39/2 (Aug 2004).
[167] Ibid, 25 (Feb 2003), 27 (Apr 2003). See, generally, W Merricks, 'The Jurisprudence of the Ombudsman' (2001) *JBL* 654–60.
[168] Failure to notify amounts to a rejection: FSMA, s 228(6), DISP 3.8.3(4).
[169] FSA & FOS, *FSMA 2 Year Review: Financial Ombudsman Service: Feedback on CP04/12 and Supplementary FOS Consultation on Procedural Rules* (FSA & FOS, March 2005).

3

Insurance Intermediaries

1. Introduction

As with the conduct of commerce generally, insurance transactions are conducted through the medium of intermediaries and as such they play a pivotal role in the creation of insurance contracts.[1] The term 'insurance intermediary' is necessarily broad brush and covers, inter alia, brokers, independent agents, employees of insurance companies and their 'tied' agents. Even where, as is more and more common, the proposer deals directly with the insurance company, the issue of agency still arises given that the company, as an artificial person, has to conduct business through its human agents.[2] Agency refers to the relationship in which one person (the agent) acts for another (the principal) in effecting a transaction with another (the third party) whereby the agent is authorised to establish privity of contract between the principal and the third party. There is no statutory definition of agency, nor is there an all-embracing judicial definition, although in *Harvest Trucking Co Ltd v Davis*,[3] Judge Diamond QC stated that: '[a] broker or other insurance intermediary is employed to act as a middle man between the person employing him – normally the person requiring insurance – on the one hand, and the proposed insurer or insurers on the other.'[4]

---

[1] See further, A McGee, *The Law and Practice of Life Assurance Contracts* (London, Sweet & Maxwell, 1995).

[2] See *Houghton v Northard, Lowe* [1928] AC 1 at 18, *per* Lord Sumner.

[3] [1991] 2 Lloyd's Rep 638.

[4] Ibid, at 643. A number of commentators have attempted to define the relationship. In GHL Fridman, *The Law of Agency* (London, Butterworths, 2003), Professor Fridman states: 'Agency is the relationship that exists between two persons when one, called the *agent*, is considered in law to represent the other, called the *principal*, in such a way as to be able to affect the principal's legal position in respect of strangers to the relationship by the making of contracts or the disposition of property.' Professor FMB Reynolds in *Bowstead and Reynolds on Agency* (London, Sweet & Maxwell, 2001), defines agency as 'the fiduciary relationship which exists between two persons, one of whom expressly or impliedly consents that the other should act on his behalf, and the other of whom similarly consents so to act or so acts.'

As has been seen in chapter 2, the issue of financial services regulation and those involved in marketing financial products, including life policies and investment products, has in recent times attracted the close scrutiny of the FSA and the EU.[5] One of the major mischiefs to which the current regime, instituted by the Financial Services and Markets Act 2000 (hereafter, FSMA 2000), is directed is the scandal surrounding the misselling of pensions by commission hungry insurance intermediaries during the 1980s.

In this chapter we consider the various types of insurance intermediaries, their authority, and their common law duties. As commented above, the subject of regulation is examined in chapter 2 but the old schemes are mentioned below as a means of demonstrating how the various categories of insurance intermediary came about and to illustrate the complexity of the pre-FSMA 2000 regime. In general terms, there are two types of insurance intermediary: independent intermediaries and tied agents. Insurance intermediaries may be categorised as follows:

- Independent agents (commonly termed independent financial advisors (IFAs)) who were registered as 'insurance brokers' pursuant to the Insurance Brokers (Registration) Act 1977 and were regulated by the Insurance Brokers Registration Council established by that Act. The Council published rules including a Code of Conduct. The 1977 Act was repealed by FSMA 2000 and the Council was abolished on 30 April 2001.
- Lloyd's Brokers accredited at Lloyd's, who place business at Lloyd's by virtue of their exclusive access to the underwriting room. Other insurance intermediaries may place business at Lloyd's by acting through a Lloyd's broker for this purpose.[6] Lloyd's brokers were regulated by the 1977 Act (above). The current regulatory regime is to be found in the Lloyd's Act 1982 (as supplemented by FSMA 2000) together with byelaws issued by the Council of Lloyd's.
- Independent intermediaries who did not call themselves 'insurance brokers', opting instead for titles such as 'insurance advisers', 'insurance agent' or 'insurance consultants', were outwith the Insurance Brokers (Registration) Act 1977. Such agents were subject to a self-regulatory scheme issued by the Association of British Insurers: *General Insurance Business–Code of Practice for all Intermediaries (Including Employees of Insurance Companies) other than Registered Insurance Brokers* (the revised version took effect in January 1989). The ABI Code also applied to tied agents and, as its title suggests, to employees of particular insurers. It also encompassed incidental intermediaries such as building societies, banks, travel agents, car dealers, utility companies, retailers, and others who sold insurance incidentally to the carrying on of their principal business. Further, incidental agents such as solicitors and accountants who sold investment products were required by the Financial Services Act 1986 to be independent or linked only to one insurer or marketing group. They could gain authorisation by a Recognised Professional Body provided their investment business did not exceed a certain threshold figure based on a percentage of their total business. The FSMA 2000

---

[5] See, eg, the 1991 Recommendation on Insurance Intermediaries, 92/48/EEC, 18 December 1991, OJL 28.1.92.
[6] See R Hodgin, 'Insurance Intermediaries' in R Hodgin (ed), *Professional Liability: Law and Insurance* (London, Lloyd's Press of London Ltd, 1996) 425.

(Designated Professional Bodies) Order 2001 recognises, among others, the Law Society, the Institute of Chartered Accountants and the Association of Chartered Certified Accountants as designated professional bodies.

Nowadays, the key point is not the title an intermediary goes by, but rather the activity undertaken by him or her (see chapter 2).

---

2. Identifying the intermediary's principal

It is often critical to determine whether the agent's principal is the insured or the insurer. For example, where a material fact is disclosed by the insured to the agent, the insurer will not be able to avoid the policy for non-disclosure if it is found to be the agent's principal and the court imputes the agent's knowledge of the material fact to it. Identifying the agent's principal is also critical to the determination of to whom the agent's duties are owed.

As far as it is possible to formulate a general rule, it can be said that agents and brokers (including Lloyd's brokers) are presumed to be the agents of the insured, while company representatives (canvassing agents and employees), are deemed to be agents of the insurer.[7] That said, there are situations where a broker will be regarded as acting as the insurer's agent. This is particularly common in motor insurance where brokers have implied authority to enter into interim insurance and to issue cover notes. The issue was considered in *Stockton v Mason*,[8] where the insured, having exchanged his Ford Anglia for an MG Midget, instructed his broker to transfer his existing insurance to cover his new vehicle. The broker's clerk told him that everything would be all right and that the firm would make the necessary arrangements. The insured inferred that this meant that the same terms would apply. However, the new cover did not extend to the insured's son who negligently caused an accident while driving the car with the result that damages amounting to £46,000 were awarded to the claimant. Reversing the county court's judgment, the Court of Appeal held that the insurers were liable because the broker had implied authority as their agent to enter into contracts of interim insurance. Lord Diplock observed:

---

[7] *Rozanes v Bowen* (1928) 32 Ll L Rep 98; *McNealy v Pennine Insurance Co Ltd, West Lancashire Insurance Brokers Ltd* [1978] 2 Lloyd's Rep 18. See also, *Arif v Excess Insurance Group Ltd* 1987 SLT 473 at 474, *per* Lord Sutherland. It should be noted that in *Winter v Irish Life Assurance plc* [1995] CLC 722 at 732, Sir Peter Webster stressed that: 'the presumption can undoubtedly be rebutted and ... the determination of the particular relationship in any case depends more on the actual circumstances, including the circumstances underlying the initiation of the relationship, than on any presumption.' See further, *Goshawk v Tyser* [2005] EWHC 461. For brokers acting for both sides, see *Drake v Provident* [2003] Lloyd's Rep IR 793; [2004] Lloyd's Rep IR 277.

[8] [1978] 2 Lloyd's Rep 430. See also, *Woolcott v Excess Insurance Co* [1979] 1 Lloyd's Rep 231 (Court of Appeal), [1978] 1 Lloyd's Rep 633 (trial decision of the High Court); the retrial, ordered by the Court of Appeal, is reported at [1979] 2 Lloyd's Rep 210. See also, *Aneco v Johnson & Higgins* [2000] Lloyd's Rep IR 12.

There must be every day thousands of cases, not only in motor insurance but in other forms of non-marine insurance, where persons wishing to become insured or wishing to transfer an insurance ring up their brokers and ask for cover or ask for fresh cover or ask to transfer the cover from an existing vehicle to another. In every case they rely upon the broker's statement that they are covered as constituting a contract binding upon the insurance company. In that sort of conversation, they are speaking, in the absence of any special circumstances, to the broker as agent for the insurance company, and the broker in dealing with the matter, is acting as agent for the insurance company and not as agent for the person wishing to have insurance. Of course, there may be exceptional cases. There was nothing exceptional about this.[9]

It would be going too far to attempt to distil a principle of general application from the decision in *Stockton*. The broker's implied authority was clearly material to the court's finding. In the absence of actual authority, whether express or implied, an insured should therefore assume that a broker or agent lacks apparent authority to bind the insurer. It is to the notions of actual and apparent authority to which we now turn.

---

3. The scope of an agent's authority

At law a principal is bound by the acts of an agent with respect to those matters over which the agent has either *actual* or *apparent* authority to conduct on behalf of the principal. Similarly, a principal will be bound by the acts of an agent by virtue of the doctrine of ratification.

3.1 Actual authority

An agent's actual authority will depend upon the agreement between him and the principal.[10] Additionally, an agent may also have implied authority to carry out certain acts on behalf of the principal as where, for example, the principal issues the agent with blank cover-notes from which it can be implied that the agent is authorised to effect interim insurance contracts.[11] Essentially, where a principal has expressly authorised an agent to enter into a transaction (actual authority), this is taken to include all those acts by the agent which are reasonably incidental and necessary to enable the agent to effect that transaction (implied authority). In *Zurich General Accident Liability Insurance Co Ltd v Rowberry*,[12] the insured instructed his brokers to arrange air travel insurance for his trip to France. The brokers erroneously notified the insurers that the destination was Paris. In fact, the insured was travelling

---

[9] Ibid, at 432.
[10] See the judgment of Diplock LJ in *Freeman and Lockyer v Buckhurst Park Properties (Mangal) Ltd* [1964] 2 QB 480, at 504.
[11] See *Stockton v Mason*, above n 8.
[12] [1954] 2 Lloyd's Rep 55.

to Nice. The insured disputed the insurers' claim for the premium arguing that due to mistake, there was never a contract between them. The Court of Appeal held that the insured was liable on the basis that his instructions to the brokers to arrange insurance cover on his behalf without specifically stating that Nice was his destination, impliedly authorised them to nominate Paris as the entry point into France. Sir Raymond Evershed MR was of the view that:

> it is quite plain from the course which was adopted that the agents ... were authorised, from the beginning of the negotiations to the end, to negotiate on behalf of the principal [the insured] the precise form of policy to be issued in response to this proposal within, of course, the broad limits of the proposal terms. More precisely, I think it was clearly within the authority of the agents to nominate for the purposes of the policy, and if the policy so required, the airport in France to which and from [the insured] intended to travel.[13]

It is evident from this passage that an agent who is authorised to arrange insurance cover has implied authority to agree the content and scope of the policy. In *Murfitt v Royal Insurance Co*,[14] the agent had given an oral assurance to the claimant that he would be covered against fire pending a final decision by the insurance company. A fire occurred shortly thereafter and the company refused cover, albeit in ignorance of the loss, on the ground that they were not interested in fire insurance of this type. McCardie J held that the claimant could recover against the insurers on the ground that as the branch manager had on previous occasions permitted the agent to give temporary cover, he therefore had implied authority to do so on this occasion. An agent's implied authority has also been held to extend to his disclosure of all information necessary for effecting cover and to the disclosure of all facts material to the risk.[15]

3.2 Apparent authority

In practice a third party, whether insured or insurer for present purposes, will rely upon an agent's apparent (sometimes termed ostensible) authority rather than upon his actual authority as to which the third party is generally ignorant. Often actual authority and apparent authority, although independent of one another, will co-exist but the respective scope of each may be different. It has been said that apparent authority is the authority of an agent 'as it *appears* to others.'[16] Apparent authority was defined by Diplock LJ in *Freeman and Lockyer v Buckhurst Park Properties (Mangal) Ltd*,[17] as the 'legal relationship between the principal and [third party] created by a representation made by the principal to the [third party], intended to be and in fact acted on by the [third party], that the agent has authority.'[18] At its root, apparent authority rests upon estoppel so that the representor (the principal) is estopped from asserting that he is not bound by the insurance contract effected by the agent.

---

[13] Ibid, at 57.
[14] (1922) 38 TLR 334.
[15] *Allen v Universal Automobile Insurance Co Ltd* (1933) 45 Ll L R 55; *Bancroft v Heath* (1901) 17 TLR 425.
[16] *Hely-Hutchinson v Brayhead Ltd* [1968] 1 QB 549, at 583, *per* Lord Denning.
[17] Above n 10.
[18] Ibid. See also the speech of Lord Keith in *Armagas Ltd v Mundogas SA (The Ocean Frost)* [1986] AC 717.

There are therefore two constituent elements to apparent authority. First, a representation made by the principal. Secondly, reliance upon that representation by the third party. The representation to the effect that the agent has authority can, of course, be made by words, but it generally arises from some form of conduct on the part of the principal as where, for example, the principal holds the agent out as entitled to act on his behalf. In either case, it must be made by a person possessing actual authority in the matter. The point was succinctly stated by Lord Denning MR in *Eagle Star Insurance Co Ltd v Spratt*,[19] a complex reinsurance decision in which the broker's knowledge of certain flaws in the execution of a policy was imputed to his principals: 'If you find conduct–standing by–of the principal, even though it is not communicated to the other party–and this conduct leads the other party to believe that the agent has authority, that is enough to bind the principal.'[20] Reliance upon the representation can be refuted by establishing that the third party had either actual or constructive knowledge of the agent's lack of authority. Constructive knowledge can be inferred from previous dealings between the parties in the same way that knowledge of an exclusion or limitation clause in any contract can be found to exist.[21]

Examples of apparent authority abound,[22] but it must be stressed that the decisions always depend upon their particular facts. In *Berryere v Fireman's Fund Insurance Co*,[23] the claimant applied for motor insurance but was told by the agent that because of a previous accident his application would have to be referred to the defendant insurer for approval. Before the insurer had decided the matter the claimant asked the agent whether approval had been given. The agent told him it had and thereupon issued him with a cover note. The agent was knowingly acting contrary to his instructions in binding the defendant and misleading the claimant into believing that insurance had been arranged. An accident occurred before the insurer had reached a decision. The Manitoba Court of Appeal, by a majority decision,[24] held that although the principal had limited the actual authority of the agent, nevertheless as regards a third party acting in good faith, the authority which the agent has is that which he is reasonably believed to have, having regard to all the circumstances. The agent was held out by the defendant insurer as having the authority to communicate with the claimant their decision and as such, he had ostensible authority which bound the insurer. Schultz JA (Monnin JA concurring) summarised the position as follows:

> The rule would seem to be that assuming there is good faith throughout by the third party then, as between principal and agent, it will be the agent's ostensible authority, not his actual authority, that will determine the extent to which he may bind his principal. The basis of the rule is that when a third party deals in good faith with an agent, relying upon credentials entrusted to such agent by his principal and which credentials are reasonable

---

[19] [1971] 2 Lloyd's Rep 116.
[20] Ibid, at 128.
[21] See further, J Beatson, *Anson's Law of Contract* (Oxford, Oxford University Press, 2002) 165 *et seq.*
[22] See, by way of examples, *Stone v Reliance Mutual Insurance Society Ltd* [1972] 1 Lloyd's Rep 469, considered below at p 66; *Kelly v London and Staffordshire Fire Insurance Co* (1883) Cab & E 47 (an agent's apparent authority to receive premiums); *Brook v Trafalgar Insurance Co* (1946) 79 Ll L Rep 365 (an agent's notice of loss binding the insurer); *Wing v Harvey* (1854) 5 De G M & G 265, considered below at p 67.
[23] (1965) 51 DLR (2d) 603.
[24] Guy JA dissenting.

indicia of the agent's authority, the principal is estopped from denying the agent's authority.[25]

Where an agent appoints a sub-agent, the latter will not bind the principal unless three factors can be established. First, that the agent had either express or implied authority from the principal to delegate his authority to a sub-agent. Secondly, the agent was authorised to create a binding agency relationship between the principal and sub-agent. Thirdly, the agent and sub-agent intended to create the agency with the principal.[26]

3.3 Ratification[27]

A principal may ratify an act of an agent even though it was performed outside the scope of the agent's actual or apparent authority. For ratification to be effective the agent must have purported to act on behalf of the principal,[28] although the principal need not necessarily be identified.[29] Where an agent, acting ultra viresly, effects an insurance policy on behalf of an unnamed principal/insured, ratification is possible provided the principal possessed insurable interest at the time of the contract and the agent was able to disclose all material facts relating to the risk.[30]

Ratification is retroactive,[31] so that it relates back to the time when the contract is purported to be concluded by the agent. The effect of ratification is to place the principal in the same position as if he had been the original contracting party (*omnis ratihabitio retrotrahitur mandato aequiparatur*). As will be seen in chapter 6, whether it is possible in non-marine insurance to ratify after a loss has occurred is a matter of some controversy. Although the decision in *Grover & Grover Ltd v Mathews*,[32] is authority for the proposition that ratification is not possible after the occurrence of the loss where the principal has knowledge of the loss, nevertheless in *National Oilwell (UK) Ltd v Davy Offshore Ltd*,[33] Colman J doubted whether he would have followed it. The judge saw no reason in principle why the marine insurance position, which permits ratification after a loss has taken place, should not be of general application in insurance law.

---

[25] Above n 23, at 609.

[26] *O'Keefe v London and Edinburgh Insurance Co Ltd* (1928) NI 85. See also, *Pangood Ltd v Barclay Brown & Co Ltd* [1999] Lloyd's Rep IR 405.

[27] See further ch 6 below, and the discussion of *National Oilwell (UK) Ltd v Davy Offshore Ltd* [1993] 2 Lloyd's Rep 582, at p 174.

[28] *Re Tiedemann and Ledermann Frères* [1899] 2 QB 66. See generally, *Keighley, Maxsted & Co v Durant* [1901] AC 240.

[29] It has been held that though not named, the principal should be capable of being ascertained at the time of the contract: see *Eastern Construction Co Ltd v National Trust Co Ltd and Schmidt* [1914] AC 197 at 213.

[30] *Lyell v Kennedy* (1889) 14 App Cas 437.

[31] *Bolton Partners v Lambert* (1888) 41 Ch D 295; *Presentaciones Musicales SA v Secunda* [1994] .2 All ER 737.

[32] [1910] 2 KB 401.

[33] Above n 27.

4. Imputing an agent's knowledge

As commented earlier, a finding that an insurer is an agent's principal gives rise to the important question as to the extent to which the agent's knowledge can be imputed to it. The question has assumed particular significance in pre-contractual situations where an agent has completed the proposal form on behalf of the insured before passing it to him for signature. If a written answer in the proposal form fails to disclose a material fact made known to the agent at the time of its completion because the agent either innocently, negligently or fraudulently transcribed an incorrect answer, the issue arises whether the agent's actual knowledge can be imputed to the insurer. If it cannot, it follows that the insurer will be able to repudiate the contract for non-disclosure of a material fact. On the other hand, the insured will claim that the insurer should be deemed to have known of the material fact by virtue of its agent's knowledge. In *Blackley v National Mutual Life Association of Australia Ltd*,[34] Turner P observed that where knowledge is disclosed to an agent in reliance upon his ostensible authority to receive it, such knowledge will be imputed to the principal on the basis of the doctrine of estoppel. Although the agent may lack actual authority to receive the disclosure, if the agent has been held out by the principal as having such authority, the latter will be estopped from denying knowledge of the disclosed facts. However, the principal will not be estopped where the third party knew the true position, or did not believe the representation and therefore did not place reliance on it.[35]

Recently, the Court of Appeal has been called upon to consider whether the knowledge of an agent of an insured who has been defrauding his principal can be imputed to the insured. In *P.C.W. Syndicates v P.C.W. Underwriters*,[36] and *Groupe Josi Re v Walbrook Insurance Co Ltd*,[37] an agent acting on behalf of the reinsured was charged with the duty of procuring reinsurance, and a broker was instructed by the agent. The agent had in fact been guilty of serious frauds at the reinsured's expense, and the reinsurer sought to avoid liability on the basis that such fraud was material and ought to have been disclosed. The Court of Appeal held that the reinsured was obliged only to disclose such facts as he knew or ought to have known in the ordinary course of business, and that earlier cases were incorrect insofar as they assumed that the knowledge of an agent could be imputed to his principal. The court concluded that the rule, codified by the Marine Insurance Act 1906, section 19 that an 'agent to insure' must disclose to the insurer all facts known to the agent, did not defeat the reinsured in the present case, as, first, the agent in question was not an 'agent to insure', as that description applied only to the last agent in the chain, ie the broker who places insurance; and secondly, that even if the agent had been a placing broker, the information which has to be disclosed under section 19 is confined to that which the agent has obtained while acting as the insured's agent and did not extend to information obtained in some other capacity, for example, because the agent was defrauding the insured. In *P.C.W.* Staughton LJ said:

[34] [1972] NZLR 1038.
[35] Ibid, at 1049. See also the judgment of Macarthur J, at 1056.
[36] [1996] 1 All ER 774.
[37] [1996] 1 All ER 791.

I do not find in the authorities any decision that an agent to insure is required by s 19 to disclose information which he has received otherwise than in the character of an agent for the insured; and certainly none where the information was as to the agent's own fraud on his principal.[38]

4.1 The agent who completes the proposal form

On its face, the case law on imputation of an agent's knowledge to the insurer appears to be inconsistent and in a confused state. The guiding principle followed by the judges seems to be that a person is bound by the contents of a document that he has signed unless *non est factum* can be pleaded.[39] For the plea to succeed in the context of a proposal for insurance, the court must be satisfied that the signed proposal form is entirely different from that which the insured intended to sign, and that his mistake was not due to carelessness.[40]

It is only in exceptional cases that the courts are prepared to deviate from the rule that a signed document is binding. For example, in *Bawden v London, Edinburgh and Glasgow Assurance Co*,[41] the insurer's agent completed the proposal form for accidental injury insurance on behalf of the proposer who was illiterate and had lost an eye. The form contained a warranty that the applicant was free from any physical infirmity. This was patently untrue, and did not escape the agent's notice. The insured was later involved in an accident in which he lost his other eye. The Court of Appeal held that the agent's knowledge of the insured's condition at the time of the proposal was imputed to the insurer, with the result that the insured could claim under the policy. Lord Esher MR,[42] concluded that the agent having 'authority to negotiate and settle the terms of a proposal... went to a man who had only one eye, and persuaded him to make a proposal to the [insurance] company, which the company might then either accept or reject... The proposal must be construed as having been negotiated and settled by the agent with a one eyed man. In that sense the knowledge of the agent was the knowledge of the company.'[43]

However, the decision in *Bawden* cannot be taken to represent a rule of general application for it has been distinguished in a range of later decisions.[44] For example, in *Biggar v Rock Life Assurance Co*,[45] false answers were given to questions in the proposal form which was completed by the agent even though the insured had given him correct information. The insured failed to check the accuracy of the answers before signing the proposal form. It was held that the insurers were not liable. By

---

[38] Above n 36, at 785.

[39] *L'Estrange v Graucob Ltd.* [1934] 2 KB 394; *Norwich & Peterborough Building Society v Steed (No 2)* [1993] 1 All ER 330. See, J Beatson, *Anson's Law of Contract,* above n 21 at 332 *et seq.*

[40] See further CHS Fifoot, *History and Sources of the Common Law, Tort and Contract* (London, Stevens & Sons, 1949). But see JE Adams, 'More Nails for the Coffin of "Transferred Agency"' [1999] *JBL* 215.

[41] [1892] 2 QB 534.

[42] Lindley and Kay LJJ concurring. Kay LJ, at 542, took the view that: 'The condition that the statements in the proposal are to form the basis of the contract do not apply at all, because knowledge is to be imputed to the company of the fact that Bawden only had one eye.'

[43] Above n 41, at 539.

[44] It is tenable to conclude that because of the insured's disabilities, *Bawden* is really an example of the plea of *non est factum.*

[45] [1902] 1 KB 516.

signing the proposal form the insured was taken to have adopted it.[46] In *Newsholme Bros v Road Transport and General Insurance Co Ltd*,[47] a proposer for a motor insurance policy orally gave correct answers to questions relating to previous losses to the insurers agent. The agent, who was not authorised to complete proposal forms, deliberately recorded untrue answers in the proposal form which was then signed by the proposer, warranting the truth of the statements contained therein. The proposal form also contained a basis of the contract clause. The Court of Appeal held that the agent's knowledge that the answers were false could not be imputed to the insurers. Scrutton LJ stated that:

> If the answers are untrue and [the agent] knows it, he is committing a fraud which prevents his knowledge being the knowledge of the insurance company. If the answers are untrue but he does not know it, I do not understand how he has any knowledge which can be imputed to the insurance company. In any case, I have great difficulty in understanding how a man who has signed, without reading it, a document which he knows to be a proposal for insurance, and which contains statements in fact untrue, and a promise that they are true and the basis of the contract, can escape from the consequences of his negligence by saying that the person he asked to fill it up for him is the agent of the person to whom the proposal is addressed.[48]

Greer LJ, while noting the agency point in issue,[49] also focused upon the parol evidence rule forbidding the admission of oral evidence of what the agent actually knew in order to vary the terms of the written contract, ie the proposal form. The agent's lack of authority to complete proposal forms or to issue cover notes was, it is suggested, material to the court's reasoning. The decision in *Bawden* was distinguished by the court on the basis that it did not apply where the insured instructed the agent to complete the proposal form.

On the other hand, the decision in *Newsholme* was distinguished in *Stone v Reliance Mutual Insurance Society Ltd*.[50] The insured was visited by an inspector (employed by the insurers) in order to reinstate a lapsed fire policy. The proposal form asked for details of lapsed policies and the insured's claims history. The inspector, who completed the form on the instructions of his employers, did not ask the insured for details but answered incorrectly that there were none. The proposal form was signed by the insured's wife without reading it. Notwithstanding that the proposal form expressly stated that should it be completed by any person other than the

---

[46] In his reasoning, Wright J cited at length from the judgment of the Supreme Court in *New York Life Assurance Co v Fletcher* 117 US 519 (1885). See also, *Winter v Irish Life Assurance plc*, above n 7 at 726, in which Sir Peter Webster observed: 'To the extent that the [insureds] signed the form when the answers to some of the questions had not been inserted, they must be taken to have adopted any answers inserted later by somebody else, whether by written additions to the form in writing or by answers received orally from or through [their authorised agent].' On the other hand, in *Keeling v Pearl Assurance Co Ltd* [1923] All ER Rep 307 at 309, Bailache J distinguished the decision in *Biggar*, preferring the *Bawden* line of cases, on the basis that the agent in question was more than a mere collector but an inspector 'whose business it is ... to fill up these forms for people who cannot fill them up for themselves... .'
[47] [1929] All ER Rep 442. For a recent example, see *Hazel for Lloyd's Syndicate 260 (trading as KGM Motor Policies at Lloyd's) v Whitlam* [2004] EWCA Civ 1600.
[48] Ibid, at 451.
[49] Ibid, at 454.
[50] [1972] 1 Lloyd's Rep 469.

insured, that person does so as agent of the insured,[51] the Court of Appeal, approving *Bawden,* held that the insurers could not avoid the policy. The decision is readily explainable on the basis of the inspector's actual and ostensible authority to complete proposal forms on behalf of prospective policyholders. Lord Denning MR, clearly influenced by the fact that the insurers could have discovered the true situation from their records of the insured, stated:

> No doubt it was Mrs Stone's mistake too. She ought to have read through the questions and answers before she signed the form: but she did not do so. Her mistake, however, was excusable, because she was of little education, and assumed that the agent would know all about previous policies and that there had been claims under them.[52]

The commercial reality, of course, is that intermediaries frequently complete proposal forms on behalf of their customers and in this respect the decisions in *Bawden* and *Stone* clearly accord with the expectations of the ordinary insured.[53] However, it should be stressed that these decisions should be viewed as being decided on their own particular facts. *Newsholme Bros v Road Transport and General Insurance Co Ltd,*[54] therefore continues to represent the orthodox position in English law.[55]

4.2 Waiver

As has been seen, in finding for the insured where information disclosed to an agent has not been transmitted to the insurer, the courts have also had recourse to the principle of waiver (or estoppel) as a means of holding an insurer liable.[56] The effect is to estop the insurer asserting breach of warranty. For example, in *Wing v Harvey,*[57] an agent continued to accept premiums on behalf of the insurers knowing that the assured was in breach of warranty. It was held that the insurers could not repudiate liability. By accepting the premiums through their authorised agent, the insurers affirmed the policy thereby waiving the assured's breach.[58] In *Holdsworth v Lancashire and Yorkshire Insurance Co,*[59] the claimant effected employer's liability cover through the agent of the insurers. The claimant told the agent that he was a joiner and builder but the agent, who completed the proposal form, described him only as a joiner. The claimant signed the proposal form without reading it. When the policy document was received he noticed the mistake and refused to take up the policy. Thereupon the agent, with the consent of the chief clerk at the insurance

---

[51] In *Facer v Vehicle and General Insurance Co Ltd* [1965] 1 Lloyd's Rep 113, the court viewed a similar clause stating that the agent is to be regarded as the insured's agent as conclusive of the issue. See also, *M'Millan v Accident Insurance Co Ltd* 1907 SC 484.

[52] Above n 22, at 474.

[53] See the judgment of Diplock LJ in *Stockton v Mason,* above n 8, in which his Lordship adopts a pragmatic view of the relationship between an insured and an intermediary.

[54] Above n 47.

[55] Yet other Anglo-Commonwealth jurisdictions have not felt so constrained. In *Blanchette v C.I.S. Ltd* (1973) 36 DLR (3d) 561 the Supreme Court of Canada refused to follow *Newsholme,* as did the High Court of Australia in *Deaves v CML Fire and General Insurance Co Ltd* (1979) 53 ALJR 382.

[56] See *Blackley v National Mutual Life Association of Australia Ltd,* above n 34.

[57] Above, n 22.

[58] See also, *Ayrey v British Legal and United Provident Assurance Co* [1918] 1 QB 136.

[59] (1907) 23 TLR 521.

company's branch office, altered the policy by inserting the words 'and builder'. The claimant then paid the first premium. The head office was not informed of the addition to the policy and when the claimant claimed, the insurers repudiated liability. Bray J, applying *Wing v Harvey*, held that the insurers were estopped from denying their agent's authority because they had received the premiums with constructive knowledge of the facts. The knowledge of the agent was therefore imputed to the insurers.

---

5. Duties owed by an agent to the principal

In addition to the obligations imposed on agents by the FSA (see chapter 2), an agent is also subject to the duties imposed by the general law of tort, contract and, as a person occupying a fiduciary position, equity. It is settled that an agent may be liable concurrently in tort and contract and so an action for breach of the duty to exercise reasonable care in the performance of a service can be brought in either.[60] However, whether the principal sues in tort or in contract has practical implications because different rules on limitation of actions apply to the different causes of action. For contract, the six-year limitation period laid down by the Limitation Act 1980 accrues when the breach occurs. The fact that damage is not suffered by the claimant until some later date does not extend the limitation period. If, on the other hand, the agent's breach gives rise to an action in negligence, the cause of action accrues when damage is in fact sustained so that the limitation period starts to run at a later date in tort.[61] The decision of the House of Lords in *Henderson v Merrett Syndicates Ltd*,[62] affords a clear example of this logistical consideration. The claimants were Names in the Lloyd's insurance market and were members of syndicates managed by the defendant underwriters as agents. Having suffered considerable financial losses in respect of a number of policies underwritten by their syndicates, the claimants sued the defendants for the negligent mismanagement of their financial affairs. The action for breach of contract against those defendants with whom there was privity, was time barred by virtue of the Limitation Act. However, the action in negligence which was founded upon the principle in *Hedley Byrne & Co Ltd v Heller & Partners*,[63] succeeded.

---

[60] *Forsikringsaktieselskapet Vesta v Butcher* [1988] 1 Lloyd's Rep 19 at 23, *per* O'Connor LJ. In *Henderson v Merrett Syndicates Ltd* [1995] 2 AC 145 at 194, Lord Goff stated: 'unless his contract precludes him from doing so, the claimant, who has available to him concurrent remedies in contract and tort, may choose that remedy which appears to him to the most advantageous.' See also, *Midland Bank Trust Co Ltd v Hett, Stubbs & Kemp* [1979] Ch 384; *Youell v Bland Welch & Co Ltd, The Superhulls Cover Case (No 2)* [1990] 2 Lloyd's Rep 431.

[61] The Limitation Act 1980, s 14A (inserted by the Latent Damage Act 1986) provides an alternative three year period based on discoverability. See further, D Oughton, J Lowry and R Merkin, *Limitation of Actions* (London, Lloyd's of London Press, 1998).

[62] [1995] 2 AC 145.

[63] [1964] AC 464.

5.1 Agent's liability in tort

In tort, liability can arise either in deceit or negligence. To support an action in deceit it must be proved that the agent made a fraudulent statement which caused loss to the claimant. The defendant must either know his statement to be false or else must be reckless, ie without knowing whether his statement is true or false he must be consciously indifferent as to its truth.[64] An award of damages for deceit will cover all the losses flowing directly from the tort so that, in contrast with the tort of negligence, they need not be foreseeable.[65]

For a claim in negligence to succeed, the claimant will need to prove that the agent owed him a legal duty of care, that the agent broke that duty, that the loss suffered was caused by the breach,[66] and the consequent damage was reasonably foreseeable.[67] The normal rules apply so that where the loss is purely economic, not arising from a negligent misstatement, no action will lie.[68] The scope of the duty of care owed by an intermediary to an insured-principal was considered by Cantley J in *Cherry Ltd v Allied Insurance*.[69] The defendant brokers had acted for the claimants for over 50 years. The claimants were aggrieved at the amount charged by way of premiums given their low claims record. They therefore decided to place their business elsewhere and instructed the defendants to terminate their policies. The defendants duly cancelled most of the policies but informed the claimants that the insurers of their consequential loss policy refused to cancel mid-term. Not wishing to be doubly insured, the claimants cancelled their new policy without notifying the defendants. Subsequently, the original insurer agreed to cancel but the defendants failed to pass this information on to the claimants who were now left uninsured in respect of this risk. The claimants then suffered a loss and successfully sued the defendant brokers in negligence for failing to inform them of the cancellation of the policy by the original insurers. Although there was a failure of communication on the part of both parties, nevertheless it was held that the cause of the loss was the defendants' negligence.

The court awarded damages for the amount which would have been recoverable under the original policy. Cantley J laid emphasis on the duty of care and skill expected of the defendants as professional insurance advisors. The judge said that '[t]hey were giving information within their specialised knowledge and they knew or

---

[64] *Derry v Peek* (1889) 14 App Cas 337.

[65] See *Doyle v Olby (Ironmongers) Ltd* [1969] 2 QB 158 at 167, in which Lord Denning MR said: 'the defendant is bound to make reparation for all the actual damages directly flowing from the fraudulent inducement ... it does not lie in the mouth of the fraudulent person to say that [damage] could not reasonably have been foreseen.' The Court of Appeal relied on the discussion in Mayne and McGregor, *Damages* (12th edn) (London, Sweet & Maxwell) at paras 955–7. See also, *Smith Kline v Long* [1988] 3 All ER 887.

[66] See, eg, *Fraser v B. Furman (Productions) Ltd* [1967] 2 Lloyd's Rep 1.

[67] Where the intermediary knows that the policy is to be assigned, the duty of care will extend to the assignee. See, eg, *Punjab National Bank v De Boinville* [1992] 3 All ER 104.

[68] See *Murphy v Brentwood DC* [1991] 1 AC 398; and *Henderson v Merrett Syndicates Ltd*, above n 60, at 182, *per* Lord Goff. Note the tripartite test promulgated by Lord Bridge in *Caparo Industries plc v Dickman* [1990] 2 AC 605, at 617. See also, *Hedley Byrne & Co Ltd v Heller & Partners Ltd*, above n 63, at 502–3, *per* Lord Morris (considered below at n 72), and 514, *per* Lord Hodson; and *Williams v Natural Life Health Foods Ltd* [1998] 2 All ER 577, at 581, *per* Lord Steyn. See generally, J Murphy, *Street on Torts* (London, LexisNexis, 2003), chs 11 and 12; NJ McBride and R Bagshaw, *Tort Law* (Harlow, Longman, 2005) ch 5.

[69] [1978] 1 Lloyd's Rep 274. See also, *Osman v J. Ralph Moss* [1970] 1 Lloyd's Rep 313.

ought to have known that it would be taken seriously and acted upon in a transaction of importance.'[70] In his reasoning, Cantley J cited the following passage from the speech of Lord Morris of Borth-y-Gest in *Hedley Byrne & Co Ltd v Heller & Partners Ltd,*[71] describing his Lordship's formulation as representing the orthodoxy to be applied to the facts before him:

> I consider that it follows and that it should now be regarded as settled that if someone possessed of a special skill undertakes, quite irrespective of contract, to apply that skill for the assistance of another person who relies upon such skill, a duty of care will arise. The fact that the service is to be given by means of or by the instrumentality of words can make no difference. Furthermore, if in a sphere in which a person is so placed that others could reasonably rely upon his skill or upon his ability to make careful inquiry, a person takes it upon himself to give information or advice to, or allows his information or advice to be passed on to, another person who, as he knows or should know, will place reliance upon it, then a duty of care will arise.[72]

In *Hedley Byrne*, of course, it was held that the defendants' disclaimer effectively excluded liability for negligence. Such exclusion clauses are now subject to the test of reasonableness contained in the Unfair Contract Terms Act 1977, section 2(2).[73]

5.1.1 Liability for negligent misstatement: the current judicial thinking on Hedley Byrne

The basis of liability for economic loss arising from negligent misstatement has been the subject of far reaching review in three House of Lords decisions. In *Spring v Guardian Assurance plc,*[74] Lord Goff of Chieveley said that the principle in *Hedley Byrne* is not limited to the provision of information and advice but extends to include the performance of other services. This, then, can be taken to include the services performed by insurance intermediaries in addition to the general information and specialist advice they provide to their clients. Lord Goff went on to add that where the claimant can demonstrate that he entrusted the defendant with the conduct of his affairs, the defendant may be held to have assumed responsibility to the claimant where the latter relied on the defendant to exercise due skill and care in respect of such conduct.[75] In the opinion of Lord Goff and Lord Woolf sufficient proximity will be found to exist between the parties where their relationship is equivalent to contract.[76]

In *Henderson v Merrett Syndicates Ltd,*[77] Lord Goff subjected the speeches in *Hedley Byrne* to considerable analysis and concluded that the principle is pivoted upon a relationship between the parties 'which may be general or specific to the particular transaction, and which or may not be contractual in nature.'[78] Significantly,

---

[70] Ibid, at 280.
[71] Above, n 63.
[72] Ibid, at 502–3.
[73] See further J Beatson, *Anson's Law of Contract*, above n 21, at 185 *et seq.*
[74] [1995] 2 AC 296.
[75] Ibid, at 318.
[76] See, eg, *Pangood Ltd v Barclay Brown & Co Ltd* [1999] Lloyd's Rep IR 405.
[77] Above, n 62.
[78] Ibid, at 180.

Lord Goff went on to add that in cases falling within the *Hedley Byrne* principle, there is no need to inquire 'whether it is "fair, just and reasonable" to impose liability for economic loss.'[79]

Finally, in *White v Jones*,[80] it was held that two beneficiaries who lost their intended legacies as a result of the negligence of the testator's solicitor, could sue the solicitor in negligence. Lord Browne-Wilkinson thought that proximity for the purposes of *Hedley Byrne* depended upon 'a conscious assumption of responsibility for the task rather than a conscious assumption of legal liability to the claimant for its careful performance.'[81] It can therefore be posited that where an intended beneficiary of an insurance policy suffers loss because an agent negligently fails to effect the contract, the duty of care owed to the insured may now be extended to the disappointed beneficiary.[82] The measure of damages awarded to the beneficiary will be based on the sum which would have been received from the insurer in the absence of the agent's breach of duty.[83]

These landmark decisions were reviewed by Lord Steyn in *Williams v Natural Life Health Food Ltd.*[84] He summarised the current position thus:

> First, in *Henderson* it was settled that the assumption of responsibility principle enunciated in *Hedley Byrne & Co Ltd v Heller & Partners Ltd* is not confined to statements but may apply to any assumption of responsibility for the provision of services. The extended *Hedley Byrne* principle is the rationalisation or technique adopted by English law to provide a remedy for the recovery of damages in respect of economic loss caused by the negligent performance of services. Secondly, it was established that once a case is identified as falling within the extended *Hedley Byrne* principle, there is no need to embark on any further inquiry whether it is 'fair, just and reasonable' to impose liability for economic loss. Thirdly, and applying *Hedley Byrne*, it was made clear that 'reliance upon [the assumption of responsibility] by the other party will be necessary to establish a cause of action (because otherwise the negligence will have no causative effect).' Fourthly, it was held that the existence of a contractual duty of care between the parties does not preclude the concurrence of a tort duty in the same respect.[85]

Given that liability under the *Hedley Byrne* principle extends to the negligent performance of services, an agent who advises on the suitability of a particular policy should be able to explain its terms.[86] This may assume particular importance in relation to any conditions precedent to the insurer's liability. For example, in *JW Bollom & Co Ltd v Byas Mosley & Co Ltd*,[87] the insured, JWB, having suffered several false alarms, left the alarm to their premises switched off over a weekend. A fire occurred

---

[79] Ibid, at 181. Commenting upon Lord Goff's disavowal of the control mechanism afforded by the 'fair, just and reasonable' test, Mr Weir laments that this 'is rather a strong thing to say in an opinion which discounted the importance of reliance, and equated not only speech with action but commission with omission (which in the case of speech means silence): (1995) 111 *LQR* 357 at 361.

[80] [1995] 2 AC 207.

[81] Ibid, at 274.

[82] See also, *Ross v Caunters* [1980] Ch 297.

[83] *Cherry Ltd v Allied Insurance*, above, n 69. The measure of damages is therefore the same irrespective of whether the claimant sues in tort or contract: *Charles v Altin* (1854) 15 CB 46.

[84] Above, n 68.

[85] Ibid, at 581.

[86] *Harvest Trucking Co Ltd v Davis*, above n 3.

[87] [2000] Lloyd's Rep IR 136.

causing some £8 million worth of damage. The insurers repudiated liability on the basis of a breach of condition precedent requiring the maintenance and use of the alarms. The claim was settled at £5 million. JWB successfully sued their brokers for £3 million arguing that they had failed to take reasonable steps to bring the clauses to their, ie the insured's, attention. In *Alexander Forbes Europe Ltd v SBJ Ltd*,[88] the action was brought by a firm of brokers against their former professional indemnity brokers, SBJ. The dispute arose out of pension mis-selling claims and SBJ were held liable for failing to make a 'blanket' notification on behalf of the claimants. David Mackie QC, sitting as a Deputy High Court Judge, found for the claimants. The defendant brokers had not been entitled to rely upon the supposed expertise of the claimant so as to lower their standard of care. The judge stated that: 'Brokers owe duties going beyond those of a post box. It was for the brokers to get a grip on the proposed notification, to appraise it and to ensure that the information was relayed to the right place in the correct form.'[89]

It should be noted that absent any circumstances giving rise to a special relationship between the insured's agent and the insurer, it has been held that no independent duty will be owed by the agent to the insurer on the basis that the agent is merely a conduit of information between the parties. In any event, the insurer's remedy for non-disclosure or misrepresentation lies against the insured by way of avoidance of the policy. But an independent duty is owed by an agent to the insurer in the limited circumstances of s 19 of the Marine Insurance Act 1906.[90]

5.1.2 Duty to disclose material facts when completing the proposal form

It has been seen that it is common practice for brokers to complete proposal forms on behalf of their clients. It has also been noted that the courts are loath to impute knowledge to the insurers which the broker may possess about the insured risk.[91] However, where a broker fails to question the insured about facts material to the risk, or where a broker omits to pass on to the insurer material facts made known to him by the insured, or misrepresents such information, the issue arises whether the broker will be held to be in breach of duty. Brokers are independent, but it is settled that in all matters relating to the placing of insurance the broker acts as the agent of the insured,[92] so that if the broker is aware of material facts but does not disclose them to the insurer, the insurer has the right to avoid the policy and the insured must therefore look to the broker for indemnification.

To be able to recover against the broker, the insured must prove that his loss resulting from the insurer's avoidance of the policy arose as a result of the broker's breach of duty and that the breach caused the loss suffered. In *O'Connor v B.D.B. Kirby & Co*,[93] the claimant arranged motor car insurance through the defendant broker. The

---

[88] [2003] Lloyd's Rep IR 432.
[89] Ibid, at [32].
[90] *Adams-Eden Furniture Ltd v Kansa General International Insurance Co Ltd* [1997] 6 Re LR 352 (Court of Appeal of Manitoba), applying *Gran Gelato Ltd v Richliff (Group) Ltd* [1992] 2 WLR 867; *HIH v Chase Manhattan Bank* [2003] Lloyd's Rep IR 230.
[91] See, eg, *Newsholme Bros v Road Transport and General Insurance Co Ltd*, above n 47.
[92] *Rozanes v Bowen* (1928) 32 Ll L Rep 98 (CA). See also, *Winter v Irish Life Assurance plc*, above n 7; *Hazel v Whitlam* [2005] Lloyd's Rep IR 168.
[93] [1972] 1 QB 90. See also, *First National Commercial Bank plc v Barnet Devanney (Harrow) Ltd* [1999] Lloyd's Rep IR 43.

proposal form was completed by the broker on the basis of answers supplied by the claimant but it wrongly stated that the car was garaged when, in fact, it was parked on the street. The insurers avoided liability and the claimant sued the broker. It was held that the broker's duty was to take reasonable care in the circumstances and did not extend to guaranteeing the accuracy of the answers. In any case, there was no evidence as to how the mistake arose and the claimant's failure to notice the inaccuracy when signing the form would have operated to break the chain of causation which flowed from the alleged negligence.

But each case must be taken on its facts and so where the insured does not have sight of the proposal form, the broker may be liable for any misrepresentations contained therein. In *Warren v Henry Sutton & Co*,[94] the claimant sought to add a friend to his policy as an additional driver for a touring holiday in France. The friend was represented as having a clean driving record which was patently not the case. They were involved in an accident while on holiday and when the claimant claimed, the insurers avoided liability on the ground of misrepresentation.[95] The claimant sued the brokers for damages arguing that they had failed to ask about the friend's claims history. The Court of Appeal held that because the brokers had told the insurers in a telephone conversation that the friend had 'no accidents, convictions, or disabilities' without first confirming this with the claimant, they were liable. The majority of the court concluded that the misrepresentation arose as a result of the brokers' failure to ask the claimant the relevant questions.[96] In providing their services the brokers were under a duty to make such enquiries as were necessary in the circumstances. Similarly, where a broker answers questions in a proposal form incorrectly but the relevant information falls within the broker's knowledge, the broker will be liable to place the insured in the same position he or she would have been in had the policy been valid.[97]

The breadth of the duty of care owed by a broker to an insured was also examined in *McNealy v Pennine Insurance Co Ltd*.[98] The claimant, who was a property repairer and a part-time musician, instructed his brokers to effect comprehensive insurance on his motor car. The insurers offered low premium rates but their underwriting instructions, of which the brokers were aware, contained a list of professions which were not acceptable and which included part-time musicians. The brokers stated the claimant's principal occupation but failed to check that he had a part-time occupation. When the claimant was involved in an accident the insurers repudiated liability on the ground of non-disclosure. It was held that the brokers were liable to the claimant for the full amount of the claim. Waller LJ said that it was the duty of the broker:

> to make as certain as he reasonably could that the [claimant] ... came within the categories acceptable to the Pennine Insurance Co, and the only way in which he could properly do that, in my opinion, was to show him the list and probably go through it with him to make sure that the [claimant] understood that he had to be outside those particular risks ...

---

[94] [1976] 2 Lloyd's Rep 276.
[95] But see now the Road Traffic Act 1988, considered in ch 13, below.
[96] Lord Denning MR dissented on the ground that the claimant was under a duty to disclose to the brokers the additional driver's record.
[97] *Dunbar v A & B Painters Ltd* [1986] 2 Lloyd's Rep 38.
[98] [1978] 2 Lloyd's Rep 18.

However, the Court of Appeal stressed that where the broker is not in possession of material facts and there are no special circumstances putting the broker on notice, there is no corresponding duty to warn the insured of his or her duty of disclosure.[99]

5.2 Agent's contractual liability

Determining the contractual liability of an agent is, of course, dependent upon the construction of the express or implied agreement entered into with the principal. It is settled that an agent is under a legal duty to exercise reasonable care and skill in the conduct of his contractual obligations.[100] This encompasses the timely discharge of the client's instructions. In *London Borough of Bromley v Ellis*,[101] the first defendant, E, was involved in car accident with a stationary Rolls-Royce which was used by the Mayor of Bromley. E discovered that at the time of the accident he was uninsured and so he joined the brokers as a third party. E had purchased his car from its original owner and the agreement between them was that the motor insurance should be transferred to him. E therefore instructed the brokers to arrange the transfer. A proposal form was completed and he was issued with a 30-day cover note. However, some four months elapsed before the brokers got around to sending the proposal form to the insurers and, in fact, they had to issue two more cover notes in the interim. Upon receipt of the proposal form the insurers raised a minor query about an answer contained therein which related to E's accident record. The brokers did not contact E about the query and did nothing to clear it up. In consequence the insurers subsequently instructed the brokers not to issue any more cover notes. E was not told of this until after the accident when he contacted the brokers. The Court of Appeal held that although the brokers were not E's agents, nevertheless they were under a duty of care to look after E's interests. They were therefore under a duty to arrange the transfer with reasonable care so as to ensure that he was protected. Lord Denning MR, who delivered the principal judgment,[102] said that the brokers:

> failed in many respects, one after the other. They ought to have sent off the proposal form straightaway to the insurance company - or, at all events, sent it within the first 30 days of the cover note. They did not do so... Then, when the query was raised, they did not do anything about it. It is clear to me that this want of due care was the reason why he was not insured...[103]

In determining the scope of an agent's duty of care the court have paid heed to the codes of practice governing insurance intermediaries, for example, that issued by the British Insurance Association.[104] No doubt this will now extend to the rules contained in the relevant FSA Handbooks. Further, in *The Superhulls Cover Case*,[105] Phillips J accepted counsel's submission that a broker's duties could be distilled into the following three propositions: (i) he must ascertain his client's needs by instruction

---

[99] See also, *Kapur v JW Francis & Co* [2000] Lloyd's Rep IR 361.
[100] *Forsikringsaktieselskapet Vesta v Butcher*, above n 60.
[101] [1971] 1 Lloyd's Rep 97.
[102] Phillimore LJ and Goff J concurring.
[103] Above n 101, at 99.
[104] *Harvest Trucking Co Ltd v Davis*, above n 3, at 643–4, *per* Judge Diamond QC.
[105] Above, n 60.

or otherwise; (ii) he must use reasonable skill and care to procure the cover which his client has asked for either expressly or by necessary implication; and (iii) if he cannot obtain what is required, he must report in what respects he has failed and seek his client's alternative instructions.[106]

5.3 Fiduciary duties

As with agents generally, an insurance agent is subject to the full rigour of fiduciary duties. For present purposes, these can be distilled into two propositions. First, to act bona fide in the interests of the principal. Secondly, to avoid a conflict of interests.[107] The situation becomes complex in insurance because the insured's agent will generally receive commission on the policy from the insurer which can give rise to issues of conflict of interest. As with fiduciaries generally, provided the principal has knowledge that commission is paid to the agent no breach arises because the principal will be taken to have consented to the payment.[108] In *Anangel Atlas C.N.S.A. v Ishikawajima-Harima Heavy Industries Co Ltd*,[109] the court took this to mean that knowledge of the amount was not necessary. This view may be doubted given that fully informed consent must include knowledge of all material facts.[110]

Although it is common practice for an insurance agent to act for more than one principal, the issue which arises is whether or not such an agent will be in breach of the duty to avoid a conflict of interest and duty. Not surprisingly, Megaw J in *Anglo-African Merchants Ltd v Bayley*,[111] took a strict view of the duty borne by insurance intermediaries. A claim made under a theft policy was met with the defence of non-disclosure. The insured's brokers had made their files available to the underwriters and their solicitors during the inquiry into the claim, but denied the insured's solicitors similar access. It was argued that in all matters relating to the placing of the risk, the broker was the agent of the insured but that once a claim arose, the broker became the agent of the underwriters. Megaw J stressed, albeit by way of *obiter*, that where an agent wishes to act for another principal, which on the facts of the case were the underwriters, the agent can only do so if he first obtains the fully informed

---

[106] Ibid, at 445, citing *McGillivray & Parkington,* Insurance Law (London, Sweet & Maxwell, 1988) para 385; *Callendar v Oelreichs* (1838) 5 Bing N C 58; *Hood v West End Motor Car Parking Co* [1917] 2 KB 38 at 47, *per* Scrutton LJ; *Mitor Investment (Pty) Ltd v General Accident Fire & Life Assurance Corporation* (1984) WAR 365; *Eagle Star Insurance Co Ltd v National Westminster Finance Australia Ltd* (1985) 58 ALR 165 at 183 (PC).

[107] *Keech v Sandford* (1726) Cas Temp King 61; *Bray v Ford* [1896] AC 44; *Boardman v Phipps* [1967] 2 AC 46. See generally, RP Meagher, WMC Gummow and JRF Lehane, *Equity Doctrines and Remedies* (Sydney, LexisNexis, 2002) ch 5. In *Companhia de Seguros Imperio v Heath (REBX) Ltd* [1999] Lloyd's Rep IR 571, the Court of Appeal, dismissing an appeal against the decision of Langley J, held that in an action for breach of fiduciary duty the same limitation periods as for any action in contract or tort apply. See also, the duty to avoid a conflict of interests contained in the GISC Private Customer Code and the GISC Commercial Code, reproduced in J Lowry and P Rawlings, *Insurance Law: Cases and Materials* (Oxford, Hart Publishing, 2004) ch 3. It should be noted, however, that the GISC ceased operation on 13 January 2005 when the FSA took over its role. See now the Principles for Business, 1 and 8, together with ICOB 4.6.IR.

[108] Such consent may be express or implied: *Workman & Army & Navy Cooperative Supply Ltd v London & Lancashire Fire Insurance Co* (1903) 19 TLR 360 at 362, *per* Kekewich J.

[109] [1990] 1 Lloyd's Rep 167.

[110] *N.Z. Netherlands Society v Kuys* [1973] 2 All ER 1222; *B.L.B. Corp of Australia Establishment v Jacobsen* (1974) 48 ALJR 372.

[111] [1970] 1 QB 311.

consent of the insured. The judge concluded that 'in the absence of such express and fully informed consent it would be a breach of duty on the part of the insurance broker so to act.'[112]

The issue arose again in *North and South Trust v Berkeley*,[113] in which the insured demanded delivery up of an assessor's report from the broker. The underwriter, claiming that the information was confidential, petitioned for an injunction preventing the broker from releasing the report. Donaldson J questioned the propriety of the practice of Lloyd's, and of the insurance industry generally, of using brokers to instruct assessors to investigate a claim. Nevertheless, and somewhat curiously, the judge held that the contents of the assessors report need not be disclosed to the insured. No doubt the learned judge was influenced by the fact that this practice was of common usage in the insurance industry, and so neither the broker nor the underwriter knew that this arrangement was improper.[114] However, Donaldson J did go on to express surprise at the failure of the Committee of Lloyd's to change this practice in the light of Megaw J's criticisms expressed in *Bayley*.[115] These criticisms were recently echoed by David Steel J in *Callaghan v Thompson*,[116] who confirmed that the broker remained the agent of the insured and was therefore in breach of the no-conflict rule by obtaining reports from loss adjusters on behalf of the underwriters.

[112] Ibid, at 323, applying the views of Scrutton LJ expressed in *Fullwood v Hurley* [1928] 1 KB 498, at 502: 'No agent who has accepted an employment from one principal can in law accept an engagement inconsistent with his duty to the first principal ... unless he makes the fullest disclosure to each principal of his interest, and obtains the consent of each principal to the double employment.'
[113] [1971] 1 WLR 470.
[114] For a detailed examination of the judge's reasoning see, BAK Rider, 'The Fiduciary And The Frying Pan' [1978] *Conv* 114, at 117–21. See also M Kay and D Yates, 'An Unremedied Breach of Fiduciary Duty' [1972] *MLR* 78.
[115] Somewhat belatedly, this was addressed by the Lloyd's Code of Practice for Lloyd's Brokers (November 1988), para 9.6: 'a Lloyd's broker should not, without the fully informed consent of both parties, act for both the client and insurers during the claims settling process if by doing so he would be undertaking duties to one principal which are inconsistent with those owed to the other. In any event, a Lloyd's broker who receives or holds on behalf of the insurers concerned an adjuster's report or similar document relating to an insurance claim made by his client should only do so on the basis that the information in the report may be imparted to the client.'
[116] [2000] Lloyd's Rep IR 125.

4

Utmost Good Faith:
The Duty of Disclosure
and Misrepresentation

This chapter is concerned with both the duty of disclosure and the duty to refrain from misrepresentation when negotiating an insurance contract. While each is treated as distinct and separate topics, there is a fine line between the two and they are frequently treated as one and the same thing by the judges.[1] This is no doubt due to the common practice of insurers of raising both by way of defence to a claim. However, there are significant distinctions. For example, non-disclosure is concerned with the insured's duty to volunteer material facts whereas misrepresentation concerns the insured's duty to answer questions accurately that are raised by the insurer generally in proposal forms.[2] The difficulty of drawing a bright line between non-disclosure and misrepresentation in insurance contracts can be seen in relation to an insured's failure to answer a specific question raised by the insurer. Such failure will be deemed to be a negative answer, that is, a misrepresentation (cf. the general law of contract where misrepresentation must take a positive form so that mere silence will not constitute misrepresentation).

---

1. The doctrine of *uberrimae fidei*

Whereas under the general law of contract there is no positive duty of disclosure, contracts of insurance are a species of contracts *uberrimae fidei* (of utmost good

---

[1] Indeed, in *HIH Casualty and General Insurance Co* v *Chase Manhattan Bank* [2003] Lloyd's Rep IR 230, the House of Lords noted that 'pure' non-disclosure is relatively rare. The fine distinction between non-disclosure and misrepresentation in insurance law is clearly and colourfully illustrated by Professor Clarke who observes: 'If I describe the shandy that I have just bought you as lemonade, is that non-disclosure of part, the beer, or misrepresentation of the whole?' See M Clarke, 'Rescission: Inducements and Good Faith' [2004] *CLJ* 286 at 288.

[2] If the insured's answers are made the 'basis of the contract' they are converted into warranties in which case the issue of misrepresentation does not arise, see ch 7, below.

faith).[3] Consequently, both parties, the proposer and the insurers, are bound to disclose every material fact affecting the risk to the other before the contract is concluded.[4] The duty of utmost good faith, in so far as it applies to contracts of insurance was explained over two centuries ago by Lord Mansfield CJ in *Carter v Boehm*.[5] The case concerned an insurance policy effected by the Governor of Sumatra, George Carter (the insured), against a French attack on Fort Marlborough. The insurers sought to avoid the contract when the insured claimed under the policy contending that he had failed to disclose the fort's weakness and the likelihood of it being attacked by the French. Although the defence failed, Lord Mansfield took the opportunity to explore the scope of the duty of disclosure borne by proposers of insurance. He stated:

> Insurance is a contract of speculation. The special facts upon which the contingent chance is to be computed lie most commonly in the knowledge of the assured only; the underwriter trusts to his representation, and proceeds upon confidence that he does not keep back any circumstance in his knowledge to mislead the underwriter into a belief that the circumstance does not exist. ... Although the suppression should happen through mistake, without any fraudulent intention, yet still the underwriter is deceived and the policy is void; because the *risque* run is really different from the *risque* understood and intended to be run at the time of the agreement. ... Good faith forbids either party, by concealing what he privately knows, to draw the other into a bargain from his ignorance of the fact, and his believing the contrary.[6]

It is self evident that the deliberate failure to disclose facts which misleads the insurer is a fraudulent concealment which renders the contract void for want of good faith. However, it is noteworthy that in this passage from his speech, Lord Mansfield went further by adding that even non-fraudulent suppression of material facts has the same result. The effect, therefore, is that a proposer bears a heavy burden of disclosure when completing a proposal form and when subsequently renewing the insurance contract. This is typically explained by virtue of the fact that insurers are wholly dependent upon the proposer providing full disclosure of all circumstances

---

[3] See the Marine Insurance Act 1906 s17, which, codifying the common law, states that: 'A contract of marine insurance is a contract based upon the utmost good faith, and, if the utmost good faith is not observed by either party, the contract may be avoided by either party.' Notwithstanding the title of the 1906 Act, utmost good faith applies to all branches of insurance including reinsurance. Other examples of contracts of utmost good faith (ie contracts requiring a positive duty of disclosure as opposed to a mere duty not to misrepresent facts) include, contracts of guarantee or surety (see *Hamilton v Watson* (1845) 12 Clark & Fin 109); partnership agreements (see *Law v Law* [1905] 1 Ch 140); contracts to takes shares in public companies–regulated by the Financial Services and Markets Act 2000 (see ss 84 and 85) and the Public Offers of Securities Regulations 1995 (as amended); and family settlements (see *Wales v Wadham* [1977] 2 All ER 125 at 140, *per* Tudor Evans J).
[4] As will be seen below, the mutuality of the duty was recognised by Lord Mansfield in *Carter v Boehm* (1766) 3 Burr 1905 (and is laid down in s 17 of the Marine Insurance Act 1906, ibid). See *Banque Financière de la Cité SA v Westgate Insurance Co Ltd* [1991] 2 AC 249 (HL), affirming the Court of Appeal, [1990] 1 QB 665, discussed below. See also, *Britton v Royal Insurance Co* (1866) 4 F & F 905, at 909.
[5] Ibid.
[6] Ibid, at 1909. As pointed out by Lord Mustill in *Pan Atlantic Insurance Co v Pine Top Insurance Co* [1995] 1 AC 501, Lord Mansfield was attempting to introduce into English law a general principle of good faith; see also *Manifest Shipping Co Ltd v Uni-Polaris Shipping Co Ltd (The Star Sea)* [2001] 2 WLR 170, (Lord Hobhouse).

pertinent to the calculation of the risk underwritten by them.[7]

That said, it has, however, been questioned whether such an onerous duty on the insured was actually envisaged by Lord Mansfield. It has been convincingly argued that this celebrated passage from Lord Manfield's speech has been taken out of context with the result that, read in isolation from the rest of his speech in the case, and indeed his views expressed in subsequent cases, a far stricter duty than was intended by him has been wrongly fashioned by successive English courts.[8] Professor Hasson contends that the effect of this 'lop-sided' reading of the judgment has been to distort the duty of disclosure so that it seems that the insurer's role in the process is entirely passive. Yet, Lord Mansfield framed the duty in narrower terms so that the insured's duty of disclosure arises only with respect to facts that the insured 'privately knows, and the [insurer] is ignorant of, and has no reason to suspect.'[9] On the facts of *Carter v Boehm*, Lord Mansfield was of the view that:

> The underwriter knew the insurance was for the governor. He knew the governor must be acquainted with the state of the place. He knew the governor could not disclose it, consistently with his duty. He knew the governor, by insuring, apprehended, at least, the possibility of an attack. With this knowledge, without asking a question, he underwrote. By so doing, he took knowledge of the state of the place upon himself. It was a matter, as to which he might be informed in various ways: it was not a matter, within the private knowledge of the governor only.[10]

---

2. The juridical roots of the duty of disclosure

Tracing the origins of the duty has given rise to much academic and judicial debate.[11] The argument is pivoted upon whether the duty arises from some implied term of the

---

[7] See further the judgment of Channell J in *Re Yager* (1912) 108 LT 28. The policy underlying the duty seems not to rest upon the need to prevent harm to the insurer but upon the need for a true and fair agreement whereby risk is transferred from one party (the proposer) to the other (the insurer). This objective depends on equality of information. See further, *HIH Casualty and General Insurance Co v Chase Manhattan Bank,* above n 1, Lord Hobhouse.

[8] See RA Hasson, 'The Doctrine of Uberrima Fides in Insurance Law–A Critical Evaluation' [1969] *MLR* 615.

[9] Above n 4, at 1911.

[10] Above n 4, at 1915.

[11] For a thorough survey of the various views expressed on the source of the duty, see Paul Matthews, 'Uberrima Fides in Modern Insurance Law' in FD Rose (ed), *New Foundations For Insurance Law, Current Legal Problems* (London, Stevens & Sons, 1987). See also, TJ Schoenbaum, 'The Duty of Utmost Good Faith in Marine Insurance Law: A Comparative Analysis of American and English Law' (1998) 29 *JMLC* 1; J Fleming, 'Insurer's breach of good faith–a new tort?' [1992] *LQR* 357; ADM Forte, 'Good Faith and Utmost Good Faith: Insurance and Cautionary Obligations in Scots Law' in ADM Forte (ed), *Good Faith in Contract and Property* (Oxford, Hart Publishing, 1999); and HN Bennett, 'Mapping the Doctrine of Utmost Good Faith in Insurance Law' [1999] *LMCLQ* 165. In terms of judicial opinion, Lord Watson stated in *Blackburn, Low & Co v Vigors* (1887) 12 App Cas 531 at 539 that: 'It is in my opinion a condition precedent of every contract of marine insurance that the insured shall make a full disclosure of all facts materially affecting the risk which are within his personal knowledge at the time when the contract is made.'

contract,[12] or is rooted in a fiduciary relationship of the parties,[13] or whether it is based in some tortious duty. The issue is significant and extends beyond the boundaries of mere academic argument. For example, for the purposes of determining the relevant limitation period the question assumes immense practical importance.[14] Also, a claim for a particular remedy is, of course, dependent upon whether the cause of action is legal or equitable.

Although the opportunity arose in *Banque Financière de la Cité S.A. v Westgate Insurance Co Ltd*,[15] for the Court of Appeal and the House of Lords to subject the juridical basis of the disclosure requirement to thorough examination, the respective courts failed to grasp the nettle. Both the Court of Appeal, and by adoption, the House of Lords rejected the notion that the duty of disclosure arose from some implied contractual term. Both courts also refused to accept the point that the duty arose from some tortious obligation, preferring instead to attribute its roots to equity. Given that Lord Mansfield CJ presided over common law courts and, ironically, his civilian antecedence, this conclusion is open to challenge. Yet, in a recent pronouncement by the House of Lords on the issue, the court also attributed the duty to equitable foundations.[16]

It is apparent that the task of properly ascribing the source of the duty to be of utmost good faith is problematic. Only by extensive and authoritative judicial consideration of the issue will the theoretical basis of the duty be properly framed. The solution may well lie in holding that the respective parties to an insurance contract are so-called 'fact-based' fiduciaries whereby the fiduciary duties arise not by virtue of the particular status of the individual concerned (as with, for example, company directors, and trustees) but out of the factual situation underlying the particular relationship.[17] The model for this can be found in many jurisdictions in the United States where the received wisdom underlying the jurisprudence is that since both parties to an insurance contract have an advantage over the other so that there is, in effect, a mutual vulnerability, they must therefore stand in a fiduciary relationship.[18] Transplanting this approach into English law would not present any insurmountable theoretical problems given that there are situations where the English courts are prepared to find a fiduciary relationship where the relation between two parties is

---

[12] See, eg, , *Blackburn Law & Co v Vigors* (1886) 17 QBD 553, at 578, *per* Lindley LJ and at 583, *per* Lopes LJ. For criticism of the implied term theory see, eg, GL Williams, 'Language And The Law–IV' (1945) 61 *LQR* 384 at 401. See also, *Merchants and Manufacturers Insurance Co v Hunt* [1941] KB 295, at 313, *per* Scott LJ and *March Cabaret Club v London Assurance* [1975] 1 Lloyd's Rep 169, at 174, in which May J observed: 'Even the common law duty of disclosure I find difficult to explain fully on the theory of its resting only on an implied term of the contract. If it did, it would not arise until the contract had been made; and then its sole operation would be to unmake the contract.'

[13] As was argued in *Banque Keyser Ullmann S.A. v Skandia (UK) Insurance Ltd* [1987] 1 Lloyd's Rep 69. See P Matthews, above n 11.

[14] See DW Oughton, JP Lowry and RM Merkin, *Limitation Of Actions* (London, Lloyd's of London Press, 1998), chs 8, 12, 18, and 23.

[15] Above, n 4.

[16] See *Pan Atlantic Insurance Co v Pine Top Insurance Co* [1995] 1 AC 501, discussed below at p 89.

[17] See R Flannigan, 'The Fiduciary Obligation' [1989] *OJLS* 285. See also, The Law Commission's Consultation Paper No 124, *Fiduciary Duties and Regulatory Rules* (London, HMSO, 1992).

[18] See, eg, the North American case law cited by P Matthews, above n 11, at 42–3. See further the judgment of Woodhouse J in *Coleman v Myers* [1977] 2 NZLR 225, at 325. See also, Finn, *Fiduciary Obligations* (Sydney, Law Book Co, 1977) para 467.

founded upon trust.[19] Indeed, recent English decisions have taken the view that the duty is equitable in nature.[20]

3. Determining the materiality of non-disclosed facts

In summary, the duty of utmost good faith requires the insured to disclose every material fact relating to the risk before the contract is concluded. It is settled that the duty applies to all classes of insurance, whether the contract is for fire, life, marine insurance, or reinsurance.[21] Further, the common law duty of disclosure as formulated by Lord Mansfield has been codified by the Marine Insurance Act 1906 s 18. Despite the title of the statute, this section is of general application in insurance law.[22] Section18(1) provides:

> Subject to the provisions of this section, the assured must disclose to the insurer, before the contract is concluded, every material circumstance which is known to the assured, and the assured is deemed to know every circumstance which, in the ordinary course of business, ought to be known by him. If the assured fails to make such disclosure, the insurer may avoid the contract.

Whether or not a fact is one that should be known to the insured in the ordinary course of business is itself a question of fact.[23] The purely innocent insured who fails to disclose a fact he has no reason to believe exists, and it is not one which ought to be known to him in the ordinary course of business, is not placed under a duty to investigate whether there are, indeed, any material facts in existence. The judges have long recognised that 'you cannot disclosure what you do not know.'[24] Rejecting the argument that insureds should be under a duty to make extensive inquiries prior to concluding a contract of insurance, McNair J observed in *Australia and New Zealand Bank Ltd v Colonial and Eagle Wharves Ltd*,[25] that:

---

[19] See, eg, *Tate v Williamson* (1866) 2 LR Ch App 55, at 61, *per* Lord Chelmsford LC.

[20] See *Strive Shipping v Hellenic* [2002] Lloyd's Rep IR 669 and *Drake v Provident* [2004] Lloyd's Rep IR 277.

[21] *London Assurance v Mansel* (1879) 41 LT 225, at 227, *per* Jessel M.R. See *Joel v Law Union* (1908) 99 LT 712. In *The Good Luck* [1988] 1 Lloyd's Rep 514 at 546, Hobhouse J described the duty as 'an incident of the contract of insurance.'

[22] Although s1 of the 1906 Act appears to limit the Act to marine insurance, the leading cases on non-disclosure proceed on the assumption that the statute codified the common law on non-disclosure so that s18 applies to all types of insurance contract. See *Lambert v Co-operative Insurance Society* [1975] 2 Lloyd's Rep 485; *Container Transport International Inc v Oceanus Mutual Underwriting Association (Bermuda) Ltd* [1984] 1 Lloyd's Rep 476; *Pan Atlantic Insurance Co Ltd v Pine Top Insurance Co Ltd*, above, n 16; and *PCW Syndicates v PCW Reinsurers* [1996] 1 WLR 1136.

[23] See *Economides v Commercial Union Insurance plc* [1997] 3 All ER 636, discussed below at p 112. See also, the first instance decision in *WISE Underwriting Agency Ltd v Grupo Nacional Provincial SA* [2003] EWHC 1706 (Comm). The Court of Appeal's decision is considered below, at p 120.

[24] *Joel v Law Union and Crown Insurance*, above n 20, *per* Fletcher-Moulton LJ. See also, *Economides v Commercial Union Assurance Co plc*, ibid.

[25] [1960] 2 Lloyd's Rep 241. See also, *Economides v Commercial Union Insurance plc*, above n 22; discussed below, at p 113.

To impose such an obligation upon the proposer is tantamount to holding that insurers only insure persons who conduct their business prudently, whereas it is commonplace that one of the purposes of insurance is to cover yourself against your own negligence or the negligence of your servant.[26]

The test for determining the materiality of any 'circumstance' is laid down by s 18(2) which provides that: 'Every circumstance is material which would influence the judgment of a prudent insurer in fixing the premium, or determining whether he will take the risk.'[27] The test of 'prudent insurer', or in other words, reasonable insurer or underwriter, is the objective yardstick against which the materiality of the non-disclosed fact is to be tested so that the view of the particular insurer is irrelevant.[28] There have been attempts by the courts to modify this requirement by substituting the test of the reasonable insured's opinion for that of the prudent insurer. For example, the approach adopted by Fletcher Moulton LJ in *Joel v Law Union and Crown Insurance Co*,[29] when considering the measure of the insured's duty of disclosure, proceeds on the basis that: 'If a reasonable man would have recognised that the knowledge in question was material to disclose, it is no excuse that you did not recognise it.'[30] But this approach has not been followed in more recent cases, the courts preferring to apply the literal words of the Act, namely the 'judgment of a prudent insurer.'[31]

---

4. The consequences of non-disclosure

4.1 Avoidance

An insurer who seeks to rely upon non-disclosure when repudiating a claim bears the burden of proof to establish, on a balance of probabilities, that the insured failed to

---

[26] Ibid, at 252.

[27] The 'prudent insurer' test was first formulated by Blackburn J in *Ionides v Pender* (1874) LR 9 QB 531 at 538. In *Lambert v Co-operative Insurance Society*, above n 21, Cairns LJ stated: 'I see no reason why the rule should be different for fire or burglary or all risks insurance from that which has been laid down by statute for marine insurance. ... In providing by statute that the test should be that of the insurer in marine insurance cases, I think that Parliament was doing no more than inserting in its code of marine insurance law what it regarded as the general rule of all insurance law.' See also, *Becker v Marshall* (1923) 12 Ll LR 113 at 114, *per* Scrutton LJ. See further, *Mutual Life Insurance Co of New York v Ontario Metal Products Co Ltd* [1925] AC 344, PC; *Zurich General Accident and Liability Insurance Co v Morrison* [1942] 2 KB 53; *Pan Atlantic Insurance Co Ltd v Pine Top Insurance Co Ltd*, above n 16. See also the definition of materiality in the Road Traffic Act 1988, s 152(2).

[28] *Container Transport International Inc v Oceanus Mutual Underwriting Association (Bermuda) Ltd* [1984] 1 Lloyd's Rep 476; discussed below, at p 88.

[29] Above, n 20.

[30] Ibid, at 718.

[31] See, eg, *Lambert v Co-operative Insurance Society Ltd*, above n 21 and *Pan Atlantic Insurance Co Ltd v Pine Top Insurance Co Ltd*, above n 16. Cf the position in Scotland where in life insurance the test is the opinion of the reasonable insured, but in fire insurance the test is the prudent insurer's judgment: *Samuel Hooper v Royal London General Insurance Co Ltd* 1993 SLT 679.

disclose the existence of a fact known to him when effecting the policy.[32] The consequence of non-disclosure, whether at the time of the original proposal or upon the
renewal of the insurance (other than a policy for life insurance which is presumed to
be entire) is to render the insurance contract voidable,[33] thereby entitling the insurer
to avoid it *ab initio*. It has been said that non-disclosure 'terminates the contract, puts
the parties in *statu quo ante* and restores things, as between them, to the position in
which they stood before the contract was entered into.'[34] A cogent summary of the
consequences of non-disclosure was recently provided by Lord Hobhouse in *HIH
Casualty and General Insurance Co* v *Chase Manhattan Bank*[35]:

> it means that if an assured or his agent has failed to make full disclosure to the underwriter
> of all facts, which he knows or ought in the ordinary course of business to know, material
> to the risk, the underwriter can avoid the policy. In other words the policy becomes value-
> less to the assured. This negates the purpose of insurance which is to provide a secure and
> certain financial safeguard against losses caused by the insured risks. It makes the safeguard
> insecure.[36]

Any premium paid is returnable to the insured except in cases of fraud.[37] In this
regard s 84(3)(a) of the 1906 Act provides:

> Where the policy is void, or is avoided by the insurer, as from the commencement of the
> risk, the premium is returnable, provided that there has been no fraud or illegality on the
> part of the assured…

The insurer must avoid the policy within a reasonable time of becoming aware of
the insured's non-disclosure. Further, the court does not have discretion to vary the
relief. In *Brotherton* v *Aseguradora Colseguros SA (No 2)*,[38] the Court of Appeal
rejected the earlier reasoning of Colman J in *Strive Shipping Corp* v *Hellenic Mutual
War Risks Association (Bermuda) Ltd, (The Grecia Express)*,[39] to the effect that
avoidance is an equitable remedy that is discretionary. Mance LJ explained that the
right to avoid is a self-help remedy that can be exercised without the court's
authorisation. The judge stated that avoidance for non-disclosure or misrepresentation should be treated in the same way as rescission for misrepresentation under the
general law of contract which is 'by act of the innocent party operating independently of the court.'[40]

Marine insurance applies a forfeiture rule where the policy is avoided on the basis
of the insured's fraud. Thus, the insured forfeits the premium paid for the

---

[32] *Butcher v Dowlen* [1981] 1 Lloyd's Rep 310.
[33] For misrepresentation, see s 20(1) of the Marine Insurance Act 1906, discussed below.
[34] *Abram v Westville* [1923] AC 773 at 781, *per* Lord Atkinson. See also, *Glasgow Assurance Corporation v
Symondson* (1911) 16 Com Cas 109 at 121, where Scrutton J suggests that the only remedy available for
non-disclosure is avoidance of the contract.
[35] Above, n 1.
[36] Ibid, at [85].
[37] *Chapman v Fraser* B R Trin 33 Geo III.
[38] [2003] EWCA Civ 705. This is a significant decision and the reasoning of Mance LJ is discussed more
fully below.
[39] [2002] 2 Lloyd's Rep 88.
[40] Above, n 38 at [27]. Although note the criticism of this reasoning by M Clarke, above n 1, at 287. See
generally, P Macdonald Eggers, 'Remedies for the failure to observe the utmost good faith' [2003]
LMCLQ 249.

insurance.[41] Whether or not this applies to non-marine insurance is less clear, the case law being inconsistent on this point. That said, it seems tenable to conclude that since insurance is a contract *uberrimae fidei* the forfeiture rule would also allow insurers to retain the premium where avoidance is exercised in a non-marine contract for fraudulent non-disclosure.[42]

The Insurance Ombudsman, now part of the Financial Ombudsman Service, has attempted to mitigate the draconian consequences of 'inadvertent' non-disclosure by, for example, requiring insurers to pay a proportion of a claim that the premium actually fixed bears to the premium that would have been charged had the fact been disclosed. In his annual report for 1994, the Ombudsman states[43]:

> (vii) Where the insurer's underwriting guide or other evidence satisfies me that the facts withheld or misrepresented would have had a bearing on the premium or acceptance of risk, I may apply the principle of proportionality. This involves my requiring the same proportion of the claim to be met as the premium paid…if the premium would have been loaded by 50%, my award will be two thirds of the amount otherwise payable. The House of Lords confirmed that so far as the common law is concerned the principle of proportionality has no application in these cases, but *dicta* suggest that it may not be inappropriate in the field of consumer insurance. The observations on this point of Sir Donald Nicholls VC in the Court of Appeal in *Pan Atlantic* were not disapproved of in the House of Lords [above]. He made a strong indictment of the harshness of the 'all or nothing' result of the English common law rules, and provided an affirmation of the essential fairness of the principle of proportionality in appropriate cases.

However, the strict legal position continues so that avoidance of the policy operates without regard to notions of fairness. In this regard, Rix LJ observed in *Drake Insurance plc* v *Provident Insurance plc*,[44] that: 'On the whole English commercial law has not favoured the process of balancing rights and wrongs under a species of what I suppose would now be called a doctrine of proportionality. Instead it has sought for stricter and simpler tests and for certainty.'[45]

---

[41] Marine Insurance Act 1906, s 84(1) and (3)(a), above.

[42] See, *MacGillivray on Insurance Law* (10th edn) (London, Sweet and Maxwell, 2003) 207, 305.

[43] See also, the Insurance Ombudsman's Annual Report, 1989 para 2.17. See also 'Ombudsman News' April 2003, Issue 27:http://www.financial-ombudsman.org.uk/publications/ombudsman-news/27/27. Although calls for reform go back some 50 years (see the Law Reform Committee's Fifth Report *(Conditions and Exceptions in Insurance Policies)* (Cmnd 62, 1957); the Proposed EC Directive relating to insurance contracts, 31/12/79 OJ C355, amended in 1980, 31/12/80 OJ C255/30; the Law Commission's Report No 104, *Insurance Law: Non-Disclosure and Breach of Warranty,* Cmnd 8064 (London, HMSO, 1980); *Insurance Law Reform–The case for a review of insurance Law* (London, National Consumer Council, 1997); and the Report of the Sub-Committee of the British Insurance Law Association, *Insurance Contract Law Reform* (London, 2002), the prospect of statutory reform seems unlikely in the immediate future. That said, the Law Commission will be embarking on another review of insurance law shortly. It is noteworthy that the 1980 Law Commission Report rejected the principle of proportionality contained in the proposed Directive (which was based on French law) as unworkable. See J Lowry and P Rawlings, *Insurance Law: Cases and Materials* (Oxford, Hart Publishing, 2004) ch 4. See further, P North, 'Law Reform: processes and problems' [1985] *LQR* 338; and J Birds, 'The reform of insurance law' [1982] *JBL* 449.

[44] [2003] EWCA Civ 1834; [2004] Lloyd's Rep IR 277.

[45] Ibid, at [88].

4.2 Proving materiality: the role of expert evidence

In non-consumer insurance contracts the prudent insurer's judgment, assessed by the court on the basis of expert evidence of the particular type of insurance in question, is the pervasive test. The approach to be taken by the court towards expert evidence was considered by McCardie J in *Yorke* v *Yorkshire Insurance Co Ltd*,[46] who said:

> Expert evidence may frequently afford great assistance to the Court upon questions of novelty or doubt. ...[but] Judges are always free to test and revise any form of expert testimony. It may be said, however, ... in ... marine insurance cases ...expert evidence has usually been given by those actually engaged in the occupation of insurers. ... But it must be pointed out that in questions of life insurance the matters at issue are usually physiological, medical, or neuropathic. The directors of insurance companies, however, are but rarely medical men. ... The importance or otherwise of that which should be disclosed to a life insurance company may well be appreciated only by doctors or surgeons. Medical men may, therefore, often give a more useful opinion than the directors themselves as to what is or is not material and important.[47]

Expert evidence is therefore admitted merely to assist the court in its determination of the prudent insurers judgment, and not to decide the issue of whether or not a particular fact should have been disclosed by the insured. In *Roselodge Ltd v Castle*,[48] the insurers rejected the claimant's claim who, as diamond merchants, had insured diamonds against all risks. The insurers defence was founded upon non-disclosure in so far that first, the principal director of the insured company had been convicted of bribing a police officer in 1946 and second, that the insured's sales manager had been convicted of smuggling diamonds into the United States in 1956. According to one of the expert witnesses called by the insurer, a person who stole apples when aged 17 is much more likely to steal diamonds at the age of 67 even if he had led a blameless life for 50 years, than someone who had led a totally blameless life. This did not convince McNair J who held that the 1946 conviction was not a material fact, it having 'no direct relation to trading as a diamond merchant.'[49] However, the judge did go on to hold that the 1956 smuggling conviction was a material fact.

---

5. Qualifying the duty of disclosure: the position of the consumer and small trader

Before we proceed further with examining the content of the duty of disclosure, it should be noted at this particular juncture that the duty may operate differently depending upon whether the proposer is insuring in a private capacity (or in a capacity akin to such) on the one hand, or in a commercial capacity, on the other. In an

---

[46] [1918–19] All ER Rep 877.
[47] Ibid, at 881.
[48] [1966] 2 Lloyd's Rep 113. See also, *Reynolds v Phoenix Assurance Co Ltd* [1978] 2 Lloyd's Rep 440.
[49] Ibid, at 132.

attempt to counter the argument that the prudent insurer test works injustice, especially where the proposer is contracting in a non-business capacity (ie as a consumer), insurers who were members of Lloyd's or the Association of British Insurers issued two statements of practice in 1977 dealing with Long-Term Insurance and General Insurance. These were both updated in 1986 and the Statement on General Insurance Practice was revised in 1995.[50]

Paragraph 2(b) of the Statement of General Insurance Practice provided that an insurer will not repudiate a contract if the non-disclosed fact is one which 'a policyholder could not reasonably be expected to have disclosed'; or where any misrepresentation by the insured is innocent.[51] However, paragraph 3(a) of the *Long-Term Statement* stated somewhat obtusely that:

> An insurer will not unreasonably reject a claim. In particular, an insurer will not reject a claim or invalidate a policy on grounds of non-disclosure or misrepresentation of a fact unless:
> (i)   it is a material fact; and
> (ii) it is a fact within the knowledge of the proposer; and
> (iii) it is a fact which the proposer could reasonably be expected to disclose.
> (It should be noted that fraud or deception will, and reckless or negligent non-disclosure or misrepresentation of a material fact may, constitute grounds for rejection of a claim.)[52]

While the honest or innocent proposer therefore had nothing to fear, it should be borne in mind that the Statements were not binding in law.[53] It is also noteworthy that in non-business insurance contracts the reasonable insured's opinion is now viewed by the Insurance Ombudsman as the decisive factor.[54] Further, non-compliance with the Statements may be taken into account by the Ombudsman (or in any case referred to arbitration) so as to deny the insurer the right to avoid the contract for non-disclosure.[55]

It is thus important to bear in mind that the following discussion, particularly in relation to the harshness of the disclosure duty, is chiefly directed towards the position of the commercial policyholder. That said, it is noteworthy that the Financial Ombudsman Service state in their news report (Issue 39, August 2004) that 'it does not always seem fair and reasonable to us to ignore totally the principles of the *Statement* when we look at commercial insurance disputes.' Elaborating on this point

---

[50] For a thorough analysis of the 1986 Statements see, A Forte, 'The revised Statements of Insurance Practice' [1986] *MLR* 754. See also, J Birds, 'Self-regulation and insurance contracts' in FD Rose (ed), *New Foundations For Insurance Law,* above n 11. It should be noted that as from 14 January 2005, the Statement of General Insurance Practice was replaced by the regulatory powers of the FSA.

[51] Misrepresentation is discussed below.

[52] See now the approach adopted by the Court of Appeal to the issues of non-disclosure and misrepresentation in *Economides v Commercial Union Assurance Co plc,* above, n 22; considered below, at p 112. The Statements are based on the recommendations of the Law Commission's Report No 104, *Insurance Law: Non-Disclosure and Breach of Warranty,* Cmnd 8064 (London, HMSO, 1980). See further, J Lowry and P Rawlings, *Insurance Law: Cases and Materials,* ch 4.

[53] Although it should be noted that parts of the Statements have been incorporated into the Code of Business Conduct Rules by the Financial Services Authority (FSA). This entered into force on 14 January 2005 when the FSA assumed responsibility for regulating the marketing of general insurance. See Ombudsman News, June 2005

[54] See the Insurance Ombudsman's Annual Report 1989, para 2.16. The Insurance Ombudsman is now part of the Financial Ombudsman Service, regulated by Part XVI of the Financial Markets and Services Act 2000.

[55] There are also clear signs of a more consumer friendly approach being taken by the courts; see, eg, *Drake Insurance plc v Provident Insurance plc* [2003] EWCA Civ 1834 , discussed below.

further, they add: 'Is it fair, for example, to say that a self-employed (sole trading) contractor should benefit from the protection given by the *Statement* when he insures his house contents, but not when he insures the tools he uses to carry out his job?' In general:

> If the policyholder's circumstances and, in particular, their likely understanding of the relevant insurance issues, appear to us to be similar to those of most private customers, then we would be more likely to think it appropriate to apply the principles of the *Statement*. This is especially likely if the dispute involves something that is commonly covered under personal insurance.

This situation may arise where a commercial policyholder is self-employed, lacks experience in financial and legal matters and lacks easy access to expert advice. But, a policyholder who uses the services of a broker will be taken to have the benefit of access to expert advice. It is stated that the Ombudsman is unlikely to conclude that the principles of the Statement should apply if the commercial policyholder is 'a limited company; employs a number of staff; and/or could reasonably be expected to have a greater understanding of business issues than a private individual.' Even with respect to small traders the Ombudsman therefore looked at all the surrounding circumstances before deciding whether the Statement of Practice applied. A subjective approach is adopted so that account will be taken of the policyholder's personal background and level of knowledge. A further dilution of the doctrine of utmost good faith for cases within the jurisdiction of the Financial Ombudsman was introduced in January 2005 by the addition to the FSA's Handbook of ICOB 7.3.6 which states:

> An insurer must not:
> 1. unreasonably reject a claim made by a customer;
> 2. except where there is evidence of fraud, refuse to meet a claim made by a retail customer on the grounds:
> (a) of non-disclosure of a fact material to the risk that the retail customer could not reasonably be expected to have disclosed;
> (b) of misrepresentation of a fact material to the risk, unless the misrepresentation is negligent.'

As is commented below, the ABI Statements will continue to inform the approach of the Ombudsman (see *Ombudsman News*, June 2005).

---

6. The duty of disclosure: defining the term 'influence' contained in S 18(2)

The Report of the Law Reform Committee observed that 'it seems that a fact may be material to insurers ... which would not necessarily appear to a proposer for insurance, however honest and careful, to be one which he ought to disclose.'[56] While the Marine Insurance Act 1906 attempts to lay down the guiding principle governing materiality of facts, it does not address the critical issue of how to define the term 'influence' contained in s 18(2). Determining whether a particular circumstance influenced someone is a nebulous exercise for there is no absolute standard. Degrees of influence are limitless. It is clear that a fact will be regarded as material if it relates either to the physical hazard of the subject matter of the insurance or to its moral hazard. For example, whether or not inflammable substances are stored in a building is obviously highly relevant to a proposal for fire insurance. Similarly, in car insurance non-standard modifications carried out to increase the vehicle's performance will be considered pertinent to the assessment of risk. Thus, if an enthusiast removes the factory fitted engine from his small family saloon car, and fits a supercharged model in its place, the premium payable will obviously be much greater to reflect the increased risk of accident. As will be seen, moral hazard centres on the circumstances surrounding the particular proposer and will include the proposer's claims history, previous refusals of cover and criminal record.[57]

The question of ascribing some meaning to the term 'influence' received extensive consideration in *Container Transport International Inc v Oceanus Mutual Underwriting Association (Bermuda) Ltd.*[58] Maintaining the balance firmly in favour of insurers, the Court of Appeal held that an insured is bound to disclose those material facts which *might* influence the judgment of a prudent insurer in deciding whether to accept the risk or in setting the premium. Kerr LJ stressed that 'judgment' as used in s 18(2) should be given its Oxford English Dictionary definition so as to be construed as meaning 'the formation of an opinion.' Thus, to prove the materiality of an undisclosed circumstance, the particular insurer must satisfy the court on a balance of probability that the 'judgment' (in the sense of formation of opinion) of a prudent insurer might have been influenced if the circumstance in question had been disclosed. This approach was adopted by Steyn J in *Highlands Insurance Co v Continental Insurance Co,*[59] to non-marine misrepresentations. Under this test, insurers are placed in a particularly strong position for it is not necessary to prove that the 'influence' was decisive. Nor, under this particular test, is it necessary for the actual insurer to prove that the misrepresentation or non-disclosure had induced the contract of insurance.[60]

At its simplest level, the duty of disclosure on a prospective insured is seemingly boundless since the parameters of the requirement of 'influence' were left open. At the extreme, the consequence is that all information (without necessarily taking into account what the reasonable insured considers relevant) will have to be disclosed on the basis that the prudent insurer might want to know it even if ultimately, it does not

---

[56] Law Reform Committee Fifth Report *(Conditions and Exceptions in Insurance Policies)* (Cmnd 62, 1957).
[57] See, eg, *Locker and Woolf Ltd v Western Australian Insurance Co Ltd* (1936) 54 Ll LR 211; and *Lambert v Co-operative Insurance Society,* above n 21, discussed below.
[58] Above, n 27.
[59] [1987] 1 Lloyds Rep 109.
[60] *Zurich General Accident and Liability Insurance Co Ltd v Morrison* [1942] 2 KB 539. Although the requirement of inducement was introduced by the House of Lords in *Pan Atlantic Insurance Co Ltd v Pine Top Insurance Co* [1995] 1 AC 501, considered below.

affect the insurer's decision as to the risk.[61] However, the Court of Appeal's view in *Container Transport International (CTI)* that it had correctly interpreted precedent on this issue, is open to question. In *Mutual Life Insurance Co v Ontario Metal Products Co Ltd*,[62] Lord Salveson accepted the submission of the insurers counsel that 'the test was whether, if the fact concealed had been disclosed, the insurers would have acted differently, ... by declining the risk at the proposed premium ... .'[63] Yet in *CTI*, the Court of Appeal distinguished this decision on the basis that the Privy Council was concerned with the interpretation of the phrase 'material misrepresentation' contained in an Ontario statute. However, the particular statute in question was a codification of the English law, and the Privy Council opined that there was no difference between the law in England and Ontario.[64]

---

7. The requirement of 'inducement'

The opportunity for a complete and authoritative review of the duty of disclosure came before the House of Lords in *Pan Atlantic Insurance Co Ltd v Pine Top Insurance Co*.[65] The issues were first, should materiality be measured by reference to whether its 'influence' on the prudent insurer's judgment was 'decisive', or should some lesser degree of impact be sufficient? Secondly, where there has been non-disclosure of a material fact, must it *induce* the actual insurer to enter into the contract?

With respect to the first issue Lord Mustill (with whom Lords Goff and Slynn concurred), could see no good reason for departing from the principle formulated by Lord Mansfield in *Carter v Boehm* and which had guided insurance law for more than two hundred years. Lord Mustill stated: 'I can see no room within [the principle] ... for a more lenient test expressed solely by reference to the decisive effect which the circumstance would have on the mind of the prudent underwriter.'[66] On the question of statutory interpretation, the majority view was that since Parliament had left the word 'influence' in s18(2) unadorned by phrases such as *decisively* or *conclusively*, it must bear its ordinary meaning. His Lordship stated that:

---

[61] Some limits can be ascribed to the insured's duty of disclosure, see below, at p 102.

[62] [1925] AC 344.

[63] Ibid, at 351. Support for this approach can be found in a number of early English insurance decisions, examples of which include, *Seaman v Fonnereau* (1743) 2 Strange 1133; *Rickards v Murdock* (1830) 10 B & C 527; *Elton v Larkins* (1832) 5 C & P 385; *Stribley v Imperial Marine Insurance Co* (1875) 1 QBD 507.

[64] See M Clarke, 'Failure to Disclose and Failure to Legislate: is it Material ?–II' [1988] *JBL* 298, who also points out that the Board's definition of materiality was adopted as a statement of the English position by the Law Reform Committee Fifth Report *(Conditions and Exceptions in Insurance Policies)* (Cmnd 62, 1957). See further, H Brooke QC, 'Materiality in insurance contracts' [1985] *LMCLQ* 437; A Hamilton QC, 'Avoidance of liability on the grounds of misrepresentation and non-disclosure, or, the rise and rise of avoidable reinsurance' *Insurance and Reinsurance Law*, September 1985, 131; Steyn J, 'The Role of Good Faith and Fair Dealing in Contract Law: A Hairshirt Philosophy?' [1991] *Denning LJ* 131; and H Bennett, 'The Duty to Disclose in Insurance Law' [1993] *LQR* 513.

[65] Above, n 6. See NJ Hird, '*Pan Atlantic–Yet More To Disclose*' [1995] *JBL* 608.

[66] Ibid, at 536. Lord Mustill went on to add, at 550, that a circumstance may be material 'even though a full and accurate disclosure of it would not in itself have had a decisive effect on the prudent underwriter's decision whether to accept the risk and if so at what premium.'

this expression clearly denotes an effect on the thought processes of the insurer in weighing up the risk, quite different from words which might have been used but were not, such as 'influencing the insurer *to take* the risk.[67]

The majority decision therefore was to reject the 'decisive influence' test, and in reaffirming the Court of Appeal's decision in *CTI*, the position remains that a circumstance is material and must be disclosed even though the prudent insurer, had he known of the fact, would have insured the risk on the same terms. On this issue, the insured thus remains in a highly vulnerable position.[68] On the other hand, Lord Lloyd in a powerful dissent, agreed with the appellants' submission that there should be a twofold test under which the insurer must show that a prudent insurer, if aware of the undisclosed fact, would either have declined the risk or charged a higher premium and that the actual insurer would have declined the risk or required a higher premium.[69] The simplicity of the logic here clearly appealed to Lord Lloyd who stated:

> But if the prudent insurer would have accepted the risk at the same premium and on the same terms, it must be because, so far as he is concerned, the risk is the same risk. How, as a matter of ordinary language, can a circumstance be described as material, when it would not have mattered to the prudent insurer whether the circumstance was disclosed or not?[70]

In his Lordship's opinion, the appellants' submission '...does full justice to the language of s 18 of the 1906 Act. It is well defined, and easily applied. It does something to mitigate the harshness of the all-or-nothing approach which disfigures this branch of the law ... .'[71]

In relation to the second issue, the House of Lords unanimously held that the non-disclosure of a material fact, as with misrepresentation, must *induce* the particular insurer to enter into the contract.[72] In reaching this conclusion, their Lordships were clearly influenced by the argument that the 1906 Act codified the common law, and given that inducement was a requirement under the general law which provides for rescission of a contract, the Act must be taken as having the same effect. Accordingly, Lord Mustill stated that:

> ... I conclude that there is to be implied in the 1906 Act a qualification that a material misrepresentation will not entitle the underwriter to avoid the policy unless the misrepresentation induced the making of the contract, using 'induced' in the sense in which it is used in the general law of contract.[73]

---

[67] Ibid, at 531. See also the speech of Lord Goff, ibid at 517.
[68] See J Birds and N Hird, 'Misrepresentation and Non-disclosure in Insurance Law–Identical Twins or Separate Issues?' [1996] *MLR* 285.
[69] Above n 16, at 553.
[70] Ibid, at 557.
[71] Ibid, at 560.
[72] In essence, the House of Lords were injecting into the law on non-disclosure a requirement of causation analogous to the 'but for' test familiar to tort lawyers. See Lord Mustill's reference to causative effect, ibid at 551.
[73] Ibid, at 549. Where there is a material misrepresentation, there is a rebuttable presumption of inducement: see *Redgrave v Hurd* (1882) 20 Ch D 1 at 21; *Smith v Chadwick* (1884) 9 App Cas 187 at 196. Lord Mustill went on to add, at 551, that: 'As a matter of common sense, however, even where the underwriter is shown to have been careless in other respects the assured will have an uphill task in persuading the court that the witholding or mistatement of circumstances satifying the test of materiality has made no difference.' See also, *Svenska Handelsbanken v Sun Alliance and London Insurance plc* [1996] CLC 833.

The assimilation of non-disclosure with misrepresentation for the purposes of requiring inducement is curious. Inducement for the purposes of misrepresentation has always taken an active form, in other words, silence cannot, without more, constitute misrepresentation.[74] However, Lord Mustill does admit that the proposition that non-disclosure must induce the contract may well involve the House in making new law.[75] Clearly, it did.

Lord Goff, concurring, thought that the need to show inducement on the part of the actual insurer addresses the criticisms directed against the *CTI* decision. He reasoned that it was the absence of this requirement that prompted the call for the test of materiality to 'be hardened into the decisive influence test.'[76] It is suggested that practical considerations render this a hollow victory for the critics,[77] and Lord Lloyd's approach in favouring the 'decisive influence' test is to be preferred since it would provide an objective assessment of materiality. The costs involved in seeking disclosure of documents required for an insured to establish *non-inducement* are likely to be immense and will therefore stand as an effective deterrent against such claims, and the matter is made more difficult from the insured's point of view by the adoption by Lord Mustill (vigorously opposed by Lord Lloyd) of a 'presumption of inducement', whereby proof of materiality by the insurer casts upon the insured the burden of proving that the insurer was not in fact induced by the non-disclosed fact. That said, whether or not a non-disclosed fact is material, is, as seen above,[78] a question of law which will be decided in the light of expert evidence. If materiality is not established in the first place, inducement becomes a *non sequitur*. While the House recognised the iniquity of the test propounded by the Court of Appeal in *CTI*, Lord Mustill considered that the question of reform along the lines argued for by *Pan Atlantic* must be left to Parliament.

A line of cases since *Pan Atlantic* suggests that there is a lack of judicial consensus on the inducement requirement. For example, in *Marc Rich & Co AG v Portman*,[79] Longmore J narrowed the scope of inducement so that it would only trigger where the insurers were unable, with good reason, to give evidence. The judge stressed that in cases where the court is in doubt, the defence of non-disclosure should fail because '[a]t the end of the day it is for the insurer to prove that the non-disclosure did induce the writing of the risk ...'[80] In *Insurance Corporation of the Channel Islands v Royal Hotel Ltd*,[81] however, the presumption operated in favour of the insurers notwithstanding that they did not give direct evidence to substantiate inducement.[82] But in

---

[74] See *Bell v Lever Bros Ltd* [1932] AC 161 at 227, *per* Lord Atkin.
[75] Above, n 16, at 549.
[76] *Ibid*, at 518.
[77] But see A McGee, 'Utmost Good Faith In The Third Millennium' in D Feldman and F Meisel (eds), *Corporate And Commercial Law: Modern Developments* (London, Lloyd's of London Press Ltd, 1996), who questions whether *Pine Top* really does fundamentally change the law to the extent assumed.
[78] See p 85, above.
[79] [1996] 1 Lloyd's Rep 430. See also, *Sirius v International Insurance Group Corp v Oriental Insurance Corp* [1999] Lloyd's Rep IR 343 where, in relation to misrepresentation, Longmore J also stressed that it is for the insurer to prove inducement. The judge did, however, recognise that the onus of proof is difficult to discharge.
[80] Ibid, at 442.
[81] [1998] Lloyd's Rep I R 151.
[82] See also, *Aneco Reinsurance Underwriting Ltd v Johnson & Higgins* [1998] 1 Lloyd's Rep 565; see also, *International Management v Simmonds* [2004] Lloyd's Rep IR 247.

Assicurazioni Generali SpA v Arab Insurance Group (BSC),[83] the Court of Appeal took the view that although the non-disclosed or misrepresented fact need not be the sole inducement operating on the insurer,[84] it must be effective in *causing* the actual insurer to enter into the contract. Significantly, the majority of the court followed earlier decisions to the effect that the insurer must give evidence as to his state of mind. This, therefore, gives the insured the opportunity to cross-examine the insurer with the view to demonstrating that he was not induced by the non-disclosed fact but would have entered into the contract on the same terms had there had been full disclosure of all material facts. Clarke LJ summarised the position thus:

1. In order to be entitled to avoid a contract of insurance or reinsurance, an insurer... must prove on the balance of probabilities that he was induced to enter into the contract by a material non-disclosure or by a material misrepresentation.
2. There is no presumption of law that an insurer... is induced to enter in the contract by a material non-disclosure or misrepresentation.
3. The facts may, however, be such that it is to be inferred that the particular insurer... was so induced even in the absence from evidence from him.
4. In order to prove inducement the insurer or reinsurer must show that the non-disclosure or misrepresentation was an effective cause of his entering into the contract on the terms on which he did. He must therefore show at least that, but for the relevant non-disclosure or misrepresentation, he would not have entered into the contract on those terms. On the other hand, he does not have to show that it was the sole effective cause of his doing so.[85]

As seen from Clarke LJ's summary, the insurers must establish that the non-disclosed or misrepresented fact was an effective cause, although not necessarily the only cause, of their agreement to underwrite the risk. Inducement is, therefore, a question of fact. In *Drake Insurance plc v Provident Insurance plc*,[86] a motor insurance case, the insured had failed to disclose a speeding conviction and the insurer sought to avoid the policy on the basis that, taking an earlier accident that had been disclosed together with the non-disclosed conviction, it would have charged a higher premium. The majority of the Court of Appeal, Pill LJ dissenting, held that even if the conviction had been disclosed and the insurer sought to charge a higher premium, information would have come to light that the earlier accident had not been the insured's fault and this would have resulted in the premium being reduced to the normal level.[87] Rix and Clarke LJJ thus took the view that in deciding whether the non-disclosed fact had induced the insurer to enter the contract, it is necessary to examine what would have happened had full disclosure been made. The court thus speculates as to what the position would have been had the fact been disclosed.[88]

---

83 [2003] 1 WLR 577.
84 Following the decision in *St Paul Fire and Marine Insurance Co v McConnell Dowell Constructors Ltd* [1995] 2 Lloyd's Rep 116.
85 [2003] 1 WLR 577, at [64].
86 Above, n 54. See the comments of R Merkin, *Insurance Law Monthly* (2004) Vol 16 No 2.
87 Professor Merkin, ibid, notes that the decision 'means that an assured who has failed to disclose a material fact is given the opportunity at a later stage to assert that its disclosure would have made no difference to the insurer, as its response to the proposal might have led to a reformulation of the application and its acceptance on the same terms. This comes perilously close to allowing a court to underwrite the policy itself.'
88 See, eg, *Bonner v Cox Dedicated Corporate Member* [2004] EWHC 2963 (Comm).

The somewhat unsettled and inconsistent approach taken towards the requirement of inducement seen in the recent cases only serves to support the conclusion that Parliament should take up Lord Mustill's challenge and swing the pendulum back some way towards finding the optimum balance between the need to protect the insurer on the one hand, and the insured on the other. Indeed, Lord Mustill's call for legislative intervention together with Rix LJ's views, among others,[89] is indicative of an emerging judicial consensus over the question of reform, the momentum of which has persuaded the Law Commission of the need to revisit insurance law in the near future.

---

8. The ambit of the insured's duty of disclosure

As we have seen, it is apparent from the language of the Marine Insurance Act 1906, s 18 that, put simply, the general rule can be expressed as requiring the insured to disclose all circumstances which are material to the insurers' (ie the underwriters) determination of the risk which are either known or presumed to be known by the insured, but not known or presumed to be known by the insurers. Conversely, an insured need not disclose any circumstance which is known or presumed to be known by the insurer, or any circumstance the fact of which is waived by the insurer. In *Joel v Law Union and Crown Insurance Co*,[90] Fletcher-Moulton LJ emphasised the point that '[T]he obligation to disclose, therefore, necessarily depends on the knowledge you possess.'[91]

The critical test is therefore whether a reasonable person, with no specialist knowledge of any kind, would have appreciated that he was possessed of knowledge material to the insurers calculation of risk.[92] Summarising the case law on the point, Colman J stated in *Strive Shipping Corp v Hellenic Mutual War Risks Association (Bermuda) Ltd (The Grecia Express)*,[93] that 'the attribute of materiality of a given circumstance has to be tested at the time of the placing of the risk and by reference to the impact which it would then have on the mind of a prudent insurer.' He went on:

---

[89] See, eg, Sir Andrew Longmore (Lord Justice of Appeal), 'An Insurance Contracts Act for a new century?' [2001] *LMCLQ* 356.
[90] Above, n 20.
[91] Ibid, at 718. See *Economides v Commercial Union Ass Co plc*, n 23, above, discussed at p 112 *et seq*.
[92] See also, *Lindenau v Desborough* (1828) 8 B & C 586, at 592, in which Bayley J said: 'I think that in all cases of insurance, whether on ships, houses, or lives, the underwriter should be informed of every material circumstance within the knowledge of the assured; and that the proper question is, whether any particular circumstance was in fact material? and not whether the party believed it to be so. The contrary doctrine would lead to frequent suppression of information, and it would often be extremely difficult to show that the party neglecting to give information thought it material. But if it be held that all material facts must be disclosed, it will be in the interest of the assured to make a full and fair disclosure of all the information within their reach.' See further, *London General Omnibus v Holloway* [1912] 2 KB 72, at 86 Kennedy LJ; and *Godfrey v Britannic Assurance Co Ltd* [1963] 2 Lloyd's Rep 515, at 532.
[93] [2002] 2 Lloyd's Rep 88, at 131.

In this connection it is for present purposes necessary to distinguish between three types of circumstances:

(1)   allegations of criminality or misconduct going to moral hazard which had been made by the authorities or third persons against the proposer and are known to him to be groundless;

(2)   circumstances involving the proposer or his property or affairs which may to all outward appearances raise a suspicion that he has been involved in criminal activity or misconduct going to moral hazard but which he knows not to be the case;

(3)   circumstances involving him or his business or his property which reasonably suggest that the magnitude of the proposed risk may be greater than what it would have been without such circumstances.[94]

In short, decisions illustrating the breadth of the duty typically centre upon either the insured's claims history, previous refusals of cover, or the insured's criminal convictions: these facts are said to signal moral hazard; or on facts which increase the risk of loss, termed physical hazard. In this section, we first consider these categories in detail. Secondly, we examine the duty of disclosure borne by the insured's agent. We then consider non-disclosure in composite insurance and, finally, the limits of, and the statutory exceptions to, the disclosure duty.

8.1 Moral hazard: the insured's claims history and prior refusals of cover

Material facts which can be classified as relating to moral hazard concern the character of the insured and, as commented above, will include matters such as his claims history, previous refusals of cover and criminal record. Further, the state of an insured's finances may also be a material fact given that there are instances where an impecunious insured has brought about a loss in order to defraud the insurers. The materiality of an insured's financial history is obvious where the cover sought is business interruption insurance and property insurance.[95] However, it has been held that the fact that the insured was in arrears with his premiums on another policy was not a material fact. Late payment could be due to a number of reasons and was not sufficient to substantiate an allegation that he might lack the financial resources to maintain the subject matter of the policy (a vessel) in a satisfactory condition.[96]

In relation to claims history, the fact that the business of the insured may have substantially changed since the previous claims because, for example, the management has been replaced, or its place of business has been relocated and the work force is different, will not necessarily excuse the non-disclosure. In *Marene Knitting Mills Pty Ltd v Greater Pacific General Insurance Ltd*,[97] the trial judge, Yeldham J, commented that:

---

[94] Ibid.

[95] *James* v *CGU General Insurance plc* [2002] Lloyd's Rep IR 206. See also, *McCormick v National Motor & Accident Insurance Union Ltd* (1934) 49 Ll L Rep 361.

[96] *O'Kane v Jones* [2004] Lloyd's Rep IR 389.

[97] [1976] 2 Lloyd's 631, PC. See also, *Buse v Turner* (1815) 6 Taunt 338; *Rozanes v Bowen* (1928) 32 Ll L Rep 98, at 102–3, *per* Scrutton LJ; and *New Hampshire Insurance Co v Oil Refineries Ltd* [2002] 2 Lloyd's Rep 463.

It is clear that in asking whether 'the business' had any prior losses or claims for the purpose of determining the question of materiality of facts which were not disclosed...it is not necessary to have regard to the niceties of corporate structure...[98]

There are numerous examples from the case law where an insured has failed to disclose a prior refusal of cover. For example, in *Locker and Woolf Ltd v Western Australian Insurance Co Ltd*,[99] the insured was asked in the proposal form for fire insurance: 'Has this or any other insurance of yours been declined by any other company?' The insured answered 'No'. In fact, two years previously a proposal for motor insurance was refused by another company by reason of non-disclosure. A fire occurred and the insurers repudiated liability for non-disclosure of a material fact. It was held that they were entitled to do so. Slesser LJ stated:

> In my view, it is quite impossible in the present case to say that the non-disclosure of the fact that the person proposing to take out an insurance policy for fire has had a motor policy declined on the grounds of misrepresentation, untrue answers, and non-disclosure is not one which is very material for the respondent insurance company to know. It is, in fact, a non-disclosure of the fact that the person who seeks to enter into the insurance has already been overtly discovered to be a person who tells untruths, conceals matters material, ...and was a highly undesirable person with whom to have any contractual relations whatever.[100]

Similarly, in *London Assurance v Mansel*,[101] the proposer for life insurance when answering the question on the proposal form: 'Has a proposal ever been made on your life at any other office or offices? If so, when?' – failed to disclose that he had made proposals for life insurance to five insurance companies which had been declined although passed as fit by the companies' medical examiners. The insurers successfully repudiated liability on the ground of non-disclosure of a material fact.

8.2 Moral hazard: the insured's criminal record and integrity

The question of moral hazard in relation to an insured's criminal history arose in *Lambert v Co-operative Insurance Society*.[102] The proposer effected an 'all risks' insurance policy on her own and her husband's jewellery in April 1963. At this time she was not asked about previous criminal convictions and she did not disclose that her husband had been convicted some years earlier of receiving stolen cigarettes. The insurers issued the policy which provided that it would be *ipso facto* void if there should be an omission to state any fact material for estimating the risk. The policy was renewed every year. In December 1971 the proposer's husband was again convicted of a criminal offence and sentenced to 15 months' imprisonment. This fact was not disclosed when the insured renewed her policy for the year 1972, and in April she

---

[98] Ibid, at 639, citing *Arterial Caravans Ltd v Yorkshire Insurance Co Ltd* [1973] 1 Lloyd's Rep 169, where it was held that the insured should have disclosed a previous claim for fire suffered by the enterprise in a former corporate guise.

[99] (1936) 54 Ll LR 211. See also, *Glicksman v Lancashire & General Assurance Co* [1927] AC 139.

[100] Ibid, at 215.

[101] Above, n 21.

[102] Above, n 22.

claimed £311.00 for items of jewellery which had been lost. The insurers successfully repudiated the claim on the basis that the insured had failed to disclose a material fact relating to moral hazard at the time of applying for the original policy and at its subsequent renewals.[103]

Similarly, in *Schoolman v Hall*,[104] the insured, who effected a jeweller's block policy, had his claim for a burglary loss rejected by the insurers on the ground that he had failed to disclose his criminal record. Fifteen years prior to effecting the policy he had been convicted of larceny, shopbreaking and receiving. The court upheld the insurers' defence despite the fact that the insured's record related 'to a dim and remote past.'[105] In *March Cabaret Club & Casino Ltd v London Assurance*,[106] the insureds, a husband and wife, had effected a fire policy covering the premises of a club and restaurant owned by them. When the policy was renewed in April 1970 the husband failed to disclose that he had committed the offence of dishonestly handling stolen goods in June 1969 for which he was convicted at the Old Bailey in June 1970. He was fined £2,000. A fire occurred at the premises and the insurers successfully repudiated liability on the ground of non-disclosure of a material fact. May J observed that: 'Be it noted also that whereas there is a presumption that matters dealt with in a proposal form are material, there is no corresponding presumption that matters not so dealt with are not material. If any authority were required for that proposition one can find it in the case of *Schoolman* v *Hall*… .' [107]

There is, however, an important exception to the duty to disclose a conviction. Section 4(3) of the Rehabilitation of Offenders Act 1974 relieves an insured of the duty to disclose a conviction which has become 'spent'. Convictions that carry custodial sentences of less than six months become spent after seven years and those that carry sentences of between six months and two and a half years become spent after ten years. A conviction which carries a sentence of two and a half years' imprisonment or more can never become spent. Where a conviction is 'spent', s 4(2) of the Act provides that any question in a proposal form regarding previous convictions is to be treated as not referring to such a conviction. However, s 7(3) of the Act confers discretion on the court to admit evidence as to spent convictions if the court is satisfied that 'justice cannot be done in the case except by admitting it.'

Facts relating to the integrity of the insured, such as his fraudulent conduct when effecting a policy, will obviously be material to the insurers in deciding whether to accept the proposal.[108] In *Insurance Corporation of the Channel Islands v Royal Hotel Ltd*,[109] a hotel owner who effected a fire insurance policy falsified the hotel's occupancy rates in order to inflate the sums that would be payable under the policy's business interruption cover. Mance J held that this was a material fact which would be taken into account by a prudent insurer. The requirement of inducement was

---

[103] Note the effect of the Rehabilitation of Offenders Act 1974, discussed below.
[104] [1951] 1 Lloyd's Rep 139.
[105] Ibid, 143 *per* Asquith LJ. See also, *Regina Fur Co v Bossom* [1951] 2 Lloyd's Rep 139.
[106] Above, n 12.
[107] Ibid, at 176.
[108] In *Locker & Wolf Ltd v Western Australian Insurance Co*, above n 56, it was held that a previous refusal of motor insurance was a material fact which should have been disclosed in a proposal for fire insurance. Such a refusal related to the integrity of the insured: see above, n 99, at 414, *per* Slesser LJ.
[109] [1998] Lloyd's Rep IR 151. The issues of affirmation and estoppel which arose on the facts are considered below.

satisfied because it was unlikely that an insurer would insure the hotel had the conduct of its owners been known to it.[110] On the issue of inducement the judge concluded:

> Looking at all the material before me, I am satisfied that all the underwriting personnel within ICCI and Mr Walpole as its managing director would have taken a serious view of Royal Hotel's conduct, and that ICCI would have been unlikely to offer renewal if it had known of such conduct before renewal ... I also consider that this is the attitude which any reputable and experienced insurer (like the present insurers) would have been likely to adopt in the face of dishonest conduct such as Royal Hotel's here.[111]

The severe results which the sheer breadth of the insured's duty of disclosure is capable of producing can be seen from the decision in *Woolcott v Sun Alliance & London Insurance.*[112] The insured, who proposed a fire insurance policy on his house through the building society to which he was applying for a mortgage, did not disclose a robbery conviction he had received 12 years previously. Caulfield J held that the insurers could avoid the policy on the basis of moral hazard even though there appeared to be no connection between the insured's criminal conviction and the building's fire risk.

The insured must also disclose any material information in his possession that relates to the honesty of an employee given that this may increase the risk to be underwritten. However, 'idle rumours' need not be disclosed. In *Brotherton v Aseguradoa Colseguros SA,*[113] Columbian media reports carried allegations of serious misconduct and related investigations involving the business activities of a senior employee of the insured bank. It was reported that he had been accused by the bank and government agencies of misappropriating the bank's assets. These reports had not been disclosed when applying for a bankers' blanket bond policy to provide cover against losses resulting from the fraud of employees. There were two issues in this appeal: (a) the materiality of the media reports and investigations, and (b) whether the validity of the reinsurers' avoidance of the policy for their non-disclosure depended upon the correctness of the allegations. The appeal was heard before the trial set for determining whether there was in fact non-disclosure of material facts. Mance LJ drew the distinction between material intelligence that might ultimately be demonstrated as unfounded but which should nevertheless be disclosed and immaterial 'loose or idle rumours' which need not be disclosed by an insured or his agent. Counsel for the reinsurers had argued, inter alia, that materiality, at least in cases of moral hazard, must depend on the known existence of actual moral hazard rather than the possession of information which merely suggested the possibility of moral hazard. Mance LJ, however, rejected this contention on the basis that as 'a matter of principle, and in the light of the authorities...it is difficult to see any reason why, if

---

[110] The insurers were, however, estopped from avoiding the policy as to which see ch 7.
[111] Above, n 108 at 161. See also, *James v CGU General Insurance plc* [2002] Lloyd's Rep IR 206, in which the fact that the insured, a garage owner, had defrauded customers and was in dispute with the Inland Revenue and the Customs and Excise Commissioners was held to be material to the insurers.
[112] [1978] 1 All ER 1253.
[113] [2003] EWCA Civ 705. See R Gay, 'Non-disclosure and Avoidance: Lies, Damned Lies, and "Intelligence"' [2004] *LMCLQ* 1. See also, *North Star Shipping Ltd v Sphere Drake Insurance plc* [2005] EWHC 665.

the evidence satisfies the court that a prudent underwriter would have regarded the information suggesting the possibility of moral hazard as material…that should not suffice.'[114] He concluded:

> I cannot see that the decision in *Pan Atlantic* that avoidance depends on inducement as well as materiality lends support to a conclusion that avoidance for non-disclosure of otherwise material information should depend upon the correctness of such information, to be ascertained if in issue by trial…[115]

The issue of whether there had been non-disclosure of material facts was heard by Morison J.[116] He held that the media reports were, in fact, material on the basis that they did not have the appearance of 'gossip' but seemed to be reporting hard fact. Further, the reports were concerned with specific matters involving an identified individual. The judge also thought that it would be too extreme to conclude that everything reported in the newspapers was wrong.

8.3 Physical hazard

Any fact which increases the risk of loss of the insured subject matter is said to relate to its physical hazard. For example, in life insurance material facts will include the age, health, occupation and hobbies of the life insured. Needless to say, if the insured engages in dangerous pastimes such as sky-diving this may be taken to increase the likelihood of accidental death and will need to be disclosed. With respect to property insurance, material facts will include the age and condition of the subject matter; how it will be used, its location and security arrangements. Thus, in motor insurance for example, insurers will typically want to know whether the vehicle is kept in a locked garage or parked in the road. The nature of the subject matter to be covered will be material,[117] and insurers will want to know about measures taken to prevent loss and whether it is substantially over-insured.

Physical hazard can pose problems especially in life or health insurance because an insured may not be aware that a particular condition is symptomatic of a more serious health risk. In *Joel v Law Union and Crown Insurance Co*,[118] Fletcher-Moulton LJ gave the following example:

> I will suppose that a man has, as is the case with almost all of us, occasionally had a headache. It may be that a particular one of these headaches would have told a brain specialist of hidden mischief, but to the man it was an ordinary headache indistinguishable from the rest. Now, no reasonable man would deem it material to tell an insurance company of all the casual headaches he had had in his life, and if he knew no more as to this particular

---

[114] Ibid, at [21]. In support of his reasoning Mance LJ cited the following passage from Phillips J's judgment in *Inversiones Manria SA v Sphere Drake Insurance Co plc (The Dora)* [1989] 1 Ll R 69: 'When accepting a risk underwriters are properly influenced not merely by facts which, with hindsight, can be shown to have actually affected the risk but with facts that raise doubts about the risk.'

[115] Ibid, at [28].

[116] [2003] Lloyd's Rep IR 762.

[117] See *WISE Underwriting Agency Ltd v Grupo Nacional Provincial SA* [2003] EWHC 1706 (Comm), reversed [2004] EWCA (Civ) 962; discussed below, at p 120.

[118] Above, n 21. See also, *Cook v Financial Insurance Co Ltd* [1998] 1 WLR 1765.

headache, there would be no breach of his duty towards the insurance company in not disclosing it.[119]

8.4 The agent's duty of disclosure

Section 19 of the Marine Insurance Act 1906 goes on to lay down a separate duty of disclosure by intermediaries (agents or brokers). Their duty has two limbs. First, s 19(a) provides that agents must disclose every material circumstance actually known to them or which in the ordinary course of business ought to be known by, or to have been communicated to, them. Secondly, s 19(b) provides that they must disclose every material circumstance which the insured is bound to disclose (unless it comes to the knowledge of the insured too late). However, as will be seen, the duty of disclosure, whether that borne by the insured or by his intermediary, does not apply to any circumstance as to which information is waived by the insurer.[120]

In placing an independent and personal duty on the agent to disclose material facts known to him irrespective of whether they were known to the insured, s 19 gives due recognition to the practical realities of the market place where facts which might not come to the attention of the insured (for example, refusals by other insurers to cover the risk), are known to the broker. Further, where the insured employs a broker to present a risk to the insurer, and the broker fails to disclose a material fact known to him alone, it is logical that the broker, being the wrongdoer, should incur liability. Further, in *Blackburn Low & Co v Vigors*,[121] the House of Lords, examining the scope of the duty, held that it was only the knowledge of the broker who effected the insurance that is relevant so that the knowledge of a broker who had previously been charged with effecting the policy is of no consequence.[122] In *PCW Syndicates v PCW Insurers*,[123] the claimants, who were members of Lloyd's syndicates that had reinsured their liabilities with the defendants, had been defrauded by their underwriting agent. The reinsurance policies were placed by brokers acting on behalf of the fraudster. The reinsurers sought to avoid the policies on the basis that the fraud of the underwriting agent was a material fact that ought to have been disclosed by the underwriting agent. The Court of Appeal held that the reinsurers could not avoid the policy. Saville and Rose LJJ stated that the duty under s 19(a) of the 1906 Act only applied to an 'agent to insure,' ie on the facts, to the placing broker and not to any intermediate agent. Therefore, the duty did not apply to the claimants' underwriting agent. Both Staughton and Rose LJJ agreed that it would be fanciful to believe that an agent would disclose his own fraud and, therefore, a reinsurer could not avoid a contract if an agent to insure failed to disclose that he had defrauded the insured.

The consequence of a breach of the duty of disclosure by an agent is that the insurer may avoid the policy. Where a broker or agent is guilty of misrepresentation the policy is voidable at the election of the insurers. If the insurers do not avoid, or are unable to do so, the broker or agent may be liable in damages. The general common law principles apply. Thus, there is no liability in damages for innocent

---

[119] Ibid, at 718.
[120] Marine Insurance Act 1906, s 18(3) and s 19. See below, p 117.
[121] (1887) 12 App Cas 531.
[122] See also, *HIH Casualty and General Insurance Ltd v Chase Manhattan Bank*, above n 1.
[123] [1996] 1 Lloyd's Rep 241.

misrepresentation. If the misrepresentation is negligent, section 2(1) of the Misrepresentation Act 1967 applies; alternatively there may be liability under the principle laid down in *Hedley Byrne & Co v Heller & Partners*.[124] Where the misrepresentation of a material fact is fraudulent, liability can be founded on the tort of deceit.[125]

8.5 Non-disclosure in composite insurance

In construction insurance, for example, it is not uncommon for one policy to cover the separate interests of a head contractor and all the sub-contractors involved in a building project. Similarly, one policy will often cover the separate interests of a mortgagor and mortgagee in the same property. The issue that arises in such co-insurance situations is whether the non-disclosure or misrepresentation on the part of one co-insured will entitle the insurer to avoid the contract as against all parties (ie, including the innocent co-insureds) or merely against the guilty co-insured. The solution depends upon whether the policy is construed as separate contracts or as a single contract. In *Arab Bank plc v Zurich Insurance Co*,[126] Browne was the managing director of John D Wood Commercial Ltd, an incorporated firm of professional estate agents and valuers. He was at all material times a substantial shareholder in the company. Browne prepared valuations for banks which were fraudulently high in that the valuation figures were deliberately or recklessly provided and did not represent the open market value of the properties: the figures were in each case grossly in excess of the true open market value and/or recent sale price. On occasions he was assisted by another director and (relatively minor) shareholder, Pitts. The company received the fees. The other directors of the company were innocent and free of any fraudulent conduct or intent to deceive. The claimants, Arab Bank and Banque Bruxelles Lambert SA, obtained judgments against the company in negligence but when the company went into liquidation they sought to enforce those judgments directly against the company's underwriters, Zurich, under the Third Parties (Rights against Insurers) Act, 1930. Zurich argued that Browne's fraud relieved them from liability.

The indemnity insurance in question had been effected in August 1990. Browne had completed the proposal form. Question 14(a) of the proposal asked:

> 'Is any Partner, Director, Principal, Consultant or employee, AFTER ENQUIRY, aware of any circumstances/incidents which might:
> (i)   give rise to a claim against the Proposer or his predecessors in business or any of the present or former Partners, Directors, Principals?...
> (iii) otherwise affect the consideration of this proposal for Professional Indemnity insurance?'

Browne answered yes to question (i), but no to question (iii), and in explanation of his answer to question (i) merely referred to a minor issue concerning a possible loss

---

[124] [1964] AC 465. See further, J Murphy, *Street on Torts* (London, LexisNexis, 2003) ch 12.
[125] See generally, J Beatson, *Anson's Law of Contract* (Oxford, OUP, 2002) 243 *et seq*. For the meaning of fraud at common law, see *Derry v Peek* (1889) 14 App Cas 337, discussed below, at p 112.
[126] [1999] 1 Lloyd's Rep 262.

of rent and a possible claim under £10,000. This was irrelevant to the present disputes. The proposal concluded as follows:

'I/We warrant that the above statements made by me/us or on my/our behalf are to the best of my/our knowledge true and complete and I/we agree that this proposal shall be the basis of the contract between me/us and the Insurer.

I/We further warrant that no higher limits(s) Insurance have been, or will be, effected by me/Us unless agreed.'

The insurers contended that Browne had failed to disclose material facts and that his answers constituted a breach of warranty. It was material that the proviso in the 'basis of the contract clause' that the answers were true to the best of Browne's knowledge meant that they were warranties of opinion not absolute guarantees as to their accuracy.

Part I of the policy defined 'the insured' as the 'firm', including its directors and employees with the proviso that 'such definition of the term "Insured" shall NOT be construed to mean that the Company shall indemnify any person knowingly committing, making or condoning any dishonest, fraudulent or malicious act or omission.' Other conditions in the policy included, among others, a fraudulent claim clause (condition 1), a waiver of the insurers rights in the event of innocent non-disclosure (condition 2), a waiver of subrogation (condition 5) and a term requiring notification of any circumstance arising during the currency of the policy which might give rise to a claim (condition 6).

The primary issue was whether the company, the principal insured, could recover under its professional indemnity policy on the basis that the dishonest mind and knowledge of its managing director could not be attributed to it. It was held by Rix J that composite policies should be viewed prima facie as a bundle of separate contracts between the insurers and the co-insureds so that, therefore, dishonesty by one co-insured did not permit the insurers to avoid the policy against all the other parties.

Rix J's reasoning that all such policies ought to be (prima facie) viewed as consisting of several contracts is questionable. It goes too far and was not necessary to support his decision given the terms of the particular policy in question. Nevertheless, the judge's approach has implicitly been endorsed by the Court of Appeal in *FNCB Ltd v Barnet Devanney (Harrow) Ltd.*[127]

The issue has also arisen in the context of groups of companies. The question here is whether the non-disclosure by one insured company in a group will necessarily entitle the insurers to avoid the policies against other companies in the group. In *New Hampshire Insurance Co v MGN Ltd; Maxwell Communications plc v New Hampshire Insurance Co,*[128] fidelity insurance policies were issued to companies in the Maxwell group. Robert Maxwell dishonestly transferred assets from some of the companies, and used them to benefit the financial position of other companies in the group. When claims on the policies were made by the companies for losses suffered as a result of these transfers, the insurers repudiated liability on the basis that the breach of utmost good faith by one company in the group corrupted all the insured

---

[127] [1999] Lloyd's Rep IR 459.
[128] [1997] LRLR 24.

companies in that group. The Court of Appeal held that the companies which made up the Maxwell group had separate interests to insure and not a joint interest in the same property, a fact that must have been known to the insurers given the companies' different business activities. Staughton LJ said 'that all the contracts of insurance were composite in nature, there being more than one insured and each being insured separately.'[129] Accordingly, the breach of duty by one of the insured companies did not entitle the insurers to avoid the policies of the others.

8.6 The limits of the disclosure duty

Against the background of s 18 of the 1906 Act, the judges have long sought to delineate the contours of the insured's duty of disclosure. As we have already commented, at the pre-contractual stage the object of disclosure is directed towards ensuring the accurate presentation of material facts (the risk) to the insurers.[130] Insurers are presumed to know their business and must, therefore, rely on their own expertise. The point was made by Hobhouse J in *Iron Trades Mutual Insurance Co Ltd v Companhia de Seguros Imperio*[131] that:

> The insurer is presumed…to be able to form his own judgment of the risk as it is presented to him…the proposer is under no duty to offer the insurer advice. The duty relates to facts not opinions. The duty is essentially a duty to make a fair presentation of the risk to the insurer.[132]

The issue was again picked up by Moore-Bick J in *Glencore International AG v Alpina Insurance Co Ltd*,[133] who stated that:

> The duty of disclosure requires the insured to place all material information fairly before the underwriter, but the underwriter must also play his part by listening carefully to what is said to him and cannot hold the insured responsible if by failing to do so he does not grasp the full implications of what he has been told.[134]

There are, of course, limits to the insured's duty of disclosure. Section 18(3) of the 1906 Act provides that:

> 'In the absence of inquiry the following circumstances need not be disclosed, namely:
> (a)   any circumstance which diminishes the risk;
> (b)   any circumstance which is known or presumed to be known to the insurer.
>
> The insurer is presumed to know matters of common notoriety or knowledge, and matters which an insurer in the ordinary course of his business as such, ought to know;
> (c)   any circumstance as to which information is waived by the insurer;

---

129 Ibid, at 57. In support of its decision the Court of Appeal cited *P Samuel & Co Ltd v Dumas* [1924] AC 431, HL.
130 Above, n 7.
131 [1991] 1 Re LR 213.
132 Ibid, at 217.
133 [2004] 1 Lloyd's Rep 111.
134 Ibid, at 143, [122].

(d) any circumstance which it is superfluous to disclose by reason of any express or implied warranty.'

(a) Any circumstance which diminishes the risk

Such facts are clearly material in that they would influence the prudent insurer and would impact upon the premium charged. However, the vulnerability of the insurer is not adversely affected where such facts are not disclosed. For example, in fire insurance it is not necessary to disclose that an extensive sprinkler system has been installed. Similarly, an insured need not disclose that comprehensive security measures have been installed to protect the subject matter of the insurance. The court will pay no heed to the argument that such measures suggest that the insured thought the insured vessel was at risk.[135]

(b) Facts within the actual or presumed knowledge of the insurers

Lord Mansfield in his original formulation of the duty of disclosure in *Carter v Boehm* had expressed this particular qualification to the insured's duty of disclosure:

> The question therefore must always be whether there was, under all the circumstances at the time the policy was underwritten, a fair representation; or a concealment; fraudulent, if designed; or, though not designed, varying materially the object of the policy, and changing the risqué understood to be run. The underwriter at London, in May 1760, could judge much better at the probability of the contingency, than Governor Carter could at Fort Marlborough, in September 1759. He knew the success of the operations of the war in Europe. He knew what naval force the English and French had sent to the East Indies. He knew, from a comparison of that force, whether the sea was open to any such attempt by the French. He knew, or might know everything which was known at Fort Marlborough in September 1769, of the general state of affairs in the East Indies, or the particular conditions of Fort Marlborough, by the ship which brought the orders for the insurance. He knew that ship must have brought many letters to the East India Company; and, particularly, from the governor. He knew what probability there was of the Dutch committing or having committed hostilities…[136]

A modern illustration is provided by *Glencore International AG v Alpina Insurance Co Ltd*.[137] The insured, G, claimed against its insurers for the loss of stored crude oil. The policy covered all risks of loss, damage and transit, wherever the oil was located. G had provided the insurers with details of expected throughput of stored oil, but had omitted to do so for the policy year 1996–7. During late 1997 and early 1998, a storage operative misappropriated large quantities of G's oil and G's claim under the policy for USD 250 million was rejected on the ground of non-disclosure and misrepresentation. It was held that an insurer who covers a commodity trader must be taken to know the whole range of circumstances affecting the business of the insured. Thus, the insurer must appreciate that market prices are volatile, that commodities are transported, placed in storage, subject to the forces of nature and can be dangerous. The insured's failure to give a throughput estimate for 1996 –7 was a

---

[135] *Decorum Investments Ltd v Atkin (The Elena G)* [2002] Lloyd's Rep IR 450. See also, *Johnson and Perrott Ltd v Holmes* [1925] 21 Ll L Rep 330.
[136] Above, n 4.
[137] Above, n 133.

misrepresentation, but it had not induced the insurers to accept the risk because the quantity covered by the estimate was a very percentage of the total risk. Moore-Bick J agreed with counsel's submission that:

> when an insurer is asked to write an open cover in favour of a commodity trader he must be taken to be aware of the whole range of circumstances that may arise in the course of carrying on a business of that kind. In the context of worldwide trading the range of circumstances likely to be encountered is inevitably very wide. That does not mean that the insured is under no duty of disclosure, of course, but it does mean that the range of circumstances that the prudent underwriter can be presumed to have in mind is very broad and that the insured's duty of disclosure, which extends only to matters which are unusual in the sense that they fall outside the contemplation of the reasonable underwriter familiar with the business of oil trading, is correspondingly limited.[138]

(c) Any circumstance the disclosure of which is waived by the insurers

The insurer may waive the right to information by the way in which questions contained in the proposal form are framed. For example, in *Revell v London General Insurance Co Ltd*,[139] it was held that where questions are directed towards specific motoring convictions the insurer can be taken to have waived disclosure of other convictions. Such questions may, therefore, be construed *contra proferentum*. Waiver and affirmation are considered in more detail below.[140]

An important matter that has come before the courts is the extent to which the parties can exclude or vary the duty of utmost good faith by a contract term.[141] This gives rise to a conceptual problem given that it is settled that the juridical basis of the duty of disclosure, as seen above,[142] does not originate from an implied contractual term. Nevertheless, as with the general law of contract, it is possible for a contract of insurance to contain exemption clauses that seek to restrict the rights of a party. In the context of insurance, such clauses may, in effect, dilute the insured's strict duty of disclosure by, for example, restricting the insurer's right to avoid the contract in the event of the insured breaching the duty of utmost good faith. For example, as we have seen, in *Arab Bank plc v Zurich Insurance Co*,[143] there was an 'Innocent Non-disclosure' clause which excluded the insurer's right to avoid for non-disclosure or misrepresentation where the assured could establish that 'such alleged non-disclosure, misrepresentation or untrue statement was innocent and free of any fraudulent conduct or intent to deceive.'

In practice such clauses appear because the particular policy may have been devised by the broker and so the contract seeks to shift the risk of non-disclosure or misrepresentation on the part of the broker to the insurers. This may be achieved by deeming the broker to be the agent of the insurers. Also, the term in question may be framed so as to eliminate the insurers' right to avoid the policy following

---

[138] Ibid, at 132, [41].
[139] (1934) 50 Ll LR 114. See also, *Doheny v New India Assurance Co Ltd* [2004] EWCA Civ 1705.
[140] See p 116 *et seq*. It is noteworthy that in *Doheny v New India Assurance Co Ltd*, ibid, the Court of Appeal rejected the submission that waiver was confined to 'consumer' insurances. Note particularly the discussion of *WISE Underwriting Ltd v Grupo* [2004] EWCA (Civ)962 at pp 120 *et seq*.
[141] See, eg, the judgment of Steyn LJ in *Pan Atlantic Insurance Co Ltd v Pine Top Insurance Co* [1993] 1 Lloyd's Rep 496, CA.
[142] See n 12 above, and associated text.
[143] [1999] 1 Lloyd's Rep 262. See p 101, above.

non-disclosure or misrepresentation by either the insured or the broker. Needless to say, the scope of such clauses is always a question of construction. In *HIH Casualty and General Insurance Ltd v Chase Manhattan Bank*,[144] the policies (time variable cover policies, hereafter TVC) related to high risk film finance insurance and were issued to the bank by HIH. TVC insurance had been devised and sold by London brokers Heaths in order to facilitate such financing arrangements. The policies contained exclusion clauses (termed 'truth of statement' clauses) which provided, inter alia, that '[3]...any misstatement...shall not be the responsibility of the insured or constitute a ground for avoidance of the insurers' obligations under the Policy' and that '[6]...[the insured] will not have any duty or obligation to make any representations, warranty of disclosure of any nature express or implied...[7]...and shall have no liability of any nature to the insurers for any information provided by any other parties and [8]...any such information provided by or non-disclosure by other parties...shall not be a ground or grounds for avoidance of the insurers' obligations under the Policy...'

It was held by the House of Lords that Heaths' duty of disclosure under section 19 of the 1906 Act was wholly independent from that imposed upon the bank. Accordingly, where the Truth of Statement clause sought to relieve the insured from its obligations the clause did not extend to Heaths' own duty of disclosure. The Truth of Statement clause did not operate to remove from Heaths the authority to speak on behalf of the bank. Paragraph 6 of the clause merely recognised that Heaths alone would be negotiating with HIH, and purported to relieve the bank from its own obligation to make disclosure. It did not relieve Heaths from its independent obligation to disclose material facts. Significantly, their Lordships held that paragraph 7 of the clause relieved the bank from any claim for damages as a consequence of negligent non-disclosure and misrepresentation by itself or by Heaths, and this was so even though the word 'negligence' had not been used in the clause.[145] But, it was not possible as a matter of public policy for the clause to entitle the bank to be granted relief from the consequences of its own fraud.

Various opinions were expressed by their Lordships as to whether the particular clause could as a matter of law protect the bank against the fraud of Heaths. Lord Hobhouse was of the view that this was not possible while Lord Scott thought that it was possible and that the words used were sufficient to achieve that objective. Lords Bingham, Steyn and Hoffmann thought that even if it was possible to exclude liability for the fraud of a broker the clause in question had not done so. Finally, it was held that paragraph 8 of the clause prevented the insurers from avoiding the contract in the case of misrepresentation or non-disclosure by the bank itself or by Heaths, whether innocent or negligent.

Notwithstanding the conceptual difficulties noted above, it seems, therefore, that it is possible for the parties to include a clause in the contract that has the effect of excluding the insurers remedy of avoidance–provided, of course, the insured's breach of the duty of disclosure was non-fraudulent. Such was clause must, however, be expressed in unequivocal terms.

---

144 Above, n 1.
145 Cf *Toomey v Eagle Star Insurance Co Ltd* [1995] 2 Lloyd's Rep 88, in which Colman J took the view that such a clause could not exclude the insurers right of avoidance where the non-disclosure was negligent.

(d) Any circumstance which it is superfluous to disclose by reason of any express or implied warranty

Any circumstance, whether material or not, that is incorporated into the policy by way of an express or implied warranty need not be disclosed by the insured. The reason for this is simple. If the underwriter has protected him or herself by way of warranty he does not need the protection of the duty of disclosure. Of course, in addition to the warranty, it is open to the insurer to specifically raise a question about the matter in which case the insured is bound by the duty of good faith to answer truthfully.[146]

---

9. The duration of the duty of utmost good faith

The duty of disclosure operates more harshly in general insurance than in life insurance. General insurance policies, such as motor or household insurance, are normally short-term contracts that are typically renewed annually–at which time a new contract is entered into. The duty, therefore, bites at each renewal.[147]

Where there is a change of circumstance between the submission of the proposal form and its formal acceptance, the insured must disclose the change to the insurer. For example, if a proposer falls ill after submitting a proposal for private medical insurance, but fails to disclose this prior to acceptance, the insurers will be able to avoid the policy since an offer to provide insurance is generally made conditional upon there being no material change in the risk between the time when the offer was made and the time of acceptance.[148] Thus, in *Looker v Law Union and Rock Insurance Co Ltd*,[149] a policy for life assurance contained a clause which stipulated that: 'The risk of the company will not commence until receipt of the first premium; and the directors meanwhile reserve the power to alter or withdraw the acceptance.' The insured fell ill after submitting his proposal but before cover had commenced and failed to give notice of his illness to the insurers. He sent a cheque for the first premium which was dishonoured and died from pneumonia four days after the illness began. It was held that the insurers could avoid the policy since the duty of disclosure continued up until payment of the first premium. Acton J stated 'that the acceptance is made in reliance upon the continued truth of the representations, and the proposer had failed to disclose the change in his state of health.'[150]

Unless there is an express term to the contrary, the insured is under no duty to disclose a change of circumstance which occurs during the operation of the insurance

---

[146] *Haywood v Rodgers* (1804) 4 East 590.
[147] *Hearts of Oak Building Society v Law Union & Rock Insurance Co* [1936] 2 All ER 619; see also, *Lambert v Co-operative Insurance Society*, above n 21.
[148] See *Canning v Farquhar* (1886) 16 QBD 727.
[149] [1928] 1 KB 554.
[150] Ibid, at 559.

contract.[151] The point was graphically made by Lord Pollock in *Baxendale v Harvey*,[152] who said:

> If a person who insures his life goes up in a balloon, that does not vitiate his policy ... A person who insures may light as many candles as he please in his house, though each additional candle increases the danger of setting the house on fire.[153]

Further, in *Kausar v Eagle Star Insurance Co Ltd*,[154] a clause in the policy which stated: 'You must tell us of any change of circumstances after the start of the insurance which increases the risk of injury or damage...' was restrictively construed by Saville LJ so as not to impose a continuing duty of disclosure on the insured:

> [A]ll that this Condition does is to state the position as it would exist anyway as a matter of common law, namely that without the further agreement of the insurer, there would be no cover where the circumstances had so changed that it could properly be said by the insurers that the new situation was something which, on the true construction of the policy, they had not agreed to cover. The mere fact that the chances of an insured peril operating increase during the period of the cover would not, save possibly in most extreme of circumstances, enable the insurers properly to say this, since the insurance bargain is one where, in return for the premium, they take upon themselves the risk that an insured peril will operate.[155]

It has been argued that where a policy contains a cancellation clause giving the insurer the right of cancellation at any time, this has the effect of placing the insured under a continuing duty of disclosure. Such a view was roundly rejected by the Court of Appeal in *New Hampshire Insurance Co v MGN Ltd; Maxwell Communications plc v New Hampshire Insurance Co*,[156] in which Staughton LJ said: 'We should hesitate to enlarge the scope for oppression by establishing a duty to disclose throughout the period of a contract of insurance, merely because it contains (as is by no means uncommon) a right to cancellation for the insurer.'[157]

However, a duty to disclose a change of circumstances can arise by virtue of a so-called 'increase of risk' clause. Generally such clauses, which are frequently found in fire policies, only operate to require disclosure of changes which are permanent in nature. In *Dobson v Sotheby*,[158] a barn was insured against fire and the policy stated that no fire or hazardous goods are to be kept on the premises. When the premises required tarring, a fire was lighted and a tar barrel was brought into the building. The tar boiled over and the premises were destroyed by the ensuing fire. Lord Tenterden CJ considered that 'the condition must be understood as forbidding only the habitual use of fire, or the ordinary deposit of hazardous goods, not their occasional introduction, as in this case, for a temporary purpose connected with the occupation of

---

[151] *Pim v Reid* (1843) 6 M & G 1; *Kausar v Eagle Star Insurance Co Ltd* [2000] Lloyd's Rep 154; *Manifest Shipping Co Ltd v Uni-Polaris Shipping Co Ltd (The Star Sea)*, [1997] 1 Lloyds Rep 360.
[152] (1859) H & N 449.
[153] Ibid, at 452. See also, *Commercial Union v The Niger Co Ltd* (1922) 13 Ll L Rep 75 at 82, in which Lord Sumner said that a continuing duty of disclosure 'would turn what is an indispensable shield for the Underwriter into an engine of oppression against the insured.'
[154] [2000] Lloyd's Rep 154.
[155] Ibid, at 159.
[156] [1999] Lloyd's Rep IR 459.
[157] Ibid, at 61.
[158] (1827) M & M 90.

the premises. The common repairs of a building necessarily require the introduction of fire upon the premises.'[159] And so an insured who brings into his house some device which by its nature is inherently dangerous, for example a blow torch for the purpose of redecorating, will not need to notify the insurers unless a clause in the policy expressly imposes such a duty in relation to temporary changes.[160]

While it is settled that the doctrine of utmost good faith as codified by s 17 of the 1906 Act applies to the formation of the insurance contract (including renewals), it is a controversial question whether the doctrine applies post-contractually and, more particularly, during the claims process. The critical question here is whether a fraudulent claim entitles the insurer to avoid the contract *ab initio*. This issue has recently attracted considerable judicial debate and is considered in chapter 10, below.

---

10. The scope of the insurers' duty of good faith

The fact that s 17 of the 1906 Act states that the duty of utmost good faith is borne by both parties to the contract, the insured and the insurer, has already been noted.[161] Although in practice it is rare for the issue of the insurer's duty to arise in litigation, at least in far as it applies to the pre-contractual relationship, nevertheless in *Banque Financière de la Cité SA v Westgate Insurance Co Ltd*,[162] the courts were afforded the opportunity to consider the scope of the duty as it applies to insurers. At first instance,[163] Steyn J re-affirmed the mutuality of the disclosure duty by holding that the insurers owed a duty of disclosure to the insured. The Court of Appeal and the House of Lords affirmed this element of the trial judge's decision, but reversed his finding that the remedy against the insurer for breach was damages,[164] confining it to avoidance of the contract and return of the premiums only on the basis that the court's power to grant relief arose from its equitable jurisdiction.

The test to be applied in determining materiality from the insurers perspective was, in Steyn J's opinion, whether 'good faith and fair dealing require disclosure' to the insured.[165] However, the Court of Appeal, notably Slade LJ, criticised this formulation as being far too broad and vague as a test for determining the existence of the

---

[159] Ibid, at 92–3.
[160] *Shaw v Robberds* (1832) 6 A & E 75; *Glen v Lewis* (1853) 8 Ex 607.
[161] See n 4, above. On the question of the mutuality of the disclosure obligation, Lord Mansfield stated in *Carter v Boehm,* above n 4, at 1909, that '[T]he policy would equally be void, against the underwriter, if he concealed; as, if he insured a ship on her voyage, which he privately knew to be arrived: and an action would lie to recover the premium.' See also the judgment of Rix LJ in *WISE (Underwriting Agency) Ltd v Grupo Nacional Provincial SA* [2004] EWCA (Civ) 942, discussed at p 120, below. See further, T Yeo, 'Of reciprocity and remedies: duty of disclosure in insurance contracts' (1991) 11 *LS* 131.
[162] [1990] 1 QB 665, CA; [1991] 2 AC 249, HL.
[163] Sub nom *Banque Keyser Ullman SA v Skandia Insurance Co* [1987] 1 Lloyd's Rep 69.
[164] Steyn J had concluded, ibid at 96, that: 'In my judgment justice and policy considerations combine in requiring me to rule that in principle an insured can claim damages from an insurer arising from loss suffered by the insured as a result of a breach of the obligation of the utmost good faith by the insurer.'
[165] Ibid, at 94.

duty which might arise 'even in the absence of any dishonest or unfair intent.'[166] For Slade LJ the insurer's duty of disclosure should:

> extend to disclosing facts known to him which are material either to the nature of the risk sought to be covered or the recoverability of a claim under the policy which a prudent insured would take into account in deciding whether to place the risk for which he seeks cover with that insurer.'[167]

The House of Lords approved Slade LJ's reasoning in this respect. It is unfortunate that the opportunity for a thorough and authoritative assessment of the insurers' duty of good faith was not taken up.

The narrow approach adopted by the Court of Appeal in *Westgate* towards the insurers' duty of good faith was recently applied in *Aldrich v Norwich Union Life Insurance Co Ltd.*[168] Norwich Union had sold certain 'property backed guarantee plans' to Lloyd's names whereby guarantees were given in respect of their liabilities. Calls by Lloyd's exhausted the guarantees and Norwich Union sought to enforce the security provided by the names. The security included the assignment of endowment and life policies to the insurer. The Court of Appeal upheld the striking-out of claims that Norwich Union had failed to disclose its knowledge that the syndicates to which the names belonged were likely to incur substantial losses. It was held that there was no obligation on Norwich Union to disclose matters relating to the risk of losses at Lloyd's because this particular risk was not covered by the endowment and life policies; the only issue material to such policies related to the insureds' (ie, the Names's) lives.

While the pre-contractual duty of good faith borne by insurers is surprisingly narrow, and seems to be settled as such for the time being, nevertheless, the judges in a number of recent cases have taken the opportunity to consider whether an insurer, in exercising its right to avoid a contract for non-disclosure, is subject to the good faith duty. In *Brotherton v Aseguradora Colseguros SA (No 2)*,[169] Mance LJ considered what he identified as the first 'strand' in Colman J's reasoning in *The Grecia Express*,[170] that the right to avoid is conditional upon the consistency of any such avoidance with 'good faith and conscience.'[171] We have already seen that Mance LJ rejected Colman J's view 'that the court has a role in permitting (or refusing to permit) insurers to avoid a policy for non-disclosure.'[172] Mance LJ also roundly rejected the second 'strand' implicit in Colman J's reasoning 'that an insured is, if necessary, entitled to litigate the issue of the truth or falsity of known but undisclosed intelligence, in order to argue that, if it is shown to be incorrect, the insurer would be acting in bad faith or unconscionably in avoiding.'[173] The judge thought that it would be an 'unsound step' to introduce into English law a principle enabling an insured:

---

166 [1990] 1 QB 665 at 772.
167 Ibid.
168 [2000] Lloyd's Rep IR 1.
169 [2003] EWCA Civ 705.
170 [2002] 2 Lloyd's Rep 88.
171 [2003] EWCA Civ 705, at [26].
172 Ibid. See p 83, above.
173 Ibid.

either not to disclose intelligence which a prudent insurer would regard as material or subsequently to resist avoidance by insisting on a trial, in circumstances where:

(i) if insurers never found out about the intelligence, the insured would face no problem in recovering for any losses which arose – however directly relevant the intelligence was to the perils insured and (quite possibly) to the losses actually occurring; and

(ii) if insurers found out about the intelligence, then (a) they would in the interests of their syndicate members or shareholders have normally to investigate its correctness, and (b) the insured would be entitled to put its insurers to the trouble, expense and (using the word deliberately) risk of expensive litigation, and perhaps force a settlement, in circumstances when insurers would never have been exposed to any of this, had the insured performed its prima facie duty to make timely disclosure.[174]

A somewhat more open-textured and, as has been commented above, more insured-friendly approach was adopted by the majority of the Court of Appeal in *Drake Insurance plc v Provident Insurance plc*.[175] It will be recalled that it was held that the non-disclosure did not induce the insurers to accept the risk and therefore they were not entitled to avoid the policy. Rix LJ observed that the doctrine of good faith should be capable of limiting the insurer's right to avoid in circumstances where that remedy, which has been described in recent years as draconian, would operate unfairly.[176] He went on to note that in recent years there appears to have been a realisation that in certain respects English insurance law has developed too stringently. Citing *Pan Atlantic* in which, it will be recalled, the House of Lords superimposed the requirement of inducement onto the statutory materiality test, Rix LJ stated that leading modern cases show that the courts are willing to find means to introduce safeguards and flexibilities which had not been appreciated before. Significantly, the judge felt inclined to say that it would not be in good faith to avoid a policy without first giving the insured an opportunity to address the reason for the avoidance.[177] By way of conclusion, he remarked that nowadays not all insurance contracts are made by those who engage in commerce and that the existence of widespread consumer insurance presents new problems: 'It may be necessary to give wider effect to the doctrine of good faith and recognize that its impact may demand that ultimately regard must be had to a concept of proportionality implicit in fair dealing.'[178] Both Rix and Clarke LJJ stated that insurers must not ignore facts which they know, or of which they have Nelsonian blindness. Pill LJ went further by requiring insurers to act in good faith and to make enquiries of the insured before taking the drastic step of avoiding the policy.

Brotherton and *Drake* represent two different approaches of the Court of Appeal to the issue of good faith in so far as it applies to insurers. Of the two, the reasoning in *Brotherton* is to be preferred. Mance LJ proceeded on the basis of case law[179] and, as has been noted above,[180] he took the view that avoidance for non-disclosure or misrepresentation is akin to rescission for misrepresentation under the general law of contract. Although, as such, this self-help remedy is not generally constrained by

---

[174] Ibid, at [31].
[175] [2003] EWCA Civ 1834.
[176] Ibid, at [87].
[177] Ibid, at [92].
[178] Ibid, at [89]
[179] Rix LJ in *Drake* did acknowledge, however, that no authority supported his stance.
[180] See p 83, above.

considerations of good faith and conscience. Moreover, as indicated above, the recent decisions on the disclosure duty are of major significance because they show that modern judges are engaged in a process of eroding the harshness of the duty of utmost good faith. This recent trend can be traced to the creation of the requirement of inducement in *Pan Atlantic.* The precise nature of the requirement came to the fore in the recent cases considered above and is likely to be subjected to further examination by the Law Commission. A further line of judicial attack, particularly by Rix LJ, has taken place via the principle of waiver, considered below.

11. Misrepresentation

Put simply, a misrepresentation can be defined as an untrue statement of a material fact made by one party to the contract to the other party which induces the contract but which is not a contractual term.[181] As with non-disclosure, where the insurer is induced to enter into the contract on the basis of some misrepresentation made by the insured, the insurer is entitled to avoid the contract. As commented above, given the breadth of the disclosure duty the law of misrepresentation has played a relatively minor part in insurance compared with the law of contract more generally. This is because first, insureds are under a positive duty to disclose material facts and so misrepresentation frequently becomes a question of non-disclosure; and secondly, because of the 'basis of the contract clause',[182] the insured's answers to questions in the proposal form are converted into contractual terms (warranties), thereby pre-empting the issue of misrepresentation arising. Although, following the Statement of General Insurance Practice,[183] basis clauses are no longer used against consumers (non-business insureds), they are still found in non-consumer insurance policies. For consumer insurance therefore, misrepresentation in insurance contracts may now assume greater significance. Yet the case law on misrepresentation in insurance contracts is far from satisfactory, the judicial language often confusing the lines of demarcation between non-disclosure and misrepresentation.

Because misrepresentation is generally subsumed under non-disclosure there has been little judicial consideration of section 2(2) of the Misrepresentation Act 1967. This provision holds the potential to prevent insurers avoiding the contract by granting the court the discretion to award damages in lieu of recission or avoidance. Although this power is unlikely to be exercised in commercial insurance,[184] it may assume greater significance in consumer insurance in the light of the Court of Appeal's decision in *Economides v Commercial Union Assurance Co plc.*[185] Further, in his Annual Report for 1990, paragraph 2.3, the Insurance Ombudsman noted that in

---

[181] See generally, J Beatson, *Anson's Law of Contract* (Oxford, Clarendon Press, 2002) ch 6. See also, M Bridge, 'Innocent Misrepresentation in Contract' [2004] *CLP* 272.
[182] See ch. 7, below.
[183] Para 1(b).
[184] *Highlands Insurance Co v Continental Insurance Co* [1987] 1 Lloyd's Rep 109.
[185] Above, n 23; discussed below.

consumer insurance most so-called non-disclosures arise *via* inaccurate answers to questions in proposal forms (in reality, misrepresentations) and that in such cases (by analogy with section 2(2) of the 1967 Act) he would not allow insurers to avoid the policy but restrict them to partially or wholly avoiding a claim.

11.1 Fraudulent misrepresentation

The House of Lords in *Derry v Peek*,[186] established that a lack of honest belief on the part of the representor is central to an allegation of fraud. Lord Herschell defined fraudulent misrepresentation as a false statement 'made (1) knowingly, or (2) without belief in its truth, or (3) recklessly, careless whether it be true or false.'[187] If a false statement is made on grounds that would not necessarily convince a reasonable person, it may be negligent, but in the absence of dishonest intent, it will certainly not be fraudulent. However, being economical with the truth by deliberately giving a false impression by making an incomplete statement may constitute fraudulent misrepresentation. Even though the several parts of the statement, if severed from the rest, are not actually false, nevertheless it is the impression designed to be conveyed to the recipient of the statement which is the critical factor. The point was forcefully made by Lord Halsbury in *Aaron's Reefs Ltd v Twiss*,[188] who, rejecting the contention that no specific element of the statement in question had been proved to be false, said:

> I protest ... against that being the true test. I should say taking the whole thing together, was there a false representation? I do not care by what means it is conveyed, by what trick or device, or ambiguous language, all those are expedients by which fraudulent people seem to think they can escape from the real substance of the transaction. If by a number of statements, you intentionally give a false impression, and induce a person to act upon it, it is not the less false, although, if one takes each statement by itself, there may be a difficulty in showing that any specific statement is untrue.[189]

A fraudulent misrepresentation renders the contract voidable and the insurer can retain premiums paid under the policy. The insurer may also bring an action for damages against the misrepresentor in the tort of deceit.[190]

11.2 Non-fraudulent misrepresentation

The law of misrepresentation in the context of insurance contracts is codified by the Marine Insurance Act 1906, s 20 which also applies to non-marine insurance. Section 20(1) provides that every material representation made by the proposer for insurance in negotiating the contract must be true, if it be untrue the insurer may avoid the contract. The test for materiality is laid down in s 20(2) which, echoing s 18(2), provides that a representation is material if it 'would influence the judgment of a prudent insurer in fixing the premium, or determining whether he will take the risk.' Section

---

[186] (1889) 14 App Cas 337.
[187] Ibid, at 374.
[188] [1886] AC 273.
[189] Ibid, at 280.
[190] See further, J Murphy, *Street on Torts* (London, LexisNexis, 2003) ch 8.

20(4) stipulates that a statement of fact is true 'if it be substantially correct, that is to say, if the difference between what is represented and what is actually correct would not be considered material by a prudent insurer.'

Section 20(3) of the 1906 Act provides that a representation may be either a representation as to a matter of fact, or as to a matter of expectation or belief. Indeed, paragraph 1(a) of the Statements of General Insurance Practice provided that for the non-business proposer the declaration at the foot of the proposal form should state that it is completed according to his knowledge and belief. Thus, when a proposer represents his own belief this is not a representation of 'fact' in the strict sense other than the fact of the proposer's belief. If the belief was not in fact held by him or her an action for misrepresentation may lie.[191] Conversely, merely because the representor's belief turns out to be wrong will not, of itself, amount to an actionable misrepresentation.[192] In *Economides v Commercial Union Assurance Co plc*,[193] the Court of Appeal took the opportunity to subject s 20 of the 1906 Act to detailed scrutiny. A material issue was whether or not an insured had to show reasonable grounds to support a representation of opinion. The insured, E, an 18 year old student, had effected a household contents policy with the defendants in 1998. The total sum insured was £12,000 (index linked) and the maximum recoverable for valuables (as defined in the policy) was one-third of that amount. The proposal form which was completed and signed by him stated that the answers given were true to the best of his knowledge and (notwithstanding the Statements of Practice, in force at that time) that it formed the basis of the contract between him and the insurers. At that time the answers given by the insured were true. In 1990 E's parents left Cyprus and came to live permanently in England. They moved in with him bringing with them a considerable quantity of valuables including jewellery worth some £30,000. E, now aged 21, saw some of the jewellery when his mother wore it, but showed little interest. However, his father, a retired police divisional commander, advised him to increase his contents policy by approximately £3,000. The insured contacted the insurers and instructed them to increase cover to £16,000. The next renewal invitation, which contained a disclosure warning modelled on the Statements of Practice stated that this was the sum insured.

In 1991 E's flat was burgled and property worth some £31,000 was stolen, the bulk of which was the parents' valuables. When he claimed under the policy it became clear that the value of his parents property was £30,970 which exceeded the sum insured. Further, the valuables in question exceeded one third of the total sum insured or the total value of the contents which was now estimated to be £40,000. The insurers avoided liability on grounds of misrepresentation and non-disclosure of material facts. It was held by the Court of Appeal, that a statement of belief, if given in good faith, does not need to be supported by reasonable grounds for that belief, but the existence or lack of reasonable grounds for such belief may be taken into account by the court in determining whether the representor has acted in good faith. Further, the duty on the insured, when representing the full contents value to be £16,000 was solely one of honesty.

---

[191] *Anderson v Pacific Fire and Marine Insurance Co* (1872) LR 7 CP 65, at 69, *per* Willes J.
[192] *Pawson v Watson* (1778) 2 Cowp 785, at 788, *per* Lord Mansfield CJ.
[193] Above, n 23. See N Hird, 'How to Make a Drama Out of a Crisis' [1998] *JBL* 279; HN Bennett, 'Statements of Fact and Statements of Belief in Insurance Contract Law and General Contract Law' [1998] *MLR* 886.

At first instance, the judge found for the insurers on the basis that although E may have honestly believed his valuation to be correct, honesty was not enough in the absence of reasonable grounds on which he could have based the representation. The judge said: 'it would have been necessary for him to make substantially more inquiries than he did make before he could be said to have reasonable grounds for his belief.'[194] E's statement was therefore an actionable misrepresentation. Further, the trial judge went on to find that since E had been informed by his parents of the presence of the jewellery and silverware in the flat but had wilfully closed his eyes ('Nelsonian blindness') to the true nature and value of these items, the insurers were entitled to avoid the policy on the ground of non-disclosure. The judge was of the view that once these items were introduced into the flat by his parents, E should have made further inquiries, and such inquiries would have led him to the conclusion that material facts had not been disclosed. E appealed.

Taking the defence of misrepresentation first, the issue before the Court of Appeal was whether for the purposes of insurance law a representor had to show objectively reasonable grounds for his belief,[195] or whether honesty alone was sufficient. Distinguishing the authorities relied on by counsel for the insurers,[196] both Simon Brown and Peter Gibson LJJ concluded that the duty on E when representing the full contents value to be £16,000 was solely one of honesty. They both thought that the Marine Insurance Act 1906, s.20(5) which provides that '[A] representation as to a matter of expectation or belief is true if it be made in good faith' provided the conclusive answer to the point,[197] and thus:

> given that the appellant was at the time aged 21, given that the figure for the increase in cover was put forward by his father, and given that father was a retired senior police officer, inevitably better able than the appellant himself to put a valuation on the additional contents, there would seem to me every reason to accept the appellant's honesty.[198]

On the issue of non-disclosure, the Court of Appeal agreed that the governing principle is to be found in the Marine Insurance Act 1906, s 18(1).[199] The true scope

---

[194] Ibid, at 641, *per* Mr Recorder Hockman QC, cited by Simon Brown LJ.
[195] In so holding the trial judge applied *Smith v Land & House Property Corp* (1884) 28 Ch D 7 at 15, *per* Bowen LJ; *Brown v Raphael* [1958] Ch 636 at 644, *per* Lord Evershed MR; *Credit Lyonnais Bank Nederland v Export Credit Guarantee Dept* [1996] 1 Lloyd's Rep 200; *Ionides v Pacific Fire and Marine Insurance Co* (1871) LR 6 QB 674; and *Highlands Insurance Co v Continental Insurance Co* [1987] 1 Lloyd's Rep 109.
[196] Simon Brown and Peter Gibson LJJ stressed that in all five decisions relied on by the respondents it had to borne in mind who had made the representation in question–either a professional who made an unqualified statement of belief or an individual who blindly ignored the true state of affairs–whereas in the present case the statement was made by a layman with no relevant skills.
[197] As has been seen this is one of a number of sections of the 1906 Act which it is now firmly established apply equally to non-marine as to marine insurance contracts, see further *PCW Syndicates v PCW Reinsurers*, above n 22. See further, *Rendall v Combined Insurance Co of America* [2005] EWHC 678 (Comm) in which it was held, applying *Economides*, that in insurance a representation of expectation or belief could not, consistently with s 20(5), carry an implicit representation that it was based on reasonable grounds.
[198] Above, n 23 at 646, *per* Simon Brown LJ. Peter Gibson LJ, at 652–3, stressed that: 'Once statute deems an honest representation as to a matter of belief to be true, I cannot see that there is scope for inquiry as to whether there were objectively reasonable grounds for that belief. Of course the absence of reasonable grounds for belief may point to the absence of good faith for that belief. But in a case such as the present where the bad faith of the plaintiff is not alleged, I can see no basis for the implication of a representation of reasonable grounds for belief.'
[199] See p 81, above.

of the words in the section 'deemed to know' has in fact long been settled. Simon Brown LJ stressed that where the insured is a private individual not acting (in the words of the section) 'in the ordinary course of business,' he 'must disclose only material facts known to him; he is not to have ascribed to him any form of deemed or constructive knowledge.'[200] In support of this proposition he cited Saville LJ's summary of the legal position in *Deutsche Ruckversicherung AG v Walbrook Insurance Co*[201]:

> The distinction is expressly drawn between knowledge and deemed knowledge. The latter type of knowledge is then carefully circumscribed. To suggest that there is to be found in the section another and unexpressed type of deemed knowledge which is not so circumscribed seems to me simply to contradict the words used, and to destroy the very distinction that has been expressly drawn ... .[202]

Accordingly, the Court of Appeal in allowing the appeal, held that the test for non-disclosure was the same as that for misrepresentation, namely that of honesty. Just as there was no duty on E to make further inquiries to establish reasonable grounds for his belief in the accuracy of his representation concerning valuation, so too he was not under a duty to inquire into the facts so as to discharge the obligation of disclosure of all material facts known to him.

The decision of the Court of Appeal on the issue of misrepresentation does, however, seem to inject an element of inconsistency in the way misrepresentation operates in insurance contracts as compared with general contract law. Limiting the duty on the proposer/insured to one of 'honesty' would appear to eliminate innocent misrepresentation from insurance law. As pointed out by Hird,[203] if the insured is dishonest then quite clearly this will amount to fraudulent misrepresentation. Where, on the other hand, the insured is honest this will not amount to misrepresentation because there is no implied requirement for the insured to show 'objectively reasonable grounds' for his belief. For the non-business insured, innocent misrepresentation does not operate because, as commented above, the Statements of Practice provided that the proposer's answers to questions on the proposal form are 'to the best of his knowledge and belief.' And so, in the words of Simon Brown LJ, the 'sole obligation' borne by the insured is that of honesty.[204] Further, in the absence of any duty of care to show 'objectively reasonable grounds' for the belief in a representation, it seems that the non-business insured also enjoys immunity from negligent misrepresentation.

Although the ICOB has replaced the Statements of Practice, the principles in the ABI statements 'remain useful examples of good industry practice' (*Ombudsman News*, June 2005).

---

[200] Above, n 22 at 647. It will be recalled that this was the position at common law. See, eg, *Blackburn Low & Co v Vigors,* above n 11 at 543 (Lord Macnaghten).
[201] [1996] 1 WLR 1152.
[202] Ibid, at 1169.
[203] See N Hird, 'How to Make a Drama Out of a Crisis' [1998] *JBL* 279.
[204] Above, n 22 at 646.

12. The consequences of misrepresentation by the insurer

Where, as must be rare, the insured is induced by some fraudulent misrepresentation of fact by the insurers to pay the premium, he is entitled to recover it on the basis of money had and received. In *Kettlewell v Refuge Assurance Co Ltd*,[205] the insured, having paid one year's premium for a life policy, notified the insurer's agent that she wished to let the insurance policy lapse. The agent induced her to continue paying the premiums for four more years by saying that she would then obtain a free policy. The Court of Appeal held that the insured was entitled to recover the premium money which she had paid to the insurers. Sir Gorell Barnes P, having noted that there was a clear misrepresentation of fact, rejected the insurers' contention that the premiums could not be repaid because the company had been at risk until the insured elected to avoid the policy. The judge said:

> I myself do not take the view of the matter as presented by [counsel for the insurers] as being correct. It seems to me in all cases where the contract can be declared void – in other words, is voidable – at the option of one side, the other side is under a liability until that option is exercised; but the mere fact that the liability exists will not prevent the person who has the option from declaring the contract void and suing for what he has paid on the basis of it being a good contract ... this money can be recovered as money had and received by the defendants.[206]

The effect of the Court of Appeal's reasoning is that the insurer's coming on risk is not a bar to rescission. As such, the insurer's exposure to the insured risk does not constitute performance.[207] Further, Lord Alverstone CJ went on to express the view that the money was also recoverable by way of damages in an action in deceit.[208]

13. Affirmation, waiver and estoppel

We have seen that s 18(3)(c) of the Marine Insurance Act 1906 removes from the duty to disclose 'any circumstance as to which information is waived by the insurer.' Further, it will be recalled that s 18(3)(b) provides that an insured need not disclose 'any circumstance which is known or presumed to be known to the insurer. The insurer is presumed to know matters of common notoriety or knowledge, and matters which an insurer in the ordinary course of his business as such, ought to know...' The issues of affirmation and waiver have attracted considerable judicial attention in recent times.

---

[205] [1908] 1 KB 545; affirmed [1909] AC 243.
[206] Ibid, at 547.
[207] Ibid, at 549.
[208] Ibid, at 550.

13.1 Affirmation

Insurers may lose their right to avoid the policy by reason of their conduct after the loss has occurred. This can occur either by affirmation, or by estoppel. The two are very similar. Affirmation arises where the insurers with full knowledge of the non-disclosure or misrepresentation make it clear to the insured by word or conduct that they do not intend to avoid the contract.[209] Estoppel arises where the insurers' conduct induces the insured to believe that they do not intend to avoid the contract and the insured has acted accordingly. Thus, affirmation must to be communicated to the insured but, unlike estoppel, it is not necessary to prove that some representation by words or conduct was made by the insurer which was relied upon by the insured to his detriment.

In *Moore Large & Co Ltd v Hermes Credit & Guarantee plc*,[210] it was held that affirmation can occur where insurers have defended legal proceedings on the basis of coverage or terms of the policy knowing that an utmost good faith defence might exist. On the facts, the insurers had sought to rely on the insured's breach of the disclosure duty at a late stage in the proceedings. Further, the insurers had the benefit of legal advice and it is not open to them to argue that they are not bound by the tactical decisions of their legal advisers. The Court of Appeal has also expressed the view that where the insurer, having purported to avoid a motor policy, failed to cancel a direct debit mandate for the collection of premiums and generally acted inconsistently with the idea that the relationship had been terminated, the defence of waiver may be available to the insured.[211]

Insurance Corporation of the Channel Islands v The Royal Hotel Ltd,[212] is a paradigm case not only on the question of affirmation, but on the repercussions of tactical decisions taken during the litigation process which can result in a finding of issue estoppel or abuse of process in a subsequent action between the parties on the policy. It will recalled that the insured hotel had been damaged in a series of fires and had to close in June 1992. Its owner claimed under two fire insurance policies effected with the claimant company, ICCI. The first policy covered material damage to the buildings and the second policy covered business interruption losses. In an action commenced in 1994, Mance J considered claims by ICCI and the Royal Hotel and counterclaims by the Royal Hotel arising out of the fires and the conduct of the subsequent claims.[213] He held that the Royal Hotel had forfeited all benefit (some £950,000) under the second policy (business interruption) because its director and company secretary had used fraudulent means to promote the hotel's occupancy rate so as to inflate the sums recoverable under the business interruption policy. The insurers now sought to avoid the first policy (material damage) on the ground of material non-disclosure.

The issues before the court concerned materiality, inducement, affirmation and cause of action or issue estoppel. Materiality and inducement were evidentially straightforward in the light of the insured's undisclosed moral hazard and the judge

---

[209] See, eg, *Spriggs v Wessington Court School Ltd* [2004] EWHC 1432 (QB).
[210] [2003] Lloyd's Rep IR 315.
[211] *Drake Insurance plc v Provident Insurance plc* [2003] EWCA Civ 1834.
[212] [1998] Lloyd's Rep I R 151. Applied in *Spriggs v Wessington Court School Ltd*, above n 208.
[213] Reported [1997] LRLR 20.

found in the insurers' favour.[214] However, on the remaining issues, Mance J held that the evidence established that the insurers first became aware of the insured's fraudulent conduct in 1993, yet their conduct of the 1994 action proceeded on the basis that the material damage policy was valid and as such they could be taken to have affirmed the policy. Further, the insurers should have raised the issue of material non-disclosure during the 1994 action, and their failure to do so resulted in them being precluded from seeking to avoid the policies in the present action on the basis of issue estoppel and abuse of process.'

13.1.1 The elements of affirmation: (a) knowledge

Addressing the question of the knowledge required for effective affirmation, the judge noted that there had to be an informed choice to treat the contract as continuing despite its breach. He rejected counsel's argument that constructive knowledge was sufficient, [215] viewing the authorities relied upon to support the proposition as cases on estoppel, rather than election.[216] Mance J did accept, however, that determining the exact nature of someone's knowledge is a nebulous exercise. He said:

> knowledge is not to be equated with absolute certainty, itself an ultimately elusive concept. The impossibility of doubt which Descartes found only in the maxim 'I think, therefore I exist' is not the criterion of legal knowledge. For practical purposes, knowledge pre-supposes the truth of the matters known, and a firm belief in their truth, as well as sufficient justification for that belief in terms of experience, information and/or reasoning. The element of regression or circularity involved in this description indicates why knowledge is a jury question.[217]

13.1.2 The elements of affirmation: (b) an unequivocal representation of affirmation

The second component of affirmation in the context of insurance, that of making an unequivocal communication to the insured of the insurer's choice not to avoid, was also problematical in terms of determining what exactly the communication should evidence. The judge queried whether, on the one hand, it is sufficient that there is knowledge of the breach and a communication (by words or conduct) which demonstrates that an unequivocal choice has been made, or whether, on the other hand, the communication itself or the surrounding circumstances demonstrating such knowledge, would suffice. On this issue Mance J concluded that for the purposes of affirmation the latter approach was correct:

---

[214] The issues of moral hazard and non-disclosure arising from the facts of this decision are discussed at p 96, above.
[215] The contention was based on a sentence in *Chitty on Contracts* (27th edn) vol 1 para 24-006 that '[in] cases of waiver by election the party who has to make the choice must either know or have obvious means of knowledge of the facts giving rise to the right...'
[216] The cases cited, *Bremer Handelsges mbH v C Mackprang Jr* [1979] I Lloyd's Rep 221 and *Avimex SA v Dewulf & Cie* [1979] 2 Lloyd's Rep 53 and *Cerealmangimi SpA v Toepfer (The Eurometal)* [1981] 1 Lloyd's Rep 337, all pre-date *The Kanchenjunga*, [1990] 1 Lloyd's Rep 391 and the Court of Appeal decision in *Peyman v Lanjani* [1985] Ch 457, both of which are considered in ch 7.
[217] [1998] Lloyd's Rep I R 151, at162.

The communication itself or the circumstances must demonstrate objectively or unequivocally that the party affirming is making an informed choice. In the context of estoppel, where knowledge is not a pre-requisite (though reliance is), it is in contrast the appearance of choice with which the law is concerned.[218]

Therefore the question whether there has been an unequivocal representation has to be considered in the light of the insured's knowledge about what the insurers actually knew. As such, where it is argued that a party's conduct amounts to an unequivocal representation, the impact such conduct has on the other party to the contract has to be objectively assessed. Mance J therefore posited that in affirmation, as distinct from estoppel, the actual state of the other party's mind is not the test because affirmation 'depends on the objective manifestation of a choice.'[219] The difficulty lies with determining what knowledge can be objectively ascribed to the insured, for it is from his perspective that some choice has to be seen to have been exercised by the insurer. On the facts of the case, Mance J was of the opinion that where the choice lies between whether or not to avoid the policy on the ground of non-disclosure of material facts (ie, Royal Hotel's fraudulent conduct), it has to be determined how far a reasonable person in the insured's position would be aware of what matters were material to a prudent insurer and how, in the absence of such awareness, the reasonable person could regard any conduct of the insurers as unequivocal. Given the severity of Royal Hotel's undisclosed conduct, it must have been clear and obvious to its director that his conduct would induce the contract. The insured must also have realised that the dishonest conduct in question had been discovered by the insurers if only on the basis of a common sense consideration of the documents which had been supplied to them during the pre-trial proceedings in 1994.[220]

On the evidence, the judge took the view that the insurers' solicitors, Herbert Smith, became suspicious of the fraud during 1993 and were convinced of it by 1994 but decided on so-called 'tactical' grounds not to raise the issue of avoidance during the 1994 trial. For Mance J therefore, this amounted to affirmation because 'they did for present purposes "know" the real position, however much Royal Hotel continued to brazen it out with implausible denials or evasions.'[221] The fact that the insured continued to deny dishonest conduct on their part, even during the earlier trial, did not preclude a finding that the insurers had the relevant knowledge and knew that the insured's denials were unsustainable.

The insurers had also continued to observe the arbitration clauses in the policies up until 1995 and as such had been a party to the ensuing arbitration proceedings. Taking this, together with the insurers' conduct of the 1994 litigation which, as has been seen, proceeded on the basis that the material damage policy was valid, the court was able to find what amounted to unequivocal conduct by the insurers from which it could be inferred that they recognised the continuing validity of the policy 'despite their and legal advisers' unannounced internal intention not to do so.'[222]

---

[218] *Ibid,* citing the judgment of Slade LJ in *Payman v Lanjani* [1985] Ch 457, in support of his finding.
[219] [1998] Lloyd's Rep I R 151, at 163.
[220] Ibid, at 174.
[221] Ibid, at 171.
[222] Ibid, at 175.

More recently, the opportunity for a thorough review of the defences of affirmation and waiver arose in *WISE Underwriting Ltd Agency Ltd v Grupo Nacional Provincial SA*.[223] The defendants, a Mexican insurer (GNP), appealed to the Court of Appeal against a decision of Simon J that the claimants, WISE, the reinsurers, were entitled to avoid a reinsurance contract on the basis of non-disclosure. In essence, the facts were that P, a retailer of luxury goods in Cancun, Mexico, imported stock from Miami. The consignment in question was delivered to P's warehouse where it was left outside overnight. The container was broken into and a number of cartons containing watches were stolen. The total value of the loss was US $817,797.00 of which US $700,390.00 represented the value of Rolex watches which made up part of the consignment. P had effected a goods in transit policy with GNP which, in turn, reinsured the risk ultimately through WISE. The slip presentation which was in Spanish referred to Rolex watches. However, the English translation which was prepared for the reinsurers referred, by mistake, to clocks. When GNP claimed under the reinsurance policy the reinsurers sought to avoid it arguing that the nature of the goods to be covered was misrepresented and that the presence of high-value brands of watches together with the fact that regular shipments would be made was not disclosed to them. GNP claimed that the reinsurers had impliedly waived the non-disclosure and, in the alternative, had affirmed the policy by giving 60 days' notice of its cancellation knowing of their right to avoid for non-disclosure. In terms of waiver, GNP argued that WISE knew that Cancun was a high class resort; that the slip had originally been prepared in Spanish with the consequent risk of imprecision in translation; that the shipment of goods from the USA to Mexico ought to have caused them to examine the risk closely; and they knew that the goods included jewellery but failed to investigate its nature or the security arrangements for its shipment. GNP also argued that WISE had not been induced by the non-disclosure or misrepresentation.

The Court of Appeal, by a majority, held that GNP were entitled to recover. Although it was unanimously held that WISE had been induced by the presentation of the risk, Rix and Peter Gibson LJJ held that the reinsurers had affirmed the policy, notwithstanding the breach of the duty of disclosure, by giving notice of its cancellation. Such notice was inconsistent with any claim to avoid the policy *ab initio*. Both judges took the view that the trial judge had overlooked a vital email which showed that WISE were unequivocal in cancelling the policy.[224]

With respect to the issue of waiver under s 18(3) of the 1906 Act, Longmore LJ, with whom Peter Gibson LJ agreed, held that there was no waiver of the duty of disclosure. Reviewing the case law, in particular *Container Transport International Inc v Oceanus*,[225] Longmore LJ thought that:

> The doctrine of waiver…has therefore come to be invoked in cases where it can be said that, if an insurer does not ask an obvious question, he will have waived disclosure of any material fact which would have been revealed by the answer. That in turn lets in the concept of a prudent insurer since, if such a question would have been obvious to such insurer, the actual insurer cannot be heard to say that such question would not have been obvious to him.[226]

---

223 [2004] EWCA (Civ) 962.
224 Longmore LJ dissented on the basis that the judge's findings of fact could not be reversed.
225 [1984] 1 Lloyd's Rep 476. On the issue of non-disclosure in this case, see p 88 above.
226 [2004] EWCA (Civ) 962, at [108].

Longmore LJ therefore took the view that deciding whether there was waiver involved a two-fold process. First, it had to be determined whether a material fact had not been disclosed. Secondly, it had to be established whether the insurer 'was put on inquiry by the disclosure of facts which would raise in the mind of the reasonable insurer at least the suspicion that there were other circumstances which would or might vitiate the presentation.'[227] On the facts he held that while there had been a material non-disclosure there was nothing in the presentation of the risk that could be said to have raised the suspicion that Rolex watches were to be included in the consignment. Longmore LJ concluded by noting that:

> Mr Kealey's [counsel for the reinsures] argument in the present case has more than an echo of the submissions he made in *Marc Rich v Portman*, [1996] 1 Lloyd's Rep 430, 442. He there submitted that the insurer could and should have asked an (obvious) question about the loss experience of the assured; now he submits the insurer could and should have asked an (obvious) question about the unlikelihood of clocks being shipped to Cancun. I rejected the argument then and the Court of Appeal held I was right to have done so [1997] 1 Lloyd's Rep 225, 234. For my part I would reject it again.[228]

Rix LJ, dissenting on this issue, placed particular emphasis on the mutuality of the duty of utmost good faith, and stated that the only relevant question was whether the presentation was fair:

> Ultimately, it seems, the question is: Has the insurer been put fairly on inquiry about the existence of other material facts, which such inquiry would necessarily have revealed? The test has to be applied by reference to a reasonably careful insurer rather than the actual insurer, and not merely by reference to what such an insurer is told in the assured's actual presentation but also by reference to what he knows or ought to know, ie his s 18(3)(b) [of the 1906 Act] knowledge. The reasonably careful underwriter is neither a detective on the one hand nor lacking in common-sense on the other hand. Mere possibilities will not put him on inquiry, and very little if anything can make up for non-disclosure of the unusual or special. Overriding all, however, is the notion of fairness, and that applies mutually to both parties, even if the presentation starts with the would-be assured.[229]

Applying this to the facts, Rix LJ concluded that a reasonably careful insurer would have been fairly put on inquiry, given what he knew from GNP's presentation and his general s 18(2)(b) knowledge. He went on to state that:

> If the question is instead the overriding question: Is the ultimate assessment of GNP's presentation that it is unfair, or would it be unfair to allow the reinsurers a remedy of avoidance in such a case? I would answer that the presentation was fair, and that it would be unfair to allow reinsurers to take advantage of an error of translation in a case where, on the evidence, an exclusion of watches would seem to have been the obvious solution.[230]

For Rix LJ the duty of utmost good faith and, more particularly, its content insofar as it applies to insurers or reinsurers, requires them to play a pro-active role in the disclosure process rather than relying solely upon the insured's presentation.[231]

---

[227] Ibid, at [111].
[228] Ibid, at [117].
[229] Ibid, at [64].
[230] Ibid, at [67].
[231] See the comments of R Merkin, *Insurance Law Monthly* (2004) Vol 16 No 10.

13.2 Issue estoppel/*res judicata* and abuse of process: *ICCI* continued

Given the insurers' failure to raise the issue of avoidance of the policies in the 1994 action, the question arose whether they could now be precluded from doing so on grounds of issue estoppel or abuse of process. Where an action is found to be an abuse of process, the court can take this by way of defence and strike the action out. On the facts of the case the judge pointed to the obvious overlap between issue estoppel or abuse of process and affirmation. While affirmation requires knowledge and a manifested election, estoppel or abuse is dependent only upon the existence of a point which might with due diligence have been raised in earlier litigation between the parties. Counsel for the insured cited *Henderson v Henderson*,[232] in which Wigram V-C said:

> The plea of *res judicata* applies, except in special cases, not only to points upon which the court was actually required by the parties to form an opinion and pronounce a judgment, but to every point which properly belonged to the subject of litigation, and which the parties, exercising reasonable diligence, might have brought forward at the time.[233]

Mance J noted that the terminology used in the authorities is not entirely consistent, some cases proceeding on the basis of *res judicata* or issue estoppel while in others emphasis is placed on the wider concept of abuse of process. For example, in *Greenhalgh v Mallard*,[234] Somervell LJ ascribed a broad meaning to the term *res judicata* and regarded it as being synonymous with abuse of process so that in effect, the one encompassed the other.[235]

Applying this wider meaning of *res judicata* or issue estoppel to the facts of the present action, the issue became whether the court was now precluded from considering the voidability of the material damage policy which could have been raised during the earlier action, but which for tactical reasons was not. It is settled law that where a point is so fundamental that it can be said to go to the very root of a prior action and as such would have been decisive, a party cannot raise it in any subsequent action. The Privy Council's decision in *Yat Tung Co v Dao Heng Bank*,[236] was therefore taken by Mance J as recognising that there are situations where a party will be expected to make any case on avoidance at the time when reliance is placed on the contract, and a party's failure to do so will result in him being precluded from doing so in subsequent proceedings.

In the insurance law context avoidance may occur either automatically or may depend upon some formal act of the party for it to be effective. Where the insured is

---

[232] (1843) 3 Hare 100.
[233] Ibid, at 114. See also, *Yat Tung Co v Dao Heng Bank* [1975] AC 581 PC at 590–1, cited by Mance J, in which Lord Kilbrandon said: 'The shutting out of a "subject of litigation"–a power which no court should exercise but after a scrupulous examination of all the circumstances– is limited to cases where reasonable diligence would have caused a matter to be earlier raised; moreover, although negligence, inadvertence, or even accident will not suffice to excuse, nevertheless "special circumstances" are reserved in case justice should be found to require the non-application of the rule...'
[234] [1947] 2 All ER 255.
[235] Somervell LJ said, ibid at 257: '... *res judicata* for this purpose is not confined to the issues which the court is actually asked to decide, but ... it covers issues or facts which so clearly could have been raised that it would be an abuse of the process of the court to allow a new proceeding to be started in respect of them.'
[236] [1975] AC 581.

in breach of warranty the insurer is automatically discharged from liability.[237] Accordingly, Mance J observed that as responses to a claim, breach of warranty, avoidance, failure to perform a condition precedent to liability or an allegation of a fraudulent claim are all generally considered 'and where arguable, either deployed or rejected in litigation, without attention to whether they depend on some formal act which has effect in contract or equity outside the insurers' pleading.'[238] On the other hand, avoidance for non-disclosure is dependent upon some formal act of the innocent party. The judge rejected the insurers' claim that they could reserve their right to avoid until a later time without running the risk of being met with *res judicata*. He thought that this simply did not fit with the practical realities of claims handling and litigation or indeed with the wider meaning of *res judicata*.

Finding there there were no special circumstances which should pre-empt the wider principle in *Henderson v Henderson* from applying to the facts before him, the judge held that the voidability of the material damage policy was integral to the 1994 litigation and so the insurers' could not now raise it. Mance J did, however, recognise that his finding involved some extension to the scope of the *Henderson* principle into the field of substantive rights. But, in his view, such an extension was inevitable in the context of the voidability of insurance contracts and merely reflected the practical and commercial realities of the litigation process such as existed in the 1994 action between the parties 'where the insurance contracts had no continuing significance save in respect of claims already paid or being pursued under them.'[239]

---

[237] See the speech of Lord Goff in *Hellenic Mutual War Risks Association v Bank of Nova Scotia* [1992] 2 AC 233 at 262, construing the Marine Insurance Act 1906, s 33(3).
[238] [1998] Lloyd's Rep I R 151, at 178.
[239] Ibid.

5

Formation of the Insurance Contract

1. Offer and acceptance

Although special rules apply to insurance contracts, such as the duty of disclosure, they do share much common ground with other types of contracts. A contract is a legally enforceable agreement: it is 'a promise or set of promises for the breach of which the law gives a remedy, or the performance of which the law in some way recognises as a duty.'[1] The test of whether an agreement exists and what are its terms is objective: in other words, even though the judges speak about the parties' intention, this intention is discovered not by attempting to understand what the parties themselves believed they had done, but by the appearance of their words and actions. For an insurance contract there must be agreement between the parties on the principal terms, [2] which would presumably include the risk to be covered, the insured subject matter, the duration of the cover, the premium and the benefit due in the event of a covered loss. Nevertheless, at the root of the courts' approach to contract is the desire to facilitate rather than obstruct agreements, at least where commercial parties are involved and especially where they acted as though a contract existed:

> Where…there is a clear intent to create legal relations and the transaction or transactions are clearly of a commercial character, English law is perfectly ready to recognize the con-tractual relations that the parties so clearly intend and will not frustrate them on account of some difficulty of analysis.[3]

---

[1] American Law Institute, *Restatement Second of the Law of Contracts*, s 1.
[2] *Allis-Chalmers Co v Fidelity and Deposit Company of Maryland* (1916) 114 LT 433; *Murfitt v Royal Insurance Co* (1922) 38 TLR 334 at 336, per McCardie J; *Kirby v Cosindit Societa per Azioni* [1969] 1 Lloyd's Rep 75.
[3] *General Accident Fire and Life Assurance Corpn Ltd v Tanter: The 'Zephyr'* [1984] 1 Lloyd's Rep 58 at 72, per Hobhouse J.

Where an insurance contract included a clause which, among other things, declared that the agreement 'shall be interpreted as an honourable engagement rather than as a legal obligation,' it was, nevertheless, held on a reading of the agreement as a whole that the parties had not intended to make the contract unenforceable through the courts, but had merely wished to restrict the application of particular rules of law, which they were entitled to do.[4]

To determine whether an agreement has been concluded the courts typically look for an offer and a matching acceptance. In insurance the offer will usually be made by the prospective insured completing a proposal form and sending it to the insurers.[5] An offer continues until it is accepted or rejected by the offeree, or a reasonable period of time has passed, or it has been revoked by the offeror prior to acceptance.[6] Clearly, there can be no acceptance if the offeree is unaware of the existence of the offer since the parties could hardly be said to have come to an agreement.[7]

The acceptance must match the offer and be unconditional, otherwise it may be regarded as a counter offer, which will be a rejection of the original offer and will begin the whole process over again. It is important to distinguish a counter offer from a mere inquiry about the terms of the offer, which does not amount to a rejection.[8] This distinction is not easily made and will depend on the particular circumstances. For example, where in response to a proposal by the prospective insured the insurer sends out a policy that includes a term of which the prospective insured was previously unaware, this might constitute a counter-offer.[9] On the other hand, where the insurer responds with a policy in standard form, then as long as it is not inconsistent with the proposal, it may be held to be a valid acceptance even though it includes terms not expressly communicated, if the insured could reasonably be expected to know that there would be such terms.[10]

In the case of a new contract of insurance (as opposed to a renewal), it is likely that the offer is made by the prospective insured completing the proposal form. Generally, the acceptance of the offer must be communicated to the offeror, unless the offeror waives this requirement.[11] It may be possible to infer acceptance from conduct, such as where the insured pays, or the insurers accept, the premium.[12] If the offer is made by the insurer, the communication of an acceptance to a third party, such as a broker, is insufficient unless the broker is the agent of the insurer, which is not usually the case. Where the insurers offer to renew an annual motor policy by issuing a cover note that extends the old policy, the motorist will accept by driving on

---

[4] *Home Insurance Co, and St Paul Fire and Marine Insurance Co v Administratia Asigurarilor De Stat* [1983] 2 Lloyd's Rep 675 at 677, per Parker J.
[5] *General Accident Insurance Co v Cronk* (1901) 17 TLR 233; *Rust v Abbey Life Insurance Co Ltd* [1979] 2 Lloyd's Rep 334.
[6] The parties may have entered a separate contract under which the offeror is obliged to keep the offer open for a period of time.
[7] *Taylor v Allon* [1966] 1 QB 304. An authority to the contrary seems illogical and anyway the facts of the case are not clearly reported: *Gibbons v Proctor* (1891) 64 LT 594.
[8] *Hyde v Wrench* (1840) 3 Beav 334; *Stevenson v McLean* (1880) 5 QBD 346.
[9] *Canning v Farquhar* (1886) 16 QBD 727 at 733, per Lindley LJ, but see the different analyses of the issues presented by Lord Esher MR and Lopes LJ.
[10] See below and ch 8.
[11] *Carlill v Carbolic Smoke Ball Co* [1893] 1 QB 256 at 262, per Lindley LJ; *Brinkibon Ltd v Stahag Stahl und Stahlwarenhandelsgesellschaft mbH* [1983] 2 AC 34 at 41, per Lord Wilberforce and 48, per Lord Brandon.
[12] *Canning v Farquhar* (1886) 16 QBD 727 at 731, per Lord Esher MR.

the basis of that offer.[13] In *Rust v Abbey Life Assurance Co*,[14] Rust, having been given advice both by the insurers and by her own advisors, completed a proposal form and sent it to the insurance company. This action was treated by the Court of Appeal as an offer that the insurers accepted by sending out a policy, so the parties were bound. However, the court went on to say that, even if the insurer's action in sending out the policy was merely a counter offer because it included terms not previously seen by Rust, her delay in taking seven months to object to those terms amounted to an acceptance. The court was not saying that silence amounts to an acceptance–it is a general rule that it does not[15]–but merely that acceptance can, in appropriate circumstances, be inferred from conduct. In view of the context of this case and in particular the extensive advice Rust had received, it was 'an inevitable inference from the conduct of the plaintiff in doing and saying nothing for seven months that she accepted the policy as a valid contract between herself and the first defendants.'[16] A case in which the insurers were bound in spite of not having communicated acceptance is *Roberts v Security Co Ltd*.[17] Roberts completed a proposal form for burglary insurance, which stated that he agreed to the usual terms applying. Subsequently, the company completed and sealed a policy, but did not deliver it to Roberts. He then suffered a loss through a burglary. The Court of Appeal held the insurers liable since their act of writing the policy signified acceptance even though they had not notified this fact to Roberts.

It is a general principle of contract law that once an offer has been accepted and an agreement formed neither party may unilaterally withdraw.[18] The contract may, of course, give the parties the right to cancel the contract. Where a policy contains a term allowing cancellation by the insurer, it will usually also provide for a portion of the premium to be repaid to the insured. There is old authority to the effect that the breadth of such clauses is not a matter in which the courts will interfere: so a clause giving the insurer an unfettered right to cancel will be enforced.[19] However, at least in consumer insurance contracts, such a term might be deemed unfair, and therefore not binding under the provisions of the Unfair Terms in Consumer Contracts Regulations 1999. The insured also has certain statutory rights to cancel an insurance contract, which are independent of that contract.[20]

If the parties have subjected the operation of their agreement to the fulfilment of a condition precedent that is never fulfilled, there will be no contract. On the other hand, where there is a suspensive condition, the contract exists and neither party can unilaterally withdraw, but its operation is suspended until the condition is fulfilled.[21] It is common for an agreement on insurance to specify that it will not commence until

---

[13] *Taylor v Allon*, see above n 7.

[14] [1979] 2 Lloyd's Rep 334.

[15] *Felthouse v Bindley* (1862) 11 CBNS 869; *De Mezey v Milwaukee Mechanics' Insurance Co* [1945] 12 ILR 122 (Alberta).

[16] See above n 14, at 340, per Brandon LJ.

[17] [1897] 1 QB 111.

[18] AH Hudson, 'Retraction of Letters of Acceptance' (1966) 82 *LQR* 169. There are situations in which one of the parties can avoid an insurance contract: for instance, as will be seen later, a failure by the insured to fulfil the duty of disclosure will entitle the insurers to treat the contract as void: see ch 4.

[19] *Sun Fire Office v Hart* (1889) 14 App Cas 98.

[20] See, eg, Financial Services Authority *Handbook, Insurance: Conduct of Business Rules*, ICOB 6. The Handbook is discussed in ch 2.

[21] Such conditions should be distinguished from 'promissory' conditions, which are terms of an operative contract whose breach entitles the innocent party to a remedy. On conditions and warranties in insurance contracts (and in particular the confusion in terminology), see ch 7.

a specified requirement is met, such as the payment of the premium or the completion of a satisfactory medical examination, or for the courts to imply such a stipulation. In *Canning v Farquhar*,[22] between completing the proposal form for life assurance and his agent tendering the first premium, Canning fell from a cliff and sustained an injury from which he later died. The Court of Appeal held that the insurers were not liable. Lord Esher MR and Lopes LJ decided that the offer was made when the premium was tendered and what came before that time was merely pre-contractual negotiation. Since this represents the majority opinion it is the ratio decidendi of the case, but Lindley LJ reached the same conclusion by a different method. While he agreed that what went on before the tendering of the premium did not amount to a binding contract, he believed it was important since only by referring to what the other judges called negotiations could the terms of the contract be determined. He regarded the offer by the insurers as represented by the proposal plus the extra terms, such as the amount of the premium, which were mentioned later. That offer had been made on the basis of a statement in the proposal that Canning was in good health and since this was no longer true at the time the premium was tendered, the offer had lapsed and could no longer be accepted. On this analysis, if Canning's health had not changed, acceptance would have been by the prospective insured tendering the premium and not by the insurers accepting it since the offer by the insurers must be capable of acceptance by the prospective insured and this can only be the case if the act of acceptance is tendering the premium.[23]

2. Premium

Each party to an insurance contract must provide consideration: the insured agrees to pay a premium and the insurers promise to provide a benefit in the event of a loss arising that falls within the terms of the policy. The premium will be set by the insurers at a level that attracts business, but that also both reflects the risk of a claim by this insured and, across the business as a whole, is likely to result in a profit.[24] The premium will be either a single payment or a series of payments: for instance, the car owner takes out motor insurance for a year and typically pays in one lump sum, whereas the premium for a life insurance policy is often paid in monthly instalments.

The premium is an important aspect of the agreement, and if one has not been agreed by the parties this may indicate that they have not concluded a contract.

---

[22] (1886) 16 QBD 727. See also, *Harrington v Pearl Life Assurance Co* 30 Times LR 613; *Looker v Law and Union Rock Co Ltd* [1928] 1 KB 554.

[23] In some jurisdictions there are presumptions concerning the formation of the contract and the payment of the premium: in Alberta, for example, the policy will bind where it has been delivered irrespective of whether the premium has been paid (Insurance Act, RSA 1980, s 208(1); *McDowell v Wawanesa Mutual Insurance Co* 102 DLR (3d) 561 (Alberta)); in the US, the courts in most states impose liability on the insurer where the insured has completed a proposal and paid the premium and there has been an unreasonable delay by the insurer in responding (J Lowry and P Rawlings, *Insurance Law: Cases and Materials* (Oxford, Hart Publishing, 2004) 236–8). See also, *Elite Builders Ltd v Maritime Life Assurance Company* [1984] ILR 1-1798 (British Columbia), and, in Australia, the Insurance Contracts Act 1984 (Cth), s 75.

[24] Insurers do not, of course, simply rely on premium income to meet their obligations. Premium income is invested and insurers also pass on risk through reinsurance contracts (on which see ch 17).

Where an 'agreement' for insurance on building work specified 'a reasonable premium,' it was held that there was no contract since 'it cannot be said that there is a sum which can be defined and described as being undisputed.'[25] Yet, the failure to set the amount of the premium may not be fatal. In the case of a normal risk, such as involved in burglary insurance or motor vehicle liability, the amount of the premium is set according to the insurer's usual tariff. Indeed, the Marine Insurance Act 1906, section 31(1) recognises the common practice of effecting marine insurance at a premium 'to be arranged' (generally shortened to TBA). If the parties never specify what that premium is, then 'a reasonable premium is payable,' which means one calculated at the prevailing market rate.[26]

The premium will usually be a payment of money,[27] but can take almost any form as long as there is, in the words of Lush J when speaking of consideration more broadly,[28] 'some right, interest, profit, or benefit accruing to the one party, or some forbearance, detriment, loss, or responsibility given, suffered, or undertaken by the other.' For instance, the Marine Insurance Act 1906, section 85(2) recognises mutual marine insurance agreements under which members do not pay a premium but agree to contribute to losses suffered by fellow members as and when they occur.[29]

Offers of 'free insurance' are sometimes made by a variety of businesses from credit card issuers to newspapers as a way of enticing potential customers to buy products or as a means of acquiring marketing information about customers. In such cases, even though there is no premium in the form of money, it is not usually difficult to discover consideration. For instance, an agreement to provide insurance might be collateral to an agreement to open a credit card account: in exchange for the promise to provide insurance, the consumer promises to enter into the main agreement. *Imperial Tobacco Ltd. v Attorney-General*,[30] while not on the issue of insurance, gives some indication of the willingness of the courts to surmount this problem of consideration in appropriate cases. Purchasers of a certain brand of cigarettes obtained the chance of winning a cash prize, and the House of Lords ruled that, although no extra was charged for the cigarettes, there was consideration for the chance: 'where a person buys two things for one price, it is impossible to say that he had paid only for one of them and not for the other. The fact that he could have bought one of the things at the same price as he paid for both, is in my view immaterial.'[31] In *Fuji*

---

[25] *Kirby v Cosindit Societa per Azioni*, see above n 2, at 79, per Megaw J.

[26] See also Marine Insurance Act 1906, s 31(2), which allows the parties to provide for an additional premium in the event that circumstances specified in the agreement occur by which the risk has increased. See *Gliksten v State Assurance* (1922) 10 Ll L Rep 604. The court may refuse to set a premium where the increase in risk has made it uninsurable in the market: *Liberian Insurance Agency Inc v Mosse* [1977] 2 Lloyd's Rep 560.

[27] *Lion Mutual Marine Insurance Association Ltd v Tucker* (1883) 12 QBD 176 at 187, per Brett MR.

[28] *Curry v Misa* (1875) LR Ex 153 at 162.

[29] Such agreements have played an important role in providing protection and indemnity cover (P. & I. cover) for ships in circumstances where it is difficult to obtain insurance from commercial insurers, such as when trading in war zones: *The Standard Steamship Owners' Protection and Indemnity Association (Bermuda) Ltd v Gann* [1992] 2 Lloyd's Rep 528; HN Bennett, *The Law of Marine Insurance* (Oxford, Clarendon Press, 1996) 236–45 and Appendix III; T Coghlin, 'Protection and Indemnity Clubs' (1984) *LMCLQ* 403; M Tilley, 'The Origin and Development of the Mutual Shipowners' Protection & Indemnity Associations' (1986) 17 *JMLC* 261; M Tilley, 'Protection and Indemnity Club Rules and Direct Actions by Third Parties' (1986) 17 *JMLC* 427.

[30] [1981] AC 718.

[31] Ibid, at 739, per Viscount Dilhorne.

Finance Inc v Aetna Life Insurance Co Ltd,[32] Nicholls V-C did express the view that if there was no attempt to link the amount of the premium to the risk this might indicate that the agreement was not an insurance contract. This might exclude 'free insurance' offers since even if it is possible to find consideration it will not be based on an actuarial calculation. It seems better to use the lack of a link between the consideration and the risk as an indicator rather than as conclusive evidence that there is no insurance contract, and to be fair this seems to have been what Nicholls V-C was himself suggesting. In *Nelson and Co. v Board of Trade*,[33] Nelson, a firm of tea merchants, offered an annuity for life to customers who were widowed (the offer was only open to women) and who could establish a record of tea-purchases from the company. The customers did not pay a premium, and the funds for the annuity came out of the company's general profits. There was no policy only a card on which purchases were recorded, but the court found no difficulty in concluding that this was insurance business. However, the issue of the premium was not specifically raised. That case was not followed by the Court of Appeal in *Hampton v Toxteth Co-operative Provident Society Limited*.[34] The society ran a general shop and advertised the offer of 'free life assurance.' Death benefits proportionate to a member's expenditure were to be paid out of what was called an 'Insurance Fund'. The majority of the judges took the view that the lack of either a policy or a premium and the apparent power the society had to stop allocating money to the fund showed that this was not life insurance but merely an allocation of the society's profits that could be terminated at any time.[35]

Payment of the premium to a broker is not payment to the insurer, unless the contract is for marine insurance,[36] or, contrary to the normal situation, the broker is the agent of the insurers.[37] In marine insurance, the insurers are not bound to issue the policy until the premium has been tendered,[38] which has important consequences since, under the Marine Insurance Act 1906, section 22, a contract of marine insurance is unenforceable unless embodied in a policy document.[39] Typically, an insurance contract stipulates that the insurers will not be on risk until the premium is paid,[40] although this requirement can be waived. In a case concerning burglary insurance, the policy document stated that the premium had been paid, so even though it had not, the insurers were taken to have waived the condition for prepayment of the premium and it was, therefore, held that the insurers were on risk.[41] If the contract

---

[32] [1995] Ch 122. The decision was reversed on appeal, but the issue discussed here was not mentioned: [1997] Ch 173.

[33] (1901) 84 LT 564.

[34] [1915] 1 Ch 721, although see the strong dissenting judgment by Phillimore LJ, who mentioned the case, as did counsel.

[35] Lord Cozens-Hardy MR did refer to the use of the words 'free insurance' in the society's advertising as 'inaccurate, misleading, and highly improper': [1915] 2 Ch 721 at 733. It is worth noting that the case concerned whether the company's offer brought it within the terms of the Assurance Companies Act 1909, which regulated insurance and which only applied if a policy had been issued (s 1). See also, *Hall D'Ath v British Provident Association for Hospital and Additional Services* (1932) 48 TLR 240.

[36] Marine Insurance Act 1906, s 53(1) *Carvill America Incorp v Camperdown UK* [2005] EWCA Civ645.

[37] On intermediaries, see ch 15. .

[38] Marine Insurance Act 1906, s 52.

[39] See also, Statute of Frauds 1677, s 4, with regard to guarantee policies.

[40] *General Accident Insurance Co v Cronk*, see above n 5.

[41] *Roberts v Security Co Ltd*, see above n 17. But see *Equitable Fire and Accident Office Ltd v The Ching Wo Hong* [1907] AC 96.

does not require the premium to be prepaid, the insured's promise to pay the premium will be sufficient consideration and, assuming all other requirements for a contract are present, the insurers will be on risk.[42]

The insurers are not entitled to retain the premium unless the risk has begun to run.[43] Indeed, in marine policies, 'where the risk has not been run, whether its not having been run was owing to the fault, pleasure, or will of the insured, or to any other cause, the premium shall be returned.'[44] The premium will be repayable where the insurers avoid the contract because of an innocent misrepresentation or non-disclosure by the insured,[45] or where there is a mistake of fact or law which renders the contract void, as, for instance, would be the case if both parties entered into a life insurance contract in the mistaken belief that the insured life was alive.[46] Where the risk has attached, even if for a shorter period than contemplated by the policy, then no part of the premium is returnable,[47] although of course the contract can expressly provide for a refund in specified circumstances, such as where the policy is cancelled before its normal expiry date.[48] If the insured has a number of policies each covering the same subject-matter for the full amount of the loss, then, although the insured cannot claim more than an indemnity and so can only claim on one policy,[49] the insurers who do not pay out are not required to return the premiums received because they have been on risk.[50] Similarly, the insurers do not have to return the premium merely because the circumstances in which the loss occurs renders the policy unenforceable. For example, where the insured life commits suicide there may be no claim under a life insurance policy,[51] but the premium will not be repayable because the insurers would have been liable had the insured died from a cause which was covered.

3. Benefit

The consideration supplied by the insurers is the promise to provide a benefit in exchange for the premium. That benefit is normally cash, but need not be. The policy may, for instance, oblige the insurers to reinstate the house if it burns down or to replace stolen items.

---

[42] *Roberts v Security Co Ltd*, ibid.

[43] *Thomson v Weems* (1884) 9 App Cas 671 at 682, per Lord Blackburn.

[44] *Tyrie v Fletcher* (1777) 2 Cowp 666 at 668, per Lord Mansfield CJ. See Marine Insurance Act 1906, s 84(1), (2), (3). This rule does not apply to non-marine policies: *Wolenberg v Royal Co-operative Collecting Society* (1915) 84 LJKB 1316 at 1319, per Lush J.

[45] On these issues, see ch 4.

[46] See below.

[47] Except in the highly unlikely event that the contract is not entire and apportionment is possible: *Stevenson v Shaw* (1761) 3 Burr 1237; Marine Insurance Act 1906, s 84(2).

[48] Marine Insurance Act 1906, s 83. For an example, see Institute Time Clauses (Hull), cl 5, on which see ch 16. If an insured exercises a right to cancel under the FSA's rules on cooling off periods, the premium must be returned, although some portion may be retained if, for instance, the insurer has been on risk or has incurred expenses: see above n 20. See also, *Swiss Reinsurance Co v United India Insurance Co Ltd* [2005] EWHC 237 (Comm).

[49] This is because of the principle of indemnity, see ch 10.

[50] *Wolenberg v Royal Co-operative Collecting Society* (1915) 84 LJKB 1316 at 1319, per Lush J.

[51] *Beresford v Royal Insurance Co Ltd* [1938] AC 586.

For an agreement to amount to a contract of insurance the insured must have a legal right to the benefit if the claim falls within the terms of the agreement, and the benefit must have some value. In *Department of Trade and Industry v St Christopher Motorists' Association,*[52] motorists made an annual payment in exchange for which the association promised to provide a driver if the motorist became unable to drive as a result of injury or disqualification. This was held to amount to an insurance contract since there was an obligation to provide a benefit and that benefit, although not a cash payment, had value.[53]

On that reasoning, an agreement will not be an insurance contract where the alleged insurers are not obliged to provide the benefit, but have a discretion whether to do so, or where the benefit is not of value. In *Medical Defence Union v Department of Trade and Industry,*[54] the union provided a scheme for indemnifying members where damages were awarded against them in connection with their medical practices, but while members had a right to advice and to have their claim considered, they had no right to demand indemnification, although in practice proper claims were met. Megarry V-C held that this did not amount to insurance. He regarded the right to a benefit as one of the distinguishing features of an insurance contract: 'When a person insures, I think that he is contracting for the certainty of payment in specified events.'[55] Furthermore, while the benefit under an insurance policy could be in 'money or money's worth...or the provision of services to be paid for by the insurer,' he believed it was important not to adopt too broad a view of what these phrases meant otherwise 'money's worth' could stretch to cover a whole host of benefits: 'from matters such as peace and quiet to the pleasure of listening to the arguments of counsel in this case, and much else besides.' In his view, the benefit to which the member had a right needed to be more than merely the right to have a claim considered for the agreement to amount to insurance. He, therefore, decided that this scheme did not amount to insurance because members had no legal right to a benefit of value. In reaching this conclusion he seems to have been influenced by a concern that to find otherwise would create difficulties by making a wide range of professional bodies subject to the system of statutory regulation applicable to insurance business. In the circumstances of this case, he believed, 'one is in a different world from the world of insurance.'[56] This decision was not directly on the issue of contract formation, but it seems likely that, while in Megarry's view the arrangement did not amount to insurance, there was a contract. The members' rights to have advice and to have their application considered were of value: certainly, they were in a better position than people who were not part of the scheme.

---

[52] [1974] 1 WLR 99.
[53] See *Card Protection Plan Ltd v Customs and Excise Commissioners* [1994] STC 199 at 207, per Balcombe LJ.
[54] [1980] Ch 82.
[55] *Medical Defence Union Ltd v Department of Trade,* ibid, at 95. See also, *Hampton v Toxteth Co-operative Provident Society Ltd,* see above n 34, at 742–3; *CVG Siderurgica del Orinoco SA v London Steamship Owners' Mutual Insurance Association Ltd (The 'Vainqueur José')* [1979] 1 Lloyd's Rep 557.
[56] *Medical Defence Union Ltd v Department of Trade,* ibid, at 95 and 97.

4. Mistake

What happens if one or both of the parties is mistaken about some aspect of the agreement? In broad terms, contract law will not intervene. However, where one party misrepresents a fact to another and the other is induced by that misrepresentation to enter into a contract, the innocent party may be able to rescind the contract or obtain damages or both. If there has been no such misrepresentation, there will be no remedy where one party is in error about the nature of the bargain, unless the contract is vitiated by mistake. The position is, of course, more complicated with respect to insurance contracts because they are contracts of utmost good faith, which, as has been seen, places both parties under a duty of disclosure. It is important, therefore, to bear this obligation in mind when considering the operation of the doctrines of misrepresentation and mistake.

The easiest type of mistake to deal with is the clerical error or 'misnomer': for instance, during the typing up of the policy the name of the insured is incorrect spelt, or the numbers of a car's registration plate are transposed, or a particular business activity is described as being undertaken by A Ltd when A Ltd has been taken over by B Ltd.[57] In such cases the court can construe the contract as if the error had not been made. However, the error must be minor. The test is:

> how would a reasonable person receiving the document take it? If, in all the circumstances of the case and looking at the document as a whole, he would say to himself: 'Of course it must mean me, but they got my name wrong,' then there is a case of mere misnomer. If, on the other hand, he would say: 'I cannot tell from the document itself whether they mean me or not and I shall have to make inquiries,' then it seems to me that one is getting beyond the realm of misnomer.[58]

Of more gravity is the situation where a document, which purports to record the agreement, does not in fact do so. The equitable remedy of rectification enables the courts to amend a contractual document, [59] although this comes up against the rule that if the parties have put their agreement into writing the court should not look outside the four corners of the document.[60] The court will not alter the original agreement, it merely alters the document because it does not accurately represent that agreement: 'Courts of Equity do not rectify contracts; they may and do rectify instruments purporting to have been made in pursuance of the terms of contracts.'[61] The courts, therefore, exercise caution in ordering rectification: 'Men must be careful if they wish to protect themselves; and it is not for this Court to relieve them from the consequences of their own carelessness.'[62] The court will not order rectification merely because one party is in some way unhappy with the original agreement or

---

[57] *Nittan (UK) Ltd v Solent Steel Fabrication Ltd Trading as Sargrove Automation and Cornhill Insurance Co. Ltd* [1981] 1 Lloyd's Rep 633 at 637, per Lord Denning MR, and 639, per Brightman LJ.

[58] *Davies v Elsby Brothers Ltd* [1961] 1 WLR 170 at 176, per Devlin LJ.

[59] J Cartwright, *Unequal Bargaining: A Study of Vitiating Factors in the Formation of Contracts* (Oxford, Clarendon Press, 1991) 52–7.

[60] See ch 8.

[61] *Mackenzie v Coulson* (1869) 8 LR Eq 368 at 375, per James VC.

[62] Ibid.

alleges a mistake occurred in that agreement, nor will it do so if, on an objective view, the document does accurately represent the agreement.[63] The conditions required for rectification to be granted are:

> First, there must be common intention in regard to the particular provisions of the agreement in question, together with some outward expression of accord. Secondly, this common intention must continue up to the time of execution of the instrument. Thirdly, there must be clear evidence that the instrument as executed does not accurately represent the true agreement of the parties at the time of its execution. Fourthly, it must be shown that the instrument, if rectified as claimed, would accurately represent the true agreement of the parties at that time.[64]

The mistake must 'be proved with a high degree of conviction.'[65] The only situation in which the court will order rectification where only one party is mistaken is if the other party knew the document did not comply with the terms of the agreement and also knew the innocent party believed that it did.[66] Finally, rectification will be barred by lapse of time.

There are two other types of mistake which cause rather more difficulty. The first is where the mistake throws into doubt the existence of the contract; the second is where it is alleged that, while an agreement was reached, it has been vitiated by a later mistake. If the mistake is such that there was never any real agreement, then the court will declare the so-called contract void and order the return of any premium paid.[67]

The fact that one party to a contract realises that the other party is mistaken does not by itself impose a duty to point out that mistake, unless failing to do so would be a breach of the duty of disclosure, or there is an element of misrepresentation or fraud in the concealment.[68] This is because contracts are about parties making their own bargains and using their own judgement. Therefore, mistakes about the quality of an item or its value are not operative mistakes. It is otherwise if Bill knows or suspects Jane is mistaken, and, although Bill has not induced the mistake, he then makes misleading statements to divert Jane's attention so that she will not discover the mistake. In such a case the contract is taken to have the meaning which the innocent party believed it had since that is the meaning which the other party intended and

---

[63] *Frederick E. Rose (London) Ltd v William H. Pym Jnr & Co Ltd* [1953] 2 QB 450.

[64] *Agip SpA v Navigazione Alta Italia SpA* [1984] 1 Lloyd's Rep 353 at 359, per Slade LJ. Also, *Establissements Georges et Paul Levy v Adderley Navigation Co Panama SA (The 'Olympic Pride')* [1980] 2 Lloyd's Rep 67 at 72. The Marine Insurance Act 1906, s 89 allows rectification of a policy where it does not correspond with the terms in the slip; also *Symington and Co. v Union Insurance Society of Canton Ltd (No 2)* (1928) 34 Com Cas 233 at 235, per Scrutton LJ (but see HN Bennett, 'The Role of the Slip in Marine Insurance' [1994] *LMCLQ* 94). For examples of situations in which rectification was ordered, see *Wilson, Holgate & Co Ltd v Lancashire & Cheshire Insurance Corpn Ltd* (1922) 13 Ll L Rep 487; *Eagle Star & British Dominions Insurance Co Ltd v A V Reiner* [1927] 27 Ll L Rep 173.

[65] *Establissements Georges et Paul Levy v Adderley Navigation Co Panama SA (The 'Olympic Pride')*, ibid, at 73, per Mustill J. See also *Pindos Shipping Corpn v Frederick Charles Raven (The 'Mata Hari')* [1983] 2 Lloyd's Rep 449 at 452, per Bingham J.

[66] *Establissements Georges et Paul Levy v Adderley Navigation Co Panama SA (The 'Olympic Pride')*, ibid, at 73–4.

[67] *Fowler v The Scottish Equitable Life Insurance Society and Ritchie* (1858) 28 LJ Ch 225.

[68] *Container Transport International Inc and Reliance Group Inc v Oceanus Mutual Underwriting Association (Bermuda) Ltd* [1984] 1 Lloyd's Rep 476 at 512, per Parker LJ.

which a reasonable person would understand it to have.[69] Of course, this situation might simply be characterised in terms of a breach of the duty of disclosure or a misrepresentation. Where Mary knows that Ted is mistaken as to the promise she is making, then there will be no agreement,[70] and indeed it may be that in such a case Mary is acting fraudulently. In *The Prince of Wales, &c Association v Palmer*,[71] evidence was brought to show that William Palmer had induced his brother, Walter, to take out a life insurance policy on his own life with the intention of later persuading Walter to assign the benefit of that policy to William and then, in the rather understated words of Romilly MR, 'precipitating, by his own act, the period at which those insurances were to become claims on the insurance offices.' William was later accused by a coroner's jury of murdering Walter, but never convicted of that crime, although he was hanged for the murder of John Parsons Cobb. In an action on the policy on Walter's life, the court concluded that the contract had been entered into for fraudulent purposes, and was, therefore, void.[72]

It may be that there is genuine agreement and no misunderstanding between the parties, but they share a mistaken belief about the existence of a particular state of affairs which is fundamental to the contract: that the person whose life is being insured is alive, the ship is afloat, or the house is standing when, in fact, she is dead, the ship is at the bottom of the sea and the house is a pile of ashes.[73] The House of Lords in the leading case of *Bell v Lever Brothers Ltd*[74] clearly wished to limit the possibility of pleading this type of mistake. The case has caused considerable difficulty and attracted much criticism,[75] but can be more easily understood if it is recognised that the courts take as their starting point that 'the law ought to uphold rather than destroy apparent contracts,'[76] although admittedly this begs the question of how one recognises an 'apparent' contract. The decision was by a majority of three to two, and there were some differences in the views of the majority, but they did agree that in order to vitiate a contract the mistake had to be common to both parties and fundamental: 'something which both must necessarily have accepted in their minds as an essential and integral element of the subject-matter,[77] or 'must render the subject matter of the contract essentially and radically different from the subject matter which the parties believed to exist.'[78] Shortly after the decision in *Bell*, Lord Wright, delivering the opinion of the Privy Council in an insurance case, said:

> It is…essential that the mistake relied on should be of such a nature that it can be properly described as a mistake in respect of the underlying assumption of the contract or

---

[69] *Commission for the New Towns v Cooper (Great Britain) Ltd* [1995] Ch 259. For an example, see *Fletcher v Board of Trade* (1923) 16 Ll L Rep 55.

[70] *Smith v Hughes* (1871) LR 6 QB 597.

[71] (1855) 25 Beav 605.

[72] This must be distinguished from the more common situation where the life insurance policy was entered into without the intention of murdering the insured life and claiming. In that case the contract is valid but unenforceable by the murderer. In the *Palmer* case the contract was void *ab initio* for fraud.

[73] *Galloway v Galloway* (1914) 30 TLR 531; *McRae v Commonwealth Disposals Commission* (1951) 84 CLR 377. See ch 9.

[74] [1932] AC 161.

[75] For a vigorous defence of the decision, see *Associated Japanese Bank (International) Ltd v Credit Du Nord S.A.* [1989] 1 WLR 255.

[76] *Associated Japanese Bank (International) Ltd* v *Credit Du Nord SA*, ibid, at 268, per Steyn J.

[77] *Bell v Lever Brothers Ltd*, see above n 74, at 235, per Lord Thankerton.

[78] *Associated Japanese Bank (International) Ltd* v *Credit Du Nord SA*, see above n 75, at 268, per Steyn J.

transaction or as being fundamental or basic. Whether the mistake does satisfy this description may often be a matter of great difficulty.[79]

In *Bell*, the company reached an agreement which provided compensation to two employees whose contracts were being terminated. It was later discovered that the employees had committed breaches of their contracts which would have enabled the company to terminate them without compensation. The House of Lords decided that there was not a fundamental mistake and, therefore, the agreement was not void because the main objective had been to terminate the contracts so as to facilitate a merger and this had been achieved.[80]

In *Pritchard v Merchants' and Tradesmen's Mutual Life Assurance Society*,[81] the insurers accepted the renewal of an annual life insurance policy without requiring proof of the good health of the insured life, although the terms of the agreement allowed them to demand it. Neither the insurers nor the person renewing the policy was aware that the insured life had already died. The court held that the payment of the premium and its acceptance were founded on a mistake. The court reasoned that the continued good health of the insured life must have been regarded by the parties as central to the contract, otherwise it would have been pointless to mention it.[82] Similarly, in *Scott v Coulson*[83] the sale of a life assurance contract was void for mistake because both parties wrongly believed the person whose life was the subject of the contract was still alive. The difficulty with that decision is that it could be seen as a case in which the mistake was not fundamental in that the contract was concerned with the sale of a life assurance contract and the mistake was only about how much that contract was worth. *Bell* does not preclude the possibility of such mistakes being sufficient to make a contract void, although *Scott* does show that it is difficult to draw the boundaries around the *Bell* decision. In *Strickland v Turner*,[84] a contract for the sale of an annuity on the life a man who, unknown to both parties, was already dead was held to be void because there was a total failure of consideration, the purchaser having received nothing in exchange for the price paid.

The decision in *Bell v Lever Brothers Ltd* has been both praised and criticised for narrowing the possibility of the doctrine of mistake: praised because it created certainty and protected innocent third parties who may have acquired the property that had passed under the original contract; criticised because it lacked flexibility. It was the latter criticism that Denning LJ sought to address in *Solle v Butcher* by devising the doctrine of mistake in equity.[85] This doctrine was wider and more flexible than common law mistake, which he claimed to be the basis of the decision in *Bell*. There were two difficulties: the first was to determine the difference between the circumstances in which common law and equitable mistake operated; the second was that one had to be prepared to accept Denning LJ's proposition that the House of Lords

---

[79] *Norwich Union Fire Insurance Society Ltd* v *WH Price Ltd* [1934] AC 455 at 463.
[80] *Associated Japanese Bank (International) Ltd v Credit Du Nord SA*, see above n 75, at 267, per Steyn J.
[81] (1858) 3 CB (NS) 622.
[82] The contract obliged the insurer to accept the renewal if the premium was paid within thirty days. If the premium was paid outside that period but within three months the insurance might be revived 'on satisfactory proof of health.' Payment arrived two days outside the thirty-day period.
[83] [1903] 2 Ch 249.
[84] (1852) 7 Exch 208.
[85] [1950] 1 KB 671.

in *Bell* neglected to consider the possibility of mistake in equity so that their decision was *per incuriam*. In *Magee v Pennine Insurance Co*,[86] an agreement to compromise an insurance claim was made on the mistaken belief of both parties that the policy was binding when, in fact, it was voidable because of an innocent misrepresentation by the insured. The Court of Appeal held that the insurers could avoid the contract for mistake in equity. The problem with the decision is that it is difficult to distinguish from the facts in *Bell*, and indeed Winn LJ dissented on that ground. The majority took the view that in *Bell* the House of Lords had, indeed, been only concerned with mistake at common law, whereas here the issue was one of mistake in equity. This left one wondering why it did not occur to the House of Lords in *Bell* to use the equitable doctrine, and the most plausible reason seemed to be that it was not invented until *Solle v Butcher*.[87] Recently, in *The Great Peace* the Court of Appeal has rejected the decision in *Solle* as inconsistent with the House of Lords decision in *Bell*.[88] Lord Phillips MR took the view that the effect of *Solle* 'is not to supplement or mitigate the common law: it is to say that *Bell v Lever Bros Ltd* was wrongly decided.' He therefore concluded that it was 'impossible to reconcile' the two decisions: 'If coherence is to be restored to this area of our law, it can only be by declaring that there is no jurisdiction to grant recession of a contract on the ground of common mistake where that contract is valid and enforceable on ordinary principles of contract law.'[89] The Court of Appeal did not overrule *Solle*, but this was, of course, the effect of saying that it was inconsistent with *Bell*. This was not to say that Lord Phillips had no sympathy for Lord Denning's dislike of *Bell*, and indeed he contemplated the idea of legislation along the lines of the Law Reform (Frustrated Contracts) Act 1943, which might provide greater flexibility to mistake than is possible under the common law. Interestingly, Lord Phillips thought the decision in *Scott v Coulson* remained good law, in spite of *Bell*, because the policy in that case was not a nullity. He took the view that the explanation for that decision was that a life policy before the death of the insured life was fundamentally different from the same policy after the death: 'the contractual consideration no longer existed, but had been replaced by something quite different—ergo the contract could not be performed.'[90]

The party pleading that there has been a mistake will not succeed 'where the mistake consists of a belief which is entertained by him without any reasonable grounds for such belief.'[91] Moreover, the court may find that one party took on the risk that the state of affairs was not as both had believed.[92] Often the insured will be required to sign a warranty in the proposal that the subject matter exists, the effect of which is that no claim can be made if, in fact, it did not exist. Before the advent of telecommunications, it might well have been the case that the owner of cargo on a ship, who wished to arrange insurance after the vessel had sailed, would have no means of knowing whether the ship was afloat or had sunk. This led to the development of the

---

[86] [1969] 2 QB 507.
[87] See above n 85. The issue rarely came before the courts, although see *Associated Japanese Bank (International) Ltd v Credit Du Nord SA*, above n 75.
[88] *Great Peace Shipping Ltd v Tsavliris Salvage (International) Ltd* [2003] QB 679. See (2003) 62 *CLJ* 29; (2003) 119 *LQR* 177, 180.
[89] In other words, there is no mistake as defined in *Bell v Lever Brothers Ltd*, above n 74.
[90] See also, *Bell v Lever Brothers Ltd*, ibid, at 236 per Lord Thankerton.
[91] *Associated Japanese Bank (International) Ltd v Credit Du Nord SA*, see above n 75, at 268, per Steyn J.
[92] *McRae v Commonwealth Disposals Commission* (1950) 84 CLR 377.

'lost or not lost' policy, under which, if unbeknown to both parties the ship had been lost before the contract, the insured would pay the premium and the insurers would pay for the loss.[93] Similarly, in reinsurance, where one insurer takes on part or all the risk entered into by another insurer with an insured, the agreement may be made on a 'lost or not lost' basis so that the second insurer will be liable for all losses incurred by–but not known to–the first insurer at the time of the reinsurance contract.[94] The 'lost or not lost' policy seems to be confined to these types of risk.[95] The normal rules about disclosure apply to such policies, so that if, for example, the insured does know that the loss has already occurred there is a duty to disclose that knowledge.

Mistake as to the identity of the person with whom a contract is being made has always caused difficulty. The key is that the person asking for relief must show that the intention to contract with a particular person and no other, and that the person with whom the alleged contract was made was not that person. It is not sufficient to show that, while Allen intended to contract with Kay, Allen would not have done so had he known more about Kay. In *Mackie v The European Assurance Society*,[96] the insured did not realise that the agent, through whom he was arranging insurance and who had previously dealt with one insurer, was now dealing with a different insurer. The court would not hold the contract void for mistake since the insured intended to obtain insurance through this agent and that is what happened. The identity of the insurer was regarded as irrelevant or at best a secondary matter.

Finally, the House of Lords has ruled that where money has been paid under a mistake, then even where it is a mistake of law rather than merely of fact, there is no general principle precluding recovery for unjust enrichment, subject to the defences that are available.[97] According to Lord Hope, the claimant must be shown to have acted under a mistake which led payment to be made to someone who is not legally entitled to receive it. The Lords also held that it was no defence for the payee to allege that the payment was made in accordance with the law as it was understood at the time and that only subsequently has the law changed. Nor is it a defence to show that the payee acted in the honest belief that he was entitled to the payment.

---

5. Insurance contracts at Lloyd's

Lloyd's does not provide insurance, it is a market in which insurance is arranged

---

[93] Marine Insurance Act 1906, s 6(1).

[94] See ch 17.

[95] There is no reason why, in theory, there could not be a 'dead or alive' provision in a life policy, but life policies normally require some proof or statement as to the health of the insured life and this will, by implication, exclude such a possibility: *Pritchard v Merchants' and Tradesmen's Mutual Life Assurance Society*, see above n 81; *Strickland v Turner*, see above n 84.

[96] (1869) 21 LT 102.

[97] *Kleinwort Benson Ltd v Lincoln City Council, Birmingham City Council, Southwark London Borough Council and Kensington and Chelsea Royal London Borough Council* [1998] 3 WLR 1095 at 1149–50, per Lord Hope.

according to particular rules.[98] An insured cannot deal directly in the Lloyd's market, but must act through a Lloyd's broker, although in some areas, such as motor and life insurance, much of the business is placed with outside agents who are guaranteed by a Lloyd's broker. The broker, who is the agent of the prospective insured, writes a slip outlining the risk and approaches an underwriter who specialises in the particular risk (the lead underwriter). An underwriter, who agrees to take on the risk, will initial the slip. Usually the lead underwriter takes on only part of the risk, but that person's expertise in the particular field of insurance may make it easier for the broker to persuade others to subscribe. The slip will be initialled by these other underwriters who, by that action, enter into a contract. Once the slip is fully subscribed, a policy may then be issued by Xchanging Ins-sure Services.[99] This practice of writing the policy from the information on the slip and of regarding the policy as the formal embodiment of the contract means that the slip is the contract and not merely evidence of a contract. To take the view that the slip was not the contract would be to admit the possibility that the terms of the agreement might be found elsewhere, which would make it impossible to be sure that the policy accurately embodies the agreement. Furthermore, underwriters subscribe to a slip on the basis of the subscriptions of earlier underwriters and must be able to have confidence that those subscriptions are on the terms set out in the slip.[100] However, once the contract has been embodied in a policy, a court will not look at the slip as an aid to interpretation of that policy, although if the policy differs from the slip and what is being sought is rectification of the policy, reference can be made to the slip.[101]

One problem that arises from the practice of the Lloyd's market involves the number of contracts that have been formed. Is there a single contract to which all those underwriters who subscribe to the slip are parties, or are there separate contracts with each underwriter? If there are several contracts relating to the same risk, each underwriter could negotiate different terms and if a claim were made the underwriters would not be required to take a common position: 'some may contest it, some may compromise it and others may decide to pay in full.'[102] These 'absurd consequences' led Donaldson J to take the view that the contract was not concluded until

---

[98] *General Reinsurance Corpn v Forsakringsaktiebolaget Fennia Patria* [1983] QB 856; *General Accident Fire and Life Assce Corpn v Tanter (The 'Zephyr')* [1984] 1 Lloyd's Rep 58; [1985] 2 Lloyd's Rep 529; *American Airlines v Hope* [1974] 2 Lloyd's Rep 301 at 304, per Lord Diplock; HN Bennett, 'The Role of the Slip in Marine Insurance Law' [1994] *LMCLQ* 94; HN Bennett, *The Law of Marine Insurance* (Oxford, Clarendon Press, 1986) 29–35. Cresswell J provides a useful outline of the history and operation of Lloyd's in *Society of Lloyd's v Clementson* [1997] LRLR 175. See also, IUA/Lloyd's Forum & LIBC, London Market Principles 2001 (2001).

[99] This replaced the Lloyd's Policy Signing Office in 2001.

[100] *General Accident Fire and Life Assce Corpn v Tanter (The 'Zephyr')*, see above n 98, at 69 (reversed on different grounds: [1985] 2 Lloyd's Rep 529); but see *American Airlines v Hope*, above n 98, at 304, per Lord Diplock.

[101] *Symington & Co v Union Insurance Society of Canton Ltd (No 2)*, see above n 64, at 235, per Scrutton LJ; *Youell v Bland Welch & Co Ltd* [1992] 2 Lloyd's Rep 127. Under Marine Insurance Act 1906, s 89, 'Where there is a duly stamped policy, reference may be made, as heretofore, to the slip or covering note, in any legal proceeding.' The use of 'heretofore' means that reference can be made to the law before 1906 and the law before 1906 restricted the use of the slip: see *Ionides v The Pacific Marine & Fire Insurance Co* (1871) LR 6 QB 674 at 685, per Lord Blackburn; HN Bennett, 'The Role of the Slip in Marine Insurance Law' above n 98, at 107–9. See, *HIH Casualty & General Insurance Ltd v New Hampshire Insurance Co* [2001] EWCA Civ 735.

[102] *General Reinsurance Corporation v Forsakringsakringsaktiebdaget Fennia Patria*, see above n 98, 856 at 864, per Kerr LJ.

the slip was fully subscribed.[103] The Court of Appeal, however, was less convinced of their absurdity and rejected his approach.[104] The Court held that a contract exists once the slip is initialled by the underwriter, and therefore each such subscription amounts to a separate contract. A contract (or contracts) exists even where the slip never becomes fully subscribed and the underwriter will be liable if, before the slip is fully subscribed, a covered loss occurs. The market does recognise the difficulty of having each underwriter negotiating different terms and, in practice, this does not happen, particularly in view of the willingness to defer to the lead underwriter's expertise. Indeed, it is common to include in the slip 'the leading underwriter clause,' under which the underwriters initial or scratch the slip even though it does not contain all the terms and do so on the understanding that negotiation over those terms will be conducted between the broker and the lead underwriter at a later date. Moreover, the leading underwriter clause will usually be drawn up in such a way as to restrict the amendments to the slip which can be made.[105]

If the slip is over-subscribed, that is, the underwriters taken together have agreed to cover more than the size of the risk, their liability (and the premium due to each underwriter), by a custom recognised by the courts by way of exception to the general rule, will be reduced in the proportion that their part of the risk bears to the whole.[106] This means that at the point of the subscription it will not be clear what is the underwriter's share of the risk or premium. The broker can approach the underwriters with an estimate as to the likely size of the over-subscription ('a signing down indication') and hence the final percentage of the risk which each underwriter will bear, although the broker is probably not liable if the indicated level of signing down is not obtained.[107] The obverse of over-subscription is where the broker fails to obtain complete cover. This does not entitle the insured (or, of course, the underwriter) to cancel the contracts already agreed between the broker and the underwriters who have initialled the slip, although the underwriters might not resist such a request from the broker since they may take the view that to do so would undermine the goodwill between brokers and underwriters on which the market depends.[108]

There is also the problem that statements made by the insured's broker to the lead underwriter will not be actionable as misrepresentations by later underwriters,

---

[103] *Jaglom v Excess Insurance Co Ltd* [1972] 2 QB 251 at 257.

[104] *General Reinsurance Corporation v Forsakringsakringsaktiebdaget Fennia Patria*, see above n 98 at 866, per Kerr LJ. See also the Court of Appeal's rejection of the different approach to this problem by Staughton J at first instance. He argued that, while there was a contract at the time of initialling, the custom of the market gave the broker the right to cancel up to the time when the slip was fully subscribed. The Court of Appeal recognised that, while underwriters might well allow a broker to cancel in order to maintain the good business relations, the broker has no legal right to require them to do so. See also *Touche Ross & Co v Baker* [1991] 2 Lloyd's Rep 230 (affirmed by the House of Lords [1992] 2 Lloyd's Rep 207).

[105] But not always, *Roadworks (1952) Ltd v J R Charman* [1994] 2 Lloyd's Rep 99; *American International Marine Agency of New York v Dandridge* [2005] EWHC 829 (Comm).

[106] *General Reinsurance Corporation v Forsakringsakringsaktiebdaget Fennia Patria*, see above n 98; *Ionides and Chapeaurouge v Pacific Fire and Marine Insurance Co* (1871) LR 6 QB 674 at 684–5, per Blackburn J; *Morrison v Universal Marine Insurance Co* (1872) LR 8 Ex 40 at 45 and (1873) LR 8 Ex 197 at 199; *Eagle Star Insurance Co Ltd v Spratt* [1971] 2 Lloyd's Rep 116; Marine Insurance Act 1906, s 21.

[107] *General Accident Fire and Life Assce Corpn v Tanter (The 'Zephyr')*, see above n 98, at 531–2, per Mustill LJ.

[108] *General Reinsurance Corporation v Forsakringsakringsaktiebolaget Fennia Patria*, above n 98, at 874, per Slade LJ. A broker, who is unsure whether there is sufficient interest in the market, may circulate a quotation slip, which is not an offer, but may reveal any difficulties and will, for instance, enable the broker to adjust the terms of the slip.

because while statements made by the broker may have induced the lead underwriter to enter the contract, this will not have been the case with those subsequent under-writers.[109] Finally, there is the less substantial difficulty of what happens in a contract for marine insurance where the loss occurs after the scratching of the slip, but before the written policy is issued. Under section 22 of the Marine Insurance Act 1906, 'a contract of marine insurance is inadmissible in evidence unless it is embodied in a marine policy.' The lack of a policy does not prevent the insurer from choosing to pay a claim, and indeed to take advantage of their strict legal position might not be regarded as either ethical or good business practice. Moreover, it may be that the slip is sufficient for the purposes of the Act.[110] Even if litigation is contemplated by the insured, the section may not prevent such an action because it goes on to say that the policy may be executed 'either at the time when the contract is concluded, or after-wards,' so that Lloyd's can–and, in practice, will–issue a policy.

---

6. Formalities

There is no general rule requiring insurance contracts to be written,[111] indeed there has recently developed a huge market in insurance by telephone. Suggestions in *Hampton v Toxteth Co-operative Provident Society Ltd* [112] that a contract of insur-ance required the existence of a written policy should be treated as confined to the special circumstances of that case, which concerned a statutory provision–long since repealed–that precluded regulation of contracts not embodied in a policy. An insur-ance contract may be formed orally and 'can be made in informal, colloquial language.'[113]

Yet, in the case of some types of insurance a written policy or written evidence of the existence of a contract is necessary for certain purposes. As has been seen, a marine insurance contract is inadmissible unless embodied in a policy.[114] The Life Assurance Act 1774 states that 'it shall not be lawful' to make any life policy without inserting the name of the person who is to benefit, which suggests that a written doc-ument is required (section 2).[115] In relation to some other types of insurance it may be a criminal offence not to have a particular document, but such a failure does not necessarily affect the enforceability of the contract itself. The insurance contract which is mandatory under the Employers' Liability (Compulsory Insurance) Act

---

[109] *General Accident Fire and Life Assce Corpn v Tanter (The 'Zephyr')*, see above n 98.

[110] HN Bennett, 'The Role of the Slip in Marine Insurance' above n 98, at 118.

[111] *Murfitt v Royal Insurance Co Ltd* (1921-2) 38 TLR 334 at 335, per McCardie J.

[112] See above n 34. See also, *Hall D'Ath v British Provident Association for Hospital and Additional Ser-vices*, above n 35.

[113] *Stockton v Mason and the Vehicle and General Insurance Co Ltd and Arthur Edward (Insurance) Ltd* [1978] 2 Lloyd's Rep 430 at 432, per Lord Diplock.

[114] Marine Insurance Act 1906, ss 21 and 22.

[115] The assumption that the word 'policy' means a written document is commonplace: *Hall D'Ath v Brit-ish Provident Association for Hospital and Additional Services*, see above n 35. However, it has been held that the word 'policy' includes any insurance contract, whether written or not: *Re Norwich Equitable Fire Assurance Society Royal Insurance Co's Claim* (1887) 57 LT 241 at 246, per Kay J.

1969[116] does not have to be written, but a certificate of insurance must be issued by the insurers and displayed by the insured (section 4). That Act also refers to the employer insuring 'under one or more approved policies' (section 1), which might suggest the need for a document, although probably the word 'policies' is simply used as a synonym for contract of insurance. It is an offence under the Road Traffic Act 1988 to use a motor vehicle unless it is covered by 'a policy of insurance,' and 'a policy' will have no effect for the purposes of the Act until the insurers have delivered to the insured 'a certificate of insurance' in a particular form.[117] Moreover, a motorist commits an offence by failing to produce such a certificate when required to do so by a police officer.[118]

7. Renewals and extensions

Where an insurance is for a limited period – such as a motor vehicle policy, which usually is for twelve months – and the parties choose to renew the cover at the expiration of that period, they enter a fresh contract on the same or different terms. This is a renewal and must be distinguished from an extension in which the contract permits the parties to extend the period for which it operates: here the old contract continues to be effective rather than being replaced, as is the case with a renewal.[119]

Some insurance contracts, such as most life policies, are automatically renewed or, more accurately, are continued by the payment of a premium, which the insurer cannot refuse. This does not amount to a new contract so the duty of disclosure does not revive.[120] Other insurance contracts, such as motor and buildings insurance, are for a limited period at the end of which a new contract may be entered into if both parties agree. With this latter type, the insurer in sending a notice of renewal makes an offer, which the insured may accept or reject.[121] A new contract is likely to be agreed with a minimum of formality and the insured may not even be asked to complete any forms, but all the requirements for the conclusion of a contract of insurance must be observed: for instance, the duty of disclosure revives so a motorist must reveal any relevant convictions that have occurred during the preceding period of insurance. In a renewal, unless new terms have been incorporated into the new policy, the old terms will apply.[122]

---

[116] Also Employers' Liability (Compulsory Insurance) Regulations SI 1998/2573.

[117] Road Traffic Act 1988, ss 143, 145 and 147. If for some reason the policy is voidable, there is no offence of driving without insurance since the policy is valid until it is avoided: *Goodbarne v Buck* [1940] 1 KB 771. See ch 13.

[118] Road Traffic Act 1988, s 165.

[119] *CE Heath Underwriting & Insurance (Australia) Pty Ltd v Edwards Dunlop & Co Ltd* (1993) 176 CLR 535 (High Court of Australia).

[120] *Pritchard v Merchant's Life and Tradesman's Mutual Life Assurance Society*, above n 81, at 643, per Willes J.

[121] Contrast this with the normal position in the case of new insurance where the offer is made by the prospective insured completing a proposal form: above.

[122] *GNER v Avon Insurance plc* [2001] 2 All ER (Comm) 526.

There is no substance to the commonly held belief that cover automatically continues for a period after a policy has expired; furthermore, there is no obligation on the insurer to issue a notice to the effect that the cover is about to expire, even if it would seem to be good business practice for them to do so.[123] A contract of insurance can expressly allow days of grace for payment during which cover will continue. This is common in contracts of life assurance where what is at issue is not the renewal of the contract, but the continuation of the existing policy subject to cancellation in the event of the premium not being paid. If a loss should occur within the days of grace the insured will be able to recover, although the premium must still be paid. Where a term of the contract allows days of grace and states that the policy will remain in force for a specified period 'from the date upon which the last premium became due,' that period runs from the date when the premium was due and not from the end of the days of grace.[124]

8. Cover notes

It often happens that pending the writing of a policy or a decision over renewal, the insurers issue a cover note. This amounts to a contract of insurance and is particularly common in those areas of insurance where the law requires some form of documentary evidence of cover, such as is the case with motor insurance under the Road Traffic Act 1988.[125] It is well established that an agent, who has been supplied by the insurer with blank cover note forms, has implied authority to bind the insurers by the issue of a cover note.[126] Insurers commonly authorise brokers to enter into provisional contracts, and where such an arrangement exists the broker will be agent for both parties and will have express authority to bind the insurers.[127] Of course, where the broker is not authorised by the insurer and has not been provided with blank forms there will usually not be any implied authority to contract as agent for the insurer.[128]

The normal analysis of contract formation applies: the offer will have been made by the prospective insured, usually through the completion of a proposal form, and acceptance is by the insurer issuing the cover note. In the case of a renewal, the cover note usually accompanies, but is separate from, an offer to renew for the next full period and its purpose is simply to allow both parties an opportunity to consider a fresh contract without the danger of there being a gap in insurance cover. In this

---

[123] *Mobil Pty Ltd v FM Insurance Ltd* (1986) 4 ANZ Ins Cas 60–718 (NSW). There are, however, certain regulatory requirements with respect to notification about a policy that is due to expire: see ch 2.

[124] *McKenna v City Life Assurance Co* [1919] 2 KB 491.

[125] See ch 13.

[126] *Mackie v The European Assurance Society*, above n 96; *Stockton v Mason and the Vehicle and General Insurance Co Ltd and Arthur Edward (Insurance) Ltd*, above n 113, at 431, per Lord Diplock.

[127] *Stockton v Mason and the Vehicle and General Insurance Co Ltd and Arthur Edward (Insurance) Ltd*, ibid, at 431.

[128] The decision to the contrary in *Murfitt v Royal Insurance Co*, above n 111, should be treated as an exception based on unusual facts.

situation, the insurer makes the offer to renew cover for the interim period pending agreement on a fresh contract, and it is the insured that has the choice to accept or refuse this offer.[129] Once the formal policy is issued, the cover note will terminate. Where the insurers decide during the currency of the cover note not to take on the risk, then the cover notice expires when they notify the insured of this decision and the note will usually be issued on terms entitling its cancellation.[130] The cover note will state the period during which it provides cover and it will cease to operate once that period has passed, whether or not another cover note or a full policy has been issued.

Whether what seems to be a cover note does, in fact, amount to a contract of insurance depends on it fulfilling the normal requirements for a contract: it is possible that the note is merely a receipt for money paid in advance and that there is no insurance until the company has properly considered the proposal. The case of the loquacious motorist, *Taylor v Allon*,[131] provides a salutary illustration of the contractual significance of the cover note, and in particular demonstrates that when issued by the insurer the note merely amounts to an offer which crystallises into a contract only if accepted by the prospective insured. A motorist was convicted of driving a car while not insured. His old insurance policy had expired on 5 April and the insurers sent a cover note to provide insurance for fifteen days. On 16 April the motorist obtained cover with a different company. Unfortunately, he had been stopped by the police the day before. He not only failed to produce the cover note, but told the police he was negotiating a change of insurers and that he did not realise the old policy had expired. The court upheld his conviction for driving without insurance. The cover note amounted to an offer to extend the insurance period which, since he was unaware of its existence, the motorist could not accept.[132] There was, therefore, no insurance contract and he was guilty of the offence charged. It is implicit in this case that by issuing the cover note the insurers are making an offer the acceptance of which does not have to be communicated. The motorist must still accept the offer, although the act of acceptance need only be such as would lead a reasonable person to infer that it had been accepted,[133] which might be simply driving in reliance on the offer. The offer in the renewal notice will lapse by the end of the expiration of the period specified, or earlier if either the insurer communicates their withdrawal of the offer,[134] or the insured rejects the offer.[135]

As with any contract of insurance, the insured is under a duty to disclose when the insurers agree to issue the cover note following a proposal by the insured, or, in the

---

[129] This arrangement is commonplace in motor vehicle liability insurance where the insurer will issue a cover note for a brief period pending a decision on renewal because otherwise the motorist would commit an offence under the Road Traffic Act 1988 in continuing to drive without insurance.

[130] *Stockton v Mason and the Vehicle and General Insurance Co Ltd and Arthur Edward (Insurance) Ltd*, above n 113, at 431, per Lord Diplock.

[131] See above n 7.

[132] As has been mentioned, an agreement is central to the concept of the contract, so there must be an acceptance of an offer: here the motorist was unaware of the offer and could, therefore, not accept it.

[133] *Carlill v Carbolic Smoke Ball Co*, above n 11.

[134] *Maguire v AMP Fire & General Insurance Co Ltd* (1982) ANZ Ins Cas 60–470 (New Zealand).

[135] The motorist in *Taylor v Allon* (see above) had not rejected the offer since, although he was negotiating cover with another company, at the time he was stopped he had not entered into another contract and might, therefore, have become aware of and decided to take up the offer contained in the cover note. Nevertheless, this does not help him because he had not accepted the offer in the cover note, and therefore there was no contract based on its terms.

case of a cover note sent by insurers to extend existing cover, within a reasonable period of time after receipt.[136] The cover note will not amount to a contract unless there is agreement on the material terms (risk, duration of cover, premium). It will be subject to such terms as were notified at the time it was made and any loss which occurs while it is in operation will be dealt with under its terms rather than those of any later, permanent policy, even where that policy purports to have retrospective effect.[137] If the cover note is issued following the expiration of a policy, the presumption will be that the cover is on the same terms as the old policy.[138] Where the cover note mentions terms or refers to another document which is accessible to the insured and in which terms are listed, then those terms will apply. There is likely to be no problem if the insured has completed a proposal form since that form or the accompanying literature will usually mention the terms upon which the insurers undertake insurance business. In addition, as has been seen, there are strong authorities suggesting that the insurer's standard terms will be implied, unless a contrary intention can be shown or those terms are not reasonably available for inspection.[139] On the other side is the decision in *Re Coleman's Depositories Ltd and Life & Health Assurance Association*.[140] An employer completed a proposal form for insurance to cover liability to employees injured at work and a cover note was issued on 28 December. A policy was issued on 3 January, which purported to be effective from 1 January. This was delivered to the employer on 9 January. The policy required the employer to notify the insurer immediately after an employee was injured at work, but this term had not been mentioned when the cover note was issued. The relevant accident occurred on 2 January. It was held that because the insured was unaware of the term until 9 January, it did not apply to this accident. The decision seems curious and could present problems were it not for the fact that insurers have adopted the practice of expressly referring to their usual policy terms in the cover note (much as a railway company refers to its standard terms and leaves it up to the traveller to enquire as to what they are).

---

9. Telephone insurance and e-insurance

The rapid growth in insurance arranged over the telephone has created some legal problems. Here there is no form for the insured to complete, the employee of the insurance company simply asks some questions and, on the basis of the answers provided, agrees to give insurance cover for the full period. The contract of insurance is probably made, at the latest, when the insured offers and the employee agrees to

---

[136] *Marene Knitting Mills v Greater Pacific General Insurance Ltd* [1976] 2 Lloyd's Rep 631.
[137] *Re Coleman's Depositories Ltd and Life & Health Assurance Association* [1907] 2 KB 798.
[138] *Stockton v Mason and the Vehicle and General Insurance Co Ltd and Arthur Edward (Insurance) Ltd*, above n 113, at 431, per Lord Diplock.
[139] *General Accident Insurance Co v Cronk*, above n 5; MA Clarke, 'Notice of Contractual Terms' (1976) 35 *CLJ* 51.
[140] See above n 137; also, *Neil v The South East Lancashire Insurance Co Ltd* 1932 SC 35.

accept payment, so that any document produced by the insurers is merely an attempt to put into writing the agreement made over the telephone and, in theory, cannot introduce new terms. To take the example of motor insurance, it is typically the case that the insurer's employee will have agreed to provide cover on the basis of answers to questions about the make of the car, the place where it is kept, the persons who are going to drive and their driving records and health, and whether the prospective insured has been refused insurance. It would be impossible for the representative to list off the terms under which motor insurance is offered and unwise of that person to summarise them. It is also likely that the insured will not have any literature since he will have contacted the company in response to an advertisement on the television or in a newspaper. This, of course, does not mean there are no terms. Where a renewal of an existing policy is being transacted over the telephone, then the presumption will be that the terms of the old policy apply. If there is no existing policy, then the decision in *Re Coleman's Depositories Ltd and Life & Health Assurance Association*[141] suggests that, unless there is express reference to the incorporation of particular terms contained in the insurer's policies, the courts will not imply such an incorporation in the case of a cover note. Moreover, the Unfair Terms in Consumer Contracts Regulations 1999 state that a term will be unfair where it has the effect of 'irrevocably binding the consumer to terms with which he had no real opportunity of becoming acquainted before the conclusion of the contract' (schedule 2, para 1(i)). Nevertheless, as Lord Wilberforce observed in *Liverpool City Council v Irwin*[142]:

> Where there is, on the face of it, a complete, bilateral contract, the courts are sometimes willing to add terms to it, as implied terms: this is very common in mercantile contracts where there is an established usage: in that case the courts are spelling out what both parties know and would, if asked, unhesitatingly agree to be part of the bargain.

Terms that are standard in the insurance market will be implied as a matter of trade practice or usage, as long as the parties have not agreed that they will not apply, they do not conflict with express terms and they are readily available for the prospective insured to examine.[143] Wills J went further and said that the insured 'must be taken to have applied for the ordinary form of policy issued by the company.'[144] The terms must be available, but if they are, the fact that the insured chooses not to examine them will not prevent them from applying.

Where the prospective insured completes a proposal form through the internet, it is likely that, as with traditional insurance, the offer is made by the prospective insured. The internet method certainly has great advantages over telephone insurance in that the insurer can avoid any potential difficulties over the terms of the contract by placing those terms on the website and by setting up the site so as to ensure that the prospective insured acknowledges having read and agreed to them, although merely requiring someone to signify their consent to such terms by clicking on a box will not necessarily mean those terms comply with the requirements of the Unfair Terms in Consumer Contracts Regulations 1999.

---

[141] See above n 137.
[142] [1977] AC 239 at 253.
[143] See, generally, Clarke, 'Notice of Contractual Terms,' above n 139.
[144] *General Accident Insurance Co v Cronk*, above n 5, at 233, per Wills J. See ch 2.

10. Illegality

The courts will refuse to enforce an insurance contract which has as its purpose the commission of a crime or tort, even if the parties were not aware of the illegality: a policy designed to cover property in an alien enemy,[145] or the profits expected from an illegal drugs deal would be illegal and unenforceable.[146] An insurance policy will also be void if the insured has no insurable interest under the Marine Insurance Act 1906.[147] In such circumstances any premium paid cannot be recovered.[148] If an insurance contract is made by a person in the course of carrying on insurance business who has not obtained authorisation under the Financial Services and Markets Act 2000, the contract is unenforceable against the insured and the insured is entitled to recover any premium paid.[149]

[145] *Janson v Driefontein Consolidated Mines Ltd* [1902] AC 484 at 499, per Lord Davey.
[146] More often the insurance is not taken out for an unlawful purpose, but the loss sustained involves a criminal act by the insured and the issue is whether or not the insurer is liable. This is discussed in ch 9.
[147] S 4(1); see ch 6.
[148] *Harse v Pearl Life Assurance* [1904] 1 KB 559.
[149] Financial Services and Markets Act 2000, s 26. See ch 2.

6

Insurable Interest and the Doctrine of Privity of Contract

1. The statutory requirements

Despite the fact that at common law there was no general requirement that the insured should have an insurable interest in the event against which the insurance is effected, it has become a fundamental requirement which governs the validity of an insurance contract. At its root, it is this prerequisite alone which distinguishes a contract of insurance from a wager,[1] for in a valid contract of insurance the interests of the parties go beyond the mere winning or losing of a bet.

The requirement of insurable interest arises from three sources which, depending upon the type of policy in question, will determine the validity of the contract. First, in indemnity insurance, where the level of the insured's loss determines the amount of payment recoverable under the policy, the very nature of the contract as one of indemnity will require the insured to have an insurable interest at the date of the loss. The general prohibition of gaming contracts contained in the Gaming Act 1845, s 18[2]

---

[1] In *Carlill v Carbolic Smoke Ball Co* [1892] 2 QB 484 at 490--491, Hawkins J defined a wagering contract as 'one by which two persons, professing to hold opposite views touching the issue of a future uncertain event, mutually agree that, dependent upon the determination of that event, one shall win from the other, and that other shall pay or hand over to him, a sum of money or other stake; neither of the contracting parties having any other interest in that contract than the sum or stake he will so win or lose, there being no other real consideration for the making of such contract by either of the parties.' This definition was approved by the Court of Appeal in *Ellesmere v Wallace* [1929] 2 Ch 1 at 24, 36, 48–9. See also, *Newbury International Ltd v Reliance National Insurance Co Ltd and Tyser Special Risks Ltd* [1994] 1 Lloyd's Rep 83.

[2] S 18 provides, inter alia, that: 'All contracts or agreements, whether by parole or in writing, by way of gaming or wagering, shall be null and void; and no suit shall be brought or maintained in any court of law or equity for recovering any sum of money or valuable thing alleged to be won upon any wager, or which shall have been deposited in the hands of any person to abide the event on which any wager shall have been made...' But note the effect of the Gambling Act 2005, see below.

will strike down a policy taken out by an insured who has no interest, and no reasonable expectation of obtaining an interest, in the subject matter of the policy. However, the court will lean in favour of finding insurable interest wherever possible.[3]

Secondly, the Life Assurance Act 1774 requires the proposer for life insurance to possess an insurable interest at the date of entering into the contract in order to prohibit 'a mischievous kind of gaming'(see the preamble to the Life Assurance Act 1774), but no such requirement need be shown at the date of the loss.[4] Failure to establish insurable interest at the outset will render the policy illegal with the result that the court will not order a return of the premiums to the insured.[5] The Act does not apply to marine policies,[6] nor does it apply to the insurance of 'goods and merchandises' since the latter are specifically excluded by s 4. The Gaming Act 1845 therefore applies to such policies.[7] Although the 1845 Act will be prospectively repealed by the Gambling Act 2005 (probably during 2006), so that the need to demonstrate insurable interest at the outset will be removed, this will be of little practical importance given the indemnity principle (see below). It will thus remain the case that the insured will need to demonstrate loss when the peril occurs. With respect to other types of indemnity insurance, the precise scope of the Act has been a matter of considerable judicial debate. While it is unclear from the wording of the 1774 statute whether it applies to real property insurance and liability insurance, modern case law suggests that it does not.[8] In *Mark Rowlands Ltd v Berni Inns Ltd*,[9] the insurer argued that the insured's tenant could not benefit from a building's fire insurance because he was not named in the policy as required by s 2 of the Act.[10] Kerr LJ expressed the opinion that to give the phrase 'or other event or events' contained in s 2 their literal meaning, so as to hold that the Act applies to indemnity insurance, would create 'havoc in much of our insurance law.'[11] He therefore concluded that 'this ancient statute was not intended to apply, and does not apply, to indemnity insurance, but only to insurance which provides for the payment of a specified sum

---

[3] *Re London County Commercial Reinsurance Office Ltd* [1922] 2 Ch 67 at 79, *per* Lawrence J. See also, *Mackenzie v Whitworth* (1875) 10 Exch 142 at 148, *per* Bramwell B; *Stock v Inglis* (1884) 12 QBD 564 at 571, *per* Lord Brett MR. See also, the essay by J Lowry and P Rawlings, 'Rethinking Insurable Interest' in Sarah Worthington (ed), *Commercial Law and Commercial Practice* (Hart Publishing , 2003) 335. Note also the commentary on this essay by Sir Jonathan Mance at 365.

[4] As will be seen, life policies can be validly assigned to a third party. In this respect, it is common practice for creditors, for example banks, to require a debtor to assign the benefit of a life policy to them as security for a loan.

[5] S 1 of the 1774 Act states that a contract entered into in breach of the Act 'shall be null and void to all intents and purposes whatsoever' and s 2 states that 'it shall not be lawful to make any policy' in breach of the section. See *Harse v Pearl Life Assurance Co* [1904] 1 KB 558, considered below at n 33, in which the insured sought to recover the premiums paid by him under a policy void for want of insurable interest. It is noteworthy that in contrast to the Life Assurance Act 1774, an insured's failure to establish insurable interest in marine insurance does not render the policy illegal, but void, see *John Edwards & Co Ltd v Motor Union Insurance Co* [1922] 2 KB 249.

[6] Which are governed by the Marine Insurance Act 1906, see ch 16 below.

[7] It has been held that the term 'goods' includes money so that an insurance policy covering money against loss by burglary falls outwith the scope of 1774 Act, see *Prudential Staff Union v Hall* [1947] KB 685.

[8] There is authority, albeit pre-dating the Act, in which it was held that for buildings insurance insurable interest was required at the time of the policy. See, *Sadler's Co v Badcock* (1743) 2 Atk 554. For the situation in motor insurance see ch 13, below.

[9] [1986] QB 211.

[10] Considered below.

[11] Above, n 9 at 227.

on the happening of an insured event.'[12] In a similar vein, in *Siu Yin Kwan v Eastern Insurance Ltd*,[13] Lord Lloyd of Berwick stated that:

> s. 2 must take colour from the short title and preamble to s. 1. By no stretch of the imagination could indemnity insurance be described as a 'mischievous kind of gaming'. Their Lordships are entitled to give s. 2 a meaning which corresponds with the obvious legislative intent.[14]

The view expressed by Lord Denning MR in *Re King, Robinson v Gray*,[15] that the 1774 Act did apply to buildings insurance was dismissed by Lord Lloyd on the bases that it was expressed by way of *obiter*, it is not reflected in the judgments of the other two members of the court and the point was not argued.[16] In any case, with respect to insurance on real property it should be borne in mind that the principle of indemnity operates to prevent a person who lacks insurable interest from recovering under the policy.

Thirdly, the Marine Insurance Act 1906, s. 4 provides that a contract of marine insurance is deemed to be a gaming or wagering contract and is therefore void unless the insured possesses an insurable interest as defined by s 5 of the Act. It is further provided that insurable interest must exist at the date of the loss, as a marine policy is one of indemnity. Section 5 of the Act goes on to define insurable interest in the following terms:

> (1) ... every person has an insurable interest who is interested in a marine adventure.
>
> (2) In particular a person is interested in a marine adventure where he stands in any legal or equitable relation to the adventure or to any insurable property at risk therein, in consequence of which he may benefit by the safety or due arrival of insurable property, or may be prejudiced by its loss, or damage thereto, or by the detention thereof, or may incur liability in respect thereof.

While this definition is confined to marine policies, it nevertheless provides a useful insight into the requirement of insurable interest in insurance law generally. Of particular note in this respect is the reference in s 5(2) to the insured standing in a 'legal or equitable relation' to the property at risk, so that where the insured will be prejudiced by the loss or damage of the insured property, the requirement of insurable interest will be established. In summary, insurable interest in property is satisfied where the insured has some proprietary, contractual or possessory interest in it.[17]

---

[14] Ibid, at 224. See also, *Dalby v India and London Life Assurance Co* (1854) 15 CB 365 at 387, *per* Parker B; and *Tattersall v Drysdale* [1935] 2 KB 174 at 181, *per* Goddard J. Cf the approach taken by Manning J in *Davjoyda Estates Ltd v National Insurance Co of New Zealand* (1967) 65 S R (NSW) 381 at 428.

[15] [1963] Ch 459, at 485.

[16] Lord Lloyd noted, above, n 13 at 224, that some doubt as to the correctness of *Mark Rowlands* is expressed in MacGillivray and Parkington *Insurance Law* (London, Sweet & Maxwell, 1988) para 154, but concluded that 'their Lordships do not share these doubts.'

[17] In this respect a proprietary interest encompasses an equitable interest in property even if the interest is not one which would found an action in negligence in respect of the damage to the property or goods in question: *Leigh & Sillavan v Aliakmon Shipping Co Ltd, The Aliakmon* [1986] 1 AC 785 at 812, *per* Lord Brandon. See further, P Cane, *Tort Law and Economic Interests* (Oxford, Clarendon Press, 1996) ch 10. Note the effect of the Gambling Act 2005, once in force (see above).

2. Insurable interest in lives: the Life Assurance Act 1774

2.1 Time when interest must be shown

The Life Assurance Act 1774, s 1, which, it should be noted, is unaffected by the Gambling Act 2005, provides that a policy of insurance will be 'null and void to all intents and purposes whatsoever' unless the insured has an insurable interest in the life of the assured. Section 3 of the Act goes on to restrict the amount recovered by the insured to the value of his interest. Taking the literal reading of s 1 and s 3 together, it might appear that the interest of the insured would have to be satisfied both at the time of effecting the policy and at the time of the loss as with indemnity insurance generally.[18] The question of when insurable interest has to be shown received a definitive answer in *Dalby v The India and London Life Assurance Co.*[19] The life of the Duke of Cambridge had been insured with the claimant's company, Anchor Life, for £3,000 under four policies. Anchor reinsured the risk with the defendants. When the insured subsequently cancelled the life policies, Anchor nevertheless maintained the reinsurance policy until the Duke's death at which time the claimant claimed. The defendants refused to pay on the basis that the claimant's interest in the Duke's life ceased when the insured cancelled the policies. However, the court held that the requirement of insurable interest imposed by the 1774 Act must be shown to exist at the date of effecting the policy only and that life could not be equated with indemnity insurance. Parke B construed s 3 of the 1774 Act as merely requiring the insured to 'value his interest at its true amount when he makes the contract.'[20] The judge opined that to hold to the contrary would result in the injustice of the insured paying a fixed premium over the term of the policy, only to find that he could recover some uncertain sum which depended on the value of his interest at the time of the death.[21]

The decision in *Dalby* has not escaped criticism.[22] Taking the facts of the case itself it is evident that the mischief which the 1774 Act was designed to address is undermined by the finding that insurable interest on death is not required. Indeed, once the insured cancelled his policies on the Duke of Cambridge's life, it is difficult to see what possible interest Anchor had in the Duke's life. It is certain that the company did not suffer a loss when he died because it was no longer bound to pay insurance monies to the insured. In this respect it can be seen that *Dalby* apparently has the effect of legitimising gaming. This also arises in the context of, for example, a creditor who insures the amount of a debt owing to him at the time when the insurance is effected but who continues to maintain the policy on the debtor's life after the

---

[18] As was held in *Godsall v Boldero* (1807) 9 East 72. The purpose of the 1774 Act was described by Tindal CJ in *Paterson v Powell* (1832) 9 Bing. 320, at 327, as being 'To prevent gambling under the form and pretext of a policy of insurance by parties who have no interest in the subject matter of such assurance.'

[19] Above, n 14. For a full analysis of the implications of this decision see, R Merkin, 'Gambling by insurance – a study of the Life Assurance Act 1774' (1990) 9 *Anglo-American L R* 331.

[20] Ibid, at 404. It is noteworthy that in *Feasey v Sun Life Life Assurance Corporation of Canada* [2003] EWCA (Civ) 885, Waller LJ, at [73], citing *Dalby* confirmed that: 'In a life policy the date at which the insurable interest must exist is the date of the taking out of the policy. Furthermore, that is the date for valuing the insurable interest...' *Feasey* is a significant decision and is considered in greater detail below.

[21] Ibid, at 403.

[22] See, eg, R Merkin, 'Gambling by insurance – a study of the Life Assurance Act 1774' above, n 19.

loan has been repaid. Again, this seems to be a clear example of wagering. Nevertheless, the practical justification for *Dalby* lies in the fact that insurance is commonly used as a vehicle for investment and saving and as such it has been said that 'it is desirable to give life policies the ordinary characteristics of property.'[23]

2.2 Defining Insurable interest in life policies

In contrast to the Marine Insurance Act 1906, the 1774 Act does not provide a definition of insurable interest. However, the nature of the interest required can be deduced from the language of s 3 itself which provides that 'no greater sum shall be recovered or received from the insurer or insurers than the amount of value of the interest of the insured in such life...' The inference then, is that it must be a financial or pecuniary interest. While s 1 of the 1774 Act is aimed at preventing wagering by declaring insurance without interest to be 'null and void,' the purpose of s 3 is to prevent recovery of more than the value of the interest. The interrelationship between the two provisions was recently explained by the trial judge in *Feasey (representing Syndicate 957 at Lloyd's) v Sun Life Assurance Corporation of Canada*.[24] Langley J said that:

> In my judgment there is no requirement to be found in Section 3 to enter into any detailed examination of the values of insurable interests with or without the benefit of any hindsight. Nor is it required that a court should examine and assess whether a given value was arrived at without negligence or reasonably. The underlying purpose of Section 3 is derived from Section 1: to outlaw recovery of the proceeds of what is properly to be described as gaming or wagering... .[25]

In two categories of life insurance insurable interest is presumed to exist and s 3 of the Life Assurance Act 1774 is disapplied so that there is no upper limit on the sum insured. The two exceptions are: (i) policies on the insured's own life where the insurance is for the insured's own benefit;[26] and (ii) policies on the life of a spouse.[27] The rationale underlying the presumption that spouses possess an unlimited insurable interest in their respective lives was explained by Farwell J in *Griffiths v Fleming*,[28] who said that 'a husband is no more likely to indulge in "mischievous gaming" on his wife's life than a wife on her husband's.'[29] The Insurance Ombudsman has decided that the presumption should also extend to engaged couples.[30] Section 253 of the Civil Partnerships Act 2004 extends the common law presumption in favour of 'spouses' to civil partners.[31]

---

[23] *Grigsby v Russell* 222 US 149 (1911) *per* Holmes J. See, eg, *Fuji Finance Inc v Aetna Life Insurance Ltd* [1997] Ch 173.
[24] [2002] EWHC 868 (Comm).
[25] Ibid, at [187].
[26] *Wainright v Bland* (1836) 1 M & W 32; *McFarlane v Royal London Friendly Society* (1886) 2 TLR 755, DC.
[27] See *Reed v Royal Exchange Assurance Co.* (1795) Peake Add Cas 70, in which Lord Kenyon CJ said, at 70, that 'it must be presumed that every wife had an interest in the life of her husband.'
[28] (1909) 100 L T 765.
[29] Ibid, at 769.
[30] *Annual Report* 1989, paras 2.31–2.35.
[31] See p 181 below.

2.3 Life policies on family members

As has been seen, subject to the exception of spouses, the general rule is that the proposer for life insurance must have some pecuniary interest in the insured life and, by analogy with the principle of indemnity,[32] the sum recoverable is limited to the extent the loss is capable of being quantified. With respect to family relationships the requirement of insurable interest can have particularly harsh consequences. For example, it is settled that an adult child does not have an insurable in the life of a parent. In *Harse v Pearl Life Assurance Co*,[33] the claimant effected two life policies on the life of his mother who lived with him as his housekeeper and to whom he paid an allowance. The claimant's father was alive, but being paralysed he did not work and would therefore be unable to meet the funeral expenses of his wife in the event of her predeceasing him. One of the policies stated that it was to cover funeral expenses. Upon discovering that the policies were void for want of insurable interest, there being no obligation on a child to bury his parent,[34] the claimant sued for the recovery of the premiums paid by him which now amounted to more than the original sum assured. It was held by the Court of Appeal that the claimant's lack of insurable interest rendered the policy illegal and, on the basis that money paid over under an illegal contract is irrecoverable, the insurers were not bound to return the premiums. However, if the insurers elect not to raise the 1774 Act by way of defence but choose to pay the sum insured, then on the basis of *melior est conditio possidentis*, the person in receipt of the payment can keep it.[35]

Whether a minor has an interest in the lives of his parents is doubtful because there is no common law obligation on a parent to maintain a child.[36] However, such an obligation may arise by virtue of a maintenance order compelling a parent to support a child, in which case insurable interest will exist. In practice, the principle that a child has no insurable interest in the life of its parents is generally circumvented by a parent taking insurance on his or her own life and ensuring that it is expressed to be for the benefit of the child.[37] As with co-habitees, it would seem sensible for the law to recognise that a minor has an insurable interest *qua* dependent in the life of a parent.[38]

Although it is common practice for parents to insure the lives of their children,[39] at law a parent lacks insurable interest because no financial loss results from the

---

[32] See the Life Assurance Act 1774, s 3, above.

[33] Above, n 5.

[34] Reported [1903] 2 KB 92. The Court of Appeal proceeded on the basis that the trial judge's finding on the point was correct. See also, *Howard v Refuge Friendly Society* (1886) 54 LT 644 at 646, *per* Matthew LJ.

[35] See *Worthington v Curtis* (1875) 1 Ch D 419 at 425, *per* Mellish LJ, in which a father who insured the life of his son was paid by the insurers. Mellish LJ also stated, at 424, that: 'the statute is a defence for the insurance company only if they choose to avail themselves of it. If they do not, the question who is entitled to the money must be determined as if the statute did not exist.'

[36] *Bazeley v Forder* (1868) LR 3 QB 559 at 565 (Lord Cockburn CJ); *Stopher v NAB* [1955] 1 QB 486 at 495 (Lord Goddard CJ).

[37] See the Married Women's Property Act 1882 s 11, considered below.

[38] See n 31 above and associated text. The Fatal Accidents Act 1976 extends the definition of 'dependent child' of the deceased to include a posthumous child.

[39] The obvious example being holiday insurance, although such a policy may be viewed as a contract for necessaries entered into by the parent as agent for the child. See further Lord Wilberforce's speech in *Woodar Investment Development Ltd v Wimpey Construction UK Ltd* [1980] 1 All ER 571.

child's death. In *Halford v Kymer*,[40] a father effected a policy on the life of his son, which named himself as beneficiary, should the son die before attaining the age of 21 years. In holding that the father lacked insurable interest, the court rejected the father's contention that he had a financial interest in his son's life because he expected his son to reimburse him the costs of maintenance and education at some future time. Bayley J, construing the relevant provision in the Life Assurance Act, was emphatic in his rejection of the father's claim:

> It is enacted by the third section, 'That no greater sum shall be recovered than the amount of the value of the interest of the insured in the life or lives.' Now, what was the amount or the value of the interest of the party insuring in this case? Not one farthing certainly. It has been said that there are numerous instances in which a father has effected an insurance on the life of his son. If a father, wishing to give his son some property to dispose of, make an insurance on his son's life in his (the son's) name, not for his (the father's) own benefit, but for the benefit of his son, there is no law to prevent his doing so; but that is a transaction quite different from the present; and if a notion prevails that such an insurance as the one in question is valid, the sooner it is corrected the better.[41]

At odds with the case law considered above is the decision in *Barnes v London, Edinburgh & Glasgow Life Insurance Co Ltd*,[42] in which the Court of Appeal held that a person who had undertaken to care for her infant stepsister had an insurable interest in her life to the extent of securing 'the repayment of the expenses incurred.'[43] The decision has been doubted,[44] and is unlikely to be followed by a future court.

2.4 The employer–employee relationship

An employer may have an insurable interest in the life of an employee and conversely, an employee may have insurable interest in the life of his employer. Calculating the value of the interest can be a relatively simple exercise in the straightforward employer/employee situation.[45] The starting point is generally the contract of employment between the parties, so that where an employee is employed on a weekly contract, the court will ascertain the value of one week's employment to the insured/employer.[46]

An employee who is working under a fixed term contract has an insurable interest in the employer's life up to the value of the wages to be paid during that term. In *Hebdon v West*,[47] Hebdon, a bank clerk, was employed for seven years under a fixed term contract at a salary of £600.00 per annum. The bank had also lent him £4,700 and the managing partner, Pedder, had promised him that the debt need not be repaid during his, Pedder's, lifetime. At a time when his contract had approximately five

---

[40] (1830) 10 B & C 724.

[41] Ibid, at 729. Yet, given the paucity of case law on such family policies, it would seem that insurers rarely raise the point of lack of insurable interest by way of defence to a claim.

[42] [1891] 1 QB 864.

[43] Ibid, at 866, *per* Lord Coleridge CJ.

[44] See *Griffiths v Fleming*, above n 28 and *Harse v Pearl Life Assurance Co*, above n 5.

[45] Cf employers of entertainers and professional sports men and women. See further, MA Clarke, *The Law of Insurance Contracts* (London, Lloyds of London Press, 2002) at 3–7F.

[46] *Simcock v Scottish Imperial Insurance Co* (1902) 10 SLT 286.

[47] (1863) 3 B & S 579.

years to run, Hebdon insured Pedder's life through two life companies, one policy was for £5,000 and the second policy was for £2,500. After six years Pedder died and the employment was terminated. Hebdon received £5,000 under the first policy but when the second insurers refused his claim, he sued. The first insurers had not raised the point that the value of the policy exceeded the salary due to Hebdon over the entire term. Further, as insurable interest in life policies must be found to exist at the date when the policy is effected, not at the date of the loss, they could not in any case raise the point that his employment contract had only one year left to run at the date of the death (a quantifiable loss of salary of only £600.00). However, with respect to the second life policy, Wightman J held that the promise made by Pedder not to call in the debt was gratuitous and therefore non-enforceable. This had the effect that since Hebdon's insurable interest had been amply satisfied by the first policy he therefore lacked the requisite insurable interest to enforce the second policy. Wightman J, considering the effect of the 1774 Act, said:

> We assume, then, that the plaintiff had a pecuniary interest in the life of Pedder to the extent of £2,500 at the time he effected the policy with the defendant's office. If that be so, the question then arises whether payment, after the death of Pedder, of £5,000 by another life insurance company ... is a bar to the plaintiff's claim ... Looking to the declared object of the legislature ... it was intended by the third section of the Act that the insured should in no case recover or receive from the insurers (whether upon one policy or many) more than the insurable interest which the person making the insurance had at the time he insured the life.[48]

The judgment is illuminating in so far as the judge proceeds on the basis that the effect of s 3 of the Act is to treat life policies as contracts of indemnity, the sole distinction being the time when insurable interest must exist. However, the strict orthodoxy of quantifying the pecuniary interest of the insured by reference to the terms of the employment contract is often ignored by the courts. This is apparent where, for example, the death of an employee would have serious implications for the profits and asset value of a business, and so the court will have regard to consequential losses ensuing from the death.[49]

2.5 Creditor and debtor insurance

A secured creditor has an insurable interest in the life of a debtor.[50] Such interest will ensue even after the debt has been paid because, as has been seen, the requirement of insurable interest need only be shown at the time when the life policy is effected and so a creditor can recover the whole sum insured even if the debtor dies after repaying the debt.[51] The value of the creditor's interest is the amount of the debt including

---

[48] Ibid, at 589–91.
[49] This, at least, can be deduced from *Fuji Finance v Aetna Life Insurance Co*, above n 23. On the other hand, older authorities support the restrictive view that an employer's interest does not extend to the estimated loss to the business caused by the employee's death: see *Simcock v Scottish Imperial Ins Co*, above n 46; and *Turner & Co v Scottish Provident Institution* (1896) 34 SLT 146 (involving a commercial agent rather than an employee).
[50] *Godsall v Boldero*, above n 18.
[51] *Dalby v The India and London Life Assurance Co*, above n 19.

interest payments. A debtor may have insurable interest in the life of a creditor where the latter has promised not to call in the debt during his lifetime provided such promise is binding by virtue, for example, of the doctrine of promissory estoppel.[52]

2.6 A wider approach towards insurable interest

The Court of Appeal has recently subjected insurable interest to detailed examination and has suggested that a more open textured approach should be adopted towards the requirement. In *Feasey v Sun Life Life Assurance Corporation of Canada*,[53] Steamship, a Protection and Indemnity Club, insured the liabilities of its members under a Master Lineslip Policy with Syndicate 957 for personal injury or death suffered by employees of the members on board a vessel or offshore rig. Syndicate 957 reinsured its liability with Sun Life and Phoenix. The benefit under Steamship's policy did not reflect the club's actual liability or that of its members but was intended to reflect, as closely as possible, Steamship's overall exposure. Due to changes in the Lloyd's Rules which affected liability insurance, the reinsurance became, in effect, first party as opposed to third party insurance. In an action brought by the Syndicate against the reinsurers for unpaid sums allegedly due under the reinsurance policy, Sun Life argued that Steamship had no insurable interest in the lives and wellbeing of the original persons when entering into the Master Lineslip so that the policy was rendered illegal by the Life Assurance Act 1774, s 1. By way of alternative, Sun Life and Phoenix argued that contrary to s 3 of the Act, Steamship was seeking to claim more than the value of any insurable interest it had.

Both the first instance judge,[54] and the majority of the Court of Appeal held that Steamship did posses a pecuniary interest in the losses covered by the policy and that its interest was capable of being ascertained when the policy was entered into. As a matter of construction the insurance was found to be one to pay fixed sums on the happening of certain events and, as such, it therefore fell within s 1 of the Act. In determining the issue of insurable interest Waller LJ took the view that this necessarily depended upon the construction of the particular insurance in question. Having reviewed the authorities on both life and property insurance he noted the difficulties which have faced the courts in attempting to formulate an all-embracing definition of the requirement. Indeed, on the basis of the case law Waller LJ concluded that the context and the contents of any given policy is critical. He stated:

> It is sufficient under section 5 of the Marine Insurance Act for a person interested in a marine adventure to stand in a 'legal or equitable relation to the adventure.' That is intended to be a broad concept... . In a policy on life or lives the court should be searching for the same broad concept... It may be that on an insurance of a specific identified life, it will be difficult to establish a 'legal or equitable' relation without a pecuniary liability recognised by law arising on the death of that particular person. There is however no authority which deals with a policy on many lives and over a substantial period and where it can be seen that a pecuniary liability will arise by reference to those lives and the intention is to

---

[52] *Hughes v Metropolitan Rly Co* (1877) 2 App Cas 439; *Central London Property Trust Ltd v High Trees House Ltd* [1947] KB 130. See also the observations of Goff J in *The Post Chaser* [1982] 1 All ER 19 at 27.
[53] Above, n 20.
[54] Above, n 24.

cover that legal liability... The interest in policies falling within section 1 of the 1774 Act must exist at the time of entry into the policy, and be capable of pecuniary evaluation at that time.[55]

Waller LJ therefore went on to explain that searching for insurable interest in any given policy involves the court in a broad based enquiry involving a number of questions:

> [I]t is not in my view a legitimate starting point to say that because normally such and such a type of risk would be insured in a certain way, therefore a different form of policy must be unlawful. Each case must depend on the precise terms of the policy under consideration. The questions are-what on the true construction of the policy is the subject matter of the insurance? Is there an insurable interest which is embraced within that subject matter? Is the insurable interest capable of valuation in money terms at the date of the contract? The question that will then arise under section 3 is whether the sum payable under the policy is greater than the value of the pecuniary interest valued as of the date of the policy?[56]

Rejecting the alternative contention of the reinsurers based upon s 3 of the Act, it was held that they had failed to demonstrate that Steamship was seeking to recover a sum exceeding the value of its interest as at the date of the contract.

While the decision in *Feasey* adheres to the orthodoxy in pure life policies, it is of signicance given that the issue of insurable interest is rarely litigated nowadays. It thus affords a rare insight into contemporary judicial thinking on the requirement. It also serves to highlight a range of problems left unresolved by the case law. This is particularly true with respect to the problems that the requirement has given rise to in the context of property insurance involving construction insurance.[57] Permission to appeal to the House of Lords has been granted, but the parties settled during argument.

---

3. Declaring the name of the insured in the policy document

The Life Assurance Act 1774, s 2 provides that the name or names of the person or persons interested in the policy for whose use, benefit or on whose account such policy is effected must be inserted in the policy document.[58] Failure to comply with this provision renders the contract illegal. It is designed to prevent avoidance of s 1 of the Act (requiring insurable interest), and so sections 1 and 2 are symbiotic. Section 2 serves little practical purpose particularly since often it will be the insured's next of

---

[55] Above, n 20, at [97].
[56] Ibid, at [98]. We return to consider Waller LJ's judgment in the context of property insurance below.
[57] See below at pp 163, *et seq*. It should also be noted that the Court of Appeal gave tacit approval to the factual expectation test for property insurance. It remains to be seen whether the House of Lords will at last address this thorny issue. For the approach adopted in US jurisdictions and Australia to the determination of insurable interest in life policies, see J Lowry and P Rawlings, *Insurance Law: Cases and Materials* (Oxford, Hart Publishing, 2004) ch 7.
[58] But note the Insurance Companies Amendment Act 1973, s50, considered below.

kin who benefits from the insurance and there is no requirement that their names should be specified in the policy. Also, in this respect, an insured may assign a policy of assurance during its currency to a third party who lacks the requisite insurable interest. There have been difficulties posed by this provision in respect of group policies, for example those effected by an employer or a trade union in respect of employees. This is because it is unclear from the outset exactly who will, from time to time, fall within the group. The potential problem in this situation was averted by s 50 of the Insurance Companies Act 1973, which disapplies s 2 of the 1774 Act, provided that the class of persons covered by the policy is identifiable with reasonable certainty.

At its simplest level, the mischief which s 2 is designed to prevent is the situation where, for example, X appears to effect an insurance policy on a life in which she has an insurable interest, but in reality the contract is for Y's benefit who lacks insurable interest. The object of the Act is not to prevent Y ultimately benefiting from X's policy, since X may apply the proceeds of such policy in any way she pleases. But rather to ensure that if Y is to gain immediate benefit, then Y's name must appear in the policy from the outset and, if the policy is to be valid, Y must have an insurable interest when the policy is effected.[59] The issue of whether the name of the true insured is declared in the policy is resolved by enquiring whether the contract 'is really and substantially intended for the benefit' of that named person.[60] This is amply illustrated by the decision in *Wainwright v Bland*.[61] The insured, Miss Abercromby, effected a policy on her own life in her own name. This was done on the advice of Wainwright, the claimant, with whom she lived. Previously she had taken out a number of other life policies, two of which had been assigned to Wainwright just before her death. On the evidence, it was apparent that the insured could not afford the premiums herself but had paid them with money supplied by the claimant. It is evident that the court was suspicious that the insured had been murdered by the claimant, and the jury decided that the policy was invalid. In addressing the jury, Lord Abinger CB said:

> the question in this case is, who was the party really and truly effecting the insurance? Was it the policy of Miss Abercromby? Or was it substantially the policy of Wainwright the [claimant], he using her name for the purposes of his own? If you think it was the policy of Miss Abercromby, effected by her for her own benefit, her representative is entitled to put it in force; and it would be no answer to say that she had no funds of her own to pay the premiums; Wainwright might lend her the money for that purpose, and the policy still continue to be her own. But, on the other hand, if, looking to all the strange facts which have been proved before you, you come to the conclusion that the policy was, in reality, effected to Wainwright; that he merely used her name, himself finding the money, and meaning (by way of assignment, or by bequest, or in some other way), to have the benefit of it himself; then I am of opinion such a transaction would be a fraudulent evasion of the [Life Assurance Act] and that your verdict should be for the defendants ...[62]

---

[59] See *Shilling v Accidental Death Insurance Co* (1857) 2 H & N 42, in which the premiums on a policy taken out by a father on his own life, were in fact paid by his son, the beneficiary. It was held that the insurance was the son's, and since he lacked insurance interest the policy was null and void by virtue of s 1 of the 1774 Act.

[60] *McFarlane v Royal London Friendly Society*, above n 26 at 756, *per* Pollock B.

[61] (1835) 1 Mood & R 481.

[62] Ibid, 486–7.

It has been convincingly argued that s 2 of the Act adds nothing to the requirement of insurable interest, for if the aim of the Act is to prevent gaming, that goal is amply achieved by s 1 alone.[63] The conundrum created by the s 2 requirement can be seen by returning to the example postulated above. Even if Y's name is declared in the policy, this alone will not render the policy valid because, in any case, Y lacks the requisite insurable interest. If, on the other hand, Y does have insurable interest in X's life, it should not matter that her name does not appear in the policy because the object of the Act (to prohibit 'a mischievous kind of gaming') is not violated. The decision in *Evans v Bignold*,[64] serves to illustrate the point clearly. Mr Evans, approached the trustees of his father-in-law's estate and asked them to advance him £200.00, which was the amount due to his wife under the terms of her father's will when she reached 21 years. In case she died before then, a surety was found to secure repayment of the advance, and the surety required Mr Evans to take out a life policy on Mrs Evans' life. The policy was, however, effected in her name. She did attain 21 years and so repayment of the advance was not required. Nevertheless, the policy continued and, when she died, her administrator (Mr Evans) sought to claim on the policy. The court was forced to decide that since the policy had originally been taken out for the benefit of Mr Evans and his name did not appear on the policy, it was unlawful and unenforceable. Since Mr Evans, as Mrs Evans' husband, had an insurable interest in her life, s 2 of the Act operated to defeat a policy which did not involve any element of gaming.

It is suggested that for those cases where doubt arises as to whether s 1 is satisfied, the test formulated by Baron Pollock would equip the court to ascertain the true beneficiary of the policy in order to determine whether that person has an insurable interest in the life insured.[65] Viewed on this basis, Mr Evans would recover under the policy.

Curiously, there appears to be an inconsistency in the way in which the rigour of the law is applied. For example, an insured may properly assign a policy to a person who lacks insurable interest. The rationale here is rooted in the notion of a person's right to freely dispose of property. This is particularly important given the investment value of life policies,[66] and businesses now exist which offer to purchase policies from insureds at a sum generally greater than the surrender value offered by insurers.

---

4. Insurable interest in property insurance

4.1 The requirement of proprietary interest or contractual right

The classic definition of insurable interest in property insurance was formulated by

---

[63] See J Birds and N Hird, *Birds Modern Insurance Law* (London, Sweet and Maxwell, 2004) 46–7.
[64] (1869) 4 LR QB 622. In this regard, note the response of the legislature to group policies, n 58 above.
[65] See n 60 above, and associated text.
[66] See, eg, *Fuji Finance Inc v Aetna Life Insurance Ltd*, above n 23.

Lord Eldon LC in *Lucena v Craufurd*,[67] as being 'a right in property, or a right derivable out of some contract about the property, which in either case may be lost upon some contingency affecting the possession or enjoyment of the party.'[68] Accordingly, the insured must possess some present legally enforceable right, whether legal or equitable, or a contractual right, to the insured property. This will, for example, exclude a beneficiary under a will and also an intestate's next of kin for although 'there is no man who will deny that such an heir at law has a moral certainty of succeeding to the estate; yet the law will not allow that he has any interest, or any thing more than a mere expectation.'[69] Lord Eldon justified a restrictive definition of insurable interest on the basis that it was necessary to ensure certainty and to avoid illusory insurance. His Lordship was, of course, concerned at ascertaining the limits on who could insure. Taking the facts of *Lucena v Craufurd,* which centred on ships lost at sea, Lord Eldon said:

> If moral certainty be a ground of insurable interest, there are hundreds, perhaps thousands, who would be entitled to insure. First the dock company, then the dock-master, then the warehouse-keeper, then the porter, then every other person who to a moral certainty would have any thing to do with the property, and of course get something by it.[70]

The traditional view in English law therefore is that the insured must have a proprietary right in the insured property. This is starkly illustrated by *Macaura v Northern Assurance Co Ltd*,[71] in which the insured, Macaura, was an unsecured creditor and the only shareholder in a limited company which owned a substantial quantity of timber, much of which was stored on his land. Two weeks after effecting insurance policies with several companies in his own name, the timber was destroyed by fire. A claim brought by Macaura on the policies was disallowed on the ground that he lacked insurable interest in the timber. Lord Sumner, proceeding on the basis that neither the company's debt to the insured nor his shares were exposed to fire, observed: 'the fact that he was virtually the company's only creditor, while the timber is its only asset, seems to me to make no difference ... he was directly prejudiced by the paucity of the company's assets, not by the fire.'[72] His Lordship stated that the insured 'stood in no "legal or equitable relation to" the timber at all. He had no "concern in" the subject insured. His relation was to the company, not to its goods... .'[73]

---

[67] (1806) 2 Bos & Pul (NR) 269.

[68] Ibid, at 321. In contrast to life insurance, for indemnity insurance the insured need not show insurable interest at the time of the contract but interest must be shown at the time of the loss: *Sparkes v Marshall* (1836) 2 Bing NC 761; *Howard v Lancashire Insurance Co* (1885) 11 SCR 92.

[69] Ibid, at 325. But note that a person who finds property and keeps it acquires an insurable interest in it even though a third party may have better title: *Marks v Hamiliton* (1852) 7 Exch 323. Cf *Macaura v Northern Assurance Co* [1925] AC 619, considered below at n 71, and associated text, in which it was held that an insured, a shareholder in a company, who permitted timber belonging to the company to remain on his land lacked insurable interest in it. Lord Buckmaster remarked, at 628, that: 'Nor can his claim to insure be supported on the ground that he was a bailee of the timber, for in fact he owed no duty whatever to the company in respect of the safe custody of the goods; he merely permitted their remaining upon his land.' See also, *Cowan v Jeffrey Associates* [1998] S C 496.

[70] Ibid.

[71] Above, n 69. See also the American case of *Farmers' Mutual Insurance Co* v *New Holland Turnpike Road Co* (1888) 122 Pa 37, in which it was held that a turnpike company who insured a bridge spanning a stream and which linked two sections of the company's road, lacked insurable interest in the bridge because the company had no legal or equitable interest in it. See further, n 17, above.

[72] Ibid, at 630.

[73] Ibid.

Further, as a gratuitous bailee he was not liable for the timber and therefore an interest could not be based on bailment.

The guiding principle in *Macaura* is pivoted upon the separate legal personality accorded to companies, so that a company is, in law, an entity distinct from its members. It was the company which owned the timber and therefore had a proprietary interest in it, not its shareholder. The fact that the timber was in his possession did not give him a proprietary interest. He merely had a factual expectation of loss. On the other hand, if Macaura, *qua* creditor, had insured against the company's insolvency, or *qua* shareholder, had insured his shares against depreciation due to the failure of a company venture, then the requirement of insurable interest would have been fulfilled. This decision was distinguished by Colman J in *Sharp v Sphere Drake Insurance Ltd, The Moonacre*,[74] where the sole shareholder in a company was held to have an insurable interest in a yacht purchased by the company, as the yacht was intended for his use and a power of attorney had been granted to him in respect of it.

As noted above, once the Gambling Act 2005, s 335, has entered into force the requirement of insurable interest will disappear although, of course, the indemnity principle will remain.

4.2 Towards a broader test of 'factual expectation'

The restrictive approach to insurable interest has not escaped judicial criticism in England,[75] nor has it found favour in other common law jurisdictions. For example, Lord Eldon's reasoning was emphatically rejected by Wilson J in *Constitution Insurance Company of Canada v Kosmopoulos*,[76] in which the Canadian Supreme Court adopted the more liberal 'factual expectation' test propounded by Lawrence J in *Lucena v Craufurd.*[77] Put simply, under this test a moral certainty of profit or loss is sufficient to constitute insurable interest. Thus, on very similar facts to *Macaura v Northern Assurance Co Ltd*, the insured was able to recover under the policies on the basis that as a sole shareholder of the company he 'was so placed with respect to the assets of the business as to have benefit from their existence and prejudice from their destruction. He had a moral certainty of advantage or benefit from those assets but for the fire.'[78] Addressing the concern of Lord Eldon that a broader definition of insurable interest would lead to an increase of liability of insurers upon the

---

[74] [1992] 2 Lloyd's Rep 501.

[75] In *Stock v Inglis*, above, n 3 at 571, Lord Brett MR noted that it is 'merely a technical objection ... which has no real merit ... as between the assured and the insurer.' More recently, see the comments of Waller LJ in *Feasey v Sun Life Life Assurance Corporation of Canada*, nn 53–56, above. For academic criticism see, AJ Campbell, 'Some Aspects of Insurable Interest' (1949) 27 *Can Bar Rev* 1; RA Hasson, 'Reform of the Law Relating to Insurable Interest in Property– Some Thoughts on *Chadwick v Gibraltar General Insurance*' (1983–4) 8 *Can Bus LJ* 114; and J Lowry and P Rawlings, 'Rethinking Insurable Interest' in Sarah Worthington (ed), *Commercial Law and Commercial Practice*, above n 3. For the implications for insurance law of the Gambling Bill (*Draft Gambling Bill* HL Paper 63-I, HC 139-I (London, HMSO, 2004)), see J Davey, 'The reform of gambling and the future of insurance law' [2004] *LS* 507.

[76] (1987) 1 SCR 2.

[77] Lawrence J took the view, above n 67, at 302, that a person will possess insurable interest in a thing if he will be prejudiced by its loss. He said: 'To be interested in the preservation of a thing is to be so circumstanced with respect to it as to have benefit from its existence, prejudice from its destruction. The property of a thing and the interest devisable from it may be very different: of the first the price is generally the measure, but by interest in a thing every benefit and advantage arising out of or depending on such thing may be considered as being comprehended.'

[78] Above n 76, at 30, *per* Wilson J.

occurrence of a single insured event owing to an increased number of policies covering the same risk, Wilson J said:

> But insurance companies have always faced the difficult task of calculating their total
> potential liability arising upon the occurrence of an insured event in order to judge whether
> to make a particular policy or class of policies and to calculate the appropriate premium to
> be charged. It is not for this Court to substitute its judgment for the sound business judg-
> ment and actuarial expertise of insurance companies by holding that a certain class of
> policies should not be made because it will result in too much insurance. I would have
> thought that a stronger argument could be made that there is too little insurance. Why
> should the porter in Lord Eldon's example not be able to obtain insurance against the possi-
> bility of being temporarily out of work as a result of the sinking of ships?[79] ... A
> broadening of the concept of insurable interest would, it seems to me, allow for the creation
> of more socially beneficial insurance policies than is the case at present with no increase in
> risk to the insurer. I therefore find both of Lord Eldon's reasons for adopting a restrictive
> approach to insurable interest unpersuasive.[80]

The broader 'factual expectation' test has also been adopted by the Australian legislature,[81] and has been followed in many American states. For example, Paragraph
3401 of the New York Insurance Law, art 34 defines insurable interest as including
'any lawful or substantial economic interest in the safety or preservation of property
from loss, destruction or pecuniary damage.'[82] The Wisconsin Insurance Code has
gone further by dispensing with the requirement of an insurable interest for the validity of an insurance policy. While in New Zealand, the Insurance Law Reform Act
1985 s. 7(1) abolishes the requirement of insurable interest in the case of life insurance and all contracts of indemnity insurance.[83]

The Gambling Act 2005 aside, there are also indications in recent English decisions that a wider and more liberal approach is being taken to the question of
insurable interest. In *Mark Rowlands Ltd v Berni Inns Ltd*,[84] the Court of Appeal
adopted and approved the definition propounded by Lawrence J in *Lucena v
Craufurd*,[85] despite the fact that Lord Eldon's formulation of insurable interest
formed the backdrop to the House of Lords decision in *Macaura v Northern Assurance Co Ltd*.[86] More recently, in *Petrofina (UK) v Magnaload Ltd*,[87] Lloyd J held that
each of the individual sub-contractors on a construction site had an insurable interest in the entire works despite the fact that they were working only on limited parts of
the site, their interest arising not from any ownership or possession, but from the fact
that, in the event of negligence, they would face liability for any part of the works
damaged or destroyed. Although the sub-contractors had no property interest in the

---

[79] See n 70 above, and associated text.
[80] Above n 76, at 17.
[81] The Insurance Contracts Act 1984, s 17.
[82] Referred to by Wilson J, above n 76, at 29. See further, West's Annotated California Insurance Code
(1994), §280-283, extracted in J Lowry and P Rawlings, *Insurance Law: Cases and Materials*, above n 57,
at 294.
[83] See further, D St L Kelly and M L Ball, *Principles of Insurance Law in Australia and New Zealand*
(Sydney, Butterworths, 1998) ch 3.
[84] Above, n 9.
[85] See text to n 77.
[86] Above, n 69.
[87] [1983] 2 Lloyd's Rep 91. See also, *Sharp v Sphere Drake Insurance Ltd, The Moonacre*, above n 74. See J
Birds, 'Insurable Interests' in N Palmer and E McKendrick (eds), *Interests in Goods* (London, LLP, 1998)
ch 4.

works in progress they had an insurable interest in the continued existence of those works. In so finding, the judge drew the analogy of the insurable interest possessed by a bailee in goods bailed to him. Accordingly, it was possible for a policy covering the entire works to be taken out on a co-insurance basis by the head contractor and all sub-contractors. Lloyd J reasoned that to hold to the contrary would result in commercial inconvenience as each sub-contractor would need 'to take out his own separate policy. This would mean, at the very least, extra paperwork; at worst it could lead to overlapping claims and cross claims in the event of an accident. Furthermore ... the cost of insuring his liability might in the case of a small sub-contractor, be uneconomic.'[88] The judge therefore held that the sub-contractor's insurable interest lay in a 'pervasive interest' in the entire property. In the absence of any English decision directly on the point, Lloyd J turned to the decision of the Supreme Court of Canada in *Commonwealth Construction Co Ltd v Imperial Oil Ltd*, in which de Grandpre J stated:

> On any construction site, and especially when the building being erected is a complex chemical plant, there is ever present the possibility of damage by one tradesman to the property of another and to the construction as a whole... By recognising in all tradesmen an insurable interest based on that very real possibility, which itself has its source in the contractual arrangements opening the doors of the job site to the tradesman, the Courts would apply to the construction field the principle expressed so long ago in the area of bailment. Thus all the parties whose joint efforts have one common goal, eg, the completion of the construction, would be spared the necessity of fighting between themselves should an accident occur involving the possible responsibility of one of them. [89]

This approach was adopted by Colman J in *National Oilwell Ltd v Davy Offshore (UK) Ltd*,[90] in holding that the suppliers of a subsea wellhead completion system for a floating oil production facility were co-insured's under the contractors' All Risks policy. The judge dismissed the contention that there cannot be an insurable interest based merely on potential liability arising from the existence of a contract between the insured and the owner of property. He held that that an insurable interest could be found in 'the insured's proximate physical relationship to the property in question.'[91] Citing Lloyd J's judgment in *Petrofina*, Colman J said:

> There is, in my judgment, in particular no reason in principle why such a supplier should not, and every commercial reason why he should, be able to insure against loss of or

---

[88] Ibid, at 96–7. In *Hopewell Project Management Ltd v Ewbank Preece Ltd* [1998] 1 Lloyd's Rep 448 it was held that the terms 'contractor' or 'sub-contractor' in a contractor's All Risk policy did not encompass those who gave advice in a professional capacity, which on the facts of the case were those who provided advisory engineering services in respect of the installation of gas turbines.

[89] (1976) 69 DLR (3d) 558, at 561.

[90] [1993] 2 Lloyd's Rep 582.

[91] Ibid, at 611. See also, *Stone Vickers Ltd v Appledore Ferguson Shipbuilders Ltd* [1991] 2 Lloyd's Rep 288 at 301, in which Colman J (sitting then as Mr Anthony Colman QC, a deputy judge of the High Court) stated that a risk of being 'materially adversely affected by loss of or damage to' the contract works 'by reason of the incidence of any of the perils insured against' was capable of amounting to 'a sufficient [insurable] interest in the whole contract works' (reversed by the Court of Appeal on another ground without the issue of insurable interest being considered [1992] 2 Lloyd's Rep 578). In *Hopewell Project Management Ltd v Ewbank Preece Ltd*, above, n 81 at 456, Mr Recorder Jackson QC, applying *National Oilwell UK Ltd*, stated that had the defendant contractors' satisfied the definition of 'insured' contained in the policy: 'the fact that the defendants were carrying out the professional services on site, and the fact that the defendants might incur legal liability for negligently causing damage to the contract works, gave the defendants an insurable interest in the contract works.'

damage to property involved in the common project not owned by him and not in his possession. The argument that because he has no possessory or proprietary interest in the property he can have no insurable interest in it and that his potential liability in respect of loss of or damage to it is insufficient to found such an insurable interest is in my judgment misconceived.[92]

The Court of Appeal tentatively approved of the more expansive approach to the issue of insurable interest in *Glengate-KG Properties Ltd v Norwich Union Fire Insurance Society Ltd.*[93] The court had to consider the meaning of the phrase 'the interest of the insured' in a policy covering the owner of a building against consequential loss following a fire or other insured peril. The issue for the court was whether the insured could recover for the loss of architects' drawings which were, at the time of the loss, owned by the architects although the insured might eventually have acquired them. It was held that the insured had an insurable interest in the drawings despite his lack of proprietary interest in them. Although the court saw his insurable interest as being in respect of consequential loss rather than in the actual drawings themselves, nevertheless Auld LJ and Sir Iain Glidewell, citing *Mark Rowlands Ltd v Berni Inns Ltd,* expressed the view that the insured could have insured the drawings on the basis of Lawrence J's 'factual expectation' test. [94]

While not the primary issue in these cases, the definition of insurable interest was, nevertheless, decisive in determining the rights and obligations of the parties. This line of authority can therefore be seen as amounting to some recognition of the broader conception of interest as adopted in Canada and elsewhere. However, some limit was placed upon this trend by the Court of Appeal in *Deepak Fertilisers & Petrochemical Corporation v Davy McKee (London) Ltd and ICI Chemicals and Polymers Ltd.*[95] The court did accept the broad conception of insurable interest in finding that a sub-contractor in a building contract possessed an insurable interest in the entire works during construction. This was because of the economic disadvantage which would be suffered if, in the event of the structure being damaged or destroyed, they lost the opportunity to complete the work and receive remuneration. However, once the work had been completed the court stressed that such interest came to an end.

The litigation arose out of the construction for Deepak of a methanol plant in India which exploded a few months after it was commissioned. There was a 'Marine-cum-Erection' policy under which contractors and sub-contractors were named as co-assureds. The sub-contractors included Davy McKee, a firm of consulting engineers, and ICI, who had provided expertise and technology. The critical question was whether the co-assureds had an insurable interest and were, therefore, immune from an action brought by Deepak's insurers exercising subrogation rights. At first instance, Rix J rejected the insurers' contention that the decisions in *Petrofina* and *National Oilwell Ltd* pointed to the cessation of insurable interest after completion of the works and concluded that Davy and ICI possessed the requisite interest so long as they were arguably responsible for damage to it. Since it was the insurer's case that

---

[92] Ibid.
[93] [1996] 1 Lloyd's Rep 614.
[94] Ibid, at 623–4 and 625–6 respectively.
[95] [1999] 1 Lloyd's Rep 387. See AT Olubajo, 'Pervasive insurable interest: a reappraisal' [2004] *Const LJ* 45.

Davy and ICI bore responsibility for the explosion even though it happened after completion of the plant, Rix J felt that they should 'in principle... be entitled to insure against their potential liability.'[96] In his view the question relating to any temporal limitation on a contractor's insurable interest had not arisen in the earlier case law, but he saw no reason why an architect, technical designer, or constructor should not be able to insure against liability for damage due to their fault, even though it occurred after completion of the structure.

The Court of Appeal, reversing the judge's decision, held that the insurable interests of the co-assureds ceased immediately upon completion of the works and did not continue thereafter merely because they could be exposed to potential liability at some future time. It followed that any damage to the plant after it was commissioned that was attributable to the fault of Davy could not be regarded as covered by the insurance policy. The insurers, therefore, could sue Davy. Stuart-Smith LJ stated that once the works were complete:

> Davy would only suffer disadvantage if the damage to or destruction of the property or structure was the result of their breach of contract or duty of care. In order to protect the contractor and sub-contractors against the risk of disadvantage by reason of damage or destruction of the property or structure resulting from their breach of contract or duty, they would, in accordance with normal practice take out liability insurance, or, in the case of architects, professional indemnity insurance... [W]hat they cannot do is persist in maintaining an insurance of the property or structure itself.[97]

Significantly, he did concede that the trial judge had been correct in stating that an architect, technical designer or contractor can participate in insurance under an All Risks policy because if the project were not completed due to the occurrence of an insured risk they would lose remuneration. Stuart-Smith LJ thereby adds further authority to the line of decisions beginning with *Petrofina*.[98] However, he took the view that an all risks policy on a building project is property insurance. The contractor and sub-contractors have insurable interests because they may suffer economic loss if building work ceases. Once the construction is completed, the contractors no longer have such an interest in the property and must effect a separate policy to cover any potential liability for their own negligence or breach of contract which results in damage to the building arising after completion. This maintains the distinction between property and liability insurance which, it has been argued,[99] was undermined by the decisions in *Stone Vickers* and *National Oilwell*. Indeed, on this point it was seen above that Waller LJ in *Feasey*,[100] was of the same mind.

The issue was revisited by the Court of Appeal in *Co-operative Retail Services Ltd v Taylor Young Partnership*.[101] The action arose as a consequence of a fire occurring on a construction site owned by the claimants, Co-operative Retail Services Ltd

---

[96] [1998] 2 Lloyd's Rep 139, at 158.
[97] Above n 95, at 399.
[98] Stuart-Smith LJ observed, '...Davy undoubtedly had an insurable interest in the plant under construction and on which they were working because they might lose the opportunity to do the work and to be remunerated for it if the property or structure were damaged or destroyed by any of the "all risks", such as fire or flood,' ibid.
[99] See J Birds, [2002] *JBL* 351.
[100] See p 158, above. See also, n 106, below.
[101] [2001] Lloyd's Rep IR 122.

(CRS). The main contractor was Wimpey (W), the architects were Taylor Young Partnership (TYP), the electrical engineers were Hoare Lea & Partners (HLP), and the electrical sub-contractors, who worked on the building's generator system, were Hall Electrical (H). H entered into a warranty with CRS and W in which H undertook to exercise all reasonable skill. CRS claimed that the fire was caused by negligence or breach of contract on the part of TYP and HLP. TYP and HLP argued that the fire was caused by breaches of the main contract by W and breaches of warranty by H, and they, therefore, sought contribution from them under the Civil Liability (Contribution) Act 1978. Both the trial judge and Brooke LJ referred extensively to *National Oilwell* and *Petrofina*, placing particular emphasis on Lloyd J's use of the *Commonwealth Construction* case and the notion of pervasive interest.[102] Brooke LJ accepted that CRS's insurers, acting through subrogation, could not pursue W or H because they were named as co-insureds under CRS's policy,[103] and consequently they were not liable to contribute to TYP and HLP because, as co-insureds, they were not 'other person[s] liable in respect of the same damage (whether jointly with him or otherwise)' under s 1(1) of the 1978 Act.

We saw above in relation to life policies that the Court of Appeal in *Feasey* advocated a more flexible approach towards the determination of insurable interest. The point was made that the court also took the opportunity to consider the requirement in the round and expressed views on the determination of insurable interest in property insurance. Waller LJ categorised the construction cases considered above and *The Moonacre*,[104] as 'policies in which the court has recognised interests which are not even strictly pecuniary.'[105] Having reviewed the case law he went on to summarise the authorities in the following terms:

> The principles which I would suggest one gets from the authorities are as follows: (1) It is from the terms of the policy that the subject of the insurance must be ascertained; (2) It is from all the surrounding circumstances that the nature of an insured's insurable interest must discovered; (3) There is no hard and fast rule that because the nature of an insurable interest relates to a liability to compensate for loss, that insurable interest could only be covered by a liability policy rather than a policy insuring property or life or indeed properties or lives; (4) The question whether a policy embraces the insurable interest intended to be recovered is a question of construction. The subject or terms of the policy may be so specific as to force a court to hold that the policy has failed to cover the insurable interest, but a court will be reluctant so to hold. (5) It is not a requirement of property insurance that the insured must have a 'legal or equitable' interest in the property as those terms might normally be understood. It is sufficient for a sub-contractor to have a contract that relates to the property and a potential liability for damage to the property to have an insurable interest in the property...[106]

The observations of Waller LJ on the position in property insurance are, strictly speaking, *obiter.* Nevertheless, they serve to reinforce the view that an overly strict test of insurable interest is out of line with current commercial practices. As such, it is

---

[102] Although the decision was upheld by the House of Lords, [2002] UKHL 17, it is unfortunate that reference was not made to this point.
[103] See *Simpson v Thompson* (1877) 3 App Cas 279.
[104] Above, n 74.
[105] Above n 20, at [90].
[106] Ibid, at [97].

noteworthy that the unease on the part of certain judges towards the requirement is by no means a modern phenomenon.[107] As indicated above, the courts have long been ill disposed towards allowing lack of insurable interest to be pleaded where insurers are fully cognisant of the risk covered by the policy.[108] This can be be seen in *The Capricorn*, in which Mance J observed:

> ...the present policy is not on its face one which the parties made for other than ordinary business reasons; it does not bear the hallmarks of wagering or the like. If underwriters make a contract in deliberate terms which covers their assured in respect of a specific situation, a Court is likely to hesitate before accepting a defence of lack of insurable interest.[109]

As commented above, when the Gambling Act 2005 enters into force the requirement of insurable interest will be removed (life policies excepted). Our principal focus will then be on the indemnity principle. But a problem with the 2005 Act is that no regard was given to insurance contracts during its passage through Parliament.

4.3 The measure of insurable interest

Property insurance is a contract of indemnity. It therefore follows that where an insured recovers insurance monies which exceed the value of his insurable interest, the excess will be held on trust for any third parties whose loss the policy also covers. As will be seen, this is particularly pertinent where a bailee insures goods in his possession because it has been held that any excess sum will be held on trust for the bailor/owner irrespective of whether the latter is aware of the policy.[110] To permit an insured to retain the excess money would be to offend the policy against wagering.[111]

Proof of insurable interest is not a pre-requisite to a valid claim under an insurance policy. In fact, as commented above, unless fraud is suspected, insurers will

---

[107] In fairness, it should be noted that in *Feasey* Ward LJ, dissenting, convincingly reasons that the House of Lords decisions in *Lucena v Crauford*, above n 67, and *Macaura v Northern Assurance*, above n 69, are binding, and must therefore be followed.

[108] In this respect, the position of insurers is safeguarded by the duty of disclosure: see ch 4, above. See *Feasey v Sun Life Assurance Co of Canada*, above n 24, in which Langley J, considering the rationale underlying the Life Assurance Act 1774, observed that 'in the early 19th century the law of disclosure had not been developed to provide the protection to insurers which it does today.' See further, J Lowry and P Rawlings, 'Rethinking Insurable Interest', above n 3, in which it is argued that the requirement no longer serves any useful purpose in property insurance particularly given the principle of indemnity.

[109] *Cepheus Shipping Corporation v Guardian Royal Exchange Assurance plc (The 'Capricorn')* [1995] 1 Lloyd's Rep 622 at 641. Some hundred years earlier, Lord Brett MR had observed that, 'it is the duty of a Court always to lean in favour of an insurable interest, if possible, for it seems to me that after underwriters have received the premium, the objection that there was no insurable interest is often, as nearly as possible, a technical objection, and one which has no real merit, certainly not between the assured and the insurer.' *Stock v Inglis*, above n 3, at 571. See also, *Feasey v Sun Life Life Assurance Corporation of Canada*, above n 20, in which Waller LJ stated, at [6], that 'It is not attractive to contemplate that where insurers have carefully crafted a policy which was intended to be enforceable [that]...a point on insurable interest could arise...' See further the report of the Australian Law Reform Commission, *Insurance Contracts*, No 20 (1982), ch 5; and the ALRC Discussion Paper No 63, *Review of the Marine Insurance Act* 1909, ch 7. In different context, but to the same effect, see, *Cleaver v Mutual Reserve Fund Life Association* [1892] 1 QB 147, 151, per Lord Brett MR; *Saunders v Edwards* [1987] 1 WLR 1116, at 1134 (Bingham LJ).

[110] *Waters v Monarch Life and Fire Assurance Co* (1856) 5 El & Bl 870; *Tomlinson v Hepburn* [1966] AC 451. See *Ebsworth v Alliance Marine Insurance Co* (1873) LR 8 CP 596 at 629, in which Lord Bovill CJ stated that: 'the effect of the plaintiffs' insuring and recovering in their own names would be to place them in the position of trustees for the other parties interested, as to any surplus beyond the amount of their own claim.' *Ramco (UK) Ltd v International Ins Co of Hanover Ltd* [2004] Lloyd's Rep IR 606.

[111] *Routh v Thompson* (1809) 11 East 428.

rarely raise the defence of lack of insurable interest. The received wisdom is that pleading a technical defence, having taken the premium(s) from the insured, would have an adverse effect on the public's view of the insurance industry. Indeed, where an insurer meets a claim under a policy in which the insured's interest is open to challenge, the court will not necessarily set such payment aside.[112] However, if a claim is litigated the court will have regard to the issue of insurable interest on the basis of public policy considerations prohibiting wagering. Whether the requirement of insurable interest can be waived by insurers is far from certain. In *Prudential Staff Union v Hall*,[113], the insured, an employees association (union), effected policies insuring against loss the premium monies collected by their members as agents of their employers. Although it was held that the insured lacked insurable interest, Morris J went on to hold that any sums recovered under the policies by the union would be held on trust for the union's members. By using the trust device in this way, the judge was able to avoid the consequences which would otherwise ensue from the absence of insurable interest, thereby avoiding any element of wagering or gaming.[114]

4.4 Examples from indemnity insurance

4.4.1 Sales of real property

Until such time as the conveyance of land is completed and the purchase price has been paid, the vendor will retain insurable interest in the property. In *Collingridge v Corporation of Royal Exchange Assurance Association*,[115] the insured, who had effected a fire insurance policy in respect of his premises, was served with a compulsory purchase order by the Metropolitan Board of Works. While a draft conveyance was being prepared the premises were destroyed by fire. It was held that the insured's claim was valid because at the time of his loss he had not divested himself of his insurable interest in the property. Mellor J, rejecting the insurers contention that the insured could not claim under the policy, said: 'I cannot see on what grounds the plaintiff, being as he is an unpaid vendor, and having possession and right to possession, can be held disentitled to sue ... the insurance company cannot in any event be released from a contract of which the terms are clear, and which there has been nothing to invalidate.'[116]

---

[112] *Worthington v Curtis*, above n 35.

[113] Above, n 7.

[114] Cf J Birds and N Hird, *Modern Insurance Law*, n 63 above, at 59 who conclude that the contractual undertaking by the insurer to pay the union amounted to a waiver of the requirement of insurable interest. However, M Clarke takes the view that as a matter of public interest the English decisions suggest that insurable interest cannot be waived by the parties: see *The Law of Insurance Contracts* (London: LLP, 2002) para 4.1.D, at n 9. The scope of a trust as a device for circumventing insurable interest and the privity doctrine is considered more fully below.

[115] (1877) 37 LT 525. See also, *Castellain v Preston* (1883) 11 QBD 380 at 385, *per* Brett LJ.

[116] Ibid, at 527.

The purchaser of real property will have an insurable interest in the land arising by virtue of the contract of sale. In practice, once contracts have been exchanged for the purchase of real property, the purchaser will insure the property even though possession and payment of the price is deferred until some later time, for example, 28 days. The mortgagee will, of course, require insurance to be effected from the date of exchange of contracts by virtue of the mortgagee's economic interest in the continued existence of the property as security for the mortgage debt. In the commercial context, it is common practice for a mortgagee to require the mortgagor to effect a life policy to cover the loan in the event of the mortgagor dying before the debt is repaid. The policy is then assigned to the mortgagee. The assignment can be effected in equity under s 136 of the Law of Property Act 1925, or by virtue of the Policies of Assurance Act 1867 which provides that a policy can be assigned by either endorsing the policy document itself, or by a separate document using the form of wording stipulated in the Schedule to the Act. Notice of the assignment must be given in writing to the insurer.

4.4.2 Sales of goods

In relation to contracts for the sale of goods, the general rule is that risk follows ownership, *res perit domino*. Thus, a seller who retains title in the subject matter of the contract clearly has insurable interest given that he continues to bear the risk of loss. Similarly, an unpaid seller in possession of the goods, or if parted with possession, one who has exercised the right of stoppage in transit, will have insurable interest.[117] Generally, the contract for sale will stipulate which party is under a duty to insure in which case the issue of insurable interest will be consequential on the contractual obligation. Accordingly, a buyer of goods will have insurable interest if risk has passed, and risk is not necessarily dependent upon ownership. Clearly, the buyer has an economic interest in the goods since if they are lost he or she will be liable to pay the contract price.[118]

4.4.3 Bailment

Basically, anyone who has a substantial interest in the continued existence of property at the time of its loss will have insurable interest and can validly insure the property for its full value. For example, a bailee who damages goods bailed with him will be liable to the owner and will therefore have insurable interest in the property. Similarly, where a person hires goods, for example where he takes possession of DIY equipment from a hire shop, or takes goods, such as a television, pursuant to a hire-purchase agreement, such person as hirer will have an insurable interest in the goods and can insure. The amount recoverable under the policy will be limited to the level of the insured's interest which is determined according to his or her liability to the owner of the goods in the event of their damage or destruction. In *Waters v*

---

[117] See the Sale of Goods Act 1979, ss 41 and 44–6.
[118] Sale of Goods Act 1979, s 20. See *Stock v Inglis*, above n 3; *Anderson v Morice* (1875) 10 C P 609.

Monarch Fire and Life Assurance Co,[119] the claimants were flour merchants, ware-housemen and wharfingers, whose warehouse was destroyed by an accidental fire, together with goods in it of which they were bailees. They had taken out two policies of insurance covering, under one, 'goods in trust or on commission therein' and, under the other, 'property of the assured or held by them in trust or on commission.' It was held that, as a matter of construction, the policies covered goods of third parties of which the claimants were bailees. Lord Campbell CJ, construing the words 'goods in trust,' said:

> I think that means goods with which the assured were entrusted; not goods held in trust in the strict technical sense, so that there was only an equitable obligation on the assured enforceable by a subpoena in Chancery, but goods with which they were entrusted in the ordinary sense of the word.[120]

The policies therefore covered not just the claimants' 'personal interest' in the goods but all damage and loss. Crompton J said: 'the parties meant to insure those goods with which the claimants were entrusted, and in every part of which they had an interest, both in respect of their lien and in respect of their responsibility to their bailors....'[121] As noted above, having recovered the full value of the merchandise the insureds, having deducted a sum reflecting their own interest, held the excess on trust for the owners of the goods.

The decision in *Waters* was followed in *Tomlinson (Hauliers) Ltd v Hepburn*.[122] The claimants who were road haulage carriers insured a consignment of cigarettes in respect of which they had contracted with the manufacturer to transport. The cigarettes were stolen without any fault or liability on the part of the claimants. The insurers repudiated the claim on the ground that in the absence of any liability on the part of the claimants there was no loss in respect of which they required indemnification. The House of Lords construed the contract as insurance on goods and held that the claimants, as bailees, had an insurable interest. The claimants could, therefore, retain any insurance monies covering their own loss (which on the facts of the present case was none) holding the balance on trust for the manufacturer. Lord Pearce noted that:

> The bailee of goods ... has a right to sue for conversion, holding in trust for the owner such damages as represent the owner's interest ... It would seem irrational ... if he could not also insure for their full value. Both those who have the legal title and those who have a right to possession have an insurable interest ... There seems, therefore, no reason in principle why they should not be entitled to insure for the whole value and recover it. They must, however (like [claimants] in actions of trover or negligence), hold in trust for the other parties interested so much of the moneys recovered as is attributable to the other interests.[123]

---

[119] Above, n 110.
[120] Ibid, at 880.
[121] Ibid, at 882.
[122] Above, n 110.
[123] Ibid, at 477.

The approach taken by the House of Lords is premised upon commercial convenience.[124] It prevents multiplicity of insurances on the same property and avoids the need to inquire into the nature and extent of the interests of the different parties.[125]

However, whether the insured is entitled to recover for all the goods in his possession is a question which depends upon the construction of the policy in question. In *Ramco (UK) Ltd v International Insurance Co of Hanover Ltd*,[126] fire destroyed industrial premises occupied by the insured. The all risks policy covered buildings, content and stock. The terms 'contents' and 'stock' were defined as 'property of the Insured or held by the Insured in trust for which the Insured is responsible.' The insurers admitted liability in respect of property owned by the claimants but, because some of the goods that were damaged or destroyed were bailed to the insureds, they disputed the amount recoverable. The question for the Court of Appeal was whether the addition of the words 'for which he is responsible' restricts the insurers' liability to those goods damaged in a way which imposes liability on the bailee, but not otherwise.[127] The insurers argued that case law had long recognised that the addition of these words carried that meaning and that the court should not disturb that understanding.[128] In effect, the contention was that the phrase 'for which he is responsible' excluded the application of *Waters*. The trial judge, Andrew Smith J, found in favour of the insurers, holding that the term 'responsible' referred to those goods in respect of which the insureds were legally liable. The Court of Appeal agreed. Waller LJ explained that:

> If a form of words has been in use for 80 years which describes one sort of insurance rather than the other, it would be meddlesome for this court to decide that the selected form of words do not achieve their intended purpose, unless there were some real reason for supposing that the form of words is unsatisfactory in practice. The fact that the form of words is the subject-matter of a previous decision of this court is a compelling reason why the courts should not depart from that settled meaning...[129]

---

[124] See the speech of Lord Pearce in *Hepburn*, ibid; see also the speech of Lord Reid in the same decision, at 467, who cited with approval the statement of Lord Campbell CJ in *Waters v Monarch Life and Fire Assurance Co*, above, n 110, at 881: 'It would be most inconvenient in business if a wharfinger could not, at his own cost, keep up a floating policy for the benefit of his customers.'

[125] *Ebsworth v Alliance Marine Insurance Co*, above n 87 at 612, *per* Lord Bovill CJ. But note the view expressed by Waller LJ in *Ramco (UK) Ltd v International Insurance Co of Hanover Ltd* [2004] EWCA Civ 675, at [32]: 'The principles established by *Waters* were highly convenient principles, but constituted an exception to the equally ancient common law principle that normally a claimant cannot sue for loss which he has not himself suffered; this was particularly striking where the cause of action was contractual (as a claim on an insurance policy always will be) since it appears inconsistent with the doctrine of privity of contract to enable a goods-owner to recover his loss when he is not a party to the contract. There is thus something of an anomaly in allowing a bailee to recover for a loss he has not suffered... The anomaly is much less striking now that the Contracts (Rights of Third Parties) Act 1999 is on the statute book. But enabling a party to a contract to recover for a loss he has not suffered or enabling a goods-owner to recover pursuant to a contract to which he is not a party is still the exception rather than the rule; the "exception" established in *Waters* should not itself be extended beyond its proper limits without good reason and no such reason exists in the present case.'

[126] Ibid.

[127] The Court of Appeal was not required to consider whether, if cover was so restricted, the amount recoverable was limited to the insured's liability.

[128] See, eg, *North British & Mercantile Insurance Co v Moffat* (1871) LR 7 CP 25; and *Engel v Lancashire & General Assurance Co Ltd* (1925) 21 Ll LR 327.

[129] Above n 125, at [32].

5. Insuring on behalf of third persons

It is common practice in motor insurance for the insured to effect cover on behalf of those who may also drive the insured's car, for example a spouse or sibling or son and daughter. In such situations the question arises whether the requirement of insurable interest is satisfied. The issue arose in *Williams v Baltic Insurance Association Of London Ltd.*[130] The claimant effected a motor policy on his car which covered liability to third parties for personal injuries caused by the use of the vehicle. The policy also contained a clause which stated that the insurers would indemnify the insured against 'all sums for which the insured (or any licensed personal friend or relative of the insured while driving the car with the insured's general knowledge and consent) shall become legally liable in compensation for loss of life or accidental bodily injury caused to any person' (clause 2). The claimant's sister, while driving the car with his consent, was involved in accident which resulted in her being liable to pay damages for injuries caused to third parties. The issue question which arose for Roche J's determination was whether the claimant could be indemnified on his sister's behalf. Construing clause 2 of the policy, it was plain to the judge that it was expressed to cover precisely the situation which arose on the facts of the case. On this point, Roche J using language which resonates with that of agency principles, concluded that:

> The [claimant] is the insured in the sense that he is the person who effected the insurance, but it is an insurance for himself and the other persons mentioned in cl. 2, and, accordingly, the company's contract is to indemnify all such persons in the event of those things happening against which the insurance is effected.[131]

On this basis, the third party as principal could enforce the contract effected by her agent, her brother. Responding to the insurers' contention that the claimant should not be permitted to recover under the policy because the insurance effected by him on third party risks was in effect a gaming policy, the claimant lacking the requisite interest in his sister's liability, Roche J held that the policy was one on goods to which the Life Assurance Act 1774 did not apply.[132] As such, 'there is nothing in the common law of England which prohibits insurance, even if no interest exists. It may be necessary to show interest, but there is no general prohibition in law.'[133]

---

[130] [1924] 2 KB 282.

[131] Ibid, at 290, citing *Waters v Monarch Fire and Life Assurance Co*, above n 110. Note that in *Waters*, Lord Campbell CJ, while holding that the excess insurance monies were held on trust by the bailee/insured, also approached the issue from the stand point of agency principles.

[132] See s 4 of the 1774 Act which expressly excludes goods from its ambit. S 4 provides that 'nothing herein contained shall extend or be construed to extend to insurances *bona fide* made by any person or persons on ships, goods, or merchandises, but every such insurance shall be as valid and effectual in the law as if this Act had not been made.' If the Act had applied, Roche J opined that he would have been unable to hold that the sister's name had been inserted in the policy in accordance with s 2.

[133] Above n 130, at 288.

6. The doctrine of privity of contract and third parties' rights

One issue which arises from *Prudential Staff Union v Hall*,[134] is whether a member would have been able to enforce the policy had the insurers refused a claim. The doctrine of privity of contract, which precludes a person enforcing a contract to which he is not a party,[135] obviously presents a major obstacle to such a claim. *Vandepitte v Preferred Accident Insurance Corporation of New York*,[136] is a paradigm case. The facts are analogous to *Williams v Baltic Insurance Association Of London Ltd*,[137] in so far as the insured had contracted with the insurers for an indemnity against third party risks and the policy provided that the indemnity should extend to any person driving the insured's car with his consent. Vandepitte (V), the third party, had obtained judgment against the insured's daughter (B) for personal injuries caused by her negligence while driving the insured's car with his permission. V sued the insurers to recover the amount of the unsatisfied judgment on the basis that B was insured against liability by virtue of her father's policy.[138] Counsel for V argued that because the policy extended the indemnity against third party risks to those driving the vehicle with the insured's permission, and because B habitually did so, it can be inferred that the father effected the policy upon her behalf as well as his own. By leaving the defence of the action to the insurers as required by the policy, this could be taken as ratification by B of the contract. Further, it was contended, citing *Waters v Monarch Life and Fire Insurance Co*,[139] and *Williams,* that even if B was not a party to the insurance contract, her father was trustee in relation to the additional risk covered.

Lord Wright, delivering the opinion of the Privy Council, held that the policy did not extend to cover the liability of the insured's daughter. The contracting party was B's father, and as such he lacked insurable interest in his daughter's potential liability. First, it was found that the insured did not effect the policy as agent for B. Lord Wright stated that a contract can only arise if there is *animus contrahendi* between the parties. On the facts, B was completely unaware of having entered into a contract of insurance and as such, no agency could be inferred.[140] Secondly, although the privity doctrine will be qualified where a contracting party constitutes himself a trustee for a third party of a right under the contract so that such right becomes enforceable in equity, there is no evidence that the insured intended to create a beneficial interest for B. Accordingly, because no trusteeship could be made out, the privity doctrine operated to preclude B benefiting under the contract.[141]

Judicial incursions into the privity doctrine have been limited, of particular note is the decision of the High Court of Australia in *Trident General Insurance Co Ltd v*

---

[134] Above n 7, the facts are discussed at n 113, and associated text.

[135] See *Price v Eaton* (1833) 4 B & Ad 433; *Tweddle v Atkinson* (1861) 1 B & S 393; and *Dunlop Pneumatic Tyre Co Ltd v Selfridge & Co Ltd* [1915] AC 847.

[136] [1933] AC 70.

[137] Above, n 130.

[138] Note that in *Williams* it was the insured who sued on the policy, not the third party as here.

[139] Above, n 110.

[140] Above, n 136, at 77.

[141] Ibid, at 79–81.

McNiece Bros Property Ltd,[142] in which it was held that in respect of liability insurance contracts, the doctrine of privity was not part of the common law of Australia and so a third party could bring a direct action against the insurer.[143] However, in general, the English courts have adhered to the orthodoxy of the privity doctrine.[144] That said, it is tenable to argue that there are emerging signs of a judicial shift in position.[145] The point is now largely academic in the light of the Contract (Rights of Third Parties) Act 1999. The Act, which applies to contracts made after 11 May 2000, and is based on the Law Commission's Report, *Privity of Contract: Contracts for the Benefit of Third Parties*,[146] provides for statutory abrogation of the doctrine so that a third party will be able to enforce an insurance contract. Section 1 provides:

> (1) ...a person who is not a party to a contract ('a third party') may in his own right enforce a term of the contract if:
> (a) the contract expressly provides that he may, or
> (b) subject to sub-s (2) below, the term purports to confer a benefit on him.

> (2) Sub-section (1)(b) above does not apply if on a proper construction of the contract it appears that the parties did not intend the term to be enforceable by the third party.[147]

If the above conditions are satisfied, the third party will be able to enforce the contract in the same way as if he or she was a party to the agreement (s 1(5)). Nevertheless, it should be stressed that s 1 leaves the principal parties to the contract in control and so they can decide that the provisions of the statute should not apply. Indeed, it is normal practice for insurers to exclude it. In this situation, presumably, the range of devices (both common law and statutory) which have been used in the past by the courts as a means of circumventing the doctrine may still be enlisted where circumstances so require. It is to these devices we now turn.

---

[142] (1988) 165 CLR 107. See Mr Justice Derrington, 'Recent Australian insurance law reform: the intent and the result: a model for England?' 91 *BILA Jo* 19; and I Stewart, 'Why Place Trust In A Promise?: Privity Of Contract And Enforcement Of Contracts By Third Party Beneficiaries' [1999] *ALJ* 354.

[143] See the judgments of Mason CJ, Wilson and Toohey JJ. Gauldron J, also dismissing the appeal, based his reasoning within the realms of restitution. He said, ibid at 175–6, that: 'Where the consideration is wholly executed in favour of a promisor under a contract made for the benefit of a third party a rule that the third party may not bring action to secure the benefit of the contract permits of the possibility that the promisor may be unjustly enriched to the extent that the promise is not fulfilled.' Brennan and Deane JJ thought that the doctrine was too entrenched to be side-stepped.

[144] Although the injustice caused by the privity doctrine has been frequently acknowledged by the judges. See, for example, *Midland Silicones Ltd v Scruttons Ltd* [1962] AC 446 at 476, in which Lord Reid, adhering to the orthodoxy of the doctrine, said that he did so 'with regret'. See also *Darlington B C v Wiltshier Northern Ltd* [1995] 3 All ER 895, at 903–4, in which Steyn LJ expressing reservations about the privity doctrine said: 'there is no doctrinal, logical or policy reason why the law should deny effectiveness to a contract for the benefit of a third party where that is the expressed intention of the parties.' See also Lord Denning's strident attack on the doctrine in *Smith and Snipes Hall Farm Ltd v River Douglas Catchment Board* [1949] 2 QB 500 at 514; and *Drive Yourself Hire Co (London) Ltd v Strutt* [1954] 1 QB 250 at 272.

[145] See, by way of example, *Petrofina Ltd v Magnaload Ltd*, above n 87. See further ch 11, below.

[146] Law Commission Report No 242 (London, The Stationary Office, 1996). A similar reform was proposed in 1937 by the Law Revision Committee (Sixth Interim Report), Cmnd 5449. See further, J Hanson and V Flynn, 'Cutting through confusion? The rights of third parties under insurance and reinsurance contracts' (1997) 1 *JIL* 50.

[147] There is a presumption of enforceability. For a detailed consideration of the Act, see *Privity of Contract*, R Merkin (ed) (London, LLP, 2000) ch 5 (which also includes the parliamentary debates on the Bill); M Clarke, *The Law of Insurance Contracts*, at 5-1B. See also, M Bridge [2001] *Edin LR* 85; and A Burrows [2000] *LMCLQ* 540.

6.1 Exceptions to the privity doctrine

6.1.1 Undisclosed/unnamed principal; ratification

It is apparent from Lord Wright's opinion in *Vandepitte v Preferred Accident Insurance Corporation of New York,* that where an agency relationship can be shown to exist, the agent may sue on the insurance contract in his own name on behalf of the principal.[148] With respect to the principal, the position was succinctly stated in *Lloyd's v Harper,*[149] by Lush LJ: 'It is true that the [third party principal] has a right, if he pleases, to take action himself and sue upon the contract made by the broker for him, for he is a principal party to the contract.'[150] Lord Russell of Killowen, when examining the statement of Lush LJ, considered that its rationale lies in the fiduciary relationship which arises between principal and agent.[151]

Lush LJ's formulation in *Lloyd's v Harper* as to the right of a principal to enforce a contract, is also applicable to the situation where the principal in question is undisclosed or unnamed.[152] In *Siu Yin Kwan v Eastern Insurance Co Ltd,*[153] the Privy Council took the opportunity to subject the third party principal's rights to detailed consideration. The central issue in the case, which concerned employers' liability insurance effected by shipping agents on behalf of shipowners, was the insurers contention that non-marine insurance contracts were so personal that the doctrine of undisclosed principal did not apply to them. The board rejected their argument, holding that the doctrine was of general application. The identity of the principal was a matter of indifference, it was not material to the risks insured against, ie employers liability.[154] The questions in the proposal form were completed fully as if they referred to the shipowners and the policy document did not exclude, either expressly or impliedly, the rights of the shipowners to sue as undisclosed principal.

Curiously, given that the insurers knew that the shipping agents were insuring on behalf of the owners, it is surprising that the Privy Council did not proceed on the basis of unnamed rather than undisclosed principal. However, the trial judge by ruling in favour of the latter view, precluded the Privy Council from treating it as a case of unnamed principal.

The doctrines of undisclosed principal and ratification were adopted by Colman J in *National Oilwell Ltd v Davy Offshore (UK) Ltd,*[155] in considering whether the

---

[148] See also, the speech of Lord Campbell CJ in *Waters v Monarch Life and Fire Assurance Co,* above n 110, at 881; and *Cochran & Son v Leckie's Trustee* (1906) 8 F (Ct Sess) 975.
[149] (1880) 16 Ch D 290.
[150] Ibid, at 321.
[151] *Woodar Investment Development Ltd v Wimpey Construction UK Ltd,* above n 39, at 585. Cf the approach taken by Lord Denning MR towards Lush LJ's formulation, in *Jackson v Horizon Holidays Ltd* [1975] 1 WLR 1468, at 1473: 'It has been suggested that Lush LJ was thinking of a contract in which A was trustee for B. But I do not think so. He was a common lawyer speaking of the common law.' In *Woodar* Lord Russell, disapproving of Lord Denning's view, stressed that read in context, Lush LJ proceeded on the basis that the relationship between principal and agent was fiduciary in nature.
[152] As to an unnamed insured see, *Provincial Insurance Co of Canada v Leduc* (1874) LR 6 PC 224, at 244, *per* Sir Barnes Peacock.
[153] Above, n 13.
[154] Cf an existing motor insurance policy, about which Sir Wilfred Greene MR said in *Peters v General Accident Fire & Life Assurance Corp Ltd* [1938] 2 All ER 267 at 269, that a: 'contract of that kind is in its very nature not assignable ... That appears to me to be altering *in toto* the character of the risk.'
[155] Above, n 90.

supplier, National Oilwell Ltd (NOW), as co-insured could make a direct claim under the contractors' All Risks policy. The learned judge stated that NOW could establish privity of contract with the insurers by:

> one of two routes: by establishing either that they were undisclosed or unnamed principals of DOL [Davy Offshore Ltd] or that they were entitled to and did ratify the policy. In both cases it is necessary for them to establish that at the time of effecting the policy DOL intended to effect insurance cover on behalf of NOW.[156]

Reviewing the earlier authorities,[157] Colman J held first, that where at the time the insurance contract was concluded the principal insured or other contracting party had express or implied actual authority to make the contract so as to bind some other party as co-insured and intended to bind that other party, the latter may enforce the policy as the undisclosed principal and co-insured irrespective of whether the policy described a class of co-insured of which he or she was or became a member. Secondly, on the issue of ratification Colman J stated:

> Where at the time when the contract of insurance was made the principal [insured] or other contracting party had no actual authority to bind the other party to the contract of insurance, but the policy is expressed to insure not only the principal [insured] but also a class of others who are not identified in that policy, a party who at the time when the policy was effected could have been ascertained to qualify as a member of that class can *ratify and sue* on the policy as co-assured if at that time it was intended by the principal [insured] or other contracting party to create privity of contract with the insurers on behalf of that particular party.[158]

The judge went on to explain that evidence of the requisite intention may be provided by the terms of the policy document, by the terms of any contract between the principal insured or other contracting party and the alleged co-assured, or by any other admissible material showing what was subjectively intended by the principal.

Ratification places the insured in the same position he would have been in had the agent's acts been authorised from the outset. As to the time when ratification must take place, the law seems far from settled. In marine insurance ratification can take place after the occurrence of the loss.[159] On the other hand, with respect to non-marine insurance it was held in *Grover & Grover Ltd v Mathews*, [160] that a fire policy cannot be ratified after the occurrence of the loss if at the time of the ratification the insured has knowledge of the loss. Hamilton J observed that the marine insurance exception 'was an anomalous rule which it was not, for business reasons, desirable to extend.'[161] The learned judge did not go on to explain what the 'business reasons' were. The decision in *Grover* can be criticised as being wrong in principle particularly in the light that it has long been settled that ratification has a retroactive

---

[156] Ibid, at 597.
[157] Principally, *Boston Fruit Co v British and Foreign Marine Insurance Co* [1905] 1 KB 637; *Graham Joint Stock Shipping Co v Merchants Marine Insurance Co* [1924] AC 294; and the Court of Appeal's decision in *Stone Vickers Ltd v Appledore Ferguson Shipbuilders Ltd* [1992] 2 Lloyd's Rep 578.
[158] Above n 90, at 596–7. Emphasis supplied.
[159] *Williams v North China Insurance Co* (1876) 1 CPD 757. See the Marine Insurance Act 1906, s 86.
[160] [1910] 2 KB 401.
[161] Ibid, at 404.

effect on the insurance contract.[162] Indeed, in *National Oilwell* Colman J stated, by way of *dicta*, that had it been necessary for him to decide the point he would not have followed *Grover* but would have held that NOW could ratify with knowledge of an insured loss, notwithstanding the insurance was non-marine. The judge noted that Canadian,[163] American and Australian courts have all permitted ratification of non-marine policies after the loss has occurred to the knowledge of the ratifying party. He therefore concluded that:

> I can see neither legal principle nor commercial reason why the English Courts should not take the same approach. A rule which has worked perfectly well for over a century for marine insurance can be expected to work equally well for non-marine. It is undesirable that different rules should apply to the two classes of insurance and in the absence of binding or compelling authority to the contrary the English courts should take a different view on a question of principle in insurance law from the views already established in other common law jurisdictions.[164]

It is suggested that Colman J's view is correct for it accords with principle, and the decision in *Grover* should not be followed by a future court when called upon to decide the issue.

6.1.2 Trusts

A life insured may create an express trust of the benefit of the policy in favour of a third party, often a son or daughter, and by so doing will avoid the requirement of insurable interest in the child's life. The effect of the insured declaring that he holds the proceeds of the policy on trust for a third party is that on the insured's death, or in the case of an endowment policy, the date of maturity, the insurers will make payment direct to the beneficiary rather than to the insured's personal representatives. In this way, the insurance monies do not form part of the deceased's estate for the purposes of inheritance tax, nor will they be subject to the claims of the insured's creditors. However, an insured who creates a trust will be precluded from varying its terms without obtaining the consent of the beneficiary.[165] He will also be bound to act responsibly when considering the interests of the beneficiary. Thus, the trustee/insured may lose the right to assign or surrender the policy unless such a course of action is in the best interests of the beneficiary.[166] The third party beneficiary can enforce the policy through the trustee and may only enforce it directly if he becomes legal owner. If the trustee fails to pay the insurance monies to the beneficiary, he can sue the trustee for it.

For an express trust to be completely constituted there must be (i) trust property, which in the case of life insurance is the benefit of the policy; (ii) identifiable beneficiaries; and (iii) a clear and unequivocal declaration that the insured intents to create

---

[162] *Bolton Partners v Lambert* (1888) 41 Ch D 295.

[163] See, eg, *Spencer v Continental Insurance Co* [1945] 4 DLR 593.

[164] Above n 90, at 608. Cf *Portavon Cinema Co Ltd v Price and Century Insurance Co Ltd* [1939] 4 All ER 601 at 607, in which Branson J professed to not having 'the boldness of youth' to refuse to follow *Grover*.

[165] *Re Schebsman* [1944] Ch 83.

[166] *Re Equitable Life Assurance Society of US Policy and Mitchell* (1911) 27 TLR 213.

a trust.[167] In the absence of an unambiguous declaration, the courts are loath to imply that a trust is intended because 'serious duties and obligations rest on any person claiming to be insured, which necessarily involve consent and privity of contract.'[168] Nevertheless, in accordance with the maxim that equity looks to the intent rather than the form, no particular form of language is necessary to create a trust. However, it is not sufficient if the policy merely states that it is for the benefit of a particular third party,[169] or that the proceeds of the policy should be paid to the third party.[170] Yet the court will endeavour to find a duly constituted trust. In *Re Webb, Barclays Bank Ltd v Webb*,[171] a father effected policies on the lives of his two children. The proposal form stated that he was the 'grantee' and that the insurance was effected 'on behalf of and for the benefit of the person therein named as the life assured,' ie the child. The respective policies provided that on the child's death at or after attaining 21 years of age, the proceeds would be paid to his representatives and, on each child's 21st birthday, the father's interest in the policy would cease. Up until then, the father had power to surrender the policies, assign them and recover the premiums should the child die before reaching 21 years. The policies also stated that should the father, having paid all the premiums, die before the child's 21st birthday, the policies would continue in force until the child reached 21 years. The father did in fact die before the children reached the specified age. The issue before the court was whether the policies belonged to his estate or to the children. Farwell J, stressing that 'the whole question...depends upon the construction of the particular policy,'[172] held that the father had created a trust in favour of the children. In his reasoning, the judge found that it was material that the policies provided that the father's interest would cease when the children reached 21 and that the insurance monies were not payable until the children reached that age. Accordingly, the children and not the father possessed the beneficial interest in the policies.

6.1.3 Group insurance

Just as with family arrangements, provided the language is unequivocal it is certainly possible for an employer to create a trust of a group life policy on the lives of employees. The leading case is *Bowskill v Dawson*,[173] where a company established a scheme under which the trustee effected a life policy for the company's employees. Construing the terms of the particular scheme pertaining to the 'rights' and ' claims' of the employees or their legal representatives, the Court of Appeal held that they were beneficiaries under a voluntary trust. The court noted that they had more than mere

---

[167] See, eg, *Jones v Lock* (1865) 1 Ch App 25. In *Milroy v Lord* (1862) 4 De G F & J 264, at 274 Turner LJ stated that: 'In order to render a voluntary settlement valid and effectual, the settlor must have done everything which according to the nature of the property comprised in the settlement was necessary to be done in order to render the settlement binding upon him. He may, of course do this by ... [declaring] that he himself holds it on trust for [the purposes of the settlement]...' See further AJ Oakley, *Parker and Mellows: The Modern Law of Trusts* (London, Sweet & Maxwell, 2003) ch 5.
[168] *Vandepitte v Preferred Accident Insurance Corporation of New York*, above n 136, at 81, *per* Lord Wright.
[169] *Re Foster's Policy* [1966] 1 WLR 222 at 227, *per* Plowman J.
[170] *Cleaver v Mutual Reserve Fund Life Assurance* [1892] 1 QB 147 at 152, *per* Lord Esher MR.
[171] [1941] Ch 225.
[172] Ibid, at 234.
[173] [1955] 1 QB 13. See s 50 of the Insurance Companies Act 1973, considered at p. 161 above.

expectancies. The scheme conferred upon the employees legally enforceable rights which entitled them as beneficiaries to call upon the trustees to perform the trusts of the deed under which they benefited. Romer LJ observed that:

> Indeed, it may well be that, had the insurance company refused to pay and the trustees declined to sue, the defendants themselves could have sued the [insurance] company adding the trustees as defendants.[174]

On the other hand, in *Green v Russell*,[175] where an employer effected a group accident policy on behalf of his employees named in the schedule to the policy, Romer LJ found that a trust had not been created. The terms of the policy permitted the employer to surrender it and receive back a proportionate sum of the premium. He therefore retained absolute ownership of the policy and was not bound to maintain the insurance.[176]

6.2 Statutory exceptions to the privity doctrine[177]

6.2.1 Married Women's Property Act 1882

To avoid life insurance monies being swallowed up by the debts of a deceased spouse's estate, the Married Women's Property Act 1882 (hereafter referred to as the MWPA) allows for the creation of a statutory family trust thereby avoiding the necessity of executing a trust deed. The statutory trust ensures that on the death of a married insured, the policy monies will be paid direct to the surviving spouse (and/or children) and will not form part of the deceased's estate. Thus, if the deceased is bankrupt at the time of death, the creditors cannot look to the proceeds of a life policy written under the MWPA for payment of the insured's debts provided, of course, that the trust was not created with the intention of defrauding the creditors.[178] Section 11 of the MWPA 1882 provides that a policy effected by a married man or woman on his or her own life and which is expressed to be for the benefit of the survivor or his or her children, or for the benefit of the surviving spouse and children together, shall create a trust if favour of them.[179] The monies payable under such a policy will not form part of the insured's estate and will not therefore be subject to

---

[174] Ibid, at 28.
[175] [1959] 2 QB 226.
[176] Note that under the Contract (Rights of Third Parties) Act 1999 the employees would have the statutory right to enforce such a policy.
[177] See also, the Road Traffic Act 1988 s 148(7) discussed in ch 13.
[178] Insolvency Act 1986, ss 423–5. For the meaning of 'fraud' in the context of bankruptcy proceedings, see *Re Kushler Ltd* [1948] Ch 248.
[179] A joint life policy effected by spouses may create two separate policies both of which may fall within the scope of s 11: *Re S (deceased)* [1996] 1 WLR 235 applying *Griffiths v Fleming*, above n 28, at 817–19, *per* Farwell and Kennedy LJJ. Note the reservations expressed by Robert Walker LJ in *Rooney v Cardona, The Times*, 4 March 1999 in which his Lordship said that had he been called upon to consider the issue he would have taken the view that 'the court was not bound to apply the views expressed by two members of the court in *Griffiths v Fleming* in relation to a policy which they regarded as a mistaken amalgamation of two separate contracts. The policy with which the court was concerned made no reference to s 11 of the 1882 Act. It was not expressed to be effected for the benefit of Mr Cardona or Mrs Cardona.' In the absence of any evidence as to separate proposal forms the judge would have been disposed to think that it was not within s 11 of the 1882 Act.

his or her debts. In addition to pure life policies, the statutory trust can also be applied to policies limited to accidental death and to endowment insurance which carry an element of life cover.[180] The Civil Partnerships Act 2004 seeks to ensure that parties in a same-sex relationship are treated in the same way as married couples. Section 70 of the 2004 Act extends the operation of s 11 of the MWPA 1882 to civil partners.

The purpose of this provision is to protect the insured's immediate dependants, ie spouse and/or children, although it has been held that it is not necessary for the beneficiary to prove actual dependency either at the time when the policy was effected or at the time of the insured's death.[181] All that need be shown is that the beneficiary falls within the qualifying relationship of spouse or child.[182] While a future spouse or child also qualifies, the section does not extend to co-habitees. The obvious effect of s 11 is to make the insured a trustee of the policy, the consequence being that he is under a duty to administer it in the best interests of the beneficiaries. Thus, a decision to surrender the policy must be made in the interests of the beneficiaries and any surrender value will be held on trust for them.[183]

If the policy document specifically identifies the spouse or child(ren) then the named beneficiaries acquire an immediate vested interest in the insurance. In *Cousins v Sun Life Assurance Society*,[184] the Court of Appeal refused to grant the insured a declaration that he had sole beneficial interest in the policy by virtue of his wife, who had been named in the policy, having predeceased him. It was held that the insurance monies belonged to his late wife's estate even though the insured had remarried. If, on the other hand, the policy does not specifically name the beneficiaries but merely refers, for example, to 'my wife' or 'to my children', the beneficiaries will have a contingent interest so that only those who satisfy that description at the time of the insured's death will benefit. If there is more than one beneficiary they will benefit in equal shares as joint tenants unless the policy, or the insured's will, or a deed provides to the contrary.[185] The share of any contingent beneficiary who predeceases the insured will be shared among the survivors.[186] If the purposes of the trust fail, a resulting trust arises in favour of the life insured and his estate. Should the insured divorce, the court has the power to vary any settlement, including insurance, made on the parties to the marriage.[187]

6.2.2 Fires Prevention (Metropolis) Act 1774

Generally an indemnity policy requires the insurer to pay to the insured a sum of money referable to the insured loss. However, a statutory form of reinstatement is provided by the Fires Prevention (Metropolis) Act 1774 which provides that any 'person interested' can require the insurer to reinstate irrespective of whether such a person is a party to the contract of insurance. The privity doctrine is thereby

---

[180] *Re Ioakimidis Policy Trusts* [1925] Ch 403.
[181] *Re Brownes Policy* [1903] 1 Ch 188, at 190, *per* Kekewich J.
[182] An adopted or illegitimate child also qualifies; see the Adoption Act 1976, s 39; and the Family Law Reform Act 1969, s 19(1). See further, *Re Clay's Policy* [1937] 2 All ER 548.
[183] *Re Fleetwood's Policy* [1926] Ch 48.
[184] [1933] 1 Ch 126.
[185] *Re Brownes Policy*, above n 181.
[186] *Re Seyton* (1887) 34 Ch D 511.
[187] Matrimonial Causes Act 1973, s 24; Matrimonial Proceedings and Property Act 1970, s 27.

circumvented. Section 83 of the 1774 Act authorises and requires fire insurers, upon suspicion of fraud or arson on the part of the insured, to use the insurance monies, so far as they will go, to reinstate the building instead of paying it to the insured. To avoid the danger that there may be other persons interested in the building whose 'lives and fortunes...may be lost or endangered,' s 83 also requires the insurers to reinstate if requested to do so by such person or persons. The scope of the Act is considered more fully below.[188]

6.2.3 Third Parties (Rights Against Insurers) Act 1930

Prior to the Act, where a person who had liability insurance became bankrupt, or if a company went into liquidation, an injured third party was left in an exposed position because he would have to prove in the bankruptcy proceedings as an ordinary creditor of the insured. The position at common law was that once an insured became insolvent, any insurance money paid by way of indemnity went into the pool for the benefit of all the insured's general creditors.[189] The unjust consequences this carried for the third party was compounded with the increase use of motor vehicles and the consequent rise in road traffic injuries. Against this background, Parliament intervened and the Third Parties (Rights Against Insurers) Act 1930 was passed to confer on third parties the right to claim directly against insurers of third party risks where the insured is insolvent. The Act, which is considered more fully below,[190] circumvents the privity doctrine by placing the injured person into the shoes of the wrongdoer/insured.[191]

---

[188] See ch 10, below.
[189] See *Re Harrington Motor Co Ltd* [1928] Ch 105 at 124, in which Atkin LJ, commenting on the anomaly produced by the common law position said: 'it would appear as though a person who is insured against risks and who has general creditors whom he is unable to satisfy, has only to go out in the street and to find the most expensive motor car or the most wealthy man he can to run down, and he will at once be provided with assets, which will enable him to pay his general creditors quite a substantial dividend.' See also, *Hood's Trustees v Southern Union General Insurance Co of Australasia Ltd* [1928] 1 Ch 793. See further, the observations of Lord Denning MR in *Post Office v Norwich Union Fire Insurance Society Ltd* [1967] 2 QB 363.
[190] See ch 14, below.
[191] S 1(1).

7

The Terms of the Insurance Contract

1. The perspective of the general law of contract

The law governing insurance contracts is rooted in the common law. As such, the approach adopted by the courts towards the classification of terms in contracts of insurance owes its origins to the jurisprudence which developed rapidly during the late eighteenth century and throughout the nineteenth century in response to the increasing sophistication of the commercial contract.

The common law of contract proceeds on the basis that not all obligations created by an agreement are of equal significance or importance to the parties. The orthodox classification of contractual terms categorises such obligations as either 'conditions' on the one hand, or 'warranties' on the other. A condition is an essential term of the contract and is fundamental in nature,[1] the effect of its breach is to entitle the innocent party to terminate the contract and sue for damages. A warranty, however, is a subsidiary promise, the breach of which entitles the innocent party to damages only and not to terminate the contract.[2] Indeed, those who drafted the Sale of Goods Act

---

[1] For a detailed analysis of the development of the law long these lines, see GH Treitel, *The Law Of Contract* (London, Sweet & Maxwell, 2003) ch 18; MP Furmston, *Cheshire Fifoot and Furmston's Law of Contract* (London, Butterworths, 2002) ch 6; J Beatson, *Anson's Law Of Contract* (Oxford, Oxford University Press, 2002) ch 4. See further, SJ Stoljar, 'The Contractual Concept of Condition' (1953) 69 *LQR* 485; W Montrose, 'Conditions, Warranties and Other Contractual Terms' 15 *Can Bar Rev* 323.

[2] In *Glaholm v Hays* (1841) 2 Man & G 257 at 268, the court stated that a term is a condition if the 'performance of the stipulation [went] to the very root ... of the contract.' In *Wallis, Son & Wells v Pratt and Haynes* [1910] 2 KB 1003 at 1012, Fletcher Moulton LJ observed that: 'But from a very early period of our law it has been recognised that ... [contractual] obligations are not all of equal importance. There are some which go so directly to the substance of the contract or, in other words, are so essential to its very nature that their non-performance may fairly be considered by the other party as a substantial failure to perform the contract at all. On the other hand, there are other obligations which, though they must be performed, are not so vital that a failure to perform them goes to the substance of the contract.' In determining the nature of a term which has been broken, the courts continue to have regard to the consequences of the breach. Thus, the fact that the effects of the breach are not significant may lead the court to hold that the term is not a condition; *State Trading Corporation of India v M Golodetz Ltd* [1989] 2 Lloyd's Rep 277.

1893 gave statutory legitimacy to this categorisation by defining such terms with reference to the remedies available in the event of breach.[3] Section 11(1)(b) of the Act,[4] defines a condition as a stipulation in a contract of sale, 'the breach of which may give rise to a right to treat the contract as repudiated,'[5] and a warranty as a stipulation 'the breach of which may give rise to a claim for damages but not to a right to reject the goods and treat the contract as repudiated.' Section 62 goes on to add the gloss that a warranty is 'collateral to the main purpose of the contract.'[6]

The word condition may also carry a different meaning insofar as such a term may be either a condition precedent or a condition subsequent. A condition precedent is a term 'which must be fulfilled before any contract is concluded at all.'[7] In this sense it has been described as a pre-condition, 'something which must happen or be done before the agreement can take effect.'[8] An obvious example can be drawn from the Sale of Goods Act 1979, section 9, which provides that where the parties to a contract for the sale of goods agree that the price is to be fixed by the valuation of a third party and the third party cannot or does not fix the price, the agreement is thereby avoided. As such, the valuation is the contingency upon which the obligations of both parties depends. Although the contract crystallises as soon as the parties conclude their agreement, nevertheless it is suspended until such valuation takes place. If the contingent event does not occur, the contract does not become operative.[9] It should be noted that a condition precedent is not restricted to the situation where the contract provides for a third party to perform some specified act, but may also arise where one of the contracting parties themselves is required to carry out some act.[10]

A condition subsequent operates to bring an existing contract to an end upon the occurrence of a stipulated event.[11] However, whether a particular term can be accurately designated a condition subsequent as opposed to a condition precedent is often nothing more than an etymological exercise. Nevertheless, the significance of the condition subsequent is more readily seen in the context of insurance contracts where it has become subsumed in the more appropriate terminology of the promissory warranty and clauses descriptive of risks.[12]

As is evident from much of the case law on the place of conditions and warranties in the general scheme of contract law,[13] there has been considerable judicial debate over whether the dichotomy amounts to nothing more than an over simplistic

---

[3] See now the Sale of Goods Act 1979, esp ss 12–15. See also, the Supply of Goods and Services Act 1982.
[4] The Sale of Goods Act 1979, s 11(3)
[5] The word 'condition' as used here carries its promissory sense. Cf insurance warranties, considered below, which are conditional and not promissory in nature.
[6] See now the Sale of Goods Act 1979, s 61.
[7] *Trans Trust SPRL v Danubian Trading Co Ltd* [1952] 2 QB 297 at 304, *per* Denning LJ.
[8] *L Schuler AG v Wickman Machine Tool Sales Ltd* [1974] AC 235 at 250, *per* Lord Reid. See also *Marten v Whale* [1917] 2 KB 480.
[9] *Pym v Campbell* (1856) 6 E & B 370.
[10] *Aberfoyle Plantations Ltd v Cheng* [1960] AC 115, PC; *Trans Trust SPRL v Danubian Trading Co Ltd,* above n 7.
[11] *Head v Tattersall* (1871) LR 7 Exch 7; *Thompson v Asda-MFI Group plc* [1988] Ch 241; *Gyllenhammer & Partners v Sour Brodogradevna* [1989] 2 Lloyd's Rep 403; *Brown v Knowlsey* [1986] IRLR 102. See further, SJ Stoljar, above n 1, at 506–11; LS Sealy, '"Risk" In The Law Of Sale' [1973] *CLJ* 225.
[12] See *Bank of Nova Scotia v Hellenic Mutual War Risks Association (Bermuda) Ltd, The Good Luck* [1992] 1 AC 233, considered below, at n 89.
[13] See, eg, *Hong Kong Fir Shipping Co Ltd v Kawasaki Kisen Kaisha Ltd* [1962] 2 QB 26 at 70, *per* Diplock LJ; *Cehave NV v Bremer Handelsgesellschaft mbH, The Hansa Nord* [1976] QB 44. Although the value of the distinction was staunchly defended in *The Mihalis Angelos* [1971] 1 QB 164 at 199, *per* Edmund Davies LJ, at 205, *per* Megaw LJ.

approach to determining the importance of contractual terms.[14] This has seen the recent emergence of a third category of terms, namely innominate or intermediate terms. Whether a party may terminate the contract in the event of breach of an innominate term lies within the discretion of the court. In this way, such terms operate as a flexible device whereby termination is made to depend upon the court's view of the seriousness of the consequences flowing from the breach.[15] Nevertheless, the classification of contractual terms as major (conditions) or minor (warranties) obligations has withstood the rigours of judicial challenge and continues to represent the orthodoxy.

---

2. The nature and effect of insurance warranties

The parallels between the general law of contract and the particular law applicable to insurance contracts encompasses the approach adopted towards the relative importance of contractual terms. The terms of a contract of insurance are not necessarily of equal importance in the minds of the parties, nor indeed in the eyes of the judges, and so the consequences arising from the breach of a term will depend (as with the general law) upon the nature of the term in question.

The terminology adopted in insurance law to categorise terms is curious and confusing to those schooled in general contract law. For insurance contracts, fundamental terms are classified as warranties, not as conditions. To compound the confusion, in insurance contracts the two terms are sometimes used interchangeably. Nevertheless, the strict nature of the warranty in insurance law can be seen from the statutory definition of the term contained in the Marine Insurance Act, 1906, section 33(3) which provides: 'A warranty ... is a condition which must be exactly complied with, whether it is material to the risk or not. If it be not so complied with ... the insurer is discharged from liability ... .'[16] The general applicability of this definition to non-marine insurance contracts is now beyond dispute, so that in this respect at least, marine insurance contracts can be treated as *sui generis*. This is manifest from the formulation of Viscount Finlay in *Dawsons Ltd v Bonnin*,[17] who said:

---

[14] Lord Devlin, 'The Treatment Of Breach Of Contract' [1966] *CLJ* 192.

[15] *Cehave NV v Bremer Handelsgesellschaft mbH, The Hansa Nord,* above n 13. See J Beatson, *Anson's Law of Contract,* above n 1, at 135 *et seq.*

[16] See *Pawson v Watson* [1778] 2 Cowp 785, in which Lord Mansfield said, at 787–8, 'There is no distinction better known to those who are at all conversant in the law of insurance, than that which exists, between a warranty or condition which makes part of a written policy, and a representation ... Where it is part of the written policy, it must be performed ... nothing tantamount will do, or answer the purpose; it must be strictly performed... .' It is noteworthy that s 33(1) of the 1906 Act states that: 'A warranty ... means a promissory warranty, that is to say, a warranty by which the assured undertakes that some particular thing shall or shall not be done, or that some condition shall be fulfilled, or whereby he affirms or negatives the existence of a particular state of facts.'

[17] [1922] 2 AC 413. See also the speech of Lord Goff in *The Good Luck,* above, n 12. See further *Brownlie v Campbell* (1880) 5 App Cas 925 at 954, *per* Lord Blackburn; *Moens v Heyworth* (1842) 10 M & W 147 at 157, *per* Parke B; *Seaton v Burnand* [1900] AC 135–all of which were cited by McCardie J in *Yorke v Yorkshire Insurance Co* [1918] 1 KB 662 at 667, who stated that the 1906 Act, 'may frequently be considered with advantage in cases of insurance even though they do not relate to marine risks. For in certain important respects ... the law is the same whether the insurance be life, fire, or marine.'

It is not necessary that the term 'warranty' should be used, as any form of words expressing the existence of a particular state of facts as a condition of the contract is enough to constitute a warranty. If there is such a warranty the materiality of the facts in themselves is irrelevant; by contract their existence is made a condition of the contract.[18]

Accordingly, even a minor or trivial breach of warranty is enough to terminate the risk under the insurance contract. For example, in *Overseas Commodities Ltd v Style*,[19] the insured warranted that each can of pork in a consignment had been date-stamped by the manufacturer. In fact, a number of cans had the date-stamp missing. The insured claimed due to a quantity of the cargo being swept overboard in a storm. It was held that the insurers could rely on the breach of warranty in denying the claim. The fact that the insured was blameless is, therefore, irrelevant, for liability is strict.[20] The court will not ask whether the breach was material or otherwise to the risk or to the loss sustained. The inexorable rule is that a warranty must be strictly complied with so that substantial performance is insufficient.[21]

---

3. Creating an insurance warranty

It is not necessary for any form of words to be used in order to create a warranty, the use or absence of the word 'warranty' is therefore not important. It was observed by Lord Blackburn in *Thomas v Weems*,[22] that:

> In policies of marine insurance I think it is settled by authority that any statement of fact bearing upon the risk introduced into the written policy is, by whatever words and in whatever place, to be construed as a warranty, and prima facie, at least that the compliance with that warranty is a condition precedent to the attaching of the risk. I think that on the balance of the authority the general principles of insurance law apply to all insurances, whether marine, life or fire... .'[23]

While there is no particular formula, nevertheless the language creating a warranty must be unequivocal, showing clearly that it is the intention of the parties that the term in question is viewed by them as fundamental to the contract.[24] In *HIH*

---

[18] Ibid, at 428–9.
[19] [1959] 1 Lloyd's Rep 546. *Chapman v Kadirga* [1998] Lloyd's Rep IR 377.
[20] *Philips v Baillie* (1784) 3 Doug. K B 374.
[21] See *De Hahn v Hartley* (1786) 1 TR 343, where Ashurst J stated that 'the very meaning of a warranty is to preclude all questions whether it has been substantially complied with; it must be literally so.' See also, *Mayall v Mitford* (1837) 6 Ad & El 670; *Glen v Lewis* (1853) 8 Ex 607; *Benham v United Guarantie & Life Assurance Co* (1852) 7 Ex 744. *Cf* the Australian Insurance Contracts Act 1984, s 54(2) which requires a causal connection between the breach and the loss. See also the reservations expressed by Lord Griffiths in *Vesta v Butcher* [1989] AC 852.
[22] (1884) 9 App Cas 671.
[23] Ibid, at 684. See also, *Barnard v Faber* [1893] 1 QB 340 at 343–4, *per* Bowen LJ; and *Svenska Handelsbanken v Sun Alliance and London Insurance plc* [1996] CLC 833 at 876, *per* Rix J.
[24] See, eg, the speech of Viscount Finlay in *Dawsons Ltd v Bonnin*, above n 17 at 428–31; and also Lord Blackburn in *Thomson v Weems*, above n 22, at 682. See further, *C.T.N. Cash & Carry Ltd v General Accident plc* [1989] 1 Lloyd's Rep 299; and the judgment of Morland J in *Kler Knitwear Ltd v Lombard General Insurance Co Ltd* [2000] Lloyd's Rep IR 47, discussed below.

Casualty and General Insurance Ltd v New Hampshire Insurance Co,[25] the issue was whether a term in the policy which stated that six films would be made was a warranty. Rix LJ laid down three tests for deciding the nature of a term:

> In my judgment, once the six film term is established as a term of the insurance or reinsurance contract, the grounds for holding it to be a warranty are very strong. It is a question of construction, and the presence or absence of the word 'warranty' or 'warranted' is not conclusive. One test is whether it is a term which goes to the root of the transaction; a second, whether it is descriptive of or bears materially on the risk of loss; a third, whether damages would be an unsatisfactory or inadequate remedy. As Lord Justice Bowen said in *Barnard v Faber*, [1893] 1 QB 340 at p 344: 'A term as regards the risk must be a condition.' Otherwise the insurer is merely left to a cross-claim in a matter which goes to the risk itself, which is unbusinesslike…In the present case, the six film term would seem to answer all three tests. It is a fundamental term, for even if only one film were omitted, the revenues are likely to be immediately reduced.[26]

This approach was recently applied by the Court of Appeal in *Toomey (of Syndicate 2021) v Banco Vitalicio de Espana SA de Seguros y Reasseguros.*[27] The defendants, Spanish insurers, insured a Spanish first division football club, Atletico de Madrid, against loss of income should the club be relegated. The club had been required to effect such insurance by Audivisual, (AV)which had exclusive rights to televise the club's home matches. AV had paid the club advances, a percentage of which, subject to certain conditions, was returnable in the event of relegation.The insurance policy provided security to AV for its exposure under promissory notes in the sum of Pts 2.9 billion. The insurers reinsured the risk with a number of reinsurers in London. At the end of the 1999–2000 season the club was relegated to the second division. The defendants paid the loss but the London based reinsurers, Toomey, refused to pay on the reinsurance on the basis that there was a material misrepresentation in the draft slip relating to the nature of the direct policy. At first instance, it was held to be a valued policy and not, as represented, an indemnity policy. The reinsurers exposure was therefore greater than appeared. Toulson J also held that the description in the slip of the policy was a warranty and that there was breach. The Court of Appeal agreed on both issues. With respect to the warranty issue, the Court held, applying the tests formulated by Rix LJ in *HIH*, that a term may be a warranty even though it is not expressed as such provided it goes to the root of the transaction and bears materially on the risk of loss and if damages would not be an adequate remedy. On the facts, these conditions were satisfied.

Given the harsh results which flow from the insured's breach of warranty, the courts have endeavoured to mitigate the effects by adopting the *contra proferentem* rule of construction towards such terms. Under this rule any ambiguity in the wording of such clauses will be strictly construed against the party, usually the insurer, seeking to rely on them. In a line of cases it has been stressed that insurers should express themselves in plain terms so that where the language used is ambiguous, it will be interpreted in the sense that the insured might reasonably have understood it. For example, in *Provincial Insurance Co Ltd v Morgan,*[28] the proposer stated in the

---

[25] [2001] 2 Lloyd's Rep 161.
[26] Ibid, at 182, [101].
[27] [2004] EWCA Civ 622. See also, *International Management Group v Simmonds* [2004] Lloyd's Rep IR 247.
[28] [1933] AC 240.

proposal form that the purpose for which the insured lorry was to be used was to carry coal. The proposal form was made the basis of the contract. The House of Lords held that it was not the intention of either party that the lorry should never be used for any purpose other than the carriage of coal so that the warranty was not broken by the occasional carriage of timber. Lord Wright stated:

> A policy ought to be so framed, that he who runs can read. It ought to be framed with such deliberate care, that no form of expression by which, on the one hand, the party assured can be caught, or by which, on the other, the company can be cheated, shall be found upon the face of it.[29]

The point has been made judicially that questions 'framed in a slovenly way' are 'mere traps' and will be strictly construed against the insurers who seek to rely on them.[30] In *Re Bradley and Essex and Suffolk Accident Indemnity Society*,[31] Farwell LJ surveyed the relevant authorities and stressed that:

> It is especially incumbent on insurance companies to make clear, both in their proposal forms and in their policies, the conditions which are precedent to their liability to pay, for such conditions have the same effect as forfeiture clauses, and may inflict loss and injury to the assured and those claiming under him out of all proportion to any damage that could possibly accrue to the company from non-observance or non-performance of the conditions. Accordingly, it has been established that the doctrine that policies are to be construed *'contra proferentes'* applies strongly against the company.[32]

However, an insured cannot avail himself of an apparent ambiguity where to a reasonable person its meaning would be clear. In this situation the court will follow the basic rule of interpreting the words reasonably. Thus, where an insured warrants that he has not suffered any illnesses of consequence when in fact he had attempted suicide by way of an overdose and was, as a result, critically ill, the court will construe the word 'illness' in a fair business manner so that the effects of the overdose would be covered by the term.[33] Provided due care has been taken in describing the nature of a term, that is likely to be decisive. In *Virk v Gan Life Holdings plc*,[34] Potter LJ explained that:

---

[29] Ibid, at 255, citing Lord St Leonards in *Anderson v Fitzgerald* (1853) 4 HL Cas 484, at 510. See also, *Dobson v Sotheby* (1827) M & M 90. Note also the device of construing such statements in proposal forms as clauses descriptive of risk (considered below).

[30] *Zurich General Accident and Liability Insurance Co Ltd v Morrison* [1942] 2 KB 53 at 57–8 *per* Lord Greene MR.

[31] [1912] 1 KB 415.

[32] Ibid, at 430. See also, *Kennedy v Smith and Ansvar Insurance Co Ltd* 1976 SLT 110, at 116-117, in which the Lord President stated that, 'if insurers seek to limit their liability under a policy by relying upon an alleged undertaking as to the future prepared by them and accepted by an insured, the language they use must be such that the terms of the alleged undertaking and its scope are clearly and unambiguously expressed or plainly implied, and ... any such alleged undertaking will be construed, *in dubio, contra preferentem*.' See further, *Notman v Anchor Assurance Co* (1858) 4 CB NS 476 at 481, *per* Lord Cockburn CJ; *Fowkes v Manchester and London Life Assurance and Loan Association* (1863) 3 B & S 917 at 929, *per* Blackburn J; *Cook v Financial Insurance Co Ltd* [1998] 1 WLR 1765 at 1771, *per* Lord Lloyd of Berwick; *John A Pike (Butchers) Ltd v Independent Insurance Co Ltd* [1998] LRLR 410.

[33] *Yorke v Yorkshire Insurance* [1918] 1 KB 662. See also, *Kumar v Life Assurance Corporation of India* [1974] 1 Lloyd's Rep 147, in which the insured warranted that she had never had an operation. Kerr J held that a Caesarean delivery must, as a matter of ordinary and technical usage, be taken to be an 'operation'.

[34] [2000] Lloyd's Rep IR 159.

In relation to the exercise of construction to be undertaken by the court, the question of 'labelling' is influential rather than decisive, particularly if the label…has been applied to a number of terms of differing type and practical importance. On the other hand, if care and logic appear to have been applied in the attachment of the label to one term but not to another, the label (or absence of it) is likely to be decisive…[35]

It is common practice for insurers to subdivide the policy document into separate schedules, each of which will relate to different types of risk put on cover and each containing warranties. Where this is the case, the question arises whether each schedule will be construed in isolation from the rest of the policy document of which it forms an integral part. If the policy is construed as a whole, without its schedules being treated as distinct, then a breach of warranty contained in one schedule will enable the insurers to repudiate the contract even though the particular risk in question is covered by another schedule in the policy altogether. Typically, insurers argue, of course, that where there is a single policy any breach of warranty discharges them from liability notwithstanding the fact that the policy is multi-sectioned. However, the Court of Appeal has recently held that this is not necessarily the case. In *Printpak v AGF Insurance Ltd*,[36] the insured had effected a commercial inclusive policy which covered various types of risk for loss and damage in the event of a fire at the insured's print factory. When the insured claimed for fire loss, the insurer repudiated liability alleging arson and also arguing that it was discharged from liability because the fire had started while the burglar alarm had been switched off during building work in breach of a warranty requiring the alarm to be fully operational whenever the building was closed. It was held by the Court of Appeal that while the policy should be viewed as a single contract, nevertheless it was not a seamless document. The particular policy comprised separate schedules, each dealing with a different type of risk and having different section endorsements. The section dealing with cover against theft contained the alarm warranty as an endorsement. Given that the schedules described the endorsements as 'section endorsements' and that they were 'operative only as stated in the policy schedule,' the court took the view that these words limited the warranties to the individual sections. It therefore concluded that a breach of warranty in one section did not operate to invalidate cover under the other self-standing sections. The insurers were therefore held liable in respect of the fire claim. Hirst LJ explained that:

> it does not follow from the fact that the policy is a single contract that it is to be treated as a seamless contractual instrument. On the contrary, in the present case, its whole structure is based on its division into sections…The commercial inclusive endorsements are all stated in terms to be 'operative only as stated in the policy schedules.' In my judgment those words explicitly write the warranty into the relevant section in which it appears and not into the others…[37]

Although, as will be seen below, a breach of warranty terminates the risk under insurance contract, nevertheless in contrast to the general law of contract, it does not

---

[35] Ibid, at 165.
[36] [1999] Lloyd's Rep IR 542. See J Davey, [1999] *JBL* 580. *Cf James v CGU Insurance plc* [2002] Lloyd's Rep IR 206.
[37] Ibid, at 546.

necessarily entitle the insurer to waive the breach and claim damages instead.[38] In *West v National Motor and Accident Insurance Union Ltd*,[39] the insured, who had effected a household contents policy against burglary, declared that the full value of the contents was £500.00. The proposal form also required the insured to declare the value of jewellery if it exceeded one-third of the declared value of the contents. The insured's declarations were incorporated into the policy as warranties. Following a burglary, the insured claimed £612.00, which included £530.00 in respect of jewellery. The insurers, having rejected the claim, sought to rely on an arbitration clause in the policy. Lord Goddard CJ viewed the insurer's position as untenable, it being based upon the fallacy that while the company wished to repudiate the claim, they also expected to be able to affirm the contract. The learned judge commented:

> They have said that they do not repudiate the policy; they only repudiate the claim. I find that extremely difficult. I do not know how you can repudiate a claim, if the claim falls within the clear terms of the policy, unless you can disclaim the policy. ... They say: 'We have not repudiated it; we have affirmed it. We are not going to pay: we repudiate the claim.' I do not follow that at all. ... If ... the company do not want to pay that money, they have to say that there is a breach of warranty which avoids the policy, because so long as the policy stands their obligation to pay stands. Their obligation to pay in one sense depends upon the warranty in the policy. That is to say, they can avoid the policy [for its breach]... . but then they cannot at the same time say: 'We approve the policy.' Having approved the policy, in my opinion, they are liable under the terms of the policy to pay this amount.[40]

3.1 The basis of the contract clause

As with contracts under the general law, the terms of an insurance contract may be incorporated from a number of sources. For insurance contracts these will include the completed proposal form, the policy document and any renewal notices. As commented in chapter 4, a common method of creating warranties is by the inclusion of the so-called 'basis of the contract clause' at the foot of the proposal form whereby the questions and answers contained in the form, together with the insured's declarations, are stated to be the basis of the contract. Often the policy document will also contain such a clause.[41] The effect is to make truth and accuracy condition precedents to the validity of the contract and the issue of materiality is irrelevant.[42] If an answer is false, the insurer is discharged from liability.[43] Thus, in *Dawsons Ltd. v Bonnin*,[44] the House of Lords held that the insured's inaccurate statement, albeit made inadvertently, as to where the insured lorry was garaged entitled the insurer to repudiate liability even though the statement was immaterial to the risk. The proposal

---

[38] Cf the Sale of Goods Act, 1979 s 11(2). Waiver and estoppel are considered below at p 200.
[39] [1954] 2 Lloyd's Rep 461.
[40] Ibid, at 462–3. But note the impact of *The Good Luck*, above n 12, on this decision, see n 90 below, and associated text.
[41] See *Anderson v Fitzgerald*, above n 29.
[42] *McKay v London and General Insurance Co* (1935) 51 Lloyd's Rep 201. See RA Hasson, 'The Basis of the Contract Clause in Insurance Law' (1971) 34 *MLR* 29; J Birds, 'Warranties in Insurance Proposal Forms' [1977] *JBL* 231. See also, *Unipac (Scotland) Ltd v Aegon Insurance Co (UK) Ltd* [1999] Lloyd's Rep IR 502.
[43] *The Good Luck*, above n 12, considered below.
[44] Above, n 17.

form had stated that the insured's answers to questions contained therein constituted the basis of the contract.[45] Viscount Haldane observed that in this situation if the insurers can show:

> that they contracted to get an accurate answer to this question, and to make the validity of the policy conditional on that answer being accurate, whether the answer was of material importance or not, the fulfilment of this contract is a condition of the [insured] being able to recover.[46]

Criticism of the practice of cross-incorporation of terms from different sources into the insurance contract was voiced by the House of Lords in *Provincial Insurance Co Ltd v Morgan*.[47] The insured's answers to questions contained in the proposal form for motor insurance were declared to be the basis of the contract and therefore warranties, and the subsequent policy stated that the contents of the proposal form should be deemed to be promissory in nature and effect. Lord Wright observed that:

> Though this general scheme of policy has been, as it were, sanctified by long usage, it has often been pointed out by judges that it must be very puzzling to the assured, who may find it difficult to fit the disjointed parts together in such a way as to get a true and complete conspectus of what their rights and duties are and what acts on their part may involve a forfeiture of the insurance. An assured may easily find himself deprived of the benefits of the policy because he has done something quite innocently but in breach of a condition, ascertainable only by the dovetailing of scattered portions.[48]

Despite the weight of criticism levelled against this practice it seems likely to continue unabated. More particularly, the basis of the contract clause has itself attracted ardent criticism as a trap for the unwary. For example, in *Glicksman v Lancashire & General Insurance Co Ltd*,[49] Lord Wrenbury observed that:

> I think it a mean and contemptible policy on the part of an insurance company that it should take the premiums and then refuse to pay upon a ground which no one says was really material. Here, upon purely technical grounds, they, having in point of fact not been deceived in any material particular, avail themselves of what seems to me the contemptible defence that although they have taken the premiums, they are protected from paying.[50]

The draconian effects consequent upon breach of a basis of the contract clause was also considered in *Zurich General Accident and Liability Insurance Co Ltd v Morrison*.[51] The facts are curious when viewed from a contemporary standpoint. The Court of Appeal held that the proposer's failure to disclose to the insurers the fact

---

[45] However, the scope for relying on such clauses was restricted by the Statement of Insurance Practice, see below. Basis clauses are now governed by the FSA rules.
[46] Above, n 17 at 421. See also, the speech of Lord Blackburn in *Thomas v Weems*, above n 22 at 683, which was cited by Viscount Haldane at 423.
[47] Above, n 28. See also, eg, *Dawsons Ltd v Bonnin*, above n 17.
[48] Ibid, at 252.
[49] [1927] AC 139.
[50] Ibid, at 144–5. See also, *Joel v Law Union and Crown Insurance Co* [1908] 2 KB 863 at 885, *per* Fletcher Moulton LJ; *Mackay v London General Insurance Co* [1935] 51 Lloyd's Rep 201 at 202, *per* Swift J; *Anderson v Fitzgerald*, above n 29 at 507 and 514, *per* Lord St Leonards.
[51] Above, n 30.

that he had failed his driving test was not a material fact for a policy designed specifically for inexperienced drivers. For present purposes, the interest of the case lies in the view expressed most vehemently by Lord Greene MR who described the practice of using basis clauses as 'vicious'.[52]

The Law Commission, recommending reform of this area of insurance law, described basis of the contract clauses as 'a major mischief in the present law,'[53] and called for their abolition. The Commission took the view that such clauses, at least insofar as they apply to statements of past or present fact, can be objected to on three principal grounds. First, they allow for repudiation of the policy by insurers where inaccurate answers are immaterial to the risk insured. Secondly, insurers can repudiate for objectively inaccurate statements of fact even where the insured could not reasonably be expected to know or to have the means of knowing the true facts. Thirdly, such clauses allow for 'technical' repudiation by insurers, ie because basis clauses convert all answers furnished by the insured into warranties, the effect is that any inaccuracy, however insignificant and immaterial, means that insurers can repudiate the contract even if it concerned matters beyond the insured's knowledge or means of knowledge.[54]

Yet, despite these criticisms and the broad support which the Law Commission's recommendations attracted both in and outside Parliament, time was not found to intervene by way of statutory reform. Nevertheless, by way of response to the Commission's report, the insurance industry in 1986 revised the Statements of Insurance Practice first issued in 1977. In essence the revisions reflected the Law Commission's proposals. Paragraph 1(a) of the Statement of Insurance Practice 1986 provided that: 'The declaration at the foot of the proposal form should be restricted to completion according to the proposer's knowledge and belief... .' Paragraph 1(b) goes on to provide that: 'Neither the proposal form nor the policy shall contain any provision converting the statements as to past or present fact in the proposal form into warranties. ...' Paragraph 2(b)(iii) states that an insurer will not repudiate a policy on grounds of a breach of warranty or condition where the circumstances of the loss are unconnected with the breach 'unless fraud is involved.'

Taken together these provisions mitigated the effect of the basis clause in insurance policies so that, so far as individuals are concerned (ie consumers or non-business insureds), the harshness exemplified by the decision in *Dawsons v Bonnin*, for example, has now been largely addressed. But it should be noted that only those insurance companies who were members of the Association of British Insurers or of Lloyd's were party to the Statements.[55] Further, it is significant that the Statements were

---

[52] Ibid, at 58. See also, the speech of Lord Wright in *Provincial Insurance Co Ltd v Morgan*, above n 28, at 251–2.

[53] The Law Commission Report No 104, *Insurance Law, Non-Disclosure and Breach of Warranty,* 1980 (Cmnd 8064), para 7.5. See also, the Law Reform Committee Fifth Report, *Conditions and Exceptions in Insurance Policies*, Cmnd 62 (London, HMSO, 1957); and *Insurance Law Reform–The consumer case for a review of insurance law* (London, NCC 1997). Insurance contracts were granted immunity from the statutory controls contained in the Unfair Contract Terms Act 1977 (see ch 8, below). However, standard terms of a policy, including warranties, do come within the scope of the Unfair Terms in Consumer Contracts Regulations 1999 (SI 1999/2083), see ch 8, below. See further, J Adams, 'Basis of the Contract Clauses and the Consumer' [2000] *JBL* 203.

[54] Ibid.

[55] See further, A Forte, 'The Revised Statements of Insurance Practice' (1986) 49 *MLR* 754; and J Birds, 'Self-regulation and Insurance Contracts' in FD Rose (ed), *New Foundations for Insurance Law: Current Legal Problems* (London, Stevens & Sons, 1987).

restricted to insurance contracts effected by private individuals. While large business enterprises are probably less in need of protection, the exclusion of small businesses from their ambit was seen to represent a major lacuna in the non-statutory regime. However, the Insurance Ombudsman, now part of the Financial Services Ombudsman, in addition to handling complaints from consumers can also deal with complaints from businesses with a turnover of less than £1 million per annum. The Ombudsman does not generally allow repudiation in cases where the loss is unconnected with the breach of warranty or where the breach is minor. With the demise of the ABI's Statements in January 2005, 'basis clauses' are now governed by the FSA rules (see chapters 2 and 4).

---

4. The classification of warranties in insurance contracts

Insurance warranties can be classified into three types depending upon whether the insured's promise or undertaking relates to: (i) some past or existing state of affairs; (ii) some future state of affairs (iii) a warranty of opinion by the insured as to the truth of a fact.

Generally, a warranty as to some past or existing fact will arise from the information contained in the proposal form after due completion by the insured. It is a question of construction whether it is a warranty as to present facts, or whether it also extends to the future, in which case it is termed a 'promissory warranty' or 'continuing warranty'. The distinction is critical, for if a false warranty relates to a state of affairs existing at the time of the proposal, there is an effective breach which will entitle the insurer to terminate the contract from the moment of its conclusion. The appropriate analogy here is rescission for misrepresentation. Conversely, if the insured's statement was true when made, no action will lie for breach if there is a subsequent change in the state of affairs. In practice, however, the insured is often placed under a continuing duty to notify the insurer of any subsequent changes.

In determining whether, as a question of construction, a warranty is promissory in nature the courts have regard not only to the purpose of the warranty, but the purpose of the policy itself. Thus, in *Hair v Prudential Assurance Co Ltd*,[56] Woolf J held that a warranty in a fire policy that the insured premises were occupied could not be construed as amounting to a continuing obligation but rather as 'an indication of the state of affairs which existed at the time that the answers were given [and as such] they did not amount to a warranty that no change would occur.'[57] However, where a warranty is construed as being promissory in its effect, any breach will operate to terminate the insurer's liability as from the date of the breach only.[58] In *Beauchamp v National Mutual Indemnity Insurance Co*,[59] the proposal form asked 'Are any explosives used in your business?' The insured answered that there were none. This was

---

[56] [1983] 2 Lloyd's Rep. 667.
[57] Ibid, at 672.
[58] See *Provincial Insurance Co. v Morgan*, above n 28.
[59] [1937] 3 All ER 19.

correct at the time it was made but the insured, a builder, did subsequently use explosives when, for the first time in his business, he was contracted to demolish a building. It was held, as a matter of construction, that the question and its answer related to the future. Similarly, in *Hales v Reliance Fire and Accident Insurance Co*,[60] a question in the proposal form asked: 'Are any inflammable oils or goods used or kept on the premises?' The insured answered: 'Lighter fuel'. It was held that the question and answer were a warranty as to the existence of the fact at the time of the proposal and also during the currency of the risk. Accordingly, there was a breach when the insured took delivery of a quantity of fireworks 17 days prior to 5 November. McNair J accepted that warranties in fire and burglary policies as to the condition of the premises and precautions taken to prevent loss will prima facie be construed as continuing otherwise such warranties will be of little value to the insurers.[61] But this view is now open to question in the light of Saville LJ's interpretation of *Hales* in the recent decision in *Hussain v Brown*.[62] His Lordship took the view (based on decided cases,[63] and doubting the approach of McNair J in *Hales*) that questions contained in proposal forms which are constructed in the present tense cannot be taken to import warranties as to the future. Saville LJ stated that:

> there is no special principle of insurance law requiring answers in proposal forms to be read, *prima facie* or otherwise, as importing promises to the future. Whether or not they do depends upon ordinary rules of construction, namely consideration of the words the parties have used in the light of the context in which they have used them and (where the words admit of more than one meaning) selection of that meaning which seems most closely to correspond with the presumed intentions of the parties.[64]

The futurity of a warranty must therefore be manifestly apparent from the words used, and the tense in which the question is framed will be the material factor. In *Kennedy v Smith and Ansvar Ins Co Ltd*,[65] the insured warranted in a proposal for motor insurance that: 'I am a total abstainer from alcoholic drinks ...' which was true at the time it was made. However, after a cricket match the insured drank a small quantity of beer on an empty stomach. He then drove himself and two friends home. His vehicle was involved in an accident and his two passengers were killed. He sought an indemnity from his insurers for the delictual damages he was liable to pay, but the insurers refused the claim on the basis that a continuing warranty had been broken. It was held that the warranty related to the past and was not promissory as to the future. Construing the term *contra proferentem*, the Lord President said that:

---

[60] [1960] 2 Lloyd's Rep. 391.
[61] Ibid, at 395. See further, J Birds, 'Warranties in Insurance Proposal Forms' [1977] *JBL* 231 at 236–8.
[62] [1996] 1 Lloyd's Rep 627. Noted N Hird [1996] *JBL* 404.
[63] *Weber & Berger v Employers' Liability Assurance Corporation* (1926) 24 Lloyd's Rep 15 and *Woolfall & Rimmer v Moyle* [1942] 1 KB 66.
[64] Above n 62, at 629. It is noteworthy, at least in terms of gaining some insight into contemporary judicial thinking, that Saville LJ, at 630, went on to stress that, 'it must be remembered that a continuing warranty is a draconian term. As I have noted, the breach of such a warranty produces an automatic cancellation of the cover, and the fact that a loss may have no connection at all with that breach is simply irrelevant. In my view, if underwriters want such protection, then it is up to them to stipulate for it in clear terms.' See also *Kirkbride v Donner* [1974] 1 Lloyd's Rep 549.
[65] Above, n 32. See also *Woolfall & Rimmer v Moyle*, above n 63.

The statement does not require to be given a future promissory content to make it intelligible. It is quite intelligible if it is read literally for no doubt the risk during the period of insurance is reduced if at the outset the proposer is a total abstainer since it may reasonably be hoped that he is unlikely to abandon his principles. It would have been simple to include in the statement if this had been intended, that the insured shall continue to be a total abstainer for the period of the insurance. No such statement was, however, included and in my opinion is not, without undue straining of the language used, to be implied.[66]

Where the insured is an individual (ie, a consumer) as opposed to a business entity, warranties of opinion or belief are commonly encountered in proposal forms. The effect of this type of term is that the insured warrants that the answers given in the proposal form are true to the best of his belief and knowledge. The insured must exercise due care when completing the proposal form.[67] In contrast with warranties of fact, a warranty of opinion will only be broken if the insured is dishonest or reckless. For example, in *Confederation Life Assn v Miller*,[68] the insured warranted in a life policy that to the best of his knowledge and belief he had suffered no serious injury. Gwynne J held that this would be untrue only if the answer given was wilfully false.

Further, householders who insure possessions against theft or other loss are frequently required to estimate and warrant the value of specific items. Where this is the case, it has been held that the value of a possession, a stamp collection, is a matter of opinion so that provided the insured gave a bona fide estimate, the warranty would not be broken where a subsequent expert valuation showed the original estimate to be too low.[69] As has been noted above, so far as non-business insureds (consumers) are concerned, the Statement of Insurance Practice 1986 requires the basis of the contract clause found at the foot of proposal forms to be framed as warranties of opinion only.

---

5. Terms descriptive of the risk

It is important to distinguish promissory warranties from terms which describe or limit the risk, sometimes called 'exceptions'. It is common practice for insurers to reduce the scope of the risk insured by listing excepted perils. The effect of such terms is merely to suspend the insurance cover during the period in which the insured engages in an excepted risk. Further, if the insured's loss is not proximately caused by an excepted peril, the insured may still be able to recover under the policy. It will be recalled that in *Provincial Insurance v Morgan*,[70] the proposer for a motor policy stated in the proposal form that the lorry to be insured was to be used for delivering

---

[66] Ibid, at 117.
[67] *Huddleston v R.ACV Insurance Property Ltd* [1975] VR 683. See J Birds, 'Warranties in Insurance Proposal Forms' [1977] *JBL* 231.
[68] (1887) 14 SCR 330.
[69] *Timms v Fai Insurances Ltd* (1976) 12 ALR 506.
[70] Above, n 28.

coal. The insured warranted the truth of his answers and the proposal form was made the basis of the contract. At the time of the accident, the lorry was carrying coal although earlier that day, it had been used to carry timber. The insured's claim was repudiated by the insurers who argued that there had been a breach of warranty. It was held by the House of Lords that the statement in the proposal form did not amount to a warranty but was merely descriptive of the risk insured. Lord Russell stated that the insured's statements could be read as nothing more than mere statements of 'intentions as to the use of the vehicle and the goods to be carried in it... .'[71]

Farr v Motor Traders' Mutual Insurance Society,[72] provides a clear illustration of the point. The claimant, answering a question in the proposal form which contained a basis of contract clause, stated that the insured taxi-cabs were only driven in one shift per twenty four hours. This was true at the time the statement was made. However, when one of the two cabs was off the road for repairs, the other was driven in two shifts during the day. Subsequently, when the repairs were completed and the two cabs were being driven in only one shift, one of them was involved in an accident and the insured claimed. The insurers argued that that the policy was void for breach of warranty. It was held that the claimant's answer was merely descriptive of risk and was not a promissory warranty. Although cover was suspended during the time when the vehicle was driven in two shifts, cover had resumed at the time of the accident so that the insurers were liable.

In motor insurance effected for non-business use, the policy typically restricts cover to when the vehicle is being used for 'social, domestic and pleasure' purposes only, the effect of such a clause is to suspend cover should the insured use the vehicle for some other purpose which has a business element.[73] When considering whether the insured's use of a vehicle at the time of the loss was for 'social, domestic and pleasure purposes,' the court will examine the true purpose of the journey to determine whether cover was suspended. Thus, in *Seddon v Binions*,[74] Roskill LJ observed that the court should look at the 'essential or predominant character' of the insured's use at the time of the loss.[75] In a similar vein, Megaw LJ looked to 'the primary purpose' of the relevant journey to see whether it could 'properly or fairly be described as use for social, domestic and pleasure purposes.'[76] If, therefore, the essential character of the journey was of a business nature, the loss will not be covered. Where insurance cover for a motor vehicle is restricted, for example, to when it is being used for 'social, domestic and pleasure purposes *and* for the business of the insured' and at the time of the loss the vehicle is being used by the insured's work colleague on employers business, the insured will not be covered. The words 'for the business of the insured' restricts cover to the insured's business use only, not that of her colleague.[77] But where the insured, as a courtesy, gives a lift to someone who was carrying on some business, the insured's use of the vehicle would nevertheless continue to be social even though the passenger was assisted in carrying on hisbusiness by receiving that lift.[78]

[71] Ibid, at 278.
[72] [1920] 3 KB 669.
[73] *Wood v General Accident Fire and Life Assurance Corporation Ltd* (1948) 82 Lloyd's Law Rep 77.
[74] [1978] 1 Lloyd's Rep 381. See *Caple v Sewell* [2002] Lloyd's Rep IR 627.
[75] Ibid, at 385.
[76] Ibid, at 386.
[77] *Passmore v Vulcan Boiler & General Insurance Co Ltd* (1936) 54 Ll L Rep 92.
[78] Ibid, at 94, *per* Du Parcq J.

It seems that as with the law of contract generally, the nature of a particular term is always a question of law based on the court's construction of the wording used and no doubt taking account of the consequences of the breach.[79] In *De Maurier (Jewels) Ltd v Bastion Insurance Co*,[80] an all risk policy contained a 'warranty' that the insured's vehicles would be fitted with approved locks and alarm systems. The insured suffered two losses. When the first loss occurred, the locks were not of the required type but by the time of the second loss there was compliance with the term. The insurers denied liability on the basis, inter alia, that the policy was voidable *ab initio* for breach of a promissory warranty, and was avoided by them two days after the second loss. However, during the course of the trial the insurers admitted liability in respect of the second loss. It was held by Donaldson J that as a matter of construction of the so-called 'warranty', it was merely a term describing the risk, so that the insurers were not liable for the first loss, the policy being suspended by the breach, but were right to admit liability for the second loss. In *C.T.N. Cash & Carry v General Accident*,[81] the court took the opportunity to again lay down explicit guidelines to the construction of contractual terms. A burglary insurance policy effected by the insureds on their cash and carry depots contained the term that: 'It is warranted that the secure cash kiosk shall be attended and locked at all times during business hours.' It was held that the clause was not a warranty but a term descriptive of risk. Macpherson J, having reviewed the authorities,[82] defined a warranty as a term which goes to the root of the contract, the breach of which therefore entitles the insurers to avoid liability under the policy. The fact that the insurers used the word 'warranty' was not sufficient to convert the term into one which is so fundamental to the contract, that it goes to its root.[83]

In *Kler Knitwear Ltd v Lombard General Insurance Co Ltd*,[84] the judge adopted the phrase 'suspensive condition' to describe the effect of a term in the policy which was stipulated to be a warranty. The insured, a hosiery and knitwear company with premises in Leicester, effected a policy with the defendants which contained, inter alia, the following sprinkler installations warranty: 'It is warranted that within 30 days of renewal 1998 the sprinkler installations at the Jellicoe Rd/Gough Rd/Spalding Rd locations must be inspected by a LPC approved sprinkler engineer with all necessary rectification work commissioned within 14 days of the inspection report being received.' The sprinkler installations were not inspected within the required 30 days of renewal but rather about 60 days after. The insured premises at Jellicoe Road were damaged by a storm and the claimant sought to recover under the policy for his losses arising from damage to raw materials and finished goods and from disruption of the business. The insurers rejected the claim on the basis that the sprinkler inspection clause is a true contractual warranty. Morland J, citing Saville LJ in *Hussain v*

---

[79] See *Wallis, Son & Wells v Pratt and Haynes*, above n. 2.
[80] [1967] 2 Lloyd's Rep. 550.
[81] Above, n 24.
[82] Citing, in particular, from the judgment of Bankes LJ in *Roberts v Anglo Saxon Insurance Co* [1927] KB 590.
[83] In *Roberts v Anglo Saxon Insurance Co* (1926) 26 Ll L Rep 154, at 157, MacKinnon J stated that 'nothing turns upon the use of the word "warranted" [which is] always used with the greatest ambiguity in a policy.'
[84] [2000] Lloyd's Rep IR 47.

Brown,[85] came to 'the clear and unhesitating conclusion' that the so-called 'warranty' was, on its true construction, merely a suspensive condition. However, the decision is open to doubt. General Condition 2 of the policy provided that:

> every Warranty to which this Insurance or any Section thereof is or may be made subject shall from the time the Warranty attaches apply and continue to be in force during the whole currency of this Insurance and non-compliance with any such Warranty; whether it increases the risk or not, or whether it be material or not to a claim, shall be a bar to any claim in respect of such property or item, provided that whenever this Insurance is renewed a claim in respect of Damage occurring during the renewal period shall not be barred by reason of a Warranty not having been complied with at any time before the commencement of such period.

It thus ascribed a label to the term, it stated when the warranty attached and the consequences of breach.[86] Given that this was a commercial contract, one is left wondering what else the insurers needed to do to achieve their purpose.

---

6. The consequences of a breach of warranty

The nature and effect of a breach of insurance warranty was subjected to detailed consideration by the House of Lords in *Bank of Nova Scotia v Hellenic Mutual War Risks Association (Bermuda) Ltd, The Good Luck*.[87] The facts of the case are complex but put simply, the owner of the ship, the 'Good Luck', insured it with the defendant association and effected a mortgage on the vessel through the claimant bank, to which the benefit of the insurance was assigned. The defendants undertook to notify the assignee bank promptly in the event that 'the association ceases to insure' the vessel. In breach of warranty the ship sailed into the Arabian Gulf where on 6 June 1982 it was hit by Iraqi missiles which resulted in it being a constructive total loss. Both parties knew of the attack on the ship but the defendants, having discovered the breach of warranty, failed to notify the bank. In the meantime the bank, believing that the loss was covered by insurance, made further advances to the shipowners, however, such further loans would not have been made had the bank been advised that the insurance had ceased. The bank sued the association for damages in respect of its breach of undertaking.

Lord Goff of Chieveley, delivering the principal speech,[88] took as the starting point of his analysis of the consequences of a breach of warranty the wording of sections 33 and 34 of the Marine Insurance Act 1906. Section 33(1) provides, so far as material: 'A warranty ... means a promissory warranty, that is to say, a warranty by

---

[85] Above, n 62. See also, n 64, and the text therein.
[86] See, eg, *Virk v Gan Life Holdings plc*, above n 34.
[87] Above, n 12. See H Bennett [1991] *JBL* 598; J Birds (1991) 107 *LQR* 540; M Clarke [1991] *LMCLQ* 437. See further, J Birds, 'Insurance Contracts' in J Birds, R Bradgate and C Villiers (eds), *Termination of Contracts* (Chichester, Wiley Chancery, 1995).
[88] Lord Bridge, Lord Brandon, Lord Oliver and Lord Lowry concurring.

which the assured undertakes that some particular thing shall or shall not be done, or that some condition shall be fulfilled, or whereby he affirms or negatives the existence of a particular state of facts.' As has been noted,[89] section 33(3) provides, inter alia, that where there has been a breach of warranty on the part of the insured, the insurer 'is discharged from liability as from the date of the breach of warranty, but without prejudice to any liability incurred by him before that date.' Section 34(3) states that a 'breach of warranty may be waived by the insurer.' In Lord Goff's view, the meaning of section 33(3) is unequivocal:

> Those words are clear. They show that discharge of the insurer from liability is automatic and is not dependent upon any decision by the insurer to treat the contract or the insurance as at an end; though under section 34(3), the insurer may waive the breach of warranty.[90]

Going on to cite Lord Blackburn in *Thomson v Weems*,[91] Lord Goff drew the distinction between conditions as fundamental terms of a contract and conditions precedent, noting that compliance with an insurance warranty is a condition precedent to the attaching of the risk.[92] He stressed that if an insured is in breach of a promissory warranty, the effect is to discharge the insurer from liability 'as from the date of the breach, for the simple reason that fulfilment of the warranty is a condition precedent to the liability of the insurer.'[93] Lord Goff convincingly reasoned that this conclusion is in accord with the rationale of insurance warranties, namely 'that the insurer only accepts the risk provided the warranty is fulfilled.'[94] His Lordship continued by pointing out that a promissory warranty is in effect a promissory condition precedent, non-fulfilment of which will not prevent the contract from coming into existence. Thus, since the insurer's liability is discharged from the date of the breach and the contract is not avoided *ab initio*, the result is that the insured's obligations, for example to pay a premium, may survive the insurer's discharge from liability.[95] Lord Goff also went on to explain that an insured's breach of promissory warranty does not entitle the insurer to avoid the contract of insurance, or to repudiate it. He thought that such terminology, inappropriate as it is, probably derived from the fact that an insurer can waive such a breach. Lord Goff added that 'it is only in the sense of repudiating liability (and not of repudiating the policy) that it would be right to describe him as being entitled to repudiate. ... the insurer, as the Act provides, is simply discharged from liability as from the date of the breach, with the effect that thereupon he has a good defence to a claim by the assured.'[96] The question whether breach of warranty also resulted in automatic discharge from liability in non-marine insurance was not addressed by the House of Lords. However, in *HIH Casualty and*

---

[89] See n 12, above, and associated text.
[90] Above n 12, at 262.
[91] Above, n 22.
[92] See, eg, *Gerling Konzern General Insurance Co v Polygram Holdings Inc* [1998] 2 Lloyd's Rep 544.
[93] Above, n 12, at 262–3. The burden of proof is on the insurer who alleges that there has been a breach of warranty or condition, *Barrett v Jermy* (1849) 3 Ex 535 at 542, *per* Parke B.
[94] Ibid, at 263.
[95] Non-fulfilment of a condition precedent at the time when the insurance contract is concluded prevents it taking effect because 'there is in reality no contract,' *Newcastle Fire Insurance Co v Macmorran & Co* (1815) 3 Dow 255 at 259, *per* Lord Eldon. Liability will be repudiated by the insurers by virtue of the breach of warranty which will therefore constitute 'a good defence' to the insured's claim; *per* Lord Goff, ibid, at 264. See also, *Unipac (Scotland) Ltd v Aegon Insurance Co (UK) Ltd* [1999] Lloyd's Rep IR 502.
[96] Above, n 12, at 264.

General Insurance Ltd v New Hampshire Insurance Co,[97] Rix LJ proceeded on the basis that it did:

> it is well established that a breach of warranty produces an automatic discharge of a contract of insurance from the moment of breach [citing *The Good Luck*]...Once this is appreciated, it becomes readily understandable that, if a promissory warranty is not complied with, the insurer is discharged from liability as from the date of the breach of warranty, for the simple reason that fulfilment of the warranty is a condition precedent to the liability of the insurer. This moreover reflects the fact that the rationale of warranties in insurance law is that the insurer only accepts the risk provided that the warranty is fulfilled. This is entirely understandable; and it follows that the immediate effect of a breach of a promissory warranty is to discharge the insurer from liability as from the date of the breach.[98]

Where the insurers claim to avoid the policy *ab initio* the insured is entitled to the return of premiums paid unless the insured's non-disclosure or misrepresentation was fraudulent.[99] This is because the insurer was never exposed to the risk. However, where the policy provides for forfeiture of premiums in the event of a breach of warranty because, for example, the insured gave incorrect answers to questions in the proposal form, such a term is enforceable even in the absence of fraud and notwithstanding that such a term might be construed as a penalty.[100]

---

7. Breach of warranty: the waiver–estoppel dichotomy

Section 34(3) of the 1906 Act provides that a 'breach of warranty may be waived by the insurer.' In *The Good Luck*, Lord Goff said that the effect of this provision 'is that, to the extent of waiver, the insurer cannot rely upon the breach as having discharged him from liability.'[101] However, taking the decision of the House of Lords in this case, namely that an insured's breach of warranty automatically discharges the insurer from liability as from the date of the breach, the language of waiver seems no longer appropriate. This is because waiver implies that an election is made by the insurer not to treat liability as discharged by the breach. Since liability is automatically discharged, clearly there is no election to make unless the contract itself provides for waiver. In general therefore, the terminology of estoppel is more apt so

---

[97] Above, n 25.
[98] Ibid, at 184–5, [122]. See also, *HIH Casualty and General Insurance Ltd v AXA Corporate Solutions* [2002] Lloyd's Rep IR 325, *per* Jules Sher QC. NB the curious consequences that can result from automatic termination. *Eg* if the insured is late in paying the premium, the risk discharges but the premium still has to be paid: see *Chapman v Kadirga* [1998] Lloyd's Rep IR 377.
[99] *Anderson v Fitzgerald*, above n 29.
[100] *Kumar v Life Insurance Corp of India*, above n 33, at 154, *per* Kerr J applying *Duckett v Williams* (1834) 2 Cromp & M 348; *Thomson v Weems*, above n 22; *Sparenborg v Edinburgh Life Assurance Company* [1912] 1 KB 195. The judge said that, 'These cases clearly show that it is settled law that if the provision is clear and explicit and provides for the forfeiture of a premium in the event of a proposal form or similar document being incorrectly answered, such a provision can be enforced by the insurance company even in the absence of fraud.'
[101] Above n 12, at 263.

that, strictly speaking, the insurer can be estopped from pleading breach of warranty in defence to a claim. The classic formulation of estoppel insofar as it operates in the insurance law context was made by Lord Goff in *Motor Oil Hellas (Corinth) Refineries S.A. v Shipping Corporation of India, The Kanchenjunga*,[102] who said:

> Equitable estoppel occurs where a person, having legal rights against another, unequivocally represents (by words or conduct) that he does not intend to enforce those legal rights; if in such circumstances the other party acts, or desists from acting, in reliance upon that representation, with the effect that it would be inequitable for the representor thereafter to enforce his legal rights inconsistently with his representation, he will to that extent be precluded from doing so.[103]

Thus, although the term 'waiver' is used in much of the case law, the position should now be viewed from the perspective of estoppel. Later in his speech, Lord Goff took the opportunity to explore the similarities and distinctions between the principles of waiver (where the insurer elects to affirm the contract) on the one hand, and estoppel on the other. An important point of similarity between the two being that each requires an unequivocal representation because each may result in a loss, whether permanent or temporary, of the other party's rights. There are, however, a number of distinctions between the two principles. Election applies when a party becomes entitled to exercise a right, and has to make an informed choice as to whether or not to exercise the right. Once made, the election is final and in no way depends upon reliance upon it by the other party. Turning to estoppel, Lord Goff said:

> equitable estoppel requires an unequivocal representation by one party that he will not insist upon his legal rights against the other party, and such reliance by the representee as will render it inequitable for the representor to go back upon his representation.[104]

Where the insured seeks to raise estoppel so as to prevent an insurer repudiating liability on the basis of breach of warranty, the burden of proof is on the insured. The point was stressed by Bowen LJ in *Bentsen v Taylor Sons & Co (No 2)*,[105] that: 'In order to succeed, the [claimant] must show, either that he has performed the condition precedent, the onus being on him, or that the defendants have excused the performance of the condition...'[106]

It has been seen that any representation relied upon by the insured, whether by words or conduct, must be clear and unambiguous. In practice, such representation will often arise by way of conduct so that where the insurer, with knowledge of the breach,[107] renews the policy or continues to accept premiums, or processes a claim,

---

[102] [1990] 1 Lloyd's Rep 391. See also, *Peyman v Lanjani* [1985] 1 Ch 457.
[103] Ibid, at 399, citing *Hughes v Metropolitan Railway Co* (1877) 2 App Cas 439. See also, *McCormick v National Motor & Accident Insurance Union Ltd* (1934) 49 Ll LR 361 at 371, *per* Slesser LJ.
[104] Ibid.
[105] [1893] 2 QB 274.
[106] Ibid, at 283. See also, *Brook v Trafalgar Insurance Co Ltd* (1947) 79 Ll LR 365 at 367, *per* Scott LJ.
[107] In *Hadenfayre Ltd v British National Insurance Society Ltd* [1984] 2 Lloyd's Rep 393 at 400, *per* Lloyd J, citing *CTI v Oceanus Mutual Underwriting Association (Bermuda) Ltd* [1984] 1 Lloyd's Rep 476, stressed that 'the question is whether [the insurers had] full knowledge of the relevant facts. Constructive notice is not, of course, enough; it is not enough that the defendants were put on enquiry.'

the insurer may be estopped from denying the insured's claim. The question of the insurers knowledge is critical, particularly in view of the fact that insurers operate through agents and employees, and the issue becomes one of attribution of an agent's or employee's knowledge to the insurer. For example, in *Ayrey v British Legal and United Provident Assurance Co Ltd*,[108] a clause in the proposal form for life insurance provided that if any information was withheld which should be made known to the insurer, the policy would be rendered absolutely void. The insured described himself in the proposal form as a fisherman, his usual occupation. The fact that he was also a member of the Royal Naval Reserve, which exposed him to additional risks was not disclosed. However, his wife did inform the insurer's district manager of this fact who continued to accept the premiums on behalf of the insurer. When the insured was killed at sea during a mine sweeping operation, the insurer repudiated liability. It was held that the district manager's knowledge of the true facts could be imputed to his employers. Lawrence J stated that it was 'a reasonable thing for her to assume that the making of that communication to the district manager was equivalent to informing the company's head office.'[109]

In *Evans v Employers Mutual Insurance Association Ltd*,[110] incorrect answers in the proposal form for motor insurance were warranted to be true. When the insured claimed under the policy the true facts were stated in the claims form which was given to the insurers' claims superintendent who, in accordance with office practice, passed the form together with the insured's original proposal to a clerk for the purpose of checking the statements they contained and noting any discrepancies. Although the clerk noticed the discrepancy he did not call attention to it, believing it to be of no importance. Having paid the insured but before paying out the third party claims, another employee noticed the discrepancy and the insurers sought to repudiate liability. The issue before the court was whether the insurers had knowledge of the truth. In holding that the insurers did have the requisite knowledge, Greer LJ said that:

> A limited company cannot know anything itself except through its agents or servants. The knowledge which is to be attributed to a company must be the knowledge of some agent or servant. ... If it be established by evidence that the duty of investigating and ascertaining facts has been delegated in the ordinary course of the company's business to a subordinate official, the company will in law be bound by his knowledge...[111]

Greer LJ went on to explain an alternative ground for the court's finding namely, that providing the insured communicated with the insurers in a manner laid down by them, the insurers could not then say 'they had no knowledge of its contents because no authorised official read it.'[112] The central issue then is whether the knowledge of a subordinate can be attributed to the insurers so as to estop them from asserting breach of warranty. In *Wing v Harvey*,[113] the agent of an insurance company received payments from a person outside Europe without raising the objection that the policy contained a term making it void if the insured went outside the limits of Europe without permission. The assignee of the policy, upon paying the premium to an agent

---

[108] [1918] 1 KB 136.
[109] Ibid, at 140.
[110] [1936] 1 KB 505.
[111] Ibid, at 515.
[112] Ibid, at 516. See also the judgment of Roche LJ at 521.
[113] (1854) 5 De G M & G 265.

at the place where the policy had been effected, informed him that the insured was living in Canada. The agent stated that this would not avoid the policy, and continued receiving premiums until the insured died. The premiums were, in turn, remitted to the insurers office in London which received the moneys without having notice of the insured's residence beyond the prescribed limits. It was held that the insurers could not repudiate liability. Knight-Bruce LJ was of the view that whether or not the agent had informed the insurers of the true state of affairs in which the premiums were paid to him, the directors were nevertheless affected with notice that the insured had moved to Canada.

The issue of estoppel recently arose in *HIH Casualty and General Insurance Ltd v AXA Corporate Solutions.*[114] It will be recalled that after payment had been made by HIH to the insured the Court of Appeal in *HIH Casualty and General Insurance Ltd v New Hampshire Insurance Co,*[115] held that a term in the policy which stated that six films would be made was a warranty. Following this decision, the reinsurers realised that the defence of breach of warranty was available to them. The issue of estoppel arose from the allegation that the reinsurers had, prior to HIH meeting the insured's claim, knowledge that less than six films had been made. The Court of Appeal, upholding the decision of the trial judge, could find no clear and unequivocal representation on the part of AXA so as to support a finding of waiver.[116] Since neither party had been aware of the breach of warranty, it was impossible for the reinsurers to have made a representation that they did not intend to rely on it. It was, therefore, not open to the reinsured to regard any communication from the reinsurers as amounting to such a representation.

8. Conditions

Conditions may be classified as either conditions precedent to the validity of the contract, conditions precedent to recovery or merely as collateral stipulations, although, as will be seen, the courts have recently imported the notion of 'innominate terms' from the general law of contract. A condition precedent to validity will often impose a continuing obligation on the insured, for example in motor insurance the insured will be required to maintain the vehicle in a road worthy condition and to ensure that the vehicle has a valid MOT test certificate. Breach of this type of condition will entitle the insurer to repudiate liability although the insurer may, of course, be estopped from relying on the breach, or the insurer may waive the breach and elect to affirm the contract.[117] The Court of Appeal has recently been called upon to construe a widely drafted condition precedent. In *Kazakstan Wool Processors (Europe) Ltd v*

---

[114] [2003] Lloyd's Rep IR 1.
[115] Above, n 25.
[116] For waiver in relation to a condition precedent, see, eg, *Barrett Bros (Taxis) Ltd v Davies* [1966] 1 WLR 1334.
[117] *Hain SS v Tate & Lyle* (1936) 52 TLR 619; *Jones v Provincial Insurance Co Ltd* (1929) 35 Ll LR 135; *Hemmings v Sceptre Life* [1905] 1 Ch 365; *Bentsen v Taylor* [1893] 2 QB 274; *Ayrey v British Legal and United Provident Assurance Co*, above n 108; *The Kanchenjunga* above n 102.

Nederlandsche Credietverzekering Maatschappij NV,[118] the policy contained a term, Article 13, to the effect that in the event of any breach of condition precedent the insurers would have the right to retain any premium paid and give written notice terminating the policy. Payment of premiums was stated to be a condition precedent to liability and the parties were in dispute over non-payment of premiums due. The insurers argued that Article 13 entitled them to deny liability for any claims including those that had been met when the insureds were in compliance. They therefore requested the return of an earlier payment. The insured argued, on the other hand, that it was unreasonable to construe Article 13 as permitting the insurers to retrospectively avoid liability in respect of risks that had attached prior to the breaches. The Court of Appeal rejected the insurers' contention. Peter Gibson LJ said:

> I can accept that all liability under the policy does not include liabilities which have crystallised and been paid. It is inappropriate to refer to terminating such a liability. Indeed it may be questioned whether it is a liability at all once it has been discharged. I can also accept that if a liability has accrued unconditionally, for example if the insurer has delayed payment after it became due, it will not be caught by the termination. It cannot have been contemplated that the insurer could benefit from its own breach. But it is hard to see how all future or contingent liabilities under the policy are not terminated on the plain wording of the clause...[119]

Conditions precedent to recovery generally impose requirements to be complied with by the insured when a loss arises, for example that a claim is made within a specified time limit and that the insurers receive specified particulars of the loss. Breach of such a condition does not entitle the insurer to terminate the contract but merely to avoid liability for a particular claim.[120] If the insured, in breach of such a condition, fails to notify the insurers of the particulars of a loss, but the insurers are nevertheless in possession of all relevant facts by virtue of being informed by, for example, the police, the court can excuse the insured's breach.[121] For example, in *Lickiss v Milestone Motor Policies at Lloyd's*,[122] a motor cyclist claimed an indemnity from the insurers in respect of damages he was required to pay to a third party arising from an accident caused by the insured's negligence in which he damaged a taxi-cab. The policy contained a condition which provided that 'full particulars' should be communicated to the insurance company 'as soon as possible after the occurrence of any accident ... and shall forward immediately any ... notice of intended prosecution.' The accident occurred on 17 May 1964 and the insured received a notice of intended prosecution but did not inform his insurers. In the meantime the insurers received a letter from the police, dated 18 June, notifying them of the proceedings. By letter dated 23 June the insurers wrote to the insured explaining that: 'We understand that proceedings are being taken against you on 2 July ... . It would be appreciated if you would let us know why you have not notified us of these

---

[118] [2000] Lloyd's Rep IR 371.
[119] Ibid, at 380.
[120] *Hood's Trustees v Southern Union General Insurance Co of Australasia* [1928] Ch. 793. Unless the policy contains a clause converting all such conditions into 'conditions precedent to any liability of the company to make any payment': see *Cox v Orion Insurance Co* [1982] RTR 1.
[121] *Barrett Bros.(Taxis) Ltd v Davies* [1966] 1 WLR 1334, *sub nom Lickiss v Milestone Motor Policies at Lloyd's* [1966] 2 All ER 972.
[122] Ibid.

proceedings since we will wish to arrange your defence.' Subsequently, the insurers denied liability on the basis that the insured was in breach of condition in not notifying them of the intended prosecution. It was held by the Court of Appeal that the letter of 23 June constituted a waiver by the insurers of the insured's breach. Lord Denning MR said:

> The principle of waiver is simply this: that if one party by his conduct leads another to believe that the strict rights arising under the contract will not be insisted on, intending that the other should act on that belief, and he does act on it, then the first party will not afterwards be allowed to insist on the strict rights when it would be inequitable for him to do so ... .By not asking for the documents, they as good as said that they did not want them. So he did not send them. I do not think that they should be allowed now to complain of not receiving them.[123]

In general, the courts are reluctant to construe a clause as a condition precedent to liability given the severe consequences that may flow from such a finding. Accordingly, unless the wording is absolutely clear – and for this purpose, calling a term a 'condition precedent' will not necessarily suffice – the courts will reject the argument that a condition is a 'condition precedent'.[124] *Charter Reinsurance Ltd v Fagan*,[125] is a paradigm case. The Court of Appeal held, in respect of a reinsurance policy under which the reinsurers (members of Lloyd's syndicates) were not to be liable to make payment to the reinsured until the reinsured 'shall actually have paid' its own policy-holders, that the wording of the 'to be paid clause' was sufficiently ambiguous so as not to give rise to a condition precedent, and accordingly the reinsured was entitled to recover from the reinsurer on proof of its liability to make payment rather than on having made payment. The reinsurers appealed unsuccessfully to the House of Lords. In holding that they were liable on the policy, Lord Mustill stressed that the words in question must be construed in the context of the policy as a whole. As such, the wording could not be taken to be concerned with the time of payments made by the reinsured to the insured, but rather with the quantification of the sums for which the reinsured was liable. Lord Mustill stated that:

> the purpose of 'the sum actually paid' ... is not to impose an additional condition precedent in relation to the disbursement of funds, but to emphasize that it is the ultimate outcome of the net loss calculation which determines the final liability of the syndicates under the policy.[126]

In his view therefore, term 'the sum actually paid' should be construed to mean 'the sum for which the reinsurer is liable under the reinsurance policy in the event that its liability is finally ascertained.'[127] Lord Mustill adopted a more restrictive approach than the trial judge, Mance J, the Court of Appeal and, indeed, Lord Hoffmann. In

---

[123] Ibid, at 975.
[124] See, eg, *George Hunt Cranes Ltd v Scottish Boiler & General Insurance Co Ltd* [2002] Lloyd's Rep IR 178. Further, the courts will interpret a condition precedent strictly and, in the case of ambiguity, it will be construed in favour of the insured: *Cornhill Insurance v D E Stamp Felt Roofing* [2002] Lloyd's Rep IR 648.
[125] [1997] AC 313. The House of Lords decision is noted by M Clarke [1996] *LMCLQ* 433.
[126] Ibid, at 757.
[127] Ibid, at 761.

construing the words in the context of the policy as a whole his Lordship expressly refused to take into account the underlying purpose of reinsurance contracts and the practical concerns of the reinsurance industry.

A clause in a policy which, on its construction, does not easily sit with any of the above categories will be held to be a collateral term not necessarily giving the right to repudiate the contract.[128] In *Alfred McAlpine plc v BAI (Run-Off) Ltd*,[129] the Court of Appeal enlisted the terminology of 'innominate terms' from the general law of contract in order to classify a notice of loss clause, condition 1(a), which required the insured to give notice of a claim under the policy 'as soon as possible.' Waller LJ explained that condition 1(a) was not so fundamental that its breach amounted to a repudiation of the whole contract. Citing the judgment of Giles J in *Trans-Pacific Insurance Co (Australia) Ltd v Grand Union Insurance Co Ltd*,[130] he said:

> It seems to me that condition 1(a) does not have what Giles J described as a quality of 'essentiality' for the reasons he gave in relation to the co-operation clause in that case. He said that it must have been obvious that there could be major or minor failures to co-operate, disagreement on what did or did not amount to co-operation, or breaches which could be readily rectified without any prejudice to the reinsurer. The same goes for the supply of details. Indeed this case exemplifies how a breach may be major or minor in that certainly some details were supplied to BAI and details which would have been sufficient to enable BAI to make such enquiries as it needed.[131]

If the breach of an innominate term is insufficiently serious to justify repudiation of the policy or a claim, insurers are left with the option of pursuing an action for damages. In practice such a claim will rarely be worth pursuing because any award is unlikely to be substantial and often, of course, the insured may lack sufficient means to make it worthwhile proceeding against him. However, in a significant recent case, *Friends Provident Life & Pensions Ltd v Sirius*,[132] the Court of Appeal (Waller LJ, not surprisingly, dissenting) rejected the views expressed in the *BAI* case to the effect that a breach of an innominate term in a policy might enable an insurer to defeat a claim. In *Friends Provident* the term in question was also a claims notification clause.[133] Mance LJ, delivering the leading judgment, held that Waller LJ's views in BAI were not binding because they were made obiter.[134] Agreeing with Moore-Bick J's finding that the clause in question was an innominate term, he nevertheless rejected the trial judge's conclusion that breach of such a clause, if sufficiently serious, would entitle the insurers to avoid liability for the claim. Mance LJ stated that there was no reason for the Court to construct 'a new doctrine of partial repudiatory breach'. A

---

[128] *Re Bradley and Essex and Suffolk Accident Indemnity Society* [1912] 1 KB 415.
[129] [2000] Lloyd's Rep IR 352. For criticism of the decision, see J Davey [2001] *JBL* 179.
[130] (1989) 18 NSWLR 675.
[131] Above n 128, at 444, [31]. This approach was approved by the Court of Appeal in *K/S Marc-Scandia XXXXII v Certain Lloyd's Underwriters Subscribing to Lloyd's Policy No. 25t 105487 and Ocean Marine Insurance Co Ltd (The' Mercandian Continent')* [2003] EWCA Civ 1275, *per* Longmore LJ. See also, *Friends Provident Life and Pensions Ltd v Sirius International Insurance Corp* [2004] EWHC 1799 (Comm). See further, Sir Andrew Longmore, 'Good faith and breach of warranty: are we moving forwards or backwards?' [2004] *LMCLQ* 158.
[132] [2005] Lloyd's Rep IR 135.
[133] See chapter 10, below.
[134] For the same reason Mance LJ also rejected Longmore LJ's approval of *BAI* expressed in *The Mercandian Continent* [2001] EWCA Civ 1275.

sufficiently serious breach of an innominate term could only ever lead to the discharge of the entire policy, not a particular claim. If insurers wish to make such a clause a condition precedent to their liability they must do so in unequivocal language. Mance LJ's views were not obiter, but a ruling on innominate terms by a unanimous Court of Appeal or by the House of Lords would, in the interests of certainty, be welcome.

Construing the Terms of the Insurance Contract

1. The terms of the contract

While in many areas of contract Parliament has acknowledged that consumers need protection against onerous terms or attempts to limit liability, in insurance there has been relatively little statutory intervention. Insurance contracts are not covered by the Unfair Contract Terms Act 1977, which regulates clauses that limit or exclude liability for breach,[1] and the Unfair Terms in Consumer Contracts Regulations 1999, which does apply to consumer insurance, was the product of a European directive.[2] Before the changes introduced by the Financial Services and Markets Act 2000, which were discussed in chapter 2, the bulk of the efforts to improve the position of the consumer came from the industry itself[3]: the Statements of Practice, which, among other things, sought to restrict the use by insurers of their legal rights; the regulation of intermediaries through the General Insurance Standards Council (now superseded by the Financial Services Authority)[4]; and the Insurance Ombudsman Bureau (replaced by the Financial Ombudsman Service), which among other things used an approach to settling disputes between consumers and insurers that did not simply rest on the common law and even referred to the Unfair Contract Terms Act to determine whether particular terms were unreasonable.[5]

Nevertheless, as with any contract (although, arguably, more than with some contracts, such as consumer credit or sales, in which there has been a good deal of

---

[1] Sch 1, para 1(a). The insurance industry was left out of the 1977 Act on the understanding that it would bring in codes of practice (the Statements of Practice), which were meant to reflect the essence of the Act.
[2] Discussed below.
[3] See ch 1.
[4] See ch 2.
[5] See ch 2.

statutory intervention), it is to the policy that one must turn to find the terms of an insurance agreement. Where a printed policy document has been amended in hand-writing or in typing, then the former 'must be read in the light of' the latter.[6] In many situations, however, the contract will have been formed before the policy document is issued, although invariably insurers make reference to their usual terms on the pro-posal form; indeed, this was a requirement of the Statements of Practice 1977 and 1986. As has been seen in chapter 5, there are problems in defining the terms applica-ble to various insurance contracts. Moreover, some insurance contracts may have been preceded by a good deal of discussion and negotiation between the parties, and it is important to distinguish between the terms of the contract and those statements made during the course of negotiation which are not part of the contract. The latter will not give rise to an action for breach of contract, although they could lead to other actions if, for instance, they constituted a misrepresentation, a breach of the duty of disclosure, or a breach of a collateral contract.[7] The distinction between a term and a pre-contractual representation rests on the intention of the parties: did they intend that the particular statement should be a term of the contract? This issue is resolved objectively: in other words, it is not a matter of what the parties subjec-tively intended, but what the reasonable person present at the time of the contract would have deduced from their words and actions.

---

2. Construing the terms of the insurance contract

Although the court determines the meaning of a contract, it 'cannot either re-write contracts or impose on parties to them what the Court may think would have been a reasonable contract.'[8] Its role is to determine the intention of the parties:

> When one speaks of the intention of the parties to the contract, one is speaking objectively – the parties cannot themselves give direct evidence of what their intention was – and what must be ascertained is what is to be taken as the intention which reasonable people would have had if placed in the situation of the parties. Similarly when one is speaking of aim, or object, or commercial purpose, one is speaking objectively of what reasonable persons would have in mind in the situation of the parties.[9]

Lord Hoffmann remarked that construing a contract is 'not a game with words. It is an attempt to discover what a reasonable person would have understood the parties

[6] *General Accident Fire and Life Assurance Corpn Ltd v Midland Bank Ltd* [1940] 2 KB 389 at 407, *per* Greene MR; *Eagle Star Insurance Co Ltd v Cresswell* [2004] EWCA Civ 602.
[7] A collateral contract or warranty may exist where one party makes a promise and the other party enters into the main contract in reliance on that promise. If the promise is not honoured, the aggrieved party may have an action for breach of the collateral contract: *Esso Petroleum Co Ltd v Marden* [1976] QB 801.
[8] *Sinochem International Oil (London) Co Ltd v Mobil Sales and Supply Corpn* [2000] 1 Lloyd's Rep 339, per Mance LJ.
[9] *Reardon Smith Line Ltd v Yngvar Hansen-Tangen* [1976] 1 WLR 989 at 996, per Lord Wilberforce.

to mean.'[10] He observed, in an important speech in *Investors Compensation Scheme Ltd v West Bromwich Building Society*,[11] that where a detailed analysis of the words in a commercial contract led to a conclusion that flouted 'business common sense,' 'it must be made to yield to business common sense.'[12] Previously, Lord Steyn had expressed the view that 'the law…generally favours a commercially sensible construction' since such is likely to have been the intention of the parties. In his opinion a court should be aware that a reasonable commercial person 'is hostile to technical interpretations and undue emphasis on niceties of language.'[13] Lord Hoffmann commented that: 'Interpretation is the ascertainment of the meaning which the document would convey to a reasonable person having all the background knowledge which would reasonably have been available to the parties in the situation in which they were at the time of the contract.'[14] It has been repeatedly asserted that this background knowledge is that which existed at the time of the contract and does not include reference to what occurred during the negotiations between the parties because, at that point, they were not in agreement.[15] Yet, it may only be by looking at these negotiations that a court can understand the meaning parties attach to particular words or the significant features of their background knowledge. As has been seen in chapter 5, where one party is seeking equitable rectification on the ground that the policy document does not express the common intention of the parties, the court can only address that issue by inquiring into the matters arising before the agreement was reduced to writing. In *King v Brandywine Re Insurance Co (UK) Ltd*,[16] Colman J summarised the approach taken by Lord Hoffmann in *Investors Compensation Scheme Ltd v West Bromwich Building Society*:

> In order to identify the mutually intended meaning of these words it is necessary first to investigate the possible range of dictionary meanings, secondly to investigate the setting of the words in their contractual environment and thirdly to investigate the circumstances in which the contracts were negotiated, in particular the circumstances of the parties and the mutually known features of the market in which they were negotiating.[17]

This statement needs to be treated with caution because the division between the first two steps may lead one to lose sight of the emphasis placed by Lord Hoffmann on words being defined against their background: in other words, steps one and two must be combined. Moreover, the reference to 'the circumstances in which the contracts were negotiated' may slip into issues that the court is not permitted to consider.

With these principles in mind, there are a number of tools employed by the judges in construing a contract. The words used by the parties are normally given their

---

[10] *Jumbo King Ltd v Faithful Properties Ltd* FACV000007/1999 (Hong Kong), per Lord Hoffmann.
[11] [1998] 1 WLR 896.
[12] Ibid.
[13] *Mannai Investment Co Ltd v Eagle Star Life Assurance Co Ltd* [1997] AC 749 at 770–1 citing *Antaios Compania Naviera SA v Salen Rederierna AB* [1985] AC 191 at 201, per Lord Diplock. See also, *Sirius International Insurance Co (Publ) v FAI General Insurance Ltd* [2004] UKHL 54 at (19), per Lord Steyn. But see the comment of Longmore LJ in *Dornoch Ltd v Royal and Sun Alliance Insurance plc* [2005] EWCA Civ 238 at [16].
[14] *Investors Compensation Scheme Ltd v West Bromwich Building Society*, above n 11.
[15] *Prenn v Simmonds* [1971] 2 All ER 237; *MSC Mediterranean Shipping Co SA v Polish Ocean Lines (The Tychy) (No 2)* [2001] 2 Lloyd's Rep 403.
[16] [2004] EWHC 1033 (Comm).
[17] Ibid, at (86). This passage was cited and followed in *Paine v Catlins* [2004] EWHC 3054.

'natural and ordinary meaning,'[18] but care must be employed since the parties may not have used these words in that sense.[19] Where they have defined a word the courts will use that definition. Theft policies commonly exclude liability if goods were stolen while not 'attended' or while 'left unattended.'[20] Lord Denning MR commented:

> I do not think that the words 'left unattended' are capable of any precise definition. It is a mistake for a lawyer to attempt a definition of ordinary words and substitute other words for them. The best way is to take the words in their ordinary sense and apply them to the facts.[21]

Where goods are left in a vehicle, the courts do not interpret such words as requiring someone to be in the vehicle at all times, but when left it must be locked, the driver must be away for no more than a few minutes and it must be in view most of the time. A car is 'attended' when left on a garage forecourt near the cashier's kiosk and locked, while the driver goes in to pay,[22] but not when it is out of sight for fifteen minutes with the keys in the ignition,[23] or when the driver is thirty-seven yards away urinating behind some bushes even if parts of the vehicle are always in view.[24]

The court will also apply the *ejusdem generis* rule, that is, the meaning of a word will be determined 'in the landscape of the instrument as a whole.'[25] Where a policy covered damage by 'storm, tempest or flood,' the word 'flood' was construed by reference to its juxtaposition to 'storm, tempest' and interpreted as meaning that any damage caused must be the result of a sudden and violent pouring in of water and not merely a slow seepage.[26] In another case, a policy required the insured to declare 'jewellery, watches, field-glasses, cameras, and other fragile or specially valuable articles,' and it was held that this wording did not require the insured to inform the insurers of a valuable fur coat because it was not of the same type of article as those specifically mentioned.[27] This rule is only a presumption and will not apply where the parties intended another meaning.

It has been suggested that where certain words are used in similar policies across the industry, then it makes sense to presume that those words have the same mean-

---

[18] *Wood v General Accident Fire and Life Assurance Corpn* (1948) 82 Ll L Rep 77 at 81, per Morris J. See, *Robertson v French* (1803) 4 East 130 at 135, per Lord Ellenborough CJ.
[19] See, for instance, the use of the word 'bankruptcy' in *Doheny v New India Assurance Co Ltd* [2004] EWCA Civ 1705.
[20] There are a range of different versions of this type of clause: some specify that the property must not be left unattended between particular hours, others may cover goods in unattended vehicles if they are fitted with security devices and the doors are locked and windows closed. See C Cashmore, 'Goods in Transit Insurance' (1993) 3 *Insur L & P* 93 at 97–8; J Birds, 'Reasonableness Conditions in Insurance Contracts' (1991) 1 *Insur L & P* 18; V Cowan, 'Lack of Reasonable Care Conditions' (1993) 3 *Insur L & P* 4; see above ch 7.
[21] *Starfire Diamond Rings Ltd v Angel* [1962] 2 Lloyd's Rep 217 at 219.
[22] *Langford v Legal and General Assurance Society* [1986] 2 Lloyd's Rep 103. See also *T. O'Donogue Ltd v Harding and Edgar Hamilton & Carter Ltd* [1988] 2 Lloyd's Rep 281.
[23] *Ingleton of Ilford Ltd v General Accident Fire and Life Assurance Corpn Ltd* [1967] 2 Lloyd's Rep 179.
[24] *Starfire Diamond Rings Ltd v Angel*, above n 21. For the word 'attended' in the context of a shop, see *CTN Cash and Carry Ltd v General Accident Fire and Life Assurance Corpn plc* [1989] 1 Lloyd's Rep 299.
[25] *Charter Reinsurance Co Ltd (In Liquidation) v Fagan* [1996] 2 Lloyd's Rep 113 at 117, per Lord Mustill.
[26] *Young v Sun Alliance and London Insurance Ltd* [1977] 1 WLR 104. See also, *Hitchens (Hatfield) Ltd v Prudential Assurance Co Ltd* [1991] 2 Lloyd's Rep 580; *Tektrol Ltd v International Insurance Co of Hanover Ltd* [2005] EWCA Civ 1624.
[27] *King v Travellers' Insurance Association Ltd* (1931) 48 TLR 53.

ing,[28] but some judges have urged caution: 'Authorities may determine the principles of construction, but a decision upon one form of words is no authority upon the construction of another form of words.'[29] In *De Souza v Home and Overseas Insurance Co Ltd*,[30] Mustill LJ remarked that it was 'better to withdraw a little from the authorities to the former ground of *this* policy and *these* facts, and to look critically at each authority to see whether it really leads inexorably to a solution of our present problem.'[31] He was faced with determining the meaning of the word 'accident' in a policy covering the insured against accidental death or injury. In his view the curious state of the case law had obliged the judge at first instance to reach a conclusion that did not conform to a common sense understanding of the word:

> The cases, regarded simply as decisions, are difficult if not impossible to reconcile. Some of them would, I believe, be regarded by at least some lawyers as wrong. Others would perhaps be differently decided in today's social context, and even at the time it is plain that the Judges were not all of a like mind. In many instances I venture to detect, not a chain of reasoning leading inexorably to a conclusion, but the intuitive choice of a solution, followed by efforts to rationalize it. Again, as reported case succeeds reported case even finer distinctions of language are drawn: sometimes so fine that, approaching them with all the respect due to their authors I find them either impossible to understand, or to reconcile with statements by other judges worthy of equal respect.[32]

Where a word has been used by the parties in a technical sense it will be given that meaning, unless the parties have agreed on another definition: so, 'theft' is usually defined according to its meaning in the Theft Act.[33] Although there is logic in this approach, it may work against the consumer who, unlike the insurers, will have little idea as to the law on theft and whose understanding of the word is, therefore, likely to differ from that contained in the law.[34] Yet, the use of what appear to be legal terms does not always mean they will be construed according to their legal meaning. In *Woolridge v Canelhas Comercio Importacao e Exportacao Ltda*,[35] the claimant ran a wholesale jewellery business in Sao Paulo. Its stock of jewellery was insured under policy which, in a clause headed 'Hold-Up or Robbery,' excluded liability in respect of loss by 'robbery' when the premises were open for business or when any employee was present at the premises. English law was the proper law of the contract. Members of the managing director's family were kidnapped and the managing director was

---

[28] *Dino Services Ltd v Prudential Assurance Co Ltd* [1989] 1 Lloyd's Rep 379 at 382, per Kerr LJ. This case provides an interesting illustration of the dilemma: in construing 'by forcible and violent means,' the Court of Appeal held itself bound by precedent when construing 'forcible', but that there was no precedent with regard to the word 'violent'.

[29] *In re an Arbitration between Coleman's Depositories Ltd, and The Life and Health Assurance Association* [1907] 2 KB 798, at 812, per Buckley LJ.

[30] [1995] LRLR 453.

[31] Ibid, at 456.

[32] Ibid, at 455–6. On the construction of 'accident' policies, see below chs 9 and 15.

[33] *Grundy (Teddington) Ltd v Fulton* [1981] 2 Lloyd's Rep 661 (affirmed [1983] 1 Lloyd's Rep 1); *Dobson v General Accident Fire and Life Assurance Corporation plc* [1989] 2 Lloyd's Rep 549; R. Leng, 'The Scope of "Theft" in Insurance' (1991) 1 *Insur L & P* 16; A McGee, '"Forcible and Violent" Means of Entry' (1991) 1 *Insur L & P* 36. For a case in which an armed robbery was defined as a 'riot', see *London and Lancashire Fire Insurance Co Ltd v Bolands Ltd* [1924] AC 836.

[34] For a slightly different critique, see M Wasik, 'Definitions of Crime in Insurance Contracts' [1986] *JBL* 45.

[35] [2004] EWCA Civ 984.

told that in order to get them back he had to go to the premises and obtain all the emeralds in stock. He went to the premises, got his staff to fill two bags with emeralds and then made the exchange with the kidnappers. The insurers denied liability on the ground that 'robbery' according to its legal meaning involved the taking of property using violence and this was what had occurred. The Court of Appeal held the insurers liable. Mance LJ observed that it was not appropriate to apply the strict English or Brazilian definition of robbery; instead, the court should, in accordance with Lord Hoffmann's principles, construe the clause within the context of the policy as a whole and interpret it according to the view that would be taken by 'ordinary commercial men.' He concluded that the clause was designed to exclude loss where the premises were open for business and the theft was effected by violence directed at the staff, so that there had to be a connection between the theft and the violence to staff in the shop. Here there was no violence against the managing director or the staff, and even though there was duress this came from the kidnapping of the family members, which was a different type of risk. While Mance LJ firmly rooted this approach to the meaning of 'robbery' in the Hoffmann principles, there was older authority for his view, as he briefly acknowledged. In *Algemeene Banvereeniging v Langton*,[36] where an English policy covered property in Belgium, Maugham LJ had said:

> it is quite wrong in principle to construe the words…'fire, burglary, theft, robbery, or hold-up' as if those words could only be construed in a technical sense according to English law. The Belgian bank, of course, do not know what the precise technical meaning, for instance, of the word 'larceny' is, if the word 'larceny' had been used, in England, and I imagine it is equally true to say that very few commercial men in this country are fully aware of the fact that in order entirely to apprehend the meaning of that word, you must go through more than 100 closely printed pages of 'Archbold on Criminal Pleading, Evidence and Practice,' and consult certainly more than 100 decisions going back for over 100 years. I am content with this, that in my opinion, the phrase 'lost, destroyed, or otherwise made away with by fire, burglary, theft, robbery or hold-up, whether with or without violence, and whether from within or without,' is a phrase which has to be construed as ordinary commercial men would construe it, or rather would understand it,

He noted that 'ordinary commercial men' would recognise that the offence leading to the loss would occur in Belgium and, therefore, that the words should be construed in light of the fact that the investigation and any prosecution would be undertaken under Belgian law. In any case, as Maugham LJ observed, the clause itself did not appear to have been intended to be understood in a technical way because of its use of non-legal words, such as 'made away with' and 'hold-up'. It is submitted that the conclusion in both cases is further supported by the fact that, since the parties were in England and Brazil in one policy and in England and Belgium in the other and the inquiries into the crime would take place in, respectively, Brazil and Belgium, there cannot have been an intention to apply a technical meaning drawn from the criminal law of one particular country.

Any ambiguity is construed against the party that inserted the wording – the *contra proferentem* rule.[37] This is likely to mean that the ambiguous words will be

---

[36] (1935) 51 Ll L Rep 275.
[37] *English v Western Insurance Co* [1940] 2 KB 156.

construed in favour of the insured since it is the insurers who draw up the contract: 'It is extremely important with reference to insurance, that there should be a tendency to hold for the assured than for the company, where any ambiguity arises upon the face of the policy.'[38] If, however, an ambiguous word or phrase is commonly used in particular types of contracts, the courts will seek to adopt a consistent approach to the meaning of those words rather than simply resorting to the *contra proferentem* rule.[39] Moreover, the courts will approach a document with the expectation that there are no ambiguities rather than with the intention of seeking them out, and the *contra proferentem* rule cannot be used unless there is ambiguity.[40] The general principle is that if the words have a clear meaning, the courts will give effect to that meaning even though this leads to a consequence which seems unreasonable,[41] although 'the more unreasonable the result the more unlikely it is that the parties can have intended it, and if they do intend it the more necessary it is that they shall make that intention abundantly clear.'[42] In *McGeown v Direct Travel Insurance*,[43] the insured took out holiday insurance that covered, 'a permanent physical disability which prevents you from doing any paid work (if you are not in paid work, we will provide the same cover for any permanent disability which prevents you from doing all your usual activities) – £50,000.' The insured, who was not in paid work, suffered an injury which prevented her from horse riding. At first instance, it was held that the clause was ambiguous and the claimant was, therefore, entitled to the benefit of the *contra proferentem* principle, so that the ambiguity should be resolved in her favour. The Court of Appeal overturned this decision. It held that the court should not seek ambiguity and that, in this case, there was no ambiguity when the clause was construed within the context of contract as a whole. Other clauses set down a maximum for various types of loss and the amount recoverable depended on the amount of the loss. This clause, however, provided a large lump-sum payment. Looked at against this background, it cannot have been the intention of the contract to provide the payment of £50,000 for anything but the most serious of injuries. Turning to the wording of the clause itself, the Court took the view that, since someone in work would have to be prevented from being able to do any paid work, it was appropriate to construe the second part of the clause as requiring that the disability suffered must constitute a substantial intrusion into the insured's usual activities and it was not sufficient merely to show that she could no longer pursue one particular activity.

It is a general principle of contract law that the courts will give such meaning to ambiguous words as renders the instrument valid rather than void or of no effect. In relation to insurance contracts the courts have gone beyond this principle and will avoid an interpretation of an exclusion clause that effectively removes cover from the insured, even if the words are clear and unambiguous. In *Cornish v The Accident*

---

[38] *Samuel Fitton, Administrator of John Fitton, Deceased v The Accidental Death Insurance Co* (1864) 17 CB (NS) 122 at 134–5, per Willes J.
[39] *Gan Insurance Co v Tai Ping Insurance Co* [2001] Lloyd's IR 667; *Royal and Sun Alliance Insurance plc v Dornoch Ltd* [2004] Lloyd's Rep IR 826.
[40] *Cole v Accident Ins Co* (1889) 5 TLR 736 at 737; *McGeown v Direct Travel Insurance* [2003] EWCA Civ 1606.
[41] *Joel v Law Union and Crown Insurance Co* [1908] 2 KB 863.
[42] *L Schuler AG v Wickman Machine Tool Sales Ltd* [1974] AC 235 at 251, per Lord Reid. See also, *Forsikringsaktieselskapet Vesta v Butcher* [1989] AC 852 at 910, per Lord Lowry.
[43] See above n 40.

Insurance Company,[44] a clause in a policy covering accidental death or injury purported to exclude liability where the accident was caused 'by exposure of the insured to obvious risk of injury.' The Court of Appeal took the view that since the purpose of the policy was to provide cover for accidental death or injury, it 'must not be construed so as to defeat that object, nor so as to render it practically illusory.'[45] Taken literally, the clause would exclude from cover someone who is injured crossing the street, even if that person took reasonable care. 'Such a result is so manifestly contrary to the real intention of the parties that a construction which leads to it ought to be rejected.'[46] The Court, therefore, concluded that 'a literal construction is inadmissible, and some qualification must be put on the words used.'[47] Similarly, Tucker J observed in *Amey Properties Ltd v Cornhill Insurance plc*,[48] 'the Courts have adopted different approaches to the construction of the words of exclusion clauses depending upon the nature of the policies in which they appear and in particular whether to give a wide construction would be repugnant to the whole purpose for which the policy was taken out.'[49] The difficulty lies in determining how far the courts are willing to press this principle. An insurer must be able to balance the risk covered against the premium charged and one means by which this can be achieved is through an exclusion clause. In theory, the broader the exclusion clause the lower the risk to the insurer and, therefore, the lower the premium, and an insured who wants better cover must pay a higher premium. Yet, in construing the exclusion clause the courts will, in line with general principles of contract, not assess the adequacy of the consideration (that is, the premium) and so cannot properly determine whether the insurer has written a broad exclusion clause because the premium is set at a very low level.[50]

---

3. Parol evidence rule

It is often claimed that there is a rule to the effect that if a contract has been reduced to writing, the courts will not look outside that document in order to ascertain its meaning: 'parol testimony cannot be received to contradict, vary, add to or subtract from the terms of a written contract.'[51] The rule has much to commend it since it seems logical to suppose that as the parties decided to put their agreement in writing the document represents the entirety of that agreement, and both parties know where

---

[44] (1883) 23 QBD 453. Also *Tektrol Ltd v International Insurance Co of Hanover Ltd* [2005] EWCA Civ 845.
[45] Ibid, at 456, per Lindley LJ. See below ch 9.
[46] Ibid. See also, *Morley and Morley v United Friendly Insurance plc* [1993] 1 WLR 996, below ch 15.
[47] Ibid. For a recent illustration of the application of this principle, see *Allianz Marine Aviation (France) v GE Frankona Reinsurance Ltd London* [2005] EWHC 101.
[48] [1996] LRLR 259.
[49] Ibid, at 264. See *Blackburn Rovers Football & Athletic Club plc v Avon Insurance plc* [2005] EWCA Civ 423.
[50] Although see the discussion of the Unfair Terms in Consumer Contracts Regulations 1999, below.
[51] *Bank of Australasia v Palmer* [1897] AC 540 at 545, per Lord Morris. Also *Jacobs v Batavia and General Plantations Trust Ltd* [1924] 1 Ch 287 at 295, per Lawrence J. An oral statement which is not part of the contract may, however, be actionable as a misrepresentation, see above ch 4.

to find the terms of their contract. Extrinsic evidence is, however, admissible where what is in issue is whether the document accurately represents the agreement, or whether there was any contract at all, or to demonstrate that it was voidable or void, as, for instance, where the question relates to the circumstances in which one party signed the document, or to show that an insurance contract has been entered into for illegal or fraudulent purposes.[52] Moreover, the parol evidence rule may be excluded when determining the terms of the contract and construing their meaning. This led Lord Russell CJ to suggest that:

> although when the parties arrive at a definite written contract the implication or presump-
> tion is very strong that such contract is intended to contain all the terms of their bargain, it
> is a presumption only, and it is open to either of the parties to allege that there was, in addi-
> tion to what appears in the written agreement, an antecedent express stipulation not
> intended by the parties to be excluded, but intended to continue in force with the express
> written agreement.[53]

In order to show that a document does not represent the entire agreement between the parties, there must be evidence of an antecedent agreement; evidence of negotia-tions is not enough because by their very nature negotiations do not indicate what was finally agreed.[54] A court may admit extrinsic evidence to explain ambiguities,[55] or look at documents that have been incorporated into the written contract,[56] or allow evidence to show that a word used in the contract has a meaning other than its normal meaning,[57] or admit proof of trade usage, unless it contradicts an unambigu-ous term of the contract.[58] If the parties made an agreement one part of which involved them promising to enter into a written contract of insurance on particular terms, then, while upholding the terms of the insurance contract, a court may also enforce that prior (or collateral) contract, as long as it has all the features of a con-tract. If the written insurance contract does not conform to the terms agreed between the parties in the collateral contract, an action for a breach of the collateral contract can be brought. Where the principal contract is for marine insurance and, therefore, must be written, the collateral agreement which led to that contract does not have to be written since it is only an agreement to enter into a marine insurance contract and not the marine insurance itself.[59]

The existence of such a large number of exceptions to the parol evidence rule led the Law Commission to conclude that it 'is a proposition of law which is no more than a circular statement,' namely that parol evidence will not be allowed when the parties have reduced their entire agreement to writing, or that, 'Evidence will only be

---

[52] *Bank of Australasia v Palmer*, ibid; *The Prince of Wales, &c Association v Palmer* (1855) 25 Beav 605.
[53] *Gillespie Brothers & Co v Cheney, Eggar & Co* [1896] 2 QB 59 at 62, per Lord Russell CJ.
[54] *Youell v Bland Welch & Co Ltd* [1992] 2 Lloyd's Rep 127. Although the position is different where equi-table rectification is sought: see above and ch 5.
[55] *Horden v Commercial Union Insurance Co* (1887) 56 LJPC 78.
[56] *Re George and Goldsmiths' & General Insurance Burglary Insurance Association* [1899] 1 QB 595.
[57] *American Airlines Inc v Hope* [1973] 1 Lloyd's Rep 223 at 245, per Roskill LJ.
[58] *Blackett v Royal Exchange Assurance Co* (1832) 2 C & J 244 at 249–50, per Lord Lyndhurst CB. For a failed attempt to prove a custom of the Lloyd's market see, *General Reinsurance Corpn v Forsakringsakringsaktiebdaget Fennia Patria* [1983] QB 856.
[59] This depends on analogy with a decision on a contract involving real property, *Boston v Boston* [1904] 1 KB 124.

excluded when its reception would be inconsistent with the intention of the parties.'[60] In spite of this, one should not be tempted to go too far. The fact that there are so many exceptions to the parol evidence rule does not mean that the courts have shifted from their reluctance to interfere with a written document: there remains a strong presumption that if the parties have taken the trouble to reduce their insurance agreement to writing the document is authoritative.[61]

4. Unfair Terms in Consumer Contracts Regulations 1999

An objective of the EU directive on which the Unfair Terms in Consumer Contracts Regulations 1999[62] are based is to facilitate the creation of a single market by providing consumers across the European Union with the same minimum level of protection against unfair terms, although the impact of the Statements of Insurance Practice[63] and the decisions of the Insurance Ombudsman Bureau meant that at least some of the protections afforded by the regulations were already informally in place.[64]

The regulations apply to unfair terms in contracts between a seller or supplier of services (hereafter referred to simply as the supplier), such as an insurer, and a consumer.[65] A term, which has not been individually negotiated, is unfair 'if, contrary to the requirement of good faith, it causes a significant imbalance in the parties' rights and obligations arising under the contract, to the detriment of the consumer' (regulation 5(1)). A term is regarded as not having been individually negotiated if it was drafted in advance thereby precluding the opportunity for the consumer to influence its content (regulation 5(2)), which will almost always be the case in consumer insurance contracts. Even where some terms have been individually negotiated, the regulations apply to the remainder of the contract if 'an overall assessment of it indicates that it is a pre-formulated standard contract' (regulation 5(3)). The onus is on the supplier to show that a term was individually negotiated (regulation 5(4)). The unfairness of a term is assessed according to the nature of the services provided, the

---

[60] Law Commission, *Law of Contract: The Parol Evidence Rule* (Law Com No 154, 1986) at paras 2.7 and 2.45. See also *Couchman v Hill* [1947] KB 554.

[61] *Youell v Bland Welch & Co Ltd*, above n 54. See also *St Paul Fire & Marine Insurance Co (UK) Ltd v McConnell Dowell Contractors Ltd* [1993] 2 Lloyd's Rep 503 at 517, per Potter J (the point was not considered by the Court of Appeal: see [1995] 2 Lloyd's Rep 117 at 128, per Evans LJ).

[62] SI 1999/2083. This version superseded the 1994 regulations (SI 1994/3159), which implemented the EC Directive on Unfair Terms in Consumer Contracts (93/13/EEC). See R Brownsword and G Howells, 'The Implementation of the EC Directive on Unfair Terms in Consumer Contracts–Some Unresolved Questions' (1995) *JBL* 243_63.

[63] I Cadogan and R Lewis, 'The Scope and Operation of the Statements of Insurance Practice' (1992) 2 *Insur L & P* 107.

[64] R Merkin and A Rodger, *EC Insurance Law* (London, Longman, 1997) 50.

[65] Reg 4(1). A consumer is 'any natural person who, in contracts covered by these Regulations, is acting for purposes which are outside his trade, business or profession,' and a seller or supplier of services is 'any natural or legal person who, in contracts covered by these Regulations, is acting for purposes relating to his trade, business or profession, whether publicly owned or privately owned': reg 3(1).

circumstances at the time of the contract and the other terms (regulation 6(1)).[66] With the exception of the requirement that the contract be in plain and intelligible language,[67] a term defining the main subject matter of the contract or the price of the services provided will not be deemed unfair (regulation 6(2)). The recitals add: 'the terms which clearly define or circumscribe the insured risk and the insurer's liability shall not be subject to such assessment since these restrictions are taken into account in calculating the premium paid by the consumer.'[68] This does leave some questions around the value of the regulations since much of an insurance contract is concerned with these issues, including terms defining the insured perils, excepted perils and causation. This could leave the bulk of the regulations applying only to subsidiary contract terms, such as those that specify a period within which the loss must be notified or which prevent the insured from seeking redress through the courts by requiring that any dispute be referred to arbitration.[69]

The supplier is obliged to ensure that written terms are expressed in plain, intelligible language and in the event of ambiguity the meaning most favourable to the consumer will be adopted (regulation 7).[70] As has been mentioned, this applies to all terms, including those relating to the main subject matter and the price. As Merkin and Rodger have pointed out, the problem here may be that a large number of words have acquired technical meanings when used in insurance policies,[71] but it seems unlikely that the English courts would regard the regulations as requiring that those meanings be supplanted by ordinary usage.

An unfair term is not binding on the consumer, but the remainder of the contract will be binding if it is capable of continuing in the absence of the unfair term (regulation 8). The regulations (with the exception of regulation 7) do not simply apply to written contracts since the intention of the directive was to regulate all contracts, including those concluded orally, such as telephone insurance.[72] Finally, the insurer cannot avoid the regulations by specifying that the contract is subject to the law of a non-member state since, they will apply in such a case 'if the contract has a close connection with the territory of the Member States' (regulation 9).

In addition to the remedies provided for individual consumers, the Director General of Fair Trading is empowered to act upon complaints that a term 'drawn up for general use' is unfair and may apply for an injunction (regulations 10 and 12).[73] The Office of Fair Trading has been very active in this function and has singled out particular types of terms for its attention. For example, the OFT regards as unfair those

---

[67] An indicative list of unfair terms is provided in sch 2. The list includes: terms giving the supplier power unilaterally to alter or to terminate the contract or to extend its duration; terms giving the supplier unequal rights as compared with the consumer; terms excluding or limiting the consumer's rights in particular circumstances; and terms restricting the consumer's right to bring a legal action or shifting the burden of proof. See the extensive analysis by the Office of Fair Trading: www.oft.gov.uk

[68] See below.

[69] Unfair Terms in Consumer Contracts Directive, above n 62.

[70] See the analysis of this provision by the Office of Fair Trading at http://www.oft.gov.uk/NR/rdonlyres/ 48EBC7C8-A922-4E17-944E-BDA2E27828B6/0/oft311part4.pdf. See also, Association of British Insurers, *Statement of General Insurance Practice* (1986), cl 5: 'Insurers will continue to develop clearer and more explicit proposal forms and policy documents while bearing in mind the legal nature of insurance contracts.' (Note the Statement no longer applies.) See ICOB 2.2.1 (above ch 2), and *Bankers Insurance Co Ltd v South* [2003] EWHC 380 (QB) (on application of regs to conditions precedent).

[71] Merkin and Rodger, *EC Insurance Law*, above n 64, at 48–9.

[72] Recital 11.

[73] Other 'qualifying bodies' may also consider complaints: reg 11, sch 1.

particular types of terms for its attention. For example, the OFT regards as unfair those terms known as entire agreement clauses by which suppliers seek to exclude from the contract anything said or implied by a representative or agent, unless the supplier states in plain language that it will not be responsible even if the representative or agent tells a lie and gives the consumer an opportunity to accept or reject the clause.[74]

5. Reasonable expectations

It is worth briefly considering the situation in the US where in some jurisdictions the approach to the construction of insurance contracts has differed markedly from that taken in England. According to the Restatement, Contracts (2d), only if there is ambiguity will the court adopt the meaning that 'operates against the party who supplies the words.'[75] Many states have, however, taken a slightly different approach. In California, for instance, the Civil Code states that if there is ambiguity the term 'must be interpreted in the sense in which the promisor believed, at the time of making it, that the promisee understood it.'[76] If this fails to resolve the uncertainty, the term will 'be interpreted most strongly against the party who caused the uncertainty to exist.'[77] In applying these provisions, the California courts have adopted a presumption in favour of coverage, and they have also said that they will 'generally interpret the coverage clauses of insurance policies broadly, in order to protect the objectively reasonable expectations of the insured' because the insurer typically drafts the policy, 'leaving the insured little or no meaningful opportunity or ability to bargain for modifications.'[78]

There have, however, been even more radical developments in some jurisdictions. In an important essay published in 1970, Professor Keeton argued that in many US jurisdictions the courts construe insurance contracts according to the reasonable expectations of the insured even if there is no ambiguity. He suggested that this approach was adopted where there was unconscionability (using that word in a fairly broad sense, as will be seen) in the conduct of the insurer or detrimental reliance by the insured. Unconscionable conduct might be present, for instance, where a policy provided very little cover in light of the size of the premium, or where the policyholder had little opportunity to examine the policy and discover a clause that in clear terms limited cover. Keeton saw this approach as justified on a number of grounds. First, he regarded policy documents as usually very long and complex documents,

---

[74] See Office of Fair Trading, *Unfair Contract Terms*, OFT Bulletin, Issue 1 (May 1996). The bulletin is issued regularly and summarises complaints with which OFT has dealt. On the exceptions to the parol evidence rule, see above.

[75] Restatement, Contracts (2d) §206. See, eg, *JA Brundage Plumbing and Roto-Rooter Inc v Massachusetts Bay Insurance Co* 818 F Supp 553 (US District Ct, New York, 1993).

[76] California Civil Code, §1649.

[77] Ibid, §1654.

[78] *AIU Insurance Co v Superior Court* 51 Cal 3d 808 at 822 (Calif, 1990). See also, *Montrose Chemical Corp v Admiral Insurance Co* 42 Cal Rptr2d 324 (Calif, 1995).

which as insurers knew policyholders rarely read, and which most would not be able to understand in any event. He did, however, acknowledge that insurers were beginning to meet this objection by writing policies in plain language. Secondly, policyholders, he asserted, were often not able to see the policy until after the contract and that this contributed to the disinclination of the policyholder to read the document. Thirdly, he thought that in many situations it was appropriate to protect the reasonable expectations of the insured because it would be unconscionable to allow the insurer to enforce limitations in coverage. Fourthly, he believed it appropriate to protect the reasonable expectations of the policyholder where they arose as a result of the marketing practices of the insurer (or of the insurance industry as a whole), and in particular, where the marketing made it appear that broader cover was being provided than was the case. Finally, he took the view that the reasonable expectations of the insured should be protected where they emerged from the way the insurer characterised coverage in the documentation by, for example, using words such as 'comprehensive cover plan' or placing a broad statement about the coverage in large print at the start of the policy and then limiting that statement in smaller print later on.[79] These justifications indicate the conditions under which, in Keeton's view, many courts would examine the reasonable expectations of the insured. He was not suggesting that the insurance policy be ignored, although he was arguing that its terms should only apply if they met the reasonable expectations of the insured and, that those expectations be defined in the light of matters such as the marketing strategy used by the insurer for that policy, the format of the document, the language in which its terms were expressed, the access of the insured to the policy terms at the time of the contract and the actual knowledge of the insured.

Although Keeton claimed merely to summarise the approach of the judges, it is clear that his views prompted some courts to adopt this method of construing insurance contracts. In *Atwater Creamery Co v Western National Mutual Insurance Co*,[80] the Supreme Court of Minnesota expressly acknowledged the influence of his ideas. This case concerned burglary insurance in which 'evidence of forcible entry' was required. The Court rejected the idea that the definition of burglary in the policy was ambiguous. It considered the purposes of the clause to be to protect the insurer against fraud by an inside job and to encourage insureds to secure their premises. Here there was no suggestion of fraud by the insured and the premises had been properly secured. So, adopting the literal meaning of the definition would not achieve either purpose. Adopting Keeton's approach, the Court held that the restrictions in the policy's definition of burglary did not meet the reasonable expectations of the insured in that no one would expect the policy to exclude coverage in the event of a skilful burglary by an outsider that did not leave visible marks of forcible entry. The Court was willing to adopt the reasonable expectations doctrine because of the inequality of bargaining power between the parties, which enabled the insurer to force terms on an insured, and the lack of skill of the ordinary insured when it came to understanding policy terms:

---

[79] RE Keeton, 'Insurance Law Rights at Variance with Policy Provisions' (1970) 83 *Harv L Rev* 961; RE Keeton and AI Widiss, *Insurance Law: A Guide to Fundamental Principles, Legal Doctrines and Commercial Practices* (St Paul, West Publishing, 1988) 627_46. See also, the essays on this topic collected in (1998) 5 *Connecticut Insurance Law Journal*.
[80] 366 NW2d 271 (Minn, 1985).

The reasonable-expectations doctrine gives the court a standard by which to construe insurance contracts without having to rely on arbitrary rules which do not reflect real-life situations and without having to bend and stretch those rules to do justice in individual cases. As Professor Keeton points out, ambiguity in the language of the contract is not irrelevant under this standard but becomes a factor in determining the reasonable expectations of the insured, along with such factors as whether the insured was told of important, but obscure, conditions or exclusions and whether the particular provision in the contract at issue is an item known by the public generally. The doctrine does not automatically remove from the insured a responsibility to read the policy. It does, however, recognise that in certain instances, such as where major exclusions are hidden in the definitions section, the insured should be held only to reasonable knowledge of the literal terms and conditions. The insured may show what actual expectations he had, but the factfinder should determine whether those expectations were reasonable under the circumstances.[81]

The Court rejected the idea that this approach was either pro-insured or pro-insurer and insisted that it simply required the insurer to communicate coverage and exclusions clearly and that it was limited to the insured's reasonable expectations, which were derived from the actions of the insurer.

Acceptance of the reasonable expectations doctrine by courts and academics in the US has been, to say the least, patchy, and it certainly poses some problems. The tendency – although not the intent – of the doctrine is to undercut the role of the policy document: if its terms do not meet the insured's reasonable expectations, then even when their meaning is clear, these terms may be rewritten. There is also the difficulty of determining what the reasonable expectations of the insured might be. The assumption underpinning much of the discussion is that standard form contracts are suspect and insurers must, therefore, justify them. Yet, insurers could not possibly run a mass consumer insurance business if they had to negotiate each contract. If they were required to do so, the costs and therefore the premiums, would rise. The reasonable expectations doctrine might therefore be regarded as overriding the positive side of standard form contracts, but of course for Keeton the point was that the doctrine merely required insurers to act reasonably and this did not preclude the use of standard forms.[82]

Some of this discussion will strike a chord with those who have been strongly critical of the practices of English insurers.[83] Aspects of English law may well produce the same results as might be achieved by applying Keeton's thesis: for instance, the presumption in favour of coverage,[84] the *contra proferentem* rule and the requirement in the Unfair Terms Regulations that written terms be expressed in plain, intelligible language (article 7(1)). In chapter 5, it was noted that where one party knows the other is mistaken about the nature of the contract and diverts the innocent party's attention from that mistake, the contract is construed according to the meaning which the innocent party believed it had. This opens up the pre-contractual negotiations, but where the words of the policy are clear it would be difficult to persuade an English court to countenance an argument that sought to use the insurer's marketing

---

[81] Ibid, at 278, per Wahl J.
[82] J Stempel, 'Reassessing the "Sophisticated Policyholder" Defense' (1993) 42 *Drake L Rev* 807.
[83] See the discussion in M Clarke, 'The Reasonable Expectations of the Insured in England' [1989] *JBL* 389.
[84] See above and also the discussion of accident policies in ch 9.

campaign as a means of overturning the clear words of a policy. It is, on the other hand, possible to argue that if one party in its advertising or through a statement by its agent explains the terms of a written contractual document to the other party in a way that misrepresents those terms, then the oral explanation will take priority.[85] Finally, it is worth noting that even if the courts are not prepared to accept an argument built around some sense of the insured's reasonable expectations, the Financial Ombudsman Service may be more willing to do.

Nevertheless, although these devices may produce a result for the insured, it seems unlikely that the English courts will adopt the reasonable expectations doctrine itself. For the English courts the parol evidence rule may have been reduced to a presumption, but as has been suggested, it is a strong presumption. The English courts still prioritise the contractual document and apply its terms. Keeton, on the other hand, suggested that some US courts look outside the policy to discover if it conforms to the reasonable expectations of the insured, even where its terms are clear. It might be suggested that since Lord Hoffmann's speech in *Investors Compensation Scheme Ltd v West Bromwich Building Society*,[86] the aim is to ascertain the meaning that the document would convey to a reasonable person having the background knowledge that was reasonably available to the parties and this might allow a court to consider the way the cover was presented either in advertising or in the format of the policy document itself. Yet, the practice of the English courts is more firmly concerned with construing the words of the document than Keeton suggested was the case in the US. In English law the document remains central and the background is only used to clarify its meaning. Keeton seems, at times, to convert the background into the foreground, which allows the words of the policy to be ignored. This is a step too far for the English courts, and, indeed, for most of the US courts. Stuart-Smith LJ represented the mainstream when he rejected the reasonable expectations doctrine in *Yorkshire Water Services Ltd v Sun Alliance & London Insurance plc*.[87] He took the view that the American courts were more benign in their attitude towards insureds for reasons that included the inequality in bargaining strength between the parties. He remarked: 'these notions which reflect a substantial element of public policy are not part of the principles of construction of contracts under English law.'[88] Except when required to do so by legislation, such as the Unfair Terms in Consumer Contracts regulations 1999, there is a reluctance in the English courts to countenance public policy issues in insurance contract law. Contract law is regarded as private law, and the insurance contract is therefore sustained and its meaning determined by the fiction that the parties share a common intention. This fails to acknowledge the disparity between the parties, the significance of insurance in social policy and the nature of the division between commercial and consumer insurance, discussed in chapter 1.

---

[85] *Curtis v Chemical Cleaning & Dyeing Co* [1951] 1 KB 805.
[86] See above n 11.
[87] [1997] 2 Lloyd's Rep 21. Also *Municipal Mutual Insurance Ltd v Sea Insurance Co Ltd* [1998] Lloyd's Rep IR 421; *Pilkington United Kingdom Ltd v CGU Insurance plc* [2004] Lloyd's Rep IR 891.
[88] Ibid. See also, Diplock LJ's comments in *Lavarack v Woods* [1967] 1 QB 278 at 294.

9

Causation

1. Proximate cause rule

The insured, who puts forward a claim, must show that it is more probable than not that the loss was caused by one of the perils which the insurers contracted to cover.[1] To take a simple example, if the policy covers loss of goods by fire, the insured must show that, on the balance of probabilities, fire caused the loss, and obviously there is no claim if the goods were lost by some other event, such as theft. But what if the fire is caused by the insured carelessly tossing away a cigarette, or by an act of arson committed by a third person or by the insured? What if the goods are damaged, not by the fire which has broken out in the warehouse, but by smoke, or by part of the building in which they are kept collapsing as a result of the fire, or by the water used by fire-fighters to extinguish it? What if the goods are moved from a burning building into the street to save them and are damaged by rain or are stolen? The question is, what loss have the insurers agreed to cover? If the fire has reduced the security of the warehouse and, as a result, thieves are able to enter and steal the goods, the cause of the loss is theft not fire. The result is the same if the goods are removed from a burning building and placed on the pavement from where they are stolen.[2] When a building, which was insured against fire, was damaged by a mob drawn to a fire in an adjacent property, the cause of the loss was the action of the mob not the fire.[3] On

---

[1] *Glowrange v CGU Insurance plc* 2001 WL 720222 at (14), per Colman J. On causation in general, see HLA Hart and T Honore, *Causation in the Law* (Oxford, Clarendon Press, 1985); JM Culp, 'Causation, Economists, and the Dinosaur: A Response to Professor Dray' 49 (3) *Law and Contemporary Problems* 23. On causation in insurance law, see AL Parks, 'Marine Insurance: Proximate Cause' (1979) 10 *JMLC* 519; P Muchlinski, 'Causation and Proof of Loss in Marine Insurance' in FD Rose (ed), *New Foundations for Insurance Law: Current Legal Problems* (London, Stevens & Sons, 1987); M Clarke, 'Insurance: The Proximate Cause in English Law' [1981] *CLJ* 284; J Lowry and P Rawlings, 'Proximate Causation in Insurance Law' [2005] 68 *MLR* 310.
[2] *Marsden v City and County Insurance Co* (1865) LR 1 CP 232. In practice, insurers have not contested such claims because of the fear that to do so would encourage the insured to leave goods in burning buildings. Under the California Insurance Code (2000), § 531, an insurer is liable if the loss is caused by efforts to rescue the subject matter insured, or if, while the subject matter is being rescued from an insured peril, it is lost through being exposed to a peril that is not covered.
[3] *Marsden v City and County Assurance Co*, ibid.

the other hand, a theft policy did cover the loss when a shop was burgled during an air raid because, although loss 'occasioned by hostilities' was an excepted peril, the cause was theft and the air raid merely made the burglars' task easier.[4]

The first question is, therefore, what peril have the insurers agreed to cover, which leads us back to the contract, and the second question is, was the loss caused by that peril? The focus in this chapter is on identifying the cause for the purposes of insurance law. The search could lead through a long chain of events: the death of a pedestrian might be said to have been caused by the negligence of the motorist who ran her down, or by her decision to cross the road at that moment. Indeed, the enquiry could go even further: 'it seems to me to be impracticable to go back to cause upon cause, which would lead us back ultimately to the birth of person, for if he had never been born the accident would not have happened.'[5] As Blackburn J pointed out in a marine insurance case, a loss typically occurs as the result of a series of events:

> The ship perished because she went ashore on the coast of Yorkshire. The cause of her going ashore was partly that it was thick weather and she was making for Hull in distress, and partly that she was unmanageable because full of water. The cause of that cause, viz., her being in distress and full of water, was, that when she laboured in the rolling sea she made water; and the cause of her making water was, that when she left London she was not in so strong and staunch a state as she ought to have been.[6]

As will be seen later, the parties may agree in the policy on the test for determining causation, but where they have not general principles have been formulated by the judges. In an early case, Willes J said, 'you are not to trouble yourself with distant causes, or to go into a metaphysical distinction between causes efficient and material and causes final; but you are to look exclusively to the proximate and immediate cause of the loss.'[7] This idea of proximity was later incorporated in the Marine Insurance Act 1906, section 55(1): 'Subject to the provisions of this Act, and unless the policy otherwise provides, the insurer is liable for any loss proximately caused by a peril insured against, but, subject as aforesaid, he is not liable for any loss which is not proximately caused by a peril insured against.'[8] In other words, the operative cause in insurance law is the proximate cause of the loss. This gives little assistance, and it would hardly be surprising if the courts were tempted to look at the latest cause. When Mr Lawrence was killed by a train after an epileptic seizure had led to him falling from the platform at Waterloo Station, the court decided that his death was caused not by the seizure but by the train. It was, therefore, an accident and covered by a personal accident policy.[9] This might be seen as merely choosing the latest cause,

---

4 *Winicofsky v Army and Navy General Assurance Assocn Ltd* (1919) 88 LJKB 1111.
5 *Lawrence v The Accidental Insurance Co Ltd* (1881) 7 QBD 216 at 221, per Watkin Williams J; *Coxe v Employers' Liability Assurance Corpn Ltd* [1916] 2 KB 629 at 634, per Scrutton J.
6 *Dudgeon v Pembroke* (1874) LR 9 QB 581 at 595.
7 *Ionides v The Universal Marine Insurance Co* (1863) 14 CB (NS) 259 at 289.
8 It is worth noting the use of the phrase, 'unless the policy otherwise provides' since it reinforces the importance of seeing whether the parties have agreed on a definition of causation which differs from that laid down in the section.
9 *Lawrence v The Accidental Insurance Co Ltd*, above n 5. See also *Winspear v The Accident Insurance Co Ltd* (1880) 6 QBD 42, where the insurer was held liable when Mr Winspear had a seizure and drowned in the river Rea at Edgbaston. Some US jurisdictions have adopted a test, which, while defined in terms of proximate cause, is determined by looking for the last cause in time: *Bird v St Paul Fire & Marine Insurance Co* 120 NE 86 (1918); *Queen Insurance Co v Globe & Rutgers Fire Insurance Co* 263 US 487; *Pan American World Airways, Inc v Aetna Casualty & Surety Corp* 505 F2d 989 (1974). But see the analysis in *Continental Insurance Co v Arkwright Mutual Insurance Co* 102 F3d 30 (1996).

but the decision can be justified on other grounds.[10] To say that the proximate cause is the last in time may merely be to assert that the cause that is closest in time to the loss is likely to be regarded as having a greater impact than other causes in the chain of events that lead to the loss. In 1918 Lord Shaw declared that: 'To treat proximate cause as if it was the cause which is proximate in time is … out of the question. The cause which is truly proximate is that which is proximate in efficiency.'[11] Lord Greene MR, on the other hand, was of the opinion that causation, 'is really a matter for the common sense and intelligence of the ordinary man,'[12] and Lord Denning MR referred to, 'the effective or dominant cause of the occurrence, or, as it is sometimes put, what is in substance the cause, even though it is more remote in point of time, such cause to be determined by common sense.'[13]

In *Reischer v Borwick*[14] a marine policy covered a ship against damage caused by a collision but not by perils of the sea. After the ship was holed in a collision, a temporary repair was effected so that it could be towed into a harbour. However, the motion through the sea caused by the towing led the hole to reopen and the ship sank. Even though in terms of time it might be said that the loss resulted from the motion of the sea, which was not covered, the Court of Appeal held that the proximate cause of the loss was the collision. In *Leyland Shipping Co Ltd v Norwich Union Fire Insurance Society Ltd*,[15] the *Ikaria* was insured against loss from perils of the sea but not from war. During the First World War, the ship was hit by a torpedo, which blew a hole in its side and damaged the bulkheads. It was towed into a safe harbour. While anchored a gale blew up causing the ship to bump against the harbour wall. The harbour authorities, fearing it might sink and block access, ordered the ship's removal into open sea where it grounded at each low tide. After two days of this buffeting, the bulkheads failed and the ship sank. Even though the ship would probably have been safe had it stayed in the harbour, the House of Lords took the view that the proximate cause of the loss was the torpedo. The impact of the torpedo meant it was reasonably certain that sea-water would flow into the ship and this is what happened, even if the extent of the damage caused might not have been expected.

The question would therefore seem to be, was it reasonably certain at the time of the event, which is alleged to have caused the loss, that it would lead to a loss of the type which occurred, even if the actual extent of the loss was greater than might

---

[10] The seizure caused him to fall, but it did not cause his death–after all, he might have fallen away from the track or on to the track when no train was entering the station.

[11] *Leyland Shipping Co Ltd v Norwich Union Fire Insurance Society Ltd* [1918] AC 350 at 369. In *Pink v Fleming* (1890) 25 QBD 396 at 397, Lord Esher MR distinguished between marine policies, where the court would look simply for 'the last cause,' and non-marine policies, where it would be prepared to go back further and look for the 'efficient cause'. But see *Reischer v Borwick* (1894) 2 QB 548 (particularly at 552, per Lindley LJ) where the court, while apparently agreeing with Esher, did not apply the distinction in practice. The House of Lords rejected Esher's distinction and approved of *Reischer* in *Leyland Shipping*. For a similar approach in the US see the decision of the Supreme Court of Washington in *Graham v Public Employees Mutual Insurance Co* 656 P2d 1077 (1983).

[12] *Athel Line Ltd v Liverpool & London War Risks Insurance Association Ltd* [1946] 1 KB 117 at 122.

[13] *Gray v Barr, Prudential Assurance Co Ltd (Third Party)* [1971] 2 QB 554 at 567. See *Wayne Tank and Pump Co Ltd v Employers' Liability Assurance Corpn Ltd* [1974] QB 57 at 67, per Lord Denning MR. Lord Wright, in *Yorkshire Dale SS Co Ltd v Minister of War Transport* [1942] AC 691 at 706, said: 'Causation is to be understood as the man in the street, and not as either the scientist or the metaphysician, would understand it.' In 1917 Lord Sumner had argued that: 'Proximate cause is not a device to avoid the trouble of discovering the real cause or the "common-sense cause"': *Becker, Gray and Co v London Assurance Corpn* [1918] AC 101 at 112.

[14] See above n 11.

[15] Ibid.

reasonably have been expected?[16] If it is established that a peril covered by the contract was the proximate cause of the loss, the insurer will be liable for all the consequences that flow naturally from this peril: as Malcolm Clarke has put it, the full extent of the loss 'will be recoverable, even though such extent was no more than not unlikely to occur at the time of the peril.'[17] In both *Reischer* and *Leyland* the influx of sea-water was the reasonably certain consequence of, respectively, the collision and the torpedo, and the effect of those events was still continuing and they had not been overshadowed by subsequent events. If, on the other hand, as it was being towed out to sea, the *Ikaria* had sunk following a collision with part of the harbour that had resulted from the negligence of the crew, then although the ship might not have been navigating out of the harbour had it not been for the torpedo, that event would no longer have been operating and the loss would have been proximately caused by the negligence.

The other point concerns the burden of proof. It is up to the insured to establish on a balance of probabilities that the loss was proximately caused by an insured peril.[18] If the insured does this, the burden of proof shifts to the insurers to show that another explanation was more probable: where a ship is insured against fire, then if the insured shows that the loss was caused by fire, the insurers must demonstrate, on a balance of probabilities, that fire was not the proximate cause of the loss, or that the fire was caused by an excepted peril.[19] If the insurers allege that the loss was caused deliberately by the insured or by someone else with the insured's connivance, particularly if that act was a criminal offence, the degree of proof required will be 'commensurate with the gravity of the allegation made.' That burden will not be discharged 'if the evidence fails to exclude a substantial, as opposed to a fanciful or remote, possibility that the loss was accidental.'[20]

---

2. Agreements to alter the rule of causation

Although the proximate cause rule has sometimes been called a rule of law,[21] it is merely a term that is implied into the insurance contract as representing 'the real meaning of the parties.'[22] The parties – or, in reality, the insurers who draw up policies – can alter the normal rule. However, the courts will presume that the proximate

---

[16] M Clarke, 'Insurance: The Proximate Cause in English Law,' above n 1.

[17] Ibid, at 289.

[18] *Foreign Marine Insurance Co Ltd v Gaunt* [1921] 2 AC 41; *Rhesa Shipping Co SA v Edmunds (The 'Popi M')* [1985] 1 WLR 948.

[19] *Slattery v Mance* [1962] 1 QB 676.

[20] *National Justice Compania Naviera SA v Prudential Assurance Co Ltd (The 'Ikarian Reefer')* (1995) 1 Lloyd's Rep 455 at 459, per Stuart-Smith LJ. For an illustration of the process by which the court may infer the connivance of the insured in the act of a third party which causes the loss, see *Bank of Athens v Royal Exchange Assurance: (The 'Eftychia')* (1937) 57 Ll L Rep 37 (affirmed at 59 Ll L Rep 67).

[21] *Leyland Shipping Co Ltd v Norwich Union Fire Insurance Society Ltd* [1917] 1 KB 873 at 892, per Scrutton LJ.

[22] *Becker, Gray and Co v London Assurance Corpn*, above n 13 at 112, per Lord Sumner. See also *Reischer v Borwick*, above n 11 at 550, per Lindley LJ, and *Leyland Shipping Co Ltd v Norwich Union Fire Insurance Society Ltd*, above n 11 at 369 and 370, per Lord Shaw; Marine Insurance Act 1906, s 55(1).

cause rule applies, and that presumption will only be displaced by clear words. [23] So, even though the parties choose not to use the phrase 'proximate cause,' but instead words such as 'reasonably attributable to' or 'attributable to' or 'arising from,'[24] the court will apply the proximate cause rule because these terms give no clear indication of the test to be applied.

A series of cases from the late nineteenth and early twentieth centuries involving accident policies provides an interesting illustration of such clauses. It seems clear that the aim of the companies in writing the causation clauses in these policies was to exclude liability where injury or death was linked to some cause other than the accident, and certainly insurers disputed liability in these cases on the basis that this was what the policies had done. In Mr Lawrence's case,[25] the policy rendered the insurers liable 'where such accidental injury is the direct and sole cause of death…but it does not insure in case of death…arising from fits,' but the court regarded 'direct and sole cause' as simply a restatement of the proximate cause rule. In *Fitton v Accidental Death Insurance Co*,[26] a policy insured against death resulting from various accidental injuries, but specified that the injury must be 'the direct and sole cause of death' and excluded liability for death arising from, among other things, hernia 'or any other disease or cause arising within the system of the insured before or at the time or following such accidental injury (whether causing death…directly or jointly with such accidental injury).' The insured suffered an accidental fall that led to a strangulated hernia which, in turn, resulted in his death. The insurers were held liable because the policy exempted them 'only where the hernia arises within the system' and not where it was caused by the accident.[27] Similarly, in *Isitt v Railway Passengers Assurance Co*,[28] the insurers were liable under a policy that only covered death from 'the effects' of an accidental injury. The insured suffered an accidental injury and he was confined to bed. However, the injury was so painful that he was unable to bear the weight of any bed clothing. This led him to contract pneumonia from which he died. Willes J thought an appropriate direction to the jury would be:

> Do you think that the circumstances leading up to the death, including the cold which caused pneumonia, were the reasonable and natural consequences of the injury and of the conditions under which the assured had to live in consequence of the injury? If you find that no foreign cause intervened and that nothing happened except what was reasonably to be expected under the circumstances, you may and ought to find that the death resulted 'from the effects of the injury' within the meaning of the policy.[29]

---

[23] *Coxe v Employers' Liability Assurance Corpn Ltd*, above n 5 at 634, per Scrutton J.

[24] These words appear in cls 1.1, 4.1 and 4.3 of the Institute Cargo Clauses (B) issued by the Institute of London Underwriters. Note that cl 4.5 uses the phrase 'proximately caused'.

[25] Above n 5.

[26] [1864] 17 CB (NS) 122.

[27] Ibid, at 134, per Williams J.

[28] (1889) 22 QBD 504.

[29] Ibid, at 512–13. In *Smith v Cornhill Insurance Co Ltd*, a motor policy included cover for the death of the insured caused by an accident while riding in the car. The insured crashed the car into a ravine and, as a result, she sustained brain damage. In a state of semi-consciousness she left the car, wandered around and stumbled into a stream. As a result of entering the water she had a heart attack and died. The shock would have been harmless but for her other injuries. The insurers were held liable, even though the judge thought that the death was not the natural or probable consequence of the accident, because 'the causation of events, each one the result of the preceding event, lead back to the accident': [1938] Ll L Rep 122 at 130, per Atkinson J. This does not seem a useful technique for determining the operative cause, indeed it merely returns us to the problems discussed at the beginning of this chapter. Anyway, the same result would surely have been achieved by applying more orthodox principles.

In an attempt to avoid that decision accident insurers reworded their policies to cover injury or death only where the accident was, 'the direct or proximate cause thereof, but not where the direct or proximate cause thereof is disease or other intervening cause, even although the disease or other intervening cause may itself have been aggravated by such accident, or have been due to weakness or exhaustion consequent thereon, or the death accelerated thereby.' Such a policy came before the Court of Appeal after Mr Etherington fell during a hunting expedition, became soaked, caught pneumonia and died. The Court decided that the insurers had not avoided the *Isitt* decision with the new clause. This conclusion seems to have been influenced by the view that not to hold the insurers liable would make it difficult to establish a claim, unless the insured died at the time the accident occurred, and that would make such polices of very limited utility. Vaughan Williams LJ, noting the insurer's intention to avoid the consequences of *Isitt*, said, 'though that may have been the desire of the company, they have not had what I may call the commercial courage to express as plainly as they might have done what their counsel says they intended to express.' He added, 'When the disease or other cause is dependent on the accident, I think it is right to say that the term "direct or proximate cause" covers in such a case not only the immediate result of the accident, but also all those things which may fairly be considered as results usually attendant upon the particular accident in question.'[30]

Vaughan Williams LJ can be seen as having fallen back on the proximate cause rule either because the clause was ambiguous or because he applied the principle of construction that avoids the literal meaning of a clause which would render the cover afforded by the policy illusory. Nevertheless, if the words used are clear the courts will apply them.[31] The accident policy in *Coxe* v *Employers' Liability Assurance Corpn Ltd*[32] excluded liability for death 'indirectly caused by, arising from, or traceable to' war. As part of his duties during the First World War, Captain Ewing was required to inspect sentries on a railway line that was poorly lit because of air raids and to which access was forbidden to civilians. He was hit and killed by a train. While Scrutton J took the view that the train was the proximate cause, the use in the contract of the word 'indirectly' obliged him to determine whether the loss had been indirectly caused by an excluded peril. The war had placed Ewing in a position of special danger and, therefore, was the indirect cause of his death, so the claim was refused. There must, however, be a limit and this would be in the use of the word 'caused': the cause may be indirect, but it still must be a cause, although how that is

---

[30] *In the Matter of an Arbitration between Etherington and the Lancashire and Yorkshire Accident Insurance Co* [1909] 1 KB 591 at 598, per Vaughan Williams LJ. See also *Mardorf v Accident Insurance Co* [1903] 1 KB 584. The insurers in another case did, however, escape liability. In *Smith v Accident Insurance Co* (1870) LR 5 Exch 302, the policy excluded death arising from, among other things, erysipelas 'arising within the system of the insured before or at the time of or following such accidental injury.' Mr Smith accidentally cut his foot, erysipelas set in as the result of that injury and he died. The insurers were held not to be liable. Cleasby B took the view that the clause had been inserted so that where there was a supervening cause it would not be necessary to determine whether death had been caused by a disease that arose independently, or as a result, of the injury. The majority also distinguished *Fitton* on the ground that the wording of the clause was different. Dissenting, Kelly CB could find no such difference and argued that the clause only exempted the insurers where the disease arose independently of the injury. This approach seems not only preferable but to have been adopted by the courts in the later personal accident cases. *Smith* was not referred to in *Etherington* and, while mentioned by counsel in *Mardorf*, was not referred to in the judgments.
[31] See above ch 8.
[32] See above n 5.

defined becomes uncertain. Presumably, the decision would have been different if Ewing had been standing on a platform waiting for a troop train and had died in the same way as Lawrence. In these circumstances the clause would not have excluded the insurer's liability because the war would have been merely a part of the background to the accident and not one of its causes, direct or indirect: he might not have been on the platform but for the war, however, the war did not pose the danger from which he died. In *Jason v Batten*[33] the term 'any Accident bodily injury resulting in and being – independently of all other causes – the exclusive direct and immediate cause of the … injury or disablement' excluded liability where a motorist, who had a narrowed coronary artery, sustained a severe coronary thrombosis when a car accident caused a blood clot to form which blocked that artery. It was held that if he had not had the narrowed artery, he would not have had a coronary thrombosis. The accident brought forward that thrombosis, but the court found that he would have suffered an attack within three years in any event. So, while the accident advanced the thrombosis by causing the blood clot to form, it was not 'independently of all other causes the exclusive … cause' of the thrombosis. Moreover, the thrombosis was 'directly or indirectly' caused by a pre-existing condition, namely, the narrowed artery. If, however, the accident had activated a condition that was latent and that, but for the accident, would have remained so, the insurers would have been liable.[34]

3. Multiple causes[35]

Until relatively recently, the courts seem not to have given much thought to the possibility of there being more than one proximate cause[36]; however, in 1974 Cairns LJ suggested the judges 'should [not] strain to find a dominant cause,'[37] and recently a High Court judge has been criticised for referring to the proximate cause in the singular.[38] While the courts have not suddenly begun to search out multiple causes as a matter of routine, the broader approach to causation and the practice of insurers extending the causation test to include indirect causes of loss can only increase the likelihood of a court finding that there is more than one cause.[39]

Where there are a number of perils covered, the insured need only show that the loss was proximately caused by one of them.[40] If there are two proximate causes that

---

[33] [1969] 1 Lloyd's Rep 281. See also, *Blackburn Rovers Football & Athletic Club plc v Avon Insurance plc* [2005] EWCA Civ 423
[34] *Fidelity and Casualty Co of New York v Mitchell* [1917] AC 592.
[35] Lowry and Rawlings, 'Proximate Causation in Insurance Law' (2005) 68 *MLR* 310.
[36] *Leyland Shipping Co Ltd v Norwich Union Fire Insurance Society Ltd*, above n 11 at 353, 371; *Board of Trade v Hain Steamship Co Ltd* [1929] AC 534 at 541. But see *Heskell v Continental Express* [1950] 1 All ER 1033.
[37] *Wayne Tank and Pump Co Ltd v Employers' Liability Assurance Corpn Ltd*, above n 13 at 69, per Cairns LJ.
[38] *Midland Mainline v Eagle Star Insurance Co Ltd* [2004] EWCA Civ 1042.
[39] For a recent example, see *Tektrol Ltd v International Insurance Co of Hanover Ltd* [2005] EWCA Civ 845.
[40] *Kuwait Airways Corporation v Kuwait Insurance Co* [1999] 1 Lloyd's Rep 803.

are independent of each other and each would have produced part of the loss without the contribution of the other, the insurer will be liable for that part caused by the covered peril. In *Ford Motor Co of Canada Ltd v Prudential Assurance Co Ltd*,[41] Ford was insured against loss caused by riot, but the policy excluded loss as a result of damage caused by cessation of work or by change in temperature. There was a riot which led to the factory being closed and a large amount of damage was caused by freezing. The Supreme Court of Canada held that the insurers were only liable for that part of the damage solely caused by the riot.

There are two problematic situations. In the first, there are two proximate causes of the loss, one of these is covered by the policy and the other is neither covered nor excepted. In *JJ Lloyd Instruments Ltd v Northern Star Insurance Co Ltd (The 'Miss Jay Jay')*,[42] the Court of Appeal held that a ship, *The Miss Jay Jay*, had been lost as the result of a combination of two events: the adverse condition of the sea and defects in the boat's design of which the insured was unaware. The insurance policy covered loss by adverse sea conditions, but did not mention loss by a design fault. Clearly, if the design fault had been the sole cause, there would have been no liability on the policy, but here the insurers were held liable. Slade LJ said: 'As there were no relevant exclusions or warranties in this policy the fact that there may have been another proximate cause did not call for specified mention since proof of a peril which was within the policy was enough to entitle the plaintiffs to judgment.'[43]

The second situation that creates difficulty is where there are two causes, one of which is covered by the policy, while the other falls within the terms of an exception clause. In *Wayne Tank and Pump Co Ltd v Employers' Liability Assurance Corpn Ltd*,[44] Wayne installed equipment to store and convey liquid wax in a factory. Subsequently, the factory burnt down as the result of two negligent actions by Wayne: the first was to supply plastic pipe to convey hot wax and an ineffective thermostat; and the second was to switch on the equipment and leave it unattended. The question before the Court of Appeal was whether the liability for the losses caused by Wayne's negligence was covered by a public liability policy. That policy's principal clause stated that the insurers 'will indemnify the Insured against all sums which the Insured shall become legally liable to pay as damages consequent upon... damage to property as a result of accidents as described in the Schedule...' There was an exception for 'damage caused by the nature or conditions of any goods or the containers thereof sold or supplied by or on behalf of the insured.' The Court of Appeal held that 'goods' included the pipe and thermostat. Lord Denning MR and Roskill LJ concluded that the proximate cause of the loss was the defective piping and thermostat and, therefore, the exclusion clause meant the insurers were not liable. They went on to say that even if there were two proximate causes – the defective installation, which was within the terms of the policy, and the defective goods, which was not – the insurers were not liable because having 'stipulated for freedom [from the excepted risk], the

---

[41] (1959) 18 DLR(2d) 273.

[42] [1987] 1 Lloyd's Rep 32. See also *Board of Trade v Hain*, above n 36 at 539, per Lord Buckmaster.

[43] See also *Seashore Marine SA v Phoenix Assurance plc (The 'Vergina') (No 2)* [2001] 2 Lloyd's Rep 698; *Kastor Navigation Co Ltd v AGF (Mat) (The Kastor Too)* [2003] 1 Lloyd's Rep 296 (affirmed [2004] Lloyd's Rep IR 481).

[44] Above, n 13. Also *Tektrol Ltd v International Insurance Co of Hanover Ltd*, above n 39.

only way of giving effect to it is by exempting them altogether.'[45] Cairns LJ preferred this second approach.[46]

Is this second approach right? Certainly, the courts in California have taken a different view. In *State Farm Mutual Auto Ins Co v Partridge*,[47] the insured accidentally shot and injured his friend. The court decided there had been two acts of negligence by the insured: filing down the trigger mechanism on his gun to create a 'hair trigger' and driving with the gun in his hand while his friend sat in the passenger seat. Without both of these separate actions the injury would not have happened. The problem was that the policy rendered the insurer liable if the cause was the negligence with regard to the hair trigger, but not if the cause was negligent driving. The court held that where there were two proximate causes and one was covered, the insurer was liable irrespective of the fact that the policy excluded liability for the other cause. In their book, *Insurance Law*,[48] Keeton and Widiss suggest that decisions like *Partridge* show that, 'when there are several distinct or distinguishable factors which contribute to a loss, a persuasive case can be made for the proposition that courts will apply the causation theory that will relate the loss to a covered peril.'[49] They see this as an aspect of the way courts construe policies in light of the reasonable expectations of the insured:[50] 'In many instances, decisions on causation questions involving insurance policy terms are best understood as manifestations of the judicial inclination to favor coverage either by construing ambiguous policy provisions against an insurer or by protecting the reasonable expectations of an insured.'[51] This idea has never achieved wide acceptance in the US and the courts tend only to look at the reasonable expectations of the insured where there is ambiguity in the contract.[52] However, in relation to exception clauses, US courts, generally, appear to take the view that 'exclusionary clauses are interpreted narrowly, whereas clauses identifying coverage are interpreted broadly,'[53] and do seem relatively easily persuaded that there is ambiguity in an exception clause.

The decision in *Partridge* suggests that the *Wayne* approach is not self explanatory. It is possible to argue in favour of *Wayne* that the exclusion clause in an insurance contract is central to the bargain between the parties if only because it is a key factor in determining the level of premium charged; therefore, the insurer should not be held liable in any case where one proximate cause falls within that clause. On the other hand, one might say that the application of the exception is unclear and, therefore, should be construed against the insurer. This would lead to the same result as was reached in *Partridge*. Yet, even if one preferred *Partridge* it is not necessarily appropriate simply to discard *Wayne*. Both *Wayne* and *Partridge* involved third-party

---

[45] Ibid, at 67, per Lord Denning MR.
[46] See also, *Midland Mainline v Eagle Star Insurance Co Ltd*, above n 38.
[47] 10 Cal3d 102 (1973). See also *Waseca Mutual Ins Co v Noska*, 331 NW2d 917 (1983); *US Fidelity & Guaranty Co v State Farm Mutual Automobile Ins Co* 437 NE2d 663 (1982); *LeJeune v Allstate Ins Co* 365 So2d 471 (La, 1978); *Houser v Gilbert*, 389 NW2d 626 (1986); *Lawver v Boling* 238 NW2d 514 (1976); *Scottsdale Ins Co v Van Nguyen* 763 P2d 540 (1988); *Unigard Mutual Ins Co v Abbott*, 732 F2d 1414 (1984).
[48] RE Keeton and AI Widiss, *Insurance Law: A Guide to Fundamental Principles, Legal Doctrines, and Commercial Practice* (St Paul, West Publishing, 1988).
[49] Ibid, at 557.
[50] See ch 8 above.
[51] Keeton and Widiss, above n 48, at 559.
[52] *Montrose Chemical Corp v Admiral Ins Co* 42 Cal Rptr2d 324 (1995).
[53] *Garvey v State Farm Fire and Casualty Co* 257 Cal Rptr 292 at 298 (1989).

liability policies and, while the reasoning in *Partridge* might persuade one to prefer it to *Wayne*, there may be different factors where first-party insurance is involved.[54] In property insurance the insurer promises to indemnify the insured if the property suffers a covered loss, and generally coverage is defined in terms of causation: the policy requires the loss to have been caused by a specified peril (eg, fire or theft), or the policy covers loss caused by any risk with certain exceptions. Since liability depends on a contract analysis, it seems right not to hold the insurer liable where one proximate cause is excluded, even if another is covered, because the loss would not have occurred without the action of the excluded cause. In liability policies, on the other hand, the insurer promises to indemnify an insured, who is liable to another party. The first stage in determining whether the insurer is liable is, therefore, determined by concepts of liability drawn from tort: is the insured liable in tort? Whereas the first-party insurer promises to pay for losses irrespective of fault, in liability insurance a claim only exists if the loss is caused by a degree of fault rendering the insured liable to a third party. There may, therefore, be an argument for distinguishing between liability and property insurance: holding the liability insurer, but not the property insurer, liable where one proximate cause is covered and the other is expressly excluded.

---

4. The impact of deliberate actions by the insured[55]

4.1 Actions taken to reduce loss

It is not unusual for an insured to take action which, although aimed at reducing the loss for which the insurers would be liable, leads to damage. This does not necessarily break the chain of causation. Indeed, the consequence of finding that it did might not suit insurers since it could discourage action to reduce loss: an insured might not pour water on goods to put out a fire if doing so affected a claim on a fire policy. The issue is whether the insurer can be said to have contracted for the event that caused the loss. In *Canada Rice Mills Ltd v Union Marine and General Insurance Co*,[56] the captain of the 'Segundo' closed the ventilators in the cargo hold to prevent seawater entering during rough weather and this resulted in the insured cargo of rice being damaged through overheating. The Privy Council took the view that, although sea water did not touch the cargo, the loss was caused by the rough sea, and therefore the insurers were liable on a policy that covered loss by perils of the sea: Lord Wright called the action of the ship's master, 'such a mere matter of routine seamanship necessitated by the peril that the damage can be regarded as the direct result of the peril.'[57] In other words, like the orders issued by the harbour authorities in *Leyland*

---

[54] Ibid.
[55] Sir Michael J Mustill, 'Fault and Marine Losses' (1988) *LMCLQ* 310.
[56] [1941] AC 55.
[57] Ibid, at 70.

Shipping, his action did not break the effect of the perils of the sea. Where the action taken by the insured is designed to protect the insured property from a peril covered by the policy, the test is: 'Is it a fear of something that will happen in the future or has the peril already happened and is it so imminent that it is immediately necessary to avert the danger by action?'[58] Fire insurers were held liable when a fire broke out near the insured goods and the port authorities decided to throw some of the goods into the sea and douse the rest with water to prevent the fire spreading.[59] In another such case the judge said, 'I have found that fire did not actually break out, but it is reasonably certain that it would have broken out, and the condition of things was such that there was an actual existing state of peril of fire, and not merely a fear of fire.'[60] On the other hand, the courts will not hold insurers liable for a loss for which they have not contracted. A mistake by a ship's captain in thinking that steam emerging from the cargo hold was smoke did not make the insurers liable for damage caused to the goods when water was sprayed on them. The reasonableness of the mistake was irrelevant: 'The underwriters insured against fire in fact, and if there had been a fire they would have had to pay. But why are they to pay if in fact there was no fire? They did not insure against an error of judgment on the part of the captain in deciding whether there was a peril or not.'[61]

In the case of marine policies, the Marine Insurance Act 1906, section 78(4) places the insured under an obligation to take such action to avert or to minimise loss from an insured peril as the prudent uninsured person would have taken.[62] There is no such requirement implied into non-marine policies, although an insured who unreasonably fails to mitigate their loss may be unable to claim for the additional loss if it is determined that it was proximately caused by the insured's failure because the chain of causation from the original cause has been broken.[63] In *Yorkshire Water Services Ltd v Sun Alliance & London Insurance plc*,[64] sewage escaped from a sewage works owned by Yorkshire Water Services ('YWS'). To reduce the likelihood of damage to

---

[58] *Symington & Co v Union Insurance Society of Canton Ltd* (1928) 139 LT 386 at 390, per Scrutton LJ. See also *Stanley v Western Insurance Co* (1868) LR 3 Ex Ch 71 at 74, per Kelly CB; *In the Matter of an Arbitration between Etherington and the Lancashire and Yorkshire Accident Insurance Co*, above n 30 at 599, per Vaughan Williams LJ; *Joseph Watson and Son Ltd v Firemen's Fund Insurance Co of San Francisco* [1922] 2 KB 355 at 359, per Rowlatt J; *Canadian Rice Mills Ltd v Union Marine and General Insurance Co Ltd*, above n 56 at 71, per Lord Wright. See also *Butler v Wildman* (1820) 3 B & Ald 398, where a similar principle was applied in the case of goods thrown overboard to prevent them from falling into enemy hands (although see the doubts expressed about the decision by Lord Sumner in *Becker, Gray and Co v London Assurance Corpn*, above n 13 at 116); Marine Insurance Act 1906, s 66(6).
[59] *Symington & Co v Union Insurance Society of Canton Ltd*, ibid.
[60] *The Knight of St. Michael* [1898] P 30 at 34, per Gorrell Barnes J. The same reasoning explains the decision in *Becker, Gray and Co v London Assurance Corpn*, above n 13. A voyage was abandoned because of the fear of capture, but here the House of Lords ruled that this loss was caused by the captain's voluntary decision since the threat was not imminent. According to Lord Sumner (at 114) 'mere apprehension that a restraint of princes will come into operation' is not sufficient, the abandonment has to be caused by an actual or imminent threat. But see H Bennett, 'Causation in the Law of Marine Insurance: Evolution and Codification of the Proximate Cause Doctrine' in D Rhidian Thomas (ed), *The Modern Law of Marine Insurance* (London, LLP, 1996).
[61] *Joseph Watson and Son Ltd v Firemen's Fund Insurance Co of San Francisco*, above n 58 at 359, per Rowlatt J.
[62] See the Institute Cargo Clauses (A), cl 16; also, *National Oilwell (UK) Ltd v Davy Offshore Ltd* [1993] 2 Lloyd's Rep 582 at 618, per Colman J.
[63] *British Westinghouse Electric Co Ltd v Underground Electric Rys Co of London* [1912] AC 673 at 689, per Vct Haldone LC. See *England v Guardian Insurance Ltd* [2000] Lloyd's Rep IR 404.
[64] [1997] 2 Lloyd's Rep 21.

neighbouring property and, therefore, of claims against YWS, the company under-took works costing £4 million. YWS sought to recover this expenditure under its public liability policy, which provided cover against 'legal liability for damages' and 'all other costs and expenses in relation to any matter which may form the subject of a claim.' The Court of Appeal took the view that the insurer was only required to indemnify YWS for sums due as compensation to third parties and not costs incurred by YWS in carrying out work on its own property. The suggestion that a term should be implied into the policy rendering the insurers liable for reasonable expenditure on work undertaken to alleviate loss was rejected, the Court pointing out that it would be difficult to assess what was reasonable: if the potential liability were a claim for compensation of £300,000 from the owner of neighbouring property would it be reasonable to require the insurers to meet the sum of £4 million paid for the works? This would become even more difficult if the damage to the neighbouring property had not been quantified. In the end, however, the case rested on the issue of what the insurer had agreed to cover.[65]

4.2 Loss resulting from an action of the insured

Property insurance will cover loss caused by the negligence of the insured, unless expressly excluded.[66] In *Harris v Poland*,[67] the insured lit a fire in the fireplace, forgetting that she had previously hidden her jewellery there. The court decided that, while her actions were probably negligent, she did not act intentionally, and the insurers were therefore liable under a policy which covered 'loss or damage by fire.' A requirement that the insured take 'reasonable care to avoid loss' will not necessarily relieve the insurers of liability in the event of the insured acting negligently.[68] With liability insurance, an attempt to exclude negligence would make no sense because the policy covers liability to a third party and that depends on the insured having been

---

[65] For an interesting discussion of these issues in Australia, see *Guardian Assurance Co Ltd v Underwood Construcitons Pty Ltd* (1974) 48 ALJR 307; *Re Mining Technologies Australia Pty Ltd* [1999] 1 Qd R 60. In the latter case, the insured equipment, which had been trapped underground following a mine collapse, was rescued by the insured at considerable expense (although the cost was less than half the value of the equipment). Davies JA noted that the policy contained a clause that excluded liability for loss to property which could have been avoided by the insured exercising reasonable care; therefore, he implied a term allowing the recovery of expenditure incurred by the insured in exercising such reasonable care. McPherson JA, on the other hand, did not regard it as necessary to decide whether there was an implied term because the insured could recover under a clause permitting repair of the insured property and he took the view that retrieving the equipment amounted to repair. The implied term approach was not used in *PMB Australia Ltd v MMI General Insurance Ltd* [2001] QSC 288 (affirmed at [2002] QCA 361). There the policy covered losses incurred through business interruption when an outbreak of salmonella stopped the manufacture of peanut butter; however, the clause did not cover expenditure incurred to alter the factory in order to prevent future outbreaks, and therefore future losses. At first instance, the judge said that Davies JA's approach was a minority view and that it related to property insurance. Moreover, the expenditure there had been incurred while the loss was taking place, whereas that was not the situation in this case.

[66] *Attorney-General v Adelaide Steamship Co Ltd* [1923] AC 292. The Marine Insurance Act 1906, s 55(2)(a) provides that, 'unless the policy provides, [the insurer] is liable for any loss proximately caused by a peril insured against, even though the loss would not have happened but for the misconduct or negligence of the master or crew.'

[67] [1941] 1 KB 462.

[68] JE Adams, 'Reasonable Care Provisions, the Courts and the Ombudsman' [1998] *JBL* 85.

negligent.[69] In a case on an employers' liability policy, it was held that the insurers were liable in spite of the presence of such a clause unless the conduct was reckless, which required the insured to have acted 'with actual recognition … that a danger exists, and not caring whether or not it is averted. The purpose of the condition is to ensure that the insured will not, because he is covered against loss by the policy refrain from taking precautions which he knows ought to be taken.'[70] In *Sofi v Prudential Assurance Co Ltd*,[71] a theft policy required the insured to 'take all reasonable steps to safeguard any property insured.' The insured locked jewellery worth £42,035 in the glove compartment of his car and then left the car in a car park for fifteen minutes. During this time the jewels were stolen. The insurers were liable because it could not be shown that the insured had acted recklessly in thinking that the jewels were safer in the car. Similarly, in *Cooke v Routledge*,[72] Mr Cooke wrote off his car when driving while heavily intoxicated. His insurers were held liable for the loss in spite of a clause saying that he was required to take reasonable care to safeguard the car from loss. The court took the view that the crash had not been a deliberate act and that it had been neither the inevitable nor the natural and probable consequence of his action. In any case, the term was construed as requiring Mr Cooke to safeguard the car from external threat and did not relate to the manner of his driving. On the other hand, in *Gunns v Par Insurance Brokers*[73] the insurer was not held liable because the insured's conduct was reckless. The insured, a jeweller, went away for the weekend, leaving valuables in a safe, which the insurers had previously declared to be unsatisfactory, and without activating the alarm system. In addition, shortly before the theft, he had reported a suspicion that he was being followed.

Public policy may exclude a claim that depends on a criminal act, but this does not preclude a claim by an innocent person. The court will not refuse a claim merely because there has been some illegal act.[74] Diplock LJ suggested that whether the court will refuse to assert a right, even in favour of someone who has committed an anti-social act, will depend on the nature of that act and the nature of the right.[75] If the loss is brought about by a deliberate criminal or tortious act, the insurer will be

---

[69] *Tinline v White Cross Insurance Association Ltd* [1921] 3 KB 327 at 330, per Bailhache J. See also *Shaw v Robberds, Hawkes and Stone* (1837) 6 Ad & E 75 at 84, per Lord Denman CJ; Marine Insurance Act 1906, s 55(2)(a). See the discussion of *Cornish v The Accident Insurance Company* (1883) 23 QBD 453 in ch 8 above.

[70] *Fraser v BN Furman (Productions) Ltd, Miller Smith & Partners (A Firm) Third Party* [1967] 1 WLR 898 at 906, per Diplock LJ.

[71] [1993] 2 Lloyd's Rep 559. See the comment of the Insurance Ombudsman Bureau on this case: *Annual Report 1993*, cited in P Hart (ed), *Digest of Annual Reports and Bulletins* (London, IOB, 1999). Prior to *Sofi*, the IOB had taken a view of such clauses that was more favourable to insurers than was taken by the Court of Appeal. On clauses excluding liability where the driver leaves the ignition key in the car: *Hayward v Norwich Union Insurance Ltd* [2001] 1 All ER (Comm) 545; also Financial Ombudsman Service, *Annual Review of 1 April 2001 to 31 March 2002* (London, FSA 2002).

[72] [1998] NI 174.

[73] [1997] 1 Lloyd's Rep 173. See also *Devco Holder Ltd v Legal and General Assurance Society Ltd* [1993] 2 Lloyd's Rep 567; JE Adams, 'Reasonable Care Provisions, the Courts and the Ombudsman'; above n 68. To avoid the consequences of having to prove recklessness, the insurers often require that property not be left 'unattended'. The Insurance Ombudsman was criticised for drawing too narrow a definition of terms requiring the insured to take reasonable care, but this might merely be seen as balancing the tendency of insurers to use such a term as an easy way of avoiding liability: J Birds, 'Reasonableness Conditions in Insurance Contracts' (1991) 1 *Insur L & P* 18; V Cowan, 'Lack of Reasonable Care Conditions' (1993) 3 *Insur L & P* 4.

[74] *Saunders v Edwards* [1987] 1 WLR 1116 at 1134, per Bingham LJ.

[75] *Hardy v Motor Insurers' Bureau* [1964] 2 QB 745 at 767–8.

liable if that act is committed by someone who is not a party to the insurance contract; indeed, insureds commonly seek to insure against, for instance, the loss of property through theft or arson by a stranger.[76] But what if the insured deliberately causes the loss or engages in an illegal act that leads to the loss?[77]

It has been seen that an insurer may be liable even though the loss was caused by the insured's deliberate act, as, for example, where the insured sprays water on goods to extinguish a fire: the loss is characterised as being proximately caused by the fire and not by the water. On the other hand, the insurer is not liable where the loss was caused by the intentional criminal or tortious act of the insured:

> On ordinary principles of insurance law an assured cannot by his own deliberate act cause the event upon which the insurance is payable. The insurers have not agreed to pay on that happening. The fire assured cannot recover if he intentionally burns down his house, nor the marine assured if he scuttles his ship, nor the life assured if he deliberately ends his own life. This is not the result of public policy, but of the correct construction of the contract.[78]

According to the Marine Insurance Act 1906, section 55(2)(a), 'The insurer is not liable for any loss attributable to the wilful misconduct of the assured.' Although this is rather vague, it is worth noting that the word 'proximate', which is present in section 55(1), is omitted and 'attributable' appears instead. Where the wilful misconduct leads to the loss, then even though it is not the proximate cause of that loss, a claim may be denied on the principle that 'it is against public policy to indemnify a man against the consequences of a crime which he knowingly commits.'[79]

It has been said that to allow someone to profit from their crime would remove 'those restraints operating on the minds of men against the commission of crimes, namely, the interest we have in the welfare and prosperity of our connexions.'[80] It is unrealistic to suppose that someone who is not deterred from committing a crime by the possibility of being punished will be deterred by the prospect of being refused a claim under an insurance policy.[81] Furthermore, such goals would seem more appropriately the province of the criminal law. In his important essay on public policy, Shand suggested that it has never been the purpose of contract law 'to regulate the conduct of the community at large by altering or invalidating the rights and obligations of individual parties,' nevertheless, he went on to admit that 'deterrence has become a firmly established factor in the application of public policy to contract

---

[76] *Schiffshypothekenbank Zu Luebeck AG v Compton (The 'Alexion Hope')* [1988] 1 Lloyd's Rep 311 at 317, per Lloyd LJ.

[77] *P. Samuel and Co Ltd v Dumas* [1924] AC 431.

[78] *Beresford v Royal Insurance Co Ltd* [1938] AC 586 at 595, per Lord Atkin. He added that where the person who committed suicide was insane at the time the insurers might be held liable 'if one premises that the insanity in question prevents the act from being in law the act of the assured' (ibid). But where the policy specifically excludes liability for insane as well as sane suicide, there will be no claim: *Ellinger & Co v Mutual Life Insurance Co of New York* [1905] 1 KB 31.

[79] *Tinline v White Cross Insurance Association Ltd*, above n 69 at 330–1, per Ballhache J. Also *Gray v Barr, Prudential Assurance Co Ltd (Third Party)*, above n 13, at 568, per Lord Denning MR; M Clarke, 'Illegal Insurance' (1987) *LMCLQ* 201 at 209–15.

[80] *The Amicable Society for a Perpetual Life Assurance Office v James Bolland, Joseph Hare and Matthias Koops Knight* (1830) 4 Bligh (NS) 194 at 211.

[81] *Hardy v Motor Insurers' Bureau*, above n 75 at 770, per Diplock LJ.

law.'[82] The other justification for intervention is that the courts will not lend the legal process to enforcing a claim based on the criminal act of the insured because 'no system of jurisprudence can with reason include amongst the rights which it enforces rights directly resulting to the person asserting them from the crime of that person,'[83] and, 'The human mind revolts at the very idea that any other doctrine could be possible in our system of jurisprudence.'[84]

Yet, there must be a causal connection between the crime and the loss, otherwise the motorist who deliberately drove a car without an MOT certificate would have no claim if a camera were stolen from that car. Moreover, the principle of public policy that denies the criminal's claim must be set against another principle that requires people to perform their contractual obligations. Lord Esher MR summed up the predicament:

> No doubt there is a rule that, if a contract be made contrary to public policy, performance cannot be enforced either at law or in equity; but when people vouch that rule to excuse themselves from the performance of a contract, in respect of which they have received the full consideration, and when all that remains to be done under the contract is for them to pay money, the application of the rule ought to be narrowly watched, and ought not to be carried a step further than the protection of the public requires.[85]

Bingham LJ recently restated this idea:

> Where issues of illegality are raised, the courts have (as it seems to me) to steer a middle course between two unacceptable positions. On the one hand it is unacceptable that any court of law should aid or lend its authority to a party seeking to pursue or enforce an object or agreement which the law prohibits. On the other hand, it is unacceptable that the court should, on the first indication of unlawfulness affecting any aspect of a transaction, draw up its skirts and refuse all assistance to the plaintiff, no matter how serious his loss nor how disproportionate his loss to the unlawfulness of his conduct.[86]

A boundary must be drawn between an unenforceable and an enforceable claim where the insured has committed a deliberate and criminal act. When a solicitor suffered a loss as the result of entering into a champertous contract[87] he was unable to claim under his policy because he had deliberately entered into the illegal contract

---

[82] JG Shand, 'Unblinkering the Unruly Horse: Public Policy in the Law of Contract' (1972) 30 *CLJ* 144 at 154–5. Indeed, the tendency is growing to use the civil law to control anti-social behaviour (for example, local authorities obtaining injunctions against tenants in public housing who are accused of racist threats) or to obtain damages from those who have not been convicted by a criminal court. See also, M Clarke, 'Insurance of Wilful Misconduct: The Court as Keeper of the Public Conscience' (1996) 7 *Ins LJ* 173.

[83] *Cleaver v Mutual Reserve Fund Life Association* [1892] 1 QB 147 at 156, per Fry LJ. Generally N Enonchong, *Illegal Transactions* (London, Lloyd's of London Press, 1998); W Gellhorn, 'Contracts and Public Policy' (1935) 35 *Col LR* 679.

[84] *In the Estate of Cunigunda (otherwise Cora) Crippen, Deceased* [1911] P 108 at 112, per Evans P. See also, *Holman v Johnson* (1775) 1 Cowp 341 at 343.

[85] *Cleaver v Mutual Reserve Fund Life Association* [1892] 1 QB 147 at 151.

[86] *Saunders v Edwards*, above n 74 at 1134, per Bingham LJ.

[87] An agreement under which one person promises to maintain another in the prosecution of an action in exchange for a share in any damages recovered. A champertous contract is no longer criminal or tortious: Criminal Law Act 1967, ss 13–14, but see *McFarlane v EE Caledonia Ltd (No 2)* [1995] 1 WLR 366.

and the fact that he did not realise it was a criminal offence to do so was irrelevant.[88] In *Beresford v Royal Insurance Co*, [89] when a man burdened by huge debts committed suicide, the insurers were not held liable on a life policy. Even though there was a clause which only excluded liability if suicide occurred within a year of the policy commencing and the death was outside that period, the House of Lords decided that, since at that time suicide was a crime, public policy would not allow recovery.[90] It will make no difference that, although the insured intended to commit the crime, which led to the death, there was no intention to cause the death itself. After Henry Fauntleroy was hanged in 1824 for forging a Bank of England note, his estate was unable to claim on a life policy that he had taken out nine years before, even though it can hardly be supposed that he committed the forgery with the intention of being convicted and hanged.[91]

In *Geismar v Sun Alliance and London Insurance Ltd*,[92] a claim was made on a theft policy after jewellery was stolen. The jewellery had been smuggled into the country and was, therefore, liable to confiscation, but the authorities would have had no claim on any insurance money. The court held that even though theft and not confiscation was the cause of the loss the insurers were not liable: 'if the contract of insurance purports to cover property which the law forbids him to have, then the contract is directly connected with the illegal act and is unenforceable.'[93] In contrast to this is the decision of the Court of Appeal in *Euro-Diam Ltd v Bathurst*.[94] A wholesaler of diamonds insured an export shipment to West Germany and was allowed to claim on a policy when the jewels were stolen after their arrival in that country. The wholesaler had misrepresented their value to the German customs so that the importer might avoid tax, although, unlike in *Geismar*, there had been no misrepresentation to the insurers. In addition to this act of smuggling, the transaction was illegal under West German law. The court held that the right to possess goods will be enforced even if the owner acquired them by virtue of an illegal contract, so long as it is not necessary to use the illegal contract to establish the claim.[95] This draws on a line of cases in which it has been held that an insured can claim under a theft policy even though the goods were originally bought with proceeds obtained through the sale of an illegal cargo: 'If this objection were well founded ... it would be necessary to examine and scrutinize the past conduct of the assured, in order to see whether or not, by their

---

[88] *Haseldine v Hosken* [1933] 1 KB 822.

[89] See above n 78.

[90] The inclusion of such a clause would not make the whole contract void *ab initio* because it could be severed from the rest of the contract. The Lords chose not to follow a decision of the United States Supreme Court in which it was held that, although a term not allowing a claim in the event of suicide would be implied into a life policy, where the policy mentioned the issue by, for instance, providing for payment if the suicide occurred after a certain period, then there was no general principle to prevent payment, and it was up to each state to legislate, if it chose, to preclude payment: *Northwestern Mutual Life Insurance Co v Johnson* (1920) 254 US 96. See also *Moore and Kettle v Woolsey and Knill* (1854) 4 E & B 243 at 254–5, per Lord Campbell CJ. It may be that shifts in public policy represented by a change in the criminal law on suicide mean that the case would now be decided differently: see below.

[91] *The Amicable Society for a Perpetual Life Assurance Office v James Bolland, Joseph Hare and Matthias Koops Knight*, see above n 80. For a similar approach in the USA, *Millen v John Hancock Mutual Life Insurance Co* 13 NE 2d 950 (1938), but see *Weeks v New York Life Insurance Co* 122 SE 586 (1924); *John Hancock Mutual Life Insurance Co v Tarrence* 244 F 2d 86 (1957).

[92] [1978] 1 QB 383. See M Clarke, 'Illegal Insurance', above n 79, at 212–15.

[93] Ibid, at 394, per Talbot J.

[94] [1987] 2 WLR 517.

[95] See *Bowmakers Ltd v Barnet Instruments Ltd* [1945] KB 65; *Tinsley v Morgan* [1994] 1 AC 340 at 375, per Lord Browne-Wilkinson.

former transactions in life, they had illegally acquired the funds with which the particular goods insured were purchased.'[96] Nevertheless, the problem remains of defining the precise degree of connection that must exist between the crime and the loss for the claim to be defeated. Kerr LJ in *Euro-Diam* adopted and expanded a principle developed in *Thackwell v Barclays Bank plc*,[97] according to which the court would not simply deny a remedy to the plaintiff, whose claim was based on the illegal act, but would look at the quality of that act and consider 'whether in all the circumstances it would be an affront to the public conscience' to permit the remedy sought, in the sense of 'indirectly assisting or encouraging the plaintiff in his criminal act [or encouraging others in similar criminal acts].'[98] Kerr LJ concluded that, while the issuing of a false invoice knowing it would be used to deceive the German authorities 'was undoubtedly reprehensible,'[99] it did not benefit the insured, it had no bearing on the loss and it did not involve any deception of the insurers. While in *Euro-Diam* there was no direct connection between the illegal act and the insurance contract, in *Geismar* the insured would have been better off by having the insurance money because the jewels were liable to confiscation by the British customs, so the contract was 'directly connected with the illegal act.'[100]

Subsequently, the House of Lords in *Tinsley v Milligan* disapproved of the public conscience test.[101] However, as against the minority led by Lord Goff, who wished to return to the rigidity of the rule that the property rights created by an illegal contract should be left as they were,[102] the majority opted for a solution that gave a degree of flexibility, albeit not as much as allowed by the public conscience test.[103] The majority in the Lords took the view that if an illegal contract was executed and property rights created, the claimant could recover the property, unless in order to prove those rights the claimant had to rely on evidence of the illegality. In *Tinsley* a house was acquired by two people but placed in the name of one to enable the making of fraudulent claims for social security benefit. The Lords held that when the house was acquired a resulting trust came into existence, so that the owner of the legal title became a trustee for the other person and the latter could claim under that trust without having

---

[96] *Bird v Appleton* (1800) 8 TR 562 at 566, per Lord Kenyon CJ. Clarke has suggested that the courts might be prepared to make more detailed inquiries when faced with a case in which a drug dealer uses the proceeds of heroin sales to buy a house which is then burnt down and the owner tries to claim on an insurance policy: M Clarke, 'Illegal Insurance', above n 79 at 215. This is, of course, separate from legislation that seeks to force criminals to disgorge the profits of crime (such as the Proceeds of Crime Act 2002), but doubtless Clarke's view draws strength from such legislation.

[97] [1986] 1 All ER 676 at 687–8.

[98] The words in brackets were added by Nicholls LJ in *Saunders v Edwards*, above n 74 at 1132. The Court of Appeal expanded further on the test in *Howard v Shirlstar Container Transport Ltd* [1990] 1 WLR 1292, and in *Tinsley* v *Morgan* [1992] Ch 310.

[99] See above n 94 at 528.

[100] *Geismar v Sun Alliance and London Insurance Ltd*, above n 92 at 394, per Talbot J.

[101] See above n 95 at 360, per Lord Goff. It may be that the test survives in the areas covered by the decision in *Thackwell v Barclays Bank plc*, above n 97, that is, tort actions for negligence and conversion, since the Lords did not expressly overrule the case. See RA Buckley, 'Social Security Fraud as Illegality' (1994) 110 *LQR* 3; N Cohen, 'The Quiet Revolution in the Enforcement of Illegal Contracts' 1994 *LMCLQ* 163; M Halliwell, 'Equitable Proprietary Claims and Dishonest Claimants: A Resolution?' (1994) 58 *The Conveyancer* 62; H Stowe, 'The "Unruly Horse" has Bolted: *Tinsley v Milligan*' (1994) 57 *MLR* 441.

[102] For this rule, see *Muckleston v Brown* (1801) 6 Ves Jun 52 at 69, per Lord Eldon LC. See also *Singh* v *Ali* [1960] AC 167 at 176–7, per Lord Denning.

[103] In Cohen's view the majority approach was 'presumably inspired by that very test': Cohen, 'The Quiet Revolution in the Enforcement of Illegal Contracts,' above n 101, at 171.

to rely on the original illegal contract. Moreover, the only defence to the plaintiff's claim that the other party could make would be based on an illegal agreement and, therefore, would not be countenanced by the court. In summary, the courts will not enforce an illegal contract, but will enforce property rights acquired as a result of an illegal contract provided that the claim can be made without relying on that contract or can only be defeated by reliance on that contract.[104]

4.3 Deliberate killing

4.3.1 The forfeiture rule

The forfeiture rule is 'the rule of public policy which in certain circumstances precludes a person who has unlawfully killed another from acquiring a benefit in consequence of the killing.'[105] The operation of the principle that a criminal must not be allowed to benefit from the crime can be seen in those spousal murder cases where the murderer is the beneficiary under a policy on the victim's life.[106] After Dr Crippen was hanged in 1910 for the murder of his wife, his estate was not allowed to claim as the beneficiary of a life policy on her life.[107] Unlike *The Prince of Wales, &c. Association v Palmer*,[108] where the life policy was void because it had been entered into so that Palmer could collect by murdering the insured life, in *Crippen* the contract was valid but could not be enforced by either Crippen or his estate.[109] On the other hand, a beneficiary under a life policy, who has neither committed nor connived in the criminal act that caused the death of the insured life, will be able to recover, as where a husband was the beneficiary under a policy on his wife's life and his wife was killed while she was deliberately setting fire to a house.[110] Indeed, the fact that the murderer is the first named beneficiary, and therefore cannot enforce a claim, does not mean that another beneficiary cannot. The rule does not make the policy void, it merely makes it unenforceable by the criminal.[111] After Florence Maybrick was convicted of the murder of her husband, James,[112] a claim under a policy on his life was refused by the insurers on the ground that she should not be allowed to benefit from her crime. The court agreed, but did not see why the insurers should avoid liability and ordered that Florence's claim be ignored, which meant that under the terms of the policy the proceeds went to James's estate.[113] Using this approach, *Beresford* would have been

---

[104] This would not change the outcomes in *Geismar* and *Euro-Diam*.
[105] Forfeiture Act 1982, s 1(1).
[106] B Kingree and L Turner, 'Life Insurance as Motive for Murder' (1994) 29 *Tort and Ins LJ* 761.
[107] *In the Estate of Cunigunda (otherwise Cora) Crippen, Deceased*, above n 84 at 112, per Evans P.
[108] (1855) 25 Beav 605.
[109] See also *Davitt v Titcumb* [1990] Ch 110; *Mackender v Feldia AG* [1967] 2 QB 590 at 599, per Lord Denning MR.
[110] *Brown v American International Life Co* 778 F Supp 912 (1991).
[111] *Mackender v Feldia AG*, above n 109 at 599, per Lord Denning MR. This passage was cited with approval by the Supreme Court of Canada in *Oldfield v Transamerica Life Insurance Co of Canada* 210 DLR (4th) 1 (2002).
[112] James Maybrick is one of the many men identified as the Whitechapel Murderer (Jack the Ripper).
[113] *Cleaver v Mutual Reserve Fund Life Association*, above n 83. Florence Maybrick was also precluded from taking as a beneficiary of James's estate. An American case did apply the *Cleaver* idea to allow a claim where a person was killed by the police during the commission of a serious felony and the beneficiary under a life policy was the insured's mother, although this approach has been rejected in other states: *Davis v Boston Mutual Life Insurance Company* 351 NE 2d 207 (1976); *Murphy v Culhane* [1977] QB 94.

decided differently if the beneficiary had not been the suicide's own estate.[114] In cases like *Crippen* it was a legal fiction that enabled the insurers to avoid paying while allowing them to keep the premiums, namely that Crippen's personal representatives were treated as being Crippen himself. In reality, of course, it would not have been Crippen who enjoyed the proceeds of the life policies but his beneficiaries.[115] On the other hand, it can be argued that, while the offender does not benefit, they should not be able to direct who should. This view was pressed by Lord Macmillan in *Beresford v Royal Insurance Co Ltd*[116]: 'To enforce payment in favour of the assured's representative would be to give him a benefit, namely, of having by his last and criminal act provided for his relatives or creditors. And no criminal can be allowed to benefit in any way by his crime.' In any event, this 'fiction' continues to prevent recovery.[117]

The forfeiture rule will apply not just where the claimant under a policy has been convicted of a murder, which led to the loss, but where diminished responsibility or provocation was successfully pleaded,[118] or where the defendant was not punished but was confined under the Mental Health Act,[119] although there is room for doubt as to whether it would apply where the defendant was found to be criminally insane under the Criminal Procedure (Insanity) Act 1964, section 1.[120] In *Dunbar v Plant*,[121] where the Court of Appeal extended the rule to the criminal complicity involved in a suicide pact,[122] Mummery LJ said:

> It is sufficient that a serious crime has been committed deliberately and intentionally. ...The essence of the principle of public policy is that (a) no person shall take a benefit resulting from a crime committed by him or her resulting in the death of the victim and (b) the nature of the crime determines the application of the principle. On that view the important point is that the crime that had fatal consequences was committed with a guilty mind (deliberately and intentionally). The particular means used to commit the crime (whether violent or non-violent) are not a necessary ingredient of the rule. There may be cases in which violence has been used deliberately without an intention to bring about the unlawful fatal consequences. Those cases will attract the application of the forfeiture rule. It does not follow,

---

[114] In *Beresford v Royal Insurance Co Ltd*, above n 78 at 605, Lord Atkin reserved his opinion on whether 'third parties who have bona fide acquired rights for value under such policies' would have an enforceable claim. See *Moore v Woolsey* (1854) 4 El & Bl 243; A McGee, *The Law and Practice of Life Assurance Contracts* (London, Sweet & Maxwell, 1995) 217–18. Changes in attitudes to suicide and in the criminal law (under the Suicide Act 1961; *Kirkham v Chief Constable of the Greater Manchester Police* [1990] 2 QB 283 at 296, per Farquharson LJ, but see the remarks of Lord Denning MR in *Hyde v Thameside Area Health Authority* unreported (1981), noted by Farquharson LJ at 295–6) might lead to a different decision in a case like *Beresford* today. If, as in *Beresford*, the parties agreed a time limit within which there could be no recovery in the event of suicide, then suicide (sane – although Farquharson LJ raised a doubt in *Kirkham* at 296 – or not) outside that period might be covered by the policy: see *Gray v Barr, Prudential Assurance Co Ltd (Third Party)*, above n 13 at 582, per Salmon LJ; *Dunbar v Plant* [1998] Ch 412. It also follows that if there is no term in the policy referring to suicide, there would be no claim in the case of a 'sane suicide' because the courts will construe the contract to preclude a claim where the cause of the loss was the deliberate act of the insured.

[115] *Prudential Life Insurance Co v Goldstein* 43 F Supp 765 at 767.

[116] See above n 78 at 605.

[117] *Hardy v Motor Insurers' Bureau*, above n 75 at 767, per Diplock LJ. See generally, Enonchong, *Illegal Transactions* (London, Lloyd's of London Press, 1998) 205–52; Shand, 'Unblinkering the Unruly Horse: Public Policy in the Law of Contract,' above n 82 at 160.

[118] *In re S, decd* [1996] 1 WLR 235.

[119] *Re Giles* [1972] Ch 544 at 552, per Pennycuick V-C; *Dalton v Latham* 2003 WL 18023075 at (9), per Patten J.

[120] *Dalton v Latham*, ibid.

[121] See above, n 114.

[122] Suicide Act 1961, s 2(1).

however, that when death has been brought about by a deliberate and intentional, but non-violent, act (eg poison or gas) the rule is inapplicable.[123]

Indeed, there may be no crime in the sense of a criminal conviction for the rule to operate. Lord Lane CJ was of the opinion that, 'in each case it is not the label which the law applies to the crime but the nature of the crime itself which will dictate whether public policy demands the court to drive the applicant from the seat of justice.'[124]

4.3.2 The Forfeiture Act 1982

A number of consequences flow from the forfeiture rule that might be regarded as undesirable. For instance, a wife who, after a long history of suffering abuse, kills her violent husband will be prevented from recovering under a policy on his life,[125] as would a wife who helps her terminally-ill husband to commit suicide. Parliament has, therefore, introduced flexibility into the application of the rule. Under the Forfeiture Act 1982,[126] unless the offender has been convicted of murder (section 5), the court can modify the rule if, having regard to the conduct of the offender and the victim and other material circumstances, 'the justice of the case requires' it (section 2(2)). The procedure is that once the court has decided the forfeiture rule applies, it will consider matters such as an offender's moral culpability, the financial position of an offender,[127] and any provocation.[128]

Since the Act the judges have struggled to define the level of culpability required to disqualify an offender. It was held in *Re H (Deceased)*[129] that the use of the Act to modify the rule might be appropriate even where someone was convicted of manslaughter on the grounds of diminished responsibility if the killing had not involved 'deliberate, intentional and unlawful violence or threats of violence.'[130] Yet, this seems out of line with other opinions on the rule, and, as Patten J has recently remarked, Parliament could have excluded the application of the rule where there was diminished responsibility, but chose not to do so.[131] *Re H (Deceased)* was also doubted by Judge Kolbert in *Jones v Roberts,*[132] on the ground that *Royse v Royse,*[133] a decision of the Court of Appeal that was on all fours with the facts in *Re H*, had not been cited. He also thought that allowing someone, who had been convicted of

---

[123] See above n 114 at 425.

[124] *R v Chief National Insurance Commissioner, ex parte Connor* [1981] QB 758 at 765, per Lord Lane CJ. Although this was a case on entitlement to the widow's allowance under the Social Security Act 1975, the principle applies more generally: *Gray v Barr, Prudential Assurance Co Ltd (Third Party)*, above n 13.

[125] For a different approach in the USA, see *Calaway v Southern Farm Bureau Life Insurance Co Inc* 619 SW 2d 301 (1981).

[126] The Act was introduced following *R v Chief National Insurance Commissioner, ex parte Connor*, above n 124; P Larkin, 'The Rule of Forfeiture and Bereavement Benefits' 11 (2004) *JSSL* 59. The Act applies only to the acquisition of certain types of property interest and, therefore, not to liability insurance (s 2(1)).

[127] *In re K, decd*, [1985] Ch 85 at 96.

[128] See also *Re S, decd*, above n 118.

[129] [1990] 1 FLR 441.

[130] Ibid, at 447, per Peter Gibson J.

[131] *Dalton v Latham*, above n 119.

[132] [1995] 2 FLR 422. See also *Re S, decd*, above n 118.

[133] [1984] 3 WLR 784.

manslaughter on the grounds of diminished responsibility, to benefit from their crime involved reshaping public policy to such an extent that it could only be undertaken by a higher court. Finally, Judge Kolbert said that battering someone to death with a hammer (as Jones did) was a deliberate, intentional and unlawful act of violence in spite of the finding of diminished responsibility. In *Dunbar v Plant*,[134] the Court of Appeal took a more liberal view in relation to complicity in a suicide pact. Phillips LJ said that, while the forfeiture rule applied to a killing in such circumstances, since the Director of Public Prosecutions had clearly not thought it in the public interest to permit a prosecution under Suicide Act 1961 (section 2(4)), the court should use its discretion under the Forfeiture Act. Moreover, he thought that it would be wrong to punish the survivor of a suicide pact by application of the rule where it was a rational decision, as where it involved an elderly couple both suffering from an incurable disease, or 'the product of an irrational depression or desperation.' In neither situation would the public interest be served by applying the forfeiture rule and, therefore, total relief under the Act should be given.[135]

4.3.3 Deliberate killing and liability insurance

In *Gray v Barr*,[136] Mr Barr, suspecting that his wife had restarted a love affair with Mr Gray, burst into the latter's house brandishing a shotgun. He fired into the ceiling, then made his way towards Gray who, doubtless fearing for his life, tried to grapple the gun away from Barr. During the struggle the gun went off and Gray was killed. Barr was acquitted of murder and manslaughter, but was sued by Gray's wife. On the question of whether Barr's liability for Gray's death was covered by a third-party liability policy, the Court of Appeal acknowledged that such policies were designed to cover death caused by the insured's negligence, but, nevertheless, denied the claim. Lord Denning MR offered two approaches. First, he said that if the shooting had been deliberate there would be no cover. He contrasted the facts of this case with the situation where someone out hunting unintentionally shot another person dead: that, he said, would be an accident within the terms of the policy, even if there had been such gross negligence as to lead to a conviction for manslaughter, because there had been no deliberate act directed at the person killed. In the present case, however, while the immediate cause of death was the second, unintentional shot, it could not be separated from the deliberate act of entering Gray's house with a loaded gun: 'The whole tragic sequence flows inexorably from that act.'[137] In summary, it

---

[134] See above n 114.

[135] Ibid, at 1285. Phillips LJ recognised that some suicide pacts might involve such culpability as would require the application of the rule: he hinted, for instance, that a pact prompted by one person who was afraid of the consequences of a theft which he had committed might prompt the application of the rule.

[136] See above n 13. *Gray v Barr* is a case which, while being given a thorough pounding by academics, has been admired and, what is more to the point, followed by the judiciary in England and abroad. See JA Jolowicz, 'Liability Insurance – Manslaughter – Public Policy' [1970] *CLJ* 194; JG Fleming, 'Insurance for the Criminal' (1971) 34 *MLR* 176; Shand, 'Unblinkering the Unruly Horse: Public Policy in the Law of Contract,' above n 82. For a critical discussion of the impact of the case in Canada, where it has been cited with approval in the Supreme Court, see RA Hasson, 'The Supreme Court of Canada and the Law of Insurance 1975' (1976) 14 *Osgoode Hall Law Journal* 769 at 776–8. See also, W Gellhorn, above n 83; RB Wuehler, 'Rethink Insurance's Public Policy Exclusion: California's Befuddled Attempt to Apply an Undefined Rule and a Call for Reform' (2001) 49 *UCLA L Rev* 651.

[137] See above n 13, at 567.

seems that Lord Denning required there to have been a deliberate act aimed at the person killed, which act was so closely linked to the act that led to the death to make the two actions into one event. As an alternative, Lord Denning said that a civil court was not bound by the verdict of the criminal court: in Denning's view Barr was guilty of manslaughter, and because 'his conduct is wilful and culpable, he is not entitled to recover.'[138] Phillimore LJ also thought that the two shots could not be separated. The wilful act of going into the house with the shotgun may have led to an unexpected and unintended result, but it was one which could reasonably have been anticipated and it was, therefore, not an accident. He added that 'the true question is whether people would commonly agree with Mr Barr if after describing all the circumstances as they occurred he went on to say. "It was an accident." I confess that I would not.'[139] Yet, Phillimore LJ need not have looked very far to find someone who differed with him on that view. Salmon LJ separated the two shots and concluded that the death was an accident because it occurred as the result of the second, unintended shot. But he went on to say that there was an implied term in the contract that precluded recovery where an accident occurred in the course of the insured threatening unlawful violence with a loaded gun. If, in the alternative, there was no such implied term, he would still deny the claim on the ground of public policy: 'Crimes of violence, particularly when committed with loaded guns, are amongst the worse curses of this age. It is very much in the public interest that they should be deterred.'[140]

There are some problems with this case, not least of which is the lack of a clear ratio decidendi.[141] Nevertheless, the decision would seem to be authority for the view that the court will look at the nature of the insured's act and decide if there was a deliberate criminal act directed at another person who is thereby killed, regardless of whether violence was involved or there was any criminal conviction.[142] Geoffrey Lane J provided a useful method of distinguishing between different types of manslaughter which returns us to the issue of the deliberate nature of the act:

> The logical test, in my judgment, is whether the person seeking the indemnity was guilty of deliberate, intentional and unlawful violence, or threats of violence. If he was, and death resulted therefrom, then, however unintended the final death of the victim may have been, the court should not entertain a claim for indemnity.[143]

This oft-quoted definition should be amending in the light of Mummery LJ's remarks about the stipulation that there must be violence or the threat of violence. The question remains as to whether the act must be directed at the person whose death occurs: what if A threatens B with a gun and during the ensuing struggle the

---

[138] Ibid, at 568.

[139] Ibid, at 585.

[140] Ibid, at 581. It is hard to disagree with Salmon LJ's opinion of guns, although if viewed in terms of death and injury caused the motor car could be said to be a much greater 'curse of this age.'

[141] See *Marcell Beller Ltd v Hayden* [1978] QB 694.

[142] This proposition fits in with cases in which the issue has been whether a claimant could obtain redress through the civil courts in connection with a felony where there had been no prosecution, such as *Ex parte Ball, In re Shepherd* (1879) 10 Ch D 667, and *The Midland Insurance Co v Smith and Wife* (1891) 6 QBD 561 at 576, in which Watkin Williams J said, 'it seems clear to me that the prosecution of the felon is not an absolute condition precedent to the accruing of the cause of action.' Leaving aside the role of jury equity in criminal trials, the assessment of whether there has been a crime will, in civil proceedings, be on a balance of probabilities, making such a conclusion more likely.

[143] [1970] 2 QB 626 at 640. See *In re K, decd*, above n 127.

gun is accidentally fired killing C? Although statements in *Gray v Barr* seem to suggest the act must be directed at the person killed, it seems clear that they should not be read so narrowly and, indeed, it is not part of Geoffrey Lane J's test.

4.3.4 Motor manslaughter

In spite of the lack of a general principle in insurance law in favour of ensuring that third parties receive compensation, when someone is killed or injured by a motorist the courts have seemed to focus on this objective to the exclusion of the issues that so exercised the Court of Appeal in *Gray v Barr*.[144] In *Tinline v White Cross Insurance Association Ltd*[145] a speeding motorist killed one pedestrian and injured two others as they were crossing Shaftesbury Avenue in London's West End. He was convicted of manslaughter involving gross or reckless negligence. In litigation over the liability of his insurers, Bailhache J remarked that: 'Speaking generally, it is true to say that it is against public policy to indemnify a man against the consequences of a crime which he knowingly commits.'[146] However, a motor policy covering liability to third parties must include 'negligence whether slight or great.'[147] Therefore, the insurers were liable on the policy. It is difficult to reconcile such decisions with *Gray v Barr*. Barr did not intend to kill any more than did the motorist in *Tinline*, and both Barr and the motorists committed deliberate and criminal acts which led to the deaths. The key distinction could be that in *Tinline* the deliberate act that caused death was not directed at anyone in the way that Barr's act of entering the house with a gun had been directed at Gray. Yet, this seems not to assist us with two cases where motorists directed their cars at people just as surely as Barr directed his gun (more so, perhaps). In *Hardy v Motor Insurers' Bureau*,[148] where the driver was convicted of wounding with intent to commit grievous bodily harm, and in *Gardner v Moore*,[149] where the driver was convicted of maliciously inflicting grievous bodily harm, the Court of Appeal and the House of Lords respectively decided that, although the deliberate and criminal nature of such acts meant that an insured driver, who had already paid damages to the victim, could not claim an indemnity from the insurers, if the victim could not recover compensation from the driver, the driver's insurers were liable, or the Motor Insurers' Bureau, where the driver was not insured or could not be traced.[150] Indeed, the victim in such cases would be able to claim directly against the insurer under the provisions of the Road Traffic Act 1988. Diplock LJ, in a judgment later approved by the House of Lords in *Gardner v Moore*, suggested that: 'The court has to weigh the gravity of the anti-social act and the extent to which it will be encouraged by enforcing the right sought to be asserted against the social harm

---

[144] See above n 13. It is worth recalling that a distinction exists in criminal law where the degree of negligence required to convict a motorist of manslaughter is much higher than that required to convict someone accused of manslaughter involving a weapon: compare *R v Andrews* [1937] AC 576 with *R v Larkin* [1943] KB 174.

[145] See above n 69.

[146] Ibid, at 332.

[147] Ibid, at 332. *James v British General Insurance Co Ltd* [1927] 2 KB 311.

[148] See above n 75.

[149] [1984] AC 549.

[150] See below ch 13.

which will be caused if the right is not enforced.'[151] In the same case Lord Denning MR said:

> If the motorist is guilty of a crime involving a wicked and deliberate intent, and he is made to pay damages to an injured person, he is not entitled to recover on the policy. But if he does not pay the damages, then the injured third party can recover against the insurers under s.207 of the Road Traffic Act 1960; for it is a liability which the motorist under the statute was required to cover. The injured third party is not affected by the disability which attached to the motorist himself ... The policy of insurance which a motorist is required by statute to take out must cover any liability which may be incurred by him arising out of the use of the vehicle by him. It must, I think, be wide enough to cover, in general terms, any use by him of the vehicle, be it an innocent use or a criminal use, or be it a murderous use or a playful use.[152]

These cases can only be distinguished from *Gray v Barr* on public policy grounds. But what public policy goals are achieved by the distinction which the courts make? When the judges in *Gray* said that Barr's action was dangerous they must have meant it was dangerous for third parties like Gray. They did not consider it more important to provide protection for those third parties other than to use the case to point out what was already obvious – that waving shotguns about is dangerous. Moreover, by not holding the insurers liable to indemnify the miscreant, they made the victim pay for a lesson which is unlikely to have any impact.[153] The idea that the decision in *Gray* would deter husbands from using guns to threaten those whom they believed to be their spouses' lovers seems fanciful. Even ignoring the likelihood that *Gray* is not widely known, it is unlikely that the husband who is so much out of control as to contemplate shooting the lover will be brought back to his senses by an insurance policy. As for the broader consideration that the law must not be used to indemnify people for their criminal actions, this has not outweighed the wish to compensate the victims of malicious motorists. What is the difference between someone, who has a licence to own a shotgun, waving that gun in someone's face and a licensed motorist driving on the pavement? Both are illegal ways of conducting oneself and Parliament has chosen to control them by a combination of licensing provisions and criminal offences. It seems better for the judges to leave the matter of deterring and punishing criminal behaviour to the criminal courts, and in a civil action to focus on the narrower issues between the parties, that is, the question of the victim's compensation, as they have done with injuries caused by motorists.[154] On the other hand, why should the wrong-doer be indemnified by the insurer for the consequences of their wrongdoing and is consideration of the plight of the victim relevant? Whatever sympathy we may feel for victims of criminal or tortious acts, there is no principle of public policy which requires a third party (the insurers) to compensate them (by indemnifying the insured) in circumstances not provided for in the contract of insurance. The victims

---

[151] See above n 75 at 768. See also *Geismar v Sun Alliance and London Insurance Ltd*, above n 92 at 390, per Talbot J.

[152] See above n 75 at 746 and 760.

[153] Whether Mrs Barr received compensation from Gray is irrelevant to the argument, as in most cases tortfeasors are unlikely to be able to afford to pay.

[154] See *Hardy v Motor Insurers' Bureau*, above n 75 at 769–70, per Diplock LJ. This returns us to arguments that were rehearsed earlier in the chapter when it was seen that, on occasion, the civil courts do see deterrence as part of their function.

of motorists have been made relevant by the intervention of legislation. The Road Traffic Act 1988 not only requires motorists to have a certain level of cover against third party liability, but gives the third party rights to pursue a claim against the insurers directly and restricts the ability of the insurers to limit their liability to third parties.[155] The significance of the legislation is illustrated by the Court of Appeal's decision in *Charlton v Fisher*.[156] A driver deliberately–although without an intention of causing injury–steered into another car in a car park. This caused injury to a person in the other car, but because the incident took place on private land the Road Traffic Act 1988 did not apply and the driver's insurer was held not to be liable because the injury was the result of a deliberate criminal act.

---

[155] However, even before the introduction of compulsory third-party liability insurance in 1930, the courts were seeking to protect victims of motorists: *Tinline v White Cross Insurance Association Ltd*, above n 69; see below ch 13. That the distinction does not rest simply on this issue of insurance is also suggested by the notion that the courts may apply the forfeiture rule less rigorously in motor manslaughter cases: *Jones v Roberts*, above n 132, 422 at 425, per Judge Kolbert.

[156] [2002] QB 578.

10

Claims Procedure, Measurement of Loss and Reinstatement

A. CLAIMS PROCEDURE

1. Claims

It has been seen,[1] that a policy may contain a range of conditions precedent. These generally include conditions precedent to recovery. Such conditions must be strictly complied with by the insured when claiming payment to cover an insured loss. Looked at another way, these terms may be described as conditions precedent to the liability of the insurers. Whether or not there has been a breach of such a condition is a question of construction, and in construing the particular term the court will have regard to its purpose.[2] Conditions precedent to recovery generally lay down requirements as to the requisite notice to be given to the insurers in the event of a loss; the particulars of the loss to be furnished by the insured; and, in the event of a dispute arising between the parties, that settlement should be by way of arbitration.

1.1 Notice of loss

Generally, the insured will be under a duty to notify the insurers of the loss within a

---

[1] See chs 7 and 8, above.
[2] *Stoneham v Ocean, Railway and General Accident Insurance Co* (1887) 19 QBD 237 at 239, *per* Mathew J. See also, *Welsh v Royal Exchange Assurance* [1939] 1 KB 294. But see the speech of Lord Mustill in *Charter Reinsurance Ltd v Fagan* [1996] 2 WLR 726, considered at p 205, above.

specified time limit, or if none is stipulated, within a reasonable time.[3] In liability insurance, such as an all risks policy, it is not uncommon for a term to require the insured to give notice to the insurers of the occurrence of an event that is 'likely to give rise to a claim.' The meaning of such a term was considered by the Court of Appeal in *Jacobs* v *Coster*,[4] in which it was held that 'likely' meant an event that presented at least a 50 per cent chance that a claim would result. Further, the Court took the view that the fact that a person had fallen over and sustained injury did not of itself mean that a claim was 'likely'. In this respect, the burden of proof was on the insurer.

Oral notice of a loss will suffice unless written notice is expressly stipulated. If the condition is clear and unequivocal, the duty is absolute and impossibility or ignorance will not afford a defence to the insured. In *Cassel* v *Lancashire & Yorkshire Insurance Co*,[5] the insured was involved in a canoeing accident but his injuries were latent for some eight months. His claim under an accident policy failed because he had not complied with the 14 days notice period specified in the policy. However, it has been held that where the police have communicated notice of the loss to the insurers, the insured is relieved from the duty of notifying them personally, even if personal notification is expressly required by the policy, because 'it would be a futile thing to require the [insured] himself to give them the selfsame information. The law never compels a person to do that which is useless and unnecessary.'[6]

Although notice clauses require strict compliance by the insured, the courts will nevertheless construe them strictly against the insurer. In *Verelst's Administratrix* v *Motor Union Insurance Co*,[7] a motor policy contained a condition which provided that in the event of a loss 'the insured or the insured's personal representative ... shall give notice ... to the ... company of such loss as soon as possible after it has come to the knowledge of the insured or the insured's personal representative.' While visiting India the insured was killed in a motoring accident. Her administratrix did not know of the insurance company with which the insured had effected cover until nearly a year after the accident had occurred when she came across the policy while sorting out old papers belonging to the insured. The insurers sought to repudiate liability for breach of the notice requirement. It was held that the administratrix could recover. Roche J construed the clause to mean 'as soon as possible to the legal representative under the existing circumstances which prevailed and applied.'[8]

---

[3] *Hadenfayre Ltd v British National Insurance Society Ltd* [1984] 2 Lloyd's Rep 393 at 402, *per* Lloyd J. See also, *Bankers Ins v South* [2004] Lloyd's Rep IR 1. With respect to policies issued to individual insureds, the Statements of Insurance Practice provided that an insured should not be required to report a claim and subsequent developments within a strict time limit but rather '"as soon as reasonably possible."' It will be recalled (see chs 4 and 7) that the Statements have been superseded by FSA rules; however, any term in this respect which is considered 'unfair' may now be struck down by virtue of the Unfair Terms in Consumer Contracts Regulations 1999. The Financial Ombudsman's Newsletter (Issue 39, August 2004), states that where a commercial policyholder is, effectively, in the same position as a private individual with a personal policy, it may be appropriate to apply the principles of the ABI's Statement to such a case. See Case 39/2, given by way of illustration.

[4] [2000] Lloyd's Rep IR 506. See also, *Layher Ltd v Lowe* [2000] Lloyd's Rep IR 510.

[5] (1885) 1 TLR 495. For an extreme example, see *Adamson & Sons v Liverpool & London & Globe Insurance Co Ltd* [1953] 2 Lloyd's Rep 355.

[6] *Barrett Bros (Taxis) Ltd v Davies (Lickiss and Milestone Motor Policies at Lloyd's, Third Parties)* [1966] 2 Lloyd's Rep 1 at 5, *per* Lord Denning MR.

[7] (1950) 21 Ll L Rep 227.

[8] Ibid, at 229.

Recent case law points to an insured-friendly approach being adopted by the courts. In chapter 7 we saw that in *Alfred McAlpine plc v BAI (Run-Off) Ltd*,[9] the Court of Appeal, importing the terminology of 'innominate terms' from the general law of contract, classified a notification clause, condition 1(a) in the policy, which required the insured to give notice of a claim under the policy 'as soon as possible,' as a term which fell short of a condition precedent. It is noteworthy that the clause in question was not described as a condition precedent, unlike other terms in the policy. Waller LJ explained that the clause was not so fundamental that its breach amounted to a repudiation of the whole contract. It lacked the quality of 'essentiality':

> Condition 1(a) is...an innominate term. Breach of it, however serious, would be unlikely to amount to a repudiation of the whole contract of insurance. Furthermore, it is not a term the breach of which, or any breach of which, would entitle the insurer not to pay the claim because that would simply make it a condition precedent. But, in my view, a breach which demonstrated an intention not to continue to make a claim, or which has very serious consequences for BAI, should be such as to entitle BAI to defeat the claim. If a term is a condition precedent to liability, any breach defeats liability but does not lead to a repudiation of the whole contract. I see no reason why although a term is not a condition precedent so that any breach defeats liability, it cannot be construed as a term where a serious breach defeats liability.[10]

The decision in *McAlpine* should not be taken as holding that notification clauses are to be viewed as something less than conditions precedent, for, as seen in chapters 7 and 8, the nature of a contractual term is a question of law. But see the Court of Appeal's decision in *Friends Provident v Sirius* in which Mance LJ rejected Waller LJ's reasoning in BAI (see p 206 above).

1.2 Particulars of the loss

In addition to notification, the insured will generally be under a duty to submit particulars of the loss to the insurers. The guiding principle seems to be that the insured must provide sufficient detail to enable the insurers 'to form a judgment as to whether or not he has sustained a loss.'[11] A condition that 'full particulars' of the loss must be given has been defined as meaning 'the best particulars which the assured can reasonably give.'[12] As with conditions relating to notice periods, terms in a consumer contract which stipulate the required particulars to be supplied to the insurers as proof of the loss will need to satisfy the Unfair Terms in Consumer Contracts Regulations 1999.

A so-called 'co-operation clause', frequently found in liability insurance policies,[13] will require the insured to co-operate by, for example, providing particulars of the loss (see above), or by undertaking not to settle with a third party, or by undertaking not to take any other steps which may prejudice the insurers' position. A common

---

[9] [2000] Lloyd's Rep IR 352. See p 206, above. See also, *Friends Provident Life and Pensions Ltd v Sirius International Insurance Corporation* [2004] EWHC 1799 (Comm).
[10] Ibid, at [34].
[11] *Mason v Harvey* (1853) 8 Exch 819 at 820–1, *per* Pollock CB.
[12] Ibid.
[13] See ch 14, below.

example is found in motor insurance where the insured is generally obliged not to admit liability to a third party. Breach of the insured's duty to co-operate will defeat the claim.[14]

1.3 Arbitration

It was at one time common for policies of insurance to include a condition providing for the resolution of disputes through arbitration in the first instance. This avoided the expense and delay of civil litigation through the courts. It has been held that an arbitration clause is enforceable as a condition precedent, with the result that the insured cannot sue on the policy but can bring an action only to enforce an arbitration award in his favour.[15] Following the findings by the Law Reform Committee of abuse by insurers in insisting upon arbitration,[16] particularly in the light of the unavailability of legal aid in such proceedings, the Association of British Insurers and Lloyd's announced that their members would not enforce arbitration clauses in cases where the insured indicated a desire to have the issue of liability, as opposed to *quantum*, determined by a court.[17]

An issue that arises with respect to an arbitration clause contained in an insurance contract is the question of its validity where it is claimed that the policy is vitiated as a result of, for example, non-disclosure or lack of insurable interest. In these cases an arbitration clause cannot be relied on unless it is so framed as to cover disputes going to the very validity of the policy.[18] An arbitration clause is, by virtue of s 7 of the Arbitration Act 1996, an independent undertaking in its own right, so that as long as the dispute falls within the scope of the clause, it is irrelevant whether the insurer has relied upon utmost good faith, breach of warranty or indeed any other defence. At one time there was doubt as to the position where the insurer sought to rely upon a fraudulent claim. In *Super Chem Products Ltd v American Life and General Insurance Co Ltd*,[19] the issue was whether the insurers could require compliance with the claims clauses in the policy while, at the same time, allege fraud. The insured had a material damage and business interruption policy. The factory in question was damaged by fire and the insurers pleaded, inter alia, arson. They also sought to rely on the insured's failure to commence proceedings within 12 months as stipulated by the policy. The Privy Council held that the plea of arson did not amount to a repudiation of the policy. In so holding, the board overruled the much criticised dicta of Viscount Haldane LC in *Jureidini v National British and Irish Millers Insurance Co Ltd*,[20] to the effect that an insurer who repudiates liability on the basis of fraud and arson cannot 'insist on a subordinate term of the contract still being enforced.'[21] In the light of

---

14 *London Guarantee Co v Fearnley* (1880) 5 App Cas 911.
15 *Scott v Avery* (1856) 5 HLC 811. See now the Arbitration Act 1996, s 9.
16 Fifth Report on Conditions and Exceptions in Insurance Policies (Cmnd 62, 1957).
17 Reinsurance, marine insurance and facets of aviation insurance are excluded from this undertaking. An arbitration clause in a consumer policy may now be caught by the Unfair Terms in Consumer Contracts Regulations 1999.
18 *Heyman v Darwins* [1942] AC 356 at 385, *per* Lord Wright.
19 [2004] Lloyd's Rep IR 446, PC. Noted by D Friedmann [2004] *LQR* 407.
20 [1915] AC 499.
21 Ibid, at 505. Lord Steyn in *Super Chem* was at pains to align the insurance law position with that of the general law of contract. See also, *Port Jackson Stevedoring Pty Ltd v Salmond and Spraggon (Australia) Pty Ltd* [1981] 1 WLR 138, PC.

Super Chem it would appear that a fraudulent claim will no longer affect the validity of an arbitration clause.

---

2. The insured's duty of utmost good faith and fraudulent claims

It was seen in chapter 4 that section 17 of the Marine Insurance Act 1906 provides that: 'A contract of marine insurance is a contract based upon the utmost good faith, and, if the utmost good faith is not observed by either party, the contract may be avoided by either party.' The issue that arises, and one that has generated considerable judicial debate, concerns the post-contractual scope of this duty. Unsurprisingly, this has generally come to the fore where the insured has made a fraudulent claim. We first consider the meaning of fraud before going on to examine the consequences of making a fraudulent claim.

2.1 Defining fraud

A material statement in a claim is fraudulent if the insured either knew it to be false or else was reckless as to its truth.[22] Mere carelessness will not suffice. The onus of proof is on the insurer, and given the nature of the allegation the burden will be greater than on a mere balance of probabilities.[23] A so-called 'rescession induced claim' where the insured has, with intent, destroyed the insured property is a common example of fraud in this context. The courts do, however, recognise that an exaggerated claim by an insured is a bargaining device used against insurers who frequently attempt to reduce the size of a claim. In *Ewer v National Employers' Mutual General Insurance Association*,[24] the claimant claimed the current cost price of new items of furniture to replace his second hand items which had been destroyed by fire. Mackinnon J, although describing the claim as preposterous, held that no deception was perpetuated. He said:

> I do not think [the claimant] was doing that in any way a fraudulent claim, but as a figure to start off with as a bargaining figure. We have been told that the defendant company wanted to see invoices. The invoices, of course, would show what the articles cost. As the [claimant] could not produce the invoices showing what the articles cost, I think he did the best he could in substituting for it... The [claimant] knew the claim would be discussed, and probably drastically criticised, by the assessors: he had been asked for invoices, and he started the bargaining with them by putting down the cost price of these articles as if they were new.[25]

---

[22] *Derry v Peek* (1889) 14 App Cas 337 at 371, *per* Lord Herschell. See also, *Lek v Mathews* (1927) 29 LL L Rep 141. See further, *Manifest Shipping Co Ltd v Uni-Polaris Shipping Co Ltd (The Star Sea)* [2001] UKHL 1, at [102] and [111]. See also, Mance LJ in *The Aegeon*, n 57, below.
[23] *Hornal v Neuberger Products Ltd* [1957] 1 QB 247 at 258, *per* Lord Denning MR.
[24] (1937) 157 LT 16.
[25] Ibid, at 21. See also, *Orakpo v Barclays Insurance Services* [1999] LRLR 443 at 451, *per* Hoffmann LJ.

While over-valuation is not therefore in itself sufficient to establish fraud, a grossly exaggerated claim of the true value of the loss will raise a presumption of fraud.[26] Such indulgence as displayed by MacKinnon J towards 'preposterously' exaggerated claims was not so readily accepted by Hoffmann LJ in *Orakpo v Barclays Insurance Services*,[27] although he did explain that:

> In cases where nothing is misrepresented or concealed, and the loss adjuster is in a good a position to form a view of the validity of the claim as the insured, it will be a legitimate reason that the insured was merely putting forward a starting figure for negotiation.[28]

2.2 The consequences of a fraudulent claim

In assessing the effect that a fraudulent claim has on the validity of the policy the critical question is whether the insured's duty of utmost good faith continues beyond the time when the policy is initially effected and renewed so that it also operates when an insured seeks to claim against the insurers for a loss. Until recently, it was generally thought that the duty revived at the claims stage.[29] The point was made by Mathew LJ in *Boulton v Houlder Bros & Co*,[30] that it 'is an essential condition of the policy of insurance that the underwriters shall be treated with good faith, not merely in reference to the inception of the risk, but in the steps taken to carry out the contract.'[31] The underlying rationale for this view was explained by Hoffmann LJ in *Orakpo v Barclays Insurance Services*:[32]

> I do not see why the duty of good faith on the part of the assured should expire when the contract has been made. The reasons for requiring good faith continue to exist. Just as the nature of the risk will usually be within the peculiar knowledge of the insured, so will the circumstances of the casualty; it will rarely be within the knowledge of the insurance company. I think that the insurance company should be able to trust the assured to put forward a claim in good faith.[33]

Sir Roger Parker agreed with Hoffmann LJ. The Court of Appeal therefore held that a claim which is fraudulent entitles the insurer to avoid the contact *ab initio* irrespective of whether there is a term in the policy to that effect. However, Staughton LJ

---

[26] *Goulstone v Royal Insurance Co* (1858) 1 F& F 276; *Central Bank of India v Guardian Assurance Co* (1936) 54 Ll LR 247; *Orakpo v Barclays Insurance Services*, ibid at 450, *per* Staughton LJ.
[27] Ibid.
[28] Ibid, at 451. In *Central Bank of India v Guardian Assurance Co*, ibid, a claim for some one hundred times the true value of the loss was held to be fraudulent.
[29] *Manifest Shipping v Uni-Polaris Insurance Co, The Star Sea* [1997] 1 Lloyd's Rep 360 at 372, *per* Leggatt LJ, approving the judgment of Rix J in *Royal Boskalis Westminster NV v Mountain* [1997] LRLR 523, in which the judge cited the following passage from the 2nd edn of M Clarke, *The Law of Insurance Contracts* (London, Lloyd's of London Press, 1994) 708: 'As regards insurance contracts, the duty of good faith continues throughout the contractual relationship at a level appropriate to the moment. In particular, the duty of disclosure, most prominent prior to contract formation, revives whenever the insured has an express or implied duty to supply information to enable the insurer to make a decision. Hence, it applies if cover is extended or renewed. It also applies when the insured claims insurance money: he must make "full disclosure of the circumstances of the case" [citing *Shepherd v Chewter* (1808) 1 Camp 274 at 275, *per* Lord Ellenborough].'
[30] [1904] 1 KB 784.
[31] Ibid, at 791–2. See, also, *Shepherd v Chewter*, above n 29.
[32] Above, n 25.
[33] Ibid, at 451.

differed. While he thought this should certainly be the case where the policy so provided,[34] he was not convinced this should necessarily be the case in the absence of such term:

> I do not know of any other corner of the law where the plaintiff who has made a fraudulent claim is deprived even of that which he is lawfully entitled to… True, there is distinguished support for such a doctrine[35]…But we were not told of any authority which binds us to teach that conclusion.[36]

It is settled that if the insured makes a fraudulent claim, he or she will not be able to recover.[37] The consequence is that the insured will forfeit all rights under the policy and it can therefore be terminated for breach.[38] However, the question whether the policy can be avoided *ab initio* so that the insurer can recover any payments made with respect to an earlier loss, or whether the insurer should be restricted to recovering only from the date of the fraudulent claim, has continued to vex judges and commentators alike.[39] It would seem that the degree of protection required by insurers at the inception of the contract is significantly higher than that at the time of any loss and subsequent claim, so that to allow avoidance *ab initio* seems to be particularly harsh. Yet, in *Black King Shipping Corp v Massie (The Litsion Pride)*,[40] it was held that a fraudulent claim could amount to breach of section 17 of the 1906 Act, thereby entitling the insurer to avoid the contract *ab initio*. Subsequently, in *Orakpo* the majority of the Court of Appeal was of the view that where an insured's claim is fraudulent to a 'substantial extent' it must fail.[41] The meaning of the term 'substantial' was considered by the Court of Appeal in *Galloway v Guardian Royal Exchange (UK) Ltd.*[42] The claimant's premises were burgled and he claimed under a home contents policy some £16,133.94 (the probable true value of the loss) and an additional £2,000 for a computer. In fact, there had been no loss of a computer and a receipt which the claimant produced as evidence of purchase was a forgery. Further, when completing the proposal form for this insurance some five months prior to the claim, he had failed to disclose a conviction for obtaining property by deception. Lord Woolf MR, stressing that the policy of the law must be to deter the making of fraudulent claims, stated that the phrase 'substantial':

> is to be understood as indicating that, if there is some immaterial non-disclosure, then of course, even though that material non-disclosure was fraudulent dire consequences do not

---

[34] Albeit, subject to the Unfair Terms in Consumer Contracts Regulations.

[35] Citing, inter alia, *Britton v Royal Insurance* (1866) 4 F & F 905 and *Black King Shipping Corp v Massie (The Litsion Pride)* [1985] 2 Lloyd's Rep 437.

[36] Above n 25, at 450.

[37] *Britton v Royal Insurance*, above n 35.

[38] Ibid.

[39] See, eg, *Gore Mutual Insurance Co v Bifford* (1987) 45 DLR (4th) 763; *The Litsion Pride* [1985] 1 Lloyd's Rep 437; *Reid & Co v Employers' Accident & Livestock Insurance Co Ltd* 1 F (Ct Sess) 1031. See also M Clarke, *The Law of Insurance Contracts* (London, Lloyd's of London Press, 2002) paras 27–2C2. See further, M Clarke, 'Lies, Damned Lies, and Insurance Claims: the Elements and Effect of Fraud' [2000] *New Zealand LR* 233.

[40] Above, n 35.

[41] Above, n 25 at 451, *per* Hoffmann LJ; at 452, *per* Sir Roger Parker. This is merely the application of the *de minimis* rule.

[42] [1999] Lloyd's Rep IR 209.

follow in relation to the claim as a whole; but if the fraud is material, it does have the effect that it taints the whole.[43]

For Lord Woolf MR the whole of the claim must be looked at in order to determine whether the fraud is material. On the facts of the case, the claim for £2,000 amounted to some 10 per cent of the whole. This was an amount which was substantial and it therefore tainted the whole claim. Millett LJ, however, disagreed with this reasoning. He said that the determination of whether a claim is 'substantially' fraudulent should not be tested by reference to the proportion it bears to the entire claim. To do so 'would lead to the absurd conclusion that the greater the genuine loss, the larger the fraudulent claim which may be made at the same time without penalty.'[44] In Millett LJ's view the size of the genuine claim should not be taken into account. All that matters is that the insured is in breach of the duty of good faith which leaves him without cover:

> the right approach in such a case is to consider the fraudulent claim as if it were the only claim and then to consider whether, taken in isolation, the making of that claim by the insured is sufficiently serious to justify stigmatising it as a breach of his duty of good faith so as to avoid the policy.[45]

It is suggested that Millett LJ's criticism of the 'substantially fraudulent' threshold is correct. Determining fine distinctions between what is 'substantial' or otherwise can lead to fine and arbitrary decisions. Millett LJ also went on to ctiticise the current vogue of lodging dishonest insurance claims in the belief that defrauding insurance companies is not 'morally reprehensible'. As a matter of policy, therefore, he added that he would not support any dilution of the insured's duty of good faith.

Recent decisions have taken a restrictive view towards the post-contractual application of s 17. In *Manifest Shipping* v *Uni-Polaris Insurance Co, (The Star Sea)*,[46] the trial judge had doubted the independent application of utmost good faith to the claims process. He held that even if it did operate there had to be at the very least recklessness by the insured and that the duty came to an end once legal proceedings had been commenced as after that date false statements were to be dealt with as part of the court's processes rather than as part of the claim.[47] The Court of Appeal,[48] took the view that the duty of good faith binds both the insured and the insurer when a claim is made. Leggatt LJ observed that:

> It is less clear from the cases whether there is a duty to disclose co-extensive with that which exists before the contract of insurance is entered into, as opposed to a rather different obligation to make full disclosure of the circumstances of the claim. But the distinction matters not.[49]

---

[43] Ibid, at 213.
[44] Ibid, at 214.
[45] Ibid.
[46] Above, n 22. See Sir Andrew Longmore, 'Good faith and breach of warranty: are we moving forwards or backwards?' [2004] *LMCLQ* 158, esp 166–71.
[47] [1995] 1 Lloyd's Rep 651.
[48] Above, n 29.
[49] Ibid, at 371.

Leggatt LJ went on to state that that the insured's duty of good faith requires that the claim should not be made fraudulently and that the duty 'is coincident with the term to be implied by law, as forming part of a contract of insurance, that where fraud is proved in the making of a claim the insurer is discharged from all liability.'[50] In conclusion, the judge stressed that given the draconian remedy available to insurers where a claim is made fraudulently, there should be no enlargement of the insured's duty so as to encompass claims made 'culpably'.[51]

The House of Lords, doubting the reasoning of Hirst J in *The Litsion Pride*,[52] accepted that the duty of utmost good faith continued to apply after the conclusion of the insurance contract but held that the claim of fraud had not been proved. Lord Hobhouse, noting that the right to avoid under section 17 entitles the insurer to rescind the contract *ab initio*, thought that were this remedy to apply where the breach of duty occurs post-contractually, the effect would be effectively penal. In his reasoning, Lord Hobhouse also placed emphasis on the disparity between the parties that would result if there was a continuing duty of utmost good faith:

> [The] authorities show that there is a clear distinction to be made between the pre-contract duty of disclosure and any duty of disclosure which may exist after the contract has been made. It is not right to reason…from the existence of an extensive duty pre-contract positively to disclose all material facts to the conclusion that post-contract there is a similarly extensive obligation to disclose all facts which the insurer has an interest in knowing and which might affect his conduct… An inevitable consequence in the post-contract situation is that the remedy of avoidance of the contract is in practical terms wholly one-sided. It is a remedy of value to the insurer and, if the defendants' argument is accepted, of disproportionate benefit to him; it enables him to escape retrospectively the liability to indemnify which he has previously and (on this hypothesis) validly undertaken…[53]

With respect to the majority view in *Orakpo*, Lord Hobhouse observed that the decision 'cannot be treated as fully authoritative in view of the contractual analysis there adopted' with respect to the duty of good faith.[54]

In *Kls Merc-Scandia XXXXII v Certain Lloyd's Underwriters Subscribing to Lloyd's Policy No 25t 105487 and Ocean Marine Insurance Co Ltd, The Mercandian Continent*,[55] the insured submitted a forged letter to his liability insurers to assist them in defending a claim that had been brought against the insured by a third party. The letter was found to be immaterial and the insurers were therefore held liable. The Court of Appeal, aligning the duty of disclosure during the claims process with its

---

[50] Ibid. See also, *Orakpo v Barclays Insurance Services*, above n 25 at 451, in which Hoffmann LJ stated 'any fraud in making the claim goes to the root of the contract and entitles the insurer to be discharged.' As has been seen, in *Galloway v Guardian Royal Exchange (UK) Ltd*, above n 42, the Court of Appeal held that the absence of an express condition providing that where there was a fraudulent claim the policy would be void made no difference for the duty of good faith continued long after the policy was effected and applied to the claims process.

[51] Ibid. See also, the observations made in *Diggens v Sun Alliance and London Insurance plc* [1994] CLC 1146 to the effect that the duty is not broken by an innocent or negligent non-disclosure.

[52] Above n 35. See HN Bennett, 'Mapping the doctrine of utmost good faith in insurance contract law' [1999] *LMCLQ* 165.

[53] Ibid, at [52] and [57].

[54] Ibid, at [66].

[55] [2001] Lloyd's Rep IR 802. See also *Agapitos v Agnew, 'The Aegeon'* [2002] Lloyd's Rep 42, discussed below. See, HY Yeo, 'Post-contractual good faith–change in judicial attitude?' [2003] *MLR* 425.

pre-contract counterpart, took the view that the non-disclosed or misrepresented fact must be material and it must induce the insurer to pay the claim. With respect to the remedy available to the innocent party, Longmore LJ explained that the right to avoid the contract with retrospective effect is only exercisable in circumstances where the innocent party would, in any event, be entitled to terminate the contract for breach. He went on to state that:

> [T]he giving of information, pursuant to an express or implied obligation to do so in the contract of insurance, is an occasion when good faith should be exercised. Since…the giving of information is essentially an obligation stemming from contract, the remedy for the insured fraudulently misinforming the insurer must be commensurate with the insurer's remedies for breach of contract. The insurer will not, therefore, be able to avoid the contract of insurance with retrospective effect unless he can show that the fraud was relevant to his ultimate liability under the policy and was such as would entitle him to terminate the insurance contract.[56]

As is illustrated by the facts of *The Mercandian Continent*, the issue has recently come to the fore in relation not to fraudulent claims as such, but in relation to the use of 'fraudulent devices' to promote a claim. The distinction was explained by Mance LJ in *Agapitos v Agnew, The Aegeon*[57]: 'a fraudulent claim exists where the insured claims, knowing that he has suffered no loss, or only a lesser loss than that which he claims (or is reckless as to whether this is the case).'[58] A fraudulent device, however, is 'used if the insured believes that he has suffered the loss claimed, but seeks to improve or embellish the facts surrounding the claim, by some lie.'[59] The question which Mance LJ focused upon was whether a genuine claim could become fraudulent because it was made fraudulently and whether, in consequence, the duty of utmost good faith was broken. Holding that the duty of utmost good faith did not apply to fraudulent claims so that the policy could not be avoided *ab initio*, Mance LJ went on to state the position with respect to fraudulent devices. He thought that an acceptable solution would be to 'treat the use of a fraudulent device as a sub-species of making a fraudulent claim' and to treat as relevant for this purpose:

> any lie, directly related to the claim to which the fraudulent device relates, which is intended to improve the insured's prospects of obtaining a settlement or winning the case, and which would, if believed, tend, objectively, prior to any final determination at trial of the parties' rights, to yield a not insignificant improvement in the insured's prospects – whether they be prospects of obtaining a settlement, or a better settlement, or of winning at trial.[60]

The insurer is therefore discharged from liability in respect of such a claim.[61] As indicated above, it was held that the common law rules governing the making of a fraudulent claim (including the use of fraudulent device) fell outside the scope of section 17 of the 1906 Act. Further, the Court of Appeal also went on to hold that once litigation between the insurers and the insured has commenced, the consequences of

---

[56] Ibid, at [40].
[57] Ibid.
[58] Ibid, at [30].
[59] Ibid. See also, *The 'Mercandian Continent'*, above n 55.
[60] Ibid, at [45].
[61] The reasoning of Mance LJ has recently been applied by Simon J in *Eagle Star Insurance Co Ltd v Games Video Co SA, The 'Game Boy'*, [2004] Lloyd's Rep IR 867.

making a fraudulent claim or promoting a claim with fraudulent devices are super-seded by the procedural rules governing civil litigation.[62]

The views expressed by Mance LJ in *The Aegeon* were considered by HHJ Cham-bers QC in *Interpart Comerciao e Gestao SA v Lexington Insurance Co*,[63] a marine insurance case where, inter alia, the insurers alleged that by submitting a fraudulent inspection certificate the insured had sought to enlist fraudulent means in the promo-tion of a claim. The judge, taking a restrictive view of *The Aegeon*, refused to give summary judgment. He accepted that while there was no requirement to show reli-ance or inducement in order for a fraudulent claim to fail (because the policy of the common law was to deter fraud), nevertheless the law was still developing with respect to the degree of nexus that must be established between the insured's fraud and the claim.

More recently, Mance LJ in *AXA General Insurance Ltd v Gottlieb*,[64] had occasion to consider whether under the common law rule relating to fraudulent claims an insurer could recover interim payments made prior to any fraud in respect of genuine losses incurred on the claim to which the subsequent fraud related. The judge rejected the submission of the insureds' counsel to the effect that where a genuine right to indemnity has both arisen and been subject of a payment made prior to any fraud committed in respect of the same claim, there can be no conceptual basis for requir-ing the insured to repay the sums received. Mance LJ stated that:

> If a later fraud forfeits a genuine claim which has already accrued but not been paid, the obvious conceptual basis is that the *whole* claim is forfeit... If the whole claim is forfeit, then the fact that sums have been advanced towards it is of itself no answer to their recovery[65]

The effect of counsel's argument would be to result in the anomaly that forfeiture of the whole claim should be restricted to the whole of the outstanding claim only; in other words, to any part that remains unpaid as at the date of the fraud. Mance LJ explained that the rationale of the rule relating to fraudulent claims is that an insured should not expect that, should the fraud fail, he will lose nothing. The court should not, therefore, undermine the prophylactic policy of the common law rule by holding that forfeiture should not apply to a part of a claim which is otherwise honest. Accordingly, it was held that the effect of the common law is to forfeit the whole of the fraudulent claim so that the consideration for any interim payments made on that claim fails. Such sums are thus recoverable by the insurers irrespective of whether they were paid prior to the fraud.

A further issue that has recently arisen is the position with respect to co-insurance where a fraudulent claim is made by one insured but not the other. In *Direct Line Insurance plc v Khan*,[66] the home of the co-insureds, Mr and Mrs Khan, was

---

[62] See also the explanation of Lord Hobhouse in '*The Star Sea*', above n 22, at [73]–[77]. But in *The 'Game Boy'*, ibid at [150], Simon J explained that this could give rise to anomalous consequences: 'After litigation has commenced an insured may advance false documentation and lie without the drastic consequences which follow if the deployment of false documentation and lies are less well timed.'

[63] [2004] Lloyd's Rep IR 690.

[64] [2005] EWCA Civ 115. Keene and Pill LJJ concurring,

[65] Ibid, at [27]; citing, *Galloway v Guardian Royal Exchange (UK) Ltd*, above n 42; and *Direct Line Insurance v Khan*, [2002] Lloyd's Rep IR 364 (considered below).

[66] [2002] Lloyd's Rep IR 364.

destroyed by fire. Mr Khan made a claim for rent, supported with forged documents, he allegedly paid for alternative accommodation. In fact no such rent was paid because he owned the alternative accommodation himself. The claim was held to be fraudulent and the insurers recovered all monies they had paid in respect of reinstating the damaged house, replacing its contents and the payment of rent. The trial judge rejected the argument that Mrs Khan was the sole policyholder and rejected the argument that she should be able to recover on the basis that the fraud had been committed by her husband without her knowledge. Arden LJ, dismissing her appeal, held that in joint insurance the effect of a fraudulent claim advanced by one co-insured is fatal to the claim of the other co-insureds even though they may be entirely innocent.

However, in composite insurance where more than one interest is covered in a policy,[67] each insured has a separate contract with the insurers and the fraud of one insured will not prejudice the claims of another in respect of the same loss.[68]

---

3. Waiver of conditions precedent to recovery

The notions of waiver and estoppel have been considered elsewhere when examining the nature of conditions and warranties in insurance law generally.[69] The rules applicable to waiver or estoppel in relation to non-disclosure or misrepresentation are,[70] by and large, the same with respect to the claims process. Waiver implies that a choice is made to elect not to repudiate a claim on the basis of the insured's breach of procedural condition. On the other hand, where an insurer indicates that it will not require performance of a condition precedent to recovery, it would be inequitable to allow the insurer to then seek to enforce that term. As such, it is said that the insurer will be estopped from insisting on its strict legal rights.[71]

Although knowledge of the insured's breach is necessary for waiver, it is not a prerequisite for estoppel to operate.[72] Further, waiver requires some positive conduct,[73] which must be made by the insurer or its authorised agent.[74] Mere delay in processing a claim will not amount to waiver unless the delay is such as to 'prejudice the [insured] or if in some way rights of third parties intervened or if the delay was so long that the court felt able to say that the delay in itself was of such a length as to be

---

[67] See ch 6, above.

[68] See *Arab Bank plc v Zurich Insurance Co* [1999] 1 Lloyd's Rep 262, See also, *P Samuel & Co v Dumas* [1924] AC 431.

[69] See ch 7, above.

[70] See ch 4, above.

[71] In *Motor Oil Hellas (Corinth) Refineries SA v Shipping Corporation of India, The Kanchenjunga* [1990] 1 Lloyd's Rep 391 at 399, Lord Goff explained the distinction thus: 'In the context of a contract, the principle of election applies when a state of affairs comes into existence in which one party becomes entitled to exercise a right, and has to choose whether to exercise that right or not ... On the other hand, equitable estoppel requires an unequivocal representation by one party that he will not insist upon his legal rights against the other party.' See also, *Super Chem Products Ltd v American Life and General Insurance Co Ltd*, above n 19.

[72] Ibid.

[73] *Craine v Colonial Mutual Fire Insurance Co Ltd* (1920) 28 CLR 305 at 326.

[74] See further, ch 3.

evidence that [the insurers] had in truth decided to accept liability.'[75] If, however, an insurer makes it clear that it wishes to reserve its position on the issue of an alleged breach of condition, it will not lose the right to raise the defence in any subsequent proceedings.[76]

There is an overlap between the doctrines of waiver and estoppel and the judges do not always draw the necessary distinction when considering the facts of cases before them. A clear example of waiver is afforded by *Lickiss v Milestone Motor Policies*,[77] in which the insured, a motor cyclist, had failed to notify the insurers of his claim although the police had communicated details to them. It was held by the Court of Appeal that the insurers by their subsequent correspondence with the insured could be taken to have waived the breach of condition.[78] The insurers, with knowledge of the breach, had chosen to ignore it by writing to the insured accepting liability. While this decision is clearly an example of waiver, the court nevertheless considered the effect which the correspondence would have on the reasonable man.

B. MEASUREMENT OF LOSS

1. The principle of indemnity

In indemnity insurance, for example where the subject matter of the policy is property, whether real or personal, the insured is precluded from recovering more than the value of the actual loss sustained. This is because 'indemnity' means that the insured is to be put back to the position he would have been in had the loss not occurred, less any excess which the insured has agreed to bear.[79] The position should be contrasted with contingency insurance, for example life and accident policies, where the sum recovered is fixed by the terms of the policy. Similarly, if the policy is valued, so that the sum recoverable is fixed by the contract (which is the usual position in marine insurance) the sum agreed is not open to challenge at a later date, and the insured is entitled to the full agreed value, or the relevant percentage of it in the case of a partial loss.

The governing principle was stated by Brett LJ in *Castellain v Preston*,[80] a case in which the Court of Appeal considered the nature of a fire insurance policy:

---

[75] *Allen v Robles* [1969] 1 WLR 1193 at 1196, *per* Fenton Atkinson LJ.
[76] *Donnison v Employers' Accident and Life Stock Insurance Co Ltd* (1897) 24 R 681.
[77] [1966] 2 Lloyd's Rep 1. See further ch 7.
[78] In his judgment Lord Denning MR cited *Plasticmoda Societa per Azioni v Davidsons (Manchester) Ltd* [1952] 1 Lloyd's Rep 527.
[79] See further, A Lewis, 'A Fundamental Principle of Insurance Law' [1979] *LMCLQ* 275; and J Birds, 'The Measure of Indemnity in Property Insurance' (1980) 43 *MLR* 456.
[80] [1881–5] All ER Rep 493.

Every contract of marine or fire insurance is a contract of indemnity, and indemnity only, the meaning of which is that the assured in case of a loss is to receive a full indemnity, but is never to receive more. Every rule of insurance law is adopted in order to carry out this fundamental rule, and if ever any proposition is brought forward, the effect of which is opposed to this fundamental rule, it will be found to be wrong.'[81]

The overriding requirement of indemnity can be seen to underlie the rules which operate in the event of an insured loss. We turn now to consider those rules.

1.1 Forms and measurement of loss

The 'sum insured' represents the maximum figure which the insured can recover, it is not necessarily the sum which will be received in the event of a loss. The principle was cogently stated by Cockburn CJ in *Chapman* v *Pole*,[82] when summing up for the jury: '[y]ou must not run away with the notion that a policy of insurance entitles a man to recover according to the amount represented as insured ... he can only recover the real and actual value of the goods.'[83] Accordingly, the sentimental value which an insured places on a lost item is not recoverable even if capable of quantification.

The property which is the subject-matter of the policy may be either totally or partially lost. The distinction centres on the difference between destruction and damage, the determination of which may be a question of degree. Total loss may arise where the property is damaged beyond economic repair. For example, insurers will sometimes 'write off' a motor vehicle that has suffered extensive damage in a crash where the repair bill would be greater than the value of the insured vehicle. A house which is damaged by fire may be viewed as totally lost even though the shell of its walls are left standing but are unusable. In this situation, the insurers will generally be liable for rebuilding costs.

1.1.1 Goods

Where goods have been totally lost the courts will take the market value of the items as a means of determining the sum recoverable by the insured. In assessing market value account will be taken of the time and place of the insured loss.[84] The test is what would it cost the insured to replace the lost goods.[85] If the lost item is second hand the insured will recover no more than its reasonable second hand value as at the time of the loss:

> Many an assured who has had an armchair burned to pieces has put forward the proposition: 'Well I want an armchair to sit upon. This one is destroyed and I can only get one to sit upon by buying a new one.' In some circumstances, if the law were otherwise, that might be very reasonable, but very often it is not recognised and he realises to his chagrin that all he can recover is not his armchair to sit upon, but the reasonable value of the second-hand armchair that has been destroyed.[86]

---

[81] Ibid, at 495.
[82] (1870) 22 LT 306.
[83] Ibid, at 307.
[84] *Chapman v Pole* (1870) 22 LT 306.
[85] *Rice v Baxendale* (1861) 7 H & N 96 at 100, *per* Bramwell B.
[86] *Ewer v National Employers' Mutual General Insurance Association Ltd*, above n 24, at 21, *per* Mackinnon J.

Where there is no market value as such, as in the case of a rare antique, the court will generally take the price which the item could have been sold for immediately prior to the loss. In the case of a work of art, for example a movie film, the amount recoverable may be less than the costs involved in producing it.[87] The difficulties of assessing the value of a damaged work of art can be seen in *Quorum AS v Schramm*.[88] The insured property, a Degas pastel, *La Danse Grecque*, suffered damage due to the heat and change in humidity caused by a fire at the warehouse where it was stored. After the fire the parties negotiated a new endorsement to the policy governing partial loss:

> In the event of partial loss or damage...the amount of the loss shall be the cost and expense of restoration plus any resulting depreciation in value. Underwriters' liability shall be limited to that proportion of such loss or damage which the sum insured bears to the market value of the item immediately prior to the loss and in no event shall underwriters be liable for more than the insured value of the item.

The court had to assess the value of the painting both before the fire and its value after the ensuing damage. With respect to the first issue, Thomas J stated that, as with the approach taken in relation to sale of goods and valuation for tax purposes, the task of the court is to ascertain the price that could be achieved between a willing seller and a willing buyer in the relevant market. If there is an open market price, that should be ascertained. Expert evidence should be taken into account, including evidence of prices obtained at auctions. The judge held, on the basis of the authorities and the views of expert valuers, that the court should have regard to the market where the painting was likely to obtain a higher price. On the facts, this was the dealers' market. Turning to the second issue, Thomas J was faced with conflicting expert evidence as to the level of depreciation of the damaged painting which ranged from 20 per cent to 80 per cent. He noted that the range of those interested in the painting in its damaged state would be far fewer. He also accepted that in valuing it after the fire, he needed to look at the risks of further deterioration. On the facts, it was held that the painting's value before the fire was US $3.6 million while its damaged value was US $2.2 million.

It should also be noted that 'new for old' policies are increasingly being offered by insurers whereby the replacement value rather than the market value of the insured property is covered.[89] Such policies do not accord with the notion of indemnity and insurers obviously charge a higher premium. The point to bear in mind is that the indemnity principle is contractual in origin. As such, it can be varied by an appropriate policy term.

As commented above, the value of the insured's loss is measured at the time it occurs. This, of course, may be different from the sum specified in the policy at the time of its inception or renewal. In *Re Wilson and Scottish Insurance Corporation Ltd*,[90] Ashbury J held that an insured could recover for the increase in value which had accrued since the policy's last renewal date. The policy in question covered a

---

[87] *Richard Aubrey Film Productions Ltd v Graham* [1960] 2 Lloyd's Rep 101.
[88] [2002] 1 Lloyd's Rep 249.
[89] See, eg, *Kuwait Airways Corp v Kuwait Insurance Co SAK* [2000] Lloyd's Rep IR 439.
[90] [1920] 2 Ch 28.

motor car, the value of which was stated as £250.00, its purchase price, but the policy provided that it covered the car 'up to full value'. The judge said that if the appreciation in value occurred before the last renewal date, the insured would be limited to recovering £250.00, but if it occurred since the last renewal date, the insured could recover £400.00, the value of the car at the time of its loss. The decision is curious, not least because the insured sum of £250.00 would normally be the maximum amount recoverable.

In 'valued policies' the agreed value of the item as specified in the policy will be the amount recoverable in the event of total loss.[91] The effect of a valued policy is that it excludes the principle of indemnity because the insured will recover the stated value without reference to the actual loss suffered. If the value of the property exceeds the sum insured, the difference is not recoverable. Whether or not a policy is a 'valued policy' depends upon its construction. Stating a value is not in itself conclusive of the issue. Generally, the courts will more readily find a valued policy where the subject-matter is property, the value of which might otherwise be difficult to determine. Where value is stated in a policy, the analogy which the courts draw is that of liquidated damages.[92] Where there is a partial loss the insured will recover a sum in proportion to the stated value. This is assessed by taking the ratio of the actual value of the property after loss to the actual value of the property before the loss.[93]

1.1.2 Real property

Where real property is lost, the measure of indemnity is generally determined by reference to the cost of reinstatement unless the insured has contracted to sell the property, in which case assessment will be based on market value, ie the agreed selling price. This figure may amount to less than the cost of reinstatement. For example, in *Leppard v Excess Insurance Co Ltd*,[94] the claimant purchased a cottage for the express purpose of reselling it. He insured the cottage against fire for £10,000. The proposal form stated that the sum insured represented the 'full value' of the property: 'full value' was defined as 'the amount which it would cost to replace the property in its existing form should it be totally destroyed.' Upon renewal of the policy, the sum insured was increased to £14,000. Before any sale took place the property was totally destroyed by fire. The claimant claimed the rebuilding cost, some £8,000. The insurer contested the claim, arguing that the claimant was entitled only to the market value of the property at the time of the fire. This was agreed at £3,000, ie the price at which the claimant was willing to sell less the site value. The Court of Appeal held that under the terms of the policy the insurers agreed to indemnify the insured in respect of loss or damage caused by fire. It being an indemnity contract, the claimant could not recover the cost of reinstatement but only the market value of the cottage at the date of the fire (£3,000). In their reasoning, both Megaw and Geoffrey Lane LJJ emphasised that the principle of indemnity operated to restrict the amount recoverable to the actual loss suffered by the insured and no more.[95]

---

[91] *Feise v Aguilar* (1811) 3 Taunt 506 at 507, *per* Lord Mansfield CJ.
[92] See, eg, *Elcock v Thomson* [1949] 2 KB 755 at 761, *per* Morris J.
[93] *Elcock v Thomson*, ibid, this aspect of the decision is considered further at p 268, below.
[94] [1979] 2 All ER 668.
[95] Ibid, at 674 and 676 respectively.

It has been noted that in property insurance the measure of indemnity is normally based upon rebuilding costs. However, where the insured uses his property as business premises from which income is derived, the measure of indemnity will take account of the cost of acquiring new premises if the insured would suffer loss of earnings while waiting for the original property to be rebuilt. In *Dominion Mosaics & Tile Co Ltd v Trafalgar Trucking Co Ltd*,[96] Taylor LJ stated that: '[w]here business premises are concerned, the need to carry on the business and to mitigate the loss of earnings is an important factor.'[97] On the facts of the case, the cost of rebuilding the fire damaged premises would have been greater than the cost of the new premises.[98]

In the event of partial loss which arises not only where the insured property has been damaged, but where a part of the property has been totally lost, indemnity is usually referable to the cost of reinstatement subject to any deduction for 'betterment'. The doctrine of betterment operates to take account of depreciation so that a deduction is applied to the amount recoverable where the reinstated property is improved beyond its pre-loss condition. In *Reynolds v Phoenix Assurance Co Ltd*,[99] business premises which had been purchased for £18,000 were insured for £628,000 covering the buildings (£550,000), machinery (£28,000) and stock (£50,000). A fire occurred which destroyed some seven-tenths of the buildings. Exercising their right under the terms of the policy, the insurers elected not to reinstate.[100] The claimants sued claiming an indemnity which amounted to the cost of reinstatement of the buildings. The insurers argued that the claimants' loss should be determined by the value of the buildings as used for the purposes intended by the claimants, and that this should be measured either by market value or modern replacement value. Further, the insurers claimed that reinstatement, even if genuinely intended by the claimants, was not appropriate in that no commercial man would think of spending £1¼ million in rebuilding obsolete premises if he could buy modern premises for £30,000.

It was held that the claimants' intention to rebuild the damaged premises if awarded an adequate sum to do so was genuine and was not based upon some eccentricity.[101] The sum claimed was a true indemnification but that betterment should be taken into account. Since the claimants intended to use second hand building materials and other substances of inferior quality as far as possible, the deduction for betterment would be minimal.

Forbes J explained the underlying basis of the doctrine of betterment in the following terms:

[T]he principle of betterment is too well established in the law of insurance to be departed from at this stage even though it may sometimes work hardship on the assured. It is simply that an allowance must be made because the assured is getting something new for something old.[102]

---

[96] [1990] 2 All ER 246.
[97] Ibid, at 249.
[98] *Quaere* whether if the cost of the alternative premises had been more than the rebuilding costs of the insured property, the insured would have recovered that greater sum from the insurer. See further, MClarke, *Policies and Perceptions of Insurance* (Oxford, Clarendon Press, 1997) 187 *et seq.*
[99] [1978] 2 Lloyd's Rep 440.
[100] The policy in question contained a pay, reinstate or replace clause.
[101] Cf *Exchange Theatre Ltd v Iron Trades Mutual Insurance Co* [1983] 1 Lloyd's Rep 674.
[102] Above n 99, at 453. See also, *Dominion Mosaics & Tile Co Ltd v Trafalgar Trucking Co Ltd*, above n 96 at 255.

The judge subjected the principle of indemnity as it applies to real property to detailed consideration. Citing the Irish case of *Murphy v Wexford County Council*,[103] which concerned statutory compensation to persons whose property had suffered malicious damage, Forbes J noted that the difficulty in assessing *quantum* lies in reaching a figure which does not amount to enrichment or impoverishment. He stressed that the determination of the proper measure of indemnity is a question of fact and degree to be decided on the circumstances of the case; and in its deliberations, the court take account of the factors indicated by Sir James Campbell C in *Murphy*[104]: 'Would [the insured] for any reason that might appeal to an ordinary man in his position rebuild [the premises] if he got replacement [costs] or is his claim for such [costs] a mere pretence?'[105]

Where partial loss occurs under a 'valued policy' the insurer is liable to pay a percentage of the stated value. This is calculated by determining the ratio which the actual value of the damaged property bears to the insured sum. In *Elcock v Thomson*,[106] a mansion was insured against loss or damage by fire. The agreed value was £106,850. A fire occurred which partially destroyed the property. The value of the property before the fire was £18,000 and after the fire, it stood as £12,600, which represented a depreciation of 30 per cent. The property was not reinstated, and the insured claimed under the policy. The issue for the court was how much should the insurers pay. It was held that the agreement as to value applied not just in the event of total loss but also to partial loss. The insurers were therefore liable to pay 30 per cent of £106,850, which was £32,055. Morris J, construing the policy, stated:

> The respective words 'loss' and 'damage', as used in the policy, seem to be synonymous. It would not seem to be the case that the word 'loss' is only referable to complete destruction. ... The result is that in my judgment, the percentage of actual depreciation resulting from the fire should be applied to the agreed values as set out in the policy so as to arrive at the amount recoverable.[107]

Where the insured possesses only a limited interest in the insured property recovery in the event of a loss is limited to the actual value of the interest in question. Examples include creditors who insure the value of their security interests in an asset, and tenants (lessees) who insure the value of their property. Where several creditors have security interests in the same property the total sum recoverable in the event of a loss may exceed the actual value of the property.[108]

A lessee who has covenanted to repair or insure the property against fire damage will receive the cost of reinstatement. Recovery is not limited to the market value of the lease. The point has also been taken that even in the absence of such a covenant, a tenant will recover more than the value of his interest where the loss results in the tenant losing his home.[109]

---

[103] (1921) 2 IR 230.
[104] Above n 103, at 451.
[105] (1921) 2 IR 230, at 240.
[106] Above n 92.
[107] Ibid, at 387.
[108] *Westminster Fire Office v Glasgow Provident Society* (1888) 13 App Cas 699.
[109] *Castellain v Preston*, above n 80.

2. Under insurance and the principle of average

Where the insured under values the subject-matter of the policy either at the time of its inception or upon renewal, so that the sum insured does not reflect the true value of the property, then strictly speaking the insurer may avoid the policy for non-disclosure or breach of warranty.[110] However, where a partial loss occurs to the insured property and the policy contains an 'average' clause, the insurers' liability will be limited. The result is that the insurer will pay a sum which is limited to that part of the loss which the sum insured bears to the actual value of the property. If, for example, property which is actually worth £50,000 is insured for £25,000, and as a result of a partial loss £10,000 is required to repair it, the insured will only recover £5,000. Average clauses, while common in commercial policies, are rare in domestic household policies and the courts are loath to imply the principle of average in them.[111] However, it remains to be seen whether, following the decision in *Economides v Commercial Union plc*,[112] insurers will seek to insert average clauses into household policies as a matter of course.[113]

3. The excess clause

As will be seen in chapter 13, an excess clause or deductible, commonly encountered in motor, household and reinsurance policies, provides that the insured will bear the first part of any loss. Such a clause is generally expressed by way of a sum of money or by way of a percentage of any loss. For example, the insured may agree to bear the first £100.00 of a loss, often in return for a lower premium. The insured is his own insurer for the amount of the excess.

---

[110] *Leppard v Excess Insurance Company Ltd*, above n 105. But note now the recent Court of Appeal decision in *Economides v Commercial Union* [1997] 3 All ER 636, on the issue of the insured's duty when expressing an opinion as to value (discussed in ch 4). In this case valuables worth some £31,000 were stolen. They were insured for £16,000. On the policy wording, valuables were only covered up to one third of the sum insured. The court held that the insured had been honest in representing the value of the insured property as being £16,000. He therefore recovered £7,815, being one third of £16,000.
[111] *Sillem v Thornton* (1854) 3 E & B 868. Average is specifically required in marine insurance by virtue of the Marine Insurance Act 1906, s 81.
[112] Above, n 110.
[113] As they are in contents policies issued by Lloyd's underwriters.

4. The franchise clause

Franchise clauses, commonly seen in marine insurance policies,[114] have the effect of relieving the insurer from liability completely unless the loss exceeds a stated figure in which case the insurer will be liable for the whole loss. However, separated losses falling below the stated sum cannot be aggregated in order to defeat a franchise clause.[115]

Excess and franchise clauses serve a deterrent purpose insofar as they promote risk avoidance. They also serve to reduce the administration costs of dealing with small claims. Some policies may also contain a promissory warranty to the effect that a certain percentage of the value of the insured property will be uninsured.[116]

5. Double insurance and contribution

There is no prohibition against double insurance, so a person may effect multiple policies on the same property against identical risks. In such a case, the insured is free to claim payment from whichever insurer he chooses.[117] It should be noted that the insured will not be allowed to recover more than is necessary to achieve indemnification against the loss, no matter how many policies are effected. So if the insured claims for the full loss against one particular policy, he cannot go on to recover for the same loss against other insurers who have provided the same cover.

The position of the co-insurers is governed by the equitable doctrine of contribution. The insurer who has paid the claim can require the other insurers to contribute rateably in proportion to the amount for which the insurer in question is liable. The doctrine of contribution is confined to indemnity insurance and operates to prevent the insured from being unjustly enriched. It will not apply as between an insurer and another party such as a builder who, under a construction contract, undertakes to indemnify the insured.[118]

As will be seen, contribution is generally modified by the terms of the insurance contract which commonly contain a so-called 'rateable proportion clause'. This has the effect of preventing an insured recovering all of the loss from one insurer only. Instead, the insured is required to claim rateably from each insurer.[119] For example, if property is insured with insurer A for £100.00 and with insurer B for £200.00 and the

---

[114] See, eg, *Paterson v Harris* (1861) 1 B & S 336 at 354, *per* Cockburn CJ.
[115] *Stewart v Merchant's Marine Insurance Co* (1885) 16 QBD 619.
[116] See, eg, *Trail v Baring* (1864) 4 DeGJ & S 318.
[117] See further the Marine Insurance Act 1906, s 32.
[118] *Caledonia North Sea Ltd v BT plc* [2002] Lloyd's Rep IR 261.
[119] As was explained by Rix LJ in *Drake Insurance plc v Provident Insurance plc* [2003] EWCA Civ 1834; [2004] Lloyd's Rep IR 277, at [114]: 'Of course, if the insured is forced to involve both his insurers, then there will be no need for contribution and the need for the application of the doctrine is excluded as a matter of fact.'

damage is valued at £60.00, A will be liable for £20.00 and B for £40.00.[120] The 'maximum liability' basis of contribution used in this example therefore limits the liability of the respective insurers to the proportion of the risk covered by them and which determined the level of premium charged. Where liability is unlimited, as for example in third party liability motor insurance, the liability of the insurers will be divided equally *inter se*.

5.1 The objective of the rules on double insurance

Where several people have an insurable interest in the same subject matter, they may each insure separately and, in the event of a loss, each insured is entitled to claim for that loss even if the total of those claims exceeds the value of the subject matter. On the other hand, in the case of indemnity insurance, while there is nothing to prevent one person from taking out a number of policies on the same property and risk, it is only possible to claim up to the amount of the loss. It may be that someone insures property with several insurers with the intention to defraud, and indeed Lord Mansfield CJ regarded the prevention of fraud as the purpose of the rule,[121] but it is more likely that double insurance arises quite innocently and is impossible to avoid. A motor policy or holiday insurance may include personal possessions carried in the car or taken on holiday which will also be covered in those situations by a home-contents policy, and since all of these policies are typically in a standard form, there will be no possibility of avoiding it even if the insured spots the double insurance.

In an early case, Lord Mansfield CJ declared:

> Where a man makes a double insurance of the same thing, in such a manner that he can clearly recover, against several insurers in distinct policies, a double satisfaction, …the law certainly says that he ought not to recover doubly for the same loss, but be content with one single satisfaction for it.And if the whole should be recovered from one [that is, one insurer], he ought to stand in the place of the insured, to receive contribution from the other, who was equally liable to pay the whole.[122]

There are, therefore, two aspects to double insurance: one is that the insured cannot recover more than an indemnity, but is free to choose which policy to claim on; the other is that the insurers who pay the claim are entitled to a contribution from the other insurers.

The doctrine of subrogation prevents an insured from recovering more than an indemnity,[123] and the rules on double insurance are an aspect of this, which means of course that they do not apply to contingency insurance, such as life assurance.[124] The difference between subrogation and contribution is that in the former the insurers

---

[120] See *North British & Mercantile Insurance Co v London, Liverpool & Globe Insurance Co* (1877) 5 Ch D 569.

[121] It is worth noting that if the intention to defraud was formed before entering the contract, that would render the policy void.

[122] *Godin v London Assurance Co* (1758) 1 Burr 489 at 492. See also, Marine Insurance Act 1906, s 32(1).

[123] *Godin v London Assurance Co,* ibid at 492, *per* Lord Mansfield CJ. As with the doctrine of contribution, the rationale here is to prevent unjust enrichment.

[124] For the distinction, see ch 1.

recoup the amount paid on a claim from the third party, while in the latter the insurers who have paid the insured can recoup a contribution from the other insurers.[125]

5.2 Defining double insurance

The problem of deciding whether there is double insurance is of course a question of construction of the insurance contracts: do they cover the same interests, are they effected for different insureds?[126] The courts have held there is no double insurance where the overlap between two policies is relatively minor. A ship called the *Aladdin* was insured on its voyage to Calcutta and for 30 days after arrival. When it arrived the owners effected another insurance with the same insurers to cover the ship at Calcutta and during a proposed voyage to Bombay. The ship sank in Calcutta, and the question was whether the reinsurers of the second policy (under which the claim was made) were entitled to a contribution from the insurers. The court construed the intention of the parties as being that the first policy terminated on the making of the second policy.[127]

5.3 Contribution

The insured who has double insurance can claim against any of the insurers,[128] and the insurers who pay can bring in an action in their own name for a contribution from the other insurers.[129] Plainly, this right does not depend on contract, since there is no contract between the insurers; instead, it depends 'on an equity which requires someone who has taken the benefit of a premium to share the burden of meeting the claim.'[130] It should be noted that contribution may be sought only as against an insurer who remains liable at the date of the contribution claim against it: if, therefore, the insured's failure to make a claim under the policy gives the insurers a defence, contribution cannot later be sought from them.[131]

Each insurer is bound to contribute 'rateably to the loss in proportion to the amount for which he is liable under his contract.'[132] This is the case even though the

---

[125] That insurers sometimes cannot distinguish between these two concepts is illustrated by *Austin v Zurich General Accident and Liability Insurance Co Ltd* [1945] KB 250 at 258, *per* MacKinnon LJ and Uthwatt J.

[126] Although, the doctrine nonetheless triggers where the same interest is insured by different insureds: *O'Kane v Jones, The Martin P* [2004] 1 Lloyd's Rep 389.

[127] *Union Marine Insurance Co Ltd v Martin* (1866) 35 LJCP 181. See also *The Australian Agricultural Co v Saunders* (1875) LR 10 CP 668, in which the court held that a marine policy covering the transit of goods did not cover them while in a warehouse, so there was no double insurance, but also held that, on a true construction of the policies, there was no overlap of coverage.

[128] Marine Insurance Act 1906, s 32(2).

[129] *Williams v The North China Insurance Co* (1876) 1 CPD 757 at 768, *per* Jessell MR; *Austin v Zurich General Accident and Liability Insurance Co Ltd*, above n 90 at 258, *per* MacKinnon LJ; *Legal and General Assurance Society Ltd v Drake Insurance Co Ltd* [1992] QB 887.

[130] *Legal and General Assurance Society Ltd v Drake Insurance Co Ltd*, ibid at 898, *per* Nourse LJ. See also ibid, at 891–2, *per* Lloyd LJ, and at 900, *per* Ralph Gibson LJ, who drew an analogy with co-sureties. The usefulness of this analogy had earlier been doubted in *Commercial Union Assurance Co Ltd v Hayden* [1977] 1 QB 804 at 814–5, *per* Cairns LJ.

[131] *Eagle Star Insurance Co Ltd v Provincial Insurance plc* [1993] 2 Lloyd's Rep 143.

[132] Marine Insurance Act 1906, s 80(1). See *O'Kane v Jones* [2005] Lloyd's Rep IR 174

different policies may be broader or narrower in their coverage,[133] so long as: the insurers are liable under their own policy and have paid out; the other insurers are liable under their policy and have not paid out;[134] the policies are in force,[135] and the insurers from whom a contribution is sought do not repudiate liability on the ground of, for instance, a breach of the duty of disclosure,[136] or because of a breach of a condition precedent to liability;[137] the policies cover the same subject matter,[138] the same risk which led to the loss,[139] the same interests in the subject matter and are effected by, on behalf of or provide benefit for the same insured.[140] A tenant and a lessor do not have the same interest,[141] nor do a mortgagor and a mortgagee,[142] nor a wharfinger and the owner of the goods stored on the wharf.[143] Of course, where two people insure the same property and an insurer pays on a claim by one, that insurer may be able to recoup the payment by exercising the right of subrogation. Where, for

---

[133] The doubts apparently expressed by Hamilton J in *American Surety Co of New York v Wrightson* (1910) 103 LT 663, in relation to this were, in fact, concerned with whether the two policies involved in that case covered the same risk: "The two instruments, therefore, although they have the common elements of insuring against loss by dishonesty and bad faith of the employees, differ very considerably in scope, both as regards the hazard covered and the persons and things bringing those hazards into operation" (at 665).

[134] *Williams v The North China Insurance Co*, above n 129 at 768, *per* Jessell MR; *Boag v Economic Insurance Co. Ltd* [1954] 2 Lloyd's Rep 581; Marine Insurance Act 1906, s 80(1) refers to the duty of each insurer to contribute to a loss 'for which he is liable under the contract.'

[135] *Sickness and Accident Assurance Assocn Ltd v General Accident Assurance Coprn Ltd* (1892) 19 R (Ct of Sess) 977.

[136] *Legal and General Assurance Society Ltd v Drake Insurance Co Ltd*, above n 129 at 893, *per* Lloyd LJ; *Eagle Star Insurance Co Ltd v Provincial Insurance plc*, above n 131 at 140, *per* Lord Woolf. The same logic would suggest that there will be no double insurance if the second insurer repudiates for a breach of warranty or a misrepresentation. See *Drake Insurance plc v Provident Insurance plc* [2004] Lloyd's Rep IR 277.

[137] *Monksfield v Vehicle and General Insurance Co Ltd* [1971] Lloyd's Rep 139, where in a motor insurance case, the second policy entitled the insurer not to pay if the insured failed to give notice of a potential claim as soon as possible after an accident, the insurer was not liable to contribute following payment of a claim by the first insurer. That decision was overruled by the Court of Appeal in *Legal and General Assurance Society Ltd v Drake Insurance Co Ltd, ibid,* at 895–6, *per* Lloyd LJ, and at 897, *per* Nourse LJ. But the Judical Committee of the Privy Council held that *Monksfield* was correctly decided in *Eagle Star Insurance Co Ltd v Provincial Insurance plc*, above n 131, at 142, *per* Lord Woolf. In *O'Kane v Jones*, above, n 132, the court preferred *Legal and General*.

[138] *Godin v London Assurance Co*, above n 122 at 492, *per* Lord Mansfield CJ.

[139] *Boag v Economic Insurance Co Ltd* [1954] 2 Lloyd's Rep 581, in which it was held that there was no double insurance where the same goods were covered by a transit policy and a policy on goods stored in a warehouse. In *Petrofina (UK) Ltd v Magnaload Ltd* [1984] QB 127 at 140, *per* Lloyd J, where one policy covered property and the other was a liability insurance there was no double insurance.

[140] *North British and Mercantile Insurance Co v London, Liverpool and Globe Insurance Co*, above n 120 at 577, *per* Jessell MR. In that case, the words in the policy 'covering the same property' were interpreted as meaning that the subject-matter of the insurance is the same and the interests (that is, the insureds) are the same. See *Godin v London Assurance Co*, above n 122. Where the policies appear to cover different interests but, by reason of an agreement between the two insureds, are effected to cover both interests, then there is double insurance: ER Hardy Ivamy, *General Principles of Insurance Law* (London, Butterworths, 1993) 520.

[141] *Portavon Cinema Co Ltd v Price and Century Insurance Co Ltd* [1939] 4 All ER. 601.

[142] *Nichols & Co v Scottish Union and National Insurance Co* (1885) 14 R (Ct of Sess) 1094 at 1096, *per* Cave J (report of case decided in the Queen's Bench Division).

[143] *North British and Mercantile Insurance Co v London, Liverpool, and Globe Insurance Co*, above n 120. However, the Fire Offices' Committee has a rule which means that with regard to fire policies on buildings and, in certain circumstances, their contents (but not commercial risks), where there are two or more policies taken out by different people with different interests but covering the same subject matter, the loss will be apportioned rateably among the insurers: ER Hardy Ivamy, *General Principles of Insurance Law*, at 521.

instance, wharfingers insure grain stored on their property and that grain is also insured by the owner, then there is no double insurance and if one insurer pays on a claim they cannot claim a contribution from the other insurer. However, if the loss is caused by the negligence of the wharfinger and the owner of the grain makes an insurance claim, their insurer would be able to recoup the payment from the wharfinger – and, ultimately, the loss would, depending on the terms of the policy, fall on the wharfinger's insurer.[144]

It is usual for a policy to contain terms that purport to modify rules of contribution. The first point is that these terms will, of course, be ineffective if there is no double insurance.[145] The commonest forms of such a term provide that the insurer will not be liable if the insured can claim an indemnity under another policy, or if the insured claims under any other policy,[146] or if the insured fails to give notice of a previous or subsequent policy.[147] Where there are two policies, each of which contains such a clause, the courts avoid the absurdity of the insured finding that he or she has no cover at all in spite of having paid two premiums by construing the contracts so as to nullify those clauses: 'it is unreasonable to suppose that it was intended that clauses such as these should cancel each other…[T]he reasonable construction is to exclude from the category of co-existing cover any cover which is expressed to be itself cancelled by such co-existence, and to hold in such cases that both companies are liable'.[148]

Unfortunately, this eminently sensible approach does not stretch to rateable proportion clauses.[149] A rateable proportion clause modifies the normal rule that the insured can claim for the full loss from one insurer and that insurer must claim a contribution from the other insurers. The effect of the clause is that, if an insured has more than one policy, the insurer will only liable be for a proportion of the loss.[150] The insured must claim against all the insurers and cannot simply make one claim leaving it to that insurer to seek a contribution from the others. This not only complicates the insured's claim, it means he will bear part of the loss if one of the insurers becomes insolvent. The justification given for such clauses is that they prevent fraud,

[144] *North British and Mercantile Insurance Co v London, Liverpool, and Globe Insurance Co*, above n 120.
[145] *National Employers Mutual General Insurance Ltd v Haydon* [1980] 2 Lloyd's Rep 149. A term which is not primarily concerned with the right of contribution may nevertheless have an impact on that right: for instance, a term which requires a motorist to notify the insurers as soon as possible after an accident as a precedent to liability under the policy will, if breached, enable the insurers to avoid having to contribute if there is double insurance and another insurer has paid. Generally, AA Tarr, 'The Measure of Indemnity under Property Insurance Rules' (1983) 2 *Canterbury L Rev* 107 at 119–20.
[146] *National Employers Mutual General Insurance Ltd v Haydon*, ibid.
[147] *Australian Agricultural Co v Saunders* (1875) 10 LRCP 668.
[148] *Weddell v Road Transport and General Insurance Co Ltd* [1932] 2 KB 563 at 567, *per* Rowlatt J. The difference between *Weddell* and *Gale v Motor Union Insurance Co* [1928] 1 KB 359 is that in the latter case both policies contained a rateable proportion clause, and therefore there was no double insurance. See also *Austin v Zurich General Accident Insurance Co*, above, n 125; *National Employers Mutual General Insurance Assocn Ltd v Haydon*, above, n 145 ; and *Structural Polymer Sustems Ltd v Brown* [2000] Lloyd's Rep IR 64. In *Equitable Fire and Accident Office Ltd v Ching Wo Hong* [1907] AC 96, the term requiring that the insurers be notified of the existence of another policy was not breached where the other policy had not come into effect because the premium had not been paid.
[149] *Weddell v Road Transport and General Insurance Co Ltd*, ibid; *Legal and General Assurance Society Ltd v Drake Insurance Co Ltd*, above n 129. Although for consumer insureds, such clauses may well be regarded as unfair under the Unfair Terms in Consumer Contracts Regulations 1999.
[150] *North British and Mercantile Insurance Co v London, Liverpool, and Globe Insurance Co*, above n 120 at 588, *per* Baggallay LJ; *Gale v Motor Union Insurance Co* [1932] 1 KB 359; Institute Time Clauses Freight, cl 14.2. Also D Friedmann, 'Double Insurance and Payment of Another's Debt' (1993) 109 *LQR* 51.

but, as with so much else in insurance contract law, they are likely to have a greater impact on the ordinary and honest insured who has paid a full premium calculated on the basis of full liability and who might, therefore, at least expect the insurer to chase about for the contribution.

There is a problem facing insurers in relation to rateable proportion clauses. If an insurer pays out for the full loss in ignorance of the existence of other policies, that insurer cannot claim a contribution because the clause makes the insurer only legally liable for a part of the claim, and therefore the payment above that legal liability is voluntary.[151] Yet even this may have an impact on the insured. In *Legal and General Assurance Society Ltd v Drake Insurance Co Ltd*,[152] one motorist was covered by two policies, both of which required as a condition precedent to liability that the insured should notify the insurer in the event of anything happening which might give rise to a claim. It was held that the fact that the motorist only gave notice to one insurer did not affect the right of that insurer to claim a contribution from the other insurer. Although the second insurer was not liable to the motorist because of the failure to give notice, the right of contribution was not affected by this because at the time of the loss the second insurer was '*potentially* liable',[153] and therefore there was double insurance. But the first insurer's policy contained a rateable proportion clause and this meant that the payment made on the claim exceeded that which was due. Since the excess was therefore a voluntary payment, it was not recoverable from the second insurer.[154] However, that payment could be recovered from the insured. This means that the insured who has paid two premiums might only be covered for half of the loss. It is noteworthy that in *Drake Insurance plc v Provident Insurance plc*,[155] Rix LJ expressed strident criticism of rateable proportion clauses:

> It is a matter of concern that an insurer who takes a premium to cover 100 per cent. of a risk may only be liable for 50 per cent. of a loss, on the basis that the insured can obtain the other half elsewhere, in circumstances where the insured finds that he cannot contractually do so.[156]

As noted in chapter 4, the current judicial inclination appears to be moving towards a more insured-friendly approach. There thus appears to be the emergence of two parallel streams of insurance law: one relating to consumer insurance, the other relating to commercial insurance.[157]

---

[151] *Legal and General Assurance Society Ltd v Drake Insurance Co Ltd*, above n 129. See the strong criticism of this case in *Eagle Star Insurance Co Ltd v Provincial Insurance plc*, above n 131. See D Friedmann, 'Double Insurance and Payment of Another's Debt' (1993) 109 LQR 51. In *Eagle Star* the Privy Council held that the right to contribution is to be determined as at the date of judgment against the insurer who has paid. However, in *Legal and General v Drake* the Court of Appeal held that it is to be determined at the date of the loss. It is noteworthy that in *O'Kane v Jones, The Martin P*, [2004] 1 Lloyd's Rep 389, Deputy High Court Judge Richard Siberry QC followed *Legal and General*, holding, at [190], that 'the equity which gave rise to the right to contribution…arose at the time of the loss, and could not be defeated by a later cancellation of the policy in respect of which a contribution was sought.'

[152] Above, n 129.

[153] Ibid, at 892, *per* Lloyd LJ.

[154] See also, *Bovis Construction Ltd v Commercial Union Assurance plc* [2001] 1 Lloyd's Rep 416. In *Drake Insurance plc v Provident Insurance plc* [2004] Lloyd's Rep IR 277, the Court of Appeal expressed reservations about the reasoning on this point. Clarke LJ noted that perhaps the House of Lords will one day have an opportunity to reconsider *Legal and General v Drake*.

[155] Ibid. For the facts of the case, see ch 4.

[156] Ibid, at [120].

[157] See further, ch 4, above.

6. Damages

It is perhaps self-evident that where an insurer unreasonably delays in settling a claim the consequences for an insured can be disastrous. *Sprung v Royal Insurance (UK) Ltd*,[158] is a paradigm case. The insured, Sprung (S), owned a factory which processed animal waste. He effected two insurance policies: the first covered him against theft and the second provided cover in relation to the plant and machinery against 'sudden and unforeseen damage that necessitates immediate repair of the plant before it can resume normal working.' Condition 6 of the second policy permitted him to carry out minor repairs 'without prejudice to the liability of the insurers' provided they were given notice together with a schedule of repairs, however, it was stipulated that major repairs required the prior sanction of the insurers. When vandals broke into the premises and destroyed the machinery, S submitted a claim. It was rejected by the insurers on the basis that the evidence did not point to theft and, with respect to the second policy, that cover was not provided against wilful damage. S lacked the financial resources to repair the machinery pending resolution of his dispute with the insurers and was not able to raise the necessary credit facility. The business's goodwill evaporated and he ceased trading six months later. The insurers continued to deny liability for almost four years before finally indemnifying him for the lost machinery. S, having lost his livelihood, brought an action seeking consequential damages in the sum of £75,000. Appearing in person and aided by the judges, he based his claim on two grounds: first, late payment and, second, that the insurer's failure to accept liability constituted a breach of contract.

It suffices at this point to note that Sprung's claim failed. To understand the Court of Appeal's reasoning it is necessary to appreciate the considerable weight of established legal principle that bound the court and which, therefore, operated to defeat the claim.

6.1 *Sprung:* the jurisprudential landscape

At the outset, it should be noted that an insurance claim amounts to a claim for unliquidated damages. A further foundational point which confronted the Court of Appeal was the principle of common law that interest is not payable as a head of general damages where a debt is paid late.[159] This, of course, has now been modified by legislation under which in certain situations a creditor may recover interest.[160] The House of Lords in *The Lips*,[161] has also acknowledged that the common law rule does

---

[158] [1999] 1 Lloyd's Rep IR 111. See, J Lowry and P Rawlings 'Insurers, Claims and the Boundaries of Good Faith' [2005] *MLR* 82.
[159] *London, Chatham & Dover Railway v South Eastern Railway* [1893] AC 429. See, G Treitel, *The Law of Contract* (London, Sweet & Maxwell, 2003) 994–8.
[160] Supreme Court Act 1981, s 35A. The Late Payment of Commercial Debts (Interest) Act 1998. Interest will be awarded against an insurer who wrongly delays payment and will generally be awarded from the date of the loss, unless the insured unreasonably delayed in bringing the claim: see, eg, *Quorum A/S v Schramm (No 2)* [2002] Lloyd's Rep IR 315; *Kuwait Airways Corp v Kuwait Insurance Co SAK* [2000] Lloyd's Rep IR 678.
[161] *President of India v Lips Maritime Corp* [1988] AC 395.

not prevent a damages claim for loss of interest which has been suffered and which falls within the second limb of *Hadley v Baxendale*,[162] that is, that the loss was within the reasonable contemplation of the defendant at the time of the contract.

While damages may be awarded for late payment of debt, no such remedy lies for late payment of damages. This point assumes major significance in *Sprung*. The classic statement of this rule was delivered by Lord Brandon in *The Lips*: '[t]here is no such thing as a cause of action in damages for late payment of damages. The only remedy which the law affords for delay in paying damages is the discretionary award of interest pursuant to statute.'[163] The rule has been applied to the late payment of insurance claims because, as commented above, a claim by an insured under a contract of insurance is treated as a claim for unliquidated damages for breach of contract.[164] It has long been settled that the insurer promises to hold the insured harmless and this is breached at the time of the loss, so it is at that point that liability to indemnify arises. Accordingly, in *The Fanti*,[165] a case on indemnity insurance, Lord Goff stated that:

> ...at common law, a contract of indemnity gives rise to an action for unliquidated damages, arising from the failure of the indemnifier to prevent the indemnified person from suffering damage, for example, by having to pay a third party. I also accept that, at common law, the cause of action does not (unless the contract provides otherwise) arise until the indemnified person can show actual loss...This is, as I understand it, because a promise of indemnity is simply a promise to hold the indemnified person harmless against a specified loss or expense. On this basis, no debt can arise before the loss is suffered or the expense incurred; however, once the loss is suffered or the expense incurred, the indemnifier is in breach of contract for having failed to hold the indemnified person harmless against the relevant loss or expense.[166]

Given that indemnity in insurance is characterised as damages, a claim for loss caused by late payment falls foul of the rule outlined by Lord Brandon in *The Lips*. However, the use of the term 'damages' in the context of insurance payments is curious. 'Damages' in this context is used in a sense different from its common (compensatory) meaning. As Pearson J has pointed out, 'its use is puzzling and seems to be used in a rather unusual sense, because the right to indemnity arises, not by reason of any wrongful act or omission on the part of the insurer (who did not promise that the loss would not happen or that he would prevent it) but only under his promise to indemnify the insured in the event of a loss.'[167]

[162] (1854) 9 Ex 341.
[163] *President of India v Lips Maritime Corp* [1988] AC 395, 424, *per* Lord Brandon. For the consequences on the relevant limitation period see, DW Oughton, JP Lowry and R. Merkin, *Limitation of Actions* (London, LLP, 1998) ch 12.
[164] *Jabbour v Custodian of Absentee Property for the State of Israel* [1954] 1 WLR 139; *Hardcastle v Netherwood* (1821) 5 B. & Ald. 93; *Castelli v Boddington* (1852) 1 E. & B. 66; *Luckie v Bushby* (1853) 13 CB 864; *Lloyd v Fleming* (1872) 7 QBD 299; *Pellas & Co v Neptune Marine Insurance Company* (1879) 5 CPD 34; *Swan and Cleland's Graving Dock and Slipway Co v Maritime Insurance Co and Croshaw* [1907] 1 KB 116, 123–4; *Baker v Adam* (1910) 15 Com Cas 227; *William Pickersgill & Sons Ltd v London and Provincial Marine and General Insurance Co Ltd* [1912] 3 KB 614, 622. For a recent endorsement of this principle, *see* *Callaghan v Dominion Insurance Co* [1997] 2 Lloyd's Rep 541, Sir Peter Webster (sitting as a judge of the High Court).
[165] *Firma C-Trade SA v Newcastle P & I Association (The Fanti)* [1991] AC 1.
[166] Ibid, at 35.
[167] *Jabbour v Custodian of Absentee Property for the State of Israel* [1954] 1 WLR 139, at 143.

The categorisation of an insurance claim as a claim for unliquidated damages for breach of contract gives rise to the unfortunate consequence that if an insurer wrongfully refuses to settle a claim, it will not be liable for damages for the losses suffered by the insured because of the principle laid down in *The Lips*. Recent English decisions on indemnity insurance proceed on the basis that the insurer will be in breach of its primary obligation from the time the loss or damage occurs irrespective of whether the insured has demanded payment from the insurer. This breach gives rise to the secondary obligation of the insurer to pay damages to the insured which is satisfied by meeting the insured's claim.[168]

The reasoning of Hirst J in *Ventouris v Mountain, (The Italia Express) (No 2)*,[169] is instructive. The claimant insured a vessel against war risks under an agreed value policy. While it was undergoing repairs, the vessel was totally lost when it was sunk by explosives attached to its hull. The insurers initially denied liability arguing that the loss was caused by the wilful misconduct of the claimant in procuring the sinking. On the thirty-seventh day of the trial, following rulings by the Court of Appeal on the admissibility of certain evidence relied on by the underwriters in their defence, they withdrew their allegations and submitted to judgment on liability. Judgment was entered in favour of the claimant in the sum of $4 million, the insured value of his vessel. The claimant went on to claim damages for other losses consequent upon the insurers' delay in meeting the claim: loss of income which would have been earned by a replacement vessel; loss suffered by virtue of increase in the capital value of a replacement vessel; and damages for hardship, inconvenience and mental distress. The issue which fell for determination was whether such heads of damages were recoverable as a matter of law.[170]

It was common ground between both parties that a contract of insurance is an agreement by the underwriter to hold the insured harmless against loss or damage from the peril insured against and that the remedy for breach of that obligation is a claim in damages. However, the parties diverged in their analysis of the nature of the obligation to 'hold the insured harmless.' The claimant argued that the underwriters failed to hold him harmless against the loss of his vessel in that if the $4 million was not paid immediately following the demand for payment then at that point the underwriter was in breach of contract and their secondary obligation to pay damages at large (which were not limited to $4 million) triggered. The claimant thus contended that in property insurance, as opposed to liability insurance, the underwriters were not in breach until a demand for immediate payment of the indemnity has been made. On the other hand, the underwriters argued that their primary obligation was to prevent the occurrence of the loss and that this obligation was broken the moment the vessel sunk. On this analysis, it followed that no demand for payment was necessary and that there was no subsequent separate breach of contract by the underwriter's failure to meet the claim. Thus, there was no distinction between liability and property insurance in this respect. Further, relying on section 67 of the Marine Insurance Act 1906, the underwriters argued that an agreed valued clause in the policy, is equivalent to a liquidated damages provision which limited the measure of indemnity to the agreed value of the vessel. Section 67(1) of the 1906 Act provides:

---

[168] See *Photo Production Ltd v Securicor Transport Ltd* [1980] 1 Lloyd's Rep 545 at 552, *per* Lord Diplock.
[169] [1992] 2 Lloyd's Rep 281.
[170] Assuming that the losses claimed were not, in any case, too remote: see *Hadley v Baxendale* (1854) 9 Exch 341.

The sum which the assured can recover in respect of a loss on a policy by which he is insured, in the case of an unvalued policy, to the full extent of the insurable value, or, in the case of a valued policy, to the full extent of the value fixed by the policy, is called the measure of indemnity.

This provision is a codification of the decision of the House of Lords in *Irving v Manning*,[171] in which it was stated that:

A policy of assurance is not a perfect contract of indemnity. It must be taken with this qualification, that the parties may agree beforehand in estimating the value of the subject assured, by way of liquidated damages, as indeed they may in any other contract to indemnify.[172]

Hirst J, on the basis of the statutory language, rejected the claimant's contention. He held that the underwriters were in breach of contract the moment the vessel sank, and therefore from the time when the peril occurred, they came under a secondary obligation to pay damages to the insured which were limited by the amount agreed in the policy. As a matter of law the underwriter's liability was fixed at $4 million by the policy and the claimant could not recover additional special or general damages for this would be tantamount to allowing damages for the late payment of damages. Further, Hirst J took the view that although *The Fanti* was a liability insurance decision, it was nevertheless of general application and extended to property insurance.

While strictly speaking *The Italia Express (No 2)* is an authority dealing purely with the construction of section 67 of the Marine Insurance Act 1906, it has not been viewed in this light in subsequent non-marine cases. The reasoning of Hirst J and the approach taken by Lord Goff in *The Fanti* both proved to be determinative in *Sprung*. At first sight it appears that the insured's plight in *Sprung* was caused by the insurer's failure to pay within a reasonable time. However, this was not the view taken by the Court of Appeal. Noting that they had not heard a detailed argument on the point, the court, nevertheless, dismissed Sprung's claim as amounting to no more than a claim for late payment of damages.[173] Evans LJ was prepared to hold that there was an implied term obliging the insurers to respond promptly to the insured's claim and that the defendants' delay did in fact amount to breach of that implied obligation. However, as a matter of law this did not result in any liability for consequential loss except in relation to interest for late payment. The insurer's initial denial of liability placed Sprung in a position where he was entitled, and indeed, bound to proceed as if he was uninsured. He could have reinstated or repaired the damaged property and if he had done so the insurer 'would not then be in a position to allege by way of defence that there had been a breach of condition (6) [of the policy]; in other words, they would have disqualified themselves from saying that, the repairs having been carried out without their consent, the claimant was not entitled to recover the promised indemnity under the policy.'[174] Evans LJ was thus driven to conclude that the insured became author of his own misfortune for which the insurer was in no way liable:

---

[171] (1847) 1 HLC 287.
[172] Ibid, at 306, *per* Patteson J, whose judgment was affirmed by their Lordships.
[173] [1999] 1 Lloyd's Rep IR 111, at 116, *per* Evans LJ.
[174] Ibid, at 118.

What has to be said, however hard it may seem to say it, is that in such circumstances the cause of any loss which the plaintiff suffered must be regarded as the consequence of his own decision not to proceed with repair or reinstatement, whether that decision was voluntary or not. In other words, if, unfortunately, through his own financial circumstances he is unable to do so without assistance from the defendants, he cannot allege that the defendants were in breach of contract by failing to accept liability at that stage.[175]

It was with 'undisguised reluctance' that Evans LJ held that Mr Sprung's claim should fail. Similarly, Beldam LJ felt constrained by the authorities in holding that an insured has no cause of action for damages for non-payment of damages. He thought that no distinction could be drawn between a breach of the term in the contract (condition 6) that required the insurers to inspect or give consent to the repairs promptly and a requirement that they should meet their obligations under the policy with due expedition. Thus, Beldam LJ also thought that if the insured had carried out his repairs after learning of the insurers' refusal to meet the claim or after unreasonable delay on the insurers part, the court would not entertain any argument on the insurer's part that they were not liable because of breach by the insured of the policy conditions.

In relation to the decisions cited in support of the principle underlying *Sprung* to the effect that actions for late payment against insurers sound in unliquidated damages rather than debt, Professor Clarke points out that 'in few of these cases was the description of the money as damages examined, and in none of them did the present point arise.'[176] In a detailed analysis Campbell argues that a promise to indemnify against loss might have one of three meanings: first, a promise to prevent loss from occurring; second, a promise loss will not occur; and third, a promise to compensate in the event of a loss occurring. He recognises that the weight of authority points to the first meaning. So far as property insurance is concerned he favours the third meaning on the basis that this more realistically reflects the reasonable expectations of the contracting parties. Whereas with respect to liability insurance he concludes that the first meaning is the one that most accurately reflects the intentions of the parties and accords with the authorities.[177]

Modern judges too have recognised the need for reform. In *Sprung*, Beldam LJ clearly felt sympathetic to the insured's plight and called for reform of the law. Denying that Sprung was entitled to anything other than an award for the loss under the policy together with interest, he said:

> There will be many who share Mr Sprung's view that in cases such as this such an award is inadequate to compensate him or any other assured who may have had to abandon his business as a result of insurers' failure to pay, and that early consideration should be given to reform of the law in similar cases.[178]

---

[175] Ibid.
[176] M Clarke, *The Law of Insurance Contracts* (London, LLP, 2002) at para 30–7A, n 1. It is unfortunate that in *The Pride Valley Foods Ltd v Independent Insurance Co Ltd* [1999] Lloyd's Rep IR 120, where the Court of Appeal granted leave to appeal the striking out of the insured's claim for consequential damages in the light of the range of contrary Commonwealth authorities and the criticism of *The Italia Express*, the opportunity to consider the insured's claim for damages was lost given that his claim for an indemnity failed.
[177] N Campbell, 'The nature of an insurer's obligation' [2000] LMCLQ 42.
[178] [1999] 1 Lloyd's Rep IR 111, at 119.

It is to be hoped that the House of Lords will have an opportunity to rule on the issue of consequential damages flowing from an insurers' failure or unreasonable delay to pay a valid claim.[179] This is not to say that the English judges have not sought to find a more just result. In *Grant v Co-operative Insurance Society,*[180] Hodgson J, applying general contractual principles governing remoteness,[181] awarded damages to the insureds against the insurers who had wrongfully repudiated liability under a fire policy. The insureds, a husband and wife, recovered damages for the cost of protecting their house from vandals while it remained unoccupied and for the cost of alternative accommodation. However, the decision must be regarded as wrong.

Yet other common law jurisdictions have displayed little tolerance towards insurers who fail to settle a valid claim in a timely manner. For example, the Supreme Court of Canada in *Whiten v Pilot Insurance Co,*[182] awarded $1 million by way of punitive damages against an insurer who wrongly repudiated a claim. Upholding the jury's award, Binnie J explained that:

> Insurance contracts, as Pilot's self-description shows, are sold by the insurance industry and purchased by members of the public for peace of mind. The more devastating the loss, the more the insured may be at the financial mercy of the insurer, and the more difficult it may be to challenge a wrongful refusal to pay the claim. Deterrence is required. The obligation of good faith dealing means that the appellant's peace of mind should have been Pilot's objective, and her vulnerability ought not to have been aggravated as a negotiating tactic. It is this relationship of reliance and vulnerability that was outrageously exploited by Pilot in this case. The jury, it appears, decided a powerful message of retribution, deterrence and denunciation had to be sent to the respondent and they sent it.[183]

As we have seen in chapter 4, criticisms of insurance law have had some impact on insurance practice although the response of the industry had been largely restricted to addressing issues of concern to private (ie consumer) insureds. Beginning in 1977, the Association of British Insurers (ABI) issued codes of practice which implicitly acknowledged the imbalance between the parties to insurance contracts. In essence, they provided that once liability under the policy has been established and the amount payable agreed, payment will be made by the insurer without avoidable

---

[179] The decision was inevitably followed by HHJ Chambers QC in *Normhurst Ltd v Dornoch Ltd* [2005] Lloyd's Rep IR 27. See also, *Mandrake Holdings Ltd v Countryside Assured Group* CA 26/5/2005, unreported.

[180] (1984) 134 NLJ 81. See also, *Stuart v GRE Assurance of New Zealand* (1988) 5 ANZ Ins Cases 75, 274.

[181] *Hadley v Baxendale* (1854) 9 Ex 341; *Victoria Laundry (Windsor) Ltd v Newman Industries Ltd* [1949] 2 KB 528; *Koufos v Czarnikow Ltd* [1969] 1 AC 350. See further J Beatson, *Anson's Law of Contract* (Oxford, Oxford University Press, 2002) ch 17. It should be noted that following the decision in *Clark v Ardington* [2004] 1 AC 1067, in which the House of Lords overruled *The Liesbosch* [1933] AC 449, a claimant in Mr Sprung's position may no longer be defeated by the causation rules. Now that *Liesbosch* has gone, it is not open to the insurers to argue that the cause of the insured's loss of business was not their late payment but his impecuniosity. Given that in *Sprung* Evans LJ was prepared to imply a term requiring the insurers to pay promptly, a future insured may now succeed in an action against a late paying insurer. In this regard, note also s150 FSMA 2000 which, by incorporating Schedule 5 of the ICOB, creates a statutory tort whereby an insurer who unreasonably delays payment is in breach of duty.

[182] [2002] 1 SCR 595. For a more detailed study of the approaches taken in other common law jurisdictions see, J Lowry and P Rawlings, 'Insurers, Claims and the Boundaries of Good Faith', above n 158.

[183] Ibid, at [129].

delay.[184] However, the codes did not cover the situation where the insurer unreasonably denies liability. Nor did they provide a mechanism for enforcement. The Financial Services Ombudsman's predecessor, the Insurance Ombudsman Bureau (IOB), did adopt a more decisive approach to delays in processing claims. The IOB was prepared to award compensation in cases where there had been 'unnecessary delays and oversights' in handling the claim.[185] However, the jurisdiction of the Ombudsman is limited. It is primarily a means by which consumers can challenge the decisions of insurers, and in relation to commercial insurance, it can normally only deal with complaints from small businesses with an annual turnover of less than £1 million.

C. REINSTATEMENT

Reinstatement, which applies only in property insurance, arises when the insurer pays for the replacement or repair of the subject-matter of the insurance instead of paying money to the insured. Unless the policy or a statutory provision provides otherwise, however, an insurer is bound to pay the insurance moneys to the insured, and the insured 'is quite entitled simply to put the money into pocket without in any way reinstating the building.'[186] Unless reinstatement is required by statute,[187] an insurer can only require the insured to reinstate if the policy expressly provides for it. The mischief which reinstatement is designed to address is 'the temptation to an ill minded owner to set fire to the building in order to pocket the insurance money.'[188]

---

1. Contractual reinstatement

If the policy provides that the insurer has the option to either pay insurance moneys to the insured or require him to reinstate or repair, the insurer must make an election.[189] The election must be made within the period fixed by the policy, or if none is

---

[184] Association of British Insurers, *Statements of General Insurance Practice* (London: ABI, 1986, replacing 1977), cl 2(c); Association of British Insurers, *Statements of Long Term Insurance Practice* (London: ABI, 1986), cl 3(d); Association of British Insurers, *General Insurance Claims Code* (London: ABI, 2000). It should be noted that as from 14 January 2005, the Statement of General Insurance Practice was replaced by the regulatory powers of the FSA.

[185] IOB, Bulletin 1994, 1, 4.

[186] *Reynolds v Phoenix Assurance Co Ltd*, above n 99 at 462, *per* Forbes J. See also *Rayner v Preston* (1881) 18 Ch D 1 at 6, *per* Cotton LJ, at 9–10, *per* Brett LJ; and *Re Law Guarantee Trust & Accident Society Ltd* [1914] 2 Ch 617 at 639, *per* Kennedy LJ.

[187] See the Fires Prevention (Metropolis) Act 1774, considered below.

[188] *Reynolds v Phoenix Assurance Co Ltd,* above, n 99 at 462, *per* Forbes J.

[189] *Kammins Ballrooms Co Ltd v Zenith Investments (Torquay) Ltd* [1971] AC 850 at 883, *per* Lord Diplock.

stipulated, within a reasonable time of the claim. The insurer must communicate its election to the insured in unequivocal terms; and once an election is made, it is irrevocable.[190] Merely making an offer to settle by way of payment may be viewed as a mere negotiation step and will not necessarily pre-empt the insurer from subsequently making an election should the offer be rejected by the insured.[191] In practice the election is communicated by the insurer informing the insured of its intention to reinstate or, conversely, of its intention to pay insurance money.[192]

Once an election has been made the contract is viewed as if it originally required the insurer to carry out the act so elected.[193] Thus, if the insurer elects to repair or reinstate, the policy becomes a repair or rebuilding contract, and as such the insurer will be responsible for the quality of the reinstatement carried out by the contractor. If the work is defective the insured may sue the insurer for damages to remedy the defect.[194] The obligation on the insurer is to replace like with like, even if the cost to the insurer is greater than the sum insured,[195] the insurer will be liable for any further damage caused to the property in question after it has entered into possession to reinstate.[196]

The insurer's liability to reinstate will not be discharged because the work is more expensive than anticipated.[197] Should reinstatement become impossible before an election is made, the insurer will be liable to indemnify the insured by paying the insurance moneys.[198] Where, however, impossibility occurs after the election to reinstate has been made, the doctrine of frustration may operate to discharge the obligation to repair or rebuild.[199] In this situation, the policy would convert to a contract to pay insurance moneys.[200] The insurers may plead the Law Reform (Frustrated Contracts) Act 1943,[201] so that if the insured has 'obtained a valuable benefit' before the contract was frustrated, he may be required to pay such sum as 'the court considers just, having regard to all the circumstances of the case...'[202]

---

[190] *Scarf v Jardine* (1882) 7 App Cas 345 at 360, *per* Lord Blackburn. This is now subject to the doctrine of discharge by frustration, see below.

[191] *Sutherland v Sun Fire Office* (1852) 14 D (Ct Sess) 775.

[192] *Scottish Amicable Heritable Securities Association Ltd v Northern Assurance Co* (1883) 11 R (Ct Sess) 287.

[193] *Brown v Royal Insurance Co* (1859) 1 El & El 853 at 859, *per* Lord Campbell CJ.

[194] *Robson v New Zealand Insurance Co Ltd* [1931] NZLR 35.

[195] Ibid. In *Times Fire Assurance Co v Hawke* (1858) 1 F & F 406 at 407, Channell B stated that the property, a house, must be restored 'substantially in the same state as before the fire.'

[196] *Ahmedbhoy Habbibhoy v Bombay Fire and Marine Insurance Co* (1912) 107 LT 668.

[197] *Brown v Royal Insurance Co*, above, n 193; *Carlyle v Elite Insurance Co* (1984) 56 BCLR 331.

[198] *Anderson v Commercial Union Assurance Co* (1885) 55 LJQB 146.

[199] Cf *Brown v Royal Insurance Co*, above n 193, which was decided before the courts developed the doctrine of discharge by virtue of impossibility or frustration.

[200] *Anderson v Commercial Union Assurance Co*, above n 198.

[201] S 1(1) of which provides: 'Where a contract governed by English law has become impossible of performance or been otherwise frustrated, and the parties thereto have for that reason been discharged from the further performance of the contract, the following provisions of this section shall, subject to the provisions of section two of this Act, have effect in relation thereto.'

[202] S 1(3) of the 1943 Act. Although by s 2(5)(b), the Act does not apply to contracts of insurance, it will be recalled that after the election has been made by the insurers, the policy becomes a contract to reinstate.

2. Statutory reinstatement

2.1 Fires Prevention (Metropolis) Act 1774, section 83

Generally an indemnity policy requires the insurer to pay to the insured a sum of money referable to the insured loss. However, a statutory form of reinstatement is provided by the Fires Prevention (Metropolis) Act 1774 whereby any 'person interested' can require the insurer to reinstate irrespective of whether such a person is a party to the contract of insurance. The Act is expressly designed to address the temptation to an ill minded owner to set fire to his insured building in order to pocket the insurance money. Section 83 of the 1774 Act therefore authorises and requires fire insurers, upon suspicion of fraud or arson on the part of the insured, to use the insurance monies, so far as they will go, to reinstate the building instead of paying it to the insured. To avoid the danger that there may be other persons interested in the building whose 'lives and fortunes...may be lost or endangered,' section 83 also requires the insurers to reinstate if requested to do so by such person or persons.

The Act is restricted to fire insurance and applies to 'offices for insuring houses or other buildings.' Fire insurance on personal chattels is therefore excluded from its ambit. Thus it has been held that section 83 does not apply to a tenant's trade fixtures,[203] or to the contents of buildings.[204] Despite the Act's short title, the courts have extended its application to England and Wales on the basis that the mischief addressed by the statute was not confined to London. In *ex p Gorely*,[205] where the insured property was in Dover, Lord Westbury LC reasoned that:

> when we approach the 83rd section we find, in the first place, that the enactment therein contained is heralded by a particular preamble of its own, which recites a general and universal evil as being the occasion of its being passed. We should be prepared, therefore, to infer, from the statement in that preamble of a general evil which the Legislature was desirous to redress, viz., that the enactment would, in fact, be co-extensive with the evil stated to have been intended to be redressed; and in point of fact, that general inference is confirmed by the language of the enactment itself, which is in itself general, and does not contain the words, 'within the limits aforesaid'; words which were evidently omitted, and omitted designedly. In my judgment, therefore, this particular section is intended to be of general and universal application...[206]

However, in *Westminster Fire Office v Glasgow Provident Investment Society,*[207] Earl Selborne and Lord Watson held that the Act does not apply to Scotland because it was originally introduced to amend earlier legislation which did not extend to Scotland. It should also be noted that the scope of section 83, which is expressed to apply to the 'governors or directors of the several [fire] insurance offices,' is restricted to insurance companies only and does not therefore apply to members of Lloyd's. The

---

[203] *Ex p Gorely* (1864) 4 De G J & S 477.
[204] *Sinnot v Bowden* [1912] 2 Ch 414.
[205] (1864) 4 De G J & S 477.
[206] Ibid, at 480–1.
[207] (1888) 13 App Cas 699, at 714 and 716 respectively.

point has been made that 'the corporation of Lloyd's do not insure anybody against anything. It is the underwriters who undertake the burden of insurances.'[208]

As has been noted, a 'person interested' may request reinstatement under s 83. Obviously this term encompasses a person who, while not being a party to the insurance contract, nevertheless has an insurable interest in the property, irrespective of whether such interest is full or limited. However, it excludes the insured and so the latter cannot require reinstatement.[209] The effect of section 83 is to give a 'person interested', although not a party to the contract, a statutory right to direct the insurers to expend the insurance monies in a particular way. Generally, any person with a legal or equitable interest in the building will be a 'person interested'. Such a person will include a mortgagee,[210] a tenant,[211] a lessor,[212] a purchaser of real property prior to completion,[213] and a lessee.[214] In *Lonsdale & Thompson Ltd v Black Arrow Group plc*,[215] it was held that a tenant could request the landlord's insurers to reinstate following a fire even though the landlord had contracted to sell the property before the loss and therefore no longer possessed any insurable interest in it. The court construed the policy as enuring for the tenant's benefit despite the sale of the freehold.

The request to reinstate must be distinct and it should include some reference to the statutory right. In *Simpson v Scottish Union Insurance Co*,[216] a landlord let two houses to a tenant who insured them as required to do so by his lease. When the houses were destroyed by fire, the landlord visited the insurers' offices and claimed the benefit of the policy and to have the insurance monies applied towards the rebuilding costs. Although the secretary of the insurers' agreed to his request, the insurers nevertheless settled with the tenant. The landlord, having rebuilt the houses, sued the insurers. The court held that as his request did not make reference to the Act, it amounted to nothing more than the landlord claiming to be the person interested under the insurance policy. There had been no distinct request before the settlement with the tenant.

Where an insurer fails to comply with a due and proper request to reinstate, the person interested cannot reinstate himself and claim the cost from the insurer. The redress available is probably a mandatory injunction compelling the insurer's compliance.[217] However, it has been held that the appropriate remedy is an injunction to prevent the insurer paying the insured since enforcing the mandate may prove impossible.[218]

---

[208] *Portavon Cinema Co Ltd v Price and Century Insurance Co Ltd*, above n 141 at 608, *per* Branson J.
[209] See *Reynolds v Phoenix Assurance Co Ltd*, above n 99 at 462, *per* Forbes J.
[210] *Sinnot v Bowden*, above n 204. See the Law of Property Act 1925, s 108(3).
[211] *Wimbledon Golf Club v Imperial Insurance Co* (1902) 18 TLR 815.
[212] *Matthey v Curling* [1922] 2 AC 180 at 198, *per* Atkin LJ.
[213] *Rayner v Preston*, above n 186 at 15, *per* James LJ.
[214] *Portavon Cinema Co Ltd v Price and Century Insurance Co Ltd*, above n 141.
[215] [1993] 2 Lloyd's Rep 428.
[216] (1863) 1 H & M 618.
[217] *Simpson v Scottish Union Insurance Co*, ibid at 629, *per* Sir W. Page-Wood V-C.
[218] *Wimbledon Golf Club v Imperial Insurance Co*, above n 211.

11

Subrogation

1. Subrogation and indemnity[1]

An insurer cannot refuse to pay merely on the ground that the insured has a claim against a third party: the insured 'does not receive [money from the insurers] because of the accident, but because he has made a contract providing for the contingency.'[2] Equally, the third party cannot deny liability on the ground that the insurer has or will indemnify the insured.[3] Yet it is also the case that the insured cannot recover a sum greater than the loss suffered:

> The very foundation, in my opinion, of every rule which has been applied to insurance law is this, namely, that the contract of insurance contained in a marine or fire policy is a contract of indemnity, and of indemnity only, and that this contract means that the assured, in case of a loss against which the policy has been made, shall be fully indemnified, but shall never be more than fully indemnified. That is the fundamental principle of insurance, and if ever a proposition is brought forward which is at variance with it, that is to say, which either will prevent the assured from obtaining a full indemnity, or which will give to the assured more than a full indemnity, that proposition must certainly be wrong.[4]

---

[1] SR Derham, *Subrogation in Insurance Law* (Sydney, The Law Book Company, 1985); JG Fleming, 'The Collateral Source Rule and Loss Allocation in Tort Law' (1966) 54 *Calif LR* 1478; J Birds, 'Contractual Subrogation in Insurance' [1979] *JBL* 124; R Hasson, 'Subrogation in Insurance Law: A Critical Evaluation' (1985) 5 *OJLS* 416; RC Horn, *Subrogation in Insurance Theory and Practice* (Homewood, Illinois, 1964); C Mitchell, 'Defences to an Insurer's Subrogated Action' [1996] *LMCLQ* 343; C Mitchell, *The Law of Subrogation* (Oxford, Oxford University Press, 1994); HN Sheldon, *The Law of Subrogation* (Frederick, Maryland, Beard, 2000); RM Walmsley, *Subrogation and Contribution in Insurance Practice* (London, Witherby, 2001). For the early history of the doctrine, see ML Marasinghe, 'An Historical Introduction to the Doctrine of Subrogation' [1975] 10 *Valparaiso UL Rev* 45, 275.
[2] *Bradburn v The Great Western Railway Co* (1874) LR 10 Exch 1 at 3, per Pigott B. See also, *Mason v Sainsbury* (1782) 3 Doug 61; *Yates v Whyte* (1838) *Cullen v Butler* (1816) 5 M & S 461; *Yates v Sainsbury* (1838) 1 Arn 85; 4 Bing (NC) 272; *Dickenson v Jardine* (1868) LR 3 CP 639; *Collingridge v Royal Exchange Assurance* (1877) 3 QBD 173 at 176–7; *Caledonia North Sea Ltd v British Telecommunications plc* [2002] Lloyd's Rep IR 261.
[3] *Parry v Cleaver* [1970] AC 1.
[4] *Castellain v Preston* (1883) 11 QBD 380 at 386, per Brett LJ.

Subrogation is one means by which the insured is prevented from obtaining more than a full indemnity.[5] The rights that the insurers acquire through subrogation were summarised by Brett LJ in *Castellain* v *Preston*:[6]

> as between the underwriter and the assured the underwriter is entitled to the advantage of every right of the assured, whether such right consists in contract, fulfilled or unfulfilled, or in remedy for tort capable of being insisted on or already insisted on, or in any other right, whether by way of condition or otherwise, legal or equitable, which can be, or has been exercised or has accrued, and whether such right could or could not be enforced by the insurer in the name of the assured by the exercise or acquiring of which right or condition the loss against which the assured is insured, can be, or has been diminished.

In the same case, Cotton LJ said that since an indemnity policy is designed 'only to pay for that loss which the assured may have sustained,' then, 'In order to ascertain what that loss is, everything must be taken into account which is received by and comes to the hand of the assured, and which diminishes that loss.'[7] This means that the insurers are entitled to be subrogated to the insured's rights of action against a third party,[8] but the insurers are also entitled to other benefits, such as compensation, received by the insured that relate to the loss.[9] In *Castellain* v *Preston*,[10] a house was damaged by fire after a contract of sale had been signed but before the date of completion. The vendor was paid by his insurers for the loss. The purchase was then completed and the price paid to the vendor. The insurers were allowed to recover their payment out of the sale proceeds of the house. If the insured has received a benefit in a form other than money, the insurers will be entitled to claim its value up to the amount of the claim paid: so, where a lessor insures the leased property and the tenant has a duty to repair, then if the property is damaged and the tenant repairs, the insurers may recover the value of the benefit which the lessor has received from those repairs up to the amount paid out by the insurers.[11] Of course, where the benefit handed over by the wrongdoer is for losses not covered by the insurance contract this may be retained by the insured.

In *Lord Napier and Ettrick* v *Hunter*,[12] the House of Lords asserted the equitable origins of subrogation and, broadly, rejected Lord Diplock's view that it is the result

---

[5] See also the discussion of double insurance, above ch 10.

[6] See above n 4, at 388.

[7] Ibid, at 393, per Cotton LJ.

[8] The right arises in any situation where a third party is liable for the loss and not simply where that liability arises in tort: *MH Smith (Plant Hire) Ltd v DL Mainwaring (t/a Inshore)* [1986] 2 Lloyd's Rep 244 at 246, per Kerr LJ.

[9] *Lord Napier and Ettrick v Hunter* [1993] AC 713. Discussed further below.

[10] *Castellain v Preston*, above n 4.

[11] *Darrell v Tibbits* [1880] 5 QBD 560; *West of England Fire Insurance Co v Issacs* [1897] 1 QB 227.

[12] See above n 9.

of an implied term in the insurance contract.[13] Nevertheless, rights of subrogation rest on the contract of indemnity and the parties may in that contract agree to alter or waive it.[14] Policies relating to construction projects routinely include a term by which insurers waive rights of subrogation against certain parties, such as sub-contractors. It is also common for contracts to include the right for the insurers to control proceedings against a third party even before they have indemnified the insured, or to require that the insured not admit liability without the consent of the insurers.[15] Less common is a requirement that the insured assign rights against third parties to the insurer,[16] although it is worth noting that in practice insurers, who have paid on a loss, require the insured to sign a letter of subrogation, which assigns the insured's rights of recovery against the third party.[17]

Following the judgments in *Castellain v Preston*,[18] and in the earlier case of *Darrell v Tibbits*,[19] it would seem that the right of subrogation confers three rights on the insurer. First, having met their liability under the policy through the payment of money or the reinstatement of the property, the insurer is entitled to take over any right of action that the insured has in relation to the loss. Secondly, where benefits relating to the covered loss were given by a third party to the insured before payment of the claim, then the insurer is entitled to recover the amount by which the total benefits received by the insured (that is, the payment from the insurer plus the benefit from the third-party) exceed the loss up to the amount paid by the insurer. Thirdly,

---

[13] In *Yorkshire Insurance Co Ltd v Nisbet Shipping Co Ltd* [1962] 2 QB 330 at 340, Diplock J, referring to marine insurance, said the right of subrogation was a term implied into the contract 'to give business efficacy to an agreement whereby the assured in the case of a loss against which the policy has been made shall be fully indemnified, and never more than fully indemnified.' See also, *Orakpo v Manson Investments Ltd* [1978] AC 95 at 104 and *Hobbs v Marlowe* [1978] AC 16 at 39, where Lord Diplock refers to the role of equity as only being to compel the reluctant insured to lend his name to the insurer to enforce rights to which the insurer was subrogated. For a case in which the judges in the Court of Appeal were prepared to countenance both explanations, see *Morris v Ford Motor Co Ltd* [1973] 1 QB 792 (discussed below); and see *The Yasin* [1979] 2 Lloyd's Rep 45. In *Lord Napier and Ettrick v Hunter*, above n 9, Lord Goff asserted that subrogation is an equitable principle originating in the courts of equity (see *Randal v Cockran* (1748) 1 Ves Sen 98; *White v Dobinson* (1844) 14 Sim 273) which was later recognised by the common law courts (see *Yates v White* (1838) 1 Arn 85). Lords Templeman and Browne-Wilkinson said that, while subrogation was implied in insurance contracts by the common law, this gave rise to equitable interests. For a rare instance where legislation provides for subrogation, see the Riots (Damages) Act 1886, s 2 (2); such legislation is more common in the US, see Indiana Code 27-7-5-6. In the US see, *Foremost County Mutual Insurance Co v Home Indemnity Co* 897 F 2d 754 (1990); *Welch Foods, Inc v Chicago Title Insurance Company* 17 SW3d 467 (Arkansas, 2000). Generally, Derham, *Subrogation in Insurance Law*, above n 1, at 4–22; J Birds, 'Subrogation in the House of Lords' [1993] *JBL* 294; C Mitchell, 'Subrogation and Insurance Law: Proprietary Claims and Excess Clauses' [1993] *LMCLQ* 192; A Tettenborn, *Law of Restitution in England and Ireland* (London, Cavendish Publishing, 1996) 55.

[14] See below.

[15] *Terry v Trafalgar Insurance Co Ltd* [1970] 1 Lloyd's Rep 524. Generally, Anon, 'Note: The Subrogation of the Insurer to Collateral Rights of the Insured' [1951] *Columbia L Rev* 202; J Birds, 'Contractual Subrogation in Insurance,' above n 1.

[16] *Re Miller, Gibb & Co Ltd* [1957] 1 WLR 703; *Compania Colombiana de Seguros v Pacific Steam Navigation Co* [1965] 1 QB 101. Sums paid by the wrongdoer for losses not covered by the insurance contract will, nevertheless, be due to the insured, see below.

[17] *Lord Napier and Ettrick v Hunter*, above n 9, at 714, per Lord Goff. For a rare exception, see *England v Guardian Insurance Ltd* [2000] Lloyd's Rep IR 404. The effect of the doctrine of subrogation is often compared with the assignment of the rights of the insured against the third party, although a key difference is that where the requirements of the Law of Property Act 1925, s 136, have been met the assignee is able to sue in their own name: *Graham v Entec Europe Ltd* [2003] EWCA Civ 1177 at (37), per Potter LJ.

[18] See above n 4.

[19] See above n 11.

where a benefit has been received from a third-party in compensation for the covered loss after the claim has been met, then the insurer has a right over those benefits to the extent that they exceed the amount of the loss suffered up to the amount paid by the insurer. Mitchell has cogently argued that only the first constitutes subrogation.[20] In the second situation the payment by the insurer is made under a mistake of fact, namely, the belief that the insured has not been indemnified. Here the means of recovering the excess is an action for money had and received. In the third situation the insurer has an equitable lien over the money in the hands of the insured.[21] While accepting the logic of this view, it is perhaps too late to retrieve the limited and more exact definition of subrogation in the face of more than a hundred and twenty years of judicial bad habits, so these three aspects will be dealt with together in this chapter.

Subrogation rights are not independent rights that the insurers can exercise against a wrongdoer, they merely mean that, 'the insurer and the insured are one.'[22] They arise only in relation to a contract of indemnity. As Lord Cairns put it:

> I know of no foundation for the right of underwriters, except the well-known principle of law, that where one person has agreed to indemnify another, he will, on making good the indemnity, be entitled to succeed to all the ways and means by which the person indemnified might have protected himself against or reimbursed himself for the loss. It is on this principle that the underwriters...can assert any right which the owner of the ship might have asserted against a wrongdoer for damage for the act which has caused the loss.[23]

There are no subrogation rights in the case of a contingency policy,[24] so that if a life policy names the insured life as beneficiary and that person is killed by another's negligent act, the insured's estate will be able to claim under the policy and keep any damages received from the wrongdoer. Not surprisingly, no right of subrogation exists if the insurance contract is void. A marine policy in which no proof of an insurable interest is required (a ppi contract) is void under the Marine Insurance Act 1906, section 4(1) and (2) and will not, therefore, give rise to the right of subrogation because any payment made by the insurer is not pursuant to an obligation to indemnify the insured.[25]

To avail themselves of the right of subrogation, the insurers must have discharged their liability under the policy to the insured. As one judge put it,

> the principle of subrogation is ever a latent and inherent ingredient of the contract of indemnity, but...it does not become operative or enforceable until actual payment be made by the insurer. It derives its life from the original contract. It gains its operative payment from payment under that contract. Not till payment is made does the equity, hitherto held in suspense, grasp and operate upon the assured's choses in action. In my view the essence of the matter is that subrogation springs not from payment only but from actual payment

---

[20] Mitchell, *The Law of Subrogation*, above n 1, at 68–74. See the comments of the court in an Australian case, *British Traders Insurance Co Ltd v Monson* (1964) 111 C LR 86 at 94.

[21] *Lord Napier and Ettrick v Hunter*, above n 9.

[22] *Mason v Sainsbury*, above n 2, at 65, per Buller J. As Lord Mansfield CJ put it, 'Every day the insurer is put in the place of the insured': ibid, at 64.

[23] *Simpson v Thomson, Birrell* (1877) 3 App Cas 279 at 284, per Lord Cairns LC. See also, *Castellain v Preston*, above n 4, at 401–2, per Bowen LJ.

[24] *Solicitors and General v Lamb* (1864) 1 De GJ & Sm 251. For the distinction, see above ch 1.

[25] *John Edwards and Co v Motor Union Insurance Co Ltd* [1922] 2 KB 249.

conjointly with the fact that it is made pursuant to the basic and original contract of indemnity.[26]

In *Page v Scottish Insurance Corporation*,[27] Mr Forster's car was involved in an accident as a result of the negligent driving of Mr Page, a mechanic. Both Forster's car and a car owned by a Mr Stobart were damaged. Forster's insurers agreed to let Page undertake the repairs to Forster's car, but failed to pay him. Page sued and the insurers responded by suing Page, as the wrongdoer, for a sum equivalent to the cost of the repairs. The Court of Appeal held that the insurers had no right to be subrogated to Forster's rights of action because they had not settled in full all the claims under the policy relating to the accident, including those brought by Stobart against Forster and Page jointly. Similarly, in *Scottish Union & National Insurance Company v Davis*,[28] when a Bentley car owned by Mr Davis was damaged by a coping stone falling from a building, the insurers agreed that the car should be repaired by a particular firm. The firm failed to carry out the repairs, but submitted a bill which the insurers paid. Davis then received a sum of money in settlement of a claim against the owner of the building and his insurers sought to recover that money. The Court of Appeal held that the right of subrogation only arose when the insurers settled the claim, and in this case, although they had paid out money, they had not settled because the car had not been repaired as the policy required.

The right of subrogation arises when the insurers have paid out for the loss to the extent required by the policy, even if the actual loss exceeds that figure.[29] The insurers will also acquire the right of subrogation where they have made a payment for a loss even if it is not covered by the policy, as long as that payment was 'honestly and reasonably' made. In *King v Victoria Insurance Co Ltd*,[30] an alleged tortfeasor sought in vain to defend an action by arguing that the insurers were not liable under the terms of the policy to meet the claim, and therefore they had no title to sue: 'if, on a claim being made, the insurers treat it as within the contract, by what right can a stranger say that it is not so?'[31] Moreover, the insurer's right of subrogation is not affected by the fact that the premium was paid by someone other than the person who benefits under the insurance contract.[32]

Although the insurers cannot bring an action until they have settled the insured's claim, it seems far-fetched to suppose that, pending this, there is any implied duty on an insured to commence an action against the wrongdoer, particularly since one of the reasons people take out insurance is to avoid the need to litigate. The insurers

[26] Ibid, at 254–5, per McCardie J. See also *Castellain v Preston*, above n 4 at 389, per Brett LJ; *Darrell v Tibbits*, above n 11 at 563, per Brett LJ; *Simpson v Thomson, Birrell*, above n 23 at 284, per Lord Cairns LC; *The Midland Insurance Co v Smith and Wife* (1881) 6 QBD 561; Marine Insurance Act 1906, s 79.
[27] (1929) 140 LT 571.
[28] [1970] 1 Lloyd's Rep 1.
[29] *Lord Napier and Ettrick v Hunter*, above n 9. This case also puts an end to the idea that the right of subrogation only arose when the insured had been fully compensated for the loss, which did enjoy some limited support (see *In re Driscoll, deceased, Driscoll v Driscoll* [1918] IR 152). It is clear that only a full indemnity under the policy is required.
[30] [1896] AC 250.
[31] Ibid, at 255, per Lord Hobhouse.
[32] 'Subrogation does not look to the person who paid the premium, it identifies the assured upon whose shoulders liability rests and on whose behalf the compensation payments have been made.' *CSE Aviation Ltd v Cardale Doors Ltd* QBD (Comm) unreported, 13 April 2000 at (13), per Morison J. See, *The Yasin*, above n 13.

must not reach a settlement that unreasonably prejudices the interests of the insured: for instance, the insurers are required to keep in mind the insured's interest in obtaining compensation for any uninsured loss. It is not uncommon for insurers to elect not to exercise the right of subrogation: until 1995 in motoring cases where both motorists were comprehensively insured, insurers operated the so-called 'knock-for-knock' agreement, which in essence meant that insurers met the losses of their own insured without arguing about liability.[33] Similarly, insurers have informally agreed that they will not normally pursue claims against the employees of an insured firm.[34] If the insurers decide not to pursue the third party, the insured can sue and might well decide to do so if the insurers are only liable for part of the loss, as, for instance, would be the case where there is an excess clause in the policy (that is, the insured pays for part of the loss up to an agreed amount) or the insured's loss is not fully covered (that is, the subject-matter is not insured to its full value).[35] A policy may, however, include an express term empowering the insurers to instruct the insured to cease an action against the wrongdoer

The insurer must bring the action in the name of the insured and so needs the insured's consent. However, the court may compel a reluctant insured, subject to the insurer providing an indemnity as to costs.[36] There is some doubt whether a court has any discretion to refuse to compel the insured. In *Morris v Ford Motor Co Ltd*,[37] Morris was an employee of a firm that undertook cleaning work for Ford. Under the contract between Ford and the cleaning firm, Ford was indemnified in respect of liability for injury caused by the negligence of the employees of either company. Morris was injured by the negligent act of Roberts, one of Ford's employees. Morris sued Ford as Roberts' employer, Ford sought an indemnity from the cleaning firm, and this in turn led to the argument that since the cleaning firm was obliged to provide an indemnity, there was a right to sue Roberts. The case for the cleaning firm seemed fairly strong in view of the decision of the House of Lords in *Lister v The Romford Ice and Cold Storage Co Ltd*.[38] Lord Denning MR in *Morris* did not really bother to conceal his distaste for *Lister*, which he called 'an unfortunate decision,' and he duly proceeded to ignore it. Since the two cases were not precisely similar, in that *Lister* involved two people employed by the same firm and *Morris* two people employed by different firms, he was technically able to distinguish them, although the distinction does not really stand up to scrutiny. In any event, Lord Denning formulated a very broad principle: 'where the risk of a servant's negligence is covered by insurance, his

---

[33] *Bell Assurance Association v Licenses & General Insurance Corpn & Guarantee Fund Ltd* (1923) 17 Ll L Rep 100; *Morley v Moore* [1936] 2 KB 359. Even when 'knock-for-knock' agreements existed, the insured motorist could sue the wrongdoer for any uncovered loss, such as the excess on a policy or the cost of hiring a replacement car: *Hobbs v Marlowe*, above n 13; J Birds, 'Motor Insurers and the Knock for Knock Agreements' (1978) 41 *MLR* 201.

[34] This follows the decision in *Lister v The Romford Ice and Cold Storage Co Ltd* [1957] AC 555, see below and G Gardiner, 'Lister v The Romford Ice and Cold Storage Company Ltd' (1959) 22 *MLR* 652.

[35] *Commercial Union Assurance Co v Lister* (1874) LR 9 Ch App 483; *Hobbs v Marlowe*, above n 13.

[36] *MH Smith (Plant Hire) Ltd v DL Mainwaring (t/a Inshore)* [1986] 2 Lloyd's Rep 244 at 246, *per* Kerr LJ.

[37] See above n 13. Although this action did not explicitly involve an insurer and appeared to have been brought by the cleaning company involved, it seems clear from what was said in the case that an insurer was involved and, in any event, the company's situation was identical to that of an insurer that indemnifies another for loss. In Australia, see Insurance Contracts Act 1984, ss 65–66. See also, J Birds, *Insurance Law Reform: The Consumer Case for a Review of Insurance Law* (London, National Consumer Council, 1997).

[38] See above n 34.

employer should not seek to make that servant liable for it. At any rate, the courts should not compel him to allow his name to be used to do it.'[39] His justification was simple: 'Everyone knows that such risks as these are covered by insurance. So they should be, when a man is doing his employer's work, with his employer's plant and equipment, and happens to make a mistake. To make the servant personally liable would not only lead to a strike. It would be positively unjust.'[40] He suggested that since subrogation rights were equitable the court had discretion, and in circumstances such as these Ford would not be compelled to lend its name to an action against one of its employees. Ford expected the cleaning firm to insure and it had; the insurance company had received premiums and everyone would have expected the insurers not the employee to bear the loss. In addition, it was 'not just and equitable' to endanger industrial relations by forcing Ford to sue its own employee.[41] This approach was without convincing precedent. It is not clear that the courts have a discretion, but leaving that matter aside, it seems odd to have looked not at the relationship between the insured and the insurers, but at the broader context of the impact on industrial relations. On the other hand, as the facts of the case show, there is much to be said for the flexibility of Lord Denning's approach.[42] James LJ avoided these difficulties by concluding that the rights of subrogation were excluded by an implied term in the insurance contract.

Since the insurers step into the shoes of the insured, they can have no greater rights than the insured and cannot pursue actions that could not have been undertaken by the insured.[43] This means that if the insured's right of action is barred by rules of court,[44] or the insured caused the loss, the insurers will not be able to exercise rights of subrogation. In *Simpson v Thomson, Birrell*,[45] the insurers were precluded from exercising rights of subrogation where two ships owned by the insured collided.

---

[39] See above n 13 at 801.

[40] Ibid. Lord Denning referred to the informal agreement drawn up by the insurance industry in the wake of *Lister v The Romford Ice and Cold Storage Co Ltd*, above n 34, under which employers' liability insurers would not pursue an employee, unless there was evidence of collusion or wilful misconduct by the employee. However, this agreement only applied where both the tortfeasor and the injured party were employed by the same company.

[41] Lord Denning argued in the alternative that if the right of subrogation originated in an implied term, he would not imply such a term into this contract (for the fate of the idea that subrogation arises through an implied term, see above n 13). For a discussion of this case, see *The Yasin*, above n 13.

[42] *Woolwich Building Society v Brown* [1996] CLC 625 at 629, *per* Waller J; *The Surf City* [1995] 2 Lloyd's Rep 242. See, *Patent Scaffolding Co v William Simpson Construction Co* 64 Cal Rptr 187 (California, 1967).

[43] *Castellain v Preston*, above n 4 at 388–9, per Brett LJ.

[44] *Buckland v Palmer* [1984] 1 WLR 1109.

[45] *Simpson v Thomson, Birrell*, above n 23. If the two ships are owned by different companies the result will be different, even if those companies are owned by the same person: ibid, at 294, *per* Lord Blackburn. See also, *Co-operative Retail Services Ltd v Taylor Young Partnership* [2001] Lloyd's Rep IR 122 (CA); [2002] UKHL 17 (HL). In *The Midland Insurance Co v Smith and Wife* (1881) 6 QBD 561, Mrs Smith burnt down the insured property, and the insurers responded to a claim on the policy with an action against Mr Smith, the policyholder, arguing that – as the law stood then – he was responsible for the actions of his wife. The court held that, while it might have been possible to argue that the claim by the insured was not within the terms of the policy (although the court felt it unlikely that this would have succeeded because Mr Smith was not implicated in the arson), it was not possible to assert, as the insurers were implicitly doing, that it was within the terms of the policy to pay out to Mr Smith and, at the same time, seek an indemnity from him. If the husband is responsible for the actions of his wife, then he cannot sue her since that would be the same as suing himself. For a critique of *Simpson*, see PS James, 'The Fallacies of *Simpson v Thomson*' (1971) 22 *MLR* 149; but D St L. Kelly and ML Ball, *Principles of Insurance Law in Australia and New Zealand* (Sydney, Butterworths, 1991) 490–1.

The wrongdoer can use any defence available against an action by the insured:[46] so, for example, the third party can allege the insured's contributory negligence, or *volenti non fit injuria*, or that the action has become time-barred. [47] The insured may have reached an agreement with the wrongdoer before the claim under the policy is met, and this will bind the insurers because they have no independent right of action against a wrongdoer. When a motorist sued for his uninsured loss and was compensated, that action precluded his insurers from recovering the amount they had paid out for the insured loss.[48] The courts have formulated a broad principle requiring the insured not to act to the prejudice of the rights of the insurers.[49] The insured must not reach any agreement, whether before or after indemnification, which undermines the rights of the insurers. If the insured abandons a claim against the wrongdoer, that may amount to a breach of the insurance contract which will entitle the insurers who have not paid to refuse to do so and the insurers who have paid to recover from the insured damages for the prejudice suffered.[50] Likewise, if the insured reaches a settlement with the wrongdoer which prejudices the insurers' rights, the insured incurs personal liability to the extent of that prejudice.[51] There is no breach of contract if the insured acted in good faith, although what amounts to a bona fide settlement is not clear.[52] It may simply be that if there is no collusion between the insured and the wrongdoer and, in the circumstances, the settlement is reasonable, the insurers may find it difficult to show they have been prejudiced. Since the subrogated action is that of the insured, the insured may proceed against the tortfeasor, not only before the insurer has paid, but if the insurer, having paid in full, refuses to proceed or, indeed, even if the insurer wishes to do so. It seems unlikely that an insured, who sues the wrongdoer, would succeed in claiming that, because any recovery reduces the payment due under the policy, the insurer should pay part of the legal costs.[53]

In practice, some – although plainly not all – of these problems are resolved by the inclusion in most policies of a term permitting the insurer to take control of any proceedings or even abandon them, irrespective of their having indemnified the insured, and typically there are various stipulations as to what the insured may or may not do (eg, not admit liability or not settle without the consent of the insurer). In a consumer contract such a term may be assessed against the standards of good faith in the Unfair Terms in Consumer Contracts Regulations 1999. The problem is that, in blissful ignorance of the niceties of this fairly obscure branch of insurance law and in confident possession of a comprehensive motor policy, the insured may enter a binding agreement not to pursue a claim unaware that this raises the possibility of an action by the insurers. It is not necessarily reassuring that the insurers may not regard

---

[46] *Simpson v Thomson, Birrell*, above n 23, at 286, per Lord Cairns LC.
[47] Mitchell, 'Defences to an Insurer's Subrogated Action,' above n 1.
[48] *Hayler v Chapman* [1989] 1 Lloyd's Rep 490.
[49] *Commercial Union Assurance Co Ltd v Lister*, above n 35.
[50] *West of England Fire Insurance Company v Issacs* [1897] 1 QB 227; *Horse, Carriage and General Insurance Company (Ltd) v Petch* (1917) 33 TLR 131. In marine insurance, the Institute Cargo Clauses (War Clauses and Strike Clauses) impose a duty on the insured to ensure that rights of subrogation are preserved: on the Institute clauses , see below ch 16.
[51] *Boag v Standard Marine Insurance Co Ltd* [1937] 2 KB 113 at 128, per Scott LJ; *Phoenix Assurance Co v Spooner* [1905] 2 KB 753.
[52] *Commercial Union Assurance Co v Lister*, above n 35.
[53] *Hobbs v Marlowe*, above n 13.

it as worthwhile to pursue the insured because of the adverse publicity or because the insured does not have the resources to pay.

---

2. Joint insurance and co-insurance

As has been seen, the insurer, who pays a claim, cannot seek reimbursement where the insured caused the loss,[54] but what happens where two or more parties are covered by the same policy and only one is responsible for the loss? There are three main contractual relationships involved in these types of policy: first, joint insurance, which strictly speaking only applies if the parties covered by the policy have the same interest in the insured property; secondly, where the parties have different interests in the property, as with a lessor and lessee; thirdly, co-insurance or composite insurance, where some of the parties do not have an interest in the property, but the policy purports to cover them.

In *Mark Rowlands Ltd v Berni Inns*,[55] two people both had an interest in the insured property. A tenancy agreement stipulated that the lessor insure against fire and use any insurance moneys to rebuild. The tenant was required to contribute to the premium and was relieved of any duty to repair where damage was caused by fire. The Court of Appeal held that the insurers, who paid out on the policy following a fire, could not recover against the tenant. Although the tenant was not mentioned in the policy, it was clear from the lease that it was effected on behalf of both the landlord and the tenant, he also contributed to the premium and the lease excluded the tenant's liability for fire. The insurers were not a party to this arrangement nor was it disclosed. Nevertheless the Court of Appeal held that the intention of the parties was that in the event of a fire the lessor's loss should be recouped from the insurance policy and there would be no other claim against the tenant by the lessor, or, therefore, by the lessor's insurer.[56] There are similarities between *Mark Rowlands* and *Lister* v *Romford Ice and Cold Storage Co Ltd*,[57] however, in the latter an employee failed to persuade the House of Lords that his employer's insurance company could not exercise rights of subrogation and sue him for the loss caused by his negligence.

---

[54] *Simpson v Thomson, Birrell*, above n 23.

[55] [1986] QB 211. See J Birds (1986) 6 *OJLS* 304. Where the lessor and the tenant jointly take out an insurance policy, the insurer cannot use the covenant in the lease that requires the tenant to keep the property in good repair to sue the tenant for the damage since the tenant would be entitled to claim against the policy, unless the damage was deliberately inflicted by the tenant. The tenant will not be able to claim immunity from a subrogated claim by the lessor's insurers in respect of damage to any parts of the building not covered by the lease, as, for example, where the tenant negligently sets fire to his part of the premises and that fire also damages premises occupied by another tenant of the same lessor in the same building: see *Barras v Hamilton* [1994] SLT 949. For another case in which an agreement with a third party excluded rights of subrogation: *Thomas & Co v Brown* (1899) 4 Com Cas 186. See *56 Associates ex rel Paolino* v *Frieband* 89 F Supp2d 189 (Rhode Is, 2000); *DiLullo v Joseph* 792 A2d 819 (Connecticut, 2002); Anon, 'Extension of the No Subrogation against Insured Rule' (1977) 56 *Nebraska L Rev* 765–82.

[56] An agreement entered into before the insurance contract that diminishes the insurer's right of subrogation should be revealed to the insurers under the duty of disclosure: *Tate & Sons v Hyslop* (1885) 15 QBD 368.

[57] See above n 34.

Both involved a third party seeking to defend an action brought by insurers who had paid out for a loss caused by the third party. The distinction is that, unlike *Mark Rowlands*, in *Lister* there was no express agreement between the employee and the employer that the insurance was taken out for the benefit of the employee, and the House of Lords refused to imply such an agreement into the contract of employment. The fact that the wrongdoer contributed to the insurance premium may indicate that a policy was entered into for the benefit of that person, but it is certainly not conclusive. In *Woolwich Building Society* v *Brown*[58] a mortgagor paid the premiums on a policy covering default on the loan, but that policy was entered into for the benefit of the mortgagee alone so the insurer was entitled to pursue the mortgagor.

Where there is co-insurance, the insurers will not be able to exercise rights of subrogation if the insured and the wrongdoer are both covered against the same risk on the same policy and the loss was not caused by the wilful misconduct of the wrongdoer.[59] It has been suggested that there may be an implied term in the insurance contract precluding insurers from exercising rights of subrogation against a co-assured, or a presumption that the intention of the parties to the insurance contract was to cover certain types of loss without the insurers having recourse against the wrongdoer.[60] It is common for contracts in the construction industry between contractors and sub-contractors to include a requirement that the contractor obtain a joint names policy, under which the sub-contractor is a co-assured, or that the contractor extract from the insurer a waiver of subrogation rights against the sub-contractor.[61] In *Petrofina (UK) Ltd v Magnaload Ltd*,[62] a contractor sub-contracted part of a construction project and took out insurance to cover themselves and the sub-contractors. One of the sub-contractors caused the loss and the insurers, having paid the claim, sought to exercise rights of subrogation to bring an action against that sub-contractor. Lloyd J recognised the commercial significance of such arrangements. The head contractor should be able to take out insurance to cover the whole project on behalf of the sub-contractors since, unless this were allowed, each sub-contractor would have to insure the whole project, which would create overlapping cover and might involve the sub-contractor in such expense that it would not be economically viable for them to undertake the building contract. His view was that each sub-contractor was a co-assured for the whole of the construction work, even though concerned only with a small part of that job. He also suggested that the sub-contractor had an insurable interest in the whole project so that the insurer's right to sue was defeated by circuitry of action. The insurers could not, therefore, exercise subrogation rights.[63] In *Co-operative Retail Services Ltd v Taylor Young Partnership*,[64] the Court of Appeal rejected the circuitry of action idea on the ground

---

[58] See above n 42.

[59] *National Oilwell (UK) v Davy Construction* [1993] 2 Lloyd's Rep 582 at 616, per Colman J. For a discussion of the impact of wilful misconduct on the insured's right to claim, see above ch 9.

[60] *National Oilwell (UK) v Davy Offshore*, ibid.

[61] See, eg, the contracts in *Co-operative Retail Services Ltd v Taylor Young Partnership Ltd*, above n 45, and *Scottish & Newcastle plc v GD Construction (St Albans) Ltd* [2003] EWCA Civ.

[62] [1983] 2 Lloyd's Rep 91. See Brownie J, 'Co-Insurance and Subrogation' (1991) 3 *Ins LJ* 48.

[63] Lloyd J relied on a similar line of argument employed by the Supreme Court in Canada in *Commonwealth Construction Co Ltd v Imperial Oil Ltd* (1977) 69 DLR (3d) 558. See also, *The Yasin*, above n 13; *National Oilwell (UK) v Davy Offshore*, above n 59.

[64] See above n 45; J Birds, 'Denying Subrogation in Co-Insurance and Similar Situations' [2001] *LMCLQ* 193.

that, having provided an indemnity to one of the co-assureds, the insurer has discharged its liability under the policy so that another co-assured cannot then seek to claim for those same losses. The court preferred the approach taken by Colman J in *Stone Vickers Ltd v Appledore Ferguson Shipbuilders Ltd*,[65] where he said that the exercise by the insurer of subrogation rights against a co-insured would be contrary to the objective of the insurance contract and, therefore, a term must be implied excluding those rights. Yet, although the technique used by Colman J differs from that used by Lloyd J, both, it is suggested, recognised that the insurance contracts in these cases were intended by the insurer and the insured to provide coverage for other parties and that it would be commercially inconvenient if the exercise of subrogation rights were permitted.

Where the insurers agree in the policy to waive subrogation rights in respect of someone who is not a co-assured the doctrine of privity would seem to prevent that person from enforcing the waiver.[66] In *National Oilwell (UK) v Davy Offshore*,[67] the head contractor on a construction project alleged breaches of contract by a sub-contractor for defective equipment which had delayed the work, and thereby caused loss to the head contractor. This loss was met by the insurers who sought to exercise subrogation rights against the sub-contractor. Colman J held that the sub-contractor would be a party to the contract if it could be shown to have been made on their behalf or in contemplation of benefiting such sub-contractors as later became involved in the project and those sub-contractors ratified the policy. Yet, he took the view in this case that, while the policy covered sub-contractors, it did so on terms different from those which applied to the head contractor and it did not include the sub-contractor's liability for losses incurred after the delivery of the equipment. The policy did waive subrogation rights against 'any assured and any person, company or corporation whose interests are covered by this policy,' but Colman J was of the opinion that this merely restated the normal rule, namely that there is no right of subrogation against a co-assured with respect to the same risk insured under the same policy. He thought the parties had simply been sensible in putting into the contract expressly what the law implied. The sub-contractor could not, therefore, take advantage of the waiver.[68] This construction may seem to make the clause pointless, but that is not in itself a ground for suggesting that the clause must, therefore, mean something else.

The *National Oilwell* case reinforces the point that the extent of the co-assurance will depend on the terms of the policy. The waiver clause would seem unnecessary

---

[65] [1991] 2 Lloyd's Rep 228. The decision was reversed on a point of construction which, as the Court of Appeal demonstrated in the *Co-operative Retail* case, did not affect the reasoning discussed here: [1992] 2 Lloyd's Rep 578.

[66] Such waiver clauses are common in professional indemnity policies where a firm seeks to protect its employees by obtaining from the insurer a waiver of their rights of subrogation.

[67] See above n 59. The project in this case involved off-shore construction and it was, therefore, covered by a marine insurance policy.

[68] This being a marine policy, Colman J also held that a breach by the sub-contractor of the duty imposed by the Marine Insurance Act 1906, s 78(4) to take reasonable measures to minimise loss would mean that the loss would not have been proximately caused by an insured peril, in which case it would make no difference that the sub-contractor was a party to the insurance contract. The Builders All Risks Policy (BAR), which is typically used in connection with building projects, is a good example of a policy that expressly refers to co-assurance provisions. On co-insurance, see J Birds, 'Agency and Insurance' [1994] JBL 386; LM Bowyer, 'Contracts (Rights of Third Parties) Bill and Insurance' [1997] *JBL* 230.

with regard to a risk covered by a policy where the wrongdoer is a co-assured,[69] and of course the wrongdoer who is not a co-assured will not be able to take advantage of a waiver, unless an exception to the application of the doctrine of privity applies, such as agency or the parties intended to benefit the wrongdoer according to the provisions of the Contracts (Rights of Third Parties) Act 1999. Clarke J, in *The Surf City*,[70] took the view that it would inequitable to allow insurers to exercise subrogation rights against a third party where they had previously agreed with the insurers that they would not do so, but, as has already been suggested in the discussion of *Morris v Ford Motor Co Ltd*, the authority for this approach is not strong. There is a further problem in that the co-assured must have an insurable interest. The courts in some of the co-insurance cases may have passed over this difficulty rather too easily. The issue was raised by the Court of Appeal in *Deepak Fertilisers Ltd v ICI Chemicals & Polymers Ltd*,[71] where a party named in a policy was not held to have an insurable interest – and, therefore, was not a co-assured – once their involvement in a project had ceased, even though they remained liable for damage to the project as a result of their work. The conclusion appeared to be that someone in this situation needed to take out a liability policy. This decision must, however, be read in light of the views expressed in the Court of Appeal in *Feasey v Sun Life Assurance Co of Canada*, where Waller LJ observed that there was no rule that only a liability policy was appropriate where the nature of the insurable interest was compensation for loss and that whether such cover was provided by a property insurance was a question of construction.[72]

---

3. The treatment of compensation received

A payment of compensation by a third-party does not automatically belong to the insurer. If property is not covered (as opposed to covered but under-valued), then the insured is their own insurer for the whole amount and any payment received from the wrongdoer that relates to this uninsured loss can be kept by the insured. For instance, if a motor policy does not cover the cost of hiring a replacement vehicle following an accident, then the part of any compensation received that relates to this expenditure should not be brought into the calculation for the purposes of apportionment of that compensation between the insured and the insurer. Where, on the other hand, compensation has been received that relates to the insured property there will be a difficulty if the actual loss is larger than the payment from the insurers. In the case of a valued policy (that is, one in which the parties agreed on the amount to be paid in

---

[69] *Stone Vickers Ltd v Appledore Ferguson Shipbuilders Ltd*, above n 65. In Canada the privity doctrine has been relaxed where sound commercial practice and justice require it and the third party is an intended beneficiary of the clause in the policy restricting the insurer's use of rights of subrogation: *Fraser Pile & Dredge Ltd v Can-Dive Services Ltd* [2000] 1 Lloyd's Rep 199.
[70] See above n 42.
[71] [1999] 1 Lloyd's Rep 387.
[72] [2003] EWCA Civ 885. See above ch 6

the event of a total loss), the value agreed in the policy is conclusive and on a total loss the insured will not have a prior claim to the amount by which the actual loss exceeds that value: so, for example, where the agreed value of a ship was £6000, even though its real value was £9000, and the insurers paid for a total loss, they were entitled to the whole of a payment of £5000 received as compensation from the wrongdoer.[73] This issue came before the House of Lords in *Lord Napier and Ettrick v Hunter*,[74] where the loss was £160,000, but the sum insured on a liability policy was only £125,000, of which the insured was liable for the first £25,000 of the loss (the excess). The insurer, therefore, paid £100,000 in full settlement of the claim under the terms of the policy. Compensation of £130,000 was later received from the wrongdoer. The House of Lords held that the insured was his own insurer for the first £25,000 and that he agreed to bear any loss over the insured sum of £125,000. Out of the compensation the insured was, therefore, entitled to £35,000. This was the uninsured loss of £60,000 (the first £25,000 and the amount of the loss that was not covered, which was £35,000) less £25,000, which was the amount of the excess. The insurer received the rest of the compensation, that is £95,000 (£130,000 less £35,000). The House of Lords held that the excess clause (the first £25,000 of the loss) entitled the insurers to priority over the insured's claim to be compensated for the amount of that excess.

Only Lords Templeman and Jauncey went on to look at the other aspect of the problem, the amount by which the loss exceeded the value in the contract (that is, the amount over £125,000 which was not covered by the policy: £35,000).[75] Lord Templeman said that there were three insurances: the first was for £25,000 (the excess), the second was for the next £100,000 (the part for which the insurer was liable under the policy), and the third was for the remaining £35,000 (the amount by which the actual loss exceeded that covered by the policy). The compensation is applied from the top down: that is, first, to the insurer of the last slice (£35,000), then the insurer of the second slice (£100,000) and, if any is left, to the insurer of the third slice (£25,000). This meant that the insured, who covered the top slice, received £35,000 and the insurers took the rest (£95,000). Since that came to £130,000, there was nothing left to pay the loss suffered by the insured on the excess (£25,000).[76] Lord Jauncey agreed with Lord Templeman on the outcome of the calculations, but disagreed on the method used. For him the loss that was not covered by the

---

[73] *North of England Iron Steamship Insurance Association v Armstrong* (1870) LR 5 QB 244. See also *Thames & Mersey Marine Insurance v British and Chilean Steamship Co* [1915] 2 KB 214 (affirmed at [1916] 1 KB 330), and, for a case of a valued policy where there was only a partial loss, *Goole & Hull Steam Towing Co Ltd v Ocean Marine Insurance Co Ltd* [1928] 1 KB 589. A valued policy must be distinguished from an unvalued policy in which the insured states the value of the subject matter but there is no agreement by the insurers on that valuation. A valued policy is a contract of indemnity insurance as long as the value agreed in the policy amounts to a genuine attempt to predict the loss.

[74] See above n 9. This case concerned liability insurance; for discussion of the applicability of this decision to property insurance and, in particular, marine insurance, see HN Bennett, *The Law of Marine Insurance* (Oxford, Clarendon Press, 1996) 420–1. See also MC Hemsworth, 'Subrogation: The Problem of Competing Claims to Recovery Monies' [1998] *JBL* 111; Mitchell, 'Subrogation and Insurance Law,' above n 13; *England v Guardian Insurance Ltd*, above n 17. See the discussion of some of these issues in R Keeton and A Widiss, *Insurance Law* (St Paul, Minnesota, 1988) 233–7.

[75] The insurers had conceded that the insured was entitled to this sum, so it was not necessary to decide the point.

[76] In support of Lord Templeman's approach, see *Kuwait Airways Corpn v Kuwait Insurance Co SAK* [2000] 1 Lloyd's Rep 252.

compensation from the wrongdoer was £30,000, which he arrived at by deducting £130,000 (the compensation paid) from £160,000 (the loss). Then, he deducted the excess of £25,000 from this amount and arrived at a figure of £5000, which was due to the insured from the insurers. In other words, of the £130,000 paid by the wrong-doer, the insurers receive £95,000 and the insured £35,000. 'When an insured loss is diminished by a recovery from a third party, whether before or after any indemnifica-tion has been made, the ultimate loss is simply the initial loss minus the recovery and it is that sum to which the provisions of the policy of assurance apply including any provision as to an excess.'[77]

There is a distinction between under-insurance and an uninsured loss. As has been seen, if the full amount of the loss is not covered by the policy – in other words, where there is under-insurance – the insured will be their own insurer for the amount by which the actual loss exceeds the insured loss and will have first claim on any com-pensation received: in *Napier* this was £35,000 (£160,000 minus £125,000 (£100,000 for the claim plus £25,000 for the excess)). Two other examples illustrate the way in which under-insurance is treated. In the first, in an action following the loss of an under-insured ship the owners were held partially to blame and, therefore, entitled to only five-twelfths of the ship's real value in compensation. The court held that the insurers could claim back from the owner that sum (up to the amount paid to the insured), even though it was calculated on the real – as opposed to the insured – value of the ship.[78] In another case, a ship, which was valued for the policy at £4000, required £5000 spending on repairs after a collision for which the owners were held to be 50 per cent responsible. They, therefore, received only £2500 in damages, and it was held that the insurers were only liable to pay out £1500 (£4000 less £2500).[79]

If the compensation received from the wrongdoer exceeds the payment made by the insurers, the surplus belongs to the insured because the action taken against the wrongdoer is in law that of the insured and because, although it is often said that the insured must not be allowed to make a profit, it is more accurate to say that the objec-tive of subrogation is to prevent double recovery by the insured. In *Yorkshire Insurance Co Ltd v Nisbet Shipping Co Ltd*,[80] after the insurers had paid for a total loss, a successful action was brought against the wrongdoer by the insured with the consent of the insurers. The damages were assessed in Canadian dollars, and, because of a shift in the value of that currency, this produced a sum in sterling which exceeded the payment made by the insurers. It was held that the insurers were entitled only to the amount paid to the insured and the insured could retain the surplus. Of course, the parties may avoid this consequence by providing for the distribution of such an excess in their agreement.[81]

Where the insurers exercise their right of subrogation and receive damages from a third party which exceed the payment made to the insured on the claim, then the insurers hold that surplus on trust for the insured.[82] If the insured has received com-pensation from the wrongdoer, which relates to the insured loss, before the insurers

---

[77] See above n 9, at 748, per Lord Jauncey.
[78] *Thames and Mersey Marine Insurance Co v British and Chilian Steamship Co*, above n 73.
[79] *Goole and Hull Steam Towing Company Ltd v Ocean Marine Insurance Co Ltd*, above n 73.
[80] See above n 13.
[81] *Lucas v Export Credit Guarantee Department* [1974] 1 WLR 909.
[82] *Lonrho Exports Ltd v Export Credits Guarantee Department* [1996] 2 Lloyd's Rep 649.

have met the claim,[83] then the amount due from the insurers under the policy will be reduced accordingly.[84] If the insurers have paid on a claim and compensation is later paid to the insured, the insurers can recoup their payment by a common law action for money had and received.[85] It is clear that the insurers also have an equitable interest in the compensation itself. In *Lord Napier and Ettrick v Hunter*,[86] compensation from the wrongdoer had been paid to the insured's agent. The problem was not that the insured denied the insurers' right to recoup from that fund, but that if the only remedy available to the insurer was a common law action for money had and received, then, since the insured was a Lloyd's syndicate made up of 246 individuals, an action would have to be brought against each individual and this would create certain difficulties: some of these people lived abroad in jurisdictions where there might be little sympathy for the insurers, and recovery would also be prejudiced if any were bankrupt because the insurer would not have priority over the other creditors. The House of Lords held that the insurer has an equitable lien over the compensation paid by the wrongdoer to the insured's agent up to the amount paid by the insurer to the insured in settlement of the claim under the policy. There is also a right under the contract that the insured will pay to the insurer the amount to which the insurer is entitled out of the moneys received in reduction of the loss.[87] According to Lord Templeman, equity will 'ensure that the insured person exercises his right of action against the wrongdoer in good faith and that the insurer is recouped out of the damages recovered from the wrongdoer.'[88] The lien also gives the insurers priority over other creditors in the event of an insured becoming insolvent or bankrupt.[89] The lien does avoid the need to bring actions against insureds in their country; the insurer need only pursue the money wherever it is. Moreover, the insurer's right to enforce the lien will not be undermined by an allegation of inequitable conduct because the lien is a proprietary right in the moneys, which cannot be defeated by the insurer's conduct.[90] This equitable interest in the money will be lost if the compensation has been paid to the insureds,[91] or if it has been acquired by a bona fide purchaser for value without notice.[92]

Lord Templeman also expressed the opinion that the insurers might have an equitable interest in any cause of action available to the insured, if, were that action to be successful, it would result in a fund in which the insurers would have an equitable

---

[83] The same principle applies where the compensation took the form of repairs to the property: *Darrell v Tibbits*, see above n 11.

[84] *Hamilton v Mendes* (1761) 2 Burr 1198 at 1210, per Lord Mansfield CJ; *Burnand v Rodocanachi* (1882) 7 App Cas 333 at 339, per Lord Blackburn.

[85] *Randal v Cockran*, above n 13; *Blaauwpot v Da Costa* (1758) 1 Ed 130; *Commercial Union Assurance Co v Lister*, above n 35; *Castellain v Preston*, above n 4, at 389 per Brett LJ; *Assicurazoni Generali De Trieste v Empress Assurance Corporation Ltd* [1907] 2 KB 814.

[86] See above n 9.

[87] An injunction was granted preventing the insured's agent from paying to the insured (and the insured from receiving) any part of the fund. The House of Lords decided that the money was not held on trust because this would place too onerous a duty on the insured as trustee and because it was more than was required to protect the insurers' interests: *Lord Napier and Ettrick v Hunter*, above n 9, at 744, per Lord Goff.

[88] Ibid, at 736, per Lord Templeman.

[89] *Re Miller, Gibb & Co*, above n 16.

[90] *England v Guardian Insurance Ltd*, above n 17.

[91] See above n 9, at 739, per Lord Templeman.

[92] Ibid, at 752, per Lord Browne-Wilkinson.

lien: 'promises implied in a contract of insurance with regard to rights of action vested in the insured person for the recovery of an insured loss from a third party responsible for the loss confer on the insurer an equitable interest in those rights of action to the extent necessary to recoup the insurer who has indemnified the insured person against the insured loss.'[93] The reasoning behind this rests on the principle that where there is a payment of compensation by a third-party that relates to the payment of a claim under the policy, the insurers have an equitable interest in that compensation so long as it forms a separate indentifiable fund. That led Lord Templeman to the rather radical proposition that the insurers will have an equitable interest in the cause of action that might lead to such payment of compensation. If this is right, then, where the insurers have indemnified the insured, they might have an action against a wrongdoer who, having notice of the interests of the insurers (merely knowing that the claim has been paid might be sufficient notice), settles with the insured on terms that are unfavourable to the interests of the insurers.[94]

Finally, if the insured receives a voluntary payment from a third party (a payment the insured has no legal right to demand and the third party no obligation to pay), the insurers will, nevertheless, be entitled to recoup what they have paid if the voluntary payment relates to the loss for which the insured has received an indemnity.[95] According to Lord Blackburn, 'the question is not whether the money was voluntarily paid or not voluntarily paid, but whether de facto the money which was paid did reduce the loss.'[96] The case in which he made this statement provides an illustration of a situation in which the payment did not reduce the insured loss. By an Act of Congress the government of the US agreed to compensate the owner of a ship sunk by Confederate forces during the American Civil War, but only for those losses which were not covered by insurance. The House of Lords decided that the payment could not be claimed by the insurers because by its very terms it did not relate to the indemnity. Similarly, a voluntary payment by a broker, which was prompted by the desire to retain the goodwill of the insured, was not paid in diminution of the loss since it was paid with the express purpose of retaining the insured's goodwill, and therefore it could not be recouped by the insurers.[97] Where the payment is a gift and is not made under a legal obligation connected with the loss,[98] or is made in the absence of a clear intention by the donor to benefit the insurers, it is assumed that there is no intention to so benefit them. Put another way, the question to ask is, was the intention of the donor to benefit the insured personally so that the loss was merely the context within which the gift was made, or was the intention to compensate for the loss and, therefore, to benefit whoever had suffered that loss, including the insurers if they had indemnified the insured?

---

[93] Ibid, at 736, per Lord Templeman.
[94] R Merkin (ed), *Colvinaux's Law of Insurance* (London, Sweet & Maxwell, 1997) 177.
[95] *Randal v Cockran*, above n 13; *Blaauwpot v Da Costa*, above n 85; *Burnand v Rodocanachi*, above n 84, at 339–40, per Lord Blackburn.
[96] *Burnand v Rodocanachi*, ibid, at 341, per Lord Blackburn.
[97] *Merrett v Capitol Indemnity Corp* [1991] 1 Lloyd's Rep 169. See also *Stearns v Village Main Reeft Gold Mining Co Ltd* (1905) 21 TLR 236; *Colonia Versicherung AG v Amoco Oil Co* [1995] 1 Lloyd's Rep 570.
[98] *Colonia Versicherung AG v Amoco Oil Co* [1995] 1 Lloyd's Rep 570.

4. The justifications for subrogation

It has been suggested that subrogation is justified because insurers are able to recover payments and this keeps premiums down. Yet, it is not clear how the likelihood of recouping claims enters into the calculation of premiums, and this invites the conclusion that insurers see any money they do recoup as a windfall. Moreover, since it is unlikely that insurers will pursue rights of subrogation unless they are reasonably sure not merely of winning but of being able to enforce a judgment, such rights are typically only going to be exercised if the wrongdoer is insured. In other words, subrogation is often merely a means of shifting losses from one insurer to another, and, since those insurers who sue to recoup their losses today will be paying out tomorrow, it is difficult to see how this merry-go-round can affect premiums. Subrogation may achieve other apparently desirable ends: ensuring that wrongdoers are held to account for the consequences of their behaviour and not allowed to gain the advantage of an insurance policy for which they have paid no premiums; encouraging people to take more care and so avoid the possibility of being held liable for their wrongful actions.[99] None of these arguments is particularly convincing because – once again – insurers are unlikely to see it as worthwhile to exercise rights of subrogation against an uninsured wrongdoer merely to serve public policy goals and the lessons may well be wasted on insured wrongdoers who can cheerfully pass the consequences of their actions on to their insurers, although, of course, they may feel the effect of their behaviour in the form of a higher premium, or by being refused cover. There are also the problems that are illustrated by *Lister v Romford Ice and Cold Storage*,[100] and that led to Lord Denning's pragmatic approach in *Morris v Ford Motor Co Ltd*.[101] Finally, it might be suggested that, while subrogation is meant to prevent an insured from making a profit, this principle is not applied to the insurers who, if they successfully recoup money paid out on a claim, have lost nothing and are entitled to retain the premiums. However, on assuming a risk the insurers do not know that if a loss occurs they will be able to recoup the moneys paid and the premium is consideration for assuming this uncertainty.[102]

---

[99] Bennett, *The Law of Marine Insurance*, above n 74, at 402.
[100] See above n 34.
[101] See above n 13.
[102] See the materials referred to above in n 1.

12

Conflict of Laws

1. Scope of the chapter

Many insurance agreements, particularly commercial policies and reinsurance contracts, have an international element in that the assured or reinsured is situated or established in a jurisdiction different from that of the underwriters' place of business. Further, many risks are subscribed to by a number of different insurance companies, often situated in different parts of the world. Whenever a contract does have an international dimension, and proceedings are brought in the English courts, two separate issues will inevitably arise: do the English courts have jurisdiction to resolve the dispute?; and if so, which law governs the rights of the parties? Matters have become increasingly complex in the last two decades, by reason of the adoption of jurisdictional rules purely between EU and EFTA courts, by the harmonisation of choice of law rules within the EU and by the adoption by the EU of special rules for jurisdiction and choice of law as regards insurance – but not reinsurance – agreements. This chapter will consider both jurisdiction and choice of law, and highlight the provision made for insurance contracts. Readers should note that very many commercial insurance and reinsurance disputes are resolved by arbitration: this matter is outside the scope of the present text.[1]

2. Jurisdiction

2.1 The different regimes

English jurisdictional rules determine whether an action may be brought in the English courts. England has long been a forum for the hearing of international disputes,

[1] See generally, Mustill and Boyd, *Commercial Arbitration*; Merkin *Arbitration Law*.

as English commercial judges are regarded as expert in their field. It may also be important for a person who wishes to sue or be sued under judicial procedures which are familiar to him and which he trusts. Until 1982 a single regime governed the jurisdiction of the English courts, but matters changed dramatically with the passing of the Civil Jurisdiction and Judgments Act 1982 which gave effect in English law to the Brussels Convention 1968. That Convention laid down an entirely separate set of jurisdictional rules for cases with an EU element. Matters were taken further by the UK's ratification of the Lugano Convention 1989 by the Civil Jurisdiction and Judgments Act 1991: this Convention is in very similar terms to the Brussels Convention, and lays down jurisdictional rules as between EU countries and European Free Trade Area (EFTA) countries. Finally, at the beginning of 2002 the Brussels Convention was (with one important caveat) replaced by an EU instrument, Council Regulation 44/2001. This is based on the Brussels Convention, although there are a number of significant modifications in the Regulation. The net effect of these changes is that there are now four[2] separate jurisdictional regimes which have to be considered by the English courts:

(1) if the defendant is domiciled in any EU country other than Denmark, jurisdiction is determined by Council Regulation 44/2001;

(2) if the defendant is domiciled in Denmark, jurisdiction is determined by the Brussels Convention 1968;

(3) if the defendant is domiciled in any of the EFTA countries, Switzerland, Iceland or Norway, jurisdiction is determined by the Lugano Convention 1989;

(4) in all other cases, jurisdiction is determined under pre-existing English procedural rules, set out in Parts 19 and 20 of the Civil Procedure Rules (CPR).

In this chapter regimes (1)–(3) will be treated together under the heading 'EU cases'. Regime (4) is referred to under the heading 'Non-EU cases'.

Whether the case is EU or non-EU is determined by the domicile of the defendant in the proceedings. An individual is domiciled in the UK if he is resident in the UK and the nature and circumstances of his residence indicate that he has a substantial connection with the UK.[3] A company is domiciled in the place of its registered office, its central administration or its principal place of business.

2.2 Non-EU cases

Where the defendant is domiciled outside the EU, the jurisdiction of the English courts over a dispute depends upon the procedural question of whether the claim form may be served upon him. Service is possible on a defendant who: is an individual and is within England, temporarily or otherwise;[4] is a company incorporated or with a place of business in England;[5] is not within England but has agreed that an

---

[2] Technically, five: the Brussels Convention in a modified form applies to determine jurisdiction as between the constituent parts of the United Kingdom: see the Civil Jurisdiction and Judgments Act 1982, sch 4.

[3] Civil Jurisdiction and Judgments Act 1982, s 41, as amended.

[4] *Maharanee of Baroda v Wildenstein* [1972] 2 QB 283.

[5] Companies Act 1985, ss 695 and 725.

action can be brought only in England[6] or that an action may be brought in England[7]; or is not present in England and has not agreed to be sued in England, but has nevertheless submitted to the jurisdiction of the English court by nominating solicitors to accept service or by participating in the proceedings by submitting a substantive defence.[8] Most importantly, however, the English courts have jurisdiction – generally referred to as 'exorbitant jurisdiction' – over a defendant who is not present in England and has not submitted to jurisdiction by agreement or otherwise, but where the case has a substantial connection with England. The claimant may apply to the English court under Part 20 CPR for permission to serve the claim form on the defendant outside the jurisdiction. Permission will be granted by the court if it is satisfied that the claim raises a serious question to be tried, that there is a good arguable case that there is a substantial connection with England in that one or more of 19 grounds of jurisdiction listed in CPR Part 20 has been made out, and that England is the most appropriate forum for the trial of the action.[9] For insurance and reinsurance purposes, the most important of the 19 heads of potential jurisdiction are that the claim is made in respect of: a contract made in England[10]; a contract made by or through an agent of the defendant who was trading in England;[11] a contract governed by English law[12]; or a breach of contract committed in England.[13]

Assuming that jurisdiction is made out on any of the above grounds, the court has an overriding discretion[14] to refuse to hear the action.[15] That discretion may be exercised on one of two grounds: that England is not the most appropriate forum for the action to be heard (*forum non conveniens*); or that there are proceedings in existence in some other place (*lis alibis pendens*).

The most important of these principles is *forum non conveniens*, an issue which arises in virtually every case where the jurisdiction of the English courts is contested. The basic principle is that the English court will hear the action unless the defendant can show that there is a more convenient forum which has under its domestic law

---

[6] Under an exclusive jurisdiction clause. There may be issues as to whether the dispute between the parties falls within the scope of the clause: see *IFR Ltd v Federal Trade SpA* 2001, unreported (clause extended to a dispute as to the right to avoid a contract).

[7] Under a permissive clause whereby the defendant agrees not to contest the jurisdiction of the English court if an action is brought against him in England.

[8] Appearing to contest jurisdiction is not enough: *Finnish Marine Insurance Co Ltd v Protective National Insurance Co* [1989] 2 All ER 929.

[9] See generally, *Seaconsar Far East Ltd v Bank Marzaki Jamhouri Islami Iran* [1994] 4 All ER 456.

[10] CPR r 6.20(5)(a). The balance of authority is in favour of the extension of this ground to an application to the court for a declaration that the contract is void: *DR Insurance Co v Central National Insurance Co of Omaha* [1996] 1 Lloyd's Rep 74; *HIB Ltd v Guardian Insurance Co Inc* [1997] 1 Lloyd's Rep 412.

[11] CPR r 6.20(5)(b). For this purpose it should be borne in mind that the broker is the agent of the assured and not the agent of insurers: *Lincoln National Life Insurance Co v Employers Reinsurance Corporation* [2002] Lloyd's Rep IR 853; *Tryg Baltica International (UK) Ltd v Boston Compania De Seguros SA* [2004] EWHC 1186 (Comm); [2005] Lloyd's Rep IR 40.

[12] CPR r 6.20(5)(c). See below.

[13] CPR r 6.20(6). If a sum of money is outstanding, the English rule is that – in the absence of anything in the contract as to the place of payment – the debtor must seek out the creditor, so that if the creditor is situated in England then non-payment constitutes a breach of contract in England: *Citadel Insurance v Atlantic Union Insurance* [1982] 2 Lloyd's Rep 543; *Overseas Union Insurance v Incorporated General Insurance* [1992] 1 Lloyd's Rep 439.

[14] The court is in any event obliged to stay its own proceedings where the parties have entered into a binding agreement to refer the dispute to arbitration: Arbitration Act 1996, s 9.

[15] That discretion is, however, removed where the jurisdiction of the English court is conferred by virtue of the defendant's English domicile. This is the effect of the European rules on jurisdiction: see below.

jurisdiction over the dispute and that the claimant in England would not be deprived of a legitimate juridical advantage by proceeding in some other jurisdiction. In considering these questions the courts will balance all the circumstances in the case, although a number of principles may be derived from the numerous authorities. First, the courts will other than in exceptional circumstances give effect to an exclusive jurisdiction clause which nominates the courts of a particular place: if England is nominated, then the action will be heard here[16]; if some other jurisdiction is nominated then a stay of English proceedings is all but inevitable.[17] Even if the clause simply confers an option on the claimant to sue in a given jurisdiction, once the claimant has chosen to exercise that option the defendant will not be able to argue that the jurisdiction is not a convenient forum, given that he had under the clause agreed to be sued there.[18] Secondly, in the absence of agreed jurisdiction provisions, the law applicable to the contract will be an important, although not determinative,[19] factor: if the policy is governed by English law there is a strong presumption that the dispute should be resolved in the English courts.[20] Thirdly, weight will be given to other matters, including the location of the witnesses and the documents, the fact that it may be necessary to join other parties to the proceedings and the possibility of delay in other jurisdictions. By way of example, where the dispute relates to the right of the underwriters to avoid a contract placed in the London market for breach of the duty of utmost good faith, it will normally be appropriate to hear the action in England given that the relevant evidence will be in England and the contract is almost certainly governed by English law in such circumstances.[21] By contrast, if the issue is whether the assured or reinsured was aware of facts misstated or withheld then the relevant evidence may be in some other jurisdiction and that will be the most appropriate forum,[22] and if the dispute relates to the circumstances of a loss then the place where the loss allegedly occurred is the most appropriate forum.[23]

The existence of other proceedings – *lis alibis pendens* – is a matter which will figure large in the court's ultimate conclusion as to whether the English action should be stayed. The English court will refuse to become involved if the parties have agreed

---

[16] *Youell v Kara Mara Shipping Co* [2000] 2 Lloyd's Rep 102.

[17] *Excess Insurance Ace Insurance SA-NV v Zurich Insurance Co* [2001] 1 Lloyd's Rep 504; *Burrows v Jamaica Private Power Co Ltd* [2002] Lloyd's Rep IR 466; *Groupaman Insurance Co v Channel Islands Securities Ltd* [2002] Lloyd's Rep IR 843.

[18] *Excess Insurance v Allendale Mutual Insurance Co* [2001] Lloyd's Rep IR 524; *Muncherer Ruckversicherungs Gesellschaft v Commonwealth Insurance Co* [2005] Lloyd's Rep IR 99. A non-exclusive jurisdiction clause should be distinguished from a clause whereby insurers or reinsurers agree that it may be served at a particular address, as this type of clause does not indicate any intention that the proceedings should be heard in that jurisdiction: *Travelers Casualty and Surety Co of Europe Ltd v Sun Life Assurance Co of Canada* [2004] Lloyd's Rep IR 846; *Munchener Ruckversicherungs Gesellschaft v Commonwealth Insurance Co* [2005] Lloyd's Rep IR 99.

[19] So decided by the House of Lords in *Amin Rasheed Shipping Corporation v Kuwait Insurance Co* [1983] 2 All ER 884.

[20] *Islamic Arab Insurance Co v Saudi Egyptian American Reinsurance Co* [1987] 1 Lloyd's Rep 315; *Seashell Shipping Corporation of Panama v Mutualidad de Seguros del Instituto Nacional de Insdustria* [198] 1 Lloyd's Rep 47; *Overseas Union Insurance v Incorporated General Insurance* [1992] 1 Lloyd's Rep 439; *Assicurazioni Generali v Ege Sigorta AS* [2002] Lloyd's Rep IR 480; *Brotherton v Aseguardora Colseguros SA* [2002] Lloyd's Rep IR 848.

[21] *Gan Insurance Co v Tai Ping Insurance Co* [1999] Lloyd's Rep IR 472; *Travelers Casualty and Surety Co of Europe Ltd v Sun Life Assurance Co of Canada (UK) Ltd* [2005] Lloyd's Rep IR 846; *Markel International Insurance Company Ltd and another v La Republica Compania Argentina de Seguros Generales SA* [2005] Lloyd's Rep IR 90.

[22] *Chase v Ram Technical Services* [2000] 2 Lloyd's Rep 418.

[23] *Navigators Insurance Co Ltd v Atlantic Methanol Production Co LLC* [2004] Lloyd's Rep IR 418.

that the action should be brought in that other jurisdiction or if that jurisdiction is the most convenient. The existence of other proceedings will necessarily be disregarded where the foreign action is brought in contravention of an exclusive jurisdiction clause nominating England,[24] and indeed in appropriate circumstances the court may grant an 'anti-suit' injunction against the claimant in the foreign proceedings,[25] preventing him from continuing with the action.[26] An anti-suit injunction will be granted where the action is in breach of arbitration, exclusive jurisdiction or other clause, or where the court otherwise regards the foreign action as oppressive. There are numerous illustrations of anti-suit injunctions being granted in insurance and reinsurance cases.[27]

Many insurance and reinsurance disputes come before the English courts by way of an application for 'negative declaratory relief,' ie an application by the underwriters to the English court that they have a right to avoid the policy or are otherwise not liable to meet any claim which may be made against them in future by the policyholder, almost certainly in a foreign court. At one time it was thought that this type of action was 'forum-shopping' and was frowned upon by the courts, but in the landmark decision in *New Hampshire Insurance Co v Philips Electronics North America Corporation*[28] the Court of Appeal confirmed that this type of action was perfectly valid and that the English court should entertain the action as long as it: (a) serves some useful purpose, eg answers a point of English law raised by the policy[29]; (b) does not undermine existing foreign proceedings;[30] and (c) does not require the court to answer a purely hypothetical question or a question which the claimant has only an indirect interest.[31]

---

[24] See *Akai v People's Insurance Co* [1998] 1 Lloyd's Rep 90, where the action was brought in Australia in breach of an English exclusive jurisdiction clause, and the Australian courts purported to assert jurisdiction under Australian domestic law.

[25] It is to be emphasised that the injunction is against the claimant in the proceedings, not against the foreign court itself, even though the effect of the injunction is to remove the action from the foreign court (unless the claimant is willing to face contempt proceedings in England).

[26] The requirements for the grant of an anti-suit injunction were laid down by the House of Lords in *Societe Nationale Industrielle v Le Kul Jak* [1987] 3 All ER 510 and *Donohue v Armco Inc* [2002] Lloyd's Rep IR 425.

[27] *Akai v People's Insurance Co* [1998] 1 Lloyd's Rep 90 (exclusive jurisdiction clause); *Youell v Kara Mara Shipping Co* [2000] 2 Lloyd's Rep 102 (exclusive jurisdiction clause); *XL Insurance v Owens Corning* [2000] 2 Lloyd's Rep 500 (arbitration clause); *Commercial Union Assurance Co v Simat Helliesen & Eichner* [2001] Lloyd's Rep IR172; *General Star International Indemnity Ltd v Stirling Cooke Brown Reinsurance Brokers Ltd* [2003] Lloyd's Rep IR 719 (oppression); *West Tankers Inc v Ras Riunione Adriatica di Sicurta SpA, The Front Comor* [2005] EWHC 454 (Comm) (arbitration clause); *CNA Ins Co Ltd v Office Depot International (UK) Ltd* [2005] EWHC 456 (exclusive jurisdiction clause); and *Advent Capital plc v G N Ellinas Imports-Exports Ltd* [2005] EWHC 1242 (Comm) (exclusive jurisdiction clause). Contrast: *Du Pont de Nemours v Agnew* [1988] 2 Lloyd's Rep 240; *SCOR v Reas International Ltd* [1995] 2 Lloyd's Rep 278 ; *American Speciality Lines Insurance Co v Abbott Laboaratories* [2003] 1 Lloyd's Rep 267; *Through Transport Mutual Ins Assoc (Eurasia) Ltd v New India Ass Co Ltd* [2005] 1 Lloyd's Rep 67.

[28] [1999] Lloyd's Rep IR 58.

[29] As in *Philips* itself (meaning of the policy). See also: *Lincoln National Life Insurance Co v Employers Reinsurance Corporation* [2002] Lloyd's Rep IR 881; *CGU International Insurance v Szabo* [2002] Lloyd's Rep IR 196; *Tiernan v Magen Life* 1998, unreported; *Tryg Baltica International (UK) Ltd v Boston Compania De Seguros SA* [2005] Lloyd's Rep IR 40.

[30] See *American Motorists Insurance v Cellstar Corporation* [2003] Lloyd's Rep IR 295; *Chase v Ram Technical Services* [2000] 2 Lloyd's Rep 418.

[31] As where a reinsurer seeks a declaration that the reinsured is not liable to the assured under a policy governed by some other law: *Meadows Insurance Co v Insurance Co of Ireland* [1989] 2 Lloyd's Rep 298; *Limit (No 3) Ltd v PDV Insurance Co Ltd* [2005] EWCA Civ 383; *Royal & Sun Alliance Insurance plc v Retail Brand Alliance Inc* [2005] Lloyd's Rep Ir 110.

2.3 EU cases: general rules

The general rules relating to jurisdiction as between EU Member States are laid down in Council Regulation 44/2001. Those rules have no application to 'matters relating to insurance', but remain relevant to reinsurance. It suffices to make the following points on the general rules in the Regulation:

(a)   The general principle in Article 2 is that the defendant must be sued in the place of his domicile.

(b)   There are various specialised alternatives to the domicile rule set out in Article 5, and if any of these applies then the defendant can, in the alternative, be sued in the jurisdiction pointed to by the exception.

(c)   The most important exception in the context of reinsurance is that in Article 5(1), namely that in 'matters relating to a contract,' the defendant may be sued 'in the place of the performance of the obligation in question.' There is a good deal of complex authority on Article 5(1) and its differently worded predecessor in the Brussels Convention, the general effect of which is that the obligation in question is the one upon which the action is founded and jurisdiction is conferred upon the courts of the country in which that obligation – or if more than one has allegedly been broken, the principal obligation – was to be performed.[32] The most important decision in Article 5(1) for reinsurance purposes is *Agnew v Lansforsakringsbolagens AB*,[33] in which the House of Lords by a bare majority held that a breach of the duty of utmost good faith by the reinsured constitutes a breach of an obligation, so that the reinsurers are entitled to seek negative declaratory relief in the jurisdiction[34] where the presentation of the risk was made.

(d)   If the parties have entered into an exclusive jurisdiction agreement, that agreement overrides the other jurisdiction rules in Regulation 44/2001 and the nominated court has exclusive jurisdiction (reg 23).[35] The parties may also enter into a non-exclusive jurisdiction clause, in which case the nominated court has concurrent jurisdiction with any other court which possesses jurisdiction under the Regulation. A jurisdiction clause is binding only if the parties can be shown to have reached consensus on the point.[36]

(e)   Where, as is perfectly possible under Regulation 44/2001, two or more courts have jurisdiction over a dispute involving the same subject matter, the same parties and the same issues, Article 27 of the Regulation confers exclusive juris-

---

[32] *AIG Group v The Ethniki* [2000] Lloyd's Rep IR 343.
[33] [2000] Lloyd's Rep IR 317.
[34] Almost inevitably the reinsurers' home state.
[35] See, eg, *Beazley v Horizon Offshore Contractors Inc, The Gulf Horizon* [2005] Lloyd's Rep IR 321.
[36] In particular a jurisdiction clause in the direct policy will not be regarded as having been incorporated into the reinsurance by the 'full reinsurance clause' wording – 'as original' – unless the reinsurance agreement expressly so provides: *AIG Group v The Ethniki* [2000] Lloyd's Rep IR 343; *AIG Europe v QBE International Insurance* [2002] Lloyd's Rep IR 22. See also *Standard Steamship Owners' Protection and Indemnity Association (Bermuda) Ltd v GIE Vision Bail* [2004] EWHC 2919 (Comm), where an exclusive jurisdiction clause in the rules of a P&I Club was held to have been incorporated into a contract between the Club and a third party entitled to the benefit of a policy issued by the Club.

diction upon the court 'first seised'[37] of the action and that court must hear the case. If the actions in the two courts are merely 'related', in that they overlap but involve either different parties, different subject matter or different issues, a court other than the court first seised has under Article 27 a general discretion to stay its proceedings and will do so if there is a risk of conflicting judgments in the two courts.[38] This aside, there is no power for the court to stay its proceedings on the grounds of *forum non conveniens*.[39] If there is a challenge to the jurisdiction of the court first seised, only that court may resolve the issue, and in particular it is not permissible for an English court to issue an anti-suit injunction to prevent an action being brought in a jurisdiction other than that agreed, as the jurisdiction of the court first seised is a matter for that court alone.[40] The principle that an anti-suit injunction may not be issued by the English court is, however, subject to an apparent exception where the foreign proceedings have been brought in contravention of an arbitration clause: the view accepted by the English courts[41] is that the fact that 'arbitration' is outside Regulation 44/2001 means that the first seised rule does not apply to an anti-suit injunction to restrain a party to an arbitration clause pursuing an action in breach of that clause.[42]

(f) A court will have exclusive jurisdiction even if it would not have had jurisdiction under the rules of Regulation 44/2001 if proceedings are commenced in that court and the defendant submits to the jurisdiction by defending the case on its merits rather than raising any objection.

2.4 EU cases: special insurance rules

Articles 8 to 14 of Regulation 444/2001 set out special rules on jurisdiction which affect 'matters relating to insurance', a phrase referring to any dispute between the

---

[37] The time at which this takes place varies from state to state, as civil procedure is not harmonised. The basic rule is that the relevant date is that on which the document instituting the proceedings is lodged with the court (art 30). In England, this refers to the issue of proceedings rather than – as was the case under the earlier Brussels Convention – the service of proceedings.

[38] See, eg, *Prifti v Musini Sociedad Anonima de Seguros y Reaseguros* [2004] Lloyd's Rep IR 528, where a stay of English proceedings was refused as the issues arising in Spanish proceedings between the assured and its insurers were different to those arising in England between those insurers and their reinsurers. In *Konkola Copper Mines plc v Coromin* [2005] EWHC 898 (Comm) it was held that the English courts have, despite *Owusu v Jackson*, retained their power of stay even against a defendant domiciled in England, if the parties have agreed under an exclusive jurisdiction clause that the dispute is to be held in a court outside the EU or EFTA.

[39] Where the English court has jurisdiction by virtue of the fact that the defendant is domiciled in England, under article 2 of Regulation 44/2001, but the competing court is outside the EU, the English view has long been that the power to stay on the ground of *forum non conveniens* is not removed even if the competing court is not one in the EU or EFTA. However, this view was decisively rejected by the European Court of Justice in a reference from England, Case–281/02 *Owusu v Jackson*, 1 March 2005, unreported. The position is now that if the defendant is domiciled in England, and the English court is first seised, the English court cannot stay its proceedings. The case does not deal with jurisdiction conferred by other articles of Reg 44/2001, and there is a powerful argument that jurisdiction conferred by virtue of, eg, the contract or tort rules and not by domicile, is not overriding and the power to stay in favour of a court outside the EU or EFTA remains intact.

[40] *Erich Gasser GmbH v MISAT Srl* [2004] 1 Lloyd's Rep 445; *Turner v Grovit* [2004] 2 Lloyd's Rep 216.

[41] Although not yet tested before the European Court of Justice.

[42] *Beazley v Horizon Offshore Contractors Inc, The Gulf Horizon* [2005] Lloyd's Rep IR 321; *Through Transport Mutual Insurance Association (Eurasia) Ltd v New India Assurance Co Ltd* [2005] 1 Lloyd's Rep 67.

parties arising out of a policy.[43] The rules are designed to protect the perceived weaker party – the assured – against the insurers, by restricting the jurisdictions in which the assured can be sued by the insurers and by giving the assured an extended choice of jurisdictions in which to bring an action. The phrase 'matters relating to insurance' is not, however, confined to consumer policies and extends to all insurances irrespective of the size of the assured.[44] The only exclusions are reinsurance,[45] and contribution actions between insurers.[46]

The basic rule in Article 12 is that the assured[47] may be sued only in the member state of his domicile, a provision designed to prevent the weaker party from being forced to defend an avoidance or similar claim in a foreign court. There is an exception to this principle where the claim arises out of the operations of the assured's agent, in which case the action may be brought in the member state where the agent carries on its operations (Article 5(5)). The insurers may also bring a counterclaim against the assured in the court where the assured's claim has been brought even though the assured is not domiciled in that territory (Article 12(2)).[48]

The assured, by contrast, may bring an action against the insurers in the courts of the member state in which the assured is domiciled (Article 9), in the courts of the member state in which the insurers are domiciled (Article 8),[49] or, if the insurers are not domiciled within the EU, in the courts of the member state in which the insurers' agent carried on its operations (Article 5(5)), at the assured's option. Further alternatives are given in the case of insurance on real property, in which case the assured may sue in the place where the harmful event affecting the property occurred (Article 10), and in the case of liability insurance, in which case the assured may sue in the place where the events giving rise to liability occurred (Article 10).

As a general rule the assured cannot contract out of his right to be sued only in his home member state and his right to sue the insurers in any one of the various jurisdictions open to him under the insurance rules. However, Articles 13 and 14 of Regulation 44/2001 do permit exclusive jurisdiction agreements in a variety of circumstances. The most important of these (which are alternative and not cumulative) are that:

(a)   the agreement has been entered into *after* the dispute has arisen, or the assured has otherwise submitted to the jurisdiction of the court in question, so that the assured can be seen to have acted voluntarily;
(b)   the agreement extends the rights of the assured;
(c)   the parties are both domiciled in the same member state and the agreement

---

[43] *Jordan Grand Prix Ltd v Baltic Insurance Group* [1999] Lloyd's Rep IR 93 (counterclaim by insurers to avoid policy and to seek damages for fraudulent conspiracy).
[44] *New Hampshire Insurance Co v Strabag Bau AG* [1992] 1 Lloyd's Rep 454.
[45] So held by the House of Lords in *Agnew v Lansforsakringsbolagens AB* [2000] Lloyd's Rep IR 317, and confirmed shortly afterwards by the European Court of Justice in *Group Josi Reinsurance Co SA v Universal General Insurance Co* [2001] Lloyd's Rep IR 483.
[46] *GIE v Zurich Espana and Soptrans*, Case C–77/04, May 2005, unreported.
[47] Including a beneficiary under the policy.
[48] Although the insurers may not join a third party with interests under the policy: *Jordan Grand Prix Ltd v Baltic Insurance Group* [1999] Lloyd's Rep IR 93.
[49] This provision can be used by an assured who is domiciled outside the EU: *Berisford v New Hampshire Insurance* [1990] 1 Lloyd's Rep 454.

confers exclusive jurisdiction on the courts of that member state;[50]
(d)   the assured is not domiciled within a member state;
(e)   the policy relates to transport risks[51] or to large commercial risks.

3. Applicable law

3.1 The different regimes

The law applicable to an insurance contract lays down all substantive matters in relation to the contract, including its legality, formation scope, interpretation, avoidance and breach. There is substantial variation in these matters in different legal systems, and it thus becomes of crucial importance to ascertain whether a policy is governed by English law or by some other law. No less than three sets of rules for determining the law applicable to a contract are recognised in England, and once the applicable law has been determined it is the obligation of the English court to apply that law to the policy before it.[52] First, there is the common law, although this now has a very limited ambit and applies only where the two other regimes are inapplicable: it may be disregarded for present purposes. Secondly, special rules for choice of law in insurance contracts have been developed. These form a part of the EU's structure of the regulation of insurance business, which does not make any provision for the substantive control of insurance contracts but merely regulates the solvency and conduct of business of insurers. The choice of law rules are designed to provide some measure of protection to the assured, by ensuring that contract is to be governed by the law of the assured's home state. The choice of law rules for insurance contracts are contained in the Financial Services and Markets Act 2000 (Law Applicable to Insurance Contracts) Regulations 2001,[53] and apply to insurance contracts whose risk is situated in the EU. The Regulations do not apply to reinsurance contracts. Thirdly, in respect of most forms of commercial contracts, other than insurance contracts, the applicable law is to be ascertained by the application of the Rome Convention 1980, a Convention which operates between EU member states but which is not strictly an EU legislative measure. The Convention was implemented into English law by the Contracts (Applicable Law) Act 1995. The result is that:

---

[50] See *Societe Financiere et Industrielle du Peloux v Axa Belgium* Case C–112/03, May 2005, unreported, in which the ECJ held that this exception does not apply to subsidiaries of the assured covered by the policy but domiciled in other member states.
[51] The definition is detailed and complex, and has been construed narrowly: *Charman v WOC Offshore BV* [1993] 2 Lloyd's Rep 551. See, however, *Standard Steamship Owners' Protection and Indemnity Association (Bermuda) Ltd v GIE Vision Bail* [2004] EWHC 2919 (Comm), in which it was held that a policy which applied primarily to maritime risks but which also included other elements, including employers' liability cover, could be the subject of an exclusive jurisdiction clause.
[52] The content of foreign law is a matter of fact which has to be proved by expert evidence. If there is no evidence, the court will assume that the relevant foreign law is the same as English law.
[53] SI 2001/2635, implementing the relevant provisions of the Second Non-Life Directive and the Second Non-Life Directive.

(a) choice of law rules for an insurance policy under which the risk is situated in the EEA[54] are laid down in the 2001 Regulations;
(b) choice of law rules for an insurance policy under which the risk is situated outside the EEA are laid down in the Rome Convention 1980;
(c) choice of law rules for all reinsurance agreements are laid down in the Rome Convention 1980.

It is apparent, therefore, that the starting point in any insurance case coming before the English courts is determining where the risk is situated. The matter is governed by reg 2 of the 2001 Regulations. In the case of a non-life policy, the risk is situated in the EEA state of the assured's residence or place of business, although there are special provisions for buildings (situation of building), motor vehicles (place of registration) and short-term travel risks (place where contract was entered into). In the case of a life policy, the risk is situated in the EEA state of the assured's[55] residence or place of business. These definitions are problematic, as they make no provision for the large number of policies which cover cross-border risks. A typical policy of this type is one taken out by a parent company under which the assured is itself and its worldwide subsidiaries. Two issues here arise. The first is whether each of the co-assureds is to be treated as an assured in its own right, so that different choice of law rules apply to each of them. The second is whether the Regulations are applicable where there are risks both inside and outside the EEA. These points arose in *American Motorists Insurance Co v Cellstar Corporation*,[56] a case in which a policy was taken out by a company resident in Texas but with subsidiaries both inside and outside the EEA. The Court of Appeal concluded that English law was the applicable law whether the Rome Convention or the predecessor to the Regulations governed the position so that the issues did not fall for consideration, although Mance LJ did express the view that the parent company should be regarded as the assured in order to avoid the policy being 'carved up'. Mance LJ was also prepared to assume that the Regulations applied even though the policy extended to risks both inside and outside the EEA, although it was noted that certain of the choice of law rules in the Regulations did not contemplate risks outside the EEA. The point here is that those responsible for the drafting of the Insurance Directives which are implemented by the Regulations did not take account of cross-border policies and accordingly made no provision for them.

3.2 Non-life policies: risk situated in the EEA

The choice of law rules in the 2001 Regulations for non-life contracts are complex. The basic proposition is that the parties are free to choose the law which governs their agreement, but subject to various safeguards. There is an absolute right for the parties to choose the applicable law if the policy covers 'large risks',[57] a term defined in the Regulations as referring to: railway rolling stock, aircraft, ships, goods in transit, and

---

[54] The EU and EFTA.
[55] This refers to the holder of the policy and not the life assured under it.
[56] [2003] Lloyd's Rep IR 359. See also *Travelers Casualty and Surety Co of Europe Ltd v Sun Life Assurance Co of Canada (UK) Ltd* [2005] Lloyd's Rep IR 846.
[57] Reg 4(7).

liability for ships and aircraft; credit and suretyship insurance which relates to the assured's business; and insurance in respect of land vehicles, fire and natural forces, damage to property and liability, although the assured must meet at least two of three financial critiera, namely a balance sheet total of €6.2 million, net turnover of €12.8 million, or 250 employees.

In all other cases party autonomy in respect of choice of law is limited, and whatever the applicable law may be under these rules, reg 5 of the 2001 Regulations lays down the overriding rule that if the risk is situated in the UK then the mandatory rules of the UK remain applicable. The most important mandatory rules are those set out in the Unfair Terms in Contracts Regulations 1999, which prevent reliance upon unfair policy terms. Subject to that consideration, the rights of the parties to choose the applicable law may be summarised as follows.

(a)   If the assured resides in the same EEA state as that in which the risk is situated, the applicable law is the law of that state unless that law allows the parties to choose some other law (reg 4(2)). If the relevant country is England, the parties have a free choice under English law. If the relevant law is that of some other EEA country, then whether a choice is permitted and has been made is a matter for that law.[58]
(b)   Where the assured is not resident in the same EEA state as that in which the risk is situated, the parties may choose either the law of the EEA state where the risk is situated or the law of the assured's residence (reg 4(3)).
(c)   Where the assured carries on a business, and the contract covers risks situated in different EEA states, the parties may choose the law of the EEA state of the assured's business or the law of any of the EEA states in which a risk is situated (reg 4(4)).
(d)   If the risks covered by the policy are limited to events occurring in one EEA state other than that in which the risk is situated, the parties may choose the former as providing the applicable law as well as any of the other member states indicated in rules (a)–(c) (reg 4(6)).

In determining whether the parties have entered into an agreement choosing the applicable law, the test is whether the parties have expressed their choice with reasonable certainty, the same test as is laid down in the Rome Convention 1980.[59] Assuming, however, that the parties have not entered into an agreement as to the applicable law, regs 4(8)–(9) of the Regulations lay down a presumption that the governing law is the law of the country in which the risk is situated, although that presumption can be ousted if the contract is more closely connected with some other EEA state. The presumption is not one which is easily ousted. In *Credit Lyonnais v New Hampshire Insurance Co*[60] a US insurer entered into arrangements with an international banking group with its head office in Paris under which separate policies would be issued to each of the bank's subsidiaries. In accordance with this scheme, a

---

[58] See *Evialis SA v SIAT* [2003] 2 Lloyd's Rep 377, where it was held that the contract governed by Italian law, and that there was no agreement to the contrary as a matter of Italian law.
[59] Which is applied for this purpose by reg 7 of the 2001 Regs. See below for discussion of the Rome Convention on the requirements for a choice of law clause.
[60] [1997] 1 Lloyd's Rep 191.

policy was issued to the claimant, the bank's UK subsidiary. The presumption was that English law applied, as the risk was situated in England, and the Court of Appeal held that the policy had not been ousted as the balance of relevant factors – including the place where the policy was issued and where it was to be performed – pointed to England. By contrast, in *American Motorists Insurance Co v Cellstar Corporation*,[61] the Court of Appeal held, on the assumption that the Regulations applied to a worldwide policy taken out in the US by a Texas parent company and that the relevant assured was the UK subsidiary of that company, that the presumption in favour of English law (the situation of the risk) was overridden by the consideration that the policy was a global one written in the US and that there was to be one single applicable law – the law of Texas – rather than different applicable laws relevant to each EEA subsidiary.

3.3 Life policies: risks situated in the EEA

The 2001 Regulations are here somewhat easier to apply. There is a presumption in reg 8 that the applicable law is the law of 'the EEA state of the commitment,' defined as meaning the place of the assured's residence or place of business. The parties may, however, choose a different law if the presumptive applicable law so allows, and in the case of English law there are no restrictions. Accordingly, if the assured resides in England, choice of any law is permitted. There is only one special rule of note: if the assured resides in one EEA state, but is the citizen of another EEA state, the parties may in any event choose the law of either EEA state. Once again, mandatory rules – in particular the Unfair Terms in Consumer Contracts Regulations – will prevail in the event that UK is the state of the commitment.

3.4 Risks situated outside the EEA and reinsurance agreements

The Rome Convention 1980 has two main effects. First, it allows the parties to enter into an agreement to choose the applicable law, subject to various safeguards.[62] Secondly, in the absence of any agreement on choice of law, the Convention sets out various presumptions which point towards the applicable law.

Turning first to choice of applicable law, Article 3.1 of the Convention sets out the basic principle that if the parties have chosen the governing law,[63] and their choice is 'expressed or demonstrated with reasonable certainty,' then that law governs the contracts. Different laws may be chosen for different parts of the contract, and the parties may agree that the law can be changed during the currency of the agreement,[64] although it must be possible to say from the outset which law is the applicable law: a clause which provides that applicable law is not fixed at the start and is to be

---

[61] [2003] Lloyd's Rep IR 359. See also *Travelers Casualty and Surety Co of Europe Ltd v Sun Life Assurance Co of Canada (UK) Ltd* [2005] Lloyd's Rep IR 846.

[62] Based on the predominance of the mandatory laws of the forum or some other EEA state where there has been an express choice of some other law: Rome Convention, Arts 7.2 and 3.3 respectively.

[63] Which must be the law of a country: *Shamil Bank of Bahrain v Beximco Pharmaceuticals* [2003] 2 All ER (Comm) 849.

[64] *King v Brandywine Reinsurance Co (UK) Ltd* [2004] Lloyd's Rep IR 554, affirmed on other grounds [2005] EWCA Civ 235; *Craft Enterprises (International) Ltd v Axa Insurance Co* [2005] Lloyd's Rep IR 14.

determined by later events is invalid.[65] The principle that the law must be expressed or demonstrated with reasonable certainty resembles the pre-existing common law under which a choice of law could be express or implied from the circumstances, and it is clear from the cases decided under Article 3.1 that there can be a choice of law within its terms where it is obvious from the contract itself and all the surrounding circumstances that the parties intended their agreement to be governed by English law. This conclusion is almost inevitable where the cover is placed in London on standard London market wordings and through English brokers.[66] Other indications as to implicit choice may be gleaned from an exclusive jurisdiction or arbitration clause, as it is likely that the applicable law follows that of the nominated forum.

In the absence of any express or implied choice of law, Article 4 of the Rome Convention lays down default rules. The basic proposition in Article 4.1 is that the contract is to be governed by the law of the country with which it is most closely connected. There is then a presumption in Article 4.2 that:

> the contract is most closely connected with the country where the party who is the effect the performance which is characteristic of the contract has, at the time of the conclusion of the contract, his habitual residence, or in the case of a body corporate or unincorporated, its central administration. However, if the contact is entered into in the course of that party's trade or profession, that country will be the country in which the principal place of business is situated ...

The presumption is disapplied by Article 4.5 'if it appears from the circumstances as a whole that the contract is more closely connected with another country.' The characterising performance of a contract of insurance or reinsurance is payment by the underwriters, so the presumption will typically point to the law of the country where the underwriters have their principal place of business.[67] As noted above, the English courts have consistently held that there is an implied choice of English law where the risk is placed in London using London brokers and London market wordings. In this type of case there is, therefore, no need to resort to Article 4 at all, and the courts have simply held that even if there is no implied choice of English law in these circumstances then at the very least the presumption in Article 4 points towards English law.[68] The English courts have in any event been reluctant to allow the presumption in Article 4.2 to be displaced other than in the clearest of cases.

Finally, it may be noted that if the assured is a consumer, and the contract was created following an invitation to the assured in his own country, the ordinary rules of the Rome Convention 1980 are ousted by Article 5. Instead, any express or implied choice of law is subject to the mandatory laws of the country of the assured's habitual residence, and in the absence of a choice of law the contract is presumed to be governed by the law of the country of the assured's habitual residence.

---

[65] *CGU International Insurance v Szabo* [2002] Lloyd's Rep IR 196.

[66] There are numerous cases to this effect. See: *AIG Europe SA v QBE International Insurance* [2002] Lloyd's Rep IR 22; *Assucurazioni Generali SpA v Ege Sigorta AS* [2002] Lloyd's Rep IR 480; *Gan Insurance Co v Tai Ping Insurance Co* [1999] Lloyd's Rep IR 229; *Tonicstar Ltd v American Home Assurance Co* [2005] Lloyd's Rep IR 32; *Tryg Baltica International (UK) Ltd v Boston Compania De Seguros SA* [2005] Lloyd's Rep IR 40; *American Motorists Insurance Co v Cellstar Corporation* [2003] Lloyd's Rep IR 359.

[67] This was more or less the position reached by the common law, applying a 'centre of gravity' test to the overall circumstances of the case: *Citadel Insurance Co v Atlantic Union Insurance Co SA* [1982] 2 Lloyd's Rep 543.

[68] See the authorities cited in n 59, above.

13

Motor Insurance

1. Requirements of compulsory insurance

1.1 Compulsory liability cover

In 1930 cover for third-party liability was made compulsory for all those who used a motor vehicle on a road.[1] This started a stream of legislation that led to the Road Traffic Act 1988.[2] One aim of this statute is to ensure compensation for those who are killed or injured or suffer loss of property by the negligence of drivers by requiring that all motorists have a minimum level of liability insurance. In addition, the motor insurance industry has created a scheme to compensate those who have suffered loss that is within the cover required under the 1988 Act, but where the wrongdoer is uninsured or cannot be traced. The scheme is administered by the Motor Insurers' Bureau, which also incorporates the Motor Insurers' Information Centre where information about vehicles and insurance is held to facilitate compensation for victims of motor accidents.[3]

It is a criminal offence under the Road Traffic Act 1988 for anyone to use, or cause or permit another to use, a motor vehicle on a road or other public place unless, in relation to the use of that vehicle by that person, there is in force an insurance policy in respect of certain third party risks (section 143(1), (2)).[4] The policy must be issued by an authorised insurer and must cover the person(s) specified 'in respect of any liability which may be incurred by him or them in respect of the death of or bodily injury to any person or damage to property caused by, or arising out of, the use of the

---

[1] Road Traffic Act 1930, s 35. See, generally, R Merkin and J Stuart-Smith, *The Law of Motor Insurance* (London, Sweet & Maxwell, 2004).

[2] Road Traffic Act 1988, Part VI, ss 143–62. Many recent changes result from EU directives and more are in the pipeline.

[3] Motor Vehicles (Compulsory Insurance (Information Centre and Compensation Body) Regs 2003 (2003/37), regs 3–9. This was introduced as the result of the Fourth Directive on Motor Insurance (2000/26/EEC).

[4] As amended by Motor Vehicles (Compulsory Insurance) Regs 2000 (2000/726), reg 2. There are exceptions to this provision in s 144, and s 143 does not require an insurance policy where security is provided (see ss 144(1), 146; Road Traffic Act 1991). The defences to a prosecution under s 143 are in s 143(3).

vehicle on a road or other public place in Great Britain' (section 145(3)(a)).[5] Where, as is usually the case, the policy refers to a particular vehicle, the insurers will not be liable if the insured has parted with ownership of that vehicle, even if the policy is stated to cover any car that is 'being used instead of the insured car.' Motor cover runs with the ownership of the vehicle specified in the policy, so that if the vehicle has been sold there is no 'insured car' and the policy terminates.[6] There must also be cover against liability in other EEA states[7] to the extent required in those countries (section 145(3)(b)), and cover against liability for emergency medical treatment (section 158).[8] While cover for injury or death must be unlimited, it is not required that the policy cover: liability above £250,000 for damage to the property of a third party (section 145(4)(b)); nor liability for the death of, or injury to, an employee (other than a passenger) arising out of the course of employment where there is cover under an employer's liability policy (section 145(4)(A));[9] nor damage to the vehicle mentioned in the policy (section 145(4)(c)), or to goods carried for hire or reward (section 145(4)(d)), or to property owned by a third party while that property is in the custody or under the control of the insured (section 145(e)); nor any contractual liability (section 145(4)(f)). Of course, the parties may expressly extend cover to include such matters, and frequently do, for instance, many motorists cover damage to themselves and their vehicles.

There is a policy for the purpose of the Act, even though it is voidable on account of, for instance, non-disclosure,[10] but a policy is of no effect until a certificate of insurance is delivered by the insurers to the insured (section 147). It is an offence to use the vehicle before the certificate is delivered, but that does not affect the insurers' liability under the contract to a third-party where there is a cover note[11] and a certificate is issued later in terms that backdate it to the relevant period.[12] In terms of the liability of the insurers to the insured, the certificate is not the contract of insurance and it is the terms of the latter that prevail.[13] It is worth noting that under section 154 a driver, against whom a claim is made in respect of damage required to be covered by virtue of section 145, must give on a demand made by a claimant the particulars specified in the certificate of insurance.

---

[5] As amended by Motor Vehicles (Compulsory Insurance) Regulations 2000 (2000/726), reg 2. Since what is required is cover for liability to third parties, the reference to 'any person or damage to property' does not refer to the driver or the driver's property (eg, the driver's car): see *Cooper v Motor Insurers' Bureau* [1985] QB 575, where the words 'any person' were said by the Court of Appeal to be limited by s 143(1) and this made it clear that what was being referred to was liability to third parties.

[6] *Rogerson v Scottish Automobile & General Insurance Co Ltd* (1932) 41 Ll L Rep 1; *Tattersall v Drysdale* [1935] 2 KB 174; C Parsons, 'Termination of Motor Policies: Some Issues of Law and Practice' (1993) 3 *Insur L & P* 43.

[7] That is, EU member states and the members of the European Free Trade Association (Iceland, Norway and Liechtenstein).

[8] See also, the liability of insurers to pay for hospital treatment in s 157.

[9] See the requirements of the Employers' Liability (Compulsory Insurance) Act 1969, but also the Employers' Liability (Compulsory Insurance) Regs 1998 (1998/2573).

[10] *Adams v Dunne* [1978] RTR 281. Where a contract is avoided, under the criminal law this does not mean it was void *ab initio*: *Goodbarne v Buck* [1940] 1 KB 771.

[11] On cover notes, see above ch 5.

[12] *Motor and General Insurance Co v Cox* [1990] 1 WLR 1443.

[13] *Biddle v Johnston* [1965] 2 Lloyd's Rep 121.

1.2 'Use'

The words 'caused by, or arising out of the use' of a vehicle (section 145(3)(a)) expand the scope of insurance that a driver must obtain, in that it must extend not just to losses proximately caused by driving but also to losses that 'arise out' of the use of a car. A person who runs out of petrol and causes an accident while leaving the vehicle to secure a lift to a garage is to be regarded as having incurred liability out of the use of a vehicle,[14] but a person who dashes across a road in order to obtain a lift in a minibus and is hit by an oncoming vehicle has not suffered injuries arising out of the use of the minibus.[15] It is worth noting that the offence of driving without insurance is only committed if the motor vehicle is 'used' on the road or other public place (s 143). The determinative issue here is control, not ownership.[16] A passenger who negligently opens a car door and injures a pedestrian is not in control of the vehicle,[17] but a passenger may enter into a joint enterprise with the driver to use the car.[18] Moreover, 'use' does not simply refer to the act of driving: there may be use where the engine does not work,[19] or the vehicle has been abandoned.[20]

1.3 'Cause or permit'

It is an offence to 'cause or permit any other person' to use a vehicle if that person is not insured (section 143(1)(b)). While 'cause' imports the notion of a positive command or authority to use the vehicle, the word 'permit' has been interpreted quite widely to include not just express words of permission, but circumstances in which permission can be inferred, such as where the vehicle is placed by its owner in the control of someone else in circumstances which 'carry with it a reasonable implication of a discretion or liberty to use it in the manner in which it was used.'[21] In *McLeod (or Houston) v Buchanan*,[22] a man was given a car for business and private use by his employer. The car proved unsatisfactory and the employer authorised the purchase of a van. This vehicle was insured only for business, although the driver also used it for private purposes. The court held that since the van was bought for the same purposes as the car and the employee had not been told to use it only for business, the employer had permitted its use by another without insurance. It is not just the owner who can commit this offence. Anyone who has control over the vehicle and causes or permits an uninsured person to use it commits an offence,[23] such as a commercial traveller who lends a company car to an uninsured friend. On the other hand, someone who is not the owner and does not have control over its use will not come within the offence.[24]

[14] *Dunthorne v Bentley* [1999] Lloyd's Rep IR 560.
[15] *Slater v Buckinghamshire County Council* [2004] Lloyd's Rep IR 432.
[16] *Napthen v Place* [1970] RTR 248.
[17] *Brown v Roberts* [1965] 1 QB 1.
[18] *Hatton v Hall* [1999] Lloyd's Rep IR 313; *Leathley v Tatton* [1980] RTR 21
[19] *Elliott v Grey* [1960] 1 QB 367, although not if it is immobile and beyond repair in which case it may be neither a motor vehicle, nor in 'use': *Pumbien v Vines* [1996] RTR 37.
[20] *Williams v Jones* [1975] RTR 433.
[21] *McLeod (or Houston) v Buchanan* [1940] 2 All ER 179 at 187, per Lord Wright.
[22] Ibid.
[23] *Lloyd v Singleton* [1953] 1 QB 357.
[24] *Watkins v O'Shaughnessy* [1939] 1 All ER 384.

An honest but mistaken belief that the driver is insured is no defence,[25] even if that mistake was induced by the driver's misrepresentation.[26] This means that an offence will be committed if no condition is imposed or if a condition is imposed that, as the owner knows, will be ignored. In *Lloyd-Wolper v Moore*,[27] it was alleged that the owner had been misled by the driver's representations that he was 17 years old and had a full driving licence, whereas he was 16 and had no licence. Unsurprisingly, the Court of Appeal seemed somewhat sceptical about the owner's claim not to have known the truth of these matters since the driver was his son; nevertheless, the judges held that permission to drive had been given even if the claim were true since consenting on the basis of a mistaken belief did not amount to the imposition of a condition. In *DPP v Fisher*,[28] the owner lent the car to someone who, as the owner knew, was uninsured on the condition that this person would only allow an insured person to drive. The car was lent to someone who was not known to the owner and who did not have insurance. It was held that the permission of the owner to the second person was unconditional and, therefore, amounted to the offence. This principle means that a driver who takes their car into a garage for repair and who permits it to be driven will have given unconditional permission for an uninsured mechanic to use it.[29] Yet, there are cases in which a rather softer approach has been taken.[30] Mackenna J was of the opinion that, 'Permission connotes knowledge or that which is in criminal law the equivalent of knowledge, a deliberate blindness to obvious facts which it would be inconvenient to know.'[31] It was held in *Newbury v Davis* that if the person giving permission makes it a condition of using the vehicle that the driver obtains insurance, then there will be no offence because: 'A permission subject to a condition which was not fulfilled was no permission.'[32] It was said in *DPP v Fisher*[33] that *Newbury* should be confined to its particular facts and this view is to be preferred, although in a subsequent Scottish decision, *Macdonald v Howdle*,[34] it was held that an owner would not have given permission to the driver had she not been told by her friend that his policy covered him and, therefore, her permission was conditional on the driver being insured.

1.4 'Motor vehicle'

The Act only applies to a 'motor vehicle' which is defined in section 185(1) as 'a mechanically propelled vehicle intended or adapted for use on the roads.'.[35] A motor car comes within this definition even if it is not capable of being driven because the engine has been removed, so long as its immobility is only temporary.[36] On the other hand, a car will not be regarded as a motor vehicle if it is in such disrepair or has

---

[25] *Baugh v Crago* [1976] 1 Lloyd's Rep 563.
[26] *Lloyd-Wolper v Moore* [2004] EWCA Civ 766.
[27] Ibid.
[28] [1992] RTR 93.
[29] *Lyons v May* [1948] 2 All ER 1062.
[30] *Sands v O'Connell* [1981] RTR 42.
[31] *Sheldon Deliveries Ltd v Willis* [1972] RTR 217 at 220, per MacKenna J.
[32] *Newbury v Davis* (1974) 118 *Sol Jo* 222.
[33] See above n 29.
[34] 1995 SLT 779.
[35] See s 189(1) for exemptions.
[36] *Lawrence v Howlett* [1952] 2 All ER 74, at 75, per Devlin J; *Newberry v Simmonds* [1961] 2 QB 345.

been dismantled to such an extent that there is little prospect of it ever being made mobile and it is, in reality, simply a pile of spare parts.[37] A motorcycle that can be pedalled is not a motor vehicle if essential parts of the engine have been removed.[38] The vehicle must also be 'intended or adapted for use on the roads.' It is not sufficient that it is capable of being used on the road if it was not intended or adapted for that use. However, if it is so intended or adapted, it does not matter that it is not normally used on the road. The test is 'what would be the view of the reasonable man as to the general user of this particular vehicle, not the particular user to which this particular appellant put it.'[39] This test may be satisfied by evidence that the device in question is widely used as a motor vehicle within the meaning of the Act, even if it does not conform to statutory vehicle safety standards and the manufacturer warns owners not to use it on the road.[40] A family car that is always used on a motor racing circuit will be a motor vehicle under the Act if on an occasion it is used on a road; on the other hand, a go-kart is certainly capable of being used on the road, but it is not intended for such use and will not come within the definition, unless adapted for the road.[41] The courts have also held that a vehicle which is intended for only occasional use on the road will not be within the Act, unless there is evidence that the intention is that such will be its general use: a dumper truck designed for carrying building materials which occasionally travelled short distances on the highway was not intended for general use on the road and was not, therefore, a motor vehicle.[42]

1.5 'Road or other public place'

Cover is only required where the vehicle is used on a 'road or other public place.'[43] The term 'road' is defined as 'any highway and other road to which the public has access, and includes bridges over which a road passes' (section 192(1)). It therefore includes private roads where they are used by the public in general, as opposed to a particular section.[44] The courtyard of a hotel, which was private property, but was used by the public without hindrance by the hotel's owners as a means of access to the hotel, and to cut a corner, was a 'road'.[45] A private road used only by the customers of a particular shop was not a road within the Act,[46] nor was a private road leading to a farm that was used, with permission, by anglers and picnickers and to gain access to a caravan site owned by the farmer. In both cases this was because only a restricted class of the public had access and the number of people in that class was

---

[37] *Smart v Allan* [1963] 1 QB 291.
[38] *Lawrence v Howlett*, above n 36. In *Floyd v Bush* [1953] 1 WLR 242, a similar bicycle was classified as a motor vehicle because the engine was intact and capable of propulsion, even though the engine was not being used. It will be the same where there is merely a temporary defect: *R v Tahsin* [1970] RTR 88.
[39] *Chief Constable of Avon and Somerset v Fleming* [1987] 1 All ER 318 at 322, per Glidewell LJ. See also *Burns v Currell* [1963] 2 QB 433 at 440, per Lord Parker CJ.
[40] *Chief Constable of North Yorkshire Police v Saddington* [2001] RTR 15.
[41] *Burns v Currell* [1963] 2 QB 433. In *Chief Constable of Avon and Somerset v Fleming*, above n 39, a motorcycle, which had been originally constructed in such a way as brought it within the Act, was later adapted for scrambling and taken outside the Act by those modifications.
[42] *Chalgray Ltd v Apsley* (1965) 109 *Sol Jo* 394.
[43] See s 143 and Motor Vehicles (Compulsory Insurance) Regs 2000 (2000/726).
[44] *Randall v Motor Insurers' Bureau* [1968] 1 WLR 1900.
[45] *Bugge v Taylor* [1941] 1 KB 198.
[46] *Thomas v Dando* [1951] 2 KB 620.

irrelevant.[47] Yet, public access is insufficient unless the land is also a 'road'. A public car park would only in exceptional circumstances be a road.[48] To be a road it must be clearly defined, as opposed to being an open space such as a field, it must be a means by which vehicles can travel to a destination, and it must have a surface (prepared or produced by constant use) suited to this purpose.[49] The case law now needs to be read within the context of the provisions of the Motor Vehicles (Compulsory Insurance) Regulations 2000, which adds to 'road' in section 143 the words 'or other public place.' The old case law on the meaning of 'public' in relation to roads is still relevant here, but it will only be necessary to show that the land was a 'place' rather than a 'road' to which the general public, rather than just a section of it, has access.

2. Third party claims

Where the owner has permitted use of their vehicle by an uninsured person, who causes loss and is unable to meet the damages award, the third party victim can sue the owner for breach of statutory duty.[50] Can a third party sue a driver's insurance company where that person has suffered injury or loss as a result of the use of the vehicle by the driver or by someone whom the driver has permitted to use it? On general principles, while the insured can enforce the insurance contract on behalf of a third party victim,[51] the third party cannot enforce it directly.[52] However, under section 151(1) where a certificate of insurance has been delivered to the insured,[53] judgment has been obtained against the driver, and the liability comes both within the requirements for compulsory insurance set out in the Act and is covered by the policy, the third party may enforce that judgment against the insurer. This is not dependent on the insured having defaulted on the judgment, so the third party, having obtained judgment, may proceed immediately against the insurer. There are restrictions on the defences that an insurer may use in such a case (sections 151, 152). Terms in the policy concerning cover will be ignored if they are invalid against a third party by virtue of section 148 (see below) and exclusions of liability that are permitted will be narrowly construed.[54] The insurers cannot seek to defend the action by showing that the driver was not authorised to drive the vehicle. They will also be liable even if they were entitled to, or have avoided or cancelled the policy, unless the certificate of insurance has been surrendered by the insured or proceedings for its

---

[47] *R v Beaumont* [1964] Crim LR 665.
[48] *Clarke v General Accident Fire and Life Assurance Corpn plc*; *Cutter v Eagle Star Insurance Co Ltd* [1998] 4 All ER 417.
[49] Ibid.
[50] *Monk v Warbey* [1935] 1 KB 75. While the same principle allows the third party to sue an uninsured employee's employer (*Gregory v Ford* [1951] 1 All ER 121), as has been seen already, the employer may be able to recoup from the negligent employee under *Lister v*
[51] *Williams v Baltic Insurance Association of London* [1924] 2 KB 282; above ch 6. The third party can include the insured: see, *Digby v General Accident Fire and Life Assurance Corpn* [1943] AC 212.
[52] *Vandepitte v Preferred Accident Insurance Corpn of New York* [1933] AC 70; above ch 6.
[53] See *Motor & General Insurance Co Ltd v Cox* [1990], above n 12.
[54] *Keeley v Pashen* [2004] EWCA Civ 1491.

recovery have been commenced (sections 151(5), 152(1)(c)). In the event of having paid in respect of the liability of an uninsured person, the insurer can recover that amount from anyone who is insured by the policy and who has caused or permitted the use of the vehicle which gave rise to the liability (section151(8)).

The insurers are not, however, liable to pay (section 152(1)): unless, before or within seven days after commencement of the proceedings in which the judgment was given, the insurers had notice of the bringing of the proceedings[55]; so long as an appeal is pending; if the policy was cancelled by mutual consent or by virtue of a term of the policy before the event which gave rise to the claim, and the certificate was surrendered within the time limits set out in the section or the insurers commenced proceedings to recover the certificate. The insurers are also not liable if, in an action begun before, or within three months after the commencement of the proceedings in which the judgment was given on the claim, they have obtained a declaration that, apart from any term of the policy,[56] they are entitled to avoid the policy – or have avoided it – because it was obtained by non-disclosure or misrepresentation relating to a material fact (section 152(2)).[57] In that event, the insurers must give notice to the third party before, or within seven days after taking action, to avoid the policy (section 152(3)), so as to give that person an opportunity to challenge this course of action. What amounts to a 'material' fact is specified in the statute as 'of such a nature as to influence the judgment of a prudent insurer in determining whether he will take the risk, and, if so, at what premium and what conditions' (section 152(2)). The cases indicate that the courts will treat as material the age of the driver, physical health, previous driving convictions, accidents, and a refusal by an insurer to insure or to renew a policy.[58]

An easier method is provided for the third party by the European Communities (Rights against Insurers) Regulations 2002.[59] Under these regulations the third party may proceed directly against the insurer without having first obtained judgment against the driver (reg 3(2)). The third party must be 'an entitled party,' which means a resident of one of the EEA states (reg 2(1)), and must have a right of action in tort against an insured person (reg 3(1)). That action must have arisen from an accident on a road or public place in the UK that was caused by the use of any vehicle, which is insured according to the requirements of section 145 and is normally based in the UK (reg 2). The regulations do have some disadvantages when compared with an action brought under s 151. Since the effect of the regulations is to put the third party into the same position as the insured with regard to the insurer, defences available to the insurer, which could not be used under section 151, may be available. For instance, where the third party is injured by the deliberate act of the insured, it is

---

[55] It is a general rule that in calculating such periods as specified here the day on which the relevant event occurs is not counted: *Stewart v Chapman* [1951] 2 KB 792. The notice must be clear, but no particular form is prescribed and it need not even be written: *Desouza v Waterlow* [1999] RTR 71.

[56] In other words, only such rights as arise from the general law of insurance contracts and not from a term in the particular contract itself.

[57] If the insurers have not avoided the policy in spite of being entitled to do so, the driver cannot be convicted of driving without insurance: *Durrant v Maclaren* [1956] 2 Lloyd's Rep 70; *Adams v Dunne* [1978] RTR 281.

[58] *Broad v Waland* (1942) 73 Ll L Rep 263; *James v British General Insurance Co* [1927] 2 KB 311; *General Accident Fire and Life Assurance Corpn Ltd v Shuttleworth* (1938) 60 Ll L Rep 301; *Dent v Blackmore* (1927) 29 Ll L Rep 9; *Cornhill Insurance Co Ltd v Assenheim* (1937) 58 Ll L Rep 27.

[59] SI 2002/3061, giving effect to part of the Fourth Motor Insurance Directive 2000/26/EC.

clear that the insured – and therefore the third party – has no right of action under the regulations against the insurer, but the third party will have such a right of action under section 151.[60] Similarly, if the policy has been terminated, but the certificate of insurance is still in the possession of the insured and no proceedings have been commenced for its recovery, the third party will be able to bring an action under section 151, but not under the regulations because there is no contract of insurance.[61]

3. The effect of exclusions in the policy

3.1 Third parties

Where a certificate of insurance has been delivered to the insured, any parts of the policy which purport to restrict the cover of the persons insured 'by reference to any matters mentioned in [s 148(2)] shall, as respects such liabilities as are required to be covered by a policy under section 145 of this Act, be of no effect' (section 148(1)). In short, the insurers are constrained as to the restrictions they can place in the policy with regard to cover for liability to third parties, including passengers. If a vehicle is used in a way that means it is not covered by the policy and that restriction does not fall within section 148(1), the insurers will not be liable, and even if the exclusion is within section 148(1) so that the insurers are liable to a third party, they may be able to recoup the payment from the insured if the terms of the policy allow this (section 148(6)).

The restrictions referred to in section 148(1) are (section 148(2)): (a) the age or physical or mental condition of drivers, (b) the condition of the vehicle, (c) the number of passengers the vehicle carries, (d) the weight or physical characteristics of goods the vehicle carries, (e) the times at which or the areas within which the vehicle is used, (f) the horsepower or cylinder capacity or value of the vehicle, and (g) the carrying of any particular apparatus or (h) of any means of identification other than as required under the Vehicle Excise and Registration Act 1994.[62] In addition, under section 148(5) the insurers cannot avoid their liability to third parties and passengers by making it subject to 'some specified thing being done or omitted to be done after the happening of the event giving rise to a claim.' So, the requirement in a policy that the insured must notify the insurers of an accident within a particular period of time will not defeat a claim by a third party. The logic of section 148(2) is unclear. Why have these matters been selected as ones for which the insurers should remain responsible, while others have been missed off the list? For example, why are the insurers liable if the car is in unroadworthy condition or is carrying more than the stipulated number of passengers, but not if the accident occurred while the insured, who was

---

[60] *Charlton v Fisher* [2001] 1 Lloyd's Rep IR 287. See *Hardy v Motor Insurers' Bureau* [1964] 2 QB 745; *Gardner v Moore* [1984] AC 548. See above ch 9
[61] Merkin and Stuart-Smith, *The Law of Motor Insurance*, see above n 1, 5–195.
[62] This Act consolidated legislation requiring the carrying of a valid vehicle licence (commonly known as the road tax disc) and the display of a registration mark (number plates).

covered for social and pleasure use, was driving to a business meeting. If the policy excludes liability for something that does not fall into one of the categories, then the insurers can avoid liability, which means that the motorist becomes uninsured and liability shifts to the Motor Insurers' Bureau, as will be seen below.

Liability to passengers cannot be negated or restricted or made subject to certain conditions by any antecedent agreement with the user of the vehicle (section 149(2)), nor by the passenger's voluntary acceptance of the risk of negligence (section 149(3).[63] However, the defence of contributory negligence is available,[64] and public policy considerations may affect the willingness of the court to give the passenger a remedy, such as, for instance, where the passenger participated in a criminal activity or knew the driver had been drinking and this led to the injury.[65] The insurers will not be liable if the passenger allowed himself to be carried in the vehicle knowing, or having reason to believe, that it had been stolen or unlawfully taken, and this knowledge was acquired before the journey began. If the passenger discovered the true facts after the journey began, the insurers will be liable, unless it is reasonable to expect the person to have alighted from the vehicle (section 151(4)).

Where, as is normal in a policy designed for private motorists, the insured driver is restricted by the policy to the use of the vehicle for specified purposes of a non-commercial nature, such as for social, domestic and pleasure purposes, or it excludes the use of the vehicle for hire or reward, or for business or commercial use, or for specified purposes of a business or commercial character, then with regard to the claims which are required to be covered under section 145, the use of the vehicle on a journey during which one or more passengers are carried at separate fares[66] will be treated as falling within either the specified use or outside the exclusions (section 150(1)). This will only be the case if: the vehicle is not adapted to carry more than eight passengers and is not a motor cycle; the fare or aggregate of fares does not exceed the running costs (including depreciation and general wear); and the fare arrangements were made before the journey began (section 150(2)). These provisions not only conform with the overall objective of the legislation, which is to ensure that third parties, including passengers, are covered by insurance, it also fits in with the desire of government to encourage car-sharing schemes and thereby, it is fondly hoped, reduce road congestion.[67]

3.2 The insured driver

If the insured warrants that the vehicle will be used in a particular way, a breach of that warranty does not necessarily mean that the policy is avoided, unless it can be shown that the parties agreed there would only be cover where the vehicle was used for that purpose.[68] There will also be no breach of warranty if the prospective insured

---

[63] This is designed to preclude a plea of *non volenti fit injuria*: *Gregory v Kelly* [1978] RTR 426.

[64] As, for instance, where the passenger failed to wear a seat-belt: *Gregory v Kelly*, ibid.

[65] *Ashton v Turner* [1981] QB 137; *Pitts v Hunt* [1991] 1 QB 24.

[66] As defined in Public Passenger Vehicles Act 1981, s 1(4) (Road Traffic Act 1988, s 150(4)).

[67] Since 1975 insurers have agreed not to regard contributions to petrol costs as falling within a term of the policy which excludes liability if the vehicle is used for hire or reward. The Transport Act 1980 added to the Road Traffic Act 1972 the provision which is now s 150. See PJ Taylor, TG Oliver and M Pether, *Bingham and Berrymans' Motor Claims Cases* (London, Butterworths, 1994) 824–5.

[68] *Roberts v Anglo-Saxon Insurance Association* (1927) 27 Ll L Rep 313.

expressed an intention as to use in the proposal form and, at that time, the answer given was correct: an insured, who answered a question about the nature of the goods to be carried on a lorry by saying 'coal', did not breach this warranty when, later, a mixed load of timber and coal was carried.[69] Normally, the use of the vehicle for a purpose that is not covered will not entitle the insurer to avoid the policy, but it will mean that cover is, in effect, suspended until the vehicle is once again used for a covered purpose.[70] It is worth, therefore, looking at cases that illustrate the way the courts have interpreted the meaning of some of the terms included in policies which are aimed at limiting use.

In construing a clause which stipulated that the vehicle must not be driven while in 'an unsafe or unroadworthy condition,' Goddard J drew an analogy with the warranty of seaworthiness implied into marine policies by the Marine Insurance Act 1906 and said that the condition will be satisfied if the vehicle was roadworthy at the commencement of the particular journey.[71] That analogy seems difficult to sustain—and, indeed, the Privy Council has refused to follow it[72]—if only because the discovery of a defect during a journey poses quite different problems for a car driver from those faced by a ship's crew, if only because, while the driver will usually be able to pull over, that option is not likely to be available to the ship's crew. There seems, therefore, less reason not to impose a continuing duty that the car be roadworthy while it is being driven and, in practice, the terms of modern policies specify such an obligation. The requirement that the car be roadworthy may be breached by the use of the car as well as by its condition: permitting nine passengers to travel in a car suitable for only four renders it unroadworthy.[73] It is enough that the car is unroadworthy for the term to be breached, it is irrelevant that the insured honestly believes, and has taken reasonable precautions to ensure, that the vehicle is roadworthy. If, however, the policy only requires that the insured 'shall take all due and reasonable precautions to safeguard the property insured and to keep it in a good state of repair,' the insured need only take reasonable care to ensure that the car is roadworthy. Similarly, where the policy requires the vehicle to be kept in an 'efficient condition' and a defect in the brakes can only be discovered by dismantling them, the insured will be covered,[74] unless the insurers are able to show that there was no reasonable system for periodical inspection of the vehicle.[75] Following this reasoning there was a breach where the defect related to the condition of the tyres since these could be readily inspected.[76] If the insured is in breach of such a term, the insurer may, nevertheless, be liable to an injured third party (see below), but may be able to claim for damages from the insured for that breach (section 148(4)).[77]

---

[69] *Provincial Insurance Co v Morgan* [1933] AC 240.
[70] *Farr v Motor Traders' Mutual Insurance Society Ltd* [1920] 3 KB 669; *Provincial Insurance Co Ltd v Morgan*, ibid.
[71] *Barrett v London General Insurance Co* [1935] 1 KB 238.
[72] *Trickett v Queensland Insurance* [1936] AC 159.
[73] *Clarke v General Accident Fire and Life Assurance Corpn plc*, above n 48.
[74] *Conn v Westminster Motor Insurance Association Ltd* [1966] 1 Lloyd's Rep 407; *Lefevere v White* [1990] 1 Lloyd's Rep 569.
[75] *Brown v Zurich Accident and Liability Insurance Co Ltd* [1954] 2 Lloyd's Rep 243. The insurer must show the insured (and not just an employee) was negligent: *Amey Properties Ltd v Cornhill Insurance plc* [1996] LRLR 259.
[76] *Conn v Westminster Motor Insurance Association Ltd*, above n 74; *Lefevere v White*, above n 74.
[77] There may be a remedy for breach of contract: *National Farmers' Union Mutual Insurance Society v Dawson* [1941] 2 KB 424.

It is normal to restrict cover for private motor vehicles to 'social, domestic and pleasure purposes,' although its precise meaning is not easy to convey. The words should be interpreted according to 'their natural, ordinary, normal and reasonable meaning'[78] and according to the context of the policy in which they are contained. Travelling to a meeting, at which a business deal was to be negotiated, was not covered, even though it was chosen as a comfortable (that is, a pleasurable) means of travel.[79] Indeed, travelling to work does not come within the phrase 'social, domestic and pleasure,' although policies are now routinely extended to cover such travel as well. A motorist was not covered when he helped out a friend's taxi business by picking up a customer, even though he did not charge for the journey.[80] On the other side is the decision in *Keeley v Pashen*.[81] Pashen's policy covered only 'social, domestic and pleasure including travel to and from permanent place of business' and expressly excluded 'use for hire or reward.' He used the car in a taxi business and deliberately drove at Keeley, a customer whom he had just dropped off. Keeley was killed and the insurers were held liable because at the time of the accident Pashen was not driving for hire or reward: Keeley had been dropped off and Pashen's purpose was to go home, even if in doing so he drove at Keeley in order to frighten him. In another case, the use of a local authority vehicle to transport visitors from France who had come to promote a town twinning was held to be within such cover on the grounds that the use in connection with the visit was social and voluntary and had nothing directly to do with the official duties of the local authority, in the sense of those which they were obliged to undertake by statute or by convention.[82] Where the insurance covers use of the vehicle for a particular business, there will be no cover if it is used for another type of business. Moreover, if the vehicle is used for two or more purposes simultaneously and one of those purposes is specifically excluded by the policy, the insurers will not be liable. For instance, there was no liability where a policy allowed the use for pleasure but not in connection with the motor trade, and it was driven, with permission, by a mechanic who, while taking his family for a ride, also used the journey to check the car for faults.[83] In such cases the courts look at the essential character of the journey.[84]

4. Where the driver is uninsured or cannot be traced

4.1 Motor Insurers' Bureau

In spite of the provisions of the legislation, there will be occasions on which a third party has no real remedy, such as where the driver is uninsured and has insufficient

---

[78] *Wood v General Accident Fire and Life Assurance Corpn* (1948) 82 Ll L Rep 77 at 81, per Morris J. See above ch 8.
[79] *Wood v General Accident Fire and Life Assurance Corpn*, ibid.
[80] *Orr v Trafalgar Insurance Co Ltd* (1948) 82 Ll L Rep 1.
[81] [2004] EWCA Civ 1491.
[82] *DHR Moody (Chemists) Ltd v Iron Trades Mutual Insurance Co Ltd* [1971] 1 Lloyd's Rep 386.
[83] *Browning v Phoenix Assurance Co Ltd* [1960] 2 Lloyd's Rep 360.
[84] *Seddon v Binions, Zurich Insurance Co Ltd (Third Party)* [1978] 1 Lloyd's Rep 381.

means to meet a claim, or where the driver simply cannot be traced, as in a 'hit-and-run'. In 1937 a Departmental Committee chaired by Sir Felix Cassel recommended the creation of arrangements with respect to uninsured drivers, although not the victims of hit-and-run accidents. This led to an agreement in 1945 between the government and those insurers who undertook compulsory motor insurance. The agreement was replaced in 1988 and again in 1999. In 1969 an agreement on compensating the victims of untraced drivers was also signed; this was replaced by further agreements in 1972, 1996 and 2003. The Motor Insurers' Bureau (MIB) administers the schemes. Although the agreements are made between the MIB and the government, and, technically, cannot be enforced by a victim, for obvious reasons the MIB has not argued this point to defeat claims and the courts have never raised it as an issue.[85] In any event, there is now a statutory right to claim from the MIB.[86] It was decided in *Hardy v Motor Insurers' Bureau*[87] that even if the motorist, had they been insured, could not have claimed an indemnity from their insurer because the act which caused the injury amounted to a wilful and culpable crime, the third party can still claim against the MIB. The House of Lords agreed with this view in *Gardner v Moore*,[88] pointing out that to conclude otherwise was contrary to the objective of the scheme, which is to compensate victims. The fact that this might also have the effect of benefiting the uninsured driver was regarded as incidental. Nevertheless, it should be remembered that the MIB was established to cover claims that come within the terms of the insurance required under the Road Traffic Acts, so that if, for instance, the victim is injured in a place which is not a 'road or other public place' there is no claim against the MIB.[89]

4.2 Victims of uninsured drivers

Under the agreement entitled, 'Compensation of Victims of Uninsured Drivers' (1999), the MIB is obliged to pay an eligible claimant who has obtained a judgment, which has not been satisfied. That obligation exists whether or not that judgment is covered by a contract of insurance and whatever the reason for the failure to satisfy the judgment (clause 5). Where the claimant has received compensation from the Financial Services Compensation Scheme,[90] or an insurer, or any other source, the MIB may deduct this from the payment (clause 17). Although liability for personal

---

[85] *Albert v Motor Insurers' Bureau* [1972] AC 301 at 312, per Lord Donovan. The European Court of Justice has concluded that these agreements comply with the requirements of European law and of the European Convention on Human Rights with regard to the use of a non-statutory body, the non-payment of interest and costs and the provision of a fair hearing, see *Evans v Secretary Of State for the Environment, Transport and the Regions* Case C-63/01 [2004] Lloyd's Rep IR 391.

[86] Motor Vehicles (Compulsory Insurance) (Information Centre and Compensation Body) Regs 2003 (2003/37), regs 12(3) and 13(2).

[87] See above n 60.

[88] See above n 60. Under the Criminal Justice Act 1988, s 110(7), the victim of the criminal actions of a motorist who succeeds in a claim against the Bureau cannot also make a claim under the Criminal Injuries Compensation Scheme.

[89] *Randall v Motor Insurers' Bureau*, above n 44; *Clarke v General Accident Fire and Life Assurance Corpn plc*, above n 48. On claims against the MIB, see N Jervis and J Dawson, *A Practical Guide to Handling Motor Insurers' Bureau Claims* (London, Cavendish, 2001); see also, Merkin and Stuart-Smith, *The Law of Motor Insurance*, above n 1.

[90] See above ch 2.

injury or death is not limited, the MIB will only compensate property damage up to £250,000 (clause 16) and is not liable for the first £300 (clause 1). The claimant is obliged to assign to the MIB the unsatisfied judgment (clause 15.1(a)) and must undertake to repay any sum received from the MIB if the judgment is subsequently set aside, or any sum received from any person by way of compensation, which would have been deducted under clause 17 (clause 15.1(b)).

Before the liability of the MIB is established a number of conditions must be met. The application must be made in the prescribed form (clause 7); proper notice must be given to the MIB of the bringing of the relevant proceedings before or within 14 days of their commencement (clause 9); and such further information relating to those proceedings as is required under clause 11 must be provided (see also clause 12; 'Notes for the Guidance of Victims of Road Accidents,' notes 5–7). As soon as reasonably practicable, the claimant must have demanded the information specified in section 154(1) of the 1988 Act, which concerns the insurance cover of someone against whom a claim has been made, and where such a demand is not complied with, the claimant must have made a formal complaint to the police and used all reasonable endeavours to obtain the name and address of the registered keeper of the vehicle (clause 13.1; 'Notes for the Guidance of Victims of Road Accidents,' note 4). If the MIB requires, the claimant must have taken all reasonable steps to obtain judgment against all those who may be liable, including anyone who may be vicariously liable, and the claimant must, if requested, consent to the MIB being joined as a party to the relevant proceedings (clause 14.1). Any dispute as to the reasonableness of a requirement imposed by the MIB can be referred by the claimant or the MIB to the Secretary of State, whose decision is final (clause 19(1)).

There are exceptions to the liability of the MIB (clause 6.1):

(a) a claim arising out of the use of a vehicle owned by or in the possession of the Crown, unless responsibility for the existence of a contract of insurance had been undertaken by some other person (whether or not the person liable was in fact covered by a contract of insurance), or unless the relevant liability was in fact covered by a contract of insurance;

(b) a claim arising out of the use of a vehicle which is not required to be covered under section 144,[91] unless that use is in fact covered;

(c) a claim by someone, who has not suffered the loss, in respect of a cause of action or judgment assigned to them, or pursuant to a right of subrogation or contractual or other right;

(d) a claim in respect of damage to a motor vehicle, which, as the claimant knew or ought to have known, was uninsured;

(e) a claim made in respect of a liability incurred by the owner or user of the vehicle in which the claimant was being voluntarily carried and, either before the commencement of the journey or after such commencement (if it was reasonable to expect the claimant to have alighted), the claimant knew or ought to have known that it had been stolen, or was uninsured, or was being used in the course of a crime or to avoid lawful apprehension (also clauses 6.2 and 6.5).

---

[91] This exempts from the requirement to have liability insurance those vehicles owned by someone who has deposited security with the court or by various state agencies.

Concerning the degree of knowledge required, in *White v White*,[92] the House of Lords held that the claimant must have actual knowledge or must have deliberately chosen to ignore something of which they were aware. In *Pickett v Motor Insurers' Bureau*,[93] a passenger in a car, which, when the journey commenced, she knew was uninsured, attempted to get out of the vehicle when the driver started doing handbrake turns, but he refused to stop and she was injured. The Court of Appeal held by a majority that, while consent could be withdrawn, in this case the passenger had not done so. The passenger must unequivocally repudiate the common venture, but here she had simply objected to the method of driving and the common venture, which was having fun, had not been ended. This test does seem to make it difficult for a passenger to withdraw consent, but that may be the point. Pill LJ, who dissented, took the view that the handbrake turns had changed the nature of the venture to which she had consented and her exhortation 'For God's sake to stop the car' together with her attempts to get out of the car meant that she had withdrawn consent. While the burden of proof in relation to the knowledge of the claimant is on the MIB, in the absence of evidence to the contrary, proof by the MIB of the following matters is sufficient: that the claimant was the owner or registered keeper of the vehicle or had caused or permitted its use, or knew that the user was neither its owner nor registered keeper (nor an employee of these people) nor the owner or registered keeper of any other vehicle; that the claimant knew the vehicle was being used by someone who was below the minimum age to qualify for the relevant driving licence or who was disqualified (clause 6.3). The claimant's knowledge for these purposes includes matters of which that person could reasonably be expected to have been aware, but for the self-induced influence of drink or drugs (clause 6.4).

Assuming that the application has been made in proper form, the MIB is required to give a reasoned reply to a request from the claimant regarding the claim, and as soon as reasonably practicable notify the claimant of its decision, together with reasons (clause 18). The claimant may seek an interim payment from the MIB ('Notes for the Guidance of Victims of Road Accidents,' note 8).

7.3 Victims of untraced drivers

The original MIB agreement covered only uninsured but identified drivers and not untraced or 'hit-and-run' drivers,[94] and it was only in 1969 that this anomaly was addressed. The current agreement is titled, 'Compensation of Victims of Untraced Drivers' (2003). This applies where: death, injury or damage to property has arisen out of the use of a motor vehicle on a road or other public place; the loss occurred in circumstances giving rise to a liability that is required to be covered by insurance under the 1988 Act; and it is not possible to identify all of the persons who appear to be liable (clause 4(1)(a)–(d)). The application must be made not later than three years after the relevant event where the claim involves personal injury, and not later than nine months where it involves damage to property, unless the applicant could not reasonably have been expected to have become aware of the losses in which case those

---

[92] [2001] 1 WLR 481.
[93] [2004] Lloyd's Rep IR 513.
[94] The MIB did give *ex gratia* payments in certain cases: *Adams v Andrews* [1964] 2 Lloyd's Rep 347 at 351, per Sachs J.

time limits are extended (clause 4(1)(a), (b)). The accident must have been reported to the police within specified time limits and the applicant must have co-operated with any investigation (clause 4(1)(c)-(e)).

The agreement does not apply in the following circumstances (clause 5(1)):

(a) where there is no claim for personal injury and the damage to property arose out of the use of an unidentified vehicle;

(b) where the loss occurred at a time when the vehicle was owned by or in the possession of the Crown, unless someone had undertaken responsibility for insurance;

(c) where the applicant allowed themselves to be carried in the vehicle and, before the commencement of the journey (or later if alighting could reasonably have been expected), knew or ought to have known that the vehicle had been stolen, or was uninsured, or was being used in crime (other than an offence under the Traffic Acts, except section 143 of the 1988 Act) or to avoid lawful apprehension (also clause 4.4(a), (c)). The provisions on burden of proof, including where the applicant is under the influence of drink or drugs, are the same as those that apply to the agreement on uninsured drivers (clause 4(2), (4)(b); see above);

(d) where the loss was caused by an act of terrorism;

(e) where property damaged was insured and the applicant has recovered the loss in full;

(f) where the claim is in respect of damage to a motor vehicle, which, as the claimant knew or ought to have known, was uninsured (but without prejudice to any other application for compensation);

(g) where the claim is made by someone, who has not suffered the loss, in respect of a cause of action or judgment assigned to them, or pursuant to a right of subrogation or contractual or other right.

The MIB is required, at its own expense, to take reasonable steps to investigate a claim (clause 7. There is an accelerated procedure under clauses 26–27). It is only obliged to make an award if satisfied on the balance of probabilities that the loss was caused in circumstances that indicate the unidentified person would have been held liable for that loss (clause 7(6)). In essence, the amount of the award will be equivalent to that which a court would have awarded (clauses 8, 9). Any award for property damage will have deducted £300 and will not exceed £250,000 (clause 8(3)). Where the MIB decides to make a payment, it will contribute towards the cost of certain aspects of any legal advice (clause 10). There are also provisions for apportioning liability where one of the parties responsible for the loss is identified (clauses 12–15).

The application must be made in the prescribed form and the applicant must provide such assistance as may be reasonably required to enable MIB to investigate (clause 11(1)–(3)). The applicant must, if reasonably required to do so by the MIB before its determination of the application, bring proceedings (or authorise the MIB to bring such proceedings) against anyone who may, in addition to the unidentified person, be liable in respect of the loss. In addition, the applicant must assign to the MIB any judgment obtained (subject to the MIB paying over any amount by which the judgment exceeds the original payment by the MIB) and must undertake to assign any sum received after payment by the MIB, which would have limited its liability (clause 11(4)–(6)). There are detailed provisions as to the notification of decisions and awards by the MIB (clause 17) and the treatment of appeals (clauses 18–23. There is also a procedure for referring other disputes to an arbitrator: clause 28). Any appeal is heard by a single arbitrator appointed by the Secretary of State, who can determine whether the agreement applies, remit the application to the MIB for investigation and decision, determine whether the MIB should make an award and what that award should be, determine any other question that has been referred, and make any award of costs thought to be appropriate (see schedule to the agreement). The applicant can request an oral hearing, but where the arbitrator concludes that this was unnecessary the award of any costs may be appropriately adjusted (clause 23). The applicant or anyone acting for the applicant may be liable for the arbitrator's fee where the arbitrator concludes there were no reasonable grounds for the appeal (clause 24(2)). If the arbitrator increases the award, the MIB may be ordered to contribute towards the costs of any legal representation (clause 24(4)).

14

Liability Insurance

Insurance effected against the risk of incurring tortious liability to a third party is now almost universal.[1] The fear to individuals or businesses that they may be confronted with a tort claim which could not be met out of their own resources has led to the rapid expansion of liability insurance over the last seventy years or so. To take just two major spheres of activity – motoring and employment – insurance against third party liability is compulsory. Indeed, occupiers of premises will also generally hold liability insurance against the risk of injury to a third party while on the property. A liability insurance policy is a contract of indemnity and, as explained by Fletcher Moulton LJ in *British Cash and Parcel Conveyors Ltd v Lamson Store Service Company Ltd*,[2] it can take various forms:

> Sometimes, as in the case of fire insurance or the ordinary forms of marine insurance, the indemnity is against the accidents of life. But frequently the insurance is against claims which may be made by third parties. The whole of the contracts of insurance of employers against claims by employees under the Employers' Liability Act and the Workmen's Compensation Act are of this kind, and so far from such contracts being illegal or tainted with any invalidity, the Courts are continually engaged in giving effect to them by deciding actions admittedly brought or defended by the insurance companies in the names of the insured...These instances by no means exhaust the types of contracts of indemnity against claims made by third persons. Nothing is more common than that contractors putting up machinery or carrying out engineering works should indemnify the persons employing them against claims for nuisance or trespass in connection therewith...Indeed it would be idle to attempt a complete enumeration of all the varied types of contracts of indemnity against claims by third persons, and, unless there is something improper in the nature of such a contract arising out of the circumstances attending its origin, the Courts have never shown any disapprobation of such contracts or any disinclination to enforce them.[3]

Being an indemnity contract the insured cannot recover until loss is suffered as a result of the occurrence of the risk. This, of course, is determined by reference to the terms of the policy. As will be seen below in relation to the Third Parties (Rights Against Insurers) Act 1930, the Court of Appeal has held that the insurer's liability to

---

[1] See further, P Cane, *Tort Law and Economic Interests* (Oxford, Clarendon Press, 1996) ch 9.
[2] [1908] 1 KB 1006.
[3] Ibid, at 1014–15.

indemnify triggers only when the insured's liability to the victim has been established either by a court or by an award in arbitration proceedings or by agreement.[4]

Broadly, there are two types of liability policies: claims made and losses occurring. Under a claims made policy, the insured is covered for any claim made against him by a third party during the currency of the policy, irrespective of when the events giving rise to the claim occurred. Such policies also allow the insured to notify the insurers of circumstances which may give rise to a claim and which come to the knowledge of the insured during the currency of the policy: if the circumstances are duly notified, any subsequent claim is deemed to have been made within the policy year. Professional indemnity liability policies are written on this basis. Under a losses occurring cover, which is typically used by employers and to protect against other forms of physical loss, the policy covers events which take place during the currency of the policy. In most an insured's negligence will cause immediate loss, so that there is no need to distinguish between negligence and damage in ascertaining the relevant event covered. However, in some situations the damage caused by an act of negligence may not manifest itself for many years, as in the case of exposure to harmful substances, and the policy may on its proper construction cover either the act of exposure itself or the damage inflicted.

In this chapter we examine briefly those contract terms which are commonly included in liability insurance policies. We then consider the law governing employers' liability insurance; and finally, we turn to the statutory protection afforded to a third party seeking to claim against an insolvent insured. Motor insurance is considered in chapter 13, above.

1. Standard terms in liability insurance policies

1.1 Co-operation clauses

It was commented in chapter 10 that liability policies generally contain co-operation clauses whereby the insured undertakes, inter alia, not to admit liability or to offer settlement of a claim without first obtaining the insurers' consent. Such a clause will also commonly go on to reserve to the insurer the right to take over and conduct in the name of the insured the defence or settlement of a claim. The nature of this type of term was considered in *Terry v Trafalgar Insurance Co Ltd*.[5] The claimant, who

---

[4] *Post Office v Norwich Union Fire Insurance Society Ltd* [1967] 2 QB 363 at 373, *per* Lord Denning MR; approved by the House of Lords in *Bradley v Eagle Star Insurance Co Ltd* [1989] AC 957 at 966, *per* Lord Brandon. Somewhat curiously, Colman J held in *Lumberman's Mutual Casualty Co v Bovis Lend Lease Ltd* [2005] Lloyd's Rep IR 74, that a settlement which did not quantify the insured's loss is not a settlement at all for liability insurance purposes. In so holding, Colman J agreed with the insurers' contention, based upon the decisions in *Post Office* and *Bradley*, that in liability insurance the insured can recover an indemnity 'only in respect of a legal liability which has been "ascertained" or, in the case of a settlement, proved, to exist and in an amount which has been ascertained by judgment or arbitration award or, in the case of a settlement, which does not exceed the true amount for which the assured would have been liable to the third party but for the settlement.'
[5] [1970] 1 Lloyd's Rep 524.

was involved in a motor collision with a third party, apologised to him at the scene of the accident and later that day wrote admitting liability. The claimant's policy with the defendant insurers contained the following clause: 'No liability shall be admitted or legal expenses incurred nor any offer promise or payment made to Third Parties without the Company's written consent... .' This was described in the policy as a condition precedent to the liability of the insurers. Initially, the claimant sought to settle with the third party but upon being informed that the damage to the vehicle was more severe than was first appreciated, he sought to claim on his insurance. The insurers denied liability. The claimant argued first, that the policy condition was contrary to public policy insofar as it tended to cause the insured to lie about what happened, or at least conceal the truth; and secondly, that the condition was subject to the implication that no liability should be admitted if it was to the prejudice of the insurers.

Judge Graham Rogers held that the claimant's first line of argument was based on a false premise, he said:

> this is a fanciful argument; the condition does not require the insured to lie, but to refrain from admissions of liability. There is a world of difference between giving a factual account of what happened, without giving any expression of opinion as to blame, and an admission of liability. This is and has been for many years a standard condition of motor insurance policies, and in my view it is clearly a necessary and proper one for the protection of insurance companies.[6]

With respect to the claimant's second contention, the judge held that whether the condition should be read as being subject to any proviso as to prejudice, the insurers were, in any case, certainly prejudiced by the claimant's admission of blame: '[B]y his letter, written within hours of the accident, the defendants were shut out from any negotiations, and deprived of a possible chance of a favourable settlement.'[7]

Where the insurers choose to exercise the right to defend or settle a claim,[8] they can dictate the way in which the action will be pursued provided they act bona fide in 'the common interest of themselves and the insured.'[9] Thus, although the solicitor appointed to conduct the case owes a duty of care to the insured,[10] nevertheless where, in accordance with the terms of the policy, the insurers give tactical instructions to the solicitor, the insured cannot complain.[11]

---

[6] Ibid, at 526.

[7] Ibid, at 527.

[8] Cf typical US policies under which insurers are bound to take over the insured's defence. In this regard, see the model Unfair Claims Settlement Process Act produced by the National Association of Insurance Commissioners. Most states have adopted versions of this model. For a more detailed discussion of the US position, see J Lowry and P Rawlings, 'Insurers, Claims and the Boundaries of Good Faith' [2005] *MLR* 82. See further, the judgment of Stephen J in *Distillers-Bio-Chemicals (Australia) Property Ltd* v *Ajax Insurance Co Ltd* (1973) 130 CLR 1, discussed below.

[9] *Groom* v *Crocker* [1939] 1 KB 194 at 203, *per* Lord Greene MR. See further, *Gan v Tai Ping (Nos 2 & 3)* [2001] Lloyd's Rep IR 667, CA; *Eagle Star v Cresswell* [2004] Lloyd's Rep IR 437.

[10] Ibid.

[11] Ibid.

1.2 The insurer's duty of good faith in the settlement process

The respective interests of the insured and the insurer with respect to the settlement of third party claims was considered in *Distillers-Bio-Chemicals (Australia) Property Ltd v Ajax Insurance Co Ltd.*[12] The case arose out of the thalidomide scandal of the 1970s in which drugs prescribed to pregnant women containing thalidomide caused severe physical damage to their unborn foetuses. It was alleged that Distillers were negligent in their failure to detect the side effects of the drug before releasing it for prescription. Distillers, who had public liability insurance with Ajax, wished to settle with the third parties who had commenced an action against the company in negligence. Ajax, however, refused to consent to this and also declined to conduct the company's defence. It was held by the High Court of Australia that Ajax could refuse its consent without incurring liability.

Stephen J observed that in relation to the question of whether to settle with a third party, the interests of the insured and the insurer are often tangentially opposed. While the insured will wish to settle the claim at any figure provided it is within the policy limits, the insurer may wish to use the deterrent of protracted litigation in order to negotiate a relatively low settlement figure. Where the third party's case is strong and a damage award above the sum insured is likely, the urgency of settlement will become a matter of paramount concern to the insured. Against this, the insurer's financial interest will be best served by seeking to avoid liability to indemnify altogether. In this situation it will not wish to exercise the right to defend the claim and by withholding its consent to a settlement, the insurer may well procure a breach of condition should the insured go ahead and settle without first obtaining the insurer's consent. Given the vulnerable position of the insured, the judge stressed that the insurer's power to prevent a settlement cannot be used arbitrarily but must be 'exercised in good faith having regard to the interests of the insured as well as to its interests and in the exercise of its power to withhold consent the insurer must not have regard to considerations extraneous to the policy of indemnity.'[13]

Thus, if the third party's case is strong and it is likely to succeed in any ensuing litigation, the insurer should not unreasonably withhold its consent to a settlement within the policy limits. Where consent is refused but the insured nevertheless negotiates a reasonable settlement figure with the third party, the insurer will be liable to indemnify him. But if the third party's case is weak and the insured seeks to settle in order, for example, to avoid damaging publicity, the insurer's refusal to grant its consent may, in the circumstances, be justified.

Subject to the requirement of good faith, an insurer can settle a claim without the insured's approval.[14] As far as is possible, the insurer should seek to settle within the limits of the sum insured and, in any case, should not reject an offer of settlement which falls within the policy limits. So far, the English courts have not been called upon to consider the position where an insurer has refused to settle for a sum within the policy limits and the third party has gone on to recover damages greater than the sum insured. It has been argued that the insurer would be in breach of its duty of good faith and so would, in any case, be liable to indemnify the insured for the full

---

[12] Above, n 8.
[13] Ibid, at 26–7, See also *Groom v Crocker*, above, n 9; and *Beacon Insurance Co Ltd v Langdale* [1939] 4 All ER 209, both of which were cited by Stephen J.
[14] *Beacon Insurance Co Ltd v Langdale*, ibid.

amount.[15] Against this, it may be countered that on a strict view of the typical policy, an insurer is not bound to settle or take over the insured's defence and so its maximum liability should be limited to the sum insured.

1.3 Waiver and estoppel

Where an insurer decides to exercise its right to take over and conduct the defence or settlement of a claim on behalf of the insured, it does not necessarily follow that it will be estopped from subsequently avoiding liability because, for example, it discovers that the insured is in breach of warranty or has failed to disclose a material fact.[16] In order for estoppel to operate in this context two conditions must be satisfied: first, that the insurer's conduct in taking over the defence of the claim amounted to an unequivocal representation that it was liable on the policy; and secondly, it must be shown that the insured acted upon the insurer's representation. There is dicta to the effect that simply defending the insured does not necessarily estop the insurer from subsequently denying liability, the reason being that the insurer's conduct is not in itself unequivocal. In *Soole v Royal Insurance Co Ltd*,[17] Shaw J stated that:

> the assumption of control of the proceedings is equivocal. It does not necessarily imply a representation by the insurers that they regard the claim which is the subject matter of those proceedings as one which *must* give rise to a liability to indemnify the insured. It indicates no more that it appears that it may give rise to such liability. Hence the insurers would not be estopped from asserting that the particular claim was, in the event, never within the ambit of the policy.[18]

But if, on the other hand, the insurer has knowledge of the insured's breach prior to defending him, the insured may be able to assume that the insurer has waived the breach.[19]

---

2. Employers' liability insurance

The liability of employers for industrial injuries or disease caused to employees continues to be one of the most litigated areas of the tort of negligence.[20] Operating in

---

[15] See J Birds and NJ Hird, *Birds' Modern Insurance Law* (London, Sweet & Maxwell, 2004) at 362, who argue, citing the decision of the Supreme Court of California in *Crisci v Security Insurance Co* 66 Cal (2d) 425, 426 P (2d) 173 (1967), that the insurer would be liable for the full amount. See further, J Lowry and P Rawlings, 'Insurers, Claims and the Boundaries of Good Faith' above n 8, at 92 *et seq*.

[16] See further, chs 4 and 7, above.

[17] [1971] 2 Lloyd's Rep 332.

[18] Ibid, at 339–40. Waiver has to be judged by the insurer's conduct towards the insured and not the third party claimant: see *Spriggs v Wessington Court School* [2005] EWHC 1432.

[19] See *Fraser v Furman (Productions) Ltd* [1967] 1 WLR 898 at 909, in which Diplock LJ, observed that 'one of the terms of the [liability] policy is that the insurers take over the conduct of the action, and, if they did so and failed to repudiate with knowledge of the facts, they would be estopped from doing so thereafter.' See also, *Evans v Employers' Mutual Insurance Association Ltd* [1936] 1 KB 505.

[20] See further, J Murphy, *Street on Torts* (London, Lexis Nexis, 2003) 266 *et seq*. BS Markesinis and SF Deakin, *Tort Law* (Oxford, Clarendon Press, 2003), ch 3; NJ McBride and R Bagshaw, *Tort Law* (Harlow, Longman, 2005) chs 27 and 28. See generally, N Wikely, A Ogus and E Barendt, *Law of Social Security* (London, LexisNexis, 2002).

tandem with the common law there are a range of statutory duties imposed on employers in respect of employee safety. The state scheme for industrial injuries provides for compensation without the need to prove fault. However, actions in negligence remain the preferred route for claimants because of the higher level of common law damages. As with actions against impecunious or uninsured defendants generally, little is gained from litigation if a damage award cannot be actually recovered. In order to ensure that an employee who is awarded damages for negligence against an employer receives the compensation due to him, the Employers' Liability (Compulsory Insurance) Act 1969 requires employers to insure against liability for injuries sustained by employees in the course of their employment.[21] Section 1(1) of the Act provides that subject to certain exceptions contained in s 2 and s 3,[22] 'every employer carrying on any business in Great Britain shall insure, and maintain insurance, under one or more *approved policies* with an authorised insurer or insurers against liability for bodily injury or disease sustained by his employees, and arising *out of and in the course of their employment* in Great Britain in that business, but except in so far as regulations otherwise provide not including injury or disease suffered or contracted outside Great Britain.'[23]

2.1 The ambit of the statutory duty – the course of employment

The key to determining the scope of the employers' duty to insure against liability to employees lies in the meaning of the phrase, contained in s 1(1) above, namely, 'arising out of and in the course of their employment.' This form of wording also appears in the Road Traffic Act 1988, s 145 and in the old workmen's compensation legislation. In *Moore v Manchester Liners Ltd*,[24] Lord Loreburn defined 'the course of employment' as meaning that the event, normally an accident, giving rise to the employee's claim must: 'arise when the employee is doing what a man so employed might reasonably do during a time during which he was employed and at a place where he may reasonably be during that time to do that thing.'[25]

As a general rule, an employee's journey to and from his place of work is not ordinarily in the course of employment unless the journey in question is so closely connected with the employee's work that the general principle ceases to apply.[26] In

---

[21] The Act entered into force on 1 January 1972.

[22] It should be noted that risks which must be covered under a motor insurance policy by virtue of the Road Traffic Act 1988 need not be included in an employers' liability policy: see the Employers' Liability (Compulsory Insurance) Regulations 1998, SI 1998/2573. Section 3(1) and (2) of the 1969 Act exempt certain employers from the statutory duty to insure. In general these are local authorities. See also the Employers' Liability (Compulsory Insurance) (Amendment) Regulations 2004 (SI 2004 No 2882).

[23] Emphasis inserted. An employers' liability policy, together with any tort claims, is transferred on the sale of the business: the Transfer of Undertakings (Protection of Employment) Regulations 1981; see *Martin v Lancashire CC* [2000] Lloyd's Rep IR 665.

[24] [1910] AC 498.

[25] Ibid, at 500–1.

[26] In *Smith v Stages* [1989] AC 928 at 955, Lord Lowry stated that: 'The paramount rule is that an employee travelling on the highway will be acting in the course of his employment if, and only if, he is at the material time going about his employer's business. One must not confuse the duty to turn up for one's work with the concept of already being "on duty"" while travelling to it.'

Smith v Stages,[27] an employee, M, a peripatetic lagger, had been instructed to work away from his usual workplace at the Drakelow power station in Staffordshire to undertake urgent work at Pembroke power station in Wales. As soon as the work was completed M was driven back to his home in Staffordshire on a Bank Holiday Monday by a colleague so that he could resume work at his usual place of employment the next day. During the journey the car left the road and crashed into a brick wall. Both men were seriously injured. M was paid by his employers for the day he needed to travel back on the same basis as any normal working day. The House of Lords held that at the time of the accident M was acting in the course of his employment. Lord Goff, having reiterated the fundamental principle that an employee remained in the course of his employment when he is doing what he is employed to do or anything reasonably incidental to his or her employment,[28] stressed that in determining the course of employment there are a number of factors to be taken into account,none of which are decisive.[29] In this respect, Lord Goff went on to state that:

> the fact that a man is being paid by his employer in respect of the relevant period of time is often important, but cannot of itself be decisive.... . I approach the matter as follows. I do not regard this case as an ordinary case of travelling to work... In my opinion, in all the circumstances of the case, [M] was required by the employers to make this journey...and it would be proper to describe him as having been employed to do so...the Monday, a normal working day, was made available for the journey, with full pay for that day to perform a task which he was required by the employers to perform...the journey was therefore made in the course of his employment.[30]

On the other hand, in *Vandyke v Fender*,[31] V and F, who were both employed by the same company as skilled moulders and who worked some distance from home, were provided with a car by their employer so that F could drive himself and V to their place of work. The employer also contributed towards the cost of petrol. During a journey to work they were involved in an accident caused by F's negligence in which V was seriously injured. V brought an action in negligence for damages against F and the employer. The employer joined as third party its insurers under an employers' liability policy. One of the issues before the court was whether the employers' liability policy covered this risk or whether the claim should be directed to the relevant motor insurer. It was held that the employers' liability insurer was not liable as the accident did not occur during the course of R and F's employment. Driving to work is not the same as driving at work and, in any case, V was under no obligation to travel in the car. Lord Denning MR, having reviewed the authorities,[32] observed that:

---

[27] Ibid. See also *Elleanor and Cavendish Woodhouse Ltd v Comerford* [1973] 1 Lloyd's Rep 313; and *Paterson v Costain & Press (Overseas) Ltd* [1979] 2 Lloyd's Rep 204. See further, J Murphy, *Street on Torts,* at 566, *et seq.*

[28] See *R v National Insurance Commissioner, ex p Michael* [1977] 1 WLR 109.

[29] Citing the judgment of Sir John Donaldson MR in *Nancollas v Insurance Officer* [1985] 1 All ER 833, at 836.

[30] Above, n 26, at 938–9.

[31] [1970] 2 QB 292.

[32] The two leading cases being, *St Helen's Colliery Co Ltd v Hewitson* [1924] AC 59; and *Weaver v Tredegar Iron & Coal Co Ltd* [1940] AC 955.

They show, to my mind quite conclusively, that when a man is going to or coming from work, along a public road, as a passenger in a vehicle provided by his employer, he is not then in the course of his employment – unless he is *obliged* by the terms of his employment to travel in that vehicle. It is not enough that he should have the right to travel in the vehicle, or be permitted to travel in it. He must have an *obligation* to travel in it. Else he is not in the course of his employment.[33]

Whether or not an employee was acting in the course of employment is a question of law which, as indicated by Lord Goff in *Smith,* is determined by a range of indecisive tests which have been devised by the judges on a case by case basis. The application of these legal tests to a particular case is, of course, a matter of fact. Given the sheer diversity of employment relationships these questions of fact often cause considerable difficulty with the consequence that attempting to predict a particular outcome is generally a fatuous exercise.

2.2 Approved policies

The reference in s 1(1) of the 1969 Act to 'approved policies' is defined in s 1(3) as meaning 'a policy of insurance not subject to any conditions or exceptions prohibited for these purposes by regulations.' The Employers' Liability (Compulsory Insurance) Regulations lay down four prohibited conditions 'in whatever terms.'[34] In general, any term which is a condition precedent to liability is prohibited for the purposes of the Act.[35] More particularly, Regulation 2(1) provides that:

there is prohibited in any contract of insurance any condition which provides (in whatever terms) that no liability (either generally or in respect of a particular claim) shall arise under the policy, or that any such liability so arising shall cease, if:

(a) some specified thing is done or omitted to be done after the happening of the event giving rise to a claim under the policy[36];

(b) the policy holder does not take reasonable care to protect his employees against the risk of bodily injury or disease in the course of their employment[37];

(c) the policy holder fails to comply with the requirements of any enactment for the protection of employees against the risk of bodily injury or disease in the course of their employment; or

---

[33] Above, n 31, at 305.
[34] SI 1998/2573, reg 2(1).
[35] See chs 7 and 10, above.
[36] See also the Road Traffic Act 1988, s 148(5) considered further in ch 13, above. The failure to give notice of a claim within a specified time limit or the failure to comply with a co-operation clause by, for example, admitting liability (see ch 10, above) will be caught by this provision.
[37] Obviously, as in liability insurance generally, a primary reason for effecting the policy is to cover the risk of liability arising from the tort of negligence. In *Woolfall and Rimmer Ltd v Moyle* [1941] 3 All ER 304, the Court of Appeal held that a condition which stated that 'the insured shall take reasonable precautions to prevent accidents' is not broken by a negligent act by a competent foreman selected by the employers to supervise their employees. Lord Greene MR stated, at 309: 'If the delegation was reasonable, and, if, in selecting that particular foreman to perform the task, the [insured] took reasonable precautions, their obligation under this condition was, in my opinion, at an end.' The probition in para (b) therefore confirms the common law position. However, a condition which provides that the insured's recklessness will relieve the insurers from liability may be enforceable. See further RA Hasson, 'The Employers' Liability (Compulsory Insurance) Act–A Broken Reed' [1974] *ILJ* 79.

(d)   the policy holder does not keep specified records or fails to provide the insurer with or make available to him information from such records.[38]

Regulation 2(2) prohibits any condition which requires: (a) an employee to pay, or (b) and insured employer to pay the employee, the first amount of any claim or any aggregation of claims. The Regulation expressly permits terms in a policy which require the employer 'to pay or contribute any sum to the insurer in respect of the satisfaction of any claim made under the contract of insurance by a relevant employee or any costs and expenses incurred in relation to any such claim.' A term in a policy which is not a condition precedent to liability and which gives the insurer the right to claim damages in the event of breach is therefore valid. Further, there is nothing in the statute which prevents an insurer avoiding the policy for non-disclosure, breach of warranty or misrepresentation.

Section 1(2) of the 1969 Act states that regulations may provide for the 'amount for which an employer is required by this Act to insure and maintain... .' The 1998 Regulations stipulate a sum insured of £5 million 'in respect of claims relating to any one or more of [the insured's] employees arising out of any one occurrence.'[39] The term 'occurrence' relates to the number of occasions the insured is negligent irrespective of the number of individual claimants who may sue as a result of any one occurrence.[40]

2.3 Employees to be covered

The term 'employee' for the purposes of the statutory duty borne by employers to insure against their liability for personal injury to employees is defined by s 2(1) of the 1969 Act. This provides that an employee is 'an individual who has entered into or works under a contract of service or apprenticeship with an employer whether by way of manual labour, clerical work or otherwise, whether such contract is express or implied, oral or in writing.' The duty to insure does not therefore extend to independent contractors who work under a contract for services. The distinction between a contract of service and a contract for services can be particularly narrow and it has long vexed the courts.[41]

Section 2(2) of the Act relieves the employer from insuring employees who are close relatives such as the employer's spouse, parent, grandparent, step-parent, child or grand child, step-child, and sibling including half-brother or half-sister. Employees who are not ordinarily resident in Great Britain are also excluded, subject to any regulation to the contrary.[42]

---

[38] Premiums are generally fixed by reference to an employer's wages bill and the breach of an express term requiring the maintenance of records in this respect will not, according to para (d), invalidate an employer's claim under a policy.

[39] Reg 3.

[40] *Forney v Dominion Insurance Co Ltd* [1969] 1 WLR 928.

[41] See, eg, *Stevenson Jordan & Harrison Ltd v MacDonald & Evans* [1952] 1 TLR 101 at 102, *per* Denning LJ. See also, *Ready Mixed Concrete (South East) Ltd v Minister of Pensions and National Insurance* [1968] 2 QB 497; *Market Investigations Ltd v Minister of Social Security* [1969] 2 QB 173; *Ferguson v John Dawson and Partners (Contractors) Ltd* [1976] 1 WLR 1213; and *Lane v Shire Roofing Co (Oxford) Ltd* [1995] TLR 104.

[42] The definition of 'relevant employee' is contained in reg 1(2).

2.4 Penalty for failure to insure

The 1998 Regulations stipluate that every insured employer shall be issued by the insurer with a certificate of insurance which must be displayed at the employer's place of business.[43] Section 5 of the 1969 Act provides that an employer who fails to effect liability insurance in accordance with the Act shall be liable on summary conviction to a fine of up to £1,000 per day. In *Richardson v Pitt-Stanley Ltd*,[44] the Court of Appeal, by a majority,[45] held that the statute did not confer upon the claimant, an injured employee, the right to bring a civil action against the directors and secretary of the company for their failure to effect liability insurance. The claimant had sought to claim damages from the company which, having gone into liquidation, lacked sufficient assets to satisfy the judgment he had obtained against it. The decision is curious when viewed against the mischief which the statute was clearly intended to address and, as such, it has been strongly criticised.[46]

---

3. Third Parties (Rights Against Insurers) Act 1930

It will be recalled that at common law,[47] where a person who had liability insurance became bankrupt, or if a company went into liquidation, a third party with an outstanding claim was left a vulnerable position because he would have to prove in the bankruptcy or liquidation proceedings as an ordinary creditor of the insured. The position was that once an insured became insolvent, any insurance moneys paid by way of indemnity went into the general pool for the benefit of all the insured's general creditors.[48] The common law position was manifestly unjust and so the Third Parties (Rights Against Insurers) Act 1930 was passed to confer on third parties the right to claim directly against insurers of third party risks where the insured is insolvent.

Section 1(1) of the 1930 Act, which circumvents the privity doctrine by placing the injured person into the shoes of the wrongdoer, provides:

---

[43] Regs 4, and 5.
[44] [1995] QB 123.
[45] Russell and Stuart-Smith LJJ; Sir John Megaw dissenting.
[46] See, for example, J O'Sullivan, 'Industrial Injuries And Compulsory Insurance – Adding Insult To Injury' [1995] *CLJ* 241 at 243 who argues that if Parliament leaves the issue of civil liability silent, the courts must address a policy question, which in this case was: 'Who should bear the risk that a company, which has carried on business in breach of safety regulations (so that an employee is disabled) and without compulsory insurance, goes bust unable to meet the employee's damages? Should it be the culpable controllers of that company, skulking behind the corporate veil, or the injured employee? English law saddles the employee ...'
[47] See ch 6, above.
[48] See *Re Harrington Motor Co Ltd* [1928] Ch 105 at 124, in which Atkin LJ, commenting on the anomaly produced by the common law position said: 'it would appear as though a person who is insured against risks and who has general creditors whom he is unable to satisfy, has only to go out in the street and to find the most expensive motor car or the most wealthy man he can to run down, and he will at once be provided with assets, which will enable him to pay his general creditors quite a substantial dividend.' See also, *Hood's Trustees v Southern Union General Insurance Co of Australasia Ltd* [1928] 1 Ch 793. See further, the observations of Lord Denning MR in *Post Office v Norwich Union Fire Insurance Society Ltd*, above, n 4.

Where under any contract of insurance a person ... is insured against liabilities to third parties which he may incur, then

(a) in the event of the insured becoming bankrupt or making a composition or arrangement with his creditors; or

(b) in the case of the insured being a company, in the event of a winding up order[49] [or administration order] being made ... [or of a voluntary arrangement proposed for the purposes of Part I of the Insolvency Act 1986 being approved under that Part];

if, either before or after that event, any such liability as aforesaid is incurred by the insured, his rights against the insurer under the contract in respect of the liability shall, notwithstanding anything in any Act or rule of law to the contrary, *be transferred to and vest in the third party to whom the liability was so incurred.*[50]

The Act therefore confers on the third party a right to claim the insurance monies ahead of the insured's general creditors. Further, an insured who becomes insolvent is under a duty to disclose to the third party all necessary information pertaining to a relevant policy of insurance so that the third party can ascertain whether any rights have been transferred to and vested in him by virtue of the statute.[51] Policy terms designed to frustrate the operation of the statute are declared to be of 'no effect'.[52] Similarly, any settlement between the insurers and the insolvent insured, or in the case of a company, any settlement between the insurers and the liquidated company, which is entered into after liability has been incurred, will not affect the rights of the third party under s 1 of the Act.[53] Conversely, any settlement concluded prior to the insured's insolvency will not be set aside, the third party lacking 'any legal or equitable right to prevent' such a settlement.[54] Neither can a third party prevent a settlement even though the amount agreed upon is insufficient to cover the insured's liability.[55]

The scope of the protection afforded to third parties by the Act has been criticised as being too restrictive.[56] Such criticisms stem from the line of decisions where the judges have been called upon to interpret the scope of the statute. Clearly liability for negligence is covered, but it has been doubted whether contractual liability fell within the Act.[57] However, in *Re OT Computers* Ltd,[58] the Court of Appeal held that the 1930 statute covered all forms of liability, including liabilities that are voluntarily incurred by the insured under a contract. The insured was a supplier of computing

---

[49] The Act does not apply where a company is wound up voluntarily merely for the purposes of reconstruction or of amalgamation with another company: s 1(6). The Act was designed to supplement the imposition of compulsory motor insurance by the Road Traffic Act 1930. See s 151 Road Traffic Act 1988.

[50] Emphasis supplied. The scope of s 1(1) is extended to apply to the situation where the insured dies insolvent: s 1(2).

[51] See s 2. *Re OT Computers Ltd* [2004] ch 317.

[52] See ss 1(3) and 2(1), discussed below.

[53] See s 3.

[54] *Normid Housing Association Ltd v Ralphs* [1989] 1 Lloyd's Rep 265 at 272, *per* Slade LJ.

[55] Ibid.

[56] See the joint consultation paper of the Law Commission and the Scottish Law Commission, *Third Parties (Rights Against Insurers) Act 1930,* Consultation Paper No 152 (London, The Stationary Office, 1997), considered below, at p 348. See also Sir Jonathan Mance, 'Insolvency at Sea' [1995] *LMCLQ* 34.

[57] Eg, in *Tarbuck v Avon Insurance Co* [2002] Lloyd's Rep IR 393, it was held that a policy covering liability to pay a contractual debt was outwith the statute. In *Tarbuck* the insured incurred liability to a solicitor for costs, and it was held that the solicitor could not recover from the insured's legal expenses insurers. See also, *T & N Ltd v Royal and Sun Alliance plc* [2004] Lloyd's Rep IR 144.

[58] [2004] Ch 317; [2004] Lloyd's Rep IR 669.

equipment and offered extended warranties to its customers. A finance company which provided credit for the purchase of computers was jointly and severally liable under the warranties by virtue of s 75 of the Consumer Credit Act 1974. The insured became insolvent and the finance company continued to honour the warranty claims; in so doing it thus became subrogated to the customers' claims against the insured. Relying on the 1930 Act, the finance company sought to recover its payments from the suppliers' liability insurers. Longmore LJ, in a strident dismissal of the argument that contractual liabilities were not covered by the Act, concluded:

> There is no reason in principle why the 1930 Act does not apply to contractual liabilities (whether in debt or for damages), although the actual terms of the insurance may determine whether the Act will apply in any particular case. *Tarbuck v Avon Insurance Co*...and *T & N Ltd v Royal and Sun Alliance plc*...should no longer be followed.[59]

It is settled that the liability of the insured must have been established before the insured's rights are transferred to the third party under s 1 of the Act. In *Post Office v Norwich Union Fire Insurance Society Ltd*,[60] it was alleged that a firm of contractors, who were insured under a public liability policy, damaged a cable belonging to the Post Office. The contractors disputed liability arguing that the damage was due to the fault of a Post Office engineer. The Post Office brought proceedings against the insurers, the insured having gone into liquidation, claiming as statutory assignees of the contractors by virtue of s 1(1) of the 1930 Act. The Court of Appeal, construing s 1(1), held that unless the contractors as the insured could have sued the insurers, the Post Office could not sue them. Until the insured's liability is established and the amount ascertained, whether by 'judgment of the court or by an award in arbitration or by agreement,'[61] the third party cannot sue the insurance company. For Lord Denning MR and Salmon LJ the guiding principle was stated by Devlin J in *West Wake Price & Co v Ching*,[62] who had observed that the insured 'cannot recover anything under the main indemnity clause or make any claim against the underwriters until [the insureds] have been found liable and so sustained a loss.'

The decision of the Court of Appeal in the *Post Office* case was approved by the House of Lords in *Bradley v Eagle Star Insurance Co Ltd*.[63] In *Bradley,* the claimant, who had been employed by the insured company which operated a cotton mill, developed a respiratory disease caused by the inhalation of cotton dust. The company was wound up in 1975 and dissolved in 1976. In 1984 the claimant instituted an action against her former employer's insurers. The House of Lords, applying the *Post Office* decision, held that the existence and amount of the employer's liability had not been

---

59 Ibid, at [53].
60 Above, n 4.
61 Ibid, at 373, *per* Lord Denning MR. In *Yorkshire Water Services Ltd v Sun Alliance & London Insurance plc* [1998] Env LR 204, Judge Humphrey Lloyd QC stated, at 221, that the references in the *Post Office* case 'to liability being established by agreement deal only with the time at which a claim for an indemnity might first be made... I see nothing in the judgments which suggests that a judgment, award or agreement *ipso facto* establishes liability conclusively for the purposes of the proceedings for indemnity against the insurers.' It should, however, be noted that where the third party has been awarded an interim payment against the insured this will be sufficient to establish the insured's liability: *Cox v Bankside Members Agency Ltd* [1995] 2 Lloyd's Rep 437.
62 [1957] 1 WLR 45, at 49.
63 Above, n 4.

established and since the dissolution of the company made it impossible to establish these factors, there was no right of indemnity which could be transferred to and vested in the claimant. Lord Templeman in his dissenting speech questioned whether Parliament could have intended that 'the protection afforded against a company in liquidation should cease as soon as the company in liquidation reaches its predestined and inevitable determination in the dissolution of the company.'[64]

Following the decision in *Bradley*, Parliament intervened and has now reformed the law. Under s 651 of the Companies Act 1985, as originally framed, a petition to restore a company to the register had to be brought within two years. This has now been amended by s 141 of the Companies Act 1989. Section 651(5) of the 1985 Act, as amended, disapplies the two year period to actions in respect of personal injuries or death, the effect of which is that a petition to the court to restore a dissolved company to the register can be brought at any time. It should be noted, however, that s 141(4) of the 1989 Act provides that applications cannot be made to restore companies dissolved more than twenty years before the commencement of that section (16 November 1989).[65] The amendment introduced by s 141 was made retroactive in order to allow the claimant's claim in *Bradley* to proceed.

It should be noted that during the interim period between the insured's insolvency and the establishment and quantification of his or her liability the third party is not without any rights against the insurers. According to Blackburne J's reading of the authorities in *Centre Reinsurance International Company, Muenchener Rueckver- sicherungs-Gesellschaft v Curzon Insurance Limited*,[66] the third party's inchoate or contingent rights entitle him to seek a declaration that the policy covers the loss and to seek information from both the insured and the insurers. In summary, the effect of the insured's insolvency is to confer contingent rights on the third party against the insurers. But those rights do not crystallise until the third party establishes and quantifies the insured's liability. Further, during this period, the insurers cannot alter the rights of the insured under the policy so as to prejudice the contingent rights of the third party.[67] There was no appeal against this aspect of the decision.[68]

It has been noted that the effect of s 1(1) of the 1930 Act is that the third party steps into the shoes of the insured.[69] The statutory rights of the third party derive from the insured and as such the third party must take the policy as he finds it. If, for example, the insured's liability falls within a policy exception, the third party will not acquire rights against the insurers. It is said that the third party cannot claim the benefit of a policy while rejecting its conditions.[70] In *Farrell v Federated Employers Insurance Association Ltd*,[71] the claimant, an employee of the insured, was injured at work. His employers liability insurance policy contained a condition requiring

---

[64] Ibid, at 970.

[65] See further, D Oughton, J Lowry and R Merkin, *Limitation of Actions* (London, Lloyd's of London Press, 1998) 141 *et seq.*

[66] [2004] Lloyd's Rep IR 622. The judge based his reasoning principally on *Cox v Bankside Members Agency Ltd*, above, n 61.

[67] See s 1(3) of the 1930 Act; below n 71.

[68] See *Centre Reinsurance International Co v Freakley* [2005] EWCA Civ 115.

[69] *Post Office v Norwich Union Fire Insurance Society Ltd*, above, n 4 at 373, *per* Lord Denning MR; *The Padre Island* [1984] 2 Lloyd's Rep 408 at 414, *per* Leggatt J.

[70] See *Austin v Zurich General Accident and Liability Insurance Co Ltd* [1945] 1 KB 250. Although see *Alfred McAlpine plc v BAI (Run-off) Ltd* [2000] Lloyd's Rep 352, discussed at p 253, above.

[71] [1970] 1 WLR 1400.

immediate notice being given to the insurers in the event of a writ being served on the insured. This condition was broken and in the meantime the company went into receivership. The Court of Appeal held that the claimant, standing in the insured's shoes, was bound by the condition and that as there had been a breach of the term the insurers were not liable. The insurers could rely as against a third party on any defence which would have been available to them as against the insured.[72] If the defences of, for example, non-disclosure, misrepresentation or breach of warranty/condition-precedent are available to the insurers against the insured, they will therefore be equally available against the third party's claim.[73]

Although s 1(3) of the 1930 Act ostensibly prohibits contract terms designed to avoid the protection afforded to third parties by the statute,[74] nevertheless it can in practice be avoided by the inclusion of standard clauses in the policy. The decision in *Farrell* illustrates the position in respect of notice clauses.[75] Arbitration clauses, whereby the submission of the insured's claim to arbitration is made a condition precedent to the insurer's liability, will also bind the third party. In *Smith v Pearl Assurance Co Ltd*,[76] the claimant, who was injured in a car accident caused by the insured's negligence, obtained judgment against him. When the insured became insolvent, the claimant sued the insurers on the basis that the insured's rights under the policy transferred to him by virtue of s 1(1) of the 1930 Act. The insurers applied to have the action stayed on the ground that the policy contained an arbitration clause. The claimant contended that although he could proceed with the High Court action with the assistance of aid from the Poor Persons Committee, he would not be able to go to arbitration, to which form of proceedings such assistance was not available. The Court of Appeal held that the claimant's poverty was not a ground for exercising its discretion to refuse an order to stay. Clauson LJ, who clearly had some sympathy for the claimant's plight, said:

> It is pointed out that, if the matter is to go to arbitration, he will not get any [financial assistance], and will be gravely hampered in establishing his case. This, it is to be observed, is a personal disability in no way connected with the contractual rights or obligations arising out of the contract in respect of which he has, or conceives himself to have, a cause of action… I only wish to add that, should it become necessary in the future to deal further legislatively with the matter which was dealt with in the Third Parties (Rights Against Insurers) Act, 1930, I trust that those who have to deal with the matter will carefully consider whether there are not weighty reasons why persons who have the advantage of some such legislative provision should not be freed from the restriction, which might otherwise fall upon them, of being driven to arbitration.[77]

---

[72] See now reg 2 of the Employers Liability (Compulsory Insurance) General Regulations 1998 (SI 1998/2573), which over-rules the decision in *Farrell*.

[73] *McCormick v National Motor and Accident Insurance Union Ltd* (1934) 49 Ll L R 361. Cf the Road Traffic Act 1988 s 151(1) which provides that the defences of misrepresentation and non-disclosure available to the insurer against the insured are not available against the third party.

[74] Section 1(3) states: 'In so far as any contract of insurance … in respect of any liability of the insured to third parties purports, whether directly or indirectly, to avoid the contract or to alter the rights of the parties thereunder upon the happening to the insured of any of … [insolvency event] …, the contract shall be of no effect.'

[75] See also *Hassett v Legal and General Assurance Society Ltd* (1939) 63 Ll L R 278. For claims control clauses, see *Centre Reinsurance International Co v Freakley*, above, n 68.

[76] [1939] 1 All ER 95. See also, *Freshwater v Western Australian Assurance Co* [1933] 1 KB 515.

[77] Ibid, at 98.

So-called 'pay to be paid' clauses have been the subject of recent extensive judicial consideration as to whether such terms are caught by s 1(3) of the 1930 Act. It is common practice for shipowners to enter their ships in Protection and Indemnity Associations (P and I Clubs) in order to obtain wider cover than that generally afforded by ordinary marine insurance policies. By entering a ship in a P and I Club the shipowner becomes a member of that club. These clubs operate on a system of mutual insurance under which the successful claim of one member is paid out of the contributions of, and calls made on, all the club's members including the insured; each member is thus both an insurer and an insured. It is standard practice for the rules of such clubs to contain a 'pay to be paid' provision whereby it is a condition precedent to the insurer's liability to indemnify the insured, that the latter should first discharge liability to third parties. The question which has arisen is whether such a clause will bind the third parties in the event of the insured being wound up before payment has been made. An affirmative answer was delivered by the House of Lords in *The Fanti*.[78]

Both the trial judge and the Court of Appeal rejected the argument propounded by the third parties that the 'pay to be paid' clause has the effect, either directly or indirectly, of avoiding the insurance contract or of altering the rights of the parties under the contract, upon the insured member being wound up, so as to render the clause of no effect under s. 1(3) of the 1930 Act . Lord Brandon of Oakbrook, agreeing with the conclusion of the lower courts on this point, went on to state that:

> It is abundantly clear from the express terms of the Act of 1930 that the legislature never intended, except as provided in section 1(3), which I have held not to apply to the 'pay to be paid' provisions in the clubs' rules, to put a third party in any better position as against an insurer than that of the insured himself.[79]

His Lordship stressed that the clause in question applied throughout the currency of the insurance and imposed a condition precedent to be fulfilled before any liability of the clubs to indemnify the members arose. The clause applied equally before and after the winding up of the member. Recognising that an insolvent club member would be prevented from discharging any liability to a third party and so would be unable to obtain an indemnity from the club in respect of it, Lord Brandon said that this situation 'does not result, directly or indirectly, from any alteration of the member's rights under his contract of insurance. It results rather from the member's inability, by reason of insolvency, to exercise those rights.'[80]

At a simple level, the approach of the House of Lords may appear to undermine the very purpose underlying the 1930 Act. But, addressing this line of argument, Lord Goff stated that the statutory scheme was only ever intended to transfer to the third party such rights as the insured had under the contract of insurance. On this basis, 'it is very difficult to see how it could be said that a condition of prior payment would drive a coach and horses through the Act; for the Act was not directed to

---

[78] *Firma C-Trade SA v Newcastle Protection and Indemnity Association* [1991] 2 AC 1; *Charter Reinsurance Co Ltd v Fagan* [1996] 1 Lloyd's Rep 261
[79] Ibid, at 29.
[80] Ibid, at 28–9. Similarly, Lord Goff said, at 32: 'But there is no duty on the member to make prior payment; there is simply a contractual term that, if he does not do so, he has no right to be indemnified. The statutory transferee of the member's right is in no better position than the member; and so, if the condition is not fulfilled, he too has no right to be indemnified.'

giving the third party greater rights than the insured had under a contract of insurance.'[81] His Lordship pointed to the fact that in contrast to employers and motorists, Parliament has not generally required shipowners to be compulsorily insured against liability to third parties.[82] And where compulsory insurance is required, the relevant legislation normally strikes down any contractual term which defeats the purpose of such insurance.[83]

More generally, it should, however, be noted that, absent any term to the contrary in the policy, the third party can disregard the liability of the insured to the insurers. The position was compendiously stated by Cumming-Bruce J in *Murray v Legal and General Assurance Society Ltd,* [84] where he said:

> It is not all the rights and liabilities of the insured under the contract of insurance which are transferred to the third party, only the particular rights in respect of the liability incurred by the insured to the third.[85]

For example, if premiums are unpaid, and provided the policy document does not contain a condition precedent to the liability of the insurers that all premiums were paid prior to the claim arising, the third party will be able to recover the full sum claimed without being subject to the insurers right of set-off.

Where there are competing claims and the sum insured under the policy is insufficient to meet all the claims of the third parties, the governing principle is not that of apportionment, but rather 'first past the post.' Thus, the first person who obtains a quantified judgment against the insured has the first claim on the policy.[86] Where there is a shortfall, s 1(4) of the Act preserves the right of third parties to proceed against the insured in the relevant insolvency procedure. Further, s 1(4)(b) of the Act provides that the insured remains liable to the third party, at least to the extent that the third party's rights against the insured exceed the rights which are subject of the statutory transfer. Thus, for example, the third party can enforce any claim against the insured to the extent that the amount of the claim exceeds the amount for which the insured is covered. In *Centre Reinsurance International Co v Freakley,* [87] the Court of Appeal accepted that the statute did not extinguish the insured's liability to the third party. But Chadwick LJ took the view that the implication of s 1(4)(b) is that the third party is precluded from suing the insured in respect of the insured sum. He explained:

> If that were not so, (i) there would be a risk of double recovery if the third party were to sue both insurer and insured and (ii) there would be a risk that the insured would be liable to the third party in respect of a claim in which he no longer had any right of indemnity under

---

[81] Ibid, at 38.
[82] Although there are special cases where compulsory insurance is required of shipowners, for example, the Merchant Shipping Act 1995.
[83] See, eg, ss 148–150 of the Road Traffic Act 1988 and reg 2 of the Employers Liability (Compulsory Insurance) General Regulations 1998, discussed above.
[84] [1969] 2 Lloyd's Rep 405.
[85] Ibid, at 411.
[86] *Cox* v *Bankside Members Agency Ltd,* above, n 61. Phillips J explained that while this may appear arbitrary, the alternative approach would give rise to serious delays as nothing could be paid out until all claims had been processed.
[87] [2005] EWCA Civ 115.

the policy – because his right had been transferred to the third party by the statute. It would, of course, be a strange case in which the third party chose to pursue the insolvent insured rather than the solvent insurer. But the question whether (and for what) the third party could prove in the insolvency of the insured would have to be addressed if the insurer were also insolvent.[88]

Arden LJ, however, disagreed on this point. She reasoned that if the insurers were insolvent, the third party's right to sue the insured would not be extinguished.

3.1 Reform

The Law Commission's consultation paper which examines the operation of the 1930 Act has already been alluded to.[89] The paper details a number of criticisms which can be made including, as has been seen, the fact that third parties may find their claims defeated because insurers can rely on defences which they would have had against the insured; that the third party will be bound by any settlement between the insured and the insurer before the occurrence of the insolvency; that an insurance fund which is insufficient to meet the claims of third parties is distributed to those who establish their claims first rather than rateably to all claimants;[90] and that third parties may have to establish the insured's liability in separate proceedings before they can proceed against the insurer under the Act or obtain policy information. The consultation paper provisionally makes a number of proposals for reform and it posed a range of questions for consultation, including: (a) that the ability of insurers to rely on defences (such as a condition precedent relating to notification) against third parties should be restricted;[91] (b) whether a statutory scheme of rateable distribution to multiple third party claimants should replace the current 'first past the post' system[92]; and (c) whether a third party should acquire rights under an amended Act before he or she has established the insured's liability. Such rights would arise either on the occurrence of the incident giving rise to the liability of the insured or upon the insured's insolvency.[93]

The ensuing report contained a draft Bill.[94] In 2002 the Lord Chancellor's Department (now the Department for Constitutional Affairs) published a consultation paper indicating that it may implement the Law Commission's recommendations via a Regulatory Reform Order.[95] By way of summary, the key reforms in the Law Commissions' draft Bill include the following provisions:

- clause 1 broadens the situations in which the Act will apply to include, inter alia, winding up for the purpose of reconstruction, individual voluntary arrangements and the appointment of a provisional liquidator;

---

[88] Ibid, at [39].
[89] See n 56, above.
[90] *Cox v Bankside Members Agency Ltd,* above, n 61.
[91] Above, n 56, at para 14.6.
[92] Ibid, at para 15.18.
[93] Ibid, para 12.10.
[94] Law Com No 272; Scot Law Com No 184, 2001, Cm 5217.
[95] CP 08/02.

- clause 4 provides that conditions precedent to liability will be able to be satisfied by the third party. Pay to be paid clauses are of no effect other than in marine claims not involving death or personal injury;
- clause 16 states that the Act will apply to voluntarily incurred liabilities (see now, *Re OT Computers Ltd,* (above));
- a new streamlined procedure is proposed so that a single set of proceedings will replace the current two-stage process which requires the third party to first sue the insured in order to establish liability and quantification before going on to sue the insurers under the policy. Under clause 8, the third party will proceed against the insurers only. It is then for the insurers to dispute the liability of the insured and raise any questions as to cover;
- clause 7 and Schedule 1 of the Bill provide for the third party to obtain information from the insured and from the insurers when proceedings are about to be initiated (see now, the decision in *Centre Reinsurance* (above) and *Re OT Computers Ltd* (above)).

In February 2004 the Departmental for Constitutional affairs stated that in view of the responses to the 2002 consultation process, only some of the draft Bill's provisions could be implemented by Regulatory Reform Order.[96] The reforms that could be introduced by such an Order include the new streamlined procedure contained in clause 8 and the provisions for improved access to information contained in clause 7 (although, as we have seen, in the case of the latter it seems that the judges have already grasped the issue). The draft Bill's other provisions will require primary legislation.

---

[96] See http://www.dca.gov.uk/consult/rro/tprairesp.htm

15

Fire and other Property Insurance and Accident Insurance

1. Fire policies

The same general principles apply to fire policies as apply to other types of insurance contract, with the exception of rules on reinstatement of property,[1] so this discussion will look at the nature of the insured perils and the interpretation placed upon the exceptions commonly found in such policies.

1.1 Loss by fire

In determining whether a loss was caused by fire, the court will eschew technical discussions as to the nature of fire: ignition is an essential element and damage by mere over-heating will not make the insurers liable.[2] The insurers will be liable for damage to an insured building caused by an explosion where that explosion was the result of a fire in the building, but not where the damage was the result of concussion caused by an explosion in another property.[3] In the absence of an agreement to the contrary, the cause of the fire is normally irrelevant. A fire caused by the negligence of the insured will not preclude a claim since covering this eventuality is 'one of the objects

---

[1] See the Fires Prevention (Metropolis) Act 1774, s 83; see ch 6.

[2] *Austin v Drewe* (1816) 4 Camp 360.

[3] *Everett v London Assurance* (1865) 19 CB (NS) 126; *Stanley v Western* (1868) LR 3 Ex 71; *Hobbs v Northern Assurance Co* (1886) 12 SCR 631 (approved in *Curtis and Harvey (Canada) Ltd v North British and Mercantile Insurance Co Ltd* [1921] 1 AC 303); *Re Hooley Hill Rubber and Chemical Co Ltd and Royal Insurance Co Ltd* [1920] 1 KB 257 at 272, per Scrutton LJ. Under the Institute clauses (unlike the SG Policy reproduced in the Marine Insurance Act 1906) used in modern marine policies (see ch 16) explosion is specifically covered (although not if the cause of that explosion is excepted): ITCH(95), cl 6.1.2, IVCH(95), cl. 4.1.2; and ICC(B) and (C), cl 1.1.1 (ICC(A) is an all risks policy and, therefore, covers loss by explosion). See also International Hulls Clauses 2003, cl 2.2.3.

of insurance against fire'[4]: when an insured lit a fire in her grate forgetting that she had hidden jewels there, the insurers were held liable.[5] Similarly, an act of arson will not prevent an insured from claiming, unless committed – or colluded in – by the insured in which case public policy will preclude a claim.[6]

Once a fire has ignited then consequential damage to the insured property will be covered, such as damage by smoke or by the roof collapsing on to insured goods as a result of being weakened by the fire,[7] as will ' any loss resulting from an apparently necessary and *bona fide* effort to put out a fire,'[8] such as damage caused by spraying water to extinguish the fire or by action to prevent fire spreading to the property.[9] However, the property must be affected by fire or by 'an actual existing state of peril of fire, and not merely a fear of fire.'[10] Moreover, a fire policy will not cover losses beyond the damage to the property caused by fire: fire damage may lead the insured to lose business or to incur additional cost in acquiring new premises while the building is repaired, but these losses are not covered by a fire policy and must be separately insured.[11]

1.2 Excepted perils in fire policies

1.2.1 Spontaneous combustion, heating and explosion

It is quite common for policies to exclude liability where the fire is the result of spontaneous combustion or heating process or explosion. Even without such exceptions the insurers are not liable for loss caused by an inherent vice of the subject matter[12] or, as has been seen, if the subject matter is damaged by heat without an actual ignition. Normally, although a policy on a house will exclude liability where the damage is the result of an explosion,[13] there will be a term making the insurers liable in the event of a domestic boiler or a domestic gas supply exploding.

---

[4] *Shaw v Robberds, Hawkes and Stone* (1837) 6 Ad & E 75 at 84, per Lord Denman CJ. See Marine Insurance Act 1906, s 55(2)(a) and the Institute clauses: eg, ITCH(95) renders the insurer liable for fire caused by 'negligence of the Master Officers Crew or Pilots' (cl 6.2.2).
[5] *Harris v Poland* [1941] 1 KB 462.
[6] *The Midland Insurance Co v Smith and Wife* (1881) 6 QBD 561 at 568, per Watkin Williams J. Where arson by the insured is alleged, it is necessary for the insurers to satisfy a degree of proof which, even if it is not the same as required by a criminal court, must nevertheless amount to a 'high degree of probability': *Slattery v Mance* [1962] 1 Lloyd's Rep 60 at 63, per Salmon J; *Watkins & Davis Ltd v Legal & General Assurance Co Ltd* [1981] 1 Lloyd's Rep 674 at 677, per Neill J. The insurers would need to show that 'the only probable conclusion' was that the insured committed arson 'and there is no other credible explanation': *McGregor v Prudential Insurance Co Ltd* [1998] 1 Lloyd's Rep 112 at 114, per Geoffrey Brice QC. In marine policies, while the shipowner is covered where the loss is due to the deliberate act of someone other than the assured (eg, ITCH(95), cl 6.2.4), a cargo owner insured under ICC(B) or (C) cannot recover because these policies exclude liability where the loss is caused by 'the deliberate destruction of the subject-matter insured... by the wrongful act of any person' (cl 4.7).
[7] *In re An Arbitration between Hooley Hill Rubber and Chemical Co Ltd, and Royal Insurance Co Ltd* [1920] 1 KB 257 at 271, per Scrutton LJ.
[8] *Stanley v Western*, above n 3 at 74, per Kelly CB.
[9] *Canada Rice Mills Ltd v Union Marine and General Insurance Co Ltd* [1941] AC 55; *Symington & Co v Union Insurance Society of Canton Ltd* (1928) 34 Com Cas 23.
[10] *The Knight of St Michael* [1898]) 30 at 35, per Gorell Barnes J. See further above ch 9.
[11] *Re Wright and Pole* (1834) 1 Ad & E 621.
[12] *Boyd v Dubois* (1811) 3 Camp 133 at 133, per Lord Ellenborough CJ.
[13] Although see above n 3.

1.2.2 Riot, civil commotion, war or civil war, rebellion, or insurrection, or military or usurped power

A fire policy may exclude liability where a fire is set as a result of certain types of public disorder. Riot is a common exception. Under the Public Order Act 1986, section 1, a riot occurs when twelve or more people, who are present together, threaten unlawful violence for a common purpose in such a manner as would cause a person of reasonable firmness to fear for his personal safety. This replaces the common law offence of riot which, among other things, required only three or more persons to be present,[14] and presumably the statutory definition would be applied in cases on the term 'riot' in an insurance policy.[15] The insured, who is denied recovery because of this exception, can make a claim against the local police authority under the Riot (Damages) Act 1886, section 2(1). If, the policy does not exclude riot, the insurers have the right to be subrogated to the insured's right to claim against the authority.

For a civil commotion, 'The element of turbulence or tumult is essential; an organised conspiracy to commit criminal acts, where there is no tumult or disturbance until after the acts, does not amount to civil commotion. It is not, however, necessary to show the existence of any outside organisation at whose instigation the acts were done.'[16] There need be no evidence of a revolt against the government, but 'the disturbances must have sufficient cohesion to prevent them from being the work of a mindless mob.'[17] Clearly, such would also amount to a riot, but civil commotion has been described as one of the various stages between riot and civil war.[18] So, for instance, fighting between different factions in Lebanon in the 1970s was held to be a civil commotion.[19] Where the exception in the policy relates to 'civil commotion assuming the proportions of or amounting to a popular rising,' then, while it is impossible to be precise about the meaning of these additional words, the commotion 'must involve a really substantial proportion of the populace, although obviously not all the population need participate, and . . . there should be tumult and violence on a large scale.'[20]

The exception for war will operate even if there has not been a declaration of war as long as the court determines that, in fact, a state of war exists.[21] A rebellion, such as the Irish Rebellion of 1916, may be defined as a 'war' for this purpose.[22] Typically, a policy will also expressly exclude liability for loss caused by civil war, although the word 'war' includes civil war, unless there is an indication to the contrary in the

---

[14] For a case on a burglary policy in which four armed robbers constituted a riot, see *London & Lancashire Fire v Bolands* [1924] AC 836.

[15] See Public Order Act 1986, s 10 for changes to the meaning of the words 'rioters' and 'riot' in the Marine Insurance Act 1906, sch 1, rr 8 and 10.

[16] *Levy v Assicurazioni Generali* [1940] AC 791 at 800, per Luxmoore LJ.

[17] *Spinney's (1948) Ltd v Royal Insurance Co Ltd* [1980] 1 Lloyd's Rep 406 at 438, per Mustill J.

[18] *Republic of Bolivia v Indemnity Mutual Marine Assurance Co Ltd* [1909] 1 KB 785 at 801, per Farewell LJ.

[19] *Spinney's (1948) Ltd v Royal Insurance Co Ltd*, above n 17. See also *Cooper v General Accident Fire and Life Assurance Corpn* (1922) 128 LT 481; *Motor Union Insurance Co Ltd v Boggan* (1923) 130 LT 588. Contrast with the situation in Palestine in 1936 when the civil authorities were still in control and the violence, although severe, was to some extent contained by the authorities: *Levy v Assicurazioni Generali*, above n 16.

[20] *Spinney's (1948) Ltd v Royal Insurance Co Ltd*, ibid, at 438, per Mustill J.

[21] *Kawasaki Kisen Kabushiki Kaisha of Kobe v Bantham SS Co Ltd* [1939] 2 KB 544.

[22] *Curtis & Sons v Matthews* [1919] 1 KB 425.

policy. It has been said by Mustill J that in determining whether there is a state of civil war the court must consider: whether there were opposing sides; what the objectives of those sides were and how they set about pursuing them; and what was the scale both of the conflict and of its effect on public order and on the life of the inhabitants?[23] Applying these criteria to Lebanon in 1975, he said that although the fighting was serious, it was not the case that one side was seeking to wrest political power from the other or to seize power by violence: for instance, the president had been criticised and his resignation suggested, but there had been no attempt at that time to remove him by violent means, and the prime minister enjoyed fairly broad support. Although the government was largely powerless to prevent the fighting, no faction sought to remove it. In addition, he took the view that there were no 'sides' in existence because there was a lack of common leadership or unanimity of purpose. The fighting was sporadic and incoherent. He therefore concluded that matters had not advanced from 'massive civil strife and virtual anarchy to the stage of civil war' at that time.[24]

In that same case Mustill J also considered the exceptions for rebellion and insurrection. He referred to the *Oxford English Dictionary* where rebellion is defined as 'organised resistance to the ruler or government of one's country; insurrection, revolt.' To this Mustill J added 'the purpose of the resistance must be to supplant the existing rulers or at least to deprive them of authority over part of their territory.'[25] An insurrection is 'an incipient or limited rebellion' and implies 'a lesser degree of organisation' than a rebellion. But the two shade into each other and in both cases there must be 'action against the government with a view to supplanting it.'[26] Although they would normally involve personal violence, it has been held that economic sabotage, such as the blowing up of an oil pipeline in Mozambique, can come within both exceptions.[27] This action amounted to an insurrection: there was widespread internal discontent with the Frelimo government in Mozambique; the group which committed the act, Renamo, had the aim of overthrowing that government; Renamo had substantial support from large numbers of Mozambican dissidents and from the Rhodesian and South African governments; and yet it could not be said that Renamo was merely a puppet organisation of those governments, which might have taken away the crucial element of internal strife.[28]

'Military power' is the action of invading forces from outside the country, including an air raid,[29] or the damage caused by the domestic army attempting to repel such an invasion or defeat rebels.[30] 'Usurped power' 'consists of the arrogation to itself by the mob of a law-making and law-enforcing power which properly belongs to the sovereign.'[31] In other words, there are elements of treason, organisation and leadership, and in the spectrum of violent disturbances, it is therefore closer to rebellion or civil

---

[23] *Spinney's (1948) Ltd v Royal Insurance Co Ltd*, above n 17, at 429–30, per Mustill J.
[24] Ibid, at 431–2. Mustill J did decide that the degree of disturbance brought it within the exception for 'civil commotion assuming the proportions of or amounting to a popular rising' (at 438).
[25] Ibid, at 436.
[26] Ibid, at 436–7.
[27] *National Oil Company of Zimbabwe (Private) Ltd v Sturge* [1991] 2 Lloyd's Rep 281.
[28] Ibid. Since this meant the insurers were not liable on the policy, Saville J did not consider fully whether this was an act of rebellion or civil war.
[29] *Rogers v Whittaker* [1917] 1 KB 942.
[30] *Curtis & Sons v Matthews*, above n 22.
[31] *Spinney's (1948) Ltd v Royal Insurance Co Ltd*, above n 17, at 435, per Mustill J.

war than to riot. Even if the action is not designed to overthrow the government, it will amount to a usurpation of power if it involves taking on some of the functions of government.

---

2. Burglary and theft

The terms contained in fire policies are commonly used in other forms of property insurance, including insurance against burglary and theft, and much of the discussion on the excepted perils in fire policies applies equally to these.

Where terms of art such as 'burglary' or 'theft' are used, they are given the definition ascribed to them by the criminal law unless the policy expressly provides another meaning.[32] Commonly, a burglary policy requires forcible and violent entry, so that the use of deception or the mere turning of a handle will not be sufficient even if it amounts to a criminal offence, nor will the use of force and violence which only occurs after an entry has been made.[33] The insured may be required to put in place certain security measures, or may be encouraged to do so by the offer of a reduced premium. Generally, a burglary policy will require that domestic premises are continuously occupied, although this does not mean that someone must be present at all times, so long as any period when it is unoccupied is temporary,[34] and if a dwelling-house, it is being occupied as such. Not surprisingly, since the cover will be for property within a certain building, if that property is not inside the building the insurers will be not liable: goods insured under a burglary policy while kept inside a warehouse were not covered when in a lorry parked outside the warehouse in a locked and walled compound.[35]

Marine policies, such as the Institute clauses ITCH(95), clause 6.1.3 and IVCH(95), clause 4.1.3,[36] insure against 'violent theft by persons from outside the Vessel,' which excludes clandestine theft.[37] It has been said that this formulation is designed to protect insurers in circumstances where the presumption must be that the theft would not have occurred without some default of the captain or crew.[38] The violence may be to property and not just to persons, but must have been used to effect the theft and not merely to facilitate the escape of the thieves.[39] There must also have been a dishonest intention so that where the action was committed by someone who had an honest belief that it was not theft, there was not sufficient dishonesty to

[32] See above ch 8.
[33] *Re George and Goldsmiths and General Burglary Insurance Association Ltd* [1899] 1 QB 595.
[34] *Winicofsky v Army and Navy General Assurance Association* (1919) 88 LJKB 1111; *Simmonds v Cockell* [1920] 1 KB 843.
[35] *Barnett and Block v National Parcels Insurance Co Ltd* [1942] 1 All ER 221 (affirmed [1942] 2 All ER 550).
[36] There is no coverage under the cargo policies, ICC(B) and (C), but theft is covered under the all risks policy, ICC(A), and the Institute Theft, Pilferage and Non-Delivery Clause. See also International Hulls Clauses 2003, cl 2.1.3.
[37] See also, Marine Insurance Act 1906, sch, r 9.
[38] *Steinman & Co v Angier Line* [1891] 1 QB 619.
[39] *La Fabrique de Produits Chimiques v Large* [1923] 2 Lloyd's Rep 483.

constitute loss by theft.[40] The Institute Theft, Pilferage and Non-Delivery Clause covers loss 'caused by theft or pilferage, or by non-delivery of an entire package.' This is clearly wider in its scope and covers clandestine theft. One difficulty is presented by the situation where it is unclear how the goods disappeared: they may have been stolen or simply wrongly delivered. 'Non-delivery' must be construed within its context, so although proof of loss through theft or pilferage need not be shown, the assured must, nevertheless, provide prima facie proof that the goods were not lost by any other means than theft or pilferage.[41]

3. Accident insurance

An accident policy is one which covers dying or sustaining an injury as the result of an accident or of a type of accident specified in the policy.[42] Typically, such policies provide for a fixed sum to be paid and since such a policy is not an indemnity, then, as has been seen, the insurers have no right of subrogation and the insured can recover not only under the policy, but also from the tortfeasor.[43] It is, however, not uncommon for accident policies to include a term requiring the insured to declare the existence of other policies covering the same loss. The Life Assurance Act 1774 has been held to apply to such policies.[44]

Much of the litigation on accident policies concerns the issue of whether the loss was caused by an 'accident': this involves construing the word within the terms of the contract and deciding whether the cause – as determined by common law principles unless there are express terms on causation – was accidental.[45] It has been said that 'accident' implies 'some violence, casualty, or vis major,' and that it is manifested in some external injury,[46] and indeed it is common for policies to use words such as 'outward, violent and visible means' or 'violent, accidental, external and visible means.' These phrases should be taken as a whole and not broken down into their component parts.[47] It seems that, although physical injury is required, it may be sufficient that such injury is purely internal in the sense of not being visible. Drinking poison can, therefore, amount to an accident, even though its effects do not manifest themselves externally on the body.[48] Nervous shock, on the other hand, is not an injury which comes within the terms of an accident policy, unless the shock suffered has some physical consequences: where a policy covered accidental injury which prevented the

---

[40] *Nishina Trading Co Ltd v Chiyoda Fire and Marine Insurance Co Ltd* [1969] 2. All ER 776.
[41] *Forestal Land, Timber and Railways Co Ltd v Rickards* [1940] 4 All ER 96 at 110, per Hilbery J.
[42] The issue of accidental injury or damage also arises in connection with liability policies: see above chs 13 and 14; the discussion of *Gray v Barr* [1971] 2 QB 554, above ch 9.4.4; and ch 8.
[43] See above ch 11.
[44] *Shilling v Accidental Death* (1857) 2 H & N 42.
[45] See above ch 8.
[46] *Sinclair v The Maritime Passengers' Assurance Co* (1861) 3 El & El 478 at 485, per Cockburn CJ.
[47] *De Souza v Home and Overseas Insurance Co Ltd* [1995] LRLR 453 at 462, per Mustill LJ.
[48] *Cole v Accident Insurance Co Ltd* (1889) 5 TLR 736 (the claim failed on the wording in the policy which excluded liability for death by poison).

insured from working and the nervous shock he suffered did so incapacitate him, then he was able to claim.[49]

As has been seen in chapter 9, insurers have been keen to reduce their liability for accidental injury or death by extending the search for the cause of the injury or by attempting to exclude liability where the insured has failed to take particular precautions.[50] In *Marcel Beller Ltd v Hayden*,[51] a personal accident policy covered death caused by an accident but excluded death 'directly or indirectly resulting from deliberate exposure to exceptional danger or insured's own criminal act.' The motorist, who was killed, had driven with a blood-alcohol level more than three times the permitted maximum and had crashed while taking a corner at a speed in excess of the permitted limit. Judge Edgar Fay said that the crash was an accident. It would only have not been an accident if 'the running of the danger was a conscious act of volition,'[52] and voluntarily exposing oneself to risk was not the same as deliberate exposure to risk: speeding was dangerous, but there was nothing to show that the driver had consciously taken on that risk, rather the fact that he was drunk would suggest that he would have been less aware of it.[53] However, although the judge concluded that this was an accident, the claim was defeated by the exclusion. Therefore, a criminal act of inadvertence or negligence would not have defeated the claim, but here he had driven while drunk and had driven dangerously, and these actions were, either 'directly or indirectly' causes of the accident.

On the other hand, in *Morley and Morley v United Friendly Insurance plc*,[54] where the policy excluded injury which resulted from 'wilful exposure to needless peril,' the deceased was held not to have wilfully exposed himself to needless peril by jumping on the bumper of a car driven by his fiancée. It is not enough to show that 'intentional acts done by the insured resulted in his being exposed' to needless peril. Moreover, the exposure to peril must go beyond negligent exposure to needless peril, there must be shown to have been 'a conscious act of volition, which can include recklessness, directed at the running of the risk,'[55] or else it must be shown that 'at the time of his actions the insured was mindful of a real risk of the kind of injury for which benefit was provided by the policy and that he either intended to run that risk or exposed himself to it not caring whether he sustained such injury or not.'[56] It is necessary to consider all the circumstances, but most particularly, the likelihood of the insured injury happening if the risk is taken, and the opportunity for reflection before the risk is taken. The test is to ask whether the insured 'appreciated that he was exposing himself to the risk at least of fracture of one of the major bones of the body or that he embarked on that conduct not caring whether he sustained such injury or

---

[49] *Pugh v The London, Brighton and South Coast Railway Co* [1896] 2 QB 248 (particularly, at 253, per A.J. Smith LJ).
[50] See also, the discussion of *Cornish v Accident Insurance Co Ltd* (1889) 23 QBD 453, ch 8.
[51] [1978] QB 694.
[52] Ibid, at 704.
[53] An earlier case on drunken driving was more cautious: it seemed to have made a difference that the driver had not become deliberately drunk, nor put himself deliberately into a position where he would drive while drunk, so that even though in the end he did drive, the judge regarded this as an act of folly rather than premeditation: *James v British General Insurance Co Ltd* [1927] 2 KB 311 at 325, per Roche J.
[54] [1993] 1 WLR 996.
[55] Ibid, at 1000, per Neill LJ.
[56] Ibid, at 1004, per Beldam LJ.

not.'[57] If the answer to either of these questions is yes, then the insurers are not liable. Here Beldam LJ thought the answer to both was no. It was not reasonable to infer from the momentary act of stupidity in jumping on to the bumper of the car that the deceased appreciated that he was exposing himself to the peril of any injury; after all he knew the driver was sober and that, as his fiancée, she loved him. Such an exclusion will, however, probably mean the insurers will not be liable if the insured takes part in some form of extreme sport, such as motor racing, hang-gliding or boxing, because there is an appreciable risk of injury and the insured will, presumably, have had time to reflect on that risk, but they will be liable where the insured takes part in a contact sport like football or rugby.[58]

Mustill LJ in *De Souza v Home and Overseas Insurance Co Ltd*[59] found the authorities on accident were not only confusing and contradictory, but they also led to conclusions which defied common sense. He defined accident as involving 'the idea of something fortuitous and unexpected, as opposed to something proceeding from natural causes; and injury caused by accident is to be regarded as the antithesis to bodily infirmity by disease in the ordinary course of events.'[60] However, he was, perhaps, more struck by a less technical test: referring to the heat stroke which led to the death of the insured in that case, he said, 'If one… asked an ordinary literate lay member of the public whether this sad event entailed that Mr De Souza had been the victim of an accidental bodily injury, I believe that he or she would say: – "Of course not." '[61] He concluded that there were two categories of accident.[62] The first is where 'the injury is the natural result of a fortuitous and unexpected cause.' Here 'the element of accident manifests itself in the cause of the injury,'[63] as, for instance, where the insured is hit by a train.[64] The second is where 'the injury is the fortuitous and unexpected result of a natural cause.'[65] Here 'the element of accident manifests itself, not in the cause, but in the result,' as where someone is doing something ordinary and normal which unexpectedly leads to an injury, such as the insured who, while putting on a sock, scratched his leg with a thumbnail and died as a result of the wound becoming infected.[66]

An injury is not caused by an accident, Mustill LJ said, 'when it is the natural result of a natural cause.'[67] Someone who dies as a result of an undetected heart condition is not killed by an accident, but by natural causes. It is the same if the heart attack, which kills that person, is brought on by running for a train. There was no accident when the insured, during the course of his employment, ejected a customer from licensed premises and died because this exertion strained his heart, which, unbeknown to him, was weak.[68] Here there is no element of intervening chance: the person deliberately ran for the train and the publican intended to eject the customer.

[57] Ibid.
[58] Ibid, at 1000, per Neill LJ.
[59] See above, n 47.
[60] Ibid, at 458.
[61] Ibid, at 454.
[62] Ibid, at 458–9.
[63] Ibid, at 458.
[64] *Lawrence v Accident Insurance Co Ltd* (1881) 45 LT 29.
[65] *De Souza v Home and Overseas Insurance Co Ltd,* above n 47, at 458.
[66] *Mardorf v Accident Insurance Co Ltd* [1903] 1 KB 584.
[67] *De Souza v Home and Overseas Insurance Co Ltd,* see above n 47, at 459 per Mustill LJ.
[68] *In re Arbitration between Kate Scarr and the General Accident Assurance Corpn Ltd* [1905] 1 KB 387.

There is nothing, according to the common understanding of the word, that could be described as accidental in either example. Similarly, when Mr De Souza chose to over-expose himself to the sun on holiday and as a result died of sunstroke, it was no accident.[69] It does not become an accident merely because the consequences of the deliberate action were not foreseen, and therefore not actually intended, so long as those consequences follow naturally from the deliberate action. 'A man must be taken to intend the ordinary consequences of his acts, and the fact that he did not foresee the particular consequence or expect the particular injury does not make the injury accidental if, in the circumstances, it was the natural and direct consequence of what he did, without the intervention of any fortuitous cause.'[70] So, in the case on the publican it was said, 'It is true that Scarr did not foresee the effect, but this, in my opinion, cannot make it accidental if it was the natural and direct consequence' of a deliberate act of the deceased.[71] In *Weyerhaesur v Evans*,[72] when Mr Weyerhaesur died as the result of an infection, which originated in a pimple, his estate was unable to prove that the pimple had been treated by a friend and that this was the cause of the infection, therefore, the insurers were not liable on an accident policy. Another illustration of this principle is provided by *Dhak v Insurance Co of North America (UK) Ltd*.[73] A nurse, who was covered by a personal accident insurance policy, suffered an accidental injury to her back at work. To ease the pain, she began to drink heavily and six months later died in her sleep as a result of choking on her own vomit. Neill LJ concluded that as a nurse she must have known the risks associated with heavy drinking and her deliberate assumption of those risks was the proximate cause of her death, not the accident. He said that where the insured undertook a deliberate action that led to injury, it must be asked, did she intend to inflict the injury on herself, or take a calculated risk of suffering injury, or was the injury the natural and direct consequence of a deliberate act? If the answer is yes to any of these questions, there will be no recovery, unless some fortuitous cause intervened between the deliberate act and the injury.

If some chance event does intervene, which is not the deliberate act of the insured (even though it may be the deliberate act of a third party or the negligent act of the insured) and which diverts events from their natural course, then the result may be an accident. It depends on the circumstances in which the injury is received. If the weak-hearted walker does not intend to run, but enters a field without knowing that it contains a bull and, as a result, is forced to run, then the running is not the intentional act of the insured. In *Hamlyn v Crown Accidental Insurance Co*,[74] a shopkeeper stooped to pick up a marble and because it rolled away from him, he bent forward and, in doing so, wrenched his knee. This was held to be an accident because the court took the view that he had not intended the extra exertion involved: the man did not intend to do the act which wrenched his knee.

---

[69] *De Souza v Home and Overseas Insurance Co Ltd, above* n 47.
[70] Ibid, at 459, per Mustill LJ.
[71] *In re Arbitration between Kate Scarr and the General Accident Assurance Corpn Ltd, above* n 68, at 393, per Bray J.
[72] (1932) 43 Ll L Rep 62.
[73] [1996] 1 WLR 936.
[74] [1893] 1 QB 750. See the interpretation placed on this case by Bray J in *In re Arbitration between Kate Scarr and the General Accident Assurance Corpn Ltd, above* n 68, at 394, and by Mustill LJ in *De Souza v Home and Overseas Insurance Co Ltd, above* n 47, at 461.

There are, however, some severe difficulties with this line of reasoning and, perhaps, the problem lies with the distinction between accidental results and accidental means that has been disinterred by the judges in *De Souza* and *Dhak*. It had long been supposed that the Court of Appeal in *Hamlyn* had rejected the idea of a distinction between accidental result and accidental means, and famously the American judge, Cardozo J, castigated those who would make such a distinction for plunging 'this branch of the law into way Serbian bog.'[75] Neill LJ in *Dhak* was not deterred. Drawing on the judgment of Lord Justice Mustill in *De Souza*, he maintained that the judges in *Hamlyn*, in which there was a similarly worded policy, had acknowledged this distinction. The policy in *Dhak* covered, 'bodily injury resulting in death... caused directly or indirectly by the accident,' and the words 'caused by accidental means' were construed as requiring the court to look at the cause of the injury and determine whether it was accidental, so there would be no cover if the insured's deliberate act led to the injury. The problem is that if *Dhak* is correct, then, however one reads the judgments in *Hamlyn*, its conclusion must surely be wrong in finding the insurers liable since the man deliberately bent forward to pick up the marble and that action led to the injury, which was its natural consequence. Other jurisdictions have rejected the distinction. For instance, in the Scottish case of *MacLeod v New Hampshire Insurance Co Ltd*,[76] the injury to the insured's back occurred when he threw a tire into his truck. The policy covered injury caused by 'accidental, violent, visible and external means' and the court held the insurers liable. Even though the injury was a natural and foreseeable consequence of an intentional act, this result was not intended and, therefore, according to the ordinary meaning of the word this was an accident. The word 'accidental' merely emphasised the distinction between an accidental injury and one resulting from an existing infirmity.

[75] *Landress v Phoenix Mutual Life Insurance* (1934) 54 S Ct 461 at 463. It should be pointed out that he dissented in that case.
[76] [1998] SLT 1191. See *Sargent v GRE (UK) Ltd* [2000] Lloyd's Rep IR 77, for some encouraging signs that the Court of Appeal may be moving away from the rather complex method of construing policies that has, it might be suggested, led to the difficulties of *De Souza* and *Dhak*.

16

Marine Insurance

1. Interpreting the Marine Insurance Act 1906

Many of the principles of the law of insurance contracts were developed in the context of marine insurance, so that although the Marine Insurance Act 1906 strictly applies only to marine policies, it has been used by judges in cases on non-marine policies, as has been seen throughout this book.[1]

The intention of the Act was to codify the common law and the approach taken to the interpretation of that type of legislation was established by Lord Herschell in a case on the Bills of Exchange Act 1882:

> I think the proper course is in the first instance to examine the language of the statute and to ask what is its rational meaning, uninfluenced by any considerations derived from the previous state of the law, and not to start with inquiring how the law previously stood, and then, assuming that it was probably intended to leave it unaltered, to see if the words of the enactment will bear an interpretation in conformity with this view.[2]

Viscount Finlay adopted this approach when it came to interpreting the 1906 Act, adding:

> When the law has been codified by such an Act as this, the question is as to the meaning of the code as shown by its language. It is, of course, legitimate to refer to previous cases to help in the explanation of anything left in doubt by the code, but, if the code is clear, reference to previous authorities is irrelevant.[3]

---

[1] It is not always the case that the rules which apply to marine policies will be applied to non-marine policies: see, for instance, *Euro-Diam Ltd v Bathurst* [1987] 2 WLR 517 at 531, where Kerr LJ said that the implied warranty of legality (Marine Insurance Act 1906, s 41, considered below) does not apply beyond marine insurance. On marine insurance, see HN Bennett, *The Law of Marine Insurance* (Oxford, Clarendon Press, 1996); S Hodges, *Law of Marine Insurance* (London, Cavendish, 1996); S Hodges, *Cases and Materials on Marine Insurance Law* (London, Cavendish, 1999).
[2] *The Governor and Company of the Bank of England v Vagliano Brothers* [1891] AC 107 at 144–5.
[3] *P Samuel & Co Ltd v Dumas* [1924] AC 431 at 451.

In a few instances it may be positively dangerous to refer to previous cases because the Act has changed the law: for instance, under the common law to determine whether there had been a constructive total loss where an owner had been deprived of possession of the subject-matter and was unlikely to recover it, the court merely looked at whether there was 'uncertainty of recovery,' whereas section 60(1) has made the test 'unlikelihood of recovery,' which is more difficult to satisfy.[4] It is also important to note that the Act is not a complete statement of the law on marine insurance: according to section 91(2): 'The rules of the common law including the law merchant, save in so far as they are inconsistent with the express provisions of this Act, shall continue to apply to contracts of marine insurance.'[5]

---

2. The contract of marine insurance

A contract of marine insurance is a contract whereby the insurer undertakes to indemnify the assured, in manner and to the extent thereby agreed, against marine losses, that is to say, the losses incident to marine adventure.[6]

A 'marine adventure' is one in which: any ship, goods or other moveables[7] (the 'insured property') is exposed to maritime perils; 'the earning or acquisition of any freight, passage money, commission, profit or other pecuniary benefits, or the security for any advances, loan, or disbursements is endangered by the exposure of insurable property to maritime perils'; 'any liability to a third party may be incurred by the owner of, or other person interested in or responsible for, insurable property, by reason of maritime perils' (section 3(2)). A ship includes 'the hull, materials and outfit, stores and provisions for the officers and crew, and, in the case of vessels engaged in a special trade, the ordinary fittings requisite for the trade, and, also, in the case of a steamship, the machinery, boilers, and coals and engine stores, if owned by the assured' (section 30(2), schedule 1, rule 15).[8] 'Goods' means 'goods in the nature of merchandise, and does not include personal effects or provisions and stores for use on board' (section 30(2), schedule 1, rule 17). So it does not include the food to be consumed during the voyage or the jewellery worn by the passengers, but it will

---

[4] *Polurrian Steamship Co Ltd v Young* [1915] 1 KB 922. On constructive total loss, see below. For another illustration of the Act effecting a change in the law, see *Hall v Hayman* [1912] 2 KB 5, although the application of that decision has been confined by *Carras v London and Scottish Assurance Corpn Ltd* [1936] 1 KB 291.

[5] For an example of such a common law rule: *British and Foreign Marine Insurance Co Ltd v Samuel Sanday & Co* (1916) 1 AC 650.

[6] Marine Insurance Act 1906, s 1. In marine insurance it is usual to refer to the assured rather than the insured.

[7] Moveables 'means any tangible property, other than the ship, and includes money, valuable securities, and other documents' (s 90).

[8] 'Ship' also includes hovercraft: The Hovercraft (Application of Enactments) Order 1972/971, art 4, sch 1, pt A.

include food or jewels being transported as cargo. Freight[9] does not come within the terms 'ship' or 'goods' and must, therefore, be specifically insured. By 'maritime perils' is meant perils 'consequent on, or incidental to, the navigation of the sea' (section 3(2)). The result of these definitions is that the insurances effected by the owner of a ship, the owner of goods that are being sent by sea and the shareholder in a company that is laying an electric cable on the seabed[10] are all marine insurances.

A contract of marine insurance can be extended to cover journeys on inland waters or on land 'which may be incidental to any sea voyage,' or to cover the construction of a ship (section 2(1), (2)). If goods are insured 'from the loading thereof' to the time when they are 'safely landed,' then the insurers will not be on risk until the goods are on board the ship (section 30(2), schedule 1, rule 4) and coverage will cease once the goods have been safely landed according to the customary manner of landing such goods and within a reasonable time of arrival (section 30(2), schedule 1, rule 5).[11] A transit clause may be used in a policy, for instance, to extend the cover on goods from the time they leave the warehouse in which they are stored to the time they are delivered to another warehouse,[12] or for a period of sixty days from the time the goods are discharged from the ship.[13]

---

3. The form of the marine insurance policy

A marine insurance contract does not have to be in a particular form, but it will not be admitted in evidence unless it is 'embodied in a marine policy,' although the policy can be issued at the time of the contract or afterwards (section 22), even after a loss has occurred. The policy must specify the name of the assured,[14] or the assured's agent (section 23(1)); the subject matter must be designated with reasonable certainty (section 26(1)); and it must be signed by or on behalf of the insurer, or, in the case of a corporation, it may be sealed (section 24).

The 1906 Act includes, in schedule 1, the form of policy commonly in use at the time known as the 'SG form'. The inadequacies of this policy had, however, been clear as early as the late eighteenth century when it was criticised by Lord Mansfield CJ, although it was not until the late nineteenth century that the Institute of London Underwriters produced the Institute Clauses, which were used to supplement the SG

---

[9] 'Freight' includes 'the profit derivable by a shipowner from the employment of his ship to carry his own goods or moveables, as well as freight payable by a third party, but does not include passage money' (s 90). In other words, the term means the payment by the owner of a cargo to the owner of a ship, but also includes the profit which the owner of the ship derives from using it to carry their own goods: *Flint v Flemyng* (1830) 1 B & Ad 45.

[10] *Wilson v Jones* (1867) LR 2 Exch 139.

[11] If the goods are not so discharged, then the risk ceases: s 30(2), sch 1, r 5.

[12] *In re Traders and General Insurance Association, ex parte Continental and Overseas Trading Co* [1924] 2 Ch 187.

[13] *Gladstone v Clay* (1813) 1 M & S 418. See the Institute clauses (discussed below), ICC (A) cl 8, (B) cl 8, (C), cl 8.

[14] It need not specify the nature and extent of the assured's interest in the subject matter (s 26(2); *Mackenzie v Whitworth* (1875) 1 Ex D 36), although of course the assured must have an insurable interest.

form. These clauses differ according to the type and subject-matter of the policy: so, for example, there are Institute Voyage Clauses (Hulls) (IVCH) and Institute Time Clauses (Hulls) (ITCH) for ships, and Institute Cargo Clauses (ICC) and each comes in several versions.[15] Eventually, the Companies Marine Policy and the Lloyd's Form of Marine Policy, known as the MAR forms, replaced the SG Form in the early 1980s. These are very simple, containing only basic information. To the MAR form is attached the appropriate version of the Institute Clauses. The Institute Clauses have recently been updated by the International Hulls Clauses 2003, although the latter are not as yet widely used.

The importance of these model policies cannot be understated for, as Lord Justice Scott put it, 'most of the law of marine insurance is in essence pure interpretation of the contract contained in the common form of marine policy...[T]he Act merely fixes the interpretation which it requires the Court to put on the old form of policy unless the special terms of the particular contract vary it.'[16]

4. Time and voyage policies

4.1 Time policy

A time policy, which is the commonest form of insurance on a ship, covers a specified duration (section 25(1)), such as 'from 1 January 2005 to 1 June 2005,' or 'whilst anchored in a creek off Netley.'[17] It is common to include a clause which, on notification to the insurers, extends the cover until the ship reaches its destination: ITCH(95) provide that if the ship is at sea and 'in distress or missing' or in port and 'in distress,' then as long as the insurers are notified before the policy expires, the ship will be held covered until it arrives at the next port in good safety at a pro rata premium. Under clause 5.1 of ITCH(95) cover is terminated automatically after change of the Classification Society of the vessel, or an alteration of the class within that society, or any of the Classification Society's surveys is overdue (without the society's consent). The standing of the particular society by which the vessel is classified and the class within which that vessel is placed are both important indicators of the seaworthiness of the vessel. Cover is also automatically terminated where there are certain changes in ownership or use of the ship, such as change of owner, flag or management (clause 5.2).

4.2 Voyage policy

A voyage policy covers a specified journey (section 25(1)), such as 'at and from Liverpool to Calais,' or even a journey with less precisely defined ports of departure and termination, such as 'from any port or ports place or places on the River Plate to any

---

[15] NG Hudson and JC Allen, *The Institute Clauses* (London, Lloyd's of London Press, 1999).
[16] *Kulukundis v Norwich Union Fire Insurance Society* [1937] 1 KB 1, 34. When he talks of 'the old form of policy,' Scott LJ is referring to the SG Form contained in the Marine Insurance Act 1906.
[17] *Whittle v Mountain* [1920] 1 KB 447.

port or ports place or places in France and/or the United Kingdom (final port).'[18] Where, for example, the words 'at and from Liverpool' are used, the risk will attach when the ship is at that place in good safety[19] (section 30, schedule 1, rule 3) and preparations have been made for the voyage by, for instance, beginning to load the cargo.[20] If insured 'from Liverpool,' the risk will attach when – and if – the ship starts on the voyage insured (section 30, schedule 1, rule 2). Where the policy covers freight and it is insured 'at and from' a particular place, 'the risk attaches pro rata as the goods or merchandise are shipped.' In the case of unshipped cargo that is 'in readiness which belongs to the shipowner, or which some other person has contracted with him to ship, the risk attaches as soon as the ship is ready to receive such cargo' (section 30(2), schedule 1, rule 3(d)). A mixed policy is one in which a duration and a voyage are specified (section 25(1)), such as, 'at and from the port of Liverpool to Calais, and for fifteen days whilst there after arrival.'[21] Where a voyage policy on a ship covers a voyage from Liverpool to Calais, the risk will not attach if the voyage begins from Bristol (section 43),[22] but if the voyage begins at Liverpool and at that time the intention is that it will end at Calais, the risk attaches. There is an implied condition that the voyage will commence within a reasonable period of time, unless the circumstance that caused the delay was known to the insurer before the contract was concluded or the insurer waived the condition (section 42).[23] Unless there is a lawful excuse, the voyage must be prosecuted with 'reasonable dispatch' and the insurer is discharged from the point at which any delay becomes unreasonable (section 48).[24] If, after the commencement of the risk, the destination is voluntarily changed this will amount to a change of voyage (section 45(1)).[25] The insurers are discharged from liability from 'when the determination to change [the destination] is manifested,' even if the loss happens before the ship has actually changed voyage,[26] although the insurers remain liable for losses incurred beforehand (section 45(2)). The policy may include an express term that permits a change of voyage provided notice is given immediately after receipt of advices and any amended terms and additional premium are agreed.[27] A change of voyage must be distinguished from a change of destination. The latter occurs where, although a particular destination is specified in the policy, there was never any intention to undertake that voyage. In those circumstances the risk never attaches (section 44). The distinction between a change of voyage and a change of destination rests on the point in time when the decision was made: there will be a change of destination where there is no intention at the start of the voyage to go to the specified destination so the risk never attaches

---

[18] *Marten v Vestey Brothers Ltd* [1920] AC 307.

[19] Good safety is a much lesser standard than seaworthy (see below) and, in essence, simply requires that the ship is afloat: *Parmeter v Cousins* (1809) 2 Camp 235.

[20] *Lambert v Liddard* (1814) 5 Taunt 480.

[21] *Gambles v The Ocean Marine Insurance Co of Bombay* (1876) 1 Ex D 141.

[22] A policy on goods for a voyage normally incorporates the ICC (A), (B) or (C): the risk attaches when the goods leave the warehouse specified in the policy, and there are provisions to cover change of voyage, deviation and delay, which matters are likely to be out of the control of the cargo owner (see below). *Nima SARL v The Deves Insurance Public Co Ltd (The "Prestrioka")* [2003] 2 Lloyd's Rep 3237.

[23] There is nothing in s 42 permitting the assured to excuse the delay by showing that it was involuntary or there was a lawful excuse (contrast with ss 45 and 48).

[24] *Samuel v The Royal Exchange Assurance Co* (1828) 8 B & C 119.

[25] A change of voyage will not be voluntary where, for instance, the ship is ordered into a port by the government: *Rickards v Forestal Land, Timber and Railways Co Ltd* [1941] 3 All ER 62.

[26] *Tasker v Cunninghame* (1819) 1 Bligh 87.

[27] See Institute clauses, IVCH(95), cl 2 (the held covered clause).

and a change of voyage where at some point after the risk attached it is decided to go to a different destination.[28]

The policy may specify the route to be taken, but if it does not it is implied that the customary course between the places specified will be taken (section 46(2)(b)). This is presumed to be the direct geographical route, although that presumption can be rebutted where a less direct route is not unreasonable having regard to those interested in the voyage. Put another way, the route must be 'usual and reasonable in a commercial sense.' What this means may change, for example, as fuel prices in different ports vary.[29] A deviation from the route without lawful excuse will discharge the insurers from liability, even if the ship later returns to the original route (section 46(1)). A deviation is not a change of voyage because the destination remains the same; it is a change in the route to that destination. Unlike the situation where there is a change of voyage, there must be an actual deviation, a mere intention to deviate will not discharge the insurers (section 46(3)). Once again, the insurers will be liable for losses incurred before the deviation (section 46(1)).[30] Some policies include a clause giving the ship liberty to 'touch and stay' at any port; this 'does not authorise the ship to depart from the course of her voyage from the port of departure to the port of destination' (section 30(2), schedule 1, rule 6). In other words, only those ports that are both properly on the route and visited for purposes connected to the adventure contemplated by the policy can be entered. If this were not the case, 'there can be no limit, either of time or place, to the risk described in this policy.'[31] The Marine Insurance Act 1906, section 49(1) lists deviations and delays which will be excused: where authorised by the policy; where caused by circumstances beyond the control of the master and the master's employer; where reasonably necessary to comply with a warranty or for the safety of the ship or subject-matter insured; for the purpose of saving human life or aiding a ship in distress if life may be in danger; where reasonably necessary for obtaining medical aid for anyone on board; where caused by the barratrous conduct of the master or crew, if barratry is one of the insured perils.[32] Once the excuse ceases to operate, the ship must resume course (section 49(2)), which, in the case of the ship driven off its original course, will mean

---

[28] *Wooldridge v Boydell* (1778) 1 Doug KB 16. A held covered clause will, of course, not excuse a change of destination because in such a circumstance the risk will not have attached.

[29] *Reardon Smith Line Ltd v Black Sea and Baltic General Insurance Co Ltd* [1939] AC 562 at 576, per Lord Wright.

[30] *Kewley v Ryan* (1794) 2 H B! 343· *Hare v Travis* (1827) 7 B & C 14.

[31] *Tenant v Brown* (1826) 5 B & C 208 at 219, per Abbott CJ.

[32] Barratry is typically covered by marine policies (see, eg, ITCH(95), cl 6.2.4). It 'includes every wrongful act wilfully committed by the master or the crew to the prejudice of the owner [of the ship]', or, as the case may be, the charterer' (s 30(2), sch 1, r 11). A loss caused by the wrongful act, or with the connivance, of the assured will not be covered, although a loss caused by the misconduct or negligence of the master or crew will be, unless the policy provides otherwise (Marine Insurance Act 1906, s 55(2)(a); also ITCH(95), cl 6.2.2). The act need not be criminal and need not be intended to injure the owner of the ship, but it must prejudice the owner. The question arises as to whether it is for the owner to prove lack of consent or for the insurers to prove consent. Bingham J felt that, in the absence of authority, he would have held that the owner had to prove lack of consent, but in view of a decision by the Court of Appeal in *Elfie A Issaias v Marine Insurance Co Ltd* (1923) 15 Ll L Rep 186, where it was declared to be 'the very cornerstone of British justice' that a wrongful act must be proved by the person alleging it, Bingham J felt obliged to hold that it was for the insurers to establish 'to the high standard required for proof of fraud in a civil case that the owners consented': *N Michalos & Sons Maritime SA v Prudential Assurance Co Ltd* [1984] 2 Lloyd's Rep 264 at 272. See SJ Hazelwood, 'Barratry – The Scuttler's Easy Route to the "Golden Prize"' (1982) *LMCLQ* 383.

taking the most direct route to its destination.[33] The Institute clauses expressly continue coverage in case of deviation provided that notice is given to the insurer immediately after the assured is notified and any amended terms and additional premium are agreed.[34] The insurer will be liable if the assured has complied with the notice requirement, even though this occurs after the loss.[35]

5. Warranties[36]

Before looking at express and implied warranties, it is worth recalling that, subject to contrary agreement of the parties, a breach of a warranty in marine insurance discharges the insurers from liability from the date of the breach (section 33(3)). According to Lord Goff in *The Good Luck*, 'discharge of the insurer from liability is automatic and is not dependent upon any decision by the insurer to treat the contract or the insurance as at an end.'[37]

5.1 Express warranties

An express warranty does not have to be in a particular form as long as the words used make it clear that there is an intention to warrant (section 35(1)), although it must be included in the policy or in a document that is incorporated by reference into the policy (section 35(2)). There are two types of express warranty: those that go to the scope of the cover and those that are promissory warranties, ie, involve a promise by the assured that the warranty will be fulfilled. Only promissory warranties are covered by the provisions in sections 33–41 of the Act, which are discussed below. It is important to distinguish between a promissory warranty and an exclusion clause: while in the former the assured warrants the existence of a certain state of affairs now or at some time in the future, in the latter are listed the perils (the excepted perils) which are not covered by the policy. A loss may be outside the scope of cover (for instance, the policy which covers a ship but not the cargo and the latter is lost), or it may be caused by an excepted peril (for instance, where the ship is not covered for loss by act of war and is sunk by an enemy missile). In neither case will the insurers be liable. It is common for the insurers to require the shipowner to warrant that the ship will not go to particular places at particular times of the year: 'Warranted no St Lawrence between 1 of October and 1 of April.' The assured may warrant the date on which the voyage will commence, such as, 'Warranted to sail on or before 1 of January 2005.' An express warranty of neutrality – that is, a warranty that the property is

---

[33] *Phyn v The Royal Exchange Assurance Co* (1798) 7 TR 505, where there was a deviation when the master of a ship, which had been blown off course, mistakenly took a less direct route to its destination.
[34] See IVCH(95), cl 2.
[35] *Greenock Steamship Co v Maritime Insurance Co* [1903] 1 KB 367.
[36] For a detailed discussion of warranties in insurance contracts generally, see above ch 7.
[37] *The Bank of Nova Scotia v Hellenic Mutual War Risks Assocn (Bermuda) Ltd (The 'Good Luck')* [1991] 2 Lloyd's Rep 191 at 202. See above ch 7.

not enemy property or tainted by carrying enemy property – implies that the property will be neutral at the commencement of the risk and, as far as the assured can control it, will remain neutral during the risk (section 36(1)).

5.2 Implied warranties

The Act implies certain warranties into marine policies. With the exception of the warranty of legality, an implied warranty can be excluded by the agreement of the parties expressed in clear language, or by an express warranty that is inconsistent with it (section 35(3)).[38] The insurers can also waive the breach of an implied warranty (section 34(3)), although this sits uncomfortably with the ruling in *The Good Luck* that a breach of a warranty automatically discharges the insurer from liability.

5.2.1 Warranty of seaworthiness in voyage policies

The Act implies a warranty in a voyage policy that, at the commencement of the voyage, the ship is seaworthy and reasonably fit to carry the goods to the destination specified (sections 39(1) and 40(2)), although there is no implied warranty that goods be seaworthy (section 40(1)).[39] The commencement of the voyage is, normally, when the ship leaves the port and goes out to sea without any intention of returning, even if bad weather forces a return to port.[40] It is up to the insurers to prove that the ship was unseaworthy at this point,[41] although where a ship sinks in calm weather shortly after commencing its voyage, then it is a reasonable assumption that it was unseaworthy at the time of sailing.[42] If the policy attaches while the ship is in port, there is an implied warranty that it 'shall be reasonably fit to encounter the ordinary perils of the port,' (section 39(2)) and seaworthy when it commences its sea voyage. Similarly, if the ship is undertaking a voyage in stages, such as part by river and part by sea (section 39(3)),[43] it must be seaworthy at the start of each stage. If seaworthy at the time of sailing, 'then it mattered not how soon after she became otherwise,'[44] the warranty is not breached since 'the assured makes no warranty to the underwriters that the vessel shall continue seaworthy.'[45]

What amounts to seaworthiness has been the subject of much debate. According to the Act, a ship is seaworthy 'when she is reasonably fit in all respects to encounter the ordinary perils of the seas of the adventure insured' (section 39(4)). In general terms the ship must be 'in a fit state as to repairs, equipment, and crew, and in all other respects, to encounter the ordinary perils of the voyage insured, at the time of

---

[38] *Parfitt v Thompson* (1844) 13 M & W 392; *Quebec Marine Insurance Co v Commercial Bank of Canada* (1870) LR 3 PC 234.
[39] *Koebel v Saunders* (1864) 17 CB (NS) 71. See generally, CB Anderson, 'The Evolution of the Implied Warranty of Seaworthiness in Comparative Perspective' (1986) 17 *JMLC* 1.
[40] *Price v Livingstone* (1882) 3 QBD 679 (a case on charterparties).
[41] *Pickup v The Thames and Mersey Marine Insurance Co Ltd* (1878) 3 QBD 594; *C Hoffman & Co v British General Insurance Co* (1922) 10 Ll L Rep 434 at 436, per Bailhache J.
[42] *Pickup v The Thames and Mersey Marine Insurance Co Ltd*, ibid, at 600, per Brett LJ.
[43] *Claude Bouillon et Cie v Lupton* (1863) 15 CB (NS) 113.
[44] *Parker v Potts* (1815) 3 Dow 23 at 30, per Lord Eldon LC.
[45] *Dixon v Sadler* (1839) 5 M & W 405 at 414, per Parke B.

sailing upon it.'[46] This means that the hull must be sound and able to carry cargo without endangering either the ship or the cargo,[47] the engine must function properly, and there must be an adequate level of competent crew and equipment to meet the ordinary perils of the insured voyage.[48] The ship will be unseaworthy if, although apparently seaworthy on commencing the voyage, there is some latent defect which means that it is not fit for the voyage: so, for example, insufficient fuel for the voyage will render an otherwise sound ship unseaworthy.[49] On the other hand, a ship is not rendered unseaworthy by a trivial defect that can ordinarily be remedied by a competent crew, even though the defect is not, in fact, remedied. This is because a ship's seaworthiness is assessed as it was at the time of departure and not in the light of later events.[50] Cargo will make the ship unseaworthy only if it affects the condition of the ship itself, such as it may if poorly stowed, but not if the only impact is on other cargo. A boat constructed for river use will usually not be seaworthy without modifications. It may be seaworthy, however, if it is merely being sent across the sea to a place where it will act as a river boat and, as far as was possible with a boat of that construction, temporary modifications were made to fit it for the voyage even though they 'might not make her as fit for the voyage as would have been usual and proper if the adventure had been that of sending out an ordinary seagoing vessel.'[51] This should cause no difficulties since the insurer will be aware of the risk involved in such a venture.

It does not matter who or what caused the ship to be unseaworthy or even that the assured had no way of knowing its condition.[52] In a case on the implied warranty of seaworthiness in a bill of lading, it was said that 'the shipowner contracts, not merely that he will do his best to make the ship reasonably fit, but that she shall really be reasonably fit for the voyage.'[53] In *C Hoffman & Co v British General Insurance Co*,[54] even though neither the owner, who acted honestly and reasonably, nor a professional surveyor could detect the problem, the ship's unseaworthy condition meant the insurers were relieved of liability. The insurers will also be discharged from liability even though the ship is subsequently rendered seaworthy: where a ship commenced a voyage from Cuba to Liverpool without the proper number of seamen, the fact that additional sailors were picked up shortly afterwards did not remedy the breach of the implied warranty.[55] Lord Redesdale, speaking in 1816, was clear about the reasons for the strict application of this implied warranty:

---

[46] Ibid.

[47] *Stanton v Richardson* (1875) 45 LJCP 78.

[48] *Tait v Levi* (1811) 14 East 481; *Phillips v Headlam* (1831) 2 B & Ad 380 at 383, per Parke J.

[49] *Greenock Steamship Co v Maritime Insurance Co Ltd*, see above n 35; *Thin v Richards & Co* [1892] 2 QB 141 (a case on the warranty as to seaworthiness in a charterparty).

[50] *Hedley v The Pinkney and Sons Steamship Co Ltd* [1892] 1 QB 58 (a case on the criminal offence of sending an unseaworthy ship to sea: Merchant Shipping Act 1876, s 4). Compare *Steel v The State Line Steamship Co* (1877) 3 App Cas 72 with *GE Dobell & Co v The Steamship Rossmond Co Ltd* [1895] 2 QB 408.

[51] *Burges v Wickham* 3 B & S 669 at 696. See also *Harocopos v Mountain* (1934) 49 Ll L Rep 267.

[52] *Douglas v Scougall* (1816) 4 Doug 269 at 276, per Lord Eldon LC.

[53] *The Glenfruin* (1885) 10 PD 103 at 108, per Butt J.

[54] (1922) 10 Ll L Rep 434.

[55] *Forshaw v Chabert* (1821) 3 Brod & B 158. In any event, *The Good Luck* (see above) means that the insurers are automatically discharged from liability when the implied warranty is breached.

Unless the assured were bound to take care that the vessel was in every respect seaworthy, the consequence would be most mischievous: for the effect of insurance would be to render those chiefly interested much more careless about the condition of the ship, and the lives of those engaged in navigating her.[56]

5.2.2 Seaworthiness in time policies

There is no implied warranty as to seaworthiness in a time policy. Nevertheless, the insurers will not be liable under a time policy if the assured was aware that the ship was unseaworthy at the start of the voyage and this caused the loss.[57] The owner must have had actual knowledge, or had reason to believe the ship was unseaworthy and deliberately failed to undertake an examination of the ship. Simple negligence in not taking precautions against the possibility that the ship is unseaworthy is not sufficient.[58] There must be a 'conscious realisation of the implication of the facts making the ship unseaworthy.'[59] If the ship owner honestly believes as a prudent owner that a crew of ten is sufficient then the fact that a court might regard the ship unseaworthy because it required twelve sailors does not mean the assured is in breach of the implied warranty. Where there are two defects which make the ship unseaworthy and the owner is only aware of one of these, the insurers is liable if the loss is caused by the condition of which the assured is not aware.[60]

5.2.3 Warranty of legality[61]

There is an implied warranty in all marine policies, first, that the adventure insured is lawful and, secondly, that 'so far as the assured can control the matter, the adventure shall be carried out in a lawful manner' (section 41; also section 3(1)).[62] The impact of a breach of this warranty is amply demonstrated by the decision in *Cunard v Hyde*.[63] The insured ship was allowed to sail without a certificate relating to the safe stowage of the cargo having first been obtained. The insurers were not liable when the cargo was lost even though the illegal act did not cause the loss. The reasoning behind this was explained by Tindal CJ:

---

[56] *Wilkie v Geddes* (1815) 3 Dow 57 at 60. See also *Douglas v Scougall*, above n 52 at 276, per Lord Eldon LC.

[57] *Dudgeon v Pembroke* (1877) 2 App Cas 284; Marine Insurance Act 1906, s 39(5); *Thomas v Tyne & Wear SS Freight Insurance Association* [1917] 1 KB 938.

[58] *Compania Naviera Vascongada v British & Foreign Marine Insurance Co Ltd* (1936) 54 Ll L Rep 35 at 58, per Branson J. Also *Compania Maritima San Basilio SA v Oceanus Mutual Underwriting Association (Bermuda) Ltd* [1977] 1 QB 49; *Manifest Shipping & Co Ltd v Uni-Polaris Insurance Co Ltd and La Réunion Europèene (The 'Star Sea')* [1995] 1 Lloyd's Rep 651.

[59] *Compania Maritima San Basilio SA v Oceanus Mutual Underwriting Association (Bermuda) Ltd*, ibid at 76–7, per Roskill LJ (he adopted the phrase from the argument of Mr Mustill QC).

[60] *Thomas v Tyne & Wear SS Freight Insurance Association*, see above n 57. For an example concerning ITCH, see *Martin Maritime Ltd v Provident Capital Indemnity Fund Ltd (The 'Lydia Flag')* [1998] 2 Lloyd's Rep 652.

[61] Although the Marine Insurance Act refers to this as a 'warranty', it is, at the least, unusual since unlike other warranties, the insurers cannot waive illegality.

[62] As has been seen, this warranty has not been implied in contracts of non-marine insurance: *Euro-Diam Ltd v Bathurst*, above n 1 (also ch 9).

[63] (1859) 2 El & El 11. See also *Parkin v Dick* (1809) 11 East 502.

A policy on an illegal voyage cannot be enforced; for it would be singular, if, the original contract being invalid and therefore incapable to be enforced, a collateral contract founded upon it could be enforced.[64]

Where the adventure is illegal before its commencement then the risk never attaches. If it becomes illegal after commencement, the insurers will not be liable where it can be shown that the assured could have prevented the illegality. For instance, in one case the owner ignored the smuggling activities of the crew in spite of the ship having been seized on three previous voyages, and he was not allowed to recover on a policy because his failure to take action amounted to consent.[65] If the adventure becomes illegal as a result of the outbreak of war, the voyage should be abandoned. Lord Davey laid down three rules on the effect which trading with an enemy has on an insurance policy. First, 'the King's subjects cannot trade with an alien enemy, ie, a person owing allegiance to a Government at war with the King, without the King's licence. Every contract made in violation of this principle is void.' Secondly, 'no action can be maintained against an insurer of an enemy's goods or ships against capture by the British Government.' This is so even where the insurance is taken out before the war and also where the person claiming on the policy is a neutral or British subject, if the insurance is effected for an alien enemy. Thirdly, if a loss occurs before the war, the claim is suspended until the restoration of peace.[66]

Not all illegal acts connected with a marine adventure will amount to a breach of the implied warranty. In *Redmond v Smith*,[67] a statute prohibiting the use of seamen who were not under articles was breached, but since this legislation aimed only to provide them with a better method of enforcing their contracts, it was held that the illegality did not affect the contract of insurance.

---

6. Construing the policy

Marine policies are construed in accordance with those principles that apply to contracts generally and that are discussed elsewhere.[68] Most of the provisions in the Act can be modified or excluded by the express agreement of the parties, so the court will start by looking at and construing the terms as they are used in the policy. As in other policies, the parties may agree a definition of a word that is not its ordinary meaning. For instance, in one early case Lord Ellenborough admitted witnesses to show that business people considered the Gulf of Finland to be within the Baltic, even though the two seas are regarded as separate by geographers. On that basis the court held

---

[64] *Redmond v Smith* (1844) 7 Man & G 457 at 474.
[65] *Pipon v Cope* (1808) 1 Camp 434, as explained in *Trinder, Anderson & Co v Thames and Mersey Marine Insurance Co* [1898] 2 QB 114 at 129, per Collins LJ.
[66] *Janson v Driefontein Consolidated Mines Ltd* (1902) AC 484 at 499.
[67] (1844) 7 Man & G 457.
[68] See above ch 8.

that an insurance for a voyage to any port in the Baltic covered a voyage to Reval in the Gulf of Finland.[69]

6.1 Perils of the seas

Marine policies commonly provide cover against 'perils of the seas,'[70] by which is meant 'fortuitous accidents or casualties of the seas.' According to Lord Herschell:

> It think it clear that the term 'perils of the sea' does not cover every accident or casualty which may happen to the subject-matter of the insurance on the sea. It must be a peril of the sea. Again, it is well settled that it is not every loss or damage of which the sea is the immediate cause that is covered by these words. They do not protect, for example, against that natural and inevitable action of the winds and waves, which results in what may be described as wear and tear. There must be some casualty, something which could not be foreseen as one of the necessary incidents of the adventure. The purpose of the policy is to secure an indemnity against accidents which may happen, not against events which must happen. It was contended that those losses only were losses by perils of the sea, which were occasioned by extraordinary violence of the winds or waves. I think this is too narrow a construction of the words, and it is certainly not supported by the authorities, or by common understanding. It is beyond question, that if a vessel strikes upon a sunken rock in fair weather and sinks, this is a loss by perils of the sea. And a loss by foundering, owing to a vessel coming into collision with another vessel, even when the collision results from the negligence of that other vessel, falls within the same category.[71]

The need for this element of unpredictability or fortuity means that perils of the sea do not include 'the ordinary action of the winds and waves' (section 30(2), schedule 1, rule 7), but here the adjective 'ordinary' qualifies the noun 'action' and not 'the winds and waves': the ordinary action of the weather is not a peril of the sea, but ordinary weather, which has an extraordinary effect on the vessel, may be. The fact that adverse weather was forecast does not mean that the loss is not by peril of the sea, although it is important to distinguish between normal and unusual weather: if a port is normally blocked at a particular time of year by ice, caused by this event is not caused by a peril of the sea, but where the ice occurs outside that time, it may be.[72] The insurers were not liable for damage to a cargo of opium when water entered the hold of a ship as a result of ordinary wear and tear (see (section 55(2)(b)) decaying the fabric of the hull: 'There was no weather, nor any other fortuitous circumstance, contributing to the incursion of the water; the water merely gravitated by its own weight through the opening in the decayed wood and so damaged the [cargo].'[73] Where cargo, which at the commencement of the voyage was in good condition and properly stowed, was found on arrival to have been water damaged by rough weather, the insurers were liable, even though that weather was expected on the

---

[69] *Uhde v Walters* (1811) 3 Camp 16.
[70] Eg, IVCH(95), cl 4.1.1 and ITCH(95), cl 6.1.1: 'perils of the seas rivers lakes or other navigable waters.'
[71] *Thomas Wilson, Sons & Co v The Owners of the Cargo* per *The 'Xantho'* (1887) 12 App Cas 503 at 509 (although a case on a bill of lading, Lord Herschell thought the meaning was the same in marine policies, at 510); *The Lapwing* [1940] 112 at 120–1, per Hodson J.
[72] *Popham and Willett v The St Petersburg Insurance Co* (1904) 10 Com Cas 31.
[73] *ED Sassoon & Co v Western Assurance Co* [1912] AC 561 at 563, per Lord Mersey.

particular voyage, because such damage to a large part of the cargo went beyond what would be expected: 'It is not the weather by itself that is fortuitous; it is the stoving in due to the weather, which is something beyond the ordinary wear and tear, of the voyage.'[74] A collision with another vessel, whether or not that other vessel was at fault, is a loss by perils of the seas.[75]

The loss must be of the sea, ie, as the result of being at sea, or as one judge put it, when cargo being loaded fell into the harbour as a result of the ship suddenly listing, 'it was...a peril *of* the sea and not merely a peril *on* the sea. It could not have happened on land; it was a happening which is characteristic of the sea, and of the behaviour of ships.'[76] In the *Inchmaree* case,[77] an engine used for pumping water into the main boilers of a ship was damaged because a valve, which should have been left open, was closed, either by accident or by the negligence of the engineer. The insurers were held not to be liable since the loss was of a type which could have happened on land as easily as at sea. On the other hand, where rats gnaw through a pipe and by this means seawater enters the vessel, the loss will probably be caused by a peril of the sea since damage by seawater could not have happened on land.[78]

If the loss is due to action taken to prevent a loss by a peril of the seas, then the insurers will be liable, as for instance where ventilators were closed to prevent the incursion of the sea during rough weather and this caused the cargo of rice to overheat.[79] Negligence will not preclude liability for a loss by perils of the seas since it 'provides the fortuitous circumstances which entitles the [assured] to recover under the terms of the policy.'[80] However, an act done with the intention of letting in the sea water is not fortuitous and is not, therefore, a peril of the sea,[81] but it may amount to barratry, which is typically covered.[82]

As an all risks policy, ICC (A) covers losses from all causes, including perils of the seas, with the exception of those listed in the exclusion clauses (clauses 4–7). In ICC (B) and (C) the term 'perils of the seas' does not appear and instead there are listed certain events in which the loss results from the vessel carrying the cargo being 'stranded grounded sunk or capsized' (ICC(B), clause 1.1.2), or in collision (ICC (C), clause 1.1.4), or the cargo is lost through 'jettison or washing overboard' (ICC(B), clause 1.2.2),[83] or 'jettison' (ICC(C), clause 1.2.2), or during loading or unloading (ICC(B), clause 1.3).[84]

[74] *NE Neter & Co Ltd v Licenses and General Insurance Co Ltd* [1944] 1 All ER 341 at 343, per Tucker J.
[75] *Thomas Wilson, Sons & Co v The Owners of the Cargo* per *The 'Xantho'*, above n 71.
[76] *The Stranna* [1938] P 69 at 83, per Scott LJ.
[77] *The Thames and Mersey Marine Insurance Co Ltd v Hamilton, Fraser & Co* (1887) 12 App Cas 484. See Marine Insurance Act 1906, s 55(2)(c), and also see below for a discussion of the Inchmaree Clause.
[78] *Hamilton, Fraser & Co v Pandorf & Co* (1887) 12 App Cas 518 (contract of affreightment).
[79] *Canada Rice Mills Ltd v Union Marine and General Insurance Co Ltd* [1941] AC 55.
[80] *The Lapwing* [1940] P 112 at 121, per Hodson J.
[81] *P Samuel and Co Ltd v Dumas*, above n 3.
[82] See above n 30.
[83] 'Jettison' involves a deliberate act of throwing cargo overboard, while 'washing overboard' occurs as the result of the action of the sea or weather.
[84] The facts of *The Stranna*, above n 76, would, presumably, not fit ICC(B), cl 1.1.2, but would come within ICC(B), cl 1.3.

6.2 Inchmaree clause

This clause is commonly found in marine policies and is an attempt to avoid the consequences of the House of Lords' decision mentioned above.[85] For instance, ITCH(95) seeks to limit that decision by covering 'loss or damage to the subject-matter insured caused by bursting of boilers breakage of shafts or any latent defect in the machinery or hull' (clause 6.2.1). This does not make the insurers liable for the latent defect, but only for any damage it causes. If a shaft breaks as a result of a latent defect, the insurers will not be liable for its loss, but they will be liable where a piece of it holes the hull.[86] There are some difficulties in determining what amounts to a latent defect, but it would seem to be something that cannot be discovered by 'such examination as a reasonably careful skilled man would make' and is assessed by looking at the actual state of the subject-matter, not at matters such as the role that the design work may have had in producing the defect.[87]

6.3 Sue and labour or duty of assured clause

The SG Form in schedule 1 of the Marine Insurance Act 1906 includes a term authorising the assured 'to sue, labour, and travel for, in and about the defence, safeguards, and recovery of the said goods and merchandises, and ship, &c., or any part thereof, without prejudice to this insurance; to the charges whereof we, the assurers, will contribute.'[88] It is clearly in the interest of the insurers that the assured be encouraged to avert or reduce the loss from insured perils. Indeed, under section 78(4), it is the duty of the assured and their agents 'to take such measures as may be reasonable for the purpose of averting or minimising a loss.'[89] There is a similar obligation in the Institute clauses: under ITCH(95), clause 11.1, it is the duty of the assured or their servants and agents 'to take such measures as may be reasonable for the purpose of averting or minimising a loss which would be recoverable under this insurance.' At the same time, the insurers agree to contribute to expenses reasonably incurred, with certain exceptions such as general average and salvage charges (clause 11.2; also section 78(2)).[90] A sue and labour clause covers the situation where the expenditure has been incurred to avert, as well as to minimise, loss: the cost of

---

[85] *The Thames and Mersey Marine Insurance Co Ltd v Hamilton, Fraser & Co*, above n 77; WC McAuliffe, 'The Concept of "Latent Defect" in Marine Insurance' (1980) 11 *JMLC* 475.

[86] *Oceanic Steamship Co v Faber* [1906] 11 Com Cas 179 at 187, per Walton J (on appeal (1907) 13 Com Cas 28); *Scindia Steamships (London) Ltd v The London Assurance* [1937] 1 KB 639; *Promet Engineering (Singapore) Pte Ltd v Sturge (The 'Nukila')* [1997] 2 Lloyd's Rep 146.

[87] *Prudent Tankers Ltd SA v Dominion Insurance (The 'Caribbean Sea')* [1980] 1 Lloyd's Rep 338; Hodges, *Law of Marine Insurance*, see above n 1, at 279–83. See International Hulls Clauses.

[88] Generally, AL Parks, 'Marine Insurance: The Sue and Labor Clause' (1977) 9 *JMLC* 415; BP O'Sullivan, 'The Scope of the Sue and Labor Clause' (1990) 21 *JMLC* 545; P MacDonald Eggers, 'Sue and Labour and Beyond: The Assured's Duty of Mitigation' (1998) *LMCLQ* 228.

[89] Here an agent is defined according to the legal meaning of agency as the fiduciary relationship that exists when one person consents to another acting on their behalf so as to affect their legal relationships with third parties. This probably includes the crew (in spite of authority to the contrary: *Astrovlanis Compania Naviera SA v Linard: The 'Gold Sky'* [1972] 2 Lloyd's Rep 187), but not to the builder of a ship, which has been insured by its purchaser (*State of the Netherlands v Youell and Hayward* [1998] 1 Lloyd's Rep 236), or to a salvor (*Aitchison v Lohre* (1879) 4 App Cas 755).

[90] Salvage charges can only be recovered as a loss by an insured peril and only up to the sum insured. On general average, see below.

feeding a cargo of cattle to prevent them from dying can, therefore, be recovered.[91] Measures taken to minimise a loss or to protect the subject-matter will not prejudice the rights of the assured or the insurers, which means that, for instance, they will not be considered to amount to a waiver (clause 11.3). Such clauses are distinct from the rest of the policy, so that the assured can recover both for a total loss and for expenses incurred in the circumstances covered by the clause (section 78(1)). The reason for this is 'to encourage exertion on the part of the assured.'[92] Of course, expenses incurred in respect of a loss not caused by an insured peril will not be recoverable (section 78(3)). The assured must also show that the efforts made or expenses incurred went beyond what is normal:

> The only conditions necessary to give a valid claim under [a sue and labour clause], are danger of damage to the subject insured by reason of perils insured against, and unusual or extraordinary efforts made or expenditure incurred in consequence of such efforts made to attempt to prevent such damage.[93]

The term 'charges' in such a clause includes not just payments made, but valuable rights that have been waived in order to protect the insured subject matter.[94] A clause in a policy which excludes liability for particular average,[95] and therefore covers only total loss of the subject-matter insured (section 76(1)), will not exclude liability for these expenses where there is a suing and labouring clause and they were incurred to avert the danger of a total loss caused by an insured peril. This means that the insurers will be liable for such expenses (and also for salvage charges and particular charges) even though they are not liable on the rest of the policy because a total loss was averted (section 76(2)). Once again, this is because the nature of the liability under a sue and labour clause is supplemental to the main liability under the policy.[96]

6.4 Excepted perils

The insurer is not liable for loss attributable to the wilful misconduct of the assured (section 55(2)(a)) and this cannot be excluded by agreement of the parties.[97] The policy will also typically exclude the insurers from liability in certain specified situations. Under the Marine Insurance Act 1906, section 55(2)(b), (c), unless the policy provides otherwise, the insurers are not liable for loss caused by delay, even if the delay has been caused by an insured peril, or for 'ordinary wear and tear, ordinary leakage and breakage, inherent vice or nature of the subject matter insured, or for any loss proximately caused by rats or vermin, or for any injury to machinery not proximately caused by maritime perils.' The Institute Clauses contain various exclusion clauses: a war exclusion clause, which excludes losses caused by abandoned weapons such as mines; a strikes exclusion clause, which excludes loss caused by

---

[91] *The Pomeranian* (1895) P 34.
[92] *Aitchison v Lohre*, above n 89 at 765, per Lord Blackburn.
[93] *Lohre v Aitchison* (1878) 3 QBD 558 at 567–8.
[94] *Royal Boskalis Westminster NV v Mountain* [1997] 2 All ER 929.
[95] See below.
[96] *Kidston v The Empire Marine Insurance Co Ltd* (1866) 1 LRCP 535. See also International Hulls Clauses.
[97] See above, ch 9.

strikers, rioters or terrorists; a malicious act exclusion clause, which excludes loss by an explosive or weapon of war caused by someone acting maliciously or from a political motive; a nuclear exclusion clause, which excludes loss caused by an atomic or nuclear weapon.[98] In a case where a ship was insured under a policy which excepted war risks it was said that once the assured has proved the loss then, even though the ship disappeared during war and in an area in which enemy submarines were operating, it is presumed that the loss was caused by perils of the sea and it is for the insurers to show the contrary.[99]

7. Collision

Under the Maritime Conventions Act 1911, section 1, where two ships collide and both are to blame, the loss suffered by the ships is added together and divided according to the fault attributable to each, failing which it is shared equally. This has led to insurers providing cover for third party liability, which the Marine Insurance Act 1906, section 3(2)(c) contemplates as an aspect of a marine policy. However, these clauses only cover a collision with another vessel, and, typically, provide cover for no more than three-quarters of the assured's liability.[100]

Where ITCH(95), clause 9, or IVCH(95), clause 7 applies and there is a collision with a ship owned – or partly owned – by the same owners or under the same management, the assured has the same rights as if the other vessel were owned by a different owner (also International Hulls Clauses, cl 7). The issue of the liability for the collision or the amount payable for the services rendered will be referred to an arbitrator.

8. General average

Obviously, it is in the interests of all the parties – the owners of the ship, of the cargo and of the freight, and the crew – that the captain and crew are free to act as necessary to protect the whole of the common adventure. Where expenditure is incurred or a sacrifice of something is made to save the adventure, then it is not unreasonable to expect that all those who benefit by this action should bear a proportion of the loss:

---

[98] See, eg, IVCH(95), cls 21, 22, 23. Some of these types of risk can be insured under special Institute clauses: Institute War and Strikes Clauses Hulls–Time (1995), Institute War Clauses (Cargo) (1982), Institute Strike Clauses (Cargo) (1982).

[99] *The British and Burmese Steam Navigation Co Ltd v The Liverpool and London War Risks Insurance Association Ltd and The British and Foreign Marine Insurance Co Ltd* (1917) 34 TLR 140.

[100] See, eg, ITCH(95), cl 8.1 and IVCH(95) cl 6.1. The International Hulls Clauses provide full cover for an additional premium.

for instance, if cargo is thrown overboard to prevent the ship from sinking, the others – such as, the ship's owner and the owners of the freight and the remaining cargo – benefit and should, therefore, contribute to the loss suffered by the cargo owner. This, in essence, is the purpose of the law of general average. It is a subject of broad significance in maritime law, which cannot be covered in great detail here, nevertheless, its impact on marine insurance requires that its main features be discussed.[101]

A general average loss 'is a loss caused by or directly consequential on a general average act' (section 66(1)), and there is a general average act 'where any extraordinary sacrifice or expenditure is voluntarily and reasonably made or incurred in time of peril for the purpose of preserving the property imperilled in the common adventure' (section 66(2)). According to the York-Antwerp Rules 1994, Rule A, 'There is a general average act, when, and only when, any extraordinary sacrifice or expenditure is intentionally and reasonably made or incurred for the common safety for the purpose of preserving from peril the property involved in a common maritime adventure.'[102] The captain of the ship must have voluntarily, intentionally and reasonably incurred extraordinary expenditure (a general average expenditure),[103] or made an extraordinary sacrifice of equipment or goods (general average sacrifice) to save more than one subject from a common peril which threatened both the interest claiming the contribution and the interest from whom the contribution is claimed.

In explaining why, in one case, the action taken had been extraordinary, Blackburn J said, 'this expenditure was not incurred on behalf of the master as agent of the shipowner, performing his contract to carry on the cargo to its destination and earn freight, but was an extraordinary expenditure for the purpose of saving the property at risk.'[104] Elsewhere it has been observed that 'there must be expenditure abnormal in kind or degree, and it must have been incurred on an abnormal occasion for the preservation of the property.'[105] An expenditure or a sacrifice, which might properly and ordinarily have been incurred by the captain in undertaking the contract of carriage of goods, is not general average. Moreover, there must be an intentional sacrifice: if goods are lost overboard by the action of the waves there is no obligation to contribute. The peril must actually exist and not merely be believed to exist, even if that belief is reasonable: where a master soaked the hold in the mistaken belief that there was a fire and thereby damaged the cargo, there was no general average loss.[106] On the other hand, the master does not have to wait until damage has actually occurred, although 'the peril must be imminent, which means that it must be substantial and threatening and something more than the ordinary peril of the seas.'[107] There is no right of contribution where the loss was caused by the fault of the interest

---

[101] It is often said that the first reported case in which general average is mentioned is *Birkley v Presgrave* (1801) 1 East 220, and it is from this case that the most commonly cited definition of general average comes (at 228, per Lawrence J), but see *Da Costa v Newnham* (1788) 2 TR 406. Generally, NG Hudson, *The York-Antwerp Rules* (London, Lloyd's of London Press, 1996); DJ Wilson and JHS Cooke, *Lowndes and Rudolf: The Law of General Average and The York-Antwerp Rules* (London, Sweet & Maxwell, 1997). Also J Macdonald, 'General Average Ancient and Modern' (1995) *LMCLQ* 480.

[102] The York-Antwerp Rules 2004 form a code on various aspects of general average. The rules are not compulsory, but are commonly expressly incorporated into marine policies.

[103] An example of general average expenditure would be the cost of towage and the harbour dues paid when, in order to save it from an immediate peril, the ship is towed into port.

[104] *Hingston v Wendt* (1876) 1 QBD 367 at 370.

[105] *Société Nouvell D'Armement v Spillers & Bakers Ltd* [1917] 1 KB 865 at 871, per Sankey J.

[106] *Joseph Watson and Son Ltd v Firemen's Fund Insurance Co of San Francisco* [1922] 2 KB 355.

[107] *Société Nouvell D'Armement v Spillers & Bakers Ltd*, see above n 105 at 871, per Sankey J.

claiming the contribution, so the owner of a ship that is unseaworthy at the start of the voyage cannot claim a general average contribution.[108] Similarly, if a latent defect in the cargo is the cause of the loss, as for instance, where coal spontaneously combusts and is damaged as a result of the operation to extinguish the fire, the cargo owner cannot claim a general average contribution, although a contribution may be awarded to the owners of freight lost when the damaged coal is unloaded before the destination is reached.[109]

The interest on whom a general average loss falls is entitled 'to a rateable contribution from the other parties interested,' known as the general average contribution (section 66(3)). Subject to any express term of the policy, an assured, who has incurred a general marine expenditure, can recover from insurers 'in respect of the proportion of the loss which falls upon him'; this is contrasted with the situation in general average sacrifice where the insured may recover 'in respect of the whole loss without having enforced his right of contribution from the other parties liable to contribute' (section 66(4)). An assured who has paid, or is liable to pay, a general average contribution can recover from the insurer (section 66(5)), which in other words means the insurer is liable for the assured's share of the contribution. In addition, where the assured has incurred general average expenses and the contributions of all the interested parties (including the assured's own share) fall below the expenditure, the insurer is liable for the shortfall because it is 'the proportion of the loss which falls' on the assured.[110] Although this reasoning came from a case where the shortfall was caused by a diminution in the value of the cargo, there seems no reason for not applying it more widely, so that whatever the reason for the shortfall the assured can ultimately claim from the insurer. The only difference from the position in general average sacrifice is that the other parties must be approached before a claim can be made against the insurer for the loss that does not form part of the assured's share.[111] Where the ship, freight and cargo, or any two of these, are owned by the same assured, the insurers' liability for general average loss or contributions is determined as if they were owned by different people (section 66(7)).

Insurers are only liable for losses covered by the policy, so they will not be liable for any general average loss or contribution 'where the loss was not incurred for the purpose of avoiding, or in connexion with the avoidance of, a peril insured against' (section 66(6)). However, the Institute clauses include a term covering general average incurred 'to avoid or in connection with the avoidance of loss from any cause,' with certain exceptions.[112] This means that the insurers will be liable if part of the cargo is thrown overboard to enable a ship to escape from a peril, which, while not specifically excluded, is not expressly covered.

The Marine Insurance Act 1906 makes the law of general average subject to the contrary express agreement of the parties, and the Institute Clauses all include provisions incorporating the York–Antwerp Rules 1994.[113] The adjustment of general average is determined by the policy, failing which it will be in accordance with the law of the port of destination. If the adventure ends at another port then it will be in

---

[108] *Schloss v Heriot* (1863) 14 CB (NS) 58.
[109] *Pirie & Co v Middle Dock Co* (1881) 44 LT 424.
[110] *Green Star Shipping Co Ltd v London Assurance Co (The 'Andree')* [1933] 1 KB 378.
[111] Hodges, *Law of Marine Insurance*, above n 1, at 447–8.
[112] ICC (B), (C), cl 2.
[113] Eg, IVCH(95), cl 8.3.

accordance with the law of that port and, where that port is not in the United Kingdom, the adjustment is a foreign adjustment, which will bind the assured and insurers.[114]

9. Particular average

It is important to distinguish general average loss from particular average (also called simple average) loss. In truth the use of the word 'average' in this context merely adds confusion since there is no averaging process, the loss lies where it falls. A particular average loss is 'a partial loss of the subject-matter insured, caused by a peril insured against, and which is not a general average loss' (section 64(1)). It is a partial loss that falls upon one interest (for example, the shipowner or the owner of the cargo) because there is no liability on the other interests in the adventure to contribute. Expenses incurred by the assured for the preservation of the subject-matter insured, other than general average and salvage charges, are particular charges and are not included in particular average (section 64(2)). In essence, the distinction between general average loss and particular average loss is that the former refers to a loss which is chargeable to all those interested in the common adventure because it is done for their benefit, and the latter is a loss borne by one party only, namely the owner of the property damaged, because the adventure as a whole is not imperilled.[115] In an early case Sir William Scott explained:

> General average is for a loss incurred, towards which the whole concern is bound to contribute *pro rata*, because it was undergone for the general benefit and preservation of the whole. *Simple* or *particular* average is not a very accurate expression; for it means damage incurred by or for one part of the concern, the expression is sufficiently understood, and received into familiar use. The loss of an anchor or cable, the starting of a plank, are matters of simple or particular average, for which the ship alone is liable. Should a cargo of wine turn sour on the voyage, it would be a matter of simple average, which the goods alone must bear; and there might be a simple average for which each would be severally liable under a misfortune happening to both ship and cargo at the same time, and from a common cause; as if a water-spout should fall on a cargo of sugars, and a plank from the same violence should start at the same time.[116]

Where a policy is 'warranted free from particular average,' the insurers will not be liable for a partial loss of the subject matter, unless it is a loss incurred through a general average sacrifice (section 76(1)). Such an exclusion will not preclude recovery for particular charges. Indeed, the suing and labouring clause in the SG Form, and the duty of the assured clauses in the Institute clauses, both expressly allow recovery for particular charges.[117] Where a policy is warranted free from particular average under

---

[114] ITCH(95), cl 10.2 expressly provides for this.
[115] Of course, the party incurring a particular average loss may be able to claim under an insurance policy.
[116] *The Copenhagen* (1799) 1 C Rob 289 at 293–4.
[117] Marine Insurance Act 1906, s 78, sch 1; ICC (A), (B), (C), cl 16.

a certain percentage, the insurers are liable if the loss exceeds that percentage. In the latter case, the size of the loss is determined by looking at the actual loss suffered by the insured subject matter, and any general average loss and particular charges must be excluded for the purposes of this calculation (section 76(3), (4)). The use of 'free from average' clauses is common for perishable cargoes. In the SG Form, corn, fish, salt, fruit, flour and seed are warranted free from average, so there will only be liability if there is a total loss; sugar, tobacco, hemp, flax, hides and skins are free from average under 5 per cent, which means there will only be liability if the damage is 5 per cent of the value of the cargo; all other goods, also the ship and freight are free from average under 3 per cent (in all these cases there will be full liability under the clause if the loss is the result of the ship becoming stranded or there is general average liability).

10. Salvage charges

Salvage charges are recoverable under maritime law independently of contract. While general average involves actions by someone who is a party to the common adventure, salvage is performed by someone who is not a party to that enterprise, although once paid salvage charges can be admitted as general average. Unless there is a contrary provision in the policy, salvage charges incurred in preventing a loss by an insured peril can be recovered from the insurers (section 65(1)), except where they represent the cost of services rendered 'by the assured or his agents, or any person employed for hire by them, for the purpose of averting a peril insured against.' These latter costs may, however, be recoverable as particular charges or general average loss, depending on the circumstances in which they were incurred (section 65(2)).

11. Total loss and abandonment[118]

According to the Marine Insurance Act 1906, section 56(1): 'A loss may be either total or partial. Any loss other than a total loss, as hereinafter defined, is a partial loss.' Furthermore: 'A total loss may be either an actual total loss, or a constructive total loss' (section 56(2)) and, unless the policy provides otherwise, cover against total loss includes both types (section 56(3)).

Actual total loss occurs when 'the subject-matter is destroyed, or so damaged as to cease to be a thing of the kind insured, or where the assured is irretrievably deprived

---

[118] R Khurram, 'Total Loss and Abandonment in the Law of Marine Insurance' (1994) 25 *JMLC* 95; see above ch 11.

thereof' (section 57(1)). There will be an actual total loss of goods if they have lost their character. The test is,

> whether, as a matter of business, the nature of the thing has altered...[I]f the nature of the thing is altered, and it becomes for business purposes something else, so that it is not dealt with by business people as the thing which it originally was, the question for determination is whether the thing insured, the original article of commerce, has become a total loss. If it is so changed in its nature by the perils of the sea as to become an unmerchantable thing, which no buyer would buy and no honest seller would sell, then there is a total loss.[119]

After a sunken ship had been raised, it was found that its cargo of dates was impregnated with sewage, so that, although still resembling dates in appearance and of value for distillation into spirit, they were no longer merchantable as dates. It was held that the cargo was an actual total loss.[120] But if part of the cargo survives in its original form, then there is no actual total loss. When a cargo of rice became immersed in water, but, following kiln drying, was later sold as rice, although for a much lower price than if undamaged, it was held to be a partial and not a total loss.[121] Freight is only payable if the cargo is delivered, but if the cargo is delivered, whether in part or damaged, then freight is payable. If the cargo is not delivered and that failure is caused by an insured peril, then there will be a claim for the total loss of freight.

A constructive total loss occurs if: the subject-matter insured is reasonably abandoned because its actual total loss from an insured peril appears to be unavoidable, or because the expenditure necessary to preserve it from actual total loss would exceed its value after the expenditure had been incurred (section 60(1)); or the assured is deprived of possession of ship or goods by an insured peril and it is unlikely that the ship or goods will be recovered;[122] or the cost of recovery would exceed the value when recovered (section 60 (2)(i)); or, in the case of a ship, it is so damaged by an insured peril that the cost of repair would exceed the value of the repaired ship (section 60(2)(ii))[123]; or, in the case of goods, the cost of repair and of forwarding the goods to their destination would exceed their value on arrival (section 60(2)(iii)).[124] In addition to the Act, there is also a common law rule that where goods are insured from the port of loading to the port of destination, and the voyage is frustrated by the detention of those goods for an indefinite period (not merely a temporary delay) and this occurs as the result of an insured peril, the owner can elect to recover from

---

[119] *Asfar & Co* v *Blundell* [1896] 1 QB 123 at 127, per Lord Esher MR.
[120] Ibid.
[121] *Francis v Boulton* (1895) 1 Com Cas 217.
[122] This requires the assured to show, on a balance of probabilities, that there is an 'unlikelihood of recovery': *Polurrian Steamship Co Ltd v Young*, above n 4 at 937, per Warrington J
[123] The value for the purposes of determining whether there has been a constructive total loss is the market value after repairs and not the value, if any, stated in the policy (see ss 27(4) and 60(2)). However, ITCH(95), cl 19.1, and IVCH(95), cl 17.1 exclude the rule by specifying that the value for assessing a constructive total loss will be the insured value. Moreover, cls 19.2 and 17.2 specify that in determining whether the costs of repair exceed the insured value, only the costs relating to 'a single accident or sequence of damages arising from the same accident shall be taken into account.'
[124] The two sub-sections that make up s 60 are to be treated as covering different sets of circumstances. It is not the case that s 60(1) represents a general rule that is illustrated by s 60(2): *Robertson v Petros M Nomikos Ltd* [1939] AC 371 at 382, per Lord Wright, and at 392, per Lord Porter. See also G Gauci, 'Constructive Total Losses in the Law of Marine Insurance' in D Rhidian Thomas (ed), *The Modern Law of Marine Insurance* (London, Lloyd's of London Press, 1996).

the insurers for a constructive total loss: so, in one case the owner of goods was able to claim following an indefinite interruption of the voyage by war.[125]

As might be imagined, there is plenty of scope for disputes over the boundary between an actual total loss and a constructive total loss. According to Lord Abinger CB:

> If, in the progress of the voyage [the subject-matter] becomes totally destroyed or annihilated, or if it be placed by reason of the perils against which [the insurer] insures, in such a position, that it is wholly out of the power of the assured or of the underwriter to procure its arrival, he is bound by the very letter of his contract to pay the sum insured.[126]

If a ship retains its character as a ship and could be repaired, it is not an actual total loss, but it may be a constructive total loss where the cost of those repairs would exceed its repaired value. On the other hand, when 'reduced to a mere congeries of planks, the vessel was a mere wreck, the name which you may think fit to apply to it cannot alter the nature of the thing.'[127] A pile of planks is not a ship. In one case in which it was said that a ship was not an actual total loss, Potter LJ remarked: 'Albeit it was grounded and incapable of proceeding without salvage and a degree of repair, its essential components were not so damaged or dissipated that its role and function as a dead ship susceptible of being towed away for scrap had been totally destroyed.'[128] The ship in that case was in one piece and the possibility or even probability that it might had to be broken into two in order to salvage it was irrelevant in deciding whether or not it was an actual total loss.[129] There will be an actual total loss if the ship has been missing for a reasonable time, although the assured must, of course, show on the balance of probabilities both that this loss can be presumed to have occurred within the period of the insurance and that it was caused by an insured peril. When, during the First World War, a ship disappeared rapidly in an area where there were stray British and German floating mines and German submarine patrols, the court held that the loss was by enemy action, which was not an insured peril.[130]

Where there is an actual total loss the assured does not have to give notice of abandonment to the insurers (section 57(2)), although under some of the Institute clauses notice must be given to the insurers promptly after the assured becomes – or should have become – aware of the loss so that a surveyor may be appointed and notice more than twelve months after the loss will discharge the insurers.[131] In the event of a constructive total loss, the assured has the choice to treat the loss as a partial loss or to abandon the subject matter to the insurers and treat it as if it were an actual total loss (section 61). Until that choice has been made there is no abandonment: in other words, unless the assured gives notice of abandonment to the insurers, the loss can only be treated as a partial loss (section 62(1)).[132] Notice need not take any particular form (section 62(2)), but it must be given 'with reasonable diligence

---

[125] *British and Foreign Marine Insurance Co Ltd v Samuel Sanday & Co*, above n 5. This rule applies only to goods, and is excluded in the Institute War Clauses (Cargo), cl 3.7, and the Institute Strikes Clauses (Cargo), cl 3.8.
[126] *Roux v Salvador* (1836) 3 Bing NC 266 at 286.
[127] *Cambridge v Anderton* (1824) 2 B & C 691 at 692–3, per Abbott CJ.
[128] *Fraser Shipping Ltd v Colton* [1997] 1 Lloyd's Rep 586 at 591.
[129] See also, *Barker v Janson* (1868) LR 3 CP 303.
[130] *Macbeth & Co v King* (1917) 86 LJKB 1004.
[131] Eg, ITCH(95), cl 13.
[132] For the reasoning behind these rules, see *Roux v Salvador*, above n 126 at 286–7, per Lord Abinger CB.

after the receipt of reliable information of the loss' (section 62(3)). The insurers can expressly accept the notice or such acceptance can be inferred from their conduct, although silence on its own is not acceptance (section 62(5)). The purpose of the notice of abandonment is, primarily, to give the insurers the opportunity to take action and, therefore if in the circumstances there is no possibility of the insurers taking action, notice is unnecessary (section 62(7)): the owners of the '*Kastor Too*' were excused this obligation because there was no opportunity to give such notice before the ship sank,[133] and the owners of the '*Litsion Pride*' were similarly excused when the ship sank in a war zone in the Persian Gulf after being hit by a missile because there was no possibility of salvage in that place.[134] The requirement of notice can also be waived by the insurers (section 62(8)), although the Institute clauses stipulate that actions to protect or recover the subject matter will not amount to a waiver. Until there has been an acceptance the assured can withdraw the notice of abandonment, but acceptance amounts to an admission of liability by the insurers and makes the abandonment irrevocable (section 62(6)), unless it is made or accepted under a mistake of fact, in which case the acceptance may be a nullity.[135]

It is worth making clear the difference between abandonment and notice of abandonment. Abandonment is 'a legal concept rather than an act, physical or mental. The legal concept is the cession of the ship to the insurer (see... sections 63 and 79 of the Act). That cession occurs in both forms of total loss, actual as well as constructive.... The cession, however, only occurs upon payment, and only if the underwriter is willing to accept the cession.'[136] A constructive total loss does not depend on the assured issuing a notice of abandonment: in any particular factual situation there is a single legal answer to the question, has there been a constructive total loss? Giving notice signifies the assured's election to treat it as a constructive total loss, but such notice can only be given if there has been a constructive total loss. The absence of notice is, in effect, an election by the assured to treat what amounts to a constructive total loss as merely a partial loss. Notice is an offer to cede, which, on payment of the claim, the insurer can take up or reject and which, before that time, can be withdrawn by the assured. Where notice of abandonment is not required, there still must be an election by the assured through conduct or omission to act. Unless the assured makes an election to treat the loss as a constructive total loss it will be treated as only a partial loss and while the former election is revocable up to the time of acceptance by the insurer, the latter is not.[137]

If there is a constructive total loss, which is proximately caused by an insured peril, and this is followed almost immediately by an actual total loss, which is proximately caused by an uninsured peril, the assured will be able to recover under the policy if there is sufficient evidence to show that, had the second event not occurred, the subject-matter would, nevertheless, have been a constructive total loss. Moreover, section 77 states that if a partial loss, which has not been repaired, is followed by a total loss, the insurer is only liable for the total loss because otherwise the assured

---

[133] *Kastor Navigation Co Ltd v Axa Global Risks (UK) Ltd* [2004] EWCA Civ 277.
[134] *Black King Shipping Corporation and Wayang (Panama) SA v Mark Ranald Massie* (1985) 1 Lloyd's Rep 437 at 478, per Hirst J.
[135] *Norwich Union Fire Insurance Society Ltd v WH Price Ltd* [1934] AC 455.
[136] *Kastor Navigation Co Ltd v Axa Global Risks (UK) Ltd*, above n 133, at (76), per Rix LJ.
[137] *Stringer v English and Scottish Marine Insurance Co Ltd* (1869) LR 4 QB 676.

would recover more than an indemnity, but this problem does not arise where a constructive total loss has been followed by an actual loss, and therefore the two events are not merged.[138]

On payment for total loss, the insurers are subrogated to the rights of the assured and may – but are not obliged to – take over the interest of the assured in the remains of the subject-matter insured (section 63(1)), and if the subject-matter is a ship, they are entitled to any freight which is being earned and is earned after the loss, as well as reasonable remuneration for carrying the shipowner's goods after the loss (section 63(2)).[139] The rule entitling the insurers to acquire the assured's rights in the subject matter following payment for a total loss is, like subrogation, connected to the principle of indemnity. Nevertheless, subrogation and abandonment give rise to distinct sets of rights.[140] As Lord Blackburn pointed out:

> My Lords, I have no doubt at all that where the owners of an insured ship have claimed or been paid as for a total loss, the property in what remains of the ship, and all rights incident to the property are transferred to the underwriters as from the time of the disaster in respect of which the total loss is claimed for and paid. The right to receive payment of freight accruing due but not earned at the time of the disaster is one of those rights so incident to the property in the ship, and it therefore passes to the underwriters because the ship has become their property, just as it would have passed to a mortgagee of the ship who before the freight was completely earned had taken possession of the ship…This is at times very hard upon the insured owner of the ship; he can, however, avoid it by claiming only for a partial loss, keeping the property in himself, and so keeping the right to earn the accruing freight. In such a case he recovers an indemnity for the amount of the loss actually sustained, in calculating which all the benefits incident to the property retained by the shipowner must be considered. But the right of the assured to recover damages from a third person is not one of those rights which are incident to the property in the ship; it does pass to the underwriters in case of payment for a total loss, but on a different principle. And on this same principle it does pass to the underwriters who have satisfied a claim for a partial loss, though no property in the ship passes.[141]

If the insurers accept the property in the subject matter following a total loss, they will take any rights that come with that subject matter: they will be entitled 'to every benefit to which the assured is entitled in respect of the thing to which the contract of insurance relates, but to nothing more.'[142] In *Attorney General v Glen Line Ltd*,[143] the insurers paid for a total loss following the seizure of a ship by the German government during the First World War. After the war the ship was recovered and sold for more than had been paid to the assured. It was held that the insurers were entitled to retain the whole of the proceeds of the sale. Where the insurance policy relates to a ship, the assured may keep any payments made in advance for the carriage of cargo, but the insurers are entitled to payments received after abandonment that relate to

---

[138] *Kastor Navigation Co Ltd v Axa Global Risks (UK) Ltd*, above n 133.
[139] See also s 79(1); *Yorkshire Insurance Co Ltd v Nisbet Shipping Co Ltd* [1962] 2 QB 330 at 339, per Diplock J.
[140] Marine Insurance Act 1906, s 79(1).
[141] *Simpson v Thomson, Birrell* (1877) 3 App Cas 279 at 292, per Lord Blackburn. The 'different principle' is, of course, subrogation. See also, *Page v Scottish Insurance Corporation* 140 LT 571 at 575, per Scrutton LJ.
[142] *The Sea Insurance Co v Hadden & Wainwright* (1884) 13 QB 706 at 718 per Lindley LJ.
[143] [1930] 37 Ll L Rep 55.

cargo subsequently delivered by the insurers.[144] Abandonment does not pass to the insurers the right to recover damages from a third party. Such a right is not an incident of the ownership of the property acquired by the insurers through abandonment because the property had already been damaged by the tortfeasor before the insurers acquired it.[145] So, unless the assured assigns the right to sue a third party, the insurers must take any action against the wrongdoer in the name of the assured under their right of subrogation.[146]

Accepting the abandonment can present the insurers with problems: for instance, the owner of a sunken ship which is blocking sea lanes may be required to pay for its removal.[147] It may, therefore, be that the insurers will not wish to exercise the right to acquire ownership of the subject matter. There is some authority that suggests that ownership automatically vests in the insurers, and some which suggests that unless the insurers accept the abandonment the property becomes *res nullius*, that is, it is owned by no one. The more plausible view is that ownership remains with the assured: so, for instance, the Marine Insurance Act 1906, sections 63(1) and 79(1) both refer to the insurers as being 'entitled' to take over the assured's interests, which suggests that it stays with the assured unless the insurers make use of their entitlement.[148]

---

[144] See also, *Davidson, Jones and Jenner v Case* (1820) 2 Brod & B 379; Marine Insurance Act 1906, s 63(2). The right to freight earned after abandonment is now typically expressly waived in contracts of marine insurance: eg, the Institute Time Clauses Hulls, cl 20 (on these clauses, see below ch 16); *Coker v Bolton* [1912] 3 KB 315.

[145] Anon, 'Abandonment and Subrogation in Marine Insurance' (1917) 30 *Harvard L Rev* 383 at 384.

[146] *Simpson v Thomson, Birrell*, above n 141.

[147] *Arrow Shipping Co Ltd v Tyne Improvement Commissioners (The 'Crystal')* [1894] AC 508. In that case, the House of Lords decided that the crucial time was not when the ship became an obstruction (at which time it was owned by the assured) but when the authority, under statutory powers, incurred expenses in the removal (at which time it was owned by the insurer).

[148] Hodges, *Law of Marine Insurance*, above n 1, at 11–12. But see Bennett, *The Law of Marine Insurance*, above n 1, at 353–4.

17

Reinsurance[1]

1. Introduction

Reinsurance is insurance taken out by insurers to protect themselves against exposure to a massive claims liability. By spreading risks between insurers worldwide, it becomes possible to issue cover for major and often international risks which would otherwise be uninsurable and to support national insurance markets which are too small in capacity to cover domestic risks. In practice many reinsurance contracts written on the London market cover 100 per cent of the underlying risk in respect of policies written by overseas insurers who themselves lack the sophistication or resources to underwrite the business, a practice known as 'fronting'. Reinsurance also enables insurers to protect their own solvency, and indeed, the rules made by the Financial Services Authority under the Financial Services and Markets Act 2000 requires insurers to have adequate reinsurance in place as a guarantee of their solvency margin.

Having struggled through the definition of an insurance contract, the reader will not find it too surprising to learn that it is rather difficult to arrive at an all-embracing definition of a reinsurance policy. There is no statutory definition of reinsurance, although there are statutory references to the activity, and there is no exhaustive judicial definition because of the sheer variety of different types of reinsurance. According to Lord Lowry, 'Reinsurance is prima facie a contract of indemnity…under which the reinsurer indemnifies the original insurer against the whole or against a specified amount or proportion…of the risk which the latter has himself insured.'[2] More simply, Viscount Cave LC said that, 'by a contract of reinsurance the reinsuring party insures the original insuring party against the original loss.'[3]

---

[1] See generally, *Butler and Merkin on Insurance Law*, Sweet & Maxwell, looseleaf; Barlow, Lyde & Gilbert, *Reinsurance Law and Practice,* Informa, looseleaf; O'Neill and Wolonecki, *The Law of Reinsurance* (Sweet & Maxwell, 2nd edn, 2004); Edelman, *The Law of Reinsurance* (Oxford University Press, 2005).

[2] *Forsikringsaktieselskapet Vesta v Butcher* [1989] AC 852 at 908. See also, *Travellers Casualty & Surety Co of Europe Ltd v Commissioners of Customs & Excise*, 6 May 2005, unreported, VAT Tribunal, where it was held that reinsurance is the reinsurance of the business of an insurer even though that business is not strictly insurance (eg, the issue of fidelity bonds),

[3] *Forsikringsaktieselskabet National (of Copenhagen) v Attorney-General* [1925] AC 639 at 642, per Viscount Cave LC.

Reinsurance is to be distinguished from co-insurance, insurance arranged in layers and double insurance, in each of which cases the assured has a separate contract of insurance with each underwriter. Reinsurance is also not an assignment of the direct policy by the reinsured to the reinsurers,[4] neither is it a partnership between the reinsured and the reinsurers.[5] There is no privity of contract between the assured and the reinsurers so that the assured's only action is against his own insurers,[6] although some reinsurance agreements contain cut-through clauses under which the assured is given a direct action against the reinsurers in the event of the reinsured's insolvency and in principle it is perfectly possible for reinsurers to agree to accept direct liability to the assured.[7] A cut-through clause is potentially enforceable by the assured under the Contracts (Third Parties) Act 1999, although there is some doubt as to whether a cut-through clause is valid under the English insolvency rule of equal treatment of unsecured creditors.[8]

Confusingly, however, reinsurance has in some case been regarded by the courts as a further policy on the direct subject-matter rather than as a policy covering the reinsured's liability under the primary policy: so the reinsurance of primary fire policies was described in one case as 'in effect a policy of insurance against loss by or incidental to fire,'[9] and for regulatory purposes under the 2000 Act reinsurance is deemed to be of the class of direct insurance to which the contract relates.[10] It would seem that there is no fixed rule on the subject, and that whether reinsurance is regarded as akin to a liability cover or to a further insurance on the direct subject matter depends upon the wording of the contract. In *Feasey v Sun Life of Canada*,[11] for instance, a reinsurance agreement which was drawn up as a life policy was held to be a life policy and thus subject to the rules on insurable interest in the Life Assurance Act 1774.[12]

---

[4] *Re Lancashire Plate Glass Fire and Burglary Insurance Co Ltd* [1912] 1 Ch 35.

[5] *Re Norwich Equitable Fire* (1887) 57 LT 241.

[6] Marine Insurance Act 1906, s 9(2); *In re Law Guarantee Trust and Accident Society Ltd. Liverpool Mortgage Insurance Company's Case* [1914] 2 Ch 617 at 647–8, per Scrutton J.; *Phoenix General Insurance Co of Greece SA v Halvanon Insurance Co Ltd* [1985] 2 Lloyd's Rep 599 at 614, per Hobhouse J: 'The relationship of a reassured and a reinsurer is not that of agent and principal; it is one as between principals. The reinsurer is in no sense a party to the contract of original insurance and has no rights under it.'

[7] See *Grecoair Inc v Tilling* [2005] Lloyd's Rep IR 151, where there was no evidence of any such intention even though the reinsurers took over all responsibility for handling the assured's claim.

[8] The rule in *British Eagle International Air Lines Ltd v Compagnie Nationale Air France* [1978] 1WLR 758.

[9] *British Dominion General Insurance Co Ltd v Duder* [1915] 2 KB 394 at 400, per Buckley LJ; *Forsikringsaktieselskabet National (of Copenhagen) v Attorney-General* above n 3 at 642, per Viscount Cave LC; *British Dominion General Insurance Co v Duder* [1915] 2 KB 394 at 400, per Buckley LJ; *Re NRG Victory Reinsurance* [1995] 1 All ER 533; *Toomey v Eagle StarInsurance Co Ltd* [1994] 1 Lloyd's Rep 516 at 522–4, per Hobhouse LJ. According to the Marine Insurance Act 1906, s 9(1): 'The insurer under a contract of marine insurance has an insurable interest in his risk, and may re-insure in respect of it.' But in *Charter Reinsurance Co Ltd v Fagan*[1996] 2 Lloyd's Rep 113 at 117, Lord Mustill did not rule out the possibility that there might be cases in which the reinsurance is not an insurance of the subject-matter of the primary contract. As Lord Mustill pointed out, the main issue in contention here is the regulation of insurance business, although there are other issues, such as the requirement of a policy in marine insurance under Marine Insurance Act 1906, s 22, and the applicability of the Life Assurance Act 1774.

[10] *Re NRG Victory Insurance* [1995] 1 All ER 533; *Re Friend's Provident Life* [1999] Lloyd's Rep IR 547.

[11] [2003] Lloyd's Rep IR 637.

[12] The root decision of *Dalby v India & London Life* (1854) 3 CB 364 may indeed be regarded as an early example of the same point.

For the most part the same principles apply to reinsurance policies as to insurance policies in general, and therefore in this chapter only the features which are peculiar to reinsurance will be examined.

2. Types of reinsurance contracts

Reinsurance agreements[13] may be proportional or non-proportional. Under a proportional agreement, the reinsured retains a proportion of the risk and cedes the balance to reinsurers. The premium paid to the reinsured is (minus expenses) payable to the reinsurers to reflect the parties proportions. Under a non-proportional agreement, the reinsured retains a given sum (referred to as the 'deductible', and much the same as an excess clause in a direct policy) and the reinsurers accept liability for an amount in excess of that sum up to a given maximum sum. The premium under a non-proportional agreement is not necessarily based on the direct premium. The reinsured may on occasion be required by a reinsurance of either type to retain the deductible for its own account, thereby giving the reinsurers some guarantee that the business accepted by the reinsured is of the appropriate quality, although in most cases there is no such provision and the reinsured is free to reinsure the amount of its deductible elsewhere.[14] A deductible is normally to be construed as applying to the amount of the reinsured's liability for a claim and not to the totality of the claim itself.[15]

The simplest form of reinsurance is facultative, which is the reinsurance of a single risk. By way of example, A insures a ship with B and B enters into facultative reinsurance with C to cover the liability undertaken in the first agreement. This type of reinsurance is nearly always proportional, and is written in the London market by means of a slip policy. This document is a short one and its most important provision is the 'full reinsurance' clause, of which the following is typical: 'being a reinsurance of and warranted same terms and conditions as original, and to follow the settlements.' There may be other terms, including claims provisions.

Treaty reinsurance is appropriate where the reinsured wishes to obtain cover for a portfolio of risks. The reinsurance may extend to the reinsured's entire business ('whole account' reinsurance) or it may be confined to a part of that business (eg, the marine account). A treaty is a framework arrangement under which the parties agree that all risks of the type described are to fall within the scope of the treaty. Treaties may be obligatory or non-obligatory. Under the former, any risks accepted by the

---

[13] Other than those which are pure fronting arrangements.

[14] *Great Atlantic Insurance v Home Insurance* [1981] 2 Lloyd's Rep 219; *Phoenix General Insurance of Greece v Halvanon Insurance* [1985] 2 Lloyd's Rep 599; *Societe Anonyme d'Intermediaries Luxembourgeois v Farex Gie* [1995] LRLR 116; *GE Reinsurance Corporation v New Hampshire Insurance Co* [2004] Lloyd's Rep IR 404.

[15] See *Allianz Marine Aviation (France) v GE Frankona Reinsurance Ltd London* [2005] EWHC 101 (Comm), in which the reinsured's subscription to the direct policy was 45.238%. The total loss was US$17,857,901.85, the reinsured's share being US$8,078,557. It was held that the US5,000,000 deductible was to be applied to the latter and not to the former figure.

reinsured are automatically ceded to the reinsurance without either party having any discretion in the matter: there may be an obligation on the reinsured to inform the reinsurers on a regular basis[16] of risks accepted, but failure to notify the reinsurers will not prevent the risk from attaching even if notification is not made until after the loss has occurred.[17] If the contract is non-obligatory, the reinsured has the right to decide whether to proffer a risk for acceptance, and the reinsurers have the right to refuse any particular risk. The treaty here is less a binding obligation and more of an agreed machinery for the presentation of proposals by the reinsured. A hybrid is a facultative-obligatory contract under which the reinsured has the right to decide which risks to cede but the reinsurers have no right to reject what is presented to them. This arrangement is unfavourable to reinsurers as they are more or less at the mercy of the reinsured who may decide to offload poor business on the reinsurers,[18] and a 'fac-oblig' contract imposes an obligation on the reinsured to inform the reinsurers of risks which have been ceded, as in the absence of a declaration the reinsured cannot be seen to have exercised the option to cede.[19]

Treaties come in various proportional and non-proportional forms. Quota share and surplus treaties are both proportional, the reinsured retaining an agreed proportion of each risk and the reinsurers taking the remainder. The most important form of non-proportional treaty is excess of loss, under which the reinsurers accept liability for sums in excess of the reinsured's 'ultimate net loss,' a figure defined as the total aggregate of liabilities, excluding fixed costs, arising out of an event or occurrence. Stop loss reinsurance is a guarantee of solvency, and comes into play when the reinsured's loss reach an agreed figure. Lloyd's operates reinsurance to close which enables syndicates of members to place limits on their liabilities. A syndicate's accounts for each year remain open for three years for the receipt of premiums and the payment of claims, the account is then closed and future liabilities reinsured by another Lloyd's syndicate.[20]

Where the amounts at stake are large, a combination of the various forms of reinsurance may be used. In particular there may be a number of different excess layers of reinsurance.[21] Reinsurers may themselves take out cover, known as retrocession, and there may often be a large number of contracts at different levels.

There has been some discussion as to whether all reinsurance treaties are insurance contracts. If the reinsurers are obliged to accept risks ceded to them, then there seems no difficulty in seeing this as a contract of insurance.[22] But where there is no such obligation, then this is not reinsurance, rather it is, as Gatehouse J expressed it,

---

[16] Often monthly and by the use of 'bordereaux'.
[17] *Glencore International AG v Ryan, The Beursgracht* [2002] 1 Lloyd's Rep 574.
[18] *Aneco Reinsurance Underwriting Ltd v Johnson & Higgins* [1998] 1 Lloyd's Rep 565.
[19] See *Glencore International AG v Alpina Insurance Co* [2004] 1 Lloyd's Rep 111, where it was held that a declaration could not be made after the assured (this was a direct declaration policy) had become aware that a loss had occurred.
[20] *Toomey v Eagle Star Insurance Co Ltd* above n 9 516 at 520, per Hobhouse LJ; *Baker v Black Sea and Baltic General Insurance Co Ltd* [1996] LRLR 353 at 358 and 360–1, per Staughton and Millett LJJ.
[21] For a description of the operation of the market, and the use of a 'spiral' of reinsurance contracts involving business which was loss-making but for reinsurance protection, see the important judgment of Thomas J in *Sphere Drake Insurance Ltd v Euro International Underwriting Ltd* [2004] Lloyd's Rep IR 525, where brokers were held to have engaged in a fraud by arranging a succession of unnecessary reinsurance contracts from which they derived commission.
[22] *Forsikringsaktieselskabet National (of Copenhagen) v Attorney-General* [1925] AC 639.

'simply a procedural mechanism which, if operated as both parties no doubt hoped and expected, would secure considerable commercial benefit to both sides.'[23]

Reinsurance treaties are generally long-term contracts which last for more than the one year traditional for direct policies. Three year agreements are common. Provision is made in such agreements for annual review of the contract, so that if the reinsured's losses are unusually high the reinsurers may have the right either to cancel the agreement on its anniversary date or at the very least give notice of a premium increase.[24]

3. Formation of the contract

Reinsurance is subject to all the rules applied to other insurance contracts, including the particular requirements of a marine or life policy, where appropriate. As noted above, the reinsureds' insurable interest is either the risk under the primary policy or the risk of having to indemnify the reinsured. If the insured under the primary policy has no insurable interest, the reinsureds will also have no insurable interest and neither policy will be enforceable.[25]

Reinsurance is frequently formed in advance of insurance. This raises as yet unresolved questions as to the agency of the broker appointed by the assured to place the direct policy – as it is clear that the broker cannot be acting for the assured unless he has been expressly authorised to place reinsurance[26] – and the status of the reinsurance agreement prior to direct policy being allocated to it. The courts have for the most part sidestepped these problems and have resorted to the traditional contractual analysis that an agreement to reinsure amounts to a standing offer which can be accepted by any insurer by accepting the direct risk and thus becoming entitled to the benefit of the reinsurance.[27]

Reinsurance agreements are normally the result of protracted negotiations, with formal agreement being reached by the scratching of a slip. As with other London market placements, the slip constitutes a series of bilateral contracts between the reinsured and each reinsurer. It is possible for a contract to come into existence prior to the scratching of the slip, as where the parties have reached agreement on all material points, although this is relatively unusual.[28]

---

[23] *Societe Anonyme d'Intermediaries Luxembourgeois v Farex Gie* [1995] LRLR 116 at 135.
[24] *Charman v New Cap Reinsurance Corporation Ltd* [2004] Lloyd's Rep IR 373.
[25] For instance, a ppi policy (that is, a proof of policy interest policy under which the insurers agree to pay whether or not the insured has an insurable interest) cannot be the subject of an enforceable reinsurance policy: *Re Overseas Marine Insurance Co Ltd* (1930) 36 Ll L Rep 183.
[26] *SAIL v Farex Gie* [1995] LRLR 116.
[27] *GAFLAC v Tanter, The Zephyr* [1985] 2 Lloyd's Rep 529; *Youell v Bland Welch (No 2)* [1990] 2 Lloyd's Rep 431; *Kingscroft v Nissan (No 2)* [1999] Lloyd's Rep IR 603; *Tryg Baltica International (UK) Ltd v Boston Compania De Seguros SA* [2005] Lloyd's Rep IR 40; *Bonner v Cox Dedicated Corporate Member Ltd* [2004] EWHC 2963 (Comm).
[28] See *Sun Life Assurance Co of Canada v CX Reinsurance Co Ltd* [2004] Lloyd's Rep IR 86.

The duty of disclosure applies to reinsurance,[29] although there are two important modifications to ordinary principles to be borne in mind. The first is that the facts which may be material for reinsurance purposes are quite different from those which are material under a direct policy. Material facts will include:

- the liabilities faced by the reinsured under the direct cover,[30] including the amount of the cover[31] and facts which render the direct risk a particularly acute one[32] such as the nature of the insured subject matter[33] any moral hazard affecting the direct assured[34];
- the reinsured's claims experience[35];
- the manner in which the reinsured sets aside reserves for actual and potential claims, as the figure for reserves may mislead the reinsurers into thinking that there are few outstanding claims if the reinsured adopts an unusual reserving policy which omits many potential claims[36];
- the amount of the premium charged by the reinsured.[37]

The second is that the duration of the duty depends upon the nature of the reinsurance agreement. As far as a treaty is concerned, it was held by Aikens J in *HIH Casualty and General Insurance v Chase Manhattan*[38] that no duty of utmost good faith attaches to a treaty, which is a contract *for* insurance rather than a contract *of* insurance, and that the reinsurers' remedies are those generally available at common law, including avoiding for misrepresentation. However, the nature of the treaty in that case was not in issue, and it may be that the duty of disclosure depends upon whether the treaty is obligatory or non-obligatory. If the treaty is obligatory, so that the reinsurers cannot refuse proffered declarations, it is arguable that reinsured's duty of disclosure exists when the treaty is set up, although it is clear that there is no separate duty of disclosure in respect of each individual declaration. If the treaty is non-obligatory, so that the reinsurers can refuse individual risks, then *HIH* is plainly right and the duty of disclosure applies only to declarations and not to treaty itself.[39]

---

[29] *Highlands Insurance Co v Continental Insurance Co* [1987] 1 Lloyd's Rep 109.
[30] *Abrahams v Mediterranean Insurance and Reinsurance Co* [1991] 1 Lloyd's Rep 216; *Aneco Reinsurance Underwriting Ltd v Johnson & Higgins* [2002] Lloyd's Rep IR 91.
[31] *Toomey v Banco Vitalico de Espana de Seguros y Reaseguros* [2004] EWCA Civ 622.
[32] *Property Insurance v National Protector Insurance* (1913) 108 LT 104.
[33] *WISE Underwriting Agency Ltd v Grupo Nacional Provincial SA* [2004] Lloyd's Rep IR 764.
[34] *Brotherton v Aseguradora Colseguros SA (No 3)* [2004] Lloyd's Rep IR 774.
[35] *Aiken v Stewart Wrightson* [1995] 3 All ER 449; *Groupama Insurance Co Ltd v Overseas Partners Re Ltd* [2003] EWHC 34 (Comm).
[36] *Assicurazioni Generali SpA v Arab Insurance Group* [2002] Lloyd's Rep IR 131.
[37] *Allianz Via Assurance v Marchant* 1996, unreported; *Mander v Commercial Union Assurance Co plc* [1998] Lloyd's Rep IR 93; *Markel International Insurance Company Ltd and another v La Republica Compania Argentina de Seguros Generales SA* [2005] Lloyd's Rep IR 90.
[38] [2001] Lloyd's Rep IR 191.
[39] *SA d'Intermediaries Luxembourgeios v Farex Gie* [1995] LRLR 116.

4. Express and implied terms

4.1 Express terms and incorporation of terms

As noted above, the practice of the London market in relation to the creation of facultative contracts is to use a minimal amount of wording, often no more that the full reinsurance clause. The first part of the full reinsurance clause states 'warranted terms and conditions as original' or its equivalent. The balance of authority holds that this wording is effective to incorporate the terms of the direct policy into the reinsurance, although there are some comments to the contrary. Lord Griffiths in *Forsikringsaktieselskapet Vesta v Butcher* expressed 'regret that so little thought was apparently given to the difference between a primary insurance contract and a reinsurance contract at the time the reinsurance was placed with Lloyd's,'[40] and his Lordship, dissenting on this point, concluded that the full reinsurance clause amounted to no more than a warranty by the reinsured that the terms of the direct policy disclosed to the reinsurers were accurately stated. In *Toomey v Banco Vitalico de Espana de Seguros y Reaseguros*[41] Thomas LJ speaking for the Court of Appeal refused to reach a concluded decision on the point, and instead held that there had been an express warranty to the effect that the terms of the direct policy were as represented to the reinsurers.

Assuming that the full reinsurance clause does have an incorporating effect, incorporation will plainly extend to the basic cover granted by the direct policy. However, claims conditions and other policy provisions will be incorporated only if consistent with the nature of reinsurance. The precise conditions for incorporation were laid down by David Steel J in *HIH Casualty and General Insurance v New Hampshire Insurance*[42] as follows: (i) the term must be germane to the reinsurance; (ii) the term must make sense, subject to permissible 'manipulation' of the words used, in the reinsurance agreement; (iii) the term must be consistent with the express terms of the reinsurance; and (iv) the term must apposite for inclusion in the reinsurance. Notice provisions have thus been held to be capable of incorporation only if they make sense in a reinsurance context.[43] In *Home Insurance Co of New York v Victoria-Montreal Fire Insurance Co*[44] the reinsurance agreement consisted of a slip containing special terms of reinsurance with attached to it a primary fire policy of the type issued by the original insurers, which had been amended to a minimal extent – so, for instance, the syllable 're' had been inserted before 'insure'. As might be expected, almost none of the terms of the primary fire policy were appropriate for a reinsurance policy, in particular a term which prohibited an action on the policy once twelve months had elapsed since the fire. The Privy Council approached this document on the basis that

---

[40] [1989] 1 All ER 402 at 406 (also at 420, per Lord Lowry).
[41] [2004] EWCA Civ 622.
[42] [2001] Lloyd's Rep IR 191.
[43] *Home Insurance of New York v Victoria-Montreal Fire* [1907] AC 59; *Municipal Mutual Insurance Ltd v Sea Insurance Co Ltd* [1996] LRLR 265; *CNA International Reinsurance v Companhia de Seguros Tranquilidade* [1999] Lloyd's Rep IR 289; *Prifti v Musini Sociedad Anonima de Seguros y Reaseguros* [2004] Lloyd's Rep IR 528.
[44] [1907] AC 59.

the primary fire policy was attached merely for information, as showing the origin of the liability which was the subject of the reinsurance policy. Since the reinsurers only became liable once claims had been settled and they had no control over when claims would be settled, the Privy Council concluded that the term could not apply to the reinsurance policy.

The leading authority on the point is now the decision of the Court of Appeal in *HIH v New Hampshire*,[45] In *HIH* the clause in issue was a waiver of defences clause in the underlying contract. The reinsurance was 'as original,' and it was held by both David Steel J and the Court of Appeal that the clause had been incorporated into the reinsurance by the general words of incorporation (the Court of Appeal disagreed with David Steel J that there had been incorporation by express reference in the reinsurance to a 'cancellation clause' as the clause was held by the Court of Appeal not to relate to cancellation). David Steel J held that the wording incorporated clause could be 'manipulated' so as to give it sense in the reinsurance context: accordingly, as manipulated, the clause operated as a waiver of reinsurers' rights of avoidance in the event of a breach of the duty of utmost good faith by the reinsured. The Court of Appeal rejected this analysis, and held that it was not possible to manipulate the wording of the incorporated clause as it contained references which could not be translated to the reinsurance context. The Court of Appeal's view was that the clause was incorporated only in unmanipulated form, which meant that it did not amount to a waiver of reinsurers' rights of avoidance for independent breaches of duty by the reinsured. Instead, it operated only to: (i) allow the reinsured to recover from reinsurers in circumstances where the reinsured's own right of avoidance against the assured had been lost by reason of the clause (ie, it was a form of follow the settlements clause); and (ii) allow the reinsured to recover where there had been a common presentation of the risk to the reinsured and reinsurers, so that both parties had agreed to waive their rights and the result was back-to-back cover. Rix LJ pointed out that giving the clause the wider meaning accepted by David Steel J would prevent the reinsurance from being back-to-back with the insurance, as the reinsurance would contain a waiver of rights independent of the insurance itself.

Terms which are ancillary to the direct policy will not be incorporated unless express reference is made to them in the reinsurance agreement. The most important terms which fall into this category involve dispute resolution, namely, exclusive jurisdiction clauses,[46] arbitration clauses[47] and choice of law clauses.[48] A leading underwriter clause in the direct policy is also to be regarded as ancillary to reinsurance and thus will not be incorporated by general words: reinsurers will not, therefore, be bound by variations to the direct risk agreed to by the leading direct underwriter for the other reinsureds.[49]

---

[45] [2001] Lloyd's Rep IR 702.
[46] *AIG Europe (UK) Ltd v The Ethniki* [2000] Lloyd's Rep IR 343; *Cigna Life Insurance Co of Europe SA-NV v Intercaser SA de Seguros y Reaseguros* [2001] Lloyd's Rep IR 821; *AIG Europe SA v QBE International Insurance Ltd* [2002] Lloyd's Rep IR 22; *Prifti v Musini Sociedad Anonima de Seguros y Reaseguros* [2004] Lloyd's Rep IR 528.
[47] *Pine Top Insurance v Unione Italiana* [1987] 1 Lloyd's Rep 476; *Excess Insurance v Mander* [1995] LRLR 358; *Tryg-Hansa v Equitas* [1998] 2 Lloyd's Rep 439.
[48] *Gan Insurance Co Ltd v Tai Ping Insurance Co Ltd* [1999] Lloyd's Rep IR 472.
[49] *American International Marine Agency of New York v Dandridge* [2005] EWHC 829 (Comm).

4.2 Implied terms

The limited requirement for disclosure under obligatory and facultative/obligatory treaties is justified by the implication of terms to protect the reinsurers from the reinsured's acceptance of bad risks and settling losses unreasonably: the terms were set out in *Phoenix General Insurance of Greece v Halvanon Insurance*,[50] a case involving a proportional treaty. The terms are:

(a) keeping proper records and accounts of risks accepted, premiums received and claims made or notified;

(b) investigating all claims and confirm that there is liability before liability is accepted;

(c) investigating risks offered prior to acceptance of them;

(d) keeping full and accurate accounts showing sums owing and owed;

(e) ensuring that all amounts owing are collected promptly, and that all amounts payable are paid promptly;

(f) making all documents reasonably available to RR.

The argument that there is a general obligation on the reinsured to keep the retention for its own account was rejected in *Halvanon* itself. *Baker v Black Sea*[51] held that the implied terms are not conditions precedent to the reinsurers' liability, so that if the reinsured breaks any of the terms the reinsurers remains liable. In *Bonner v Cox Dedicated Corporate Member Ltd*[52] some doubt was cast upon the width of the implied terms recognised in *Halvanon*, at least in respect of excess of loss contracts. In that case the reinsured had engaged in 'writing against' the reinsurance, ie accepting risks which were likely to give rise to net losses without reinsurance but which were perfectly profitable with reinsurance. Morison J rejected the notion that the reinsured under an excess of loss contract owes any duty of care or continuing duty of good faith to the reinsurers, and that the obligations of the reinsured were limited to implied terms in respect of: (i) exercising some judgment in the acceptance of risks (even if that judgment was misconceived); (ii) acting honestly; and (iii) accepting risks which were not intended to fall within the terms of the reinsurance (although this matter was often one of pre-contract disclosure). There were no further obligations, and the notion that 'writing against' reinsurance was a breach of duty was misconceived as the very essence of reinsurance was that this would occur. In so deciding, Morison J distinguished proportional from non-proportional reinsurance, although he did cast some doubt on the notion that even a reinsured under a proportional contract might owe various implied duties to the reinsurers, as held by Hobhouse J in *Halvanon*.

---

[50] [1985] 2 Lloyd's Rep 599.
[51] [1995] LRLR 287.
[52] [2004] EWHC 2963 (Comm).

4.3 Interpretation of reinsurance contracts: the presumption of back-to-back cover

Irrespective of incorporation, there is a general presumption that the cover granted by a proportional reinsurance agreement is 'back-to-back' with the underlying insurance, as the parties can be regarded as 'co-adventurers' even though as a matter of law they are simply contracting parties. This presumption, which is in essence a principle of construction rather than a rule of law, was emphasised in *Forsakrings Vesta v Butcher*, in order to overcome problems arising where the reinsurance and the insurance are governed by different applicable laws. In that case the direct policy, which was governed by the law of Norway, contained a warranty that the insured fish farm would be under 24 hour watch. The reinsurance, which was governed by English law, incorporated the terms of the direct policy, so that the same warranty was contained in the reinsurance. A loss occurred at a time when the assured was in breach of warranty, which under Norwegian law did not provide a defence to the insurers because it was not causative of the loss, but the reinsurers nevertheless denied liability to the insurers and relied upon the stricter English rule that a breach of warranty has an automatic discharging effect. The House of Lords was unwilling to accept the defence, and resorted to the presumption of back-to-back cover to conclude that it was appropriate to construe the reinsurance agreement in the same manner as the insurance agreement, ie in accordance with principles of Norwegian law, even though the reinsurance was governed by English law. The outcome is welcome but the reasoning is curious.[53] The back-to-back analysis has been followed on numerous occasions,[54] but has two main limitations: as a rule of construction, the notion of back-to-back cover cannot operate to strike out or override those express terms of the reinsurance agreement which are inconsistent with the underlying terms[55]; and there is no similar presumption in non-proportional reinsurance contracts, as in those cases the parties are not co-adventurers and the reinsurance premium is assessed independently of the premium paid to the reinsured.[56]

The presumption of back-to-back cover was arguably taken to extreme lengths in *Groupama Navigation et Transports v Catatumbo CA Seguros*.[57] In this case an English law reinsurance policy incorporated the terms of an underlying Venezuelan law marine policy. The insurance contained a classification warranty, and the reinsurance itself included a classification warranty, albeit similarly worded. The assured failed to comply with the class warranty, but as their breach was not causative of the loss the insurers were not discharged from liability. The reinsurers nevertheless pleaded their own warranty, and argued that the presumption of back-to-back cover had been ousted by the use of an express English law provision. The Court of Appeal

---

[53] It should be noted that the finding that the full reinsurance clause had incorporated the direct policy's terms into the reinsurance was the root cause of the problem. Had the House of Lords rejected the incorporation theory, as per Lord Griffiths, the same result could have been reached without doing violence to the rule that the applicable law governs the construction of the contract.

[54] *Commercial Union Assurance v Sun Alliance* [1992] 1 Lloyd's Rep 475; *Ace Insurance SA-NV v Zurich Insurance Co* [2001] Lloyd's Rep IR 504; *Goshawk Syndicate Management Ltd and others v XL Speciality Insurance Co* [2004] Lloyd's Rep IR 683.

[55] *Youell v Bland Welch (No 1)* [1992] 2 Lloyd's Rep 127; *Municipal Mutual Insurance Ltd v Sea Insurance Co Ltd* [1996] LRLR 265; *GE Reinsurance Corporation v New Hampshire Insurance Co* [2004] Lloyd's Rep IR 404.

[56] *Axa Reinsurance v Field* [1996] 3 All ER 517.

[57] [2001] Lloyd's Rep IR 141.

disagreed, and applied the *Vesta* case to the facts. Mance LJ, delivering the leading judgment, took the view that the reinsurance warranty had been inserted on a provisional basis only to guard against the possibility that there was no classification warranty in the direct policy, and that once it became clear that there was such a warranty then the reinsurance warranty ceased to operate and the principle of back-to-back cover applied. This case comes close to allowing a rule of construction to override the express terms of the reinsurance.

5. Losses and claims

5.1 Loss

The reinsured suffers a loss for reinsurance purposes when its liability to the direct assured is established and quantified by judgment, arbitration award or binding settlement.[58] In the absence of express wording, reinsurers are not liable for the costs incurred by the reinsured in defending claims brought by the assured.[59] The six-year limitation period under section 5 of the Limitation Act 1980 for a claim against the reinsurers will also run from the date on which liability has been established and quantified.[60] The fact that the reinsured has not made payment under the direct policy is not a relevant consideration. A problem has arisen in relation to excess of loss treaties, as many ultimate net loss clauses contain wording to the effect that the reinsured 'shall actually have paid.' Decisions of the English courts,[61] culminating in that of the House of Lords in *Charter Reinsurance v Fagan*,[62] have reached the conclusion that this type of wording does not oust the principle that payment is not required. In *Charter Re* itself the reinsured had become insolvent and was unable to make payment to its policyholders, which meant that given the wording a literal interpretation would have fortuitously relieved the reinsurers from any possible liability. The outcome has more to do with commercial considerations than with the meaning

---

[58] *Baker v Black Sea & Baltic General Insurance Co Ltd* [1995] LRLR 261; *Halvanon Insurance Co Ltd v Companhia de Seguros do Estado de Sao Paulo* [1995] LRLR 303; *North Atlantic Insurance Co Ltd v. Bishopsgate Insurance Ltd* [1998] 1 Lloyd's Rep 459; *Sphere Drake Insurance plc v Basler Versicherungs-Gesellschaft* [1998] Lloyd's Rep IR 35. This is the same test applicable to liability policies. It is possible to vary this by express wording, and to specify that the reinsurers' duty to provide an indemnity arises on the happening of a given event, which may arise where the reinsurance is on the direct subject matter rather than on liability: see *Feasey v Sun Life of Canada* [2003] Lloyd's Rep IR 637.
[59] *Baker v Black Sea and Baltic General Insurance Co Ltd* [1998] Lloyd's Rep IR 327.
[60] *North Atlantic Insurance Co Ltd v. Bishopsgate Insurance Ltd, above n 55; Sphere Drake Insurance plc v Basler Versicherungs-Gesellschaft* [1998] Lloyd's Rep IR 35.
[61] *Home Insurance Co v Mentor Insurance* [1989] 3 All ER 74; *Re A Company No 0013734 of 1991* [1992] 2 Lloyd's Rep 413.
[62] [1996] 3 All ER 46.

of the words used,[63] and it may be that clearer wording could achieve the result that the liability of reinsurers is postponed until the date of payment by the reinsured.[64]

5.2 The effect of a settlement by the reinsured

In the event that there has been a judgment or arbitration award in favour of the assured against the reinsured, there is rarely any doubt[65] that the reinsured has proved its loss and is able to claim from the reinsurers, as long of course as the loss is covered by the terms of the reinsurance agreement.[66] The position is more complex in the case of a settlement. The principle adopted by the Court of Appeal in *Commercial Union Assurance Co v NRG Victory Reinsurance Ltd*[67] is that a settlement is not binding on the reinsurers, and that the reinsured can be called upon to prove that as a matter of law it faced liability to the assured under the direct policy. The reinsured was the insurer of the Exxon Valdez, which ran aground in 1989. The assured incurred substantial losses, including clean-up costs, and sought to recover clean-up costs from the reinsured. Proceedings were commenced against the reinsured in Texas, and in the course of those proceedings the reinsured settled on the basis that it was liable for clean-up costs. The reinsurers denied liability under the reinsurance, on the basis that as a matter of law the direct policy excluded clean-up costs. Clarke J at first instance accepted that the reinsured had to prove its loss, and that required proof of actual liability to the assured it was not enough that the reinsured had reached a settlement which was bona fide and businesslike. Clarke J further ruled that, in determining legal liability, the matter should be approached not from the point of view of an English court (even though the direct insurance was governed by English law), but rather from the point of view of the court which would have determined the matter had the action against the reinsured proceeded to judgment. At the time of the settlement the matter was pending in an action in Texas, and Clarke J was satisfied by the evidence of a US lawyer that the court in Texas would in all probability have ruled in favour of the reinsured had the matter gone to a non-expert judge and to a jury, and accordingly he held that the reinsured was entitled to summary judgment. The Court of Appeal on appeal set aside the summary judgment. The Court of Appeal agreed with Clarke J on the need of the reinsured to prove its loss, but held that the learned judge had been wrong to rely upon the prediction in the evidence of the U.S. lawyer as to the outcome of the Texas proceedings, as that prediction had been based on a variety of considerations as well as legal considerations. It was necessary for the reinsured to go further and to demonstrate that there was legal liability as

---

[63] This is plain from a reading of the speech of Lord Mustill. There is a brave if unconvincing attempt in the speech of Lord Hoffmann to demonstrate that the words of the ultimate net loss clause are concerned with establishing the amount payable rather than the date of payment.

[64] This has been recognised at the direct level, in the form of 'pay to be paid' clauses in liability policies which have been construed as having this very effect: *The Fanti and the Padre Island* [1990] 2 All ER 705. Under New York law, actual payment is required of the reinsured: *Cleaver and Bodden v Delta American Reinsurance Co* [2002] Lloyd's Rep IR 167.

[65] In *Commercial Union Assurance Co v NRG Victory Reinsurance Ltd* [1998] Lloyd's Rep IR 421 the Court of Appeal raised the possibility that reinsurers might not be obliged to follow a 'perverse' judgment from an overseas court.

[66] See below.

[67] [1998] Lloyd's Rep IR 421, reversing [1998] 1 Lloyd's Rep 80.

a matter of law. The result, therefore, is that the assured cannot settle proceedings brought against it in a foreign court, and seek to recover from its reinsurers, unless the settlement is based upon the absence of any arguable defence in those proceedings: it is not enough that the settlement is advantageous to the reinsured, in that it limits costs and removes the possibility of a large award of punitive damages by a foreign court, or that the foreign court may well find against the reinsured for reasons other than the strict application of the law applicable to the insurance agreement.[68]

More recently, it has also been decided, in *Lumberman's Mutual Casualty Co v Bovis Lend Lease Ltd*,[69] a direct liability case, that a global settlement which encompasses various claims and cross-claims can be taken into account only if it contains a clear allocation of sums to each of the various items within its scope. In the absence of such allocation, the settlement has no legal effect on the reinsurers and there can be no claim under the reinsurance even if the reinsured is able to prove its liability as a matter of law. The decision is widely regarded as unsupportable, given that global settlements very rarely seek to allocate sums in this way[70] and because a settlement which purports to apportion liabilities will almost inevitably result in the reinsured breaking its obligation not to admit liability. It is particularly curious that the reinsured is deprived of the right to establish its liability as a matter of law simply because such a settlement has been entered into.

5.3 Follow the settlements

To overcome the problems raised by the principles recognised in *Commercial Union v NRG Victory*, most facultative reinsurance agreements today contain 'follow the settlements' clauses, normally as the second part of the 'full reinsurance clause' referred to earlier. These clauses originally appeared in facultative agreements in the 1930s, in order to prevent the reinsurers from reopening the reinsured's settlements. In the leading authority, *Insurance Co of Africa v Scor (UK) Reinsurance*,[71] the Court of Appeal accepted the general rule that reinsurers are liable to the reinsured if, in the words of Goff LJ: (i) 'in settling the claim the insurers have acted honestly and have taken all proper and business like steps in making the settlement'; and (ii) 'the claim so recognised by [the reinsured] falls within the risks covered by the policy of reinsurance as a matter of law.'[72] The Court of Appeal went on to hold that the effect of a follow the settlements clause is to modify the first of these requirements, and that instead of having to prove its loss as a matter of law it is enough that the reinsured has settled with the assured in a bona fide and businesslike fashion.[73]

---

[68] In the subsequent trial, *King v Brandywine Reinsurance Co (UK) Ltd* [2004] Lloyd's Rep IR 554, Colman J held that the reinsured had not proved that it faced liability for clean up costs under the direct policy, so that the reinsurers were not liable to provide an indemnity.

[69] [2005] Lloyd's Rep IR 74.

[70] Reaching a settlement on that basis is a far less likely prospect as a matter of practice.

[71] [1985] 1 Lloyd's Rep 312.

[72] The two limbs in *Scor* were approved by the House of Lords in *Hill v Mercantile & General* [1996] LRLR 160.

[73] An alternative formulation used in many reinsurances, although mainly from outside England, is that the reinsurers are to 'follow the fortunes' of the reinsured. There is no English authority on this wording, and there is a difference of view among practitioners as to whether these words replicate 'follow the settlements' or whether they impose additional burdens on reinsurers.

There is little authority on the meaning of 'bona fide and businesslike,' although it is established that the burden of proof is on the reinsurers to show that the settlement was not bona fide and businesslike.[74] What is clear is that the settlement must be a genuine compromise, and that any payment by the reinsured which is purely ex gratia for its own business purposes is not within the scope of a follow settlements clause. The reinsured must also show that it has made appropriate investigations into the circumstances of the loss and has taken advice from local lawyers as to the meaning of the direct policy.[75]

There is a potential difficulty in ascertaining the relationship between the two principles in *Scor* that the settlement must be bona fide and businesslike and that the loss must fall within the scope of the reinsurance. In most cases the insurance and reinsurance will be on the same terms, either by incorporation of the terms or by reason of the 'back-to-back' cover presumption. The problem arises where the reinsured reaches a settlement on the basis of its view that it probably faces liability under the direct policy, but the reinsurers deny liability on the basis that they are not liable under the identical words in the reinsurance agreement. If the reinsurers are allowed to act in this way, the follow the settlements clause is undermined as the settlement can be indirectly reopened, but if they are not allowed to act in this way then the second condition of liability as set out in *Scor* is removed. The matter was addressed by the Court of Appeal in *Assicurazioni Generali Spa v CGU International Insurance plc*.[76] The Court of Appeal rejected the reinsurers' suggestion that they were always entitled to rely upon the incorporated wording of the reinsurance, and it also rejected the reinsured's most extreme argument that there was an automatic right to recovery if the settlement was bona fide and businesslike. Instead, the Court of Appeal adopted a middle approach,[77] namely that the reinsured was entitled to recover if: (i) the settlement was bona fide and businesslike; and (ii) the basis on which the claim was accepted by the reinsured was one which fell, or at least arguably fell, within the scope of the direct policy and the reinsurance. The effect of this reasoning is that the reinsurers cannot challenge the facts as found by the reinsured, and they cannot not challenge the reinsured's conclusions as to the coverage of the direct policy: all that they can do is to put the reinsured to proof of the basis upon which the claim had been admitted to ensure that the facts and the wording have not been disregarded.

These principles may of course be varied by the express terms of the reinsurance, and the obligations of the reinsurers may be restricted[78] or extended. However, the courts have decided that the obligation on reinsurers to follow settlements 'whether liable or not'[79] or 'without question'[80] do not vary the general rule laid down in *Assicurazioni Generali*.

---

[74] *Insurance Co of the State of Pennsylvania v Grand Union Insurance* [1990] 1 Lloyd's Rep 208.
[75] See generally *Gan Insurance v Tai Ping Insurance (No 3)* [2002] Lloyd's Rep IR 612.
[76] [2004] Lloyd's Rep IR 457.
[77] Predicated by Evans J in *Hiscox v Outhwaite (No 3)* [1991] 2 Lloyd's Rep 524.
[78] *Hill v Mercantile and General* [1996] LRLR 341.
[79] *Charman v Guardian Royal Exchange Assurance plc* [1992] 2 Lloyd's Rep 607.
[80] The formulation in *Assicurazioni* itself.

5.4 'Claims co-operation' or 'claims control' clauses

A claims co-operation clause requires the reinsured to provide information to reinsurers[81] and will generally give the reinsurers the ultimate right to consent to any settlement in order to be bound by it at the reinsurance level. A claims control clause takes negotiations with the assured out of the reinsured's hands and confers upon reinsurers the right to negotiate with the assured. These types of clauses have come into widespread use relatively recently, in order to remove the possibility that reinsurers might face liability to indemnify the reinsured in circumstances where there are valid doubts as to the veracity of a judgment, award or settlement which establishes and quantifies the reinsured's liability. Such clauses are particularly important where the insurance is simply a fronting operation for London market reinsurers, as it is obvious that the reinsured has no real interest in the outcome any claim by the assured given that the reinsurers are providing an indemnity of 100 per cent. It is apparent that the obligation of reinsurers to follow settlements can scarcely be reconciled with their right to approve settlements. The relationship between follow settlements clauses and claims clauses was authoritatively determined by the Court of Appeal in the *Scor* case, Goff LJ laying down the principle that the claims clause has priority and 'emasculates' any obligation to follow settlements. However, it was further held in *Scor* that if the claims clause is not a condition precedent then its breach will not affect the right of the reinsured to recover, provided that he can prove his loss as a matter of law, by being sued to judgment or establishing liability in proceedings against the reinsurers. By contrast, if compliance with the claims clause is a condition precedent to the liability of the reinsurers, then non-compliance with the clause is fatal, even if there is a judgment against the reinsured in favour of the assured. The reinsurers are under a duty of good faith in exercising their rights under a claims clause, and must not arbitrarily refuse to approve a settlement[82] or refuse to take over the negotiations with the assured where there can be no liability unless the negotiations are conducted by the reinsurers.[83] That the test for breach is not one of reasonableness, as this would require the court to second-guess the commercial judgment of the reinsurers: the test is whether the reinsurers have in reaching their decision taken into account considerations extraneous to the merits of the claim.

---

[81] As in *Royal and Sun Alliance Insurance plc v Dornoch Ltd* [2004] Lloyd's Rep IR 826, where it was held that the reinsured's obligation to notify direct losses of which it had knowledge was not broken until the assured's loss (under a liability policy) had actually been ascertained.
[82] *Gan Insurance Co Ltd v Tai Ping Insurance Co Ltd (Nos 2 and 3)* [2002] Lloyd's Rep IR 667.
[83] *Eagle Star Insurance Co Ltd v Cresswell* [2004] EWCA Civ 602.

Appendix

MARINE ASSURANCE ACT 1906
(6 Edw 7 c 41)

Arrangement of sections

Marine Insurance

1 Marine insurance defined

A contract of marine insurance is a contract whereby the insurer undertakes to indemnify the assured, in manner and to the extent thereby agreed, against marine losses, that is to say, the losses incident to marine adventure.

2 Mixed sea and land risks

(1) A contract of marine insurance may, by its express terms, or by usage of trade, be extended so as to protect the assured against losses on inland waters or on any land risk which may be incidental to any sea voyage.

(2) Where a ship in course of building, or the launch of a ship, or any adventure analogous to a marine adventure, is covered by a policy in the form of a marine policy, the provisions of this Act, in so far as applicable, shall apply thereto; but, except as by this section provided, nothing in this Act shall alter or affect any rule of law applicable to any contract of insurance other than a contract of marine insurance as by this Act defined.

3 Marine adventure and maritime perils defined

(1) Subject to the provisions of this Act, every lawful marine adventure may be the subject of a contract of marine insurance.

(2) In particular there is a marine adventure where—

(a) Any ship goods or other moveables are exposed to maritime perils. Such property is in this Act referred to as "insurable property_;

(b) The earning or acquisition of any freight, passage money, commission, profit, or other pecuniary benefit, or the security for any advances, loan, or disbursements, is endangered by the exposure of insurable property to maritime perils;

(c) Any liability to a third party may be incurred by the owner of, or other person interested in or responsible for, insurable property, by reason of maritime perils.

"Maritime perils" means the perils consequent on, or incidental to, the navigation of the sea, that is to say, perils of the seas, fire, war perils, pirates, rovers, thieves, captures, seisures, restraints, and detainments of princes and peoples, jettisons, barratry, and any other perils, either of the like kind or which may be designated by the policy.

Insurable interest

4 Avoidance of watering or gaming contracts

(1) Every contract of marine insurance by way of gaming or wagering is void.

(2) A contract of marine insurance is deemed to be a gaming or wagering contract –

(a) Where the assured has not an insurable interest as defined by this Act, and the contract is entered into with no expectation of acquiring such an interest; or

(b) Where the policy is made "interest or no interest", or "without further proof of interest than the policy itself", or "without benefit of salvage to the insurer", or subject to any other like term:

Provided that, where there is no possibility of salvage, a policy may be effected without benefit of salvage to the insurer.

5 Insurable interest defined

(1) Subject to the provisions of this Act, every person has an insurable interest who is interested in a marine adventure.

(2) In particular a person is interested in a marine adventure where he stands in any legal or equitable relation to the adventure or to any insurable property at risk therein, in consequence of which he may benefit by the safety or due arrival of insurable property, or may be prejudiced by its loss, or damage thereto, or by the detention thereof, or may incur liability in respect thereof.

6 When interest must attach

(1) The assured must be interested in the subject matter insured at the time of the loss though he need not be interested when the insurance is effected.

Provided that where the subject-matter is insured "lost or not lost", the assured may recover although he may not have acquired his interest until after the loss, unless at the time of effecting the contract of insurance the assured was aware of the loss, and the insurer was not.

(2) Where the assured has no interest at the time of the loss, he cannot acquire interest by any act or election after he is aware of the loss.

7 Defeasible or contingent interest

(1) A defeasible interest is insurable, as also is a contingent interest.

(2) In particular, where the buyer of goods has insured them, he has an insurable interest, notwithstanding that he might, at his election, have rejected the goods, or have treated them as at the seller's risk, by reason of the latter's delay in making delivery or otherwise.

8 Partial interest

A partial interest of any nature is insurable.

9 Re-insurance

(1) The insurer under a contract of marine insurance has an insurable interest in his risk, and may re-insure in respect of it.

(2) Unless the policy otherwise provides, the original assured has no right or interest in respect of such re-insurance.

10 Bottomry

The lender of money on bottomry or respondentia has an insurable interest in respect of the loan.

11 Master's and seamen's wages

The master or any member of the crew of a ship has an insurable interest in respect of his wages.

12 Advance freight

In the case of advance freight, the person advancing the freight has an insurable interest, in so far as such freight is not repayable in case of loss.

13 Charges of insurance

The assured has an insurable interest in the charges of any insurance which he may effect.

14 Quantum of interest

(1) Where the subject-matter insured is mortgaged, the mortgagor has an insurable interest in the full value thereof, and the mortgagee has an insurable interest in respect of any sum due or to become due under the mortgage.

(2) A mortgagee, consignee, or other person having an interest in the subject-matter insured may insure on behalf and for the benefit of other persons interested as well as for his own benefit.

(3) The owner of insurable property has an insurable interest in respect of the full value thereof, notwithstanding that some third person may have agreed, or be liable, to indemnify him in case of loss.

15 Assignment of interest

Where the assured assigns or otherwise parts with his interest in the subject-matter insured, he does not thereby transfer to the assignee his rights under the contract of insurance, unless there be an express or implied agreement with the assignee to that effect.

But the provisions of this section do not affect a transmission of interest by operation of law.

Insurable Value

16 Measure of insurable value

Subject to any express provision or valuation in the policy, the insurable value of the subject-matter insured must be ascertained as follows:

(1) In insurance on ship, the insurable value is the value, at the commencement of the risk, of the ship, including her outfit, provisions and stores for the officers and crew, money advanced for seamen's wages, and other disbursements (if any) incurred to make the ship fit for the voyage or adventure contemplated by the policy, plus the charges of insurance upon the whole:

The insurable value, in the case of a steamship, includes also the machinery, boilers, and coals and engine stores if owned by the assured, and, in the case of a ship engaged in a special trade, the ordinary fittings requisite for that trade:

(2) In insurance on freight, whether paid in advance or otherwise, the insurable value is the gross amount of the freight at the risk of the assured, plus the charges of insurance:

(3) In insurance on goods or merchandise, the insurable value is the prime cost of the property insured, plus the expenses of and incidental to shipping and the charges of insurance upon the whole:

(4) In insurance on any other subject-matter, the insurable value is the amount at the risk of the assured when the policy attaches, plus the charges of insurance.

Disclosure and Representations

17 Insurance is uberrimae fidei

A contract of marine insurance is a contract based upon the utmost good faith, and, if the utmost good faith be not observed by either party, the contract may be avoided by the other party.

18 Disclosure by assured

(1) Subject to the provisions of this section, the assured must disclose to the insurer, before the contract is concluded, every material circumstance which is known to the assured, and the assured is deemed to know every circumstance which, in the ordinary course of business, ought to be known by him. If the assured fails to make such disclosure, the insurer may avoid the contract.

(2) Every circumstance is material which would influence the judgment of a prudent insurer in fixing the premium, or determining whether he will take the risk.

(3) In the absence of inquiry the following circumstances need not be disclosed, namely:

(a) Any circumstance which diminishes the risk;

(b) Any circumstance which is known or presumed to be known to the insurer. The insurer is presumed to know matters of common notoriety or knowledge, and matters which an insurer in the ordinary course of his business, as such, ought to know;

(c) Any circumstance as to which information is waived by the insurer;

(d) Any circumstance which it is superfluous to disclose by reason of any express or implied warranty.

(4) Whether any particular circumstance, which is not disclosed, be material or not is, in each case, a question of fact.

(5) The term "circumstance" includes any communication made to, or information received by, the assured.

19 Disclosure by agent effecting insurance

Subject to the provisions of the preceding section as to circumstances which need not be disclosed, where an insurance is effected for the assured by an agent, the agent must disclose to the insurer –

(a) Every material circumstance which is known to himself, and an agent to insure is deemed to know every circumstance which in the ordinary course of business ought to be known by, or to have been communicated to, him; and

(b) Every material circumstance which the assured is bound to disclose, unless it come to his knowledge too late to communicate it to the agent.

20 Representations pending negotiation of contract

(1) Every material representation made by the assured or his agent to the insurer during the negotiations for the contract, and before the contract is concluded, must be true. If it be untrue the insurer may avoid the contract.

(2) A representation is material which would influence the judgment of a prudent insurer in fixing the premium, or determining whether he will take the risk.

(3) A representation may be either a representation as to a matter of fact, or as to a matter of expectation or belief.

(4) A representation as to matter of fact is true, if it be substantially correct, that is to say, if the difference between what is represented and what is actually correct would not be considered material by a prudent insurer.

21 When contract is deemed to be concluded

A contract of marine insurance is deemed to be concluded when the proposal of the assured is accepted by the insurer, whether the policy be then issued or not; and, for the purpose of showing when the proposal was accepted, reference may be made to the slip or covering note or other customary memorandum of the contract...

The Policy

22 Contract must be embodied in policy

Subject to the provisions of any statute, a contract of marine insurance is inadmissible in evidence unless it is embodied in a marine policy in accordance with this Act. The policy may be executed and issued either at the time when the contract is concluded, or afterwards.

23 What policy must specify

A marine policy must specify –

(1) The name of the assured, or some person who effects the insurance on his behalf.

24 Signature of insurer

(1) A marine policy must be signed by or on behalf of the insurer, provided that in the case of a corporation the corporate seal may be sufficient, but nothing in this section shall be construed as requiring the subscription of a corporation to be under seal.

(2) Where a policy is subscibed by or on behalf of two or more insurers, each subscription, unless the contrary be expressed, constitutes a distinct contract with the assured.

25 Voyage and time policies

(1) Where the contract is to insure the subject-matter "at and from", or from one place to another or others, the policy is called a "voyage policy", and where the contract is to insure the subject-matter for a definite period of time the policy is called a "time policy". A contract for both voyage and time may be included in the same policy.

(2) *(repealed)*.

26 Designation of subject-matter

(1) The subject-matter insured must be designated in a marine policy with reasonable certainty.

(2) The nature and extent of the interest of the assured in the subject-matter insured need not be specified in the policy.

(3) Where the policy designates the subject-matter insured in general terms, it shall be construed to apply to the interest intended by the assured to be covered.

(4) In the application of this section regard shall be had to any usage regulating the designation of the subject-matter insured.

27 Valued policy

(1) A policy may be either valued or unvalued.

(2) A valued policy is a policy which specifies the agreed value of the subject-matter insured.

(3) Subject to the provisions of this Act, and in the absence of fraud, the value fixed by the policy is, as between the insurer and assured, conclusive of the insurable value of the subject intended to be insured, whether the loss be total or partial.

(4) Unless the policy otherwise provides, the value fixed by the policy is not conclusive for the purpose of determining whether there has been a constructive total loss.

28 Unvalued policy

An unvalued policy is a policy which does not specify the value of the subject-matter insured, but, subject to the limit of the sum insured, leaves the insurable value to be subsequently ascertained, in the manner herein-before specified.

29 Floating policy by ship or ships

(1) A floating policy is a policy which describes the insurance in general terms, and leaves the name of the ship or ships and other particulars to be defined by subsequent declaration.

(2) The subsequent declaration or declarations may be made by indorsement on the policy, or in other customary manner.

(3) Unless the policy otherwise provides, the declarations must be made in the order of dispatch or shipment. They must, in the case of goods, comprise all consignments within the terms of the policy, and the value of the goods or other property must be honestly stated, but an omission or erroneous declaration may be rectified even after loss or arrival, provided the omission or declaration was made in good faith.

(4) Unless the policy otherwise provides, where a declaration of value is not made until after notice of loss or arrival, the policy must be treated as an unvalued policy as regards the subject-matter of that declaration.

30 Construction of terms in policy

(1) A policy may be in the form in the First Schedule to this Act.

(2) Subject to the provisions of this Act, and unless the context of the policy otherwise requires, the terms and expressions mentioned in the First Schedule to this Act shall be construed as having the scope and meaning in that schedule assigned to them.

31 Premium to be arranged

(1) Where an insurance is effected at a premium to be arranged, and no arrangement is made, a reasonable premium is payable.

(2) Where an insurance is effected on the terms that an additional premium is to be arranged in a given event, and that event happens but no arrangement is made, then a reasonable additional premium is payable.

Double Insurance

32 Double insurance

(1) Where two or more policies are effected by or on behalf of the assured on the same adventure and interest or any part thereof, and the sums insured exceed the indemnity allowed by this Act, the assured is said to be over-insured by double insurance.

(2) Where the assured is over-insured by double insurance—

(a) The assured, unless the policy otherwise provides, may claim payment from the insurers in such order as he may think fit, provided that he is not entitled to receive any sum in excess of the indemnity allowed by this Act;

(b) Where the policy under which the assured claims is a valued policy, the assured must give credit as against the valuation for any sum received by him under any other policy without regard to the actual value of the subject-matter insured;

(c) Where the policy under which the assured claims is an unvalued policy he must give credit, as against the full insurable value, for any sum received by him under any other policy;

(d) Where the assured receives any sum in excess of the indemnity allowed by this Act, he is deemed to hold such sum in trust for the insurers, according to their right of contribution among themselves.

Warranties, etc

33 Nature of Warranty

(1) A warranty, in the following sections relating to warranties, means a promissory warranty, that is to say, a warranty by which the assured undertakes that some particular thing shall or shall not be done, or that some condition shall be fulfilled, or whereby he affirms or negatives the existence of a particular state of facts.

(2) A warranty may be express or implied.

(3) A warranty, as above defined, is a condition which must be exactly complied with, whether it be material to the risk or not. If it be not so complied with, then, subject to any express provision in the policy, the insurer is discharged from liability as from the date of the breach of warranty, but without prejudice to any liability incurred by him before that date.

34 When breach of warranty excused

(1) Non-compliance with a warranty is excused when, by reason of a change of circumstances, the warranty ceases to be applicable to the circumstances of the

contract, or when compliance with the warranty is rendered unlawful by any subsequent law.

(2) Where a warranty is broken, the assured cannot avail himself of the defence that the breach has been remedied, and the warranty complied with, before loss.

(3) A breach of warranty may be waived by the insurer.

35 Express warranties

(1) An express warranty may be in any form of words from which the intention to warrant is to be inferred.

(2) An express warranty must be included in, or written upon, the policy, or must be contained in some document incorporated by reference into the policy.

(3) An express warranty does not exclude an implied warranty, unless it be inconsistent therewith.

36 Warranty of neutrality

(1) Where insurable property, whether ship or goods, is expressly warranted neutral, there is an implied condition that the property shall have a neutral character at the commencement of the risk, and that, so far as the assured can control the matter, its neutral character shall be preserved during the risk.

(2) Where a ship is expressly warranted "neutral" there is also an implied condition that, so far as the assured can control the matter, she shall be properly documented, that is to say, that she shall carry the necessary papers to establish her neutrality, and that she shall not falsify or suppress her papers, or use simulated papers. If any loss occurs through breach of this condition, the insurer may avoid the contract.

37 No implied warranty of nationality

There is no implied warranty as to the nationality of a ship, or that her nationality shall not be changed during the risk.

38 Warranty of good safety

Where the subject-matter insured is warranted "well" or "in good safety" on a particular day, it is sufficient if it be safe at any time during that day.

39 Warranty of seaworthiness of ship

(1) In a voyage policy there is an implied warranty that at the commencement of the voyage the ship shall be seaworthy for the purpose of the particular adventure insured.

(2) Where the policy attaches while the ship is in port, there is also an implied warranty that she shall, at the commencement of the risk, be reasonably fit to encounter the ordinary perils of the port.

(3) Where the policy relates to a voyage which is performed in different stages, during which the ship requires different kinds of or further preparation or equipment, there is an implied warranty that at the commencement of each stage the ship is seaworthy in respect of such preparation or equipment for the purposes of that stage.

(4) A ship is deemed to be seaworthy when she is reasonably fit in all respects to encounter the ordinary perils of the seas of the adventure insured.

(5) In a time policy there is no implied warranty that the ship shall be seaworthy at any stage of the adventure, but where, with the privity of the assured, the ship is sent to sea in an unseaworthy state, the insurer is not liable for any loss attributable to unseaworthiness.

40 No implied warranty that goods are seaworthy

(1) In a policy on goods or other moveables there is no implied warranty that the goods or moveables are seaworthy.

(2) In a voyage policy on goods or other moveables there is an implied warranty that at the commencement of the voyage the ship is not only seaworthy as a ship, but also that she is reasonably fit to carry the goods or other moveables to the destination contemplated by the policy.

41 Warranty of legality

There is an implied warranty that the adventure insured is a lawful one, and that, so far as the assured can control the matter, the adventure shall be carried out in a lawful manner.

The Voyage

42 Implied condition as to commencement of risk

(1) Where the subject-matter is insured by a voyage policy "at and from" or "from" a particular place, it is not necessary that the ship should be at that place when the contract is concluded, but there is an implied condition that the adventure shall be commenced within a reasonable time, and that if the adventure be not so commenced the insurer may avoid the contract.

(2) The implied condition may be negatived by showing that the delay was caused by circumstances known to the insurer before the contract was concluded, or by showing that he waived the condition.

43 Alteration of port of departure

Where the place of departure is specified by the policy, and the ship instead of sailing from that place sails from any other place, the risk does not attach.

44 Sailing for different destination

Where the destination is specified in the policy, and the ship, instead of sailing for that destination, sails for any other destination, the risk does not attach.

45 Change of voyage

(1) Where, after the commencement of the risk, the destination of the ship is voluntarily changed from the destination contemplated by the policy, there is said to be a change of voyage.

(2) Unless the policy otherwise provides, where there is a change of voyage, the insurer is discharged from liability as from the time of change, that is to say, as from the time when the determination to change it is manifested; and it is immaterial that the ship may not in fact have left the course of voyage contemplated by the policy when the loss occurs.

46 Deviation

(1) Where a ship, without lawful excuse, deviates from the voyage contemplated by the policy, the insurer is discharged from liability as from the time of deviation, and it is immaterial that the ship may have regained her route before any loss occurs.

(2) There is a deviation from the voyage contemplated by the policy—

(a) Where the course of the voyage is specifically designated by the policy, and that course is departed from; or

(b) Where the course of the voyage is not specifically designated by the policy, but the usual and customary course is departed from.

(3) The intention to deviate is immaterial; there must be a deviation in fact to discharge the insurer from his liability under the contract.

47 Several ports of discharge

(1) Where several ports of discharge are specified by the policy, the ship may proceed to all or any of them, but, in the absence of any usage or sufficient cause to the contrary, she must proceed to them, or such of them as she goes to, in the order designated by the policy. If she does not there is a deviation.

(2) Where the policy is to "ports of discharge", within a given area, which are not named, the ship must, in the absence of any usage or sufficient cause to the contrary, proceed to them, or such of them as she goes to, in their geographical order. If she does not there is a deviation.

48 Delay in voyage

In the case of a voyage policy, the adventure insured must be prosecuted throughout its course with reasonable dispatch, and, if without lawful excuse it is not so prosecuted, the insurer is discharged from liability as from the time when the delay became unreasonable.

49 Excuses for deviation or delay

(1) Deviation or delay in prosecuting the voyage contemplated by the policy is excused—
(a) Where authorised by any special term in the policy; or
(b) Where caused by circumstances beyond the control of the master and his employer; or
(c) Where reasonably necessary in order to comply with an express or implied warranty; or
(d) Where reasonably necessary for the safety of the ship or subject-matter insured; or
(e) For the purpose of saving human life, or aiding a ship in distress where human life may be in danger; or
(f) Where reasonably necessary for the purpose of obtaining medical or surgical aid for any person on board the ship; or
(g)   Where caused by the barratrous conduct of the master or crew, if barratry be one of the perils insured against.
(2) When the cause excusing the deviation or delay ceases to operate, the ship mustresume her course, and prosecute her voyage, with reasonable dispatch.

Assignment of Policy

50 When and how policy is assignable

(1) A marine policy is assignable unless it contains terms expressly prohibiting assignment. It may be assigned either before or after loss.
(2) Where a marine policy has been assigned so as to pass the beneficial interest in such policy, the assignee of the policy is entitled to sue thereon in his own name; and the defendant is entitled to make any defence arising out of the contract which he would have been entitled to make if the action had been brought in the name of the person by or on behalf of whom the policy was effected.
(3) A marine policy may be assigned by indorsement thereon or in other customary manner.

51 Assured who has no interest cannot assign

Where the assured has parted with or lost his interest in the subject-matter insured, and has not, before or at the time of so doing, expressly or impliedly agreed to assign the policy, any subsequent assignment of the policy is inoperative:
Provided that nothing in this section affects the assignment of a policy after loss.

The Premium

52 When premium payable

Unless otherwise agreed, the duty of the assured or his agent to pay the premium, and the duty of the insurer to issue the policy to the assured or his agent, are concurrent conditions, and the insurer is not bound to issue the policy until payment or tender of the premium.

53 Policy effected through broker

(1) Unless otherwise agreed, where a marine policy is effected on behalf of the assured by a broker, the broker is directly responsible to the insurer for the premium, and the insurer is directly responsible to the assured for the amount which may be payable in respect of losses, or in respect of returnable premium.

(2) Unless otherwise agreed, the broker has, as against the assured, a lien upon the policy for the amount of the premium and his charges in respect of effecting the policy; and, where he has dealt with the person who employs him as a principal, he has also a lien on the policy in respect of any balance on any insurance account which may be due to him from such person, unless when the debt was incurred he had reason to believe that such person was only an agent.

54 Effect of receipt on policy

Where a marine policy effected on behalf of the assured by a broker acknowledges the receipt of the premium, such acknowledgement is, in the absence of fraud, conclusive as between the insurer and the assured, but not as between the insurer and broker.

Loss and Abandonment

55 Included and excluded losses

(1) Subject to the provisions of this Act, and unless the policy otherwise provides, the insurer is liable for any loss proximately caused by a peril insured against, but, subject as aforesaid, he is not liable for any loss which is not proximately caused by a peril insured against.

(2) In particular, –

    (a) The insurer is not liable for any loss attributable to the wilful misconduct of the assured, but, unless the policy otherwise provides, he is liable for any loss proximately caused by a peril insured against, even though the loss would not have happened but for the misconduct or negligence of the master or crew;

    (b) Unless the policy otherwise provides, the insurer on ship or goods is not liable for any loss proximately caused by delay, although the delay be caused by a peril insured against;

(c) Unless the policy otherwise provides, the insurer is not liable for ordinary wear and tear, ordinary leakage and breakage, inherent vice or nature of the subject-matter insured, or for any loss proximately caused by rats or vermin, or for any injury to machinery not proximately caused by maritime perils.

56 Partial and total loss

(1) A loss may be either total or partial. Any loss other than a total loss, as herein-after defined, is a partial loss.

(2) A total loss may be either an actual total loss, or a constructive total loss.

(3) Unless a different intention appears from the terms of the policy, an insurance against total loss includes a constructive, as well as an actual, total loss.

(4) Where the assured brings an action for a total loss and the evidence proves only a partial loss, he may, unless the policy otherwise provides, recover for a partial loss.

(5) Where goods reach their destination in specie, but by reason of obliteration of marks, or otherwise, they are incapable of identification, the loss, if any, is partial, and not total.

57 Actual total loss

(1) Where the subject-matter insured is destroyed, or so damaged as to cease to be a thing of the kind insured, or where the assured is irretrievably deprived thereof, there is an actual total loss.

(2) In the case of an actual total loss no notice of abandonment need be given.

58 Missing ship

Where the ship concerned in the adventure is missing, and after the lapse of a reasonable time no news of her has been received, an actual total loss may be presumed.

59 Effect of transhipment, etc

Where, by a peril insured against, the voyage is interrupted at an intermediate port or place, under such circumstances as, apart from any special stipulation in the contract of affreightment, to justify the master in landing and re-shipping the goods or other moveables, or in transhipping them, and sending them on to their destination, the liability of the insurer continues, notwithstanding the landing or transhipment.

60 Constructive total loss defined

(1) Subject to any express provision in the policy, there is a constructive total loss where the subject-matter insured is reasonably abandoned on account of its actual total loss appearing to be unavoidable, or because it could not be preserved from actual total loss without an expenditure which would exceed its value when the expenditure had been incurred.

(2) In particular, there is a constructive total loss –

(i) Where the assured is deprived of the possession of his ship or goods by a peril insured against, and (a) it is unlikely that he can recover the ship or goods, as the case may be, or (b) the cost of recovering the ship or goods, as the case may be, would exceed their value when recovered; or

(ii) In the case of damage to a ship, where she is so damaged by a peril insured against that the cost of repairing the damage would exceed the value of the ship when repaired.

In estimating the cost of repairs, no deductions to be made in respect of general average contributions to those repairs payable by other interests, but account is to be taken of the expense of future salvage operations and of any future general average contributions to which the ship would be liable if repaired; or

(iii) In the case of damage to goods, where the cost of repairing the damage and forwarding the goods to their destination would exceed their value on arrival.

61 Effect of constructive total loss

Where there is a constructive total loss the assured may either treat the loss as a partial loss, or abandon the subject-matter insured to the insurer and treat the loss as if it were an actual total loss.

62 Notice of abandonment

(1) Subject to the provisions of this section, where the assured elects to abandon the subject-matter insured to the insurer, he must give notice of abandonment. If he fails to do so the loss can only be treated as a partial loss.

(2) Notice of abandonment may be given in writing, or by word of mouth, or partly in writing and partly by word of mouth, and may be given in terms which indicate the intention of the assured to abandon his insured interest in the subject-matter insured unconditionally to the insurer.

(3) Notice of abandonment must be given with reasonable diligence after the receipt of reliable information of the loss, but where the information is of a doubtful character the assured is entitled to a reasonable time to make inquiry.

(4) Where notice of abandonment is properly given, the rights of the assured are not prejudiced by the fact that the insurer refuses to accept the abandonment.

(5) The acceptance of an abandonment may be either express or implied from the conduct of the insurer. The mere silence of the insurer after notice is not an acceptance.

(6) Where a notice of abandonment is accepted the abandonment is irrevocable. The acceptance of the notice conclusively admits liability for the loss and the sufficiency of the notice.

(7) Notice of abandonment is unnecessary where, at the time when the assured receives information of the loss, there would be no possibility of benefit to the insurer if notice were given to him.

(8) Notice of abandonment may be waived by the insurer.

(9) Where an insurer has re-insured his risk, no notice of abandonment need be given by him.

63 Effect of abandonment

(1) Where there is a valid abandonment the insurer is entitled to take over the interest of the assured in whatever may remain of the subject-matter insured, and all proprietary rights incidental thereto.

(2) Upon the abandonment of a ship, the insurer thereof is entitled to any freight in course of being earned, and which is earned by her subsequent to the casualty causing the loss, less the expenses of earning it incurred after the casualty; and, where the ship is carrying the owner's goods, the insurer is entitled to a reasonable remuneration for the carriage of them subsequent to the casualty causing the loss.

Partial Losses (including Salvage and General Average and Particular Charges)

64 Particular average loss

(1) A particular average loss is a partial loss of the subject-matter insured, caused by a peril insured against, and which is not a general average loss.

(2) Expenses incurred by or on behalf of the assured for the safety or preservation of the subject-matter insured, other than general average and salvage charges, are called particular charges. Particular charges are not included in particular average.

65 Salvage charges

(1) Subject to any express provision in the policy, salvage charges incurred in preventing a loss by perils insured against may be recovered as a loss by those perils.

(2) "Salvage charges" means the charges recoverable under maritime law by a salvor independently of contract. They do not include the expenses of services in the nature of salvage rendered by the assured or his agents, or any person employed for hire by them, for the purpose of averting a peril insured against. Such expenses, where properly incurred, may be recovered as particular charges or as a general average loss, according to the circumstances under which they were incurred.

66 General average loss

(1) A general average loss is a loss caused by or directly consequential on a general average act. It includes a general average expenditure as well as a general average sacrifice.

(2) There is a general average act where any extraordinary sacrifice or expenditure is voluntarily and reasonably made or incurred in time of peril for the purpose of preserving the property imperilled in the common adventure.

(3) Where there is a general average loss, the party on whom it falls is entitled, subject to the conditions imposed by maritime law, to a rateable contribution from

the other parties interested, and such contribution is called a general average contribution.

(4) Subject to any express provision in the policy, where the assured has incurred a general average expenditure, he may recover from the insurer in respect of the proportion of the loss which falls upon him; and, in the case of a general average sacrifice, he may recover from the insurer in respect of the whole loss without having enforced his right of contribution from the other parties liable to contribute.

(5) Subject to any express provision in the policy, where the assured has paid, or is liable to pay, a general average contribution in respect of the subject insured, he may recover therefor from the insurer.

(6) In the absence of express stipulation, the insurer is not liable for any general average loss or contribution where the loss was not incurred for the purpose of avoiding, or in connexion with the avoidance of, a peril insured against.

(7) Where ship, freight, and cargo, or any two of those interests, are owned by the same assured, the liability of the insurer in respect of general average losses or contributions is to be determined as if those subjects were owned by different persons.

Measure of Indemnity

67 Extent of liability of insurer for loss

(1) The sum which the assured can recover in respect of a loss on a policy by which he is insured, in the case of an unvalued policy to the full extent of the insurable value, or, in the case of a valued policy to the full extent of the value fixed by the policy is called the measure of indemnity.

(2) Where there is a loss recoverable under the policy, the insurer, or each insurer if there be more than one, is liable for such proportion of the measure of indemnity as the amount of his subscription bears to the value fixed by the policy in the case of a valued policy, or to the insurable value in the case of an unvalued policy.

68 Total loss

Subject to the provisions of this Act and to any express provision in the policy, where there is a total loss of the subject-matter insured, –

(1) If the policy be a valued policy, the measure of indemnity is the sum fixed by the policy:

(2) If the policy be an unvalued policy, the measure of indemnity is the insurable value of the subject-matter insured.

69 Partial loss of ship

Where a ship is damaged, but is not totally lost, the measure of indemnity, subject to any express provision in the policy, is as follows: –

(1) Where the ship has been repaired, the assured is entitled to the reasonable cost of the repairs, less the customary deductions, but not exceeding the sum insured in respect of any one casualty:

(2) Where the ship has been only partially repaired, the assured is entitled to the reasonable cost of such repairs, computed as above, and also to be indemnified for the reasonable depreciation, if any, arising from the unrepaired damage, provided that the aggregate amount shall not exceed the cost of repairing the whole damage, computed as above:

(3) where the ship has to been repaired, and has not been sold in her damaged state during the risk, the assured is entitled to be indemnified for the reasonable depreciation arising from the unrepaired damage, but not exceeding the reasonable cost of repairing such damage, computed as above.

70 Partial loss of freight

Subject to any express provision in the policy, where there is a partial loss of freight, the measure of indemnity is such proportion of the sum fixed by the policy in the case of a valued policy, or of the insurable value in the case of an unvalued policy, as the proportion of freight lost by the assured bears to the whole freight at the risk of the assured under the policy.

71 Partial loss of goods, merchandise, etc

Where there is a partial loss of goods, merchandise, or other moveables, the measure of indemnity, subject to any express provision in the policy, is as follows: –

(1) Where part of the goods, merchandise or other moveables insured by a valued policy is totally lost, the measure of indemnity is such proportion of the sum fixed by the policy as the insurable value of the part lost bears to the insurable value of the whole, ascertained as in the case of an unvalued policy:

(2) Where part of the goods, merchandise, or other moveables insured by an unvalued policy is totally lost, the measure of indemnity is the insurable value of the part lost, ascertained as in case of total loss:

(3) Where the whole or any part of the goods or merchandise insured has been delivered damaged at its destination, the measure of indemnity is such proportion of the sum fixed by the policy in the case of a valued policy, or of the insurable value in the case of an unvalued policy, as the difference between the gross sound and damaged values at the place of arrival bears to the gross sound value:

(4) "Gross value" means the wholesale price or, if there be no such price, the estimated value, with, in either case, freight, landing charges, and duty paid beforehand; provided that, in the case of goods or merchandise customarily sold in bond, the bonded price is deemed to be the gross value. "Gross proceeds" means the actual price obtained at a sale where all charges on sale are paid by the sellers.

72 Apportionment of valuation

(1) Where different species of property are insured under a single valuation, the valuation must be apportioned over the different species in proportion to their respective insurable values, as in the case of an unvalued policy. The insured value of any part of a species is such proportion of the total insured value of the same as the

insurable value of the part bears to the insurable value of the whole, ascertained in both cases as provided by this Act.

(2) Where a valuation has to be apportioned, and particulars of the prime cost of each separate species, quality, or description of goods cannot be ascertained, the division of the valuation may be made over the net arrived sound values of the different species, qualities, or descriptions of goods.

73 General average contributions and salvage charges

(1) Subject to any express provision in the policy, where the assured has paid, or is liable for any general average contribution, the measure of indemnity is the full amount of such contribution, if the subject-matter liable to contribution is insured for its full contributory value; but, if such subject-matter be not insured for its full contributory value, or if only part of it be insured, the indemnity payable by the insurer must be reduced in proportion to the under insurance, and where there has been a particular average loss which constitutes a deduction from the contributory value, and for which the insurer is liable, that amount must be deducted from the insured value in order to ascertain what the insurer is liable to contribute.

(2) Where the insurer is liable for salvage charges the extent of his liability must be determined on the like principle.

74 Liabilities to third parties

Where the assured has effected an insurance in express terms against any liability to a third party, the measure of indemnity, subject to any express provision in the policy, is the amount paid or payable by him to such third party in respect of such liability.

75 General provisions as to measure of indemnity

(1) Where there has been a loss in respect of any subject-matter not expressly provided for in the foregoing provisions of this Act, the measure of indemnity shall be ascertained, as nearly as may be, in accordance with those provisions, in so far as applicable to the particular case.

(2) Nothing in the provisions of this Act relating to the measure of indemnity shall affect the rules relating to double insurance, or prohibit the insurer from disproving interest wholly or in part, or from showing that at the time of the loss the whole or any part of the subject-matter insured was not at risk under the policy.

76 Particular average warranties

(1) Where the subject-matter insured is warranted free from particular average, the assured cannot recover for a loss of part, other than a loss incurred by a general average sacrifice unless the contract contained in the policy be apportionable; but, if the contract be apportionable, the assured may recover for a total loss of any apportionable part.

(2) Where the subject-matter insured is warranted free from particular average, either wholly or under a certain percentage, the insurer is nevertheless liable for

salvage charges, and for particular charges and other expenses properly incurred pursuant to the provisions of the suing and labouring clause in order to avert a loss insured against.

(3) Unless the policy otherwise provides, where the subject-matter insured is warranted free from particular average under a specified percentage, a general average loss cannot be added to a particular average loss to make up the specified percentage.

(4) For the purpose of ascertaining whether the specified percentage has been reached, regard shall be had only to the actual loss suffered by the subject-matter insured. Particular charges and the expenses of and incidental to ascertaining and proving the loss must be excluded.

77 Successive losses

(1) Unless the policy otherwise provides, and subject to the provisions of this Act, the insurer is liable for successive losses, even though the total amount of such losses may exceed the sum insured.

(2) Where, under the same policy, a partial loss, which has not been repaired or otherwise made good, is followed by a total loss, the assured can only recover in respect of the total loss:

Provided that nothing in this section shall affect the liability of the insurer under the suing and labouring clause.

78 Suing and labouring clause

(1) Where the policy contains a suing and labouring clause, the engagement thereby entered into is deemed to be supplementary to the contract of insurance, and the assured may recover from the insurer any expenses properly incurred pursuant to the clause, notwithstanding that the insurer may have paid for a total loss, or that the subject-matter may have been warranted free from particular average, either wholly or under a certain percentage.

(2) General average losses and contributions and salvage charges, as defined by this Act, are not recoverable under the suing and labouring clause.

(3) Expenses incurred for the purpose of averting or diminishing any loss not covered by the policy are not recoverable under the suing and labouring clause.

(4) It is the duty of the assured and his agents, in all cases, to take such measures as may be reasonable for the purpose of averting or minimising a loss.

Rights of Insurer on Payment

79 Right of subrogation

(1) Where the insurer pays for a total loss, either of the whole, or in the case of goods of any apportionable part, of the subject-matter insured, he thereupon becomes entitled to take over the interest of the assured in whatever may remain of the subject-matter so paid for, and he is thereby subrogated to all the rights and

remedies of the assured in and in respect of that subject-matter as from the time of the casualty causing the loss.

(2) Subject to the foregoing provisions, where the insurer pays for a partial loss, he acquires no title to the subject-matter insured, or such part of it as may remain, but he is thereupon subrogated to all rights and remedies of the assured in and in respect of the subject-matter insured as from the time of the casualty causing the loss, in so far as the assured has been indemnified, according to this Act, by such payment for the loss.

80 Right of contribution

(1) Where the assured is over-insured by double insurance, each insurer is bound, as between himself and the other insurers, to contribute rateably to the loss in proportion to the amount for which he is liable under his contract.

(2) If any insurer pays more than his proportion of the loss, he is entitled to maintain an action for contribution against the other insurers, and is entitled to the like remedies as a surety who has paid more than his proportion of the debt.

81 Effect of under insurance

Where the assured in insured for an amount less than the insurable value or, in the case of a valued policy, for an amount less than the policy valuation, he is deemed to be his own insurer in respect of the uninsured balance.

Return of Premium

82 Enforcement of return

Where the premium or a proportionate part thereof is, by this Act, declared to be returnable, –
  (a) If already paid, it may be recovered by the assured from the insurer; and
  (b) If unpaid, it may be retained by the assured or his agent.

83 Return by agreement

Where the policy contains a stipulation for the return of the premium, or a proportionate part thereof, on the happening of a certain event, and that event happens, the premium, or, as the case may be, the proportionate part thereof, is thereupon returnable to the assured.

84 Return for failure of consideration

(1) Where the consideration for the payment of the premium totally fails, and there has been no fraud or illegality on the part of the assured or his agents, the premium is thereupon returnable to the assured.

(2) Where the consideration for the payment of the premium is apportionable and there is a total failure of any apportionable part of the consideration, a proportionate part of the premium is, under the like conditions, thereupon returnable to the assured.

(3) In particular –

(a) Where the policy is void, or is avoided by the insurer as from the commencement of the risk, the premium is returnable, provided that there has been no fraud or illegality on the part of the assured; but if the risk is not apportionable, and has once attached, the premium is not returnable;

(b) Where the subject-matter insured, or part thereof, has never been imperilled, the premium, or, as the case may be, a proportionate part thereof, is returnable:

Provided that where the subject-matter has been insured "lost or not lost" and has arrived in safety at the time when the contract is concluded, the premium is not returnable unless, at such time, the insurer knew of the safe arrival.

(c) Where the assured has no insurable interest throughout the currency of the risk, the premium is returnable, provided that this rule does not apply to a policy effected by way of gaming or wagering;

(d) Where the assured has a defeasible interest which is terminated during the currency of the risk, the premium is not returnable;

(e) Where the assured has over-insured under an unvalued policy, a proportionate part of the premium is returnable;

(f) Subject to the foregoing provisions, where the assured has over-insured by double insurance, a proportionate part of the several premiums is returnable:

Provided that, if the policies are effected at different times, and any earlier policy has at any time borne the entire risk, or if a claim has been paid on the policy in respect of the full sum insured thereby, no premium is returnable in respect of that policy, and when the double insurance is effected knowingly by the assured no premium is returnable.

Mutual Insurance

85 Modification of act in case of mutual insurance

(1) Where two or more persons mutually agree to insure each other against marine losses there is said to be a mutual insurance.

(2) The provisions of this Act relating to the premium do not apply to mutual insurance, but a guarantee, or such other arrangement as may be agreed upon, may be substituted for the premium.

(3) The provisions of this Act, in so far as they may be modified by the agreement of the parties, may in the case of mutual insurance be modified by the terms of the policies issued by the association, or by the rules and regulations of the association.

(4) Subject to the exceptions mentioned in this section, the provisions of this Act apply to a mutual insurance.

Supplementally

86 Ratification by assured

Where a contract of marine insurance is in good faith effected by one person on behalf of another, the person on whose behalf it is effected may ratify the contract even after he is aware of a loss.

87 Implied obligations varied by agreement or usage

(1) Where any right, duty, or liability would arise under a contract of marine insurance by implication of law, it may be negatived or varied by express agreement, or by usage, if the usage be such as to bind both parties to the contract.

(2) The provisions of this section extend to any right, duty, or liability declared by this Act which may be lawfully modified by agreement.

88 Reasonable time, etc, a question of fact

Where by this Act any reference is made to reasonable time, reasonable premium, or reasonable diligence, the question what is reasonable is a question of fact.

89 Slip as evidence

Where there is a duly stamped policy, reference may be made, as heretofore, to the slip or covering note, in any legal proceeding.

90 Interpretation of terms

In this Act, unless the context or subject-matter otherwise requires, –

"Action" includes counter-claim and set off;

"Freight" includes the profit derivable by a shipowner from the employment of his ship to carry his own goods or moveables, as well as freight payable by a third party, but does not include passage money;

"Moveables" means any moveable tangible property, other than the ship, and includes money, valuable securities, and other documents;

"Policy" means a marine policy.

91 Savings

(1) Nothing in this Act, or in any repeal effected thereby, shall affect—

(a) The provisions of the Stamp Act 1891, or any enactment for the time being in force relating to the revenue;

(b) The provisions of the Companies Act 1862, or any enactment amending or substituted for the same;

(c) The provisions of any statute not expressly repealed by this Act.

(2) The rules of the common law including the law merchant,s ave in so far as they are inconsistent with the express provisions of this Act, shall continue to apply to contracts of marine insurance.

92, 93 *(repealed)*

94 *Short title*

This Act may be cited as the Marine Insurance Act 1906.

First Schedule

Section 30

(Form of Notice omitted)

The following are the rules referred to by this Act for the construction of a policy in the above or other like form, where the context does not otherwise require: –

1. Where the subject-matter is insured "lost or not lost", and the loss has occurred before the contract is concluded, the risk attaches, unless at such time the assured was aware of the loss, and the insurer was not.

2. Where the subject-matter is insured "from" a particular place, the risk does not attach until the ship starts on the voyage insured.

3. (a) Where a ship is insured "at and from" a particular place, and she is at that place in good safety when the contract is concluded, the risk attaches immediately.

(b) If she be not at that place when the contract is concluded, the risk attaches as soon as she arrives there in good safety, and, unless they policy otherwise provides, it is immaterial that she is covered by another policy for a specified time after arrival.

(c) Where chartered freight is insured "at and from" a particular place, and the ship is at that place in good safety when the contract is concluded the risk attaches immediately. If she be not there when the contract is concluded, the risk attaches as soon as she arrives there in good safety.

(d) Where freight, other than chartered freight, is payable without special conditions and is insured "at and from" a particular place, the risk attaches pro rata as the goods or merchandise are shipped; provided that if there be cargo in readiness which belongs to the shipowner, or which some other person has contracted with him to ship, the risk attaches as soon as the ship is ready to receive such cargo.

4. Where goods or other moveables are insured "from the loading thereof", the risk does not attach until such goods or moveables are actually on board, and the insurer is not liable for them while in transit from the shore to ship.

5. Where the risk on goods or other moveables continues until they are "safely landed", they must be landed in the customary manner and within a

reasonable time after arrival at the port of discharge, and if they are not so landed the risk ceases.

6. In the absence of any further license or usage, the liberty to touch and stay "at any port or place whatsoever" does not authorise the ship to depart from the course of her voyage from the port of departure to the port of destination.

7. The term "perils of the seas" refers only to fortuitous accidents or casualties of the seas. It does not include the ordinary action of the winds and waves.

8. The term "pirates" includes passengers who mutiny and rioters who attack the ship from the shore.

9. The term "thieves" does not cover clandestine theft or a theft committed by any one of the ship's company, whether crew or passengers.

10. The term "arrests, etc, of kings, princes, and people" refers to political or executive acts, and does not include a loss caused by riot or by ordinary judicial process.

11. The term "barratry" includes every wrongful act wilfully committed by the master or crew to the prejudice of the owner, or, as the case may be, the charterer.

12. The term "all other perils" includes only perils similar in kind to the perils specifically mentioned in the policy.

13. The term "average unless general" means a partial loss of the subject-matter insured other than a general average loss, and does not include "particular charges".

14. Where the ship has stranded, the insurer is liable for the excepted losses, although the loss is not attributable to the stranding, provided that when the stranding takes place the risk has attached and, if the policy be on goods, that the damaged goods are on board.

15. The term "ship" includes the hull, materials and outfit, stores and provisions for the officers and crew, and, in the case of vessels engaged in a special trade, the ordinary fittings requisite for the trade, and also, in the case of a steamship, the machinery, boilers, and coals and engine stores, if owned by the assured.

16. The term "freight" includes the profit derivable by a shipowner from the employment of his ship to carry his own goods or moveables, as well as freight payable by a third party, but does not include passage money.

17. The term "goods" means goods in the nature of merchandise, and does not include personal effects or provisions and stores for use on board.

In the absence of any usage to the contrary, deck cargo and living animals must be insured specifically, and not under the general denomination of goods.

Index

Please note that page references to footnotes have the letter 'n' following the page number